PHILIP'S
Family
ROAD ATLAS

Contents

Kids on board...

For the journey

It is always a good idea to have a basic travel bag that's easily accessible at all times for snacks, drinks, wipes, etc.

In addition, put a soft blanket and a pillow or two in the car to keep children comfortable when napping (but not for children under 2). Seat-belt cushions are a good idea for older children.

As a general rule, try to keep the car interior as clutter free as possible, as your children will stay much more comfortable if they've got plenty of leg room to move around. Stretchy netting bags or seat-back car-tidies or a cardboard shoe box on the back seat will help to keep things tidy.

When all else fails, have an emergency supply of sweets to bring out to calm things down and generally raise morale.

Food and drink

An absolute essential on any journey – nothing raises the spirits like a tasty snack or drink. Some foods suit travelling much better than others. While there's definitely a place for crisps, chocolate and biscuits, make sure you also offer your child some healthier foods, as too much salt and sugar can make you dehydrated and irritable.

Have to hand a selection of foods that everyone likes: mini sandwiches, breadsticks, vegetable sticks, fresh bread, fresh fruit (crisp apples, easy-peel satsumas and firm pears). Choose small bananas and offer them first as they get squashed quickly.

Take plenty of still water on any journey, though it's also useful to have cartons of fruit juice with straws; flavoured waters for children who won't readily drink plain, and a flask of tea or coffee for the adults. Choose a spillproof beaker for your toddler, and sports bottles for older children.

Travel essentials for children

Babies

- bottles, your baby's usual milk and a bottle insulator, as well as food and cutlery if your baby is weaned
- changing bag, nappies and baby wipes
- changes of clothes
- dummies, if you use them
- baby moisturizing cream
- kitchen paper and supply of plastic bags
- a favourite cuddly toy

Toddlers

- potty in case you can't get to a service station in time
- a few favourite toys or cuddlies

For older children

- travel-sized versions of popular board games
- MP3 players and hand-held games (make sure they're charged before you leave or take spare batteries)
- books, including puzzle books

Other essentials

- tissues
- wipes
- medicines (keep these locked in the glove compartment)
- mobile phone
- rescue service card
- side-window sun blinds, which you should fit before you go
- CDs and talking books
- sun glasses

Pre-trip maintenance

The last thing you want to happen is to have car trouble, so it is worth spending a few minutes to make sure that nothing is wrong. Make sure that the engine and tyres are cold, that the car is on a level surface and the ignition is off. The car's handbook will tell you the correct settings for the tyre pressure, what grade oil to use and what type of fluids are needed. Don't leave these checks until the last minute.

Tyres – check the pressure (don't forget the spare) and tread.

Oil – check the reservoir is full. Top up if necessary, taking care not to overfill.

Radiator coolant – make sure that the indicator is showing 'max'.

Brakes, clutch and power-steering fluids – check that all of these are at maximum level.

Fan belts (drivebelts) – make sure that these are not loose, fraying or damaged.

Windscreen wipers – check these are not worn.

Washer reservoir – check that this is full. If there is a separate reservoir in the boot for the rear window, check that, too. If the nozzle is blocked, use a needle to clear it.

Battery – some batteries require topping up with distilled water, so check the level. Make sure that the battery connections are tight.

- Now turn the ignition on.
- Check that the lights are all working correctly. Get someone to help you check the brake lights.
- If any of the warning lights on the dashboard comes on, get this problem sorted.

Family-friendly service areas

The following motorway services have a choice of places to eat, baby-feeding stations, children's meals, play areas and parent and baby rooms.

M1 – J11-12	Toddington Services	40	B3
M1 – J38-39	Woolley Edge Services	88	C4
M4 – J2-3	Heston Services	28	B2
M4 – J11-12	Reading Services	26	C4
M4 – J13	Chieveley Services	26	B2
M4 – J17-18	Leigh Delamere Services	24	B3
M4 – J33	Cardiff West	22	B2
M5 – J3-4	Frankley Services	62	F3
M5 – J24	Bridgwater Services	22	F5
M5 – J30	Exeter Services	10	E4
M6 – J14-15	Stafford Services Northbound	75	F5
M6 – J18-19	Knutsford Services	74	B4
M6 – J32-33	Lancaster Services	92	D5
M6 – J35-36	Burton-in-Kendal Services	92	B5
M6 – J38-39	Tebay Services	99	D8
M6 – J41-42	Southwaite Services	108	E4
M9 – J9	Stirling Services	133	F7
M18 – J5	Doncaster N Services	89	C7
M23 – J11	Pease Pottage Services	28	F3
M40 – J10	Cherwell Valley Services	39	B5
M42 – J10	Tamworth Services	63	D6
M62 – J18-19	Birch Services	87	D6
M62 – J33	Ferrybridge Services	89	B5
M90 – J6	Kinross Services	134	D3
A1(M) – J34	Blyth Services	89	F7

First aid kit

Before you go, make sure your first aid box is up to date. There are lots of travel-sized kits available from any chemist but if you want to make up a basic one of your own it should contain:

- Sticking plasters, hypoallergenic ones if needed
- Antiseptic cream or wipes
- Several clean non-fluffy dressings
- Adhesive tape
- Infant paracetamol
- Rehydrating sachets
- Pain-relief spray or antihystamine cream for bites and stings
- Cotton wool
- Thermometer
- Calamine lotion
- Tweezers
- Scissors
- Gauze bandage
- Triangular bandage
- Safety pins

If your kit contains any pills or medicines, make sure it is secured in a locked glove compartment away from your children or in the boot. Be sure you have enough supplies of any prescribed medicines and don't leave packs of pills in a bag where a toddler could discover them. An empty box or plastic bag is also useful in case your child feels sick.

Child seats and cushions

On 18 September 2006, new rules were introduced making the use of the correct child restraints compulsory, with only a very few exceptions, such as in taxis or on one-off unforeseen journeys where no child restraint is available. In the former, children under 3 may be unrestrained (the only exemption for this age group). In both cases, children aged 3 and over should use an adult seat belt in the rear. No child may be carried on an adult's lap.

Check when you buy a new seat that it will fit correctly in your vehicle. Major retailers may have staff members who can help with the fitting and Road Safety Officers of many local councils offer similar services. All seats should be fitted according to the manufacturer's instructions and checked before every journey in case the seat belt has worked loose. The seat belt should be sufficiently tight that the seat cannot move. Make sure that the buckle is not touching the seat's frame. If your car has permanent ISOFix anchorage points, buy a seat that is compatible.

Rear-facing baby seats

For babies up to 13 kg (29 lb), roughly 9–12 months.

These can be fitted either in the rear seat, preferably using the central strap as this is the safest position, or in the front passenger seat. However, in vehicles with airbags, they should not be used in the front passenger seat unless the airbag has been deactivated.

Front-facing child seats

For children 9–18 kg (20–40 lb), from 9 months to 4 years.

These should be fitted on the rear seat unless there is insufficient room because of other child seats, in which case one may be fitted to the front passenger seat, which should be pushed back as far as possible. Before fitting the seat in the vehicle, adjust the shoulder and chest straps to the correct position for your child, according to the manufacturer's instructions. When you buckle your child in, make sure that you can get only two fingers between the chest strap and their chest. If it is any looser than that, the child could work their way out, or slip out under sudden braking.

Booster seats

For children 15 kg (33 lb) upwards, from roughly 4 years.

These raise the child up so that they are in the correct position for the adult seat belt to restrain them. Make sure that the lower part of the belt is correctly threaded through the base of the seat and is as low as possible across the child's stomach and that the shoulder strap is correctly positioned across their chest.

Booster cushions

For children 22 kg (49 lb) upwards, from roughly 6 years.

Make sure that the lower part of the belt is correctly threaded though the cushion and that the shoulder strap is positioned as for booster seats.

Children no longer have to use a seat or cushion once they have either reached their 12th birthday or are 135 cm (4 ft 5 in) tall, but they must wear a seat belt.

The penalty for not using the appropriate child restraint is a fixed penalty of £30. If the driver is taken to court, the fine could be as much as £500.

Travel sickness

If a child is feeling travel sick, encourage them to look ahead rather than out of side windows and don't let them read or write – it will only make them feel worse.

Travel sickness can affect adults and children alike, and may make a journey very uncomfortable. Try to prevent it before the journey starts by wearing travel wristbands, or taking a suitable medication recommended by your pharmacist. Double-check the age range it's suitable for, and how long before your journey it should be taken. Feed your children an hour before travelling to help settle their stomachs, but avoid greasy or large meals. If possible make sure there's plenty of fresh air, and that your children don't get overheated. Allow plenty of time for the journey as this helps to keep the atmosphere calm.

A child who's feeling sick may be more comfortable in the front of the car. If you can, stop the car and have a short walk outside. Iced water can relieve discomfort, as can dry biscuits, anything containing ginger, and a fresh apple. However if the worst happens, be prepared with a plastic bag, a bottle of water for rinsing and a pack of wipes. Being able to freshen up after a bout of sickness will really help your child's morale.

Safety concerns

- Never allow children to play with the controls in the car. Electric windows and sun roofs are potentially dangerous, so make sure your child is not able to operate them.
- If your car has central locking and child-locks on the windows, use them.
- Make sure you have a fully charged mobile phone with you for any emergencies. If you use pre-pay, make sure you have enough credit. If you belong to a rescue service, take your card with you and make sure your membership is up to date.

Sunlight safety

- If you're playing a game that involves looking out of the window on a sunny day, make sure you have your child's sunglasses to hand.

Sleepy?

- Many road accidents are caused by tired drivers desperate to get home. There's one golden rule – you MUST stop if you're tired. Even a few minutes walking up and down in a service station car park will help. Other things to try include: getting a passenger to talk to you; listening to a radio talk show; and having a caffeinated drink, such as coffee or cola.

Stay fresh

- Keep fresh air circulating in the car by opening the roof or taking turns to have your window open. Leaving the heater on without some fresh air can leave you all feeling heavy-headed.

Travel games for children

Every game and activity has a rough indication of the age for which it is suitable, although an older child might enjoy playing a silly one suggested for younger children and many of the games can be adapted to give younger children a head start.

Make sure that you've got all the bits and pieces needed to hand. Prepare lists for spotting games, grids for word searches and pictures for colouring in before you go.

Each child can have a clipboard, so you can clip paper for pen and paper games to it. Alternatively, lap trays that they can rest paper on might do the trick. If there's room, sit a box for pencils and crayons between the children. Intersperse different kinds of games, so that no one gets bored.

Try to think ahead: don't arrange a noisy game for busy areas where the driver needs to concentrate even harder than usual.

For pencil and paper games, attach plenty of sheets of paper to clipboards.

Games that can be prepared in advance are marked ★

★Pencil walk

4+ Sheets of paper and a pencil; coloured crayons or felt-tipped pens

Draw randomly all over a sheet of paper. Use any combination of loops, squiggles or straight lines, but do not take the pencil off the paper until the pattern is complete. Make sure the lines cross over each other to create a number of irregular shapes. Then get the children to colour in the different sections, making sure that no two adjoining sections are the same colour.

* Older children can draw the random outline themselves.

WORD GAMES

Tailor these games to your children's reading levels.

★Word search

7+ Sheets of paper and a pencil (squared paper is helpful, but not essential); felt-tipped pens

The aim of this game is to find a number of words hidden in a grid of letters. You can make the game more of a challenge by increasing the size of the grid and choosing more, or longer, words.

Draw a 64-square grid on the sheet of paper, eight squares across by eight squares down. Choose a category, such as pets, and think of five words – for example, fish, dog, cat, rabbit and mouse. Write each of these words across or down your grid, with one letter in each square. Fill in the remaining squares with random letters to disguise where the correct words are hidden. Match the words on each puzzle to each child's reading ability.

Get your children to find the words and ring round them with felt-tipped pens.

Letter sandwich

10+ A sheet of paper and a pencil for each player; an egg timer or a stopwatch

Give the children a set time to think of as many words as they can beginning and ending with the same letter.

Each player has just five minutes to write down as many words as he can that begin and end with the same letter. Each player scores a point for every word, with a bonus point for any word that no one else has thought of. Allocate extra points for longer words, too.

Sample words

● Taught ● Taut ● Rear ● Roar ● Sees ● Sausages ● Mum ● Dad ● Trumpet

Zany verses

7+ A sheet of paper and a pencil for each player

This is a poetic variation of He Said, She Said, where some pretty strange tales are read out at the end of the game, much to the amusement of the players. Here the idea is the same, only the players have to write different verses of a poem.

One player decides how many lines there will be in each verse of a poem, and whether or not they should rhyme. Then each player writes an opening verse. The players swap papers, folding

the top over so that the next player cannot see what has been written. Each player might offer a verbal clue as to the subject of her poem to ensure that it makes some sense. For example, she might say, 'It is about being in the woods at night'. Alternatively, the players might say nothing and simply see what happens next! They complete a second verse, fold the paper once more and pass it on. Four or five verses should be enough before unfolding the sheets of paper and reading out each silly poem in turn.

Join up words

9+ A sheet of paper and a pencil for each player; an egg timer or a stopwatch

In this game, the children have to think of as many two-word combinations as they can that all start with the same word.

Call out a starter word and give the children five minutes to add other words, so making as many new combinations as they can. Give an example to start them off. At the end of the time each child reads out his answers and scores one point for every word combination that no one else has thought of. The person with the most points wins.

Good starter words

● Moon ● Flag ● Ice ● Bread ● Over ● Fire ● Train ● Sea ● Egg ● Bed ● Ring ● Shoe

Telegrams

7+ A sheet of paper and a pencil for each player; an egg timer or a stopwatch

Each child in this game has to make a sentence, where each new word begins with a specially chosen letter.

Each person in the game takes a turn to call out a letter, which every player writes down on the left side of his sheet of paper. This continues until the players have up to 15 letters written down in the same order in which they were given. With just one minute to play the game, each player must write down a 'telegram' or 'sentence', using the written-down letters – in the correct order – to start each new word. For example, if the letters were H, W, P, P, O, B, T, I, A, C, B, one telegram could be: Hugh was painting pictures of blue teapots in a cardboard box.

At the end of the minute, each player reads out his version to the others and the best one wins.

Use fewer letters for younger players – even three can make a sentence. For example, C, E, G could be: Cows Eat Grass.

MAPS, MAZES AND CODES

★Lion and tiger

6+ A sheet of paper; a pencil for each player; two coloured pencils (optional)

Draw a 25-dot grid, five dots across by five dots down.

Decide who is going to be the lion and who is going to be the tiger. Each player takes it in turns to join any two adjacent dots with a straight vertical or horizontal line, until one of them draws a line that completes a square. The person who forms the square puts her initial (L for Lion, T for Tiger) inside the 'box' and joins two dots somewhere else on the grid. If this line completes another box, she gets another turn. More squares are made as the game progresses and play continues until it is impossible to complete any more squares. The lion and the tiger count up how many squares they each have, and the winner is the one with the most.

For older children, make the grid larger.

Alphabet sentences

8+ A sheet of paper and a pencil

This is a game that gets harder as it progresses and will really test your children's verbal dexterity. The idea is to add a word to a sentence, where each word begins with a consecutive letter of the alphabet. There is always a very funny story to read out at the end of the game.

The first player starts writing a 'story' by putting down a word that begins with the letter 'a'. She could either use the article A, or find another word that begins with 'a', such as Alfred, Annie, armadillos, arms or angry. She then passes the paper to the other child to write a word that begins with the letter 'b', who then passes it back for her to write a word beginning with the letter 'c'. Play continues until the players have worked through the entire alphabet to make a reasonably coherent sentence.

For younger children, discard the difficult letters.

How many legs on the pub sign?

11+ A Pencil and paper for each child

Get the children to note down pub signs (each keeping to their own side of the road) and count up the number of legs. Set a time limit to prevent the children losing interest.

Agree in advance on values, for example:

George and Dragon – 10 (assume that George is on a horse)
●Coach and Horses – 18 (assume that there are four horses and one driver) ●Cricketers – 30 (13 players and two umpires)
●Swan – 2 (even if you can't see them because they're underwater) ●King's Arms or Queen's Head – 0
●Dog and Duck – 6

Limericks

8+ A sheet of paper and a pencil for each player and a timer.

Give the children the first line of a limerick, which they have to complete within five minutes (or less if they finish early). Try to avoid first lines that will obviously lead to rude verses.

Variations

● A quicker way to play this is for the children to complete the limerick out loud, taking it in turns to add lines.

● You could also ask the children to make up Haiku (17-syllable Japanese poems) on subjects that you give them or ones they come up with for themselves.

CARD GAMES FOR ONE

Dundee or Second Guess

5+ The aim is to turn over all 52 cards in a pack without predicting one correctly

Shuffle the cards and hold the shuffled deck face down.

Before turning over each card, the player must announce a rank of card out loud, for example, 'five'.

If the card revealed is anything except a five, the player then predicts the next card. (The only rule in Dundee is that no player may predict the same rank in consecutive turns.) However, if a five is revealed, the player's go comes to an immediate end.

The play continues in this way until the player either predicts a card correctly or gets through the entire deck.

In the two-person version of the game, each player keeps the cards they win so they can count them up at the end. When one player predicts correctly, it is the other player's turn.

Aces Up or Idiot's Delight

7+ The aim is to end up with just the four Aces left at the end of the game

Deal four cards face up on to a table from a shuffled deck. Hold the remaining cards face down in your hand.

If there are two cards of the same suit in the layout, the lower card is discarded. (Aces are high.)

Deal four more cards and discard as before. If there are any gaps in the layout, they can be filled with cards from other piles.

The game continues in this way, with cards discarded and replaced until either the cards are exhausted or the game becomes blocked.

Tip

If the game becomes blocked, younger players should be given one free move; in other words they are allowed to discard the lowest-ranked card in the layout irrespective of suit. If this doesn't get the game moving again, it's time to gather up the cards, shuffle and re-deal.

CARD GAMES FOR TWO

Card games for two people can be played by older children on the central arm rest or a cardboard box between them.

Beat My Neighbour Out Of Doors

or Jack Out Of Town, Strip Jack Naked, Beggar My Neighbour

6+ The aim of the game is to win all 52 cards and leave your opponent empty-handed

A standard 52-card deck is shuffled and dealt between the two players so that each has half the pack.

The players hold their cards in a face-down stack.

The non-dealer turns over the top card of his or her stack and places it between them.

The rank of card played determines how many cards the next player must lay. If the card was a numbered pip card, the second player need only lay one of his or her cards. However, if the card was a 'pay card' (that is to say, either an Ace or a court card), he or she must lay the following cards in compensation:

For an Ace – four pip cards • For a King – three pip cards • For a Queen – two pip cards • For a Jack – one pip card

When payment is complete, the player who laid the pay card collects up the cards from the waste pile and adds them to his or her hand. They then restart the play by laying another card between them as before.

Frequently, however, a player will turn up a pay card when they are in the midst of paying their opponent for a card. When this happens, the earlier pay card is void and the previously smug opponent must compensate the other player. For example, John puts down a King and Barry begins paying him, turning over a four, a five and then a Jack. The appearance of the Jack means that John must now compensate Barry by putting down one card. He plays a five and Barry collects the cards from the waste pile and restarts the game.

Jacks are the most valuable cards as they give you the chance to win the waste pile while offering only a minimal chance that your opponent will turn up a pay card in the midst of their compensation.

The winner is the player who collects all the cards, leaving their opponent with none. However, this situation can take hours, days or weeks to achieve. In many cases, it is the player who gives up last who wins the game by default!

War

6+ The aim is to win all your opponent's cards

Shuffle a standard 52-card pack and deal out all the cards between the two players. Players do not look at their cards, which are placed face down in a pack in front of them.

Both players simultaneously turn over the top card in their respective piles and place it face up between them.

The highest-rank card wins the hand and collects the cards, placing them face down at the bottom of his or her pack. Aces are high.

If the two cards played are of equal value, the two players must now go to War. They both now place the top cards of their packs face down between them. These cards are not revealed; instead, the players return to their packs and take the new top card, turning it over and placing it face up on the table.

Whoever plays the highest card wins the hand and collects all six cards from the middle of the table, which are placed face down at the bottom of his or her pack.

If, however, the turned-up cards are of equal value, the War continues. Each player puts down another face-down card before turning over the next card in their stack.

When a player run out of cards during a War, the game comes to an end and the other player is the winner.

QUIZ

1 Which celebrity chef changed school food in the UK?

2 Which king had 6 wives?

3 Which outlaw lived in Sherwood Forest with his merry men?

4 Name the character played by Johnny Depp in the 'Pirates of the Caribbean' films.

5 What sort of fish is Nemo in 'Finding Nemo'?

6 Name the world's highest mountain.

7 What is the name of Wallace's dog?

8 Where is the Statue of Liberty?

9 How are Declan Donnelly and Anthony McPartlin better known?

10 Which planet lost its status in 2006?

11 Name Peter Rabbit's sisters.

12 Where is the Kremlin?

13 Who wrote the 'His Dark Materials' trilogy?

14 Where does the Pope live?

15 What is Hagrid's first name?

16 What is the world's tallest waterfall?

17 Which sheep has his own TV series?

18 Where is Uluru (also known as Ayers Rock)?

19 Which of Dr Who's enemies use antigravity to get up and down stairs?

20 Where is the British National Space Centre?

21 What do Tracy Beaker and her friends call the Littlewood children's home?

22 Where are the pyramids?

23 What is the biggest passenger plane?

24 Who invented television?

25 What is the capital of China?

26 What is the usual speed limit on motorways in the UK?

27 Name the home of Scottish rugby.

28 What is the name of Fern's pig in 'Charlotte's Web'?

29 What is unusual about the Dead Sea?

30 What is a young frog called?

31 Where is the Taj Mahal?

32 Where was the FA Cup final played while Wembley Stadium was being rebuilt?

33 Name Comic Relief's fund-raising day.

34 Name the famous geyser in Yellowstone Park.

35 In which animals do the males give birth?

36 What is the capital of Germany?

37 Which 'Top Gear' presenter crashed a jet-powered car at 288 miles an hour?

38 What was Gollum's real name?

39 What does Willy Wonka's factory make?

40 What is the largest mammal?

MORE WORD GAMES

Incomplete sentences

10+

The children take turns to say a word each, but must not complete a sentence: each word must leave the possibility of the sentence being completed. The sillier it gets, the better. The one who accidentally finishes the sentence loses.

Variation

- All the words must start with the same letter that you have chosen.

I'm going on a trip to America...

6 +

Start the children off by saying, 'I'm going on a trip to America, and in my case I'm going to pack...' (something that begins with the letter A, so you might say, "an armadillo"). The next person continues by adding a word that starts with B: 'I'm going on a trip to America and in my case I'm going to pack an armadillo and a banana.' The sillier, the items, the better.

Variation

Choose any other destination in the world.

Daft definitions

10+

The children must suggest alternative definitions for English words. For example, 'mummify' could be 'to become a parent and 'disappointed' could be 'lost his job'. Start off by suggesting words to the children and let them come up with their own.

Variation

- English place-names can be a rich source of amusement in this game. For example, 'Hinckley' could be 'covered in hinckles', while 'Hassocks' might be 'but can't find her shoes'. This version can be played intermittently during a journey as you come across place-names on road signs.

Word against word

9+

Start the children off with one word, and then they take it in turns to come up with words that have no connection with the previous word. It is surprisingly difficult. The children can challenge each other if they think there is a link, whether

sensible or silly, so you may need to act as judge. Each round can last until the children run out of steam. Award points for correct challenges.

Number-plates

11+

Get your children to spot the last letter of number plates in alphabetical order. Whoever spots each one first gets a point and whoever gets most points wins. Remember that some letters, such as I, are not used.

Variation

- What country? Ask your children to look out for cars with stickers or number-plates that identify which country they're from and name the country. Each correct guess earns them a point, and they get bonuses if they can tell you anything about the country. Below is a list of the European codes, some of which will be easier to spot. A few regional ones are also included.

- A–Austria ● AL–Albania ● AND–Andorra
- B–Belgium ● BIH–Bosnia Herzegovina
- BY–Belarus ● CH–Switzerland
- CY–Cyprus ● Cymru–Wales ● CZ–Czech Republic ● D–Germany ● DK–Denmark
- E–Spain ● EST–Estonia ● F–France
- FIN–Finland ● FL–Liechtenstein
- GB–United Kingdom ● GBA–Alderney
- GBG–Guernsey ● GBJ–Jersey
- GBM–Isle of Man ● GE–Georgia
- GR–Greece ● H–Hungary ● HR–Croatia
- I–Italy ● IRL–Republic of Ireland
- IS–Iceland ● L–Luxembourg
- LT–Lithuania ● LV–Latvia ● M–Malta
- MC–Monaco ● MD–Moldova
- MK–Macedonia ● MNE–Montenegro
- N–Norway ● NL–Netherlands
- P–Portugal ● PL–Poland ● RO–Romania
- RSM–San Marino ● S–Sweden
- SRB–Serbia ● SCO–Scotland
- SK–Slovakia ● SLO–Slovenia ● TR–Turkey
- UA–Ukraine ● V–Vatican City

Quiz answers

1 Jamie Oliver
2 Henry VIII
3 Robin Hood
4 Jack Sparrow
5 Clown fish
6 Mt Everest
7 Gromit
8 Liberty Island, Stadium
9 Ant and Dec
10 Pluto
11 Flopsy, Mopsy and Cottontail
12 Moscow, Russia
13 Philip Pullman
14 Vatican City, in Rome
15 Rubeus
16 Angel Falls, Venezuela
17 Shaun
18 Near Alice Springs, Australia
19 Daleks
20 Leicester
21 Dumping Ground/DG
22 Giza, Egypt
23 Airbus A380
24 John Logie Baird
25 Beijing (or Peking) (in 1924)
26 70 miles an hour
27 Murrayfield
28 Wilbur
29 It is so salty that you float
30 Tadpole
31 Near Agra, India
32 The Millennium Stadium, Cardiff
33 Red Nose Day
34 Old Faithful
35 Seahorses and pipefish
36 Berlin
37 Richard
38 Smeagol
39 Sweets, chocolates especially
40 Blue whale

TRAVEL TRIVIA

Did you know?

→ The Channel tunnel is 31 miles or 51.5 km long

→ The United Kingdom touches 1 ocean (the Atlantic), 2 seas (the Irish and the North) and 4 channels (the English, the North, Bristol and St George's).

→ The total area of the United Kingdom is 94,526 square miles or 244,820 square km.

→ The shortest distance between Lands End and John o'Groats by road is 874 miles or 1,046.5 km.

→ Clapham Junction is Britain's busiest railway station.

→ Scotland's highest mountain is Ben Nevis at 4,406 feet or 1,343 metres.

→ Wales's highest mountain is Snowdon at 3,560 feet or 1,085 metres.

→ England's highest mountain is Scafell Pike at 2,308 feet or 978 metres.

→ Northern ireland's highest mountain is Slieve Donard at 2,786 feet or 849 metres.

→ Scotland has almost 800 islands.

→ The Severn is the longest river in Britain, at 220 miles or 354 km.

→ The highest main road is the A93 at Cairnwell Pass between Braemar and the Spittal of Glenshee.

→ Spaghetti Junction (J6 of the M6) is Britain's busiest road junction.

→ In the UK, the total length of all the roads and motorways is roughly 250,000 miles or 400,000 km.

→ London Heathrow is the world's busiest airport.

→ The first speed limit in the United Kingdom, introduced in 1861, was 10 mph. Four years later this was reduced to 2 mph in towns and 4 mph in the country. A man had to walk 60 yards in front of the vehicle with a red flag or lantern to warn other road users.

→ The London to Brighton Veteran Car Run commemorates the speed limit being raised to 14 mph in 1896.

→ The oddest roundabout is the Plough Roundabout in Hemel Hempstead, which has 6 mini roundabouts around the central one and a river running through the middle. It is also known as the Magic Roundabout.

→ The longest road bridge in the UK is the Tay Road Bridge at 1.4 miles or 2.25 km, while the longest rail bridge is the nearby Tay Bridge at 2.2 miles or 3.5 km.

→ The highest vertical cliff in the British Isles is St John's Head on Orkney at 1,134 feet or 346 metres.

→ The National Rail network is about 10,260 miles or 16,420 km long, not counting sidings, etc.

→ The tallest building in the UK is One Canada Square (Canary Wharf Tower) at 771 ft (235.1 m).

→ The first traffic light was installed in London in 1868 (it exploded the following year).

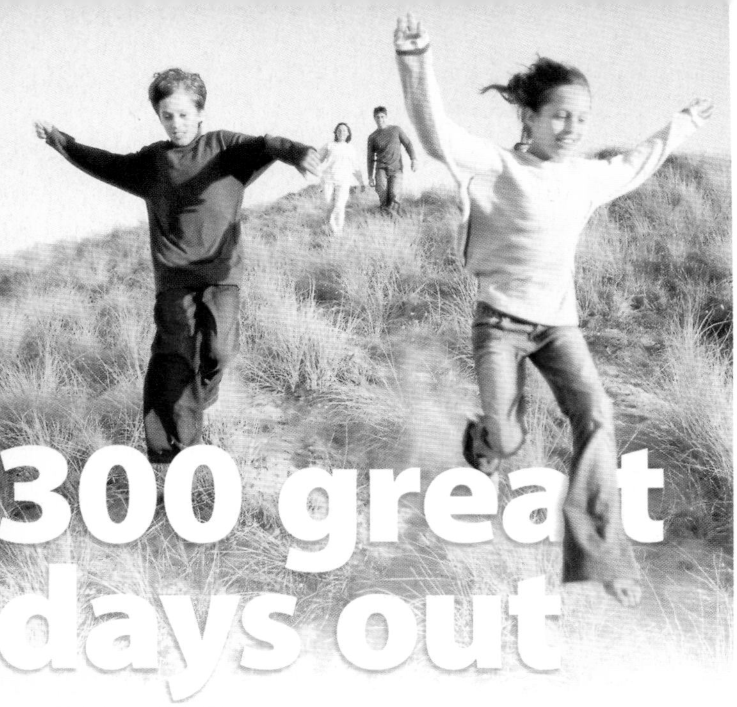

300 great days out

Key to symbols

£ Entrance fee
👪 Age range
🏃 Activity level
◐ Unusualness
🅿 Parking
🔥 Barbecue area
🍔 Burger bar
🍴 Cafe
☕ Coffee shop
🧺 Picnic area
🍺 Pub
✕ Restaurant
🥪 light snacks
🫖 tea shop

South West England

Avebury Stone Circle (EH/NT)
£ (circle) free (museum) adults £4.20, children £2.10, 2+2 £10.50 👪5+ 🏃🏃 ◐◐◐ ✕🧺🅿 public nearby

Avebury, Wiltshire Constructed 4000 years ago, originally using more than 180 stones and surrounding the village of the same name, with the Alexander Keiller Museum. Nearby are the West Kennet Avenue, West Kennet Long Barrow, Adam and Eve, the Sanctuary, Windmill Hill and Silbury Hill (all EH).
💻**www.nationaltrust.org.uk**
www.english-heritage.org.uk
☎**01672 539250** 25 C6

Avon Valley Country Park
£ adults £6.00 children (2–16) £5.50, seniors £5.50 👪2+ 🏃🏃🏃 ◐🍴🅿

Keynsham, Bath and NE Somerset Outdoor adventure playground, junior assault course, pets' corner, soft-play area, boating and places for fishing. Riverside trail, well marked with numbered signs providing information about the animals, birds and plants that can be seen along the way. ☎**0117 986 4929** 💻**www.avonvalleycountrypark.co.uk** 23 C8

Avon Valley Railway
£ (standard) adults £5.50, children (3–16) £4.00, seniors £4.50, 2+2 £15.00 👪3+ 🏃🏃 ◐◐🍴🅿

Bitton, S Gloucestershire Along former branch of old Midland Railway. Wide variety of mainline, industrial steam and diesel locomotives. ☎**0117 932 5538** 💻**www.avonvalleyrailway.co.uk** 23 B8

Beer Quarry Caves
£ adults £5.50, children (5–16) £3.95, seniors £3.95, 2+2 £16.50 👪5+ 🏃🏃🏃 ◐◐🥪🅿

Beer, Devon Caverns dating from Roman times in quarries that have provided stone for many cathedrals and important buildings. Guided tours (1hr) and exhibits. ☎**01297 680282** 💻**www.beerquarrycaves.fsnet.co.uk** 11 F7

Ben's Play World
£ adults £1.00, children (2–12) £4.50 (12+) £1.00 👪2–12 🏃🏃🏃 ◐🍴🅿

St Austell, Cornwall Adventure centre for younger children with tubes, slides, giant ballpond. 💻**www.bensplayworld.co.uk** ☎**01726 815553** 4 D5

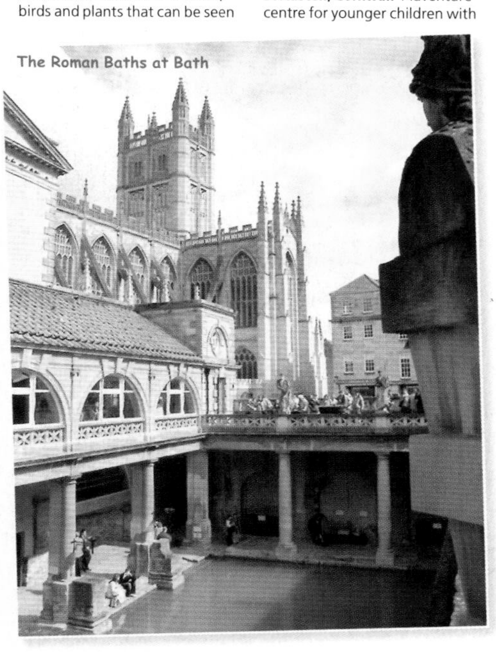

The Roman Baths at Bath

Birdland Park & Gardens
£ adults £5.25, children (4–14) £3.25, seniors £4.25, 2+2 £15.50 👪4+ 🏃🏃 ◐◐◐🍴🧺🅿 Nearby

Bourton-on-the-Water, Gloucestershire 2.8 ha (7 acres) inhabited by more than 500 birds, including flamingos, pelicans and penguins. Also tropical, temperate and desert houses. 💻**www.birdland.co.uk** ☎**01451 820480** 38 B1

Blue Reef Aquarium
£ adults £7.50, children (3–16) £5.50, seniors £6.50, 2+2 £21.99, 2+3 £25.99 👪3+ 🏃🏃 ◐🍴

Towan Parade, Newquay, Cornwall Underwater walk-through tunnels, open-top tanks, splash-pools and hands-on encounters with friendly rays. 💻**www.bluereefaquarium.co.uk** ☎**01637 838143** 4 C2

Bournemouth Oceanarium
£ adults 8, children 👪(3–15) £5.50, seniors £7.00, 2+1 £19.00, 2+2 £23.00, 2+3 £27.00 age 3+ 🏃🏃 ◐◐🍴

West Cliff Promenade, Bournemouth Ocean displays of climates and wildlife from around the world. ☎**01202 311993** 💻**www.oceanarium.co.uk** 13 E8

Brean Leisure Park
£ phone for details 👪7+ 🏃🏃 ◐✕🍴🍔🅿

Brean, Somerset Pool complex with four water shutes. Funfair. Theme park with 30 rides, roller coaster. ☎**01278 751595** 💻**www.brean.com** 22 D5

Bristol Zoo Gardens
£ adults £11.50, children (3–14) £7.25, seniors £10.00 2+2 £34.00 👪3+ 🏃🏃 ◐◐✕

Clifton, Bristol A large variety of animals including big cats, gorillas, reptiles, seals, penguins and other birds, monkeys, bugs, and bats, as well as a large aquarium. 💻**www.bristolzoo.org.uk** ☎**0117 974399** 23 B7

Brocklands Adventure Park
£ telephone for details 👪2+ 🏃🏃 ◐🍴🅿

Kilkhampton, Cornwall Adventure Park and wildlife centre. Two-seater super-carts, 'Supa Bouncer' for all ages, bumper-boats, train rides, pony rides, paddle boats, ride-on racing cars, crazy golf, trampolines and mini assault course. ☎**01288 321920** 💻**www.brocklands.com** 8 C4

Brokerswood Country Park
£ adults £3.00, children £2.50, seniors, £2.50 👪3+ 🏃🏃 ◐🍴🔥🧺🅿

Westbury, Wiltshire Set in remnant ancient forest, this park has a strong emphasis on conservation with a Woodland Heritage Centre, as well as amusements including a woodland railway, fishing, an undercover play area for toddlers and an adventure play area and play trails for older children. ☎**01373 822238** 💻**www.brokerswood.co.uk** 24 D3

Buckfast Butterflies and Dartmoor Otter Sanctuary
£ adults £6.50, children £4.95, seniors £5.95 👪3+ 🏃🏃 ◐◐🍴🅿

Buckfastleigh, Devon Tropical garden housing exotic butterflies and moths. Large landscaped otter enclosures. ☎**01364 642916** 💻**www.ottersandbutterflies.co.uk** 7 C5

Bush Farm Bison Centre
£ adults £5.50, children (4–16) £3.00 👪4+ 🏃🏃 ◐◐🅿

Mere, Wiltshire Herds of bison, wapiti and red deer. Gallery of North American wildlife and artefacts. ☎**01747 830263** 💻**www.bisonfarm.co.uk** 24 F3

Cattle Country Adventure Park
£ 5.50 👪2+ 🏃🏃 ◐◐✕🅿

Berkeley, Gloucestershire Large outdoor park and indoor slides, miniature railway, cattle, bison, miniature golf, pigs, toddler play area, zip wire and small animals. ☎**01453 810510** 💻**www.cattlecountry.co.uk** 36 E3

Charmouth Heritage Coast Centre
£ free, telephone for price of events 👪7+ 🏃🏃 ◐

Charmouth, Dorset Discover fossils with the centre's computers and displays and theatre (adults £1, children 50p) and displays. Guided walks and fossil weekends are among the events organized. ☎**01297 560772** 💻**www.charmouth.org** 11 E8

Cheddar Caves and Gorge
£ adults £14.00, children (5–15) £9.00, seniors £8, 2+3 £37.00 👪4+ 🏃🏃 ◐◐🍴🅿

Cheddar, Somerset Caves carved out by rivers over a million years. The show caves have massive stalactites and stalagmites, the Cheddar cannibal and Crystal Quest adventure. Rocksport adventure activities (age restictions apply). ☎**01934 742343** 💻**www.cheddarcaves.co.uk** 23 D6

Chedworth Roman Villa (NT)
£ adults £6.00, children £3.50, 2+2 £15.50 👪7+ 🏃🏃 ◐◐🧺🅿

Yanworth, Gloucestershire One of the largest Romano-British villas in the country. Walls and mosaics, bathhouses, hypocausts, water-shrine and latrine. Small museum. ☎**01242 890256** 💻**www.chedworthromanvilla.com** 37 C7

Coate Water Country Park
£ telephone for details 👪2+ 🏃🏃 ◐🍴🅿

Coate, Swindon, Swindon Two reservoirs, the smaller of which forms the heart of a nature reserve and SSSI with woodland and wildflower meadows. Facilities and activities on offer include pitch and putt, orienteering, fishing, cycle hire, mini golf, a paddling pool and birdwatching. Ranger centre. ☎**01793 490150** 💻**www.swindon.gov.uk/leisuresport/parksandgardens/leisureparkscoatewater.htm** 38 F1

Combe Martin Wildlife and Dinosaur Park
£ adults £12.00, children £7.00, seniors £8.00, 2+2 £34.00 👪4+ 🏃🏃 ◐◐🍴🅿

Combe Martin, Ilfracombe, Devon Safari park. 8-ha (20-acre) home to otters, gibbons, etc, with regular wildlife shows and animal handling sessions. Life-size dinosaur models including a 6.7-m (22-ft) Tyrannosaurus Rex. Train rides include an earthquake simulator. ☎**01271 882486** 💻**www.combemartinpark.co.uk** 20 E4

Cotswold Falconry Centre
£ adults £6.00, children £2.50, seniors £5.00 2+2 £15.00 👪5+ 🏃 ◐◐🥪🅿

Batsford Arboretum, Moreton-in-Marsh, Gloucs Breeding and conservation. Eagles, hawks, owls and falcons. 💻**www.cotswold-falconry.co.uk** ☎**01386 701043** 51 F6

Cotswold Water Park
£ telephone for details 👪3+ 🏃🏃 ◐✕🍴🧺🅿

South Cerney, Gloucestershire A vast complex of lakes created by gravel extraction. Activities on offer include walking, cycling, angling, sailing, canoeing, kayaking, horse riding, waterskiing, wind surfing and horse riding. Three of the lakes are designated nature reserves and have bird hides. The complex of parks includes Neigh Bridge Country Park and Keynes Country Park. ☎**01285 816459** 💻**www.waterpark.org** 37 E7

Court Farm Country Park
£ telephone for details 👪3+ 🏃🏃 ◐🫖🅿

Wolvershill Road, Banwell, North Somerset 2325 sq m (25,000 sq ft) of indoor play areas, outdoor play areas, hundreds of animals. ☎**01934 822282** 💻**www.courtfarmcountrypark.co.uk** 23 D5

Crealy Adventure Park
£ under 92 cm free, others £9.95, seniors £6.50 👪2+ 🏃🏃 ◐🍴🧺🅿

Clyst St Mary, Devon Rides including log flume and rollercoaster, go-karts, indoor adventure play centre, farm animals and parkland. ☎**01395 23320** 💻**www.crealy.co.uk** 10 E5

Crealy Great Adventure Park
£ under 92 cm free, others £9.95, seniors £6.50 👪2+ 🏃🏃 ◐🍴🧺🅿

Wadebridge, Cornwall Outdoor adventures, aerial walkways, slides, log flume, horses, farm animals and parkland. ☎**0870 1163333** 💻**www.crealy.co.uk** 4 C4

Cricket St Thomas Wildlife Park
£ adults £8.75, children (3–14) £6.50, seniors £7.50, 2+2–3 £27.00 👪3+ 🏃🏃 ◐🍺🍴🅿

Chard, Somerset Famous country estate where animals and birds live naturally. Safari trains and walks, play areas. ☎**01460 30111** 💻**www.cstwp.co.uk** 11 D8

Diggerland
£ £12.50, under-3s free, over-65s £6.25 👪3+ 🏃🏃 ◐◐◐🍴🅿

Verbeer Manor, Cullompton, Devon Adventure park with JCBs and dumper trucks. Age and height restrictions apply on some rides. ☎**0870 344437** 💻**www.diggerland.com** 10 D5

Durlston Country Park
£ up to £5.00 for parking 👪7+ 🏃🏃 ◐◐🍴🧺🅿

Swanage, Dorset Set in the beautiful Isle of Purbeck, a World Heritage Site, Durlston has 113 ha (280 acres) of spectacular countryside. There is a hugh variety of wildlife, including bottlenose dolphins offshore, large numbers of migrating birds and 34 species of butterfly. The visitor centre has video links to the seabird colonies. Guided walks with rangers, boat trips and way-marked trails. Visitor centre and shop. ☎**01929 424443** 💻**www.durlston.co.uk** 13 G8

Durrell Wildlife Conservation Trust
£ adults £11.50, children (4–16) £7.40, seniors £8.50, 2+2 £35.00 👪all ages 🏃🏃 ◐◐◐🍴🧺🅿

Trinity, Jersey Conservation zoo and breeding centre, specializing in some of the world's most endangered animals, including lemurs, giant rats, tamarins, gibbons, wolves, otters, orang-utan, gorillas, a wide variety of birds, snakes, iguanas, tortoises and frogs ☎**01534 860000** 💻**www.durrellwildlife.org** 17

Eden Project
£ adults £14, children (5–18) £5, seniors £10.00 👪5+ 🏃🏃 ◐◐✕🍴🅿

St Austell, Cornwall Specially created temperature- and humidity-controlled giant 'biomes' in a former china clay pit contain a wide range of plants and fauna from different world regions. This spectacular centre also has interactive displays celebrating the varied life on our planet. ☎**01726 811911** 💻**www.edenproject.com** 4 D5

Escot
£ adults £5.95, children (3–15) £4.95, seniors £4.95, 2+2 £18.50 👪3+ 🏃🏃 ◐◐✕🅿

Ottery St Mary, Devon Wild gardens in 101 ha (250 acres) of landscaped parkland. Has otters, wild boar and birds of prey, 3.2 ha (8 acres) of wetlands rich in wildlife, an aquatic and pet centre, a new maze and an adventure playground. ☎**01404 822188** 💻**www.escot-devon.co.uk** 11 E5

Exmoor Zoo
£ adults £7.50, children (3–15) £5.50, seniors £6.50 👪2+ 🏃 ◐🍴🧺🅿

Bratton Fleming, Devon More than 200 species of animals live in this popular zoo, including big cats, primates, wolves, otters and arctic foxes, as well as numerous small animals. Children's playground. ☎**01598 763352** 💻**www.exmoorzoo.co.uk** 21 E5

Fundays
£ adults, £1.00, under 1 £1.25, 1–3 £4.25, 4 and over, £4.75, seniors free 👪0–11 🏃🏃 ◐🍴🔥🅿

Bourton-on-the-Water, Gloucestershire Large indoor children's adventure playground with slides, soft play, ball pools, toddler play areas. ☎**01451 822999** 💻**www.fundaysplaybarn.com** 38 B1

Gus Gorilla's Jungle Playground
£ £3.95 👪0–12 🏃🏃 ◐🅿

Poole Adventure playground within Poole Park, Poole Spiral slides, aerial walkways, tube slides, Tarzan ropes, roller challenge, ball pool. Tiny tots area for smaller children (£2.50). Age/height restrictions apply to different areas. ☎**01202 717197** 💻**www.gusgorillas.co.uk** 13 E8

Hidden Valley Discovery Park
£ adults £4.95, children (5–15) £4.75, seniors £4.50 👪5+ 🏃🏃 ◐🍴🅿

Trethorne, Launceston, Cornwall Treasure hunt centre. Also a 9-hole golf course, nature reserve, farm animals, miniature railway and play area. Crystal Challenge and the Vault have age restrictions. ☎**01566 86463** 💻**www.hiddenvalleydiscoverypark.co.uk** 8 F4

Jurassic Coast
£ 👪3+ 🏃🏃 ◐◐◐

Exmouth, Devon to Swanage, Dorset The Jurassic Coast World Heritage Sites stretches from Orcombe Point in the west to Swanage (Dorset) in the east. It is an area rich in geology and wildlife and has some of the south coast's most spectacular scenery. Movements in the Earth's crust over millions of years mean that rock layers that originally formed on top of each other now lie side by side with the older rocks in the west and the younger in the

east, showing how the area's geology was formed. and, in some places, how it is being destroyed. Highlights include fossil-spotting at Charmouth, Kimmeridge Bay and Lyme Regis, the stark grandeur of Portland Bill, the beauty of Lulworth Cove and the dramatic coastal scenery of Ladram Bay, Durlston Head and Chesil Beach. There are also good beaches and walks. ⌨www.jurassiccoast.com **11 F7–12 G4**

Kent's Cavern
£ adults £7.00, children (3–15) £5.50, seniors £6.50, 2+2 £23.50
†ı†3+ 大大 ◑◐ ⑪ 🅿
Torquay, Torbay Prehistoric remains and the life of the Cavecian. Guided tours, woodland trail, children's activities. ☎01803 215136 ⌨www.kents-cavern.co.uk **7 C7**

Killarney Springs
£ telephone for details
†ı†5+ 大大大 ◑◐╳⑪🍴⇆🅿
Bude, Cornwall Adventure playground, boating lake, BMX track, basketball, fishing lake, white-water rapids, etc. ⌨www.killarneysprings.com ☎01288 331475 **8 C4**

Living Coasts
£ adults £6.75, children (3–15) £4.70, seniors £5.25, 2+2 £20.50
†ı†3+ 大大 ◑◐╳⑪🅿 public nearby
Torquay, Torbay Local and exotic marine wildlife, including seals and penguins. Opportunities to see the animals being fed. ☎01803 202470 ⌨www.livingcoasts.org.uk **7 C7**

Longleat
£ (passport tickets) adults £20.00, children (3–14) £16.00, seniors £16.00
†ı†all ages 大大大 ◑⑪🍴🅿
Warminster, Wiltshire Safari park with big cats, primates, sea lions and safari boats, and stately home. Adventure castle, miniature railways, butterfly gardens, world's longest hedge maze and pets' corner. See website for prices for individual attractions. ☎01985 844400 ⌨www.longleat.co.uk **24 E3**

Monkey Sanctuary
£ adults £6.00, children (5–16) £3.50, seniors £4.50 2+2 £16.00
†ı†5+ 大大大 ◑◐◑⑪🅿
Near Looe, Cornwall Rescue centre for monkeys and primates from all over the world. ⌨www.monkeysanctuary.org ☎01503 262532 **5 D7**

Moors Valley Country Park
£ up to £7.00 for parking
†ı†2+ 大大大 ◑╳🍴➡🅿
Ashley Heath, Dorset A 300-ha (750-acre) country park with a broad range of habitats and wildlife, a woodland adventure play area for older children, a castle and sand area for toddlers, a narrow-gauge steam railway and an 18-hole golf course. Miles of footpaths, way-marked trails and cycle trails allow visitors to explore much of the valley. Visitor centre, shop, wildlife events and cycle hire. Charges for railway, golf and cycle hire. ☎01425 470721 ⌨www.moors-valley.co.uk **14 D2**

National Marine Aquarium
£ Adults £9.50, children (4–15) £5.75, seniors £8.00 2+2 £27.00 †ı†4+ 大大大 ◑⑪🍴🅿 public nearby
Rope Walk, Coxside, Plymouth,, Plymouth Sharks, seahorses, deep reef displays, etc. The aquarium has created an offshore reef for animals to colonize by sinking the frigate Scylla. ⌨www.national-aquarium.co.uk ☎01752 600301 **6 D2**

National Seal Sanctuary
£ phone for details †ı†5+ 大大 ◑◐🅿
Gweek, Cornwall Britain's largest seal rescue facility where visitors can watch these delightful animals from above and under water. ☎01326 221361 ⌨www.sealsanctuary.co.uk **3 D6**

Newquay Zoo
£ adults £6.35, children (3–15) £4.15, seniors £5.25, 2+2 £17.35 †ı†3+ 大大大 ◑◐⑪🍴🅿
Edgecumbe Avenue, Newquay, Cornwall A wide range of exotic animals in lush surroundings. Tarzan trail, dragon maze and children's play area. ☎01637 873342 ⌨www.newquayzoo.co.uk **4 C3**

Paignton Zoo Environmental Park
£ adults £11.35, children (3–15) £7.60, seniors £9.35, 2+2 £34.10 †ı†3+ 大大大 ◑◐╳⑪🅿
Paignton, Torbay One of Britain's largest zoos, with more than 1,300 animals, and more than 300 species within 30 ha (75 acres). ☎01803 697500 ⌨www.paigntonzoo.org.uk **7 D6**

Peat Moors Visitor Centre
£ adults £2.95, children £2.45, seniors £2.45 2+2 £9.50
†ı†5+ 大大大 ◑◐╳⑪🍴🅿
Glastonbury, Somerset Reconstruction of Iron Age roundhouses, with regular craft demonstrations and hands-on wattle and daubing for children. ⌨www.somerset.gov.uk/somerset.cultureheritage/pmc ☎01458 860697 **23 E6**

Prinknash Bird and Deer Park
£ adults £5.00, children £3.50, seniors £4.50 †ı†3+ 大大大 ◑◐🦆🅿
Cranham, Gloucestershire Unusual birds from all over the world set in the grounds of Prinknash Abbey. Other animals include deer and African pygmy goats. ☎01452 812727 ⌨www.prinknash-bird-and-deer-park.com **37 C5**

Putlake Adventure Farm
£ adults £4.95, children (2+) £4.75, seniors £4.50 2+2 £18.50
†ı†2+ 大大大 ◑◐🅿
Langton Matravers, Dorset Lamb-feeding in season, picnic and play areas, farm trail, pony rides and trailer rides. Barn owls and ferret-racing. ☎01929 422917 ⌨www.putlakefarm.co.uk **13 G8**

Roman Baths, Pump Room and Baths Museum
£ adults £10.25–11.25, children (6–16) £6.50, seniors £8.75, 2+2–4 £29.00
†ı†5+ 大大大 ◑◐⑪
Abbey Churchyard, Bath, Bath & NE Somerset The baths, originally built in Roman times but with Georgian alterations, are fed by the only hot springs in Britain. The pump room is 18th-century and the museum contains finds from the baths and nearby. ⌨www.romanbaths.co.uk ☎01225 477785 **24 C2**

Seaquarium
£ adults £5.57, children £4.75, seniors £4.75 †ı†7+ 大大大 ◑🦆🅿
Marine Parade, Weston-super-Mare, North Somerset Set on its own pier, Seaquarium explores the marine life of the Severn Estuary and beyond, with displays ranging from starfish to sharks and rays to eels. ☎01934 613361 ⌨www.seaquarium weston.co.uk **22 C5**

Shaldon Wildlife Trust
£ adults £4.95, children £2.75, seniors £3.85, 2+2 £12.75 †ı†2+ 大大 ◑◐🅿
Shaldon, Devon A conservation

and breeding centre for many rare and endangered species, including butterflies, marmosets, tamarins, ocelots, lemurs, meerkats, capuchins, parrots and other birds and plenty of bugs, all set in lush gardens. ☎01626 872234 ⌨www.shaldonwildlifetrust.org.uk **7 B7**

Spirit of the West
£ adults £7.00, children £5.00, seniors £5.00, 2+2 £22.00 †ı†5+ 大大大 ◐🅿
Retallack, Winnard's Perch, near St Columb, Cornwall American themed park with silver mine and fort reconstructions. American town re-creations. (summer only) ☎01637 881160 ⌨www.wildwestthemepark.co.uk **4 C4**

Springfields Fun Park and Pony Centre
£ adults £7.20, children (2–14) £6.20, seniors £5.20, 2+2 £24.00
†ı†2+ 大大大 ◑◐🍴🅿
Near Newquay, Cornwall Large all-weather family fun centre. Pony rides and farm animals. ☎01637 881224 ⌨www.springfieldsponycentre.co.uk **4 C4**

Stonehenge (EH/NT)
£ adults £5.90, children (5–15) £3.00, seniors £4.40, 2+2–3 £14.80
†ı†5+ 大大大 ◑◐🅿
Near Amesbury, Wiltshire The great ancient stone circle of Stonehenge stands at the centre of an extensive prehistoric landscape (NT) filled with the remains of ceremonial and domestic structures and dotted with round barrows. Nearby are the remains of the Neolithic Woodhenge (EH) and Durrington Walls, recently excavated to reveal the settlement where the builders of the circles may have lived. ☎01980 624715 ⌨www.english-heritage.org.uk www.nationaltrust.org.uk **25 E6**

The Flambards Experience
£ (3–10 years) £8.25, (11 +) £12.95, seniors £6.95 2+2 £41.00
†ı†3+ 大大大 ◑⑪🅿
Helston, Cornwall Re-creation of Victorian and war-time street. Theme park with thrill rides including log flume and rollercoasters. Age/height restrictions apply on some rides. ⌨www.flambards-experience.com ☎0845 60186843 **D5**

The Milky Way Adventure Park
£ under-3s free, under 1.2m £8.00, over 1.2m £9.00, seniors £6.00
†ı†3+ 大大大 ◑◐⑪🍴🅿
Clovelly, Devon Space-themed rides, adventure play area, archery, golf driving, railway, bird and sheep-dog displays. ☎01237 431255 ⌨www.themilkyway.co.uk **8 B5**

The World of Country Life
£ adults £9.00, children (£-17) £7.50, seniors £7.50, 2+2 £30.00
†ı†4+ 大大大 ◑◐🅿
Exmouth, Devon Falconry displays, deer park safari, farm centre, pets centre and nursery. Historical exhibits and play areas. ☎01395 274533 ⌨www.worldofcountrylife.co.uk **11 F5**

Tropiquaria Animal and Adventure Park
£ adults £7.00, children £6.00, seniors £6.00 †ı†3+ 大大大 ◑⑪🍴🅿
Washford, Minehead, Somerset Indoor tropical rain forests. Exotic creatures, farm animals, pirate ship adventure playground, puppets, trampolines, etc. ☎01984 640688 ⌨www.tropiquaria.co.uk **22 E2**

Watermouth Castle and Family Theme Park
£ adults £1.50, children (3–13) £9.00, seniors £7.50 †ı†3+ 大大大 ◑◐🍴🅿
Near Ilfracombe, Devon Rides, adventure playground, mini golf, mazes, model railway, tube slides, crazy snooker, Gnomeland and swing boats. Age and height restrictions apply on some rides.

⌨www.watermouthcastle.com ☎01271 867474 **20 E4**

West Somerset Railway
£ (day rover) adults £13.00, children (5–15) £6.50, seniors £11.20, 2+2–4 £32.70 †ı†5+ 大大 🅿
Minehead, Somerset Britain's longest steam railway. Check website or telephone for details of catering. ☎01643 704996 ⌨www.west-somerset-railway.co.uk **21 E8**

Weymouth Sea Life Park
£ telephone for details
†ı†3+ 大大大 ◑⑪
Lodmoor Country Park, Weymouth, Dorset Seal sanctuary, tropical shark nursery, turtle sanctuary, seahorses, Humboldt penguins, stingrays and otter centre and splash pool, all set in a large park. ☎01305 788255 ⌨www.sealifeeurope.com/ukweymouth/home.htm **12 F4**

Wookey Hole
£ adults £12.50, children (3–14) £9.50, seniors £9.50, 2+2 £38.00 †ı†3+ 大大大 ◑◐⑪🍴🅿
Wookey Hole, Somerset Spectacular caves and legendary home of the witch of Wookey. ☎01749 672243 ⌨www.wookey.co.uk **23 E7**

World in Miniature
£ adults £6.50, children (2–14) £5.00, seniors £5.25, 2+2 21.00 †ı†2+ 大大大 ◑⑪🅿
Goonhavern, Cornwall Miniature versions of the world's landmarks, children's play area, Jurassic Trail. ☎01872 572828, 0870 4584433 ⌨www.worldinminiature.co.uk **4 D2**

▲The Eden Project

London and the South East

Birdworld and Underwater World
£ adults £11.95, children (3–14) £9.95, seniors £9.95, 2+2 £39.95 †ı†all ages 大大 ◑◐╳🅿
Holt Pound, Farnham, Hampshire A mixed zoo, with hundreds of birds, including penguins, vultures, emus and cranes, set in 26 acres of beautiful parkland and gardens. In Underwater World, attractions include a swamp with crocodiles, alligators and caimen, and other marine animals from tropical waters around the world. Jenny Wren Farm has a range of domestic animals including turkeys, cattle and sheep, as well as small pets. ☎01420 22140 ⌨www.birdworld.co.uk **00 A0**

Bletchley Park
£ adults £10.00, children (12–16) £6.00, seniors £8.00m 2+2 £22.50 †ı†12+ 大大大 ◑◐╳⑪🅿
The Mansion, Bletchley Park, Milton Keynes The home of British code-breaking during World War II, with displays including Enigma Machines, spies and spying, a wartime mini cinema, working computers, wartime toys, the Victorian mansion and a playground within the extensive parkland. ☎01908 640404 ⌨www.bletchleypark.org.uk **53 F6**

Bodiham Castle (NT)
£ adults £4.50, children £2.20, 2+2 £11.35
大大大 ◑◐◑🏰➡🅿
Bodiam, nr Robertsbridge, East Sussex Set in beautiful countryside and lying within its defensive moat, Bodiam is one of the most stunning medieval castles in Britain. There are medieval battlements, ramparts, spiral staircases, a gateway and a moat to explore, and plenty of space to let off steam. Guided tours. ☎01580 830436 ⌨www.nationaltrust.org.uk **18 C4**

British Museum
£ free †ı†5+ 大大大 ◑◐╳🍴➡
Great Russell Street, London Britain's premier ethnographic museum, with items from all of the world's major cultures and historical peoples, including a mummy gallery, exhibits on the Romans and ancient Greeks, Iron Age and Saxon Britain, including Lindow Man, a body preserved for thousands of years in a peat bog, the Mildenhall treasure. ☎020 7323 8299 ⌨www.thebritishmuseum.ac.uk **41 D6**

Chessington World of Adventures
£ adults 29.00, (1 m-12 years) £19.00, seniors 22.00, 2+2 £74.00 †ı†all ages 大大大 ◑◐⑪🍴🅿
Chessington, London The rides are divided by age group: mini adventures for toddlers, junior adventures for all the family and experienced adventures for older children and adults. Height and age restrictions apply on some rides. Attractions include Dragon's Playhouse, Sea Dragons, Sir Walter Squirtalot, a Carousel, Tiny Truckers, Bash Street Bus, Dennis's Madhouse, Canopy Capers, Rameses Revenge and Griffen's Galleon. There is also the world-famous children's zoo. ☎0870 999 0045 ⌨www.chessington.co.uk **28 C2**

Chiltern Open Air Museum
£ adults £7.50, children (5–16) £4.50, seniors £6.50, 2+2 £21.50 †ı†6+ 大大大 ◑◐🅿
Gorelands Lane, Chalfont St. Giles, Bucks Open-air museum, set in 45 acres of woods and parkland, with more than 30 historic buildings rescued from the local area to explore and learn about how they were built and how people lived in them. Victorian farmyard. ☎01494 871117 ⌨www.ww.coam.org.uk **40 E3**

Cotswold Wildlife Park
£ adults 9.50, children 7, seniors 7 †ı†7+ 大大大 ◑◐╳🅿
Burford, Oxfordshire Cotswold Wildlife Park is set in 160 acres of parkland and gardens around a listed Victorian Manor House. Among the animals here are rhinos, marmosets, big cats, exotic birds, reptiles, bugs and camels, many of which are endangered in the wild. ☎01993 823006 ⌨www.cotswoldwildlifepark.co.uk **38 D2**

Diggerland
£ £12.50, under-3s free, over-65s £6.25
†ı†3+ 大大大 ◑◐🅿
Roman Way, Medway Valley Leisure Park, Strood, Medway Adventure park with JCBs and dumper trucks. Age and height restrictions apply on some rides. Off junction 2 of the M2. ☎0870 344437 ⌨www.diggerland.com **29 C8**

Dinosaur Isle
£ adults £4.85, children (3–15) £2.85, seniors £3.60, 2+2 £13.50 †ı†3+ 大大大 ◑◐🅿
Culver Parade, Sandown, Isle of Wight A purpose-built interactive museum, Dinosaur Isle is built in the shape of a giant pterodactyl and houses the rich fossil collection of one of the best areas for dinosaurs in the British Isles, as well as full-size dinosaur models, reconstructed skeletons, an animatronic, and displays on the geology of the island. Visitors experience the world at the time of the dinosaurs through sight, sound and smell. Guided dinosaur walks are also available. ☎01983 404344 ⌨www.dinosaurisle.com **15 F7**

▼Dover Castle

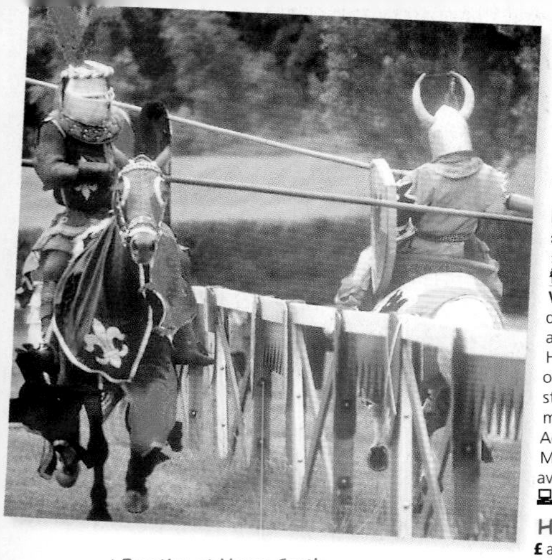

▲Jousting at Hever Castle

Dover Castle and Hellfire Corner (EH)
£ adults £9.80, children £4.90, seniors £7.40, 2+2 £24.50 👪5+ 🚶🚶🚶 ◐◐◐✕🍴🧺🅿
Dover, Kent Sited at a strategic point overlooking the narrowest stretch of the English Channel, the current castle was begun in Anglo Saxon times, and strengthened by William the Conqueror, Henry II and Henry VIII. The secret tunnels under the castle were begun in the early 19th century. Visitors can explore Winston Churchill's wartime Command Centre as well as the 1216 Siege Experience and Henry VIII's fortress. The Princess of Wales' Royal Regimental Museum and a Saxon church are also on the site. ☎**01304 211067** 💻**www.english-heritage.org.uk** 31 E7

Drusillas Park
£ adults £12.95, children (2–12) £11.95, seniors £12.95, 2+2 £47.80 👪all ages 🚶🚶🚶 ◐◐✕🍴🅿
Alfriston, East Sussex As well as hundreds of animals, Drusillas Playland has rides and activities including a shooting gallery, adventure golf, discovery centre, Thomas the Tank Engine, toddler village, under 6s play area, and a dino dig. ☎**01323 874100** 💻**www.drusillas.co.uk** 18 E2

Fishbourne Palace
£ adults £6.80, children (5–15) £3.60, seniors £5.80, 2+2 £17.40 👪6+ 🚶🚶🚶 ◐◐◐🍴🅿
Fishbourne, West Sussex This magnificent Roman palace was discovered by accident in 1960. Finds from the site are housed in the museum and the remains of the north wing of the palace are open to the public so that their magnificent frescoes can be seen. The garden is planted as it would have been in the Roman period. ☎**01243 785859** 💻**www.sussexpast.co.uk** 16 D2

Fort Victoria
£ (aquarium) adults £2.50, children (5–15) £1.50, seniors £2.20, 2+2 £7.00 (planetarium) adults £4.00, children (5–15) £2.00, seniors £3.50, 2+2 £11.00 👪7+ 🚶🚶🚶 ◐◐🧺🅿
Yarmouth, Isle of Wight Fort Victoria Country Park is home to a marine aquarium that concentrates mainly on the sea life of the area, such as sponges, cuttlefish, dogfish rays, conger eels and sea anemones, as well as a small display of a tropical reef. It also houses a planetarium that has regular shows. The park offers large areas of park, seashore and woodlandin which to ramble. ☎**01983 76086** 💻**www.fortvictoria.co.uk** 14 F4

Hever Castle
£ adults £10.50, children (5–15) £5.70, seniors £8.80, 2+2 £26.70 👪5+ 🚶🚶🚶 ◐◐✕🍴🧺🅿
Edenbridge, Kent As well as the beautiful gardens and the castle, in which Henry VIII's second wife Anne Boleyn grew up, there is an adventure playground, rowing boats to hire, a yew maze, a water maze and miniature model houses exhibition. ☎**01732 865224** 💻**www.hever-castle.co.uk** 29 E5

Historic Dockyard, Chatham
£ adults £12.50, children (5–15) £7.50, seniors £10.00, 2+2 £32.50 👪7+ 🚶🚶🚶 ◐◐✕🍴🧺🅿
Chatham, Medway Royal dockyard with more than 400 years of history. Attractions include historic warships including HMS Gannet, a Victorian naval sloop, exhibitions, historic buildings and a working ropewalk. This 80-acre site is the best-preserved dockyard from before the age of steam in the world. ☎**(0)1732 865224** 💻**www.chdt.org.uk** 29 C8

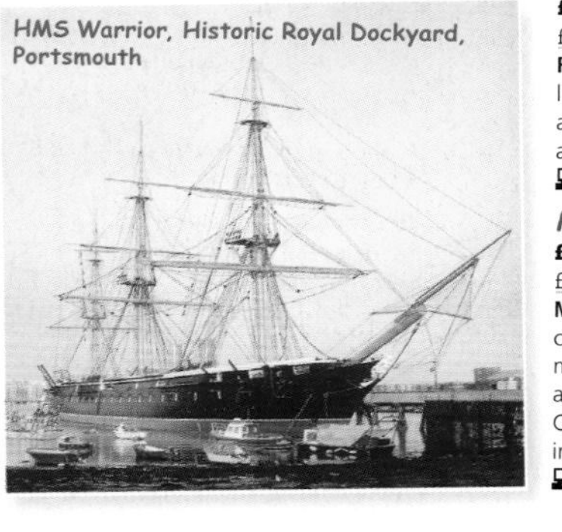

HMS Warrior, Historic Royal Dockyard, Portsmouth

Historic Royal Dockyard
£ (all inclusive ticket) adults £16.50, children (5–15) £12.00, seniors £14.00, 2+2–3 £48.00 👪3+ 🚶🚶🚶 ◐◐🍴
Victory Gate, Portsmouth The former royal dockyards have a wealth of ships from different ages, including HMS Victory, the remains of Henry III's Mary Rose and HMS Warrior. Many of the Georgian dockyard buildings, such as store houses, rope houses and officers' accommodation, survive and house attractions such as Action Stations, Dockyard Apprentice and the Mary Rose Experience. Harbour tours are also available. ☎**023 9283 9766** 💻**www.flagship.org.uk** 15 D7

HMS Belfast
£ adults £9.95, children (under 16) free, seniors £6.15 🚶🚶🚶 ◐◐◐✕🍴🅿
Morgan's Lane, Tooley Street, London A 1930s 6-in, 16-gun cruiser, which took part in many hazardous operations during World War II and also saw service during the Korean War. The ship has been preserved more or less as she was when she last saw service in the late 1960s and it is possible to explore her from the gunwhales to the bridge. ☎**0207 940 6300** 💻**http://hmsbelfast.iwm.org.uk** 41 F6

Howletts Wild Animal Park
£ adults £13.95, children (4–16) £10.95, seniors £11.95, 2+2 £42.00 👪4+ 🚶🚶🚶 ◐◐◐✕🅿
Bekesbourne, Canterbury, Kent Among the stunning array of animals here are elephants, primates, wild dogs, deer and antelope, big cats such as tigers and leopards, tapirs, wolves, rhinos, capybara, bison, anteaters and honey badgers, ☎**01227 721 286** 💻**www.portlympne.co.uk** 31 D5

Intech Science Technology Centre, nr Winchester
£ adults £ 6.75, children (3–14) £ 4.50, seniors £ 5.25, 2+2 £20.25 👪3+ 🚶🚶 ◐◐◐🍴🧺🅿
Morn Hill, Winchester, Hampshire A hands-on science and technology centre which allows children and adults alike to learn about the world around them through 100 often amusing interactive exhibits including being able to slow down a tornado, bend light, and work out how much energy it takes to power a light bulb. ☎**01962 863791** 💻**www.intech-uk.com** 15 B6

Leeds Castle
£ adults £14.00, children (4–15) £8.50, seniors £11.00 👪all ages 🚶🚶🚶 ◐◐✕🧺🅿
Maidstone, Kent One of the most beautiful castles in the world, Leeds was begun in the Norman period and altered repeatedly over its 900-year history. As well as the castle itself, attractions include the large parkland, the gardens, the aviary, falconry displays, a museum devoted to dog collars, two mazes and a grotto, vineyards, a duckery, and a pay-and-play golf course. ☎**1622 76540** 💻**www.leeds-castle.com** 30 D2

Legoland
£ adults £3.001, children £24.00, seniors £24.00 👪all ages 🚶🚶🚶 ◐◐◐✕🍴▭🅿
South of Windsor, off B3022 , Windsor Theme park with models made of Lego bricks, including city scapes of many of the world's capitals, as well as other attractions and activities including a wet play area, climbing frames, panning for gold, train rides, a ferris wheel, enchanted forest and a carousel. ☎**08705 04 04 04** 💻**www.legoland.co.uk** 27 B7

London Aquarium
£ adults (18+) £13.25, children (3–14) £9.75, (15–17) £11.25, seniors £11.25, 2+2 £44.00 👪3+ 🚶🚶🚶 ◐◐
Westminster Bridge Road, London Large aquarium with double-height tanks containing fish from both British and tropical waters, including sharks, rays, cod, mud skippers, piranhas and jacks. Touch pool. ☎**020 7967 8000** 💻**www.londonaquarium.co.uk** 28 B4

London Zoo
£ adults £16.00, children (3–15) £12.50, seniors £14.50, 2+2 £51.50 👪all ages 🚶🚶🚶 ◐◐◐🍴🅿£10.00
Regent's Park, London One of Britain's premier wildlife attractions, this important conservation zoo has a wide range of rare and endangered animals from all over the world. ☎**020 7722 3333** 💻**www.zsl.org/zsl-london-zoo** 41 F5

Madame Tussauds
£ adults £25.00, children £21.00, seniors £25.00, 2+2 £78.00 👪8+ 🚶 ◐◐◐🍴
Marylebone Road, London Wax models of current celebrities, such as footballers, pop stars and actors, many of which are interactive. The Stardome has an animated show called the Wonderful World of Stars. Chamber Live is not suitable for under-13s. Booking in advance is recommended. ☎**0870 999 0293** 💻**www.madame-tussauds.co.uk** 41 F5

Marwell Zoological Park
£ adults £14.25. children (3–16 years) £10.25, seniors £12.25, 2+2 £46.00 👪all ages 🚶🚶🚶 ◐◐🍴🧺🅿
Colden Common, Winchester, Hampshire Animals in the zoo include lemurs, penguins, giraffes, many species of bird. The animals can be viewed either on foot or from road and rail trains. Adventure playground. ☎**01962 777407** 💻**www.marwell.org.uk** 15 B6

National Motor Museum, Beaulieu
£ (entire estate) £ adults £14.75, (13–17) £8.75, children (5–12) £7.75, seniors £13.75, 2+2–3 £40.50 👪5+ 🚶🚶🚶 ◐◐🍴🅿
Beaulieu, Hampshire The collection comprises some 250 vehicles, from very early motors to world-record breakers like Golden Arrow and Bluebird. The museum is in the grounds of the Beaulieu estate, together with the palace, abbey and monorail train. For entry fees for individual attractions telephone for details. ☎**01590 612345** 💻**www.beaulieu.co.uk** 14 D4

Natural History Museum
£ free 👪3+ 🚶🚶🚶 ◐◐◐ ✕🍴🧺☕
Cromwell Road, London This museum's vast collections cover the entire history of the Earth and the life that inhabits it. Favourites include the dinosaur models, fossils, the blue whale skeleton and an earthquake simulator. ☎**0207 942 5000** 💻**www.nhm.ac.uk** 28 B3

Odds Farm Park
£ adults £6.95, children (2–16) £5.95, seniors £5.95 👪all ages 🚶🚶 ◐🅿
Wooburn Green, Buckinghamshire Farm-based attraction with the usual farmyard animals, such as goats, cows and pigs, together with rabbits, birds of prey, lamb-feeding (in season), play barn and soft play areas, ☎**01628 520188** 💻**www.oddsfarm.co.uk** 40 F2

Port Lympne Wild Animal Park and Gardens
£ adults £13.95, children (4–16) 10.95, seniors £11.95, 2 +2 £42.00 👪all ages 🚶🚶🚶 ◐◐✕🅿
Port Lympne,nr Hythe, Kent Animals in this large park include elephants, bison, wild dogs, deer and antelopes, big cats, primates, rhinos, waterbuck, tapirs, meerkats, ostrichs, Przewalski's horse, red panda and giraffe. ☎**01303 264 647** 💻**www.portlympne.co.uk** 19 B8

Royal Air Force Museum, London
£ free 👪8+ 🚶🚶 ◐◐◐ 🍴🧺
Grahame Park Way, Hendon, London Aircraft and exhibits collection with a wide range of equipment and items from all stages of aviation history, especially that of the Royal Air Force. There are more than 200 aircraft in the collection, as well as examples of hundreds of engines from the 1930s onwards, a wide range of support vehicles and weapons, as well as two flight simulators (£2.50). ☎**0208 205 2266** 💻**www.rafmuseum.org.uk** 41 F5

Science Museum
£ free 👪3+ 🚶🚶🚶 ◐◐◐✕🍴🧺
Exhibition Road, London Founded in 1857 with objects shown at the Great Exhibition held in the Crystal Palace, the Science Museum has renowned historic collections of objects relating to every aspect of science and technology, ranging from early trains to space exploration. Many of the exhibitions are hands-on. Charges apply for the Imax cinema and some exhibitions and simulators. ☎**0870 870 486** 💻**www.sciencemuseum.org.uk** 28 B3

Sea Life Aquarium, Brighton
£ telephone for details 👪5+ 🚶🚶🚶 ◐◐◐🍴🅿public
Marine Parade, Brighton Aquarium with displays of more than 50 species of fish, mainly from British waters. ☎**01273 604234** 💻**www.sealifeeurope.com** 47 B4

The Observatory Science Centre
£ adults £7.48, children (4–15) £5.50, seniors £5.78, 2+2 £25.74 👪4+ ◐◐◐🍴🧺🅿
Herstmonceux Castle, Wartling Rd, Herstmonceux, East Sussex Based in the telescope domes of the former observatory, this is an interactive centre with clear demonstrations that allow children to explore the universe around us in themed areas on force and gravity, time, Earth and optics. ☎**01323 832731** 💻**www.the-observatory.org** 18 D3

Thorpe Park
£ adults £32.00, children (1m-11 years) £20, seniors £20, 2+2 £88.00 👪all ages 🚶🚶🚶 ◐🍴🅿
Chertsey, Surrey The rides include Stealth, Colossus, Detonator, Nemesis Inferno, Quantum, Rush, Samurai, Salmmer, Tidal Wave and Vortex, Canada Creek Railway Station, Chief Ranger's Carousel, Flying Fish, Depth Charge, Ligger's Leap, Rocky Express and Storm in a Teacup. Minimum heights apply on many rides. ☎**0870 444 44** 💻**www.thorpepark.com** 27 C8

Underwater World, Hastings
£ adults, £6.60, children £4.60, seniors £5.60, 2+2 £19.50 👪all ages 🚶🚶🚶 ◐◐ ☕ 🅿public nearby
Rock-a-Nore Road, Hastings, East Sussex Marine aquarium devoted to the species of fish found in British waters. ☎**01424 444412.** 💻**www.discoverhastings.co.uk** 18 E5

Weald and Downland Open Air Museum
£ adults £8.25, children (5–15) £4.40, seniors £7.25, 2+2–3 £22.65 👪5+ 🚶🚶🚶 ◐◐▦🅿
Singleton, West Sussex A collection of almost 50 historic buildings rescued from demolition, dating back to between the 13th and 19th centuries. They include farmhouses, a market hall, a medieval shop, a Victorian School, barns and a granary. The interiors of several have also been restored, allowing a glimpse of how people lived and worked in them. The water mill operates daily, and still produces flour. There are regular demonstrations of craft skills and daily guided tours. ☎**01243 811363** 💻**www.wealddown.co.uk** 16 C2

West Wycombe Caves
£ adults £5.00, children £4.00, seniors £4.00, 2+2 £15.00 👪10+ 🚶🚶 ◐◐🍴🅿
West Wycombe, Buckinghamshire The caves consist of almost a mile of underground passages with figures depicting the life and times of the the members of the Hellfire Club. The caves were dug by hand as an enormous underground folly. An audio commentary guides visitors through the cave system. ☎**01494 533739** 💻**www.hellfirecaves.co.uk** 39 E8

Windsor Castle
£ adults £14.20, children (5–16) £8.00, seniors £12.70, 2+3 £36.50 👪5+ 🚶 ◐◐◐
Windsor, Windsor and Maidenhead Windsor Castle is the oldest and largest occupied castle in the world, with parts dating back to the time of William the Conqueror and added to over the succeeding 940 years. St George's Chapel is home to the Knights of the Garter and is the burial place of 10 monarchs. ☎**(+44) 020 7766 7304** 💻**www.royalcollection.org.uk** 27 B7

East of England

Amazonia
£ telephone for details 👪7+ 🚶🚶 ◐◐◐🍴
Marine Parade, Great Yarmouth, Norfolk The largest collection of reptiles in Britain, including a giant tortoise, pythons, turtles, iguanas, bearded dragon, an alligator and more than 50 other species. ☎**01493 842202** 💻**www.amazonia-worldofreptiles.net/home.htm** 69 D8

Banham Zoo
£ adults £11.95, children (3+) £7.95, seniors £10.95 👪3+ 🚶🚶🚶 ◐◐🍴🅿
Banham, Norfolk Lions, cheetahs, zebras, giraffes and buffalo, striped hyenas, bat-eared fox, fennec fox and lemurs. Other attractions include a safari road-train, bird of prey displays, play area, animal encounters and crazy golf. ☎**01953 887771** 💻**www.banhamzoo.co.uk** 68 F3

Barleylands Farm Museum and Visitors Centre
£ £4.00 👪3+ 🚶🚶 ◐◐🧺🅿
Billericay, Essex Farm animals, horses, chick hatchery, honey bees, duck pond, adventure play area, farming museum, steam engines, glass-blowing and blacksmith. Adventure playground. ☎**01268 290229** 💻**www.barleylands.co.uk** 42 E2

Colchester Castle and Museum
£ adults £5.10, children (5–15) £3.30, seniors £3.30 👪5+ 🚶🚶 ◐◐🧺🅿public nearby
Castle Park, High Street, Colchester, Essex Largest Norman keep in Europe. The museum's archaeological collections go back to the Romans. ☎**01206 282939** 💻**www.colchestermuseums.org.uk** 43 B6

Colchester Zoo
£ adults £13.99, children (3–14) £7.75, seniors £9.99 👪7+ 🚶🚶🚶 ◐◐◐🍴☕▭🅿
Colchester, Essex Interactive zoo with animals including elephants, snakes, leopards, chimpanzees, reptiles, monkeys, zebra, lemurs, lions, tigers, llamas, rhinos, warthogs, hyenas and birds of prey. ☎**01206 331292** 💻**www.colchesterzoo.com** 43 B5

Dinosaur Adventure Park
£ adults £8.95, children (3+) £7.95, seniors £7.95 👪3+ 🚶🚶🚶 ◐◐◐🍴🅿
Lenwade, Norfolk Theme park with dinosaur trail, Neanderthal walk, adventure playground, assault course and raptor races. ☎**01603 876210** 💻**www.dinosauradventure.co.uk** 68 C4

Easton Farm Park
£ adults £6.25, children (1–16) £4.75, seniors £5.75, 2+2 £20.00 👪1+ 🚶🚶🚶 ◐◐🍴🅿
Wickham Market, Suffolk Victorian model farm buildings, farm animals, dairy centre, pig races, cart horses, pony and cart rides, barrel train and train rides, working blacksmith's forge, pets' paddock and children's battery-operated tractors. Play barn. ☎**01728 746475** 💻**www.eastonfarmpark.co.uk** 57 D6

EcoTech
£ adults £5.00, children £3.00, seniors £4.00, 2+2 £15.00
7+
Turbine Way, Swaffham, Norfolk Environmental discovery centre, includes some of the UK's largest wind turbines, which members of the public can climb. Sensory displays and a soft play area for toddlers. Advance booking advisable.
01760 726100 **www.ecotech.org.uk** **67 D8**

Flag Fen Bronze Age Centre
£ adults £5.50, children £4.15, seniors £4.95, 2+2–3 £15.15
The Droveway, Northey Road,, Peterborough Two miles east of central Peterborough, Flag Fen is a working archaeological site dedicated to the excavation and preservation of an ancient site where people lived and worshipped over 4,000 years ago. As well as the dig itself, visitors can see the preserved timbers, the bronze museum, the heritage centre and reconstructions of Bronze Age and Iron Age roundhouses and part of a Roman road. **01733 313414** **www.flagfen.com** **66 E2**

Fritton Lake Countryworld
£ adults £6.70, children (3–15) £4.60, seniors £5.60 7+
Great Yarmouth, Norfolk Gardens and woodland walks, part of the Somerleyton Hall estate, boating on the lake, falconry centre, heavy horses, putting and 9-hole golf course, coarse fishing, pony riding, adventure playground, miniature railway and children's farm. Extra charges apply for some activities. **01493 488288**
www.somerleyton.co.uk **69 E7**

Hamerton Zoological Park
£ adults £7.50, children (3–12) £5.00, seniors £6.50 3+
Hamerton, Cambridgeshire A conservation zoo with animals, ranging from tigers, cheetahs and serval cats to capybara, lemurs, snakes, aardwolves, meerkats, mongoose, monkeys, gibbons, marmosets, Siberian weasels and many other rare mammals and a variety of birds from all over the world. Two play areas **01832 293362**
www.hamertonzoopark.com **65 F8**

Linton Zoo
£ adults £7.00, children (2–13) £4.50, seniors £6.50 2+
Linton, Cambridgeshire Set in 16 acres of gardens, this conservation zoo has leopards, lions and Amur tigers, tapirs, lemurs, giant tortoises, owls, parrots and tarantulas, among many other animals.
01223 891308 **www.lintonzoo.com** **55 E6**

Marsh Farm Country Park
£ adults £6.00, children (3–16) £3.50, seniors £4.30 2+2 £18.00
3+
South Woodham Ferrers, Essex Working farm and country park. Adventure play area, farm trail, and visitor centre.
01245 321552 **www.marshfarmcountrypark.co.uk** **42 E4**

Mole Hall Wildlife Park and Butterfly Pavilion
£ adults £6.50, children (3–15) £4.50, seniors £5.20, 2+2 £20.00
3+
Widdington, Essex Otters, wallabies, chimps, small monkeys, tropical butterfly pavilion, spiders, snakes and love birds, as well as pets' corner and play area, including a squirty maze. **01799 540400**
www.molehall.co.uk **55 F6**

National Horseracing Museum
£ adults £5.50, children £3.00, seniors £4.50, 2+2 £12.00
7+ public nearby
Newmarket, Suffolk Horses, working stables, gallops, horse simulator and equine swimming pool. **01638 667333** **www.nhrm.co.uk** **55 C7**

Norfolk Shire Horse Centre
£ adults 6.50, children £4.50, seniors £5.50 7+
West Runton, Norfolk Heavy horses working daily. Children's farm and free cart rides for children also available. West Runton riding stables located on site – accompanied hourly rides through pleasant coastal countryside or lessons in basic riding.
01263 837339 **www.norfolk-shirehorse-centre.co.uk** **81 C7**

Paradise Wildlife Park
£ telephone for details all ages
Broxbourne, Hertfordshire A large range of animals including tigers, lions, monkeys, zebras, camels and wolves, many of which can be approached closely. There are also three themed adventure playgrounds, children's rides and indoor soft play areas. In summer, children may swim in the paradise lagoon. Crazy Golf, panning for gold and Crazy Sand Cabin, tractor trailer rides and woodland railway.
:01992 470490 **www.pwpark.com** **41 D6**

Sea Life Adventure
£ adults £6.25, children (4–14) £4.75, seniors £4.95, +2+2 £18.50
4+ public nearby
Southend-on-Sea, Essex Aquarium with seahorses and tanks with fish from both UK and tropical waters, with a ray pool, breeding area and underwater walk-through tunnel.
01702 442200 **www.sealifeadventure.co.uk** **42 F4**

Sea Life Sanctuary
£ telephone for details 5+ public nearby
The Promenade, Hunstanton, Norfolk Rescue sanctuary, also houses an aquarium, penguins, otters and other sea life including rays and seahorses. **01485 533576** **www.sealsanctuary.co.uk/hunt1.html** **80 C2**

Sea Life, Great Yarmouth
£ telephone for details 3+
Great Yarmouth, Norfolk Large aquarium with sharks, an underwater walk-through tunnel, more than 50 native species of fish, including conger eels, shrimps, starfish and rays. **01493 330631**
www.sealifeeurope.com **69 D8**

Shepreth Wildlife Park
£ adults £7.95, children (2+) £5.95, seniors £6.25 7+
Shepreth, Cambridgeshire Wild and domestic animals, including wolves, monkeys, reptiles and birds. Pet's corner, pirate ship, toddler's play area, waterworld and bug city. **09066 800031**
www.sheprethwildlifepark.co.uk **54 E4**

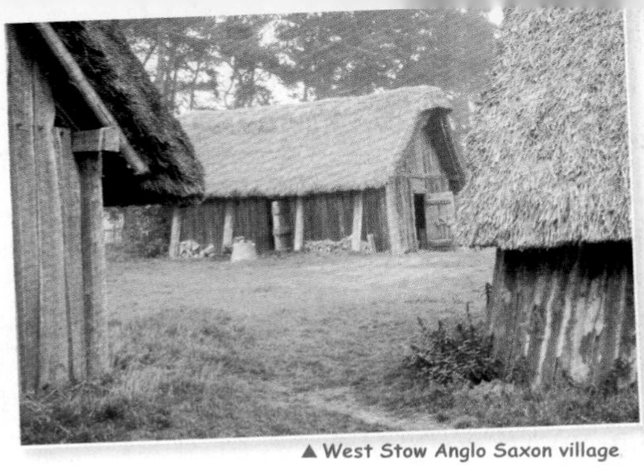

▲ West Stow Anglo Saxon village

Thrigby Hall Wildlife Gardens
£ adults £8.50, children (4–14) £6.50, seniors £7.50
4+
Filby, Norfolk Wildlife gardens with tigers, owls, primates, otters, leopards, red pandas and reptiles including crocodiles. Play areas.
01493 369477 **www.thrigbyplus.com/home.htm** **69 C7**

Tropical Butterfly World
£ telephone for details age3+
Great Ellingham, Attleborough, Norfolk 2,400 sq ft tropical gardens with hundreds of free-flying butterflies, caterpillar climbing frame, bird park and 15-acre conservation walk. **01953 453175** **68 E3**

West Stow Country Park and Anglo Saxon Village
£ adults £5.00, children (5+) £4.00, seniors £4.00 5+
West Stow, Suffolk Reconstruction of an Anglo Saxon settlement of c. 420–650, with finds from the original village, and reconstructed furniture to try out. Play area and woodland and lakeside walks.
www.stedmundsbury.gov.uk/sebc/play/weststow-asv.cfm
01284 72871855 **B8**

Whipsnade Animal Park
£ adults £16.00, children (3–15) £12.00, seniors £14.50, 2+2 £51.50 3+
P £3.50
Dunstable, Bedfordshire A wide range of animals from all round the world, including big cats, pygmy hippos, lemurs, reptiles and elephants. It is possible to bring cars into the safari areas (£13.00 extra charge).
01582 872171 **www.zsl.org/zsl-whipsnade-zoo** **40 C3**

Woburn Abbey
£ adults £17.00, children £13.00, seniors £14.50 3+
Woburn, Bedfordshire Safari park where visitors drive their own vehicles through the enclosures. Animals to be seen include rhino, eland, camels, giraffe, zebra, bison, big cats, bears, wolves, monkeys and other primates and antelopes. Activities and demonstrations include elephant encounters, sea lion displays, bird of prey demonstrations, feeding time for monkeys, penguins and lemurs. Leisure area.
01525 290407 **www.woburnsafari.co.uk** **53 F7**

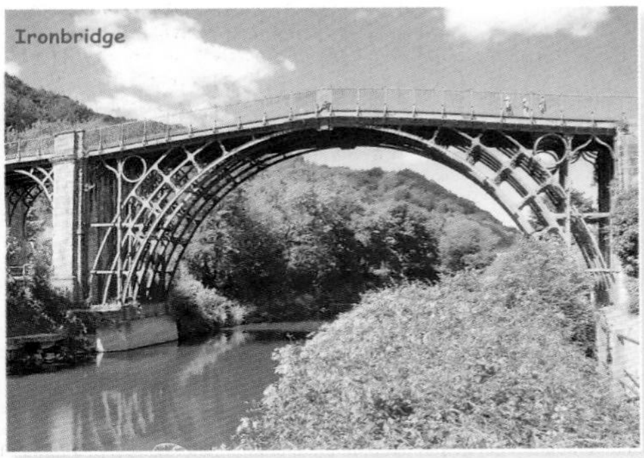

Ironbridge

The Midlands

Alton Towers
£ (theme park) adults £32.00, children £22.00, seniors £16.00, 2+2 £89.00 (water park), 5+ £12.50, 2+2 £39.50
5+
Alton, Staffordshire Known for its extreme rides, including Nemesis, Oblivion, Corkscrew, Air, Rita – Queen of Speed, Alton Towers is also a family-friendly park, with such rides as The Flume, Runaway Mine Train, Congo River Rapids, Duel, Frog Hopper, Bouncing Bugs, Cred Street Carousel and Charlie and the Chocolate Factory: the Ride, as well as many, many more. Storybook Land is aimed at toddlers. There are height and age restrictions on many of the rides. **08705 20 40 60**
www.altontowers.com **75 E7**

Battle of Britain Memorial Flight Museum
£ adults £3.80, children (5–16) £2.20, seniors £2.50, 2+2 £9.90 5+
Coningsby, Lincolnshire Guided tours around the Flight's hangar, where a Lancaster, two Hurricanes, a Dakota, two Chipmunks and five Spitfires can be seen when they are not flying. **01526 3344041**
www.lincolnshire.gov.uk/museums **78 D5**

Blue John Cavern
£ adults £7.00, children (5–15) £3.50, seniors £5.00, 2+2 £19.00 5+
Near Castleton, Derbyshire Guided tours through a complex of part natural caverns, part mine-workings, with natural chambers, fossils, stalactites and stalagmites.
www.bluejohn-cavern.co.uk
01433 620638 **88 F2**

British National Space Science Centre
£ adults £11.00, children (4–16) £9.00, seniors £9.00, 2+2 £34.00 4+
Exploration Drive, Leicester The centre's main galleries explore space hardware, deep space, planets and Earth-orbiting satellites. Tranquillity Base allows visitors to experience what life would be like on a moon base in the future. There are also usually experts on hand to answer visitors' questions about space. There is also a theatre and planetarium. **0116 261 0261**
www.spacecentre.co.uk **64 D2**

Chatsworth House
£ (house and garden) adults £11.55, children (3+) £9.35, senior £4.40, 2 + 2–4 £27.50
all ages £2.00
Bakewell, Derbyshire The Peak District's most popular tourist attraction. As well as the house itself, there is a farmyard and woodland adventure playground with daily activities, a 105-acre garden with spectacular water features and a yew maze and a 1,000-acre parkin which to to roam. Farmyard and adventure playground £5.50.
01246 582204 **www.chatsworth.org** **76 B2**

Drayton Manor Theme Park
£ adults £20.00, children (4–11) £16.95, seniors £10.00, 2+2 £66.00 4+
Tamworth, Staffordshire Rides here include StormForce 10, Shockwave, Apocalypse, Pirate Adventure, the Haunting, Splash Canyon, G-force and Maelstrom. For the less brave, rides include Buffalo Train, Wild West Shoot Out, Excalibur, Sombrero and Drunken Barrels. Younger children will enjoy Ladybirds, Arriva Crazy Bus, Flying Jumbos, Pirate Raft Ride and Froghopper. Many of the rides have age or height restrictions. **08708 725252**
www.draytonmanor.do.uk **63 D5**

Dudley Zoo and Castle
£ adults £9.95, children (3–15) £6.96, seniors £7.50
all ages £3.00!
Dudley, West Midlands A wide range of some of the most exotic and rarest animals including chimpanzees, penguins, lemurs, tigers, lions and orangutans. Also Dudley Castle. **01384 215313**
www.dudleyzoo.org.uk **62 E3**

Hatton Country World
£ £8.95 all ages
Hatton, Warwickshire Attractions and activities include maze, Bouncy Barn, Gold Rush, a runaway train, tractor trek, sheep-racing, pony rides, guinea pigs, farmyard animals, falconry displays and a country fun fair. **01926843411**
www.hattonworld.com **51 C7**

Heights of Abraham
£ adults £10.00, child (5+) £7.50, seniors £7.50, 2+2 £32.00
all ages
Matlock Bath, Derbyshire A beech-covered hilltop popular as a site for short walks, accessed via a cable car, and home to the Rutland Cavern and Great Masson Cavern, part natural caves and part lead mines. Woodland adventure park, and exhibitions on lead mining and the construction of the cable car.
01629 582356
www.heightsofabraham.com **76 D2**

Ironbridge Gorge Museums
£ (passport) adults £14.00, children (5–18) £9.50, seniors £12.50, 2+2–3 £46.00 7+
Coalbrookdale, Telford The museums located within this cradle of the Industrial Revolution include Blists Hill Victorian Town, Enginuity, Coalbrookdale Museum of Iron, Darby Houses, Jackfield Tile Museum, Coalport China Museum, Museum of the Gorge, The Iron Bridge and Tollhouse, Broseley Pipeworks and the Tar Tunnel.
01952 88439101952 884391
www.ironbridge.org.uk **61 D6**

Manor Farm
£ telephone for details all ages
East Leake, Nottinghamshire Animal centre and donkey sanctuary, with more than 50 breeds of animals and birds, including rare kune kune pigs, pygmy goats and a jersey bullock. Children are encouraged to learn about the animals, Donkey rides, nature trails, play area, adventure playground and pond dipping. **01509 852252** **64 B2**

Northcote Heavy Horse Centre
£ telephone for details 5+
Spilsby, Lincolnshire Hands-on encounters with heavy horses and horse-drawn wagon rides.
01754 830286 **www.northcote-horses.co.uk**
79 C7

Peak Cavern
£ adults £6.75, child (5–15) £4.75, seniors £5.75, 2+2 £20.00 all ages
Near Castleton, Derbyshire The only entirely natural cavern of the four Castleton caverns and the least commercialized, with an entrance that was wide enough to accommodate several small cottages. Beyond the 200ft Great Cave is the Orchestral Chamber, where village maidens sang to distinguished visitors such as Queen Victoria. Joint tickets with the Speedwell Cavern are available.
01433 620 285 **www.peakcavern.co.uk**
88 F2

Poole's Cavern
£ adults £6.75, children (5+) £4.00, seniors £5.50, 2+2–3 £20.00 all ages
Near Buxton, Derbyshire Part of the Wye system, with some impressive formations, including the 'Fitch of Bacon' stalactite and the 'Poached Egg Chamber', with formations coloured by minerals leached out of lime-tips on the hillside above. The surrounding Buxton Country Park has woodland orienteering trails. **01298 26978**
www.poolescavern.co.uk **75 B7**

Rays Farm Country Matters
£ adults £6.00, children (2–16) £4.50, seniors £5.50, 2+2 £19.00 2+
Billingsley, Bridgnorth, Shropshire A farm-based attraction with a variety of deer, other farm animals including friendly goats, and owls.
01299 841255 **www.raysfarm.com** **61 F7**

Rushmoor Country Park
£ £3.75 3+
North Cockerington, Lincolnshire Animal feeding, learning about life on the farm, small pets, ponies, wallabies, birds of prey, and ferrets, plus adventure playground.
www.tyharness.co.uk/rushmoorcountrypark/index1.htm **01507 327184** **91 F7**

Sherwood Forest Farm Park
£ adults £6.00, children (3+) £1.400, seniors £5.00, 2+2 £18.00 all ages
Edwinstowe, Nottinghamshire Sherwood Forest Farm Park is a centre dedicated to the breeding and care of rare and protected farm animals, of which there are more than 40 breeds here, as well as wildfowl, wallabies, water buffalo and kune kune pigs. .
www.sherwoodforestfarmpark.co.uk
01623 82355877 C5

Speedwell Cavern
£ adults £7.25, children (5–15) £5.25, seniors £6.25, 2+2 £25.00 all ages
Winnats Pass, near Castleton, Derbyshire A mine with several natural chambers and an underground canal, the most popular of the four Castleton caverns. Joint tickets with the Peak Cavern are available. 01433 620512 **www.sppeedwellcavern.co.uk** 88 F2

The Butterfly and Wildlife Park
£ adults £6.20, children (3–16) £4.70, seniors £5.70 2+2 £20.00 3+
Long Sutton, Lincolnshire Britain's largest indoor butterfly house. Reptile land, ant room and twice-daily bird of prey displays, water buffalo, pygmy goats, rare-breed sheep, pot-bellied pigs, small pets, possums, miniature ponies and wallabies. Mini golf, adventure playground . 01406 363833 **www.butterflyandwildlifepark.co.uk** 66 B4

Treak Cliff Cavern
£ telephone for details 5+
Castleton, Derbyshire One of the four Castleton caverns, a former mine with impressive stalactites and stalagmites and fine natural formations. 01433 620571 **www.bluejohnstone.com** 88 F2

Twinlakes Park
£ adults £8.50, children (92cm-16yrs) £8.50, seniors £4.99 all ages
Melton Mowbray, Leicestershire Eighty attractions within ten Playzones, including the indoor Labyrinth with slides and net climbs, Trauma Tower, Spinning Spiders, assault courses, bumper boats and dune buggies. Smaller children are catered for in Dolphins Bay and the Barrel Ride. Red Rooster Farm has hundreds of fascinating animals and birds. 01664 567777 **www.twinlakespark.co.uk** 64 B4

Twycross Zoo
£ adults £9.00, children £5.50, seniors £6.50, 2+2 £27.00 3+
Twycross, Leicestershire Among the animals here are lemurs, marmosets, tamarins, monkeys, gibbons, gorillas, chimpanzees, orang-utans, sloths, foxes and wild dogs, big cats, meerkats, otters, elephants, tapirs, camels, giraffes, deer, wallabies, a wide variety of exotic and endangered birds, turtles and tortoises, lizards and crocodiles. 01827 880250 **www.twycrosszoo.com** 63 D7

Warwick Castle
£ adults £17.95, children £10.95, seniors £12.95, 2+2 £48.00 £5.00
Castle Lane, Warwick, Warwickshire As well as the substantial remains of one of Britain's most spectacular medieval castles, attractions here include the mill and engine house, the river and island, a peacock garden and conservatory, and a Victorian rose garden. Extra charges may apply for events in summer. 0870 442 2000 **www.warwick-castle.co.uk** 51 C7

West Midland Safari Park
£ Adults and children (3+) £9.50
3+
Spring Grove, Bewdley, Worcestershire A 4-mile drive-through Safari, with animals including elephants, lions, rhinos, giraffes, zebras, tigers, emus, camels, gnus, yaks, llamas and Przewalski's horse. 01299 402114 **www.wmsp.co.uk** 50 B3

Wonderland Pleasure Park
£ (age 3+) 7.50, 2+2 £28.00 3+
White Post, Nottinghamshire Tropical house with butterflies, soft play, 30 outdoor activities and rides including mini diggers, sky track, trampolines, adventure fort, water fun fountain, rodeo convoy and slide mania (extra charges apply for some rides). 01623 882773 **www.wonderlandpleasurepark.com** 77 D6

Wye Valley Butterfly Zoo
£ adults £4.25, children £2.75, seniors £3.25 3+
Symonds Yat, Herefordshire A conservation zoo that allows visitors to walk among free-flying butterflies to learn about butterflies from all round the world and also how to provide habitats for them. 01600 890360 **www.butterflyzoo.co.uk** 36 C2

North West England

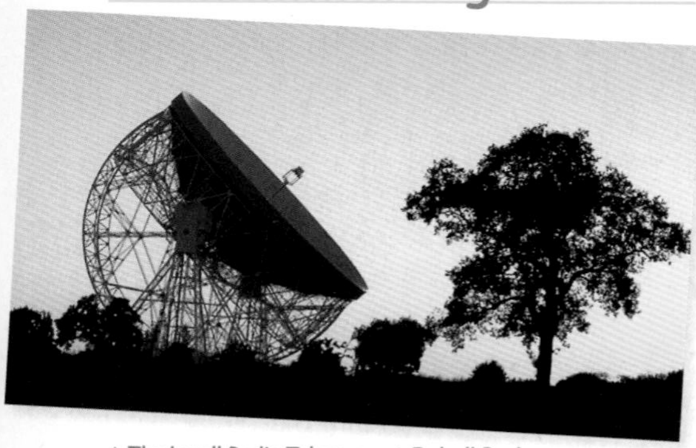

▲ The Lovell Radio Telescope at Jodrell Bank

Anderton Boat Lift
£ adults £10.25, children £7.25, seniors £8.50
2+ £2.00
Lift Lane, Anderton, Cheshire The world's first and only currently working canal boat lift, linking the Trent and Mersey Canal to the River Weaver. Trips along the river and through the lift are available. **www.andertonboatlift.co.uk** 01606 786777 74 B3

Aquarium of the Lakes
£ adults £7.50, children (3–15) £5.00, seniors £6.50, 2+2 £22.00
3+
Lakeside, Cumbria An award-winning freshwater aquarium with Britain's biggest collection of freshwater fish, a simulated lake bed, and otters and ducks. **www.aquariumofthelakes.co.uk** 015395 30153 99 F5

Arrowe Country Park
£ (park) free all ages
Arrowe Park Road, Upton, Merseyside Four hundred acres of parkland, including orienteering areas, woodland trails, a lake, and adventure playground and a golf course. Charges apply for some facilities. 0151 678 4200 **www.wirral.gov.uk** 85 F3

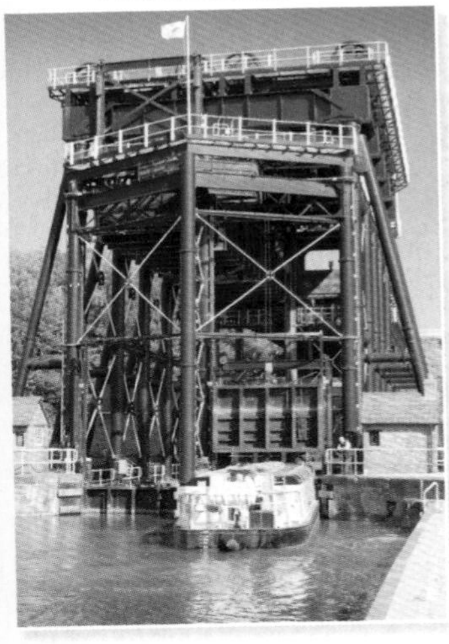

▼Anderton Boat Lift

Blackpool Pleasure Beach
£ (all-day wristband) adults £25.00, children (under 12) £15.00 all ages
Ocean Boulevard, Blackpool A huge adventure park with more than 145 rides and attractions, including the Pepsi Max Big One, the tallest and fastest rollercoaster in Europe. Height restrictions apply on some rides. 0870 444 5566 **www.blackpoolpleasurebeach.com** 92 F3

Blackpool Tower
£ adults £12.95, children (90cm – 16 years) £9.95, seniors £8.95, 2+2 £43.00 all ages
public nearby
Promenade, Blackpool The famous 518-ft tower, opened in 1894 and based on the Eiffel Tower, containing the new Blackpool Tower Circus, the Ballroom, an aquarium and Jungle Jim's indoor adventure playground. **www.blackpooltower.co.uk** 01253 622242 92 F3

Blackpool Zoo Park
£ adults £12.95, children (3–15) £8.95, seniors £10.95, 2+2 £39.00 3+
East Park Drive, Blackpool A 32-acre zoo with more than 1,500 animals, including gorillas, tigers, and orang-utans, in themed areas and a dolphin 'swimulator', children's zoo and a 'dinosaur safari'. 01253 830830 **www.blackpoolzoo.org.uk** 92 F3

Blue Planet Aquarium
£ adults £10.50, children (3–15) £7.75, seniors £7.75, 2+2 £35.50
3+
Kinsey Road, Cheshire Oaks, Ellesmere Port, Cheshire The UK's largest aquarium, with interactive displays and themed areas about different regions of the world, and with an 'aquatheatre' including one of the world's longest underwater 'safari tunnels' housing more than 20 sharks. Outdoor play park. 0151 357 8800 **www.blueplanetaquarium.com** 73 B8

Bowland Wild Boar Park
£ adults £4.50, children (2+) £3.50, seniors £3.50, 2+2 £14.00. 3+
Near Chipping, Lancashire A scenic wooded park in the Ribble Valley, with wild boar, longhorn cows, llamas, goats and deer. Children's play area, small-animal feeding and tractor-trailer rides (£1.00). 01995 61554 **www.wildboarpark.co.uk** 93 E6

Chester Zoo
£ adults £14.95, children (3–15) £10.95, seniors £13.50, 2+2 £49.50
3+
Upton-by-Chester, Chester, Cheshire The UK's most-visited zoo, famous for its conservation work, large paddocks and gardens. Highlights include the Chimpanzee Forest, 'Zoofari' monorail, rhinos, Komodo dragons and elephants. **www.chesterzoo.org** 01244 380280 73 B8

Dewa Roman Experience
£ (2006) adults £4.25, children £2.50, seniors £3.75 5+
Pierpoint Lane, Bridge Street, Chester, Cheshire Roman remains recently unearthed by archaeologists beneath the city, along with relics of Saxon and medieval life and a reconstructed Roman street and galley interior. The activity studio allows you to try on a replica suit of Roman armour, handle Roman pottery, animals bones and so on. Other Roman sites in the area include the city walls and part of the amphitheatre. 01244 343407 73 C8

East Lancashire Railway
£ telephone for details
all ages
Bolton Street Station, Bury, Greater Manchester Restored steam and diesel trains along the Irwell Valley, with stops at traditional stations buildings and the scenic market town of Ramsbottom. In summer 2003, a Heywood-Rawtenstall line opened in Rochdale. **www.east-lancs-rly.co.uk** 0161 764 7790 87 C6

Formby Squirrel Reserve (NT)
£ free all ages
Formby, Merseyside A nature reserve owned by the National Trust and home to one of the last thriving colonies of red squirrels in the UK. Pine woodland and dune walks, including the Sefton Coastal Footpath. 01704 878591 **www.nationaltrust.org.uk** 85 D3

Gulliver's World
£ adults £10.30, children (90cm+) £10.30, seniors £9.30 all ages
Old Hall, Warrington Theme park with many rides, grouped in areas such as Smuggler's Wharf, Water World, Adventure World, Count's Castle, Alice's Wonderland, the Lost World, Circus World and Western World. 01925 230088 **www.gulliversfun.co.uk** 86 E3

Haigh Hall and Country Park
£ (country park) free, (hall and model village) telephone for details all ages
Near Wigan, Greater Manchester The former manor house of the Bradshaigh family, with a 250-acre wooded parkland complete with miles of trails and containing a model village, a children's playground, a narrow-gauge steam railway and golf ranges. 01942 832895 **www.wlct.org** 86 D3

Hill Top (NT)
£ adults £5.40, children £2.70, 2+2 £13.50 7+
Near Sawrey, Cumbria Beatrix Potter's holiday home, bought in 1905 and bequeathed to the National Trust on her death in 1943 on condition that it be kept as she left it. 015394 36269 **www.nationaltrust.org.uk** 99 E5

Jodrell Bank Science Centre
£ (centre) adults £1.50, children (4–16) £1.00, (planetarium) £1.00
4+
Lower Withington, Macclesfield, Cheshire A planetarium and exhibitions on astronomy, satellites and the mysteries of the universe in the shadow of the Lovell Radio Telescope. There's also a 35-acre arboretum, an environmental discovery centre and play areas. 01477 571339 **www.jb.man.ac.uk/viscen** 74 B4

Knowsley Safari Park
£ (2006) adults £10.00, children (3+) £7.00, seniors £7.00, 2+2 £30.00
3+
Prescot, Merseyside The historic parkland surrounds Knowsley Hall, ancestral home of the Earls of Derby, now home to big-game animals. Amusement rides (small fee), farm and sea lion shows. The winner of various animal husbandry awards. 0151 430 9009 **www.knowsley.com/safari** 86 E2

Lake District Coast Aquarium
£ adults £5.00, children (4+) £3.25, seniors £4.25, 2+2 £14.75
4+
South Quay, Maryport, Cumbria An aquarium in the renovated Maryport harbour, with displays on aquatic life in British waters, particularly Cumbria's seas and coasts, including a mockup of Maryport's harbour wall and a ray pool where gentle stroking is allowed. Fish living here include conger eel, cod, sea bass and mullet, as well as more exotic animals such as seahorses and squid. Boat pool and play park. 01900 817760 **www.lakedistrict-coastaquarium.co.uk** 107 F7

Lakeland Motor Museum
£ (museum, hall and gardens) adults £11.50, children (6–15) £6.50, seniors £10.50, 2+2 £32.00
6+
Holker Hall, Cark, Cumbria Vintage vehicles and an exhibition about Sir Malcolm and Donald Campbell, who set more than 20 land and water speed records, set within the grounds of Holker Hall. 015395 58509 **www.lakelandmotormuseum.co.uk** 92 B3

Lancaster Castle
£ adults £5.00, children £4.00, seniors £44.00, 2+2 £14.00 6+
Lancaster, Lancashire One of the UK's best-preserved castles, built on the site of Roman fortifications, owned by the Queen and still used as a court and prison. Visitors can see Gillow furniture, dungeons, the Shire Hall with its 600 heraldic shields and the Crown Court from which convicts were transported to Australia. **www.lancastercastle.com** 01524 64998 92 C4

Muncaster Castle, Gardens and World Owl Trust
£ adults £9.50, children (5–15) £6.50, 2+2 £27.00
5+
Ravenglass, Cumbria An historic house with famous grounds, including the 77-acre Himalayan Gardens, the 'Meadowvolemaze' and the Terrace Walk, described by John Ruskin as the 'Gateway to Paradise'. The Owl Trust runs 'Meet the Birds' flying displays and a 'Heron Happy Hour'. Playgrounds, wildfowl pond and information centre. **www.muncaster.co.uk** 01229 717614 98 E3

National Football Museum
£ free 5+
Deepdale Stadium, Preston, Lancashire A major museum housing world-class collections and interactive exhibits relating to 'the beautiful game', including the official FIFA collection, plus social history displays. 01772 908442 **www.nationalfootballmuseum.com** 92 F5

Sea Life Centre
£ telephone for details 3+
public nearby
Central Promenade, Blackpool One of the biggest marine collections in Europe, with a tropical shark display **www.sealifeeurope.com** 01253 622445 92 F3

South Lakes Wild Animal Park
£ adults £10.50, children (3+) £7.00, seniors £7.00 7+
Crossgates, Dalton-in-Furness, Cumbria A tiger conservation centre offering walking safaris and deck areas offering views over the animals. Other residents include lions, kangaroos, rhinos, lemurs, tamarins, baboons, otters, giraffes, penguins, hippos and emus. 01229 466086 **www.wildanimalpark.co.uk** 92 B2

Southport Eco Visitor Centre
£ free 7+
Esplanade, Southport, Merseyside Exhibitions on energy, transport and tourism, with the aim of inspiring people to consider the human impact on the environment. 0845 330 1342 **www.southportecocentre.com** 85 C4

Southport Pier
£ free all ages
Southport, Merseyside Britain's second-longest pier (and its first iron pier, built in 1860), which reopened in 2002 after a £7-million restoration with family rides and Victorian merry-go-round (charges apply for rides). **www.silcock-leisure.co.uk** 0207 531 8400 85 C4

Stapeley Water Gardens
£ (The Palms) adults £4.45, children £2.60, seniors, £3.95 2+2 £12.10
3+
Nantwich, Cheshire A water garden containing the National Collection of Water Lilies and the Palms Tropical Oasis, boasting a koi pool, a 'zoo room' with a cottontop tamarin monkey family, water dragons and a baby Caiman and a stingray pool, as well as snakes and flying frogs. Angling facilities. 01270 623868 **www.stapeleywg.com** 74 D3

The Lowry
£ free 7+
Salford, Greater Manchester Voted UK building of the year in 2001, this contains the world's biggest collection of works by LS Lowry, plus galleries for contemporary exhibitions, theatres, shops, cafes and bars. 0870 787 5780 **www.thelowry.com** 87 E6

Wigan Pier Experience
£ (saver) adults £5.25, children £4.25, concession £4.25, 2+2 £14.75 all ages
Trencherfield Mill, Wigan, Greater Manchester An 8.5-acre site beside the redeveloped Leeds and Liverpool Canal, with The Way We Were Museum, depicting Wigan life in 1900, Opie's Museum of Memories tracing 20th-century British domestic life, a waterbus, the world's largest working mill steam engine and the Machinery Hall re-creating the harsh working conditions at the mill. 01942 323666 **www.wlct.org** 86 D3

Windermere Lake Cruises
£ (all-day ticket) adults £14.00, children (5–15) £7.00, 2+2–3 £36.00
all ages
Lakeside, Cumbria Trips by steamers and launches between Ambleside, Bowness and Lakeside on England's longest lake. 015395 31188 **www.windermere-lakecruises.co.uk** 99 E5

North East England

Alnwick Castle

£ telephone for details all ages

Alnwick, Northumberland In addition to the interior of the massive castle keep, rich art collection and stunning grounds and views, Alnwick's attractions include Dragon's Quest, Knights Quest, Under Siege, the Constable's Tower, the archaeological collection in the Postern Tower and the Coach House. Abbot's Tower is home to the Fusiliers Museum of Northumberland. **01665 510777** **www.alnwickcastle.com** 117 C7

Beamish Museum

£ free 7+

Stanley, Durham Set in 300 acres of beautiful countryside, Beamish re-creates life as it was in the 19th and early 20th centuries through demonstrations by costumed staff in attractions such as the 1825 Pockerley Waggonway, the town, home farm, colliery village and railway station as they were in 1913, and operational trams. Funfair (small fee). **01913 704000** **www.beamish.org.uk** 110 D5

Blue Reef Aquarium

£ adults £6.95, children (3–16) £4.95, seniors £5.95, 2+2 £19.99 all ages

Grand Parade, Tynemouth Among the animals and attractions here are otters, a variety of frogs, a shark nursery, tropical paradise and displays on predators and the octopus. The large tanks house sharks, seahorses, giant crabs and piranhas, among others. **0191 258 1032** **www.bluereefaquarium.co.uk/tynemouth.htm** 111 B6

Chesters Roman Fort (EH)

£ adults £4.0, children £2.10, seniors £3.10 5+

Chollerford, Northumberland Chesters Fort was built to guard the Roman bridge which carried Hadrian's Wall and the military road over the North River Tyne. Remains that can be seen include the main gateways, parts of the wall, the foundations of the HQ building. Nearer the river, the garrison's bath house is well preserved. Museum of Roman finds. Down by the river, the changing rooms, steam rooms and bathing areas of the garrison's bath house are extremely well preserved, as is the Roman bridge abutment on the opposite bank of the river. **01434 681379**, **www.english-heritage.org.uk** 110 B2

Diggerland

£ £12.50, under-3s free, over-65s £6.25 3+

Willowbridge Lane, Whitwood, Castleford, West Yorkshire Adventure park with JCBs and dumper trucks. Age and height restrictions apply on some rides. Off the A655 between J31 of the M62 and Castleford. **0870 344437** **www.diggerland.com** 88 B5

Eureka!

£ adults and children 3+ £7.25, toddlers (1–2) £2.25 all ages

Discovery Road, Halifax, West Yorkshire A hands-on museum with more than 400 exhibits that explore just about everything from how the body works to what makes sound. **01422 330069** **www.eureka.org.uk** 87 B8

Hartlepool's Maritime Experience

£ adults £7.50, children (5+) £4.50, seniors £5.75, 2+2 £19.50 5+

Maritime Avenue, Hartlepool A re-creation of an 18th-century seaport, which brings to life the time of Nelson, Napoleon and the Battle of Trafalgar, allowing visitors to experience life as it was in the British navy in the early 19th century. **01429 860077** **www.hartlepoolsmaritimeexperience.com** 111 F8

Housesteads Roman Fort (EH/NT)

£ adults £4.10, children £2.10, seniors £3.10 5+

Bardon Mill, Northumberland Known to the Romans as Vercovicium, the Hilly Place, Housesteads stands on the end of a crag. There are good remains of the fort, the Wall and the civilian settlement (vicus) that grew up near the fort. **01434 344363** **www.english-heritage.org.uk www.nationaltrust.org.uk** 109 C7

How Stean Gorge

£ telephone for details 7+

Lofthouse, North Yorkshire An 80ft limestone ravine with narrow paths and footbridges, containing Tom Taylor's Cave complete with dripping stalactite. Children's play area, bicycle hire **04123 755666** **www.howstean.co.uk** 94 B3

Ingleborough Show Cave

£ adults £6.00, children £3.00, 2+2 £15.00 all ages

Clapham, North Yorkshire Guided tours around one of Britain's most spectacular show caves. **www.ingleboroughcave.co.uk** **015242 51242** 93 B7

Jorvik Centre

£ adults £11.20, children £8.30, seniors £9.20, 2+2 £32.00 5+

Coppergate, York. A reconstruction of Viking-age York, complete with sounds and smells. Three exhibitions on the city at that time and demonstrations. **01904 543402** **www.jorvik-viking-centre.co.uk** 96 D2

Killhope Leadmining Centre

£ adults £6.50, children (4–16) £3.50, seniors £6.00, 2+2 £15.00 4+

Near Cowshill, Durham A fully restored 19th-century lead mine, where visitors experience the life and work of the lead mining families of the Pennine dales. Features include a huge working waterwheel, the 'mineshop', where miners lived for the week and slept three or four to a bed, and the working machinery. Under fours cannot go on the mine tour. **01388 537505** **www.http://www.durham.gov.uk** 109 E8

Kilnsey Park

£ (park) free, (trail) adults £3.50, children (5+) £2.50, seniors £2.50, 2+2 £10.00 7+

Kilnsey, North Yorkshire Situated beneath Kilnsey Crag in the Yorkshire Dales, a 'countryside experience' with a squirrel trail, a nature trail, 'goat skyway', a freshwater aquarium, fly-fishing lakes and fishing pools for children. **01756 752150** **www.kilnseypark.co.uk** 94 C2

Lightwater Valley

£ 100cm+ free, 113cm £15,95, 130cm+ £14.50, seniors £7.95, 2+2 £58.00 3+

North Stainley, Ripon, North Yorkshire Theme park with spectacular rides, including the Hornets Nest, Flying Camels, Trauma Tower, Eagles Claw and Skyrider. Some rides have height/age restrictions. Birds of Prey Centre. **0870 458 0040** **www.lightwatervalley.co.uk** 95 B5

Stump Cross Caverns

£ adults £6.00, children (4–13) £3.95 all ages

Greenhow Hill, North Yorkshire A half-million-year-old cave with stalactites and stalagmites, a video presentation and a visitor centre with a variety of animal remains. **01756 752780** **www.stumpcrosscaverns.co.uk** 94 C3

Vindolanda and Roman Army Museum

£ adults £7.50, children £4.70, seniors £6.50, 2+2 £22.00 4+

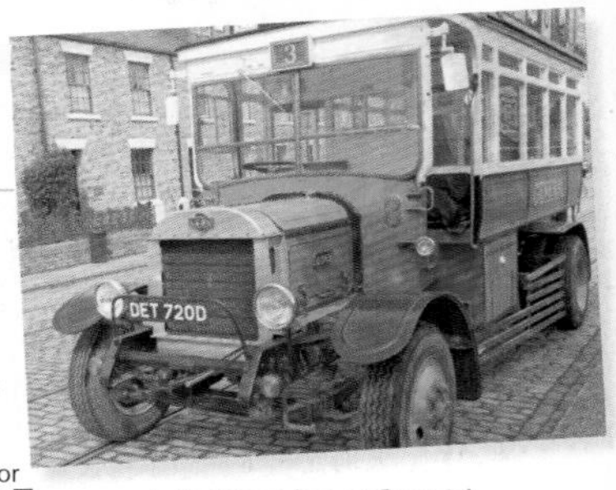

▲ A vintage bus at Beamish Museum

Bardon Mill, Northumberland Vindolanda Roman fort and settlement lies just south of Hadrian's Wall. Remains of numerous buildings survive and finds from the excavations, including footwear, coins, jewellery and armour, are displayed in the museum. Full-sized reconstructions of a Roman temple, shop and house as well as a Northumbrian croft bring the past to life, as does the full-size replica of a section of Hadrian's Wall. **(Vindolanda) 01434 344277 (museum) 016977 47485** **www.vindolanda.com** 109 C7

White Scar Cave

£ adults £7.50, children £4.50, family £21.00 4+

Ingleton, North Yorkshire A huge Ice Age cavern forming Britain's longest show cave, with underground waterfalls and stalactites. Guided tours. **01524 241244** **www.whitescarcave.co.uk** 93 B7

Wales

Afan Forest Park

£ free 5+ small charge

Afan Argoed, Cynonville, Neath Port Talbot A park containing one of south Wales' loveliest valleys, with a Visitor Centre hosting exhibitions on its history, wildlife and woodlands, facilities for walking, cycling, orienteering and pony-trekking, Glyncorrwg Ponds (three fishing lakes, plus canoeing and rowing), a Miners' Museum and Roman, Iron Age and Bronze Age remains and cairns (charges for some activities). **01639 850564** **www.npt.gov.uk/afanforestpark/welcome.cfm** 34 E2

Anglesey Model Village

£ adults £2.25, children £1.75, 2+2 £6.50 all ages

Newborough, Isle of Anglesey A scale model village featuring many of Anglesey's landmarks, in an acre of landscaped gardens with water features, play areas and the Ynys Mon Express model railway. **01248 440477** 82 E4

Anglesey Sea Zoo

£ adults £6.95, children (3–16) £5.95, seniors £5.95, 2+2 £23.80 all ages

Brynslencyn, Isle of Anglesey Award-winning displays of marine life from the surrounding waters. **01248 430411** **www.angleseyseazoo.co.uk** 82 E4

Aquadome

£ telephone for details all ages

Afan Lido, Aberavon, Neath Port Talbot A theme pool with a giant spaceship, an Inca temple, a lily pond, bubble loungers, river rides and more. **01639 871444** **www.celticleisure.org/afanlido.php** 34 E1

Bala Lake (Llyn Tegid)

£ free all ages

Bala/Y Bala, Gwynedd The largest natural body of water in Wales, at four miles in length and up to a mile wide, with watersports facilities (charges apply). Among its many species of fish is the very rare gwyniad, and there are steam trains (small charge) along its southern shore. **0207 531 8400** **www.bala.co.uk** 73 F3

Beaumaris Castle (CADW)

£ adults £3.50, children £3.00, seniors £3.00, 2+2 £10.00 4+

Castle Street, Beaumaris, Isle of Anglesey An unfinished castle intended as one of Edward I's 'Iron ring' with an ingenious symmetrical concentric design involving four successive lines of fortification. **01248 810361** **www.beaumaris.com** 83 D6

Bedford Country Park

£ free all ages

Cefn Cribwr, Bridgend A 40-acre site comprising ancient woodlands and meadows full of wildflowers and fauna, way-marked nature trails, play areas and the ruins of industrial buildings. **01658 725155** **www.bridgend.gov.uk** 34 F2

Bodelwyddan Castle

£ adults £5.00, children (5–16) £2.00, seniors £4.50, 1+2 £10.00, 2+2 £12.00 5+ tea room/picnic area

Bodelwyddan, Denbighshire A 19th-century mock-medieval castle with turrets and battlements, designed by Joseph Hansom and now an outstation of the National Portrait Gallery, with 260 acres of parkland, woodland trails, orienteering and WWI practice trenches. **0207 531 8400** **www.bodelwyddan-castle.co.uk** 72 B3

Brecon Mountain Railway

£ telephone for details 5+

Pontsticill, Merthyr Tydfil Vintage steam locomotive trips into the Brecon Beacons National Park, along Taf Fechan Reservoir to Del-y-Gaer, plus visits to the restoration workshops. **01685 722988** **www.breconmountainrailway.co.uk** 34 C4

Bryngarw Country Park

£ free, charge to park at peak times all ages

Brynmenyn, Bridgend A 113-acre site with woodlands, wetlands, formal gardens, open pastures, waymarked nature trails and an ornamental lake, plus an adventure playground. Events throughout the summer. **01656 725155** **www.bridgend.gov.uk** 34 F3

Caernarfon Castle (CADW)

£ adults £4.90, children £4.50, seniors £4.50, 2+2 £15.00 4+

Castle Street, Caernarfon, Gwynedd A commanding castle begun in 1283 as Edward I's seat of government and royal palace, with unique polygonal towers and colour-banded masonry. **01248 810361** **www.caernarfon.com** 82 E4

Caerphilly Castle (CADW)

£ adults £3.50, reduced rate £3.00, (2+3) £10.00 all ages public nearby

Castle St, Caerphilly/Caerffili, Caerphilly One of western Europe's greatest medieval castles, the biggest castle in Britain after Windsor, and the country's first truly concentric castle, built in the late 13th century by one of Henry III's most powerful barons and a masterpiece of military planning. There is a leaning tower, and impressive inner ward with an exhibition on Welsh castles. Events during summer. **01443 336000** **www.cadw.wales.gov.uk** 35 F5

Caldicot Castle and Country Park

£ adults £3.75, children (5–17) £2.50, seniors £2.50 2+3 £12.00 all ages

Church Rd, Caldicot, Monmouthshire Castle begun by the Normans, completed by the end of the 14th century and restored as a family home in the 19th century, set in 55 acres of attractive wooded parkland and gardens, with audio tours, living-history events, outdoor activities such as orienteering and pond-dipping, hands-on activities and an adventure play area. **01291 420241** **www.caldicotcastle.co.uk** 36 F1

Canolfan Bwlch Nant Yr Arian Forest Centre

£ free 6+ (small fee)

Llywernog, Ponterwyd, Ceredigion A forest centre with panoramic views down the Melindwr Valley to Cardigan Bay and through the forest to Llywernog Uchaf lake. There is live footage of nesting red kites and other birds of prey, including kestrels and buzzards, walking and orienteering trails, including the All Ability Lakeside Trail, and mountain-bike trails, a play area and daily red-kite feeding. **01970 890694** **www.forestry.gov.uk** 58 F4

Cardigan Bay Marine Wildlife Centre

£ (centre) free, (trips) adults £14.00-£40.00, under 12s £7.00–30.00 5+

2nd Floor, Patent Slip, New Quay/Ceinewydd, Ceredigion A research and public information centre about dolphins, seals and sea birds of Cardigan Bay and the Irish Sea, with interactive displays and a children's corner and activities. Trips can be booked on dolphin-surveys, lasting between 2 and 8 hours. **01545 560032** **www.cbmwc.org** 46 D2

Cardigan Island Coastal Farm Park

£ adults £3.50, children (2–13) £2.50, seniors £3.20 all ages

Gwbert, Ceredigion A farm park on a headland overlooking the nature reserve of Cardigan Island, offering sightings of Atlantic grey seals (which breed in the caves below), bottlenose dolphins and choughs (which nest on the cliffs). Shetland ponies, Vietnamese pigs, rare breed cattle and llamas also feature. Animal feeding sessions. Outdoor adventure playground and indoor play area. Tractor and trailer rides to seal-watching point (small charge). **01239 612196** **www.cardiganisland.com** 45 D3

Centre for Alternative Technology

£ adults 8.00, children (5–15) £4.00, seniors £7.00 8+

Machynlleth, Powys An award-winning centre with Europe's largest ecological exhibition, including working examples of wind, water and solar power, energy conservation, environmentally sound buildings and organic growing. **01654 705950** **www.cat.org.uk** 58 D4

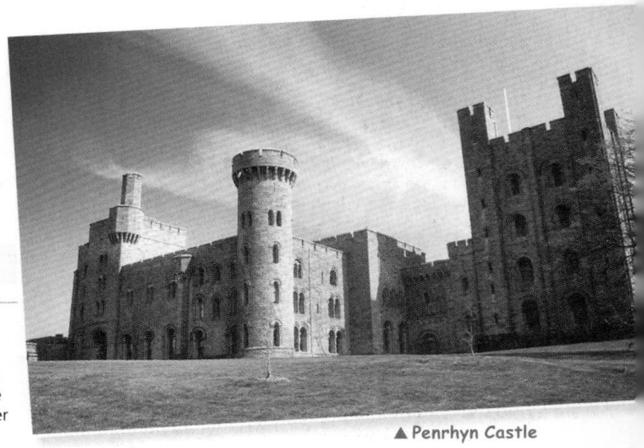

▲ Penrhyn Castle

Conwy Castle (CADW)

£ adults £4.00, others £3.50, 2 +3 £11.50 all ages

Conwy, Conwy A ruin considered to have been one of the greatest European fortresses, built by Edward I and accessed via an 1826 suspension bridge. **01492 592358** **www.conwy.com** 83 D7

Cosmeston Lakes Country Park

£ (park) free, (medieval village) adults £3.50, children £2.00, seniors £2.00, 2+2 £8.00 all ages

Lavernock Rd, Penarth, Vale of Glamorgan An attractive 200-acre site embracing woodlands, meadows, lakes, an SSSI with rare plant and animal species, nature trails, an adventure playground, a medieval village and a Visitor Centre. **029 2070 1678** **www.valeofglamorgan.gov.uk** 22 C3

Craig y Nos Country Park

£ free 5+

Brecon Road, Pen-y-cae, Powys A 40-acre country park run by the Brecon Beacons National Park, set in the historic gardens of Craig y Nos Castle, built by opera singer Dame Adelina Patti. There is a restored Victorian pavilion, a hay meadow, walking trails and a Visitor Centre. **01639 730395** **www.breconbeacons.org.uk** 34 C2

Dinosaur Park

£ adults £5.55, children (2+) £4.95, seniors £4.95 7+

Gumfreston, near Tenby/Dinbych-y-Pysgod, Pembrokeshire A dinosaur theme park with indoor and outdoor attractions, including an adventure playground, activity centre and woodland trail, diggers, a labyrinth, astra slide, jungle climb, disco boats, tractors and trampolines, and a daily programme of activities. Small charges for some rides. **01834 845 272** **www.thedinosaurpark.co.uk** 32 D2

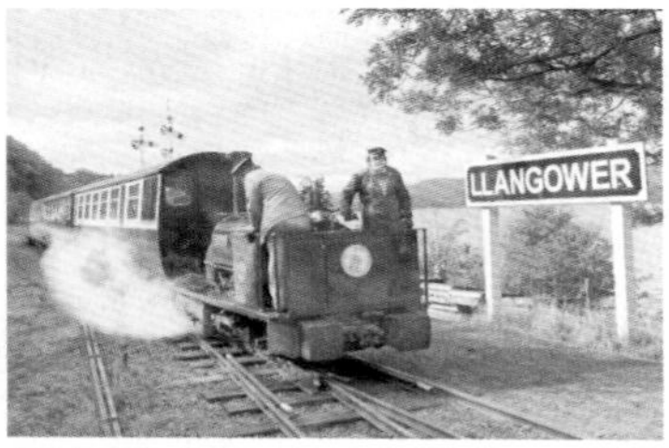

▲ Bala Lake Railway

Dolaucothi Goldmines (NT)
£ adults £3.08, child £1.54, family £3.50, underground tour £3.45, £1.71 £8.63 👪5+ 🏃🏃🏃 ◐◐◐ ☕🧺Ⓟ

Old Coach House, Pumsaint, Llanwrda, Carmarthenshire A Roman gold mine, with an exhibition of 1930s mining equipment, audio-visual presentations, an activity room where children can pan for gold, waymarked walks, cycle hire and guided tours of Roman and modern mines and Long Adit. Nearby are the remains of a wooden Flavian fort built c. 120AD to guard the mine. 📞**01558 650177** 💻**www.nationaltrust.org.uk** 47 E5

Electric Mountain Visitor Centre
£ (visitor centre) free, (power station tour) adults £7.00, children £3.50, 2+2 £19.50 👪3+ 🏃🏃🏃 ◐🍽Ⓟ

Llanberis, Gwynedd A complex on the edge of Snowdonia National Park, with interactive displays, models and exhibitions about the history of hydro-electricity. There's also a guided tour of Dinorwig Power Station and two art galleries. 📞**01286 870636** 💻**www.fhc.co.uk/electric_mountain.htm** 83 E5

Festival Park
£ free 👪all ages 🏃🏃🏃 ◐✕🍽🛍 Ⓟ

Ebbw Vale/Glyn Ebwy, Blaenau Gwent A scenic park next to the shopping centre of the same name with a tropical planthouse, ornamental gardens, woodlands, a lake, a Wetland Centre, an owl sanctuary, an oriental pavilion, a sculpture trail, a playground, a treehouse, a 'snakemaze', plus Visitor and Education Centres. 35 D5

Ffestiniog Railway
£ (all day rover) adults £16.95, others £15.30 👪all ages 🏃 ◐◐◐ Ⓟ

Harbour Station, Porthmadog, Gwynedd The world's oldest independent railway, built to carry slate from Blaenau Ffestiniog, now crossing the spectacular scenery of the Snowdonia National Park. There is a sister railway, the Welsh Highland, between Caernarfon and Waunfawr. 📞**01766 516024** 💻**www.festrail.co.uk** 71 D6

Folly Farm Adventure Park
£ adults £6.95, children (3–15) £5.95, seniors £5.95 👪all ages 🏃🏃🏃 ◐◐◐✕🍽🛍 Ⓟ

Begelly, Kilgetty, near Tenby/Dinbych-y-Pysgod, Pembrokeshire The biggest farm attraction in Wales, with a children's zoo, petting and feeding sessions, milking and falconry displays, indoor and outdoor play areas, a vintage funfair and a magic show. 📞**01834 812731** 💻**www.folly-farm.co.uk** 32 D2

Gnoll Country Park
£ free 👪all ages 🏃🏃 ◐🍽Ⓟ

Neath/Castell-nedd, Neath Port Talbot A country park based on an 18th-century landscaped garden, with lakes, waterfalls, a grotto, narrow-gauge railway, deer park, farm trail, pets' corner, a play area and adventure playground, a Visitor Interpretation Centre and forest footpaths linking to the Mosshouse Reservoir and Cefn Morfudd historical viewpoints. 📞**01639 635808** 💻**www.npt.gov.uk/gnollcountrypark** 34 E1

Great Orme Country Park
£ (park) free, (tramway) adults £5.00, children (3–16) £3.50, (copper mines) adults £5.00, children (5–16 £3.50), 2+2 £15.00 👪4+ 🏃🏃🏃 ◐◐🍽🧺Ⓟ

Llandudno, Conwy A limestone headland designated a Special Area of Conservation, SSSI and Heritage Coast, containing some famous Kashmiri goats and the Great Orme Bronze Age Copper Mines. The Visitor Centre has interactive displays and a live camera link to a seabird colony. Play area, pitch and putt. 📞**01492 874151** 💻**www.conwy.gov.uk** 83 C7

Greenfield Valley Heritage and Country Park
£ adults £3.20, children £1.95, 2+2 £9.40 👪all ages 🏃🏃 ◐◐🍽Ⓟ

Holywell/Treffynon, Flintshire A park containing St Winefride's Well, the ruins of the 12th-century Basingwerk Abbey and various mill buildings (many scheduled ancient monuments), a reconstructed Victorian school, farmhouses, five lakes, and woodland walks. There is also a farm museum and a museum about naturalist and explorer Thomas Pennant. 📞**01352 714172** 💻**www.greenfieldvalley.com** 73 F3

Greenwood Forest Park
£ adults £9.00, children £8.25, seniors £8.45, 2+2 £30.80 👪all ages 🏃🏃🏃 ◐◐◐🍽Ⓟ

Port Dinrwic/Y Feinheli, Gwynedd A family attraction with a 70m Great Green Run, the longest slide in Wales, longbow shooting, log sawing, peacock feeding, a Forest Theatre, toddlers' village, mini tractors, stiltwalking and woodland crafts and sculptures. The Visitor Centre has displays on ancient forests and modern conservation. Age restrictions apply. 📞**01248 670076** 💻**www.greenwoodforestpark.co.uk** 82 E5

Gwydyr Forest Park
£ free 👪8+ 🏃🏃🏃 ◐◐🧺Ⓟ

Betws-y-Coed, Conwy A forest park ranging across eastern Snowdonia's hills, with more than 20 miles of trails through mountain forest, plus riding, canoeing and mountain biking. 📞**01492 640578** 💻**www.forestry.gov.uk** 83 F7

Henblas Country Park
£ adults £5.00, children (2+) £4.00, seniors £4.25, 2+2 £16.00 👪2+ 🏃🏃🏃 ◐◐🍽🧺Ⓟ

Cerrigceinwen, Isle of Anglesey A family park with falconry displays, pony rides, tractor tours, farm animals and lamb feeding, sheepdog displays, a dragon train ride, a pets' corner, face painting, crazy golf and more. 📞**01407 840440** 💻**www.parc-henblas.co.uk** 82 D4

Manor House Wildlife and Leisure Park
£ adults £6.00, children (3–15) £5.00, seniors £5.00 👪3+ 🏃🏃🏃 ◐◐🍽🛍 Ⓟ

St Florence, Pembrokeshire A wild animal park with more than 200 species of mammals, birds, fish and reptiles, and a daily programme of events, including snake-handling, penguin feeding and falconry. 📞**01646 651201** 💻**www.manorhousewildanimalpark.co.uk** 32 D1

Margam Country Park
£ free 👪all ages 🏃🏃 ◐☕🧺Ⓟ£3.00

Margam, Neath Port Talbot An 850-acre parkland with historic gardens, walking trails, a Tudor-Gothic style Victorian mansion, an 18th-century orangery, a Victorian vine-house, a 12th-century chapterhouse, a narrow-gauge railway, a bird of prey rescue centre, a farm trail, a pets' corner, a deer collection, an adventure playground, a 'Fairytale Village' and a Visitor Centre. 📞**01639 881635** 💻**www.npt.gov.uk/margampark/index.cfm** 34 F2

Merlin's Hill
£ adults £3.00, children £1.50, seniors £2.50, 2+3 £9.00 👪all ages 🏃🏃 ◐◐🧺Ⓟ

Alltyfyrdden Farm, Abergwili, Carmarthenshire An Iron Age fort on a hill where, according to legend, Merlin the wizard is imprisoned, accessed via guided walks over ancient pathways. The farm on which it is located has a heritage centre dedicated to local history and agriculture, milking displays, meet-the-animals sessions and a play area. 📞**01267 237808** 💻**www.merlinshill.com** 33 B5

Moel Famau Country Park
£ free 👪4+ 🏃🏃🏃 ◐☕🧺Ⓟ

Ruthin/Rhuthun, Denbighshire One of Wales' biggest country parks, covering about 2,000 acres of uplands and containing the remains of three hillforts dating from 500BC to 43AD and a seven-mile stretch of the Offa's Dyke Trail, and providing a home to many bird of prey species. 📞**0845 604 0845** 💻**www.forestry.gov.uk** 72 C5

National Museum and Gallery
£ free 👪7+ 🏃 ◐✕🛍 Ⓟ

Cathays Park, Cardiff/Caerdydd, Cardiff A world-class museum and gallery with the world's biggest collection of Impressionist art outside France, plus archaeology and history of Wales, natural history and science displays. The Glanely Discovery Gallery allows hands-on experience of parts of the collections. 📞**029 2039 7951** 💻**www.museumwales.ac.uk/en/cardiff** 22 B3

National Wetlands Centre Wales
£ adults £5.72, children £3.49, concessions £4.50, 2+2 £14.94 👪5+ 🏃🏃 ◐◐✕🧺Ⓟ

Penclacwydd, Llwynhendy, Llanelli, Carmarthenshire An award-winning and innovative centre with ponds, lakes and reedbeds providing a habitat for thousands of ducks, swans and geese, water vole city, a maze, play area and a Millennium Wetland complex housing dragonflies, little egrets and more. 📞**01554 741087** 💻**www.wwt.org.uk** 33 E6

Oakwood Theme Park
£ telephone for details 👪all ages 🏃🏃🏃 ◐◐✕🍽☕🛍 Ⓟ

Cross Hands, Pembrokeshire A theme park with more than 40 rides and attractions, including Megaphobia, a wooden roller coaster, and many smaller rides for younger children. 📞**08712 206211** 💻**www.oakwood-leisure.com** 32 C1

Ocean Lab
£ telephone for details 👪all ages 🏃🏃 ◐◐ 🛍 Ⓟ

The Parrog, Goodwick/Wdig, Pembrokeshire An aquarium with an exhibition gallery, hands-on activities relating to the sea and shore life, a simulated submarine journey through time, computer games, ocean-themed soft play and more. 📞**01348 874737** 💻**www.ocean-lab.co.uk** 44 B4

Padarn Country Park
£ free 👪3+ 🏃🏃🏃 ◐◐◐🧺Ⓟ

Llanberis, Gwynedd Nature, woodland and industrial trails, the Welsh Slate Museum, the Llanberis steam railway, craft workshops, a watersports centre, Cwm Derwen Woodland Centre with its audiovisual displays, and an adventure playground with high-level rope walks. 📞**0207 531 8400** 💻**www.snowdonia-tourist-information-llanberis.co.uk** 83 E5

Pembrey Country Park
£ per car (winter) £2.00, (Apr-Jun, Sep) £3.50, (Jul-Aug) £5.50 👪all ages 🏃🏃🏃 ◐◐✕🍽🛍Ⓟ

Pembrey/Pembre, Carmarthenshire A country park with one of Britain's best beaches, a play area and playground, miniature railway, cycle hire, dry ski and snowboard slopes and picnic areas, as well as horse-riding at the Cowin Centre (01554 031260). Charges apply for horse-riding, cycle hire, skiing and toboggans. 📞**01554 833913** 💻**www.carmarthenshire.gov.uk** 33 D5

Penrhyn Castle (NT)
£ adults £8.00, children £4.00, 2+2 £20.00, (garden and stable block only) adults £5.40, children £2.70 👪7+ 🏃🏃 ◐☕🧺Ⓟ

Bangor, Gwynedd An exuberant early-19th-century neo-Norman Castle built by a local slate and sugar baron, with a one-ton slate bed made for Queen Victoria and old-master paintings. The stable block has two railway museums, a doll museum and two galleries. The extensive grounds include an adventure playground. 📞**01248 353084** 💻**www.nationaltrust.org.uk** 83 D6

Plantasia
£ adults £3.30, children £2.30, seniors £2.30 👪all ages 🏃🏃 ◐◐ 🛍Ⓟ

Parc Tawe, Swansea/Abertawe, Swansea A high-tech hothouse with one of Wales' best collections of plants, including giant bamboo, ferns and cacti, a butterfly house, a colony of cotton-top Tamarin monkeys and a variety of insects, reptiles and fish. There are treasure trails and children's activities and guided tours by request. 📞**01792 474555** 33 E7

Porthkerry Country Park
£ free 👪all ages 🏃🏃🏃 ◐🧺🛍Ⓟ

Barry/Y Barri, Vale of Glamorgan A 220-acre area of parkland with woods, meadows, cycle trails, nature trails leading to the beach, mini golf (small charge). 📞**01446 733589** 💻**www.valeofglamorgan.gov.uk** 22 C2

Queen Victoria
£ telephone for details 👪7+ 🏃🏃🏃 ◐✕🍽Ⓟ

Conwy Quay, Conwy River-bus trips to the Conwy Valley or round the estuary to see Puffin Island, Anglesey and the Great Orme. 📞**01492 592830** 83 D7

Rhyl Seaquarium
£ adults £6.15, children (4–16) £5.15, seniors £5.15 👪all ages 🏃🏃 ◐◐◐✕

East Parade, Rhyl/Y Rhyl, Denbighshire An aquarium with Wales' only walkthrough underwater tunnel, the Ocean Falls Cascade, the Sea at Night, with catfish and octopuses, and the Shark Encounter. 📞**01745 344660** 💻**www.seaquariumrhyl.co.uk** 72 A4

South Stack Lighthouse
£ adults £4.00, children £2.00, seniors £3.00 👪8+ 🏃🏃🏃 ◐◐◐✕Ⓟ

Holyhead, Isle of Anglesey A spectacular lighthouse on Holy Island, built in 1809 and accessed via 543 steps and a narrow bridge of the chasm separating it from the main island. The visitor centre, Ellin's Tower, has live footage of birds nesting on the cliffs during the breeding season. 📞**01248 75244** 💻**www.trinityhouse.co.uk** 82 C2

Ty Mawr Country Park
£ free 👪all ages 🏃🏃🏃 ◐🧺Ⓟ

Cae Gwilym Lane, Cafn-mawr, Wrexham A wildlife-rich, organically farmed country park on the banks of the Dee, with hay meadows, animal-feeding sessions, a play area, a Visitor Centre and panoramic views over the River Dee and the Pontcysyllte aqueduct. 📞**01978 822780** 73 E6

Welsh Mountain Zoo
£ adults £7.95, children (3–15) £5.80, seniors £8.90, 2+2 £24.95 👪all ages 🏃🏃🏃 ◐◐✕🍽Ⓟ

Colwyn Bay/Bae Colwyn, Conwy A conservation zoo in beautiful gardens above Colwyn Bay, with hundreds of animal and plant species from around the world, including Przewalski's horses, primates, rare owls, reptiles and insects, a seal rescue centre and children's farm animals. 📞**01492 532938** 💻**www.welshmountainzoo.org** 83 C8

Scotland

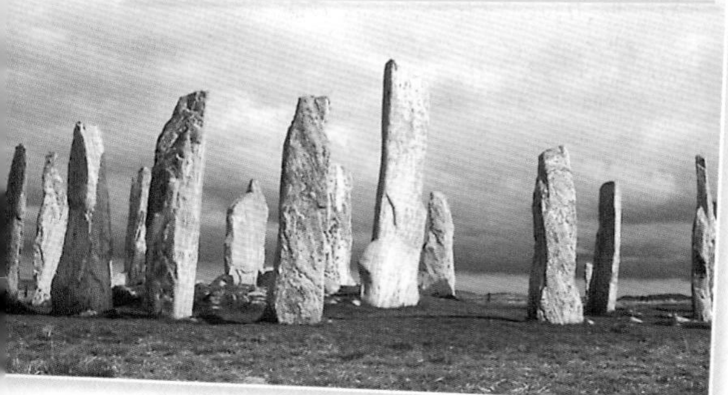

▲ Callanish Standing Stones

Alford Valley Railway
£ adults £2, children £1.00 👪all ages 🏃 ◐🧺Ⓟ

Main Street, Alford, Aberdeenshire A narrow-gauge train runs for about a mile from Alford Station to Murray Park, through the valley's wooded landscape. 📞**01975 562292** 💻**www.alfordvalleyrailway.org.uk** 150 C4

Archaeolink Prehistory Park
£ adults £5.00, children £2.40, concessions £4.50, 1+2 £11.50, 2+2 £15.25, 2+3 £18.20, 2+4 £21.00 👪7+ 🏃🏃 ◐◐✕Ⓟ

Oyne, Aberdeenshire An exploration of this area's Pictish heritage, with a reconstructed Iron Age farm, hands-on exhibits, re-enactments and craft demonstrations. Play area. 📞**01464 851500** 💻**www.archaeolink.co.uk** 151 B5

Blair Drummond Safari and Adventure Park
£ adults £10, children (3–14) £6.50, seniors 6.50 👪7+ 🏃🏃🏃 ◐◐✕🧺Ⓟ

Blair Drummond, Stirling The animal collection includes chimpanzees, elephants, monkeys, lemurs, zebras, bears, giraffes, ostriches, rhinos, camels, bison, wallabies and penguins. Sea lion displays take place regularly and other attractions include a pets' farm, boating and an adventure playground. 📞**01786 841456** 💻**www.blairdrummond.com** 133 E6

Bo'ness and Kinnell Railway
£ adults £5.00, children (5–15) £2.50, seniors £4.00, 2+2 £13.00 👪all ages 🏃 ◐ Ⓟ

Bo'ness Station, Union Street, Bo'ness, Falkirk Steam trains run in the summer months. Railway exhibition of Bo'ness Station. 📞**01506 822298** 💻**www.srps.org.uk/railway** 133 F8

Cairngorm Mountain Railway
£ adults £8.95, children (5–16) £5.95, senior £7.75, 2+2–3 £26.95. Snowsports facilities extra 👪5+ 🏃🏃 ◐◐✕🍽Ⓟ

Aviemore, Highland The funicular railway journey from the Coire Cas car park lasts about 8 minutes, giving views up the mountains and over the Cairngorm plateau and access to the ski and snow-boarding and sledging slopes in winter. There is a small mountain exhibition in the top station. 📞**01479 861261** 💻**www.cairngormmountain.com** 149 D5

Calderglen Country Park
£ free 👪all ages 🏃🏃 ◐🍽Ⓟ

Strathaven Road, East Kilbride, South Lanarkshire As well as miles of nature trails, this country park has a children's zoo with exotic animals, adventure play areas and a visitor centre. 📞**01355 236 644** 💻**www.southlanarkshire.gov.uk** 121 D6

Callanish Standing Stones and Visitor Centre
£ free 👪7+ 🏃🏃 ◐◐🍽Ⓟ

Calanais, Lewis, Western Isles A complex of standing stones. The main circle (Callanish) and the central megalith were erected about 5,000 years ago and a chambered cairn inserted within the circle. The other rows and avenue were added over the following 2,000 years. Callanish II is the remains of another circle with a cairn, Callanish III is another ring or ellipse and Callanish IV is another ring on the other side of the loch. There are also other settings of stones in the area. 📞**01851 621422** 💻**www.calanaisvisitorcentre.co.uk** 172 E5

Craig Highland Farm
£ adults £1.50, children £1.00 👪all ages 🏃🏃🏃 ◐ Ⓟ

Woodside, Plockton, Highland Set on the shore of Loch Carron, this farm has rare and traditional breeds of sheep and chickens, as well as rabbits, pigs, geese and ponies. In the surrounding area there is a chance of seeing seals, otters and pine martens. 📞**01599 544 205** 💻**www.geocities.com/t_heaviside** 155 G4

Dolphins and seals of the Moray Firth
£ free ⁜4+ 大大 ◎◎ P
North Kessock, Highland More than 100 bottlenose dolphins live in the Moray Firth. At the visitor centre in North Kessock, visitors can listen in to the dolphins' calls. Among the best viewing points is nearby Kessock Bridge. ☎01463 731866 **157 E7**

Doonies Farm
£ adults £1.00, seniors £0.50, 2+2 £2.00 ⁜all ages 大大大 ◎◎ 岡 P
Coast Road, Nigg, Aberdeen City One of the largest collections of rare-breed farm animals, including horses, goats, cattle, sheep, pigs and poultry. Children's play area. ☎01224 875 879
🖳 www.aberdeencity.gov.uk **151 D8**

Ecoventures
£ adults £20.00, children £15.00
⁜5+ (8+ in poor weather) 大大 ◎◎ 폭 P on-street parking
Harbour Workshop, Victoria Place, Cromarty, Highland Full-day trips to see the dolphins and seals in the outer regions of the Moray Firth. Booking recommended. Each child under 12 must be accompanied by an adult. ☎01381 600323 🖳 www.ecoventures.co.uk **157 C8**

Edinburgh Butterfly and Insect World
£ adults £5, children/seniors £3.85, families from £16.50 ⁜2+ 大大 ◎ X ⑪ P
Dobbies Garden World, Lasswade, Dalkeith, Midlothian Breeding butterflies from around the world, in enclosures that visitors may walk through. Small animals include leaf-cutting ants, beetles, scorpions, locusts, spiders and grasshoppers, while among the larger specimens are terrapins, snakes, an iguana and some quail.
☎0131 6634932 🖳 www.edinburgh-butterfly-world.co.uk **123 C6**

Edinburgh Zoo
£ adults £10.50, children (3–14) £7.50, concessions free, 2+2 £34.00, 2+3 £38.50
⁜3+ 大大 ◎◎ ⑪ 岡 P
134 Corstorphine Road, Edinburgh, City of Edinburgh The collection holds more than 1,500 animals, including endangered species such as snow leopards, white rhinos and pygmy hippos.
☎0131 3349171 🖳 www.edinburghzoo.org.uk **122 B5**

Eilean Bàn
£ telephone for details ⁜8+ 大大 ◎◎ P (at visitor centre)
Kyle of Lochalsh, Highland Island wildlife sanctuary under the Skye Bridge. Once the home of Gavin Maxwell, author of 'Ring of Bright Water', this sanctuary is particularly associated with otters. Guided tours must be prebooked at the Bright Water Visitor Centre in Kyleakin.
☎01599 530040) 🖳 www.eileanban.org **155 H3**

Falkirk Wheel
£ adults £8.00, children 3–16 £4.20, seniors £6.50, 2+2 £21.50
⁜3+ 大大 ◎◎◎ ⑪ P
Lime Road, Tamfourhill, Falkirk Built to reconnect the Forth and Clyde and Union canals, the Falkirk Wheel is the world's first rotating boat lift. It rises to 34.5 m, a height that would have required 11 locks, moving 600 tonnes of water to that height in 4 minutes. This visitor centre has an interactive exhibition, play area and a viewing gallery. Boat trips on the wheel can be prebooked. ☎01324 619888
🖳 www.thefalkirkwheel.co.uk **133 F7**

Glasgow Science Centre
£ adults £9.95, children/concessions £7.95 ⁜7+ 大大大 ◎◎◎ ⑪ P
50 Pacific Quay, Glasgow Science centre with hands-on displays, a planetarium, live shows and an Imax cinema. ☎0141 4205000
🖳 www.glasgowsciencecentre.org **121 C5**

Highland Wildlife Park
£ adults £10.00, children £7.50, seniors £8.00, 2+2 £23.50, 2+3 £38.00
⁜4+ 大大大 ◎◎◎ P
Kincraig, Highland This extensive park is devoted to the native fauna of the Highlands, from the whole range of habitats. Forest specialities include polecat, wildcat, red squirrel and capercaillie, while arctic fox and snowy owl prefer tundra, otters and beavers are wetland species and tawny owls, badgers and black grouse inhabit the woodlands. Some species are extinct in the wild, or have been reintroduced only in limited areas: these include lynx, white-tailed sea eagle, wolf and chough. ☎01540 651270 🖳 www.highlandwildlifepark.org **148 D4**

Iolaire
£ adults £20, children (under 14) £10.00 ⁜5+ 大 ◎◎◎
Fionnphort, Mull, Argyll & Bute Boat trips to Fingal's Cave on Staffa. Weather permitting, the boat sails right into the cave, allowing passengers to land. The hexagonal shape of the rocks that make up the cave's walls, floor and roof formed when Tertiary basalt lava flows shrank and cracked as they cooled after a volcanic eruption.
☎01681 700 358 🖳 www.staffatrips.f9.co.uk **136 F4**

Jacobite Steam Train
£ (return) adults from £28.00, children from £16.00 ⁜all ages 大大 ◎◎
Fort William Railway Station, Fort William, Highland Return trips along the West Highland Railway between Fort William and Mallaig by steam train, through scenery including Loch Shiel, over the 21 arches of the Glenfinnan viaduct, familiar from the Harry Potter films, and past the beautiful beaches of Morar. ☎01463 239026
🖳 www.westcoastrailway.com **139 B5**

Jedforest Deer and Farm Park
£ adults £4.50, children (5+) £2.50, seniors £2.50 ⁜2+ 大大大 ◎ ⑪ 岡 P
Camptown, Scottish Borders Farm with rare breeds of cattle, goats, sheep, chickens and pigs, as well as herds of red, fallow and sika deer and more exotic animals. Indoor and outdoor play areas, ranger-led walks and animal-feeding sessions are available. ☎01385 840364
🖳 www.aboutscotland.co.uk/jedforest/farm.html **116 C2**

Keith and Dufftown Railway
£ adults £9.50, children £4.50, concessions £7.50, 2+2 £23.00
⁜all ages 大 ◎ X P
Dufftown Station, Dufftown, Moray Also known as the Whisky Line, this is an 11-mile route through beautiful countryside, providing views of wildlife and spectacular scenery. The diesel trains operate during summer weekends. ☎01340 821181
🖳 www.keith-dufftown.org.uk **159 E7**

Landmark Highland Heritage and Adventure Park
£ adults £9.75, children (5–14) £7.60, seniors £7.10 ⁜2+ 大大大 ◎ X ⑪ P
Carrbridge, near Aviemore, Highland This varied site includes a water coaster, a hands-on nature centre called Microworld, where children can examine bugs under a microscope or with a magnifying glass, an

adventure trail, a timber trail that explores the timber industry, an ant city and hands-on woodcrafts. Age/height restrictions apply on some rides. ☎01479841613 🖳 www.landmark-centre.co.uk **148 B5**

Leadhills and Wanlockhead Railway
£ adults £3.00, children (3–16) £1.00, 2+2–6 £7.00 ⁜4+ 大 ◎ P
The Station, Leadhills, South Lanarkshire Diesel trains operate on this tourist railway between Leadhills and the disused lead mine at Wanlockhead, where there is a small museum and a beam engine.
☎01555 820778 🖳 www.leadhillsrailway.co.uk **113 C8**

Loch Ness 2000 Exhibition
£ adults £5.95, children (7+) £3.50, seniors £4.50, 2+1–3 £14.95
⁜7+ 大大大 ◎◎ P
Drumnadrochit, Highland This exhibition explores the history of Nessie through eyewitness accounts and the research of various expeditions to locate the monster. ☎01456 450573
🖳 www.loch-ness-scotland.com **157 F6**

Loudoun Castle Theme Park
£ under 1m free, 1–1.3 m £11.99, over 1.3m £13.99, seniors £8.99
⁜4+ 大大 ◎◎◎ ⑪ P
Loudoun Castle, Galston, East Ayrshire A family attraction with rides such as a roller coaster and pirate ship, as well as live entertainment. Height/age restrictions apply for some rides. ☎01563 822296
🖳 www.loudouncastle.co.uk **120 F5**

Macduff Marine Aquarium
£ adults £6, children £2.50 (3–15), seniors £3.00, 2+2 £13.75
⁜5+ 大大 ◎◎ P
11 High Shore, Macduff, Aberdeenshire This aquarium concentrates on the sea life of the Moray Firth, with rays, native fish, crustaceans and touch tanks. ☎01261 833369 🖳 www.macduff-aquarium.org.uk **160 B4**

Moray Firth Cruises
£ adults £12.50, children (3+) £9.00, seniors £10, 2+2–4 £55.00 ⁜3+ 大大 ◎◎
Shore Street Quay, Shore Street, Inverness, Highland Boat trips to see the dolphins and seals in the Moray Firth. ☎01463 717900
🖳 www.inverness-dolphin-cruises.co.uk **157 E7**

Museum of Flight
£ adults £5.50, children (under 12) free, seniors £4.50 ⁜6+ 大大 ◎◎ P
East Fortune, East Lothian The attractions in the old World War II hangars include more than 50 aircraft, among them a Tiger Moth, a Spitfire and a Vulcan as well as a Concorde with an accompanying exhibition. Pre-booking is essential for the Concorde boarding pass.
☎(Museum) 01620 880308 (Concorde Boarding Pass) 0870 4214299
🖳 www.nms.ac.uk/flight **123 B8**

MV Shearwater
£ adults £10.00–£16.00, children (3–10) £8.00, (11–16) £11.00 ⁜3+ 大 ◎◎ P
The Harbour, Arisaig, Highland Boat trips run by Arisaig Marine between Arisaig and various nearby islands including the nature reserve on Rum, Eigg, Muck and Canna. Whales and porpoises are sometimes seen en route. ☎01687 450 224 🖳 www.arisaig.co.uk **145 E6**

North Coast Marine Adventures
£ telephone for details ⁜5+ 大大大 ◎
Sunfield, Skarsferry by Thurso, Highland Full-day wildlife cruises in a rigid inflatable boat. Seabirds are abundant and whales and dolphins are sometimes seen. ☎01955 611797
🖳 www.northcoast.fsnet.co.uk **169 B7**

North East Falconry Centre
£ adults £4.75, children £2.75, concessions £3.75 ⁜all ages 大大 ◎◎ ⑪ 岡 P
Broadland, Carnie, Huntly, Aberdeenshire Daily demonstrations of falconry, with flying eagles and falcons. There are also owls in the collection. ☎01466 760 328 🖳 www.huntly-falconry.co.uk **159 E8**

Our Dynamic Earth
£ adults £8.95, children (5–15) £5.75, (2–4) £1.95, seniors £6.95
⁜2+ 大大大 ◎◎ ⑪ P
107 Holyrood Road, Edinburgh, City of Edinburgh A fully interactive exploration of the geological and biological history of the Earth, including aquaria, audiovisual clips, simulations of different climates on Earth from tundra to rainforests and an earthquake simulator.
☎0131 5507800 🖳 www.dynamicearth.co.uk **123 B5**

Perth, Angus, Dundee and Fife Deep Sea World
£ adults £8.75, children (3–15) £6.50, seniors £7.00, 2+2 £29.50
⁜3+ 大大 ◎◎ ⑪ P
Battery Quarry, North Queensferry, Fife Attractions include sharks, piranhas, touch pools with rays and snake-handling sessions.
☎01383 411880 🖳 www.deepseaworld.com **134 F3**

Pictavia Visitor Centre
£ adults £3.25, children (5+) and concessions £2.25, 2+2–3 £10.00
⁜5+ 大大大 ◎◎◎ X P
Brechin, Angus Interpretative centre about the Picts, who lived in Scotland about 2,000 years ago, looking at their musical instruments, their carved stones and other aspects of these little-known people's lives. ☎01307 473765 🖳 www.pictavia.org.uk **143 C5**

Royal Museum of Scotland
£ free ⁜4+ 大大 ◎ X ⑪ P
Chambers Street, Edinburgh, City of Edinburgh Exhibits include the decorative arts, geology, natural history, archaeology, ethnography, technology and science. The history of Scotland over the last 3.9 billion years is explored in six modern galleries, including its role as an independent state before Union with England in 1707 and the Industrial Revolution. ☎0131 2474422 🖳 www.nms.ac.uk/scotland **123 B5**

Satrosphere
£ adults £5.75, children (3+) £4.40, concessions £4.50 ⁜3+ 大大 ◎◎◎ ⑪ P
The Tramsheds, 179 Constitution Street, Aberdeen, Aberdeen City A series of hands-on science exhibits that will occupy children of all ages.
☎01224 640340 🖳 www.satrosphere.net **151 D8**

Scottish Crannog Centre
£ adults £5.25, children £3.50, seniors £4.25, family from £15.00
⁜6+ 大大 ◎◎◎ 폭 P
Kenmore, Perth and Kinross A museum devoted to the history of crannogs (loch-dwellings) with archaeological items from a nearby example, tours of a re-created crannog and demonstrations of Iron Age technology and crafts that visitors may try for themselves.
☎01887 830583 🖳 www.crannog.co.uk **140 E4**

▲ The Falkirk Wheel

Scottish Sea Life and Marine Sanctuary
£ adults £10.50, children £7.50, seniors £8.50 ⁜4+ 大大 ◎ X P
Barcaldine, Oban, Argyll & Bute On the southern shore of Loch Creran, this centre has plenty of sea creatures, including rays that can be stroked. Children can dip in the rock pools and learn how orphaned seal pups are rescued and returned to the wild. ☎01631 720386
🖳 www.sealsanctuary.co.uk/oban1.html **138 E3**

Scottish Seabird Centre
£ adults £6.95, concessions £4.50, 1+2 £13.95, 1+3 £17.95, 2+1 £15.95, 2+2 £13.95, 2+3 £21.95 ⁜all ages 大大 ◎◎ ⑪ P
North Berwick, East Lothian The chief feature of this centre is the close-up views of the birdlife of nearby Bass Rock, obtained via a live link to cameras there, as well as to the Isle of May. There are also games for children and exhibits on Scotland's different seabirds.
☎01620 890 202 🖳 www.seabird.org **135 F7**

Sea Life Surveys and Ecocruz
£ half-day £40.00, children £35.00, family £140.00, full day £70.00
⁜7+ 大 ◎◎ P
Tobermory, Mull, Argyll & Bute Research vessels that take passengers conducting surveys of the area's dolphins and whales. Tea and coffee are available. ☎01688 302916 🖳 www.sealifesurveys.com **137 C6**

Sea.fari Adventures
£ telephone for details ⁜5+ 大大大 ◎◎ P
Newhaven Harbour, Leith/Hawes Pier, Queensferry, City of Edinburgh Trips to see the birds and sea life of the islands in the Firth of Forth. ☎07850 882304 🖳 www.seafari.co.uk **123 B5/122 B4**

Seaprobe Atlantis
£ adults £12.50–£24.00, children (4–14) £6.50–£12.00, (2–3) £3.00–£6.00, seniors £10.50–£22.00, 2+2 £36.00–£41.00 ⁜all ages 大 ◎◎◎ P
Off Station Road, Kyle of Lochalsh, Highland Operating from the pier, this boat has viewports in the hull allowing passengers to see the wild-life under water, including seals and diving birds. Trips include a visit to seal island. ☎01471 822716 🖳 www.seaprobeatlantis.com **155 H3**

Skye Serpentarium Reptile World
£ telephone for details ⁜7+ 大大 ◎◎ P
Harrapool, Skye, Highland Reptile and amphibian rescue centre with many on display, including snakes, iguanas, monitor lizard, tree frogs and tortoises. Snake handling sessions are often held.
☎01471 8222209 🖳 www.skyeserpentarium.org.uk **155 H2**

Smoo Cave
£ entrance free, boat trip small charge ⁜5+ 大大 ◎◎ P
Durness, Highland A 200ft long complex of three caves etched into the limestone cliffs by the stream and the sea. The central cave is crossed by rubber dinghy. ☎(Durness TIC) 03452 255121
🖳 www.smoocave.org **167 C6**

St Andrews Aquarium
£ adults £6.20, children (3–15) £4.40, seniors £5.00, 2+2 £19.50, 2+3 £23.00, 2+3 £26.50 ⁜3+ 大大 ◎◎ P
The Scores, St Andrews, Fife This popular attractions holds seals, sharks, exotic fish, crustaceans, rays, octopuses, seahorses and touch-pools. ☎01334 474786 🖳 www.standrewsaquarium.co.uk **151 D8**

Strathclyde Country Park
£ entrance free, charges for activities and hire of some facilities
⁜all ages 大大 ◎ ⑪ P
336 Hamilton Road, Motherwell, North Lanarkshire Centred on Strathclyde Loch, this park consists of 1,000 acres of mature woodland, wetland, wildlife areas and open parkland. Activities include a variety of watersports, wayfaring and orienteering. ☎01698 266155 🖳 www.northlan.gov.uk/leisure+and+tourism/index.html **121 D7**

Strathspey Steam Railway
£ telephone for details ⁜7+ 大 ◎◎ X P
Dalfaber Road, Aviemore, Highland This restored railway runs through Highland scenery between Aviemore and Broomhill.
☎01479 810725 🖳 www.strathspeyrailway.co.uk **148 C5**

Sula
£ telephone for details ⁜8+ 大 ◎◎ P
North Berwick, East Lothian The boat 'Sula' provides trips around Bass Rock from North Berwick harbour. Breeding birds that may be seen include fulmars, guillemots, puffins, razorbills and terns, as well as Scotland's second biggest gannet colony. ☎01620 890181
🖳 www.north-berwick.co.uk/bassRock.asp **135 F7**

Treasures of the Earth
£ telephone for details ⁜8+ 大 ◎◎ P
Corpach, Fort William, Highland A centre dedicated to crystals, rocks and gemstones, their properties, where they come from and how they are mined. Exhibits include a re-created mine which shows the conditions under which the miners work. ☎01397 772283 **138 B4**

Vikingar!
£ telephone for details ⁜5+ 大大大 ◎◎◎ ⑪ P
Greenock Road, Largs, North Ayrshire ☎01475 689777
🖳 www.naleisure.co.uk **120 C2**

Distance table

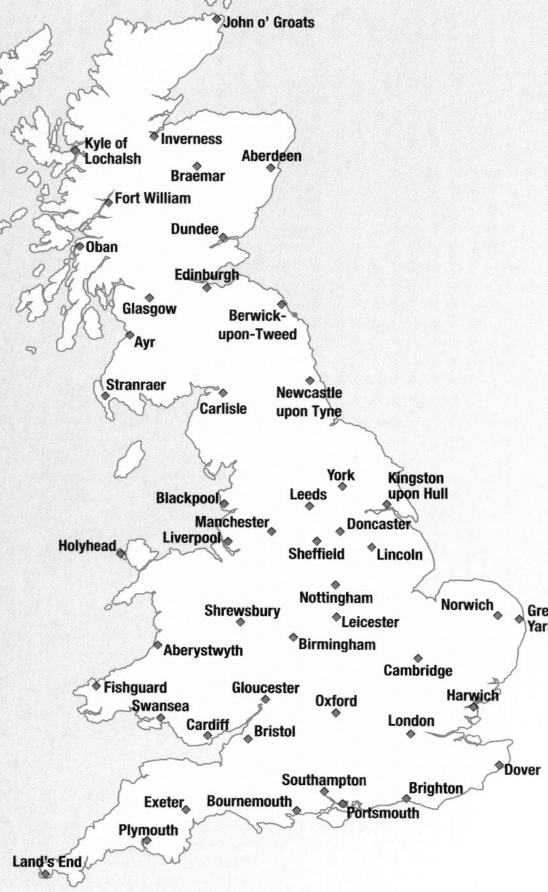

How to use this table

Distances are shown in miles and kilometres with estimated journey times in hours and minutes.

For example: the distance between Dover and Fishguard is 331 miles or 533 kilometres with an estimated journey time of 6 hours, 20 minutes.

Estimated driving times are based on an average speed of 60mph on Motorways and 40mph on other roads. Drivers should allow extra time when driving at peak periods or through areas likely to be congested.

	Fishguard	Exeter	Edinburgh	Dundee	Dover
Dundee					523 842 9:10
Edinburgh				56 90 1:30	462 744 8:10
Exeter			450 724 8:00	518 834 9:10	248 399 4:40
Fishguard		230 370 4:30	399 642 7:30	460 740 8:30	331 533 6:20
Fort William	486 782 9:30	560 901 10:20	144 232 3:30	127 204 3:10	596 959 11:00

	Swansea	Stranraer	Southampton	Shrewsbury	Sheffield	Portsmouth	Plymouth	Oxford	Oban	Nottingham	Norwich	Newcastle upon Tyne	Manchester	Liverpool	Lincoln	Leicester	Leeds	Land's End	Kyle of Lochalsh	Kingston upon Hull	John o' Groats	Inverness	Holyhead	Harwich	Great Yarmouth	Gloucester	Glasgow	Fort William	Fishguard	Exeter	Edinburgh	Dundee	Dover	Doncaster	Carlisle	Cardiff	Cambridge	Bristol	Brighton	Braemar	Bournemouth	Blackpool	Birmingham	Berwick-upon-Tweed	Ayr	Aberystwyth	Aberdeen	London
Aberdeen																																																517 832 11:20
Aberystwyth																																															445 716 8:40	211 340 4:40
Ayr																																														317 510 6:10	183 295 4:20	394 634 7:20
Berwick-upon-Tweed																																													134 216 3:00	311 501 6:20	182 293 4:40	352 567 7:30
Birmingham																																												274 441 5:30	289 465 5:30	114 183 2:50	420 676 8:30	117 188 2:50
Blackpool																																											123 198 2:40	181 291 3:50	180 290 3:30	153 246 3:20	308 496 6:20	226 364 4:30
Bournemouth																																										270 435 5:00	147 237 3:10	412 663 7:50	436 702 8:00	207 333 4:30	564 908 10:20	107 172 2:40
Braemar																																									524 843 9:30	281 452 5:20	385 620 7:10	148 238 3:20	143 230 3:00	405 652 7:50	59 95 1:30	482 776 10:30
Brighton																																								534 859 9:40	92 148 2:10	286 460 5:20	163 262 3:20	409 658 7:40	446 718 8:00	253 407 5:10	573 922 10:30	52 84 1:50
Bristol																																							147 237 4:10	477 768 8:40	82 132 2:30	204 328 3:50	81 130 2:00	362 583 6:50	370 595 6:40	125 201 3:00	493 793 9:10	122 196 2:50
Cambridge																																						169 272 3:10	116 187 2:20	438 705 7:50	154 248 3:00	208 335 3:50	100 161 2:10	306 493 5:40	357 575 6:20	214 344 4:20	471 758 10:00	54 87 1:30
Cardiff																																					190 306 3:30	45 72 1:20	182 293 3:40	483 778 8:40	117 188 3:00	209 336 4:00	103 166 2:20	368 592 7:00	382 615 7:00	105 169 2:40	505 813 9:20	157 253 3:20
Carlisle																																				289 465 5:20	264 425 4:40	277 446 5:00	370 596 6:40	196 316 3:50	343 552 6:20	87 140 1:50	196 315 3:50	87 140 2:10	93 150 2:00	224 360 4:30	221 356 4:30	301 484 5:40
Doncaster																																			142 229 3:00	209 336 4:00	116 187 2:10	175 282 3:20	236 380 4:30	310 499 5:40	235 378 4:20	94 151 1:50	94 151 2:00	184 296 3:50	235 378 4:20	176 283 3:40	344 554 6:50	171 275 3:30
Dover																																		242 390 4:30	389 626 7:00	238 383 4:30	125 201 2:30	202 325 3:50	82 132 2:20	553 890 9:50	174 280 4:30	312 502 5:40	194 312 3:50	424 683 7:50	478 769 8:30	297 478 5:50	588 947 10:40	71 114 2:00
Dundee																																	523 842 9:10	275 443 5:00	152 245 3:00	441 710 8:00	406 654 7:10	430 692 7:40	517 832 9:10	52 84 1:20	495 797 8:50	239 385 4:30	349 562 6:20	113 182 2:40	117 188 2:30	376 605 7:10	67 108 1:50	448 721 8:40
Edinburgh																																56 90 1:30	462 744 8:10	219 352 4:00	96 154 2:00	385 620 7:00	345 555 6:10	373 600 6:50	456 734 8:20	91 146 2:10	439 707 8:00	183 295 3:30	292 470 5:30	57 92 1:40	73 117 1:50	320 515 6:20	125 201 3:10	390 628 7:20
Exeter																															450 724 8:00	518 834 9:10	248 399 4:40	251 404 4:30	353 568 6:20	121 195 2:30	249 401 4:30	76 122 1:40	184 296 5:00	550 885 9:40	82 132 2:20	282 454 5:10	157 253 3:10	428 689 7:50	446 718 7:50	201 323 4:10	569 916 10:20	181 291 3:40
Fishguard																														230 370 4:30	399 642 7:30	460 740 8:30	331 533 6:20	247 398 4:50	297 478 5:40	112 180 2:40	270 435 5:10	154 248 3:20	291 468 5:40	493 794 9:10	222 357 4:40	209 336 4:10	170 274 3:40	371 597 7:20	373 600 7:00	56 90 1:30	504 811 10:10	260 418 5:20
Fort William																													486 782 9:30	560 901 10:20	144 232 3:30	127 204 3:10	596 959 11:00	357 575 7:00	206 332 4:30	485 781 9:10	479 771 9:00	486 782 9:10	575 926 10:50	125 201 3:10	539 867 10:10	296 476 6:00	392 631 7:40	190 306 4:40	133 214 3:20	430 692 8:40	149 240 3:50	510 821 9:50
Glasgow																												101 163 2:50	376 605 7:10	449 723 8:00	44 71 1:20	83 134 2:00	488 786 8:40	249 401 4:40	96 154 2:10	385 620 7:00	372 599 6:40	373 600 6:50	468 753 8:30	110 177 2:30	439 707 8:00	183 295 3:40	292 470 5:30	101 163 2:40	33 53 1:10	320 515 6:20	145 233 3:30	397 639 7:30
Gloucester																											346 557 6:10	454 731 8:30	153 246 3:10	111 179 2:10	349 562 6:10	410 660 7:10	191 307 3:30	150 241 2:50	247 398 4:20	56 90 1:20	123 198 2:20	35 56 1:00	159 256 3:10	443 713 8:00	99 159 2:40	174 280 3:10	56 90 1:20	318 512 6:00	330 531 5:50	102 164 2:30	468 753 8:30	109 175 2:30
Great Yarmouth																										225 362 4:40	419 674 8:00	527 848 10:20	366 589 7:20	335 539 6:30	386 621 7:30	484 779 9:00	185 298 4:00	167 269 3:40	320 515 6:20	284 457 5:50	82 132 2:10	275 443 5:40	180 290 4:10	477 768 9:10	240 386 5:00	252 406 5:10	180 290 4:10	345 555 7:00	402 647 7:40	294 473 6:20	517 832 10:50	128 206 3:40
Harwich																									82 132 2:10	196 316 4:00	432 695 8:10	543 874 10:30	337 542 6:40	279 449 5:20	413 665 7:40	469 755 8:40	125 201 2:50	194 312 4:00	336 541 6:20	246 396 5:00	67 108 1:50	217 349 4:30	128 206 3:00	504 811 9:20	187 301 4:00	275 443 5:20	167 269 3:40	372 599 7:20	425 684 8:00	281 452 5:50	535 861 11:20	76 122 2:20
Holyhead																								349 562 7:10	334 538 7:00	191 307 4:00	330 531 6:40	438 705 8:50	167 269 4:00	282 454 5:40	333 536 6:40	394 634 7:30	360 580 7:00	181 291 3:50	231 372 4:50	216 348 5:40	270 435 5:20	206 332 4:30	334 538 6:40	426 686 8:20	288 463 5:50	141 227 3:20	148 238 3:30	311 501 6:30	305 491 6:10	111 179 2:50	439 707 8:40	269 433 5:40
Inverness																							474 763 9:40	569 916 11:00	553 890 11:00	504 811 9:30	166 267 4:00	66 106 1:40	542 872 10:30	618 995 11:30	158 254 3:50	132 212 3:20	622 1001 11:30	383 617 7:30	262 422 5:30	549 884 10:20	505 813 9:30	539 867 10:10	617 993 11:30	75 121 2:00	597 961 11:20	348 560 7:00	458 737 9:00	215 346 5:10	199 320 4:30	486 782 9:40	105 169 2:50	550 885 10:40
John o' Groats																						129 208 3:20	603 970 12:40	693 1116 14:00	677 1090 14:00	628 1011 12:30	295 475 7:10	195 314 5:00	671 1080 13:40	744 1197 14:30	285 459 7:00	259 417 6:30	746 1201 14:40	507 816 10:30	391 629 8:40	680 1094 13:30	630 1014 12:30	668 1075 13:20	741 1193 14:40	202 325 5:00	724 1165 14:20	478 769 10:00	574 924 11:50	342 550 8:10	328 528 7:40	601 967 12:40	232 373 5:50	663 1067 13:30
Kingston upon Hull																					518 834 10:50	394 634 7:50	231 372 4:50	196 316 4:10	207 333 5:20	169 272 3:10	254 409 4:50	369 594 7:20	280 451 5:30	309 497 5:40	234 377 4:30	295 475 5:30	256 412 4:50	47 76 1:10	158 254 3:00	244 393 4:40	139 224 3:10	233 375 4:20	245 394 4:40	327 526 6:10	264 425 5:00	127 204 2:30	134 216 2:50	185 298 3:50	251 404 4:40	223 359 4:40	364 586 7:20	184 296 3:50
Kyle of Lochalsh																				445 716 9:00	189 304 4:40	84 135 2:10	514 827 10:40	611 983 12:10	602 969 12:10	528 850 10:20	179 288 4:40	79 127 2:00	567 913 11:20	628 1011 12:00	216 348 5:20	186 299 4:40	671 1080 12:50	432 695 8:40	275 443 6:10	564 908 11:10	555 893 10:50	552 888 10:50	651 1048 12:40	159 256 4:00	618 995 12:10	372 599 7:50	471 758 9:40	263 423 6:20	212 341 5:10	499 803 10:20	189 304 4:50	586 943 11:40
Land's End																			763 1228 15:10	421 678 8:20	868 1397 17:20	741 1193 14:20	405 652 8:30	390 628 8:00	446 718 9:10	235 378 5:00	573 922 10:50	686 1104 13:20	353 568 7:20	123 198 3:20	574 924 10:50	642 1033 12:00	381 613 7:40	374 602 7:20	477 768 9:10	245 394 5:20	374 602 7:20	200 322 4:40	308 496 7:50	665 1070 12:30	205 330 5:20	405 652 8:00	281 452 6:00	552 888 10:40	570 917 10:50	313 504 6:50	692 1114 13:10	297 478 6:30
Leeds																		405 652 8:00	394 634 8:20	55 89 1:30	487 784 10:20	360 579 7:10	176 283 4:00	223 359 4:30	196 315 4:20	174 280 3:20	215 346 4:10	329 530 6:40	237 381 4:40	270 435 5:00	202 325 4:00	258 415 4:50	260 418 4:50	29 47 0:50	119 192 2:30	232 373 4:20	145 233 2:50	194 312 3:50	260 419 5:00	293 472 5:30	255 410 4:50	72 116 1:40	113 182 2:30	156 251 3:20	212 341 4:00	169 272 3:40	327 526 6:50	189 304 3:50
Leicester																	95 153 2:00	320 515 6:30	500 805 9:50	102 164 2:10	588 947 11:50	461 742 8:50	190 306 4:00	147 237 3:10	140 225 3:20	85 137 1:40	314 505 5:40	422 679 8:00	209 336 4:10	196 315 3:40	296 476 5:20	349 562 6:20	185 298 3:30	74 119 1:30	206 332 3:50	154 248 3:00	68 109 1:20	120 193 2:30	166 267 3:20	389 626 7:00	158 254 3:10	140 225 2:40	39 63 1:10	252 406 5:00	299 481 5:20	153 246 3:20	414 666 7:40	97 156 2:20
Lincoln																51 82 1:20	68 109 1:50	371 597 7:30	476 766 9:40	44 71 1:20	554 892 11:30	427 687 8:30	216 348 4:40	155 249 3:30	128 206 3:20	159 256 3:10	291 468 5:30	399 642 7:50	272 438 5:30	247 398 4:40	258 415 5:00	314 505 5:50	202 325 4:00	39 63 1:10	191 307 3:40	208 335 4:10	85 137 2:20	183 295 3:40	197 317 4:00	357 575 6:40	209 336 4:10	128 206 2:40	90 145 2:10	224 360 4:40	274 441 5:10	199 320 4:20	383 616 7:20	131 211 3:10
Liverpool															129 208 2:50	130 209 2:40	75 121 1:50	361 581 7:20	407 655 8:30	130 209 2:40	511 822 10:40	382 615 7:40	102 164 2:40	265 427 5:20	240 386 5:00	140 225 2:40	216 348 4:10	329 530 6:40	160 257 3:30	237 381 4:30	216 348 4:10	286 460 5:20	299 481 5:30	86 138 1:50	120 193 2:30	169 272 3:20	194 312 3:40	161 259 3:10	272 438 5:10	318 512 6:00	234 377 4:30	49 79 1:20	93 150 2:10	219 352 4:30	213 343 4:10	104 167 2:40	341 549 6:40	202 325 4:10
Manchester														35 56 1:10	84 135 2:00	92 148 2:00	40 64 1:10	361 581 7:20	406 654 8:30	95 153 2:10	500 805 10:30	373 600 7:30	124 200 3:00	228 367 4:40	212 341 4:30	126 203 2:30	215 346 4:10	329 530 6:40	197 317 4:00	236 380 4:20	215 346 4:10	285 459 5:20	276 444 5:10	61 98 1:30	119 192 2:30	183 295 3:40	165 266 3:10	161 259 3:10	257 414 4:50	318 512 6:00	227 365 4:20	48 77 1:20	80 129 2:00	196 315 4:00	212 341 4:00	129 208 3:00	340 547 6:30	185 298 3:50
Newcastle upon Tyne													132 212 2:50	168 270 3:20	159 256 3:20	187 301 3:40	92 148 2:10	498 802 9:40	318 512 7:00	132 212 2:50	395 636 8:50	268 431 5:40	272 438 5:40	308 496 6:00	281 452 5:40	266 428 4:50	148 238 3:10	253 407 5:20	329 529 6:20	364 586 6:30	110 177 2:20	166 267 3:20	358 576 6:30	114 183 2:20	57 92 1:50	325 523 6:00	241 388 4:20	299 481 5:30	352 567 6:30	201 323 4:00	347 558 6:30	129 208 2:40	207 333 4:10	64 103 1:50	149 240 3:00	257 414 5:20	235 378 4:50	286 460 5:40
Norwich												264 425 5:20	185 298 4:30	220 354 4:40	105 169 2:50	119 192 3:20	176 283 3:50	421 678 8:40	582 937 11:50	149 240 4:00	654 1053 13:30	529 852 10:30	311 501 6:40	73 117 2:00	20 32 0:40	204 328 4:10	385 620 9:00	504 811 10:00	343 552 7:00	308 496 6:00	366 589 7:00	422 679 8:00	174 280 3:50	147 237 3:20	289 465 5:40	262 422 5:20	62 100 1:50	252 406 5:10	175 282 4:00	457 735 8:40	214 344 4:40	232 373 4:50	166 267 3:50	328 528 6:40	382 615 7:20	276 444 6:00	496 798 9:40	114 183 3:30
Nottingham											130 209 3:40	157 253 3:10	73 118 1:40	98 158 2:10	35 56 1:10	25 40 0:50	70 113 1:40	345 555 7:00	479 771 9:40	90 145 2:00	557 896 11:30	430 692 8:20	185 298 4:00	150 241 3:20	153 246 3:30	110 177 2:10	293 472 5:30	401 646 7:50	220 354 4:30	221 356 4:10	262 422 4:50	328 528 6:00	205 330 3:50	43 69 1:10	194 312 3:40	172 277 3:20	83 134 1:40	145 233 3:00	193 311 3:50	353 568 6:30	183 295 3:40	111 179 2:20	50 80 1:20	221 356 4:30	274 441 5:10	164 264 3:40	393 633 7:30	122 196 2:40
Oban										390 628 7:30	492 792 9:40	233 375 4:50	307 494 6:00	308 496 6:10	387 623 7:30	419 674 7:50	307 494 6:00	665 1070 12:50	128 206 3:10	346 557 6:40	244 393 6:10	117 188 3:00	427 687 8:30	524 843 10:00	515 829 10:00	441 710 8:10	92 148 2:30	49 79 1:20	481 774 9:10	549 884 10:00	123 198 3:00	117 188 2:50	585 942 10:40	346 557 6:40	188 303 4:00	477 768 9:00	468 753 8:40	465 748 8:40	565 910 10:30	141 227 3:30	530 853 9:50	285 459 5:40	384 618 7:30	180 290 4:20	94 151 2:20	412 663 8:10	178 286 4:20	499 803 9:30
Oxford									462 744 8:30	109 175 2:10	145 233 3:50	260 418 4:50	144 232 2:50	172 277 3:20	137 221 2:50	73 117 1:30	168 270 3:10	274 441 5:40	550 885 10:40	192 309 3:40	656 1056 13:00	532 856 10:00	238 383 4:50	145 233 3:10	200 322 4:20	52 84 1:30	356 573 6:30	472 760 9:00	205 330 4:10	156 251 3:00	372 599 6:40	433 697 7:40	141 227 2:50	145 233 2:40	260 418 4:40	108 174 2:20	83 134 1:40	74 119 1:40	108 174 2:20	465 749 8:20	90 145 2:00	187 301 3:30	64 103 1:30	324 521 6:10	353 568 6:20	154 248 3:20	483 777 8:50	57 92 1:40
Plymouth								199 320 4:00	587 945 11:00	267 430 5:10	343 552 7:00	410 660 7:40	283 455 5:30	283 455 5:30	293 472 5:50	242 389 4:40	316 509 6:00	89 143 2:20	674 1085 13:10	355 571 6:40	790 1271 15:40	664 1069 12:30	328 528 6:40	309 497 6:10	365 588 7:20	157 253 3:20	495 797 9:10	595 958 11:20	264 425 5:30	46 74 1:30	496 798 9:00	552 888 10:00	300 483 5:50	297 478 5:40	399 642 7:20	167 269 3:40	293 472 5:30	122 196 2:50	224 361 6:00	587 945 10:40	128 206 3:30	328 528 6:10	203 327 4:20	474 763 9:00	492 792 9:00	237 382 5:10	615 990 11:20	218 351 4:40
Portsmouth							176 283 4:50	77 124 1:40	545 877 10:00	191 307 3:40	207 333 4:20	337 542 6:10	236 380 4:30	254 409 4:50	201 323 4:00	162 261 3:10	257 414 4:50	259 417 5:40	633 1019 12:10	269 433 5:00	737 1186 14:30	613 987 11:30	311 501 6:10	166 267 3:40	221 356 4:40	119 192 3:00	448 721 8:10	555 893 10:20	251 404 5:00	135 217 2:40	453 729 8:10	514 827 9:00	130 209 2:50	234 377 4:20	348 560 6:10	142 229 3:00	144 232 2:50	97 156 2:10	48 77 1:40	547 881 9:50	52 84 1:30	264 425 4:50	141 227 3:00	401 645 7:30	430 692 7:40	222 357 4:40	560 901 10:10	70 113 2:00
Sheffield						230 370 4:20	283 455 5:30	135 217 2:40	339 546 6:30	37 60 1:00	146 235 3:20	125 201 2:40	38 61 1:00	72 116 1:40	46 74 1:20	62 100 1:20	33 53 1:00	361 581 7:10	427 687 8:40	65 105 1:30	520 837 10:50	393 632 7:40	168 270 3:40	187 301 3:50	166 267 3:40	126 203 2:20	248 399 4:40	348 560 6:50	215 346 4:20	237 381 4:20	235 378 4:20	291 468 5:20	245 394 4:30	18 29 0:40	152 245 3:00	194 312 3:40	120 193 2:20	161 259 3:10	226 364 4:20	320 515 6:00	216 348 4:10	86 138 1:50	76 122 1:50	190 306 4:00	245 394 4:30	159 256 3:30	360 579 6:50	159 256 3:20
Shrewsbury					82 132 2:10	207 333 3:50	225 362 4:40	106 171 2:10	364 586 7:00	93 150 2:00	205 330 4:20	201 323 3:50	69 111 1:40	58 93 1:50	133 214 2:50	84 135 1:40	109 175 2:20	303 488 6:10	451 726 9:00	169 272 3:10	567 912 11:30	438 705 8:20	113 182 2:50	240 386 4:40	225 362 4:40	77 124 1:30	272 438 5:00	382 615 7:20	145 233 3:10	179 288 3:20	274 441 5:00	330 531 6:00	251 404 4:30	109 175 2:10	176 283 3:20	111 179 2:20	159 256 3:00	103 166 2:50	226 364 4:20	371 597 6:50	185 298 3:40	98 158 2:00	45 72 1:20	265 426 5:10	269 433 5:00	77 124 2:10	399 642 7:30	160 258 3:20
Southampton				185 298 4:10	199 320 3:40	21 34 0:50	151 243 4:10	64 103 1:30	530 853 9:40	176 283 3:20	206 332 4:20	324 521 5:50	221 356 4:10	239 385 4:30	204 328 4:00	137 220 2:40	232 373 4:20	228 367 5:00	618 995 12:00	256 412 4:40	723 1164 14:10	598 963 11:10	293 472 5:50	164 264 3:30	220 354 4:40	105 169 2:40	433 697 7:40	541 871 10:00	233 375 4:40	105 169 3:00	438 705 7:50	500 805 8:50	143 230 2:50	209 336 3:50	324 521 5:50	121 195 2:30	148 238 2:50	76 122 2:20	61 98 1:50	532 856 9:30	31 50 1:00	251 404 4:40	128 206 2:40	388 624 7:10	417 671 7:30	201 323 4:10	547 880 10:00	77 124 2:00
Stranraer			445 716 8:20	277 446 5:30	263 423 5:20	461 742 8:40	500 805 9:40	379 610 7:10	148 238 3:40	290 467 5:50	403 649 8:10	158 254 3:40	220 354 4:40	221 356 4:40	298 480 6:00	330 531 6:20	220 354 4:40	585 942 11:30	263 423 6:30	259 417 5:20	379 610 9:00	262 422 6:00	338 544 7:00	410 660 8:10	426 686 8:40	343 552 6:30	84 135 2:30	195 314 4:50	392 631 7:50	454 731 8:30	124 200 3:00	167 269 3:40	496 798 9:10	257 414 5:10	101 163 2:40	390 628 7:30	379 610 7:10	378 608 7:20	475 765 9:00	194 312 4:20	444 715 8:30	188 303 4:00	297 478 6:00	170 274 4:10	51 82 1:20	325 523 6:50	228 367 5:10	402 647 7:50
Swansea		417 671 7:50	161 259 3:00	118 190 2:20	217 349 4:00	182 293 3:30	206 332 4:10	141 227 2:40	506 815 9:20	192 309 3:40	301 485 6:00	347 559 6:20	187 301 3:30	195 314 3:40	233 375 4:30	177 285 3:20	248 399 4:40	285 459 6:00	594 956 11:30	264 425 4:50	696 1120 13:40	572 921 10:40	184 296 4:50	267 430 5:10	329 530 6:30	89 143 1:50	409 658 7:20	496 798 9:20	67 108 1:50	161 259 3:00	412 663 7:20	473 761 8:20	274 441 5:00	232 373 4:10	309 497 5:30	41 66 1:10	227 365 4:10	85 137 1:50	222 357 4:20	505 813 9:00	167 269 3:20	216 348 4:00	119 192 2:30	383 616 7:10	379 610 6:50	73 117 2:00	507 816 9:20	194 312 4:00
York	272 438 5:10	222 357 4:40	258 415 5:10	133 214 2:40	52 84 1:20	278 448 5:10	333 536 6:20	181 291 3:20	309 497 6:00	77 124 1:40	181 291 4:20	84 135 2:20	64 103 1:30	99 159 2:10	75 121 1:50	108 174 2:10	24 39 0:50	411 661 8:00	407 655 8:20	37 60 1:10	479 771 10:10	352 566 7:00	204 328 4:20	228 367 4:40	201 323 4:20	189 304 3:30	217 349 4:10	330 531 6:30	261 420 5:10	287 462 5:10	194 312 3:40	250 402 4:40	282 454 5:10	34 55 1:00	121 195 2:30	244 393 4:40	165 266 3:10	222 357 4:10	275 443 5:10	285 459 5:20	269 433 5:00	96 154 2:00	130 209 2:40	148 238 3:10	214 344 4:00	195 314 4:10	319 513 6:10	207 333 4:10

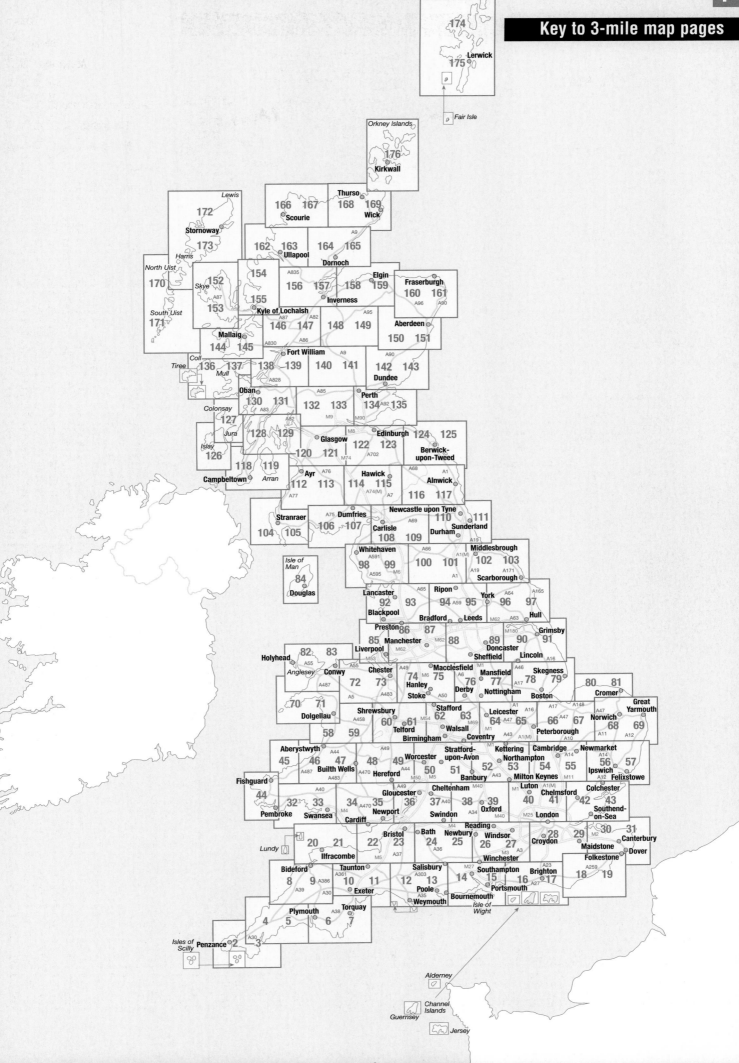

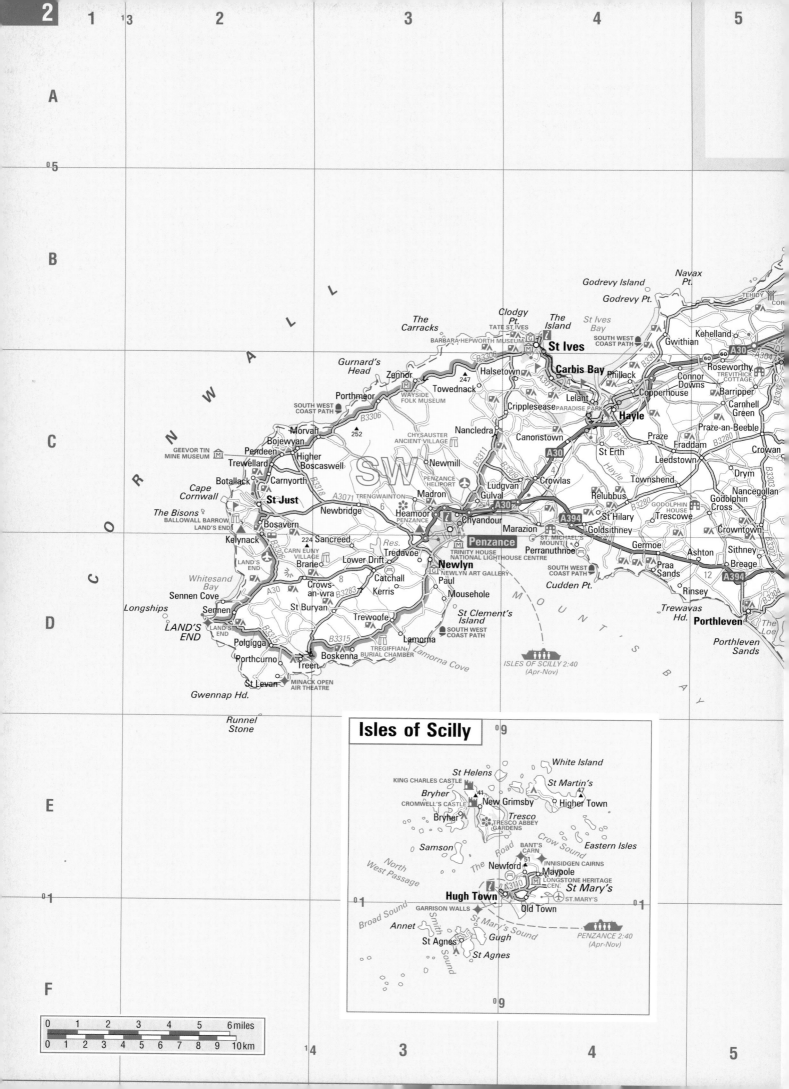

A

B

C

D

E

F

CORNWALL

Godrevy Island   Navax Pt.
Godrevy Pt.
TEHIDY
COR

The Carracks
Clodgy Pt.
TATE ST IVES
The Island
St Ives Bay
SOUTH WEST COAST PATH
Gwithian
Kehelland
A30

Gurnard's Head
Zennor
BARBARA HEPWORTH MUSEUM
St Ives
Halsetown
Carbis Bay
Phillack
Roseworthy
TREVITHICK COTTAGE
Connor Downs
Barripper

Porthmeor
247
Towednack
Lelant
Copperhouse
Carnhell Green

WAYSIDE FOLK MUSEUM
SOUTH WEST COAST PATH
B3306
Cripplesease
PARADISE PARK
Hayle
Praze-an-Beeble

Morvah
252
Nancledra
Canonstown
Praze
Crowan

Bojewyan
CHYSAUSTER ANCIENT VILLAGE
Newmill
St Erth
Fraddam
Leedstown

Pendeen
GEEVOR TIN MINE MUSEUM
Higher Boscaswell
SW
PENZANCE HELIPORT
Ludgvan
Crowlas
Townshend
Drym

Trewellard
Carnyorth
Madron
Gulval
A30
Relubbus
Nancegollan

Botallack
TRENGWAINTON
Heamoor
A394
St Hilary
GODOLPHIN HOUSE
Godolphin Cross

Cape Cornwall
A3071
PENZANCE
Chyandour
Goldsithney
Trescowe

St Just
Newbridge
6
Marazion
ST. MICHAEL'S MOUNT
Germoe
Crowntown

The Bisons
BALLOWALL BARROW
LAND'S END
Bosavern
Penzance
Perranuthnoe
Ashton
Sithney

Kelynack
224
Sancreed
Res.
TRINITY HOUSE NATIONAL LIGHTHOUSE CENTRE
SOUTH WEST COAST PATH
Praa Sands
Breage
A394

CARN EUNY VILLAGE
Tredavoe
Newlyn
Cudden Pt.
Rinsey
12

Whitesand Bay
Brane
Lower Drift
NEWLYN ART GALLERY
Paul
Trewavas Hd.

Sennen Cove
Crows-an-wra
Catchall
8
Mousehole
Porthleven

Longships
Sennen
B3283
Kerris
St Clement's Island
Porthleven Sands
The Loe

LAND'S END
LAND'S END
St Buryan
Trewoofe
SOUTH WEST COAST PATH

Polgigga
B3315
Boskenna
Lamorna
Lamorna Cove
ISLES OF SCILLY 2:40 (Apr-Nov)

Porthcurno
Treen
TREGIFFIAN BURIAL CHAMBER

St Levan
MINACK OPEN AIR THEATRE

Gwennap Hd.

Runnel Stone

MOUNT'S BAY

Isles of Scilly

9

St Helens
White Island

KING CHARLES CASTLE
St Martin's
47

Bryher
41
Higher Town

CROMWELL'S CASTLE
New Grimsby

Bryher
Tresco
TRESCO ABBEY GARDENS
Eastern Isles

Samson
Crow Sound

The Road
BANT'S CARN
INNISIDGEN CAIRNS

North West Passage
Newford
51
Maypole
LONGSTONE HERITAGE CEN.

1
Hugh Town
St Mary's
ST.MARY'S

1
GARRISON WALLS
Old Town

Broad Sound
Annet
Gugh
PENZANCE 2:40 (Apr-Nov)

St Agnes
Smith Sound

St Agnes
St Mary's Sound

9

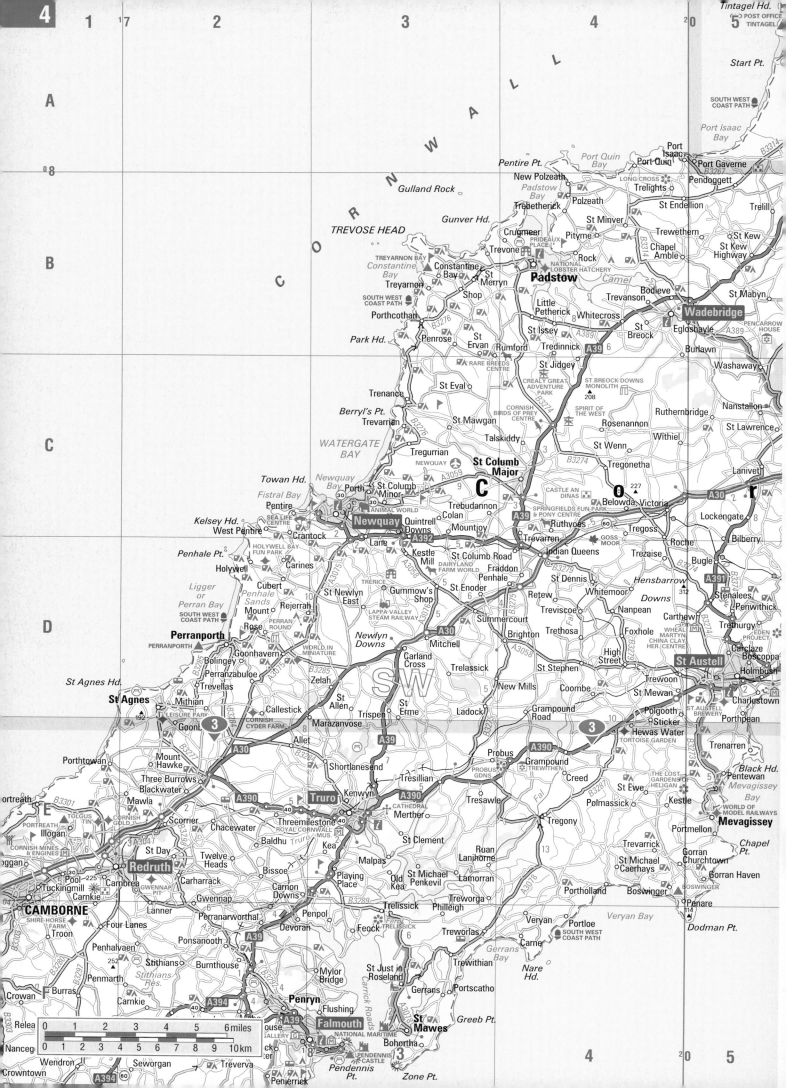

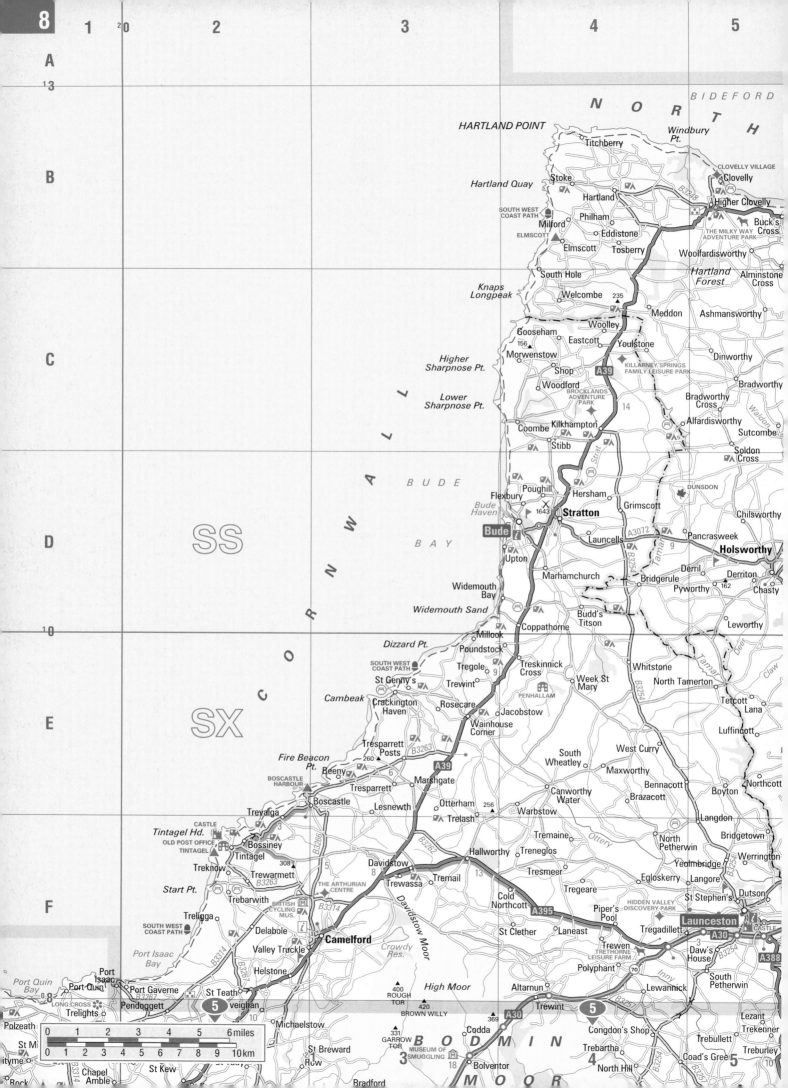

Jersey
3½ miles to 1 inch

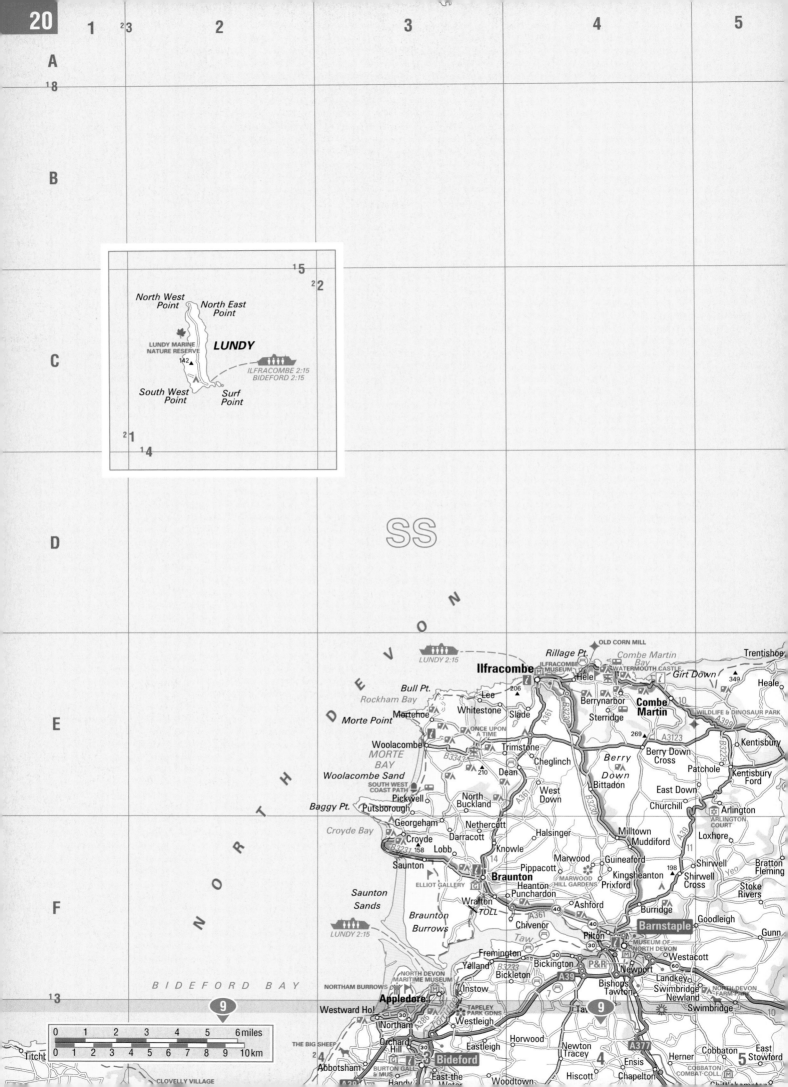

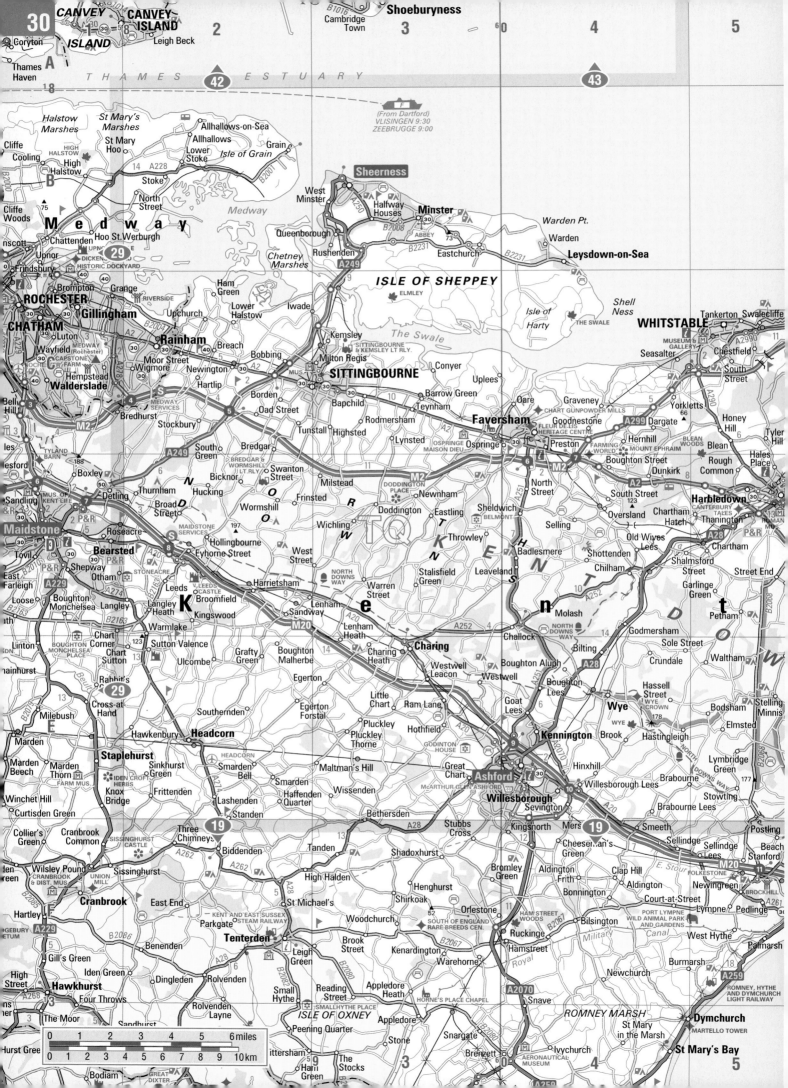

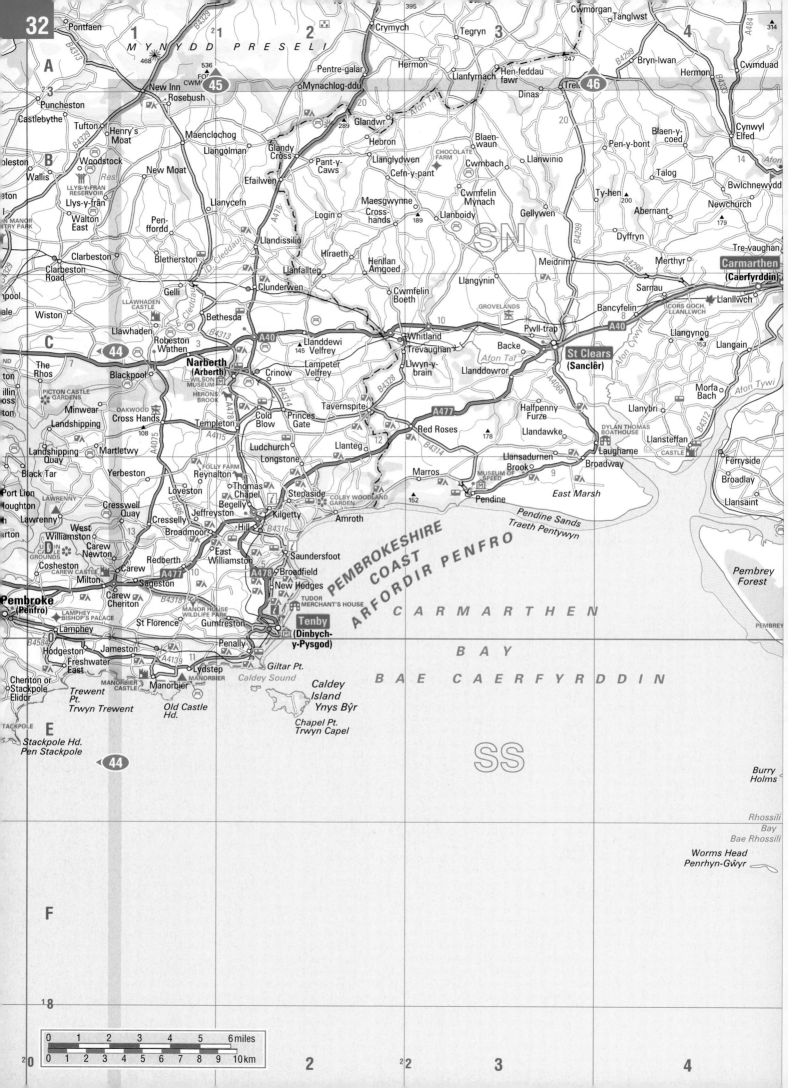

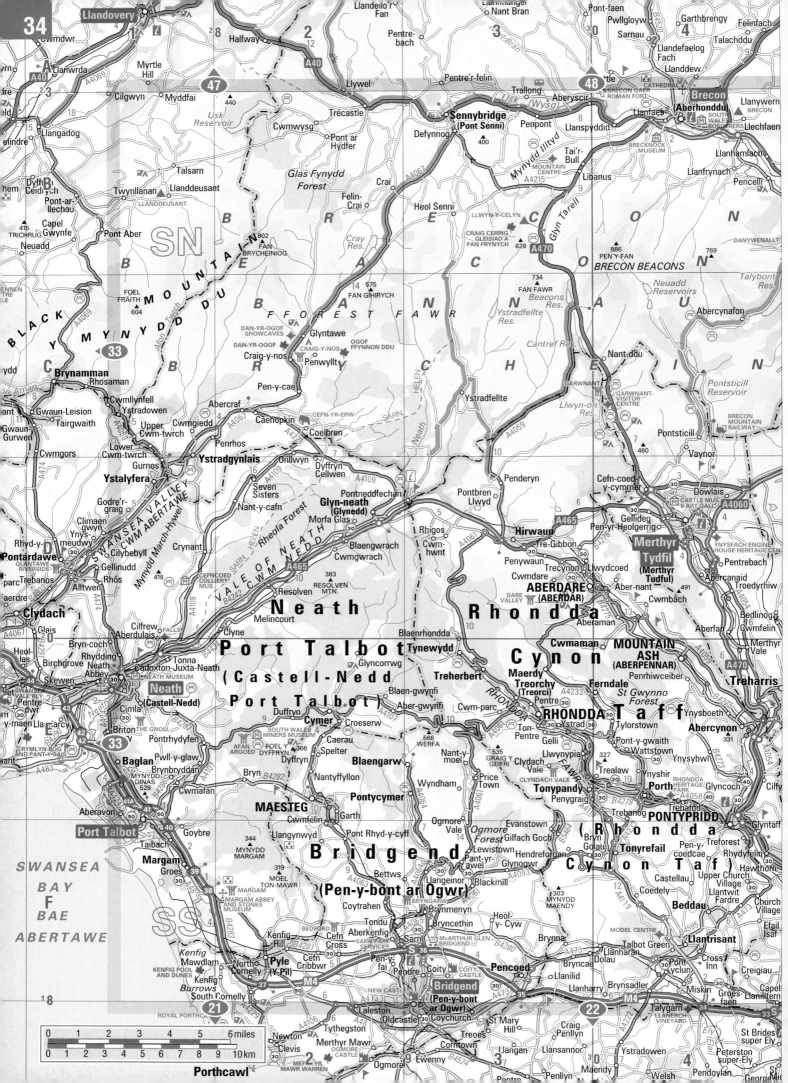

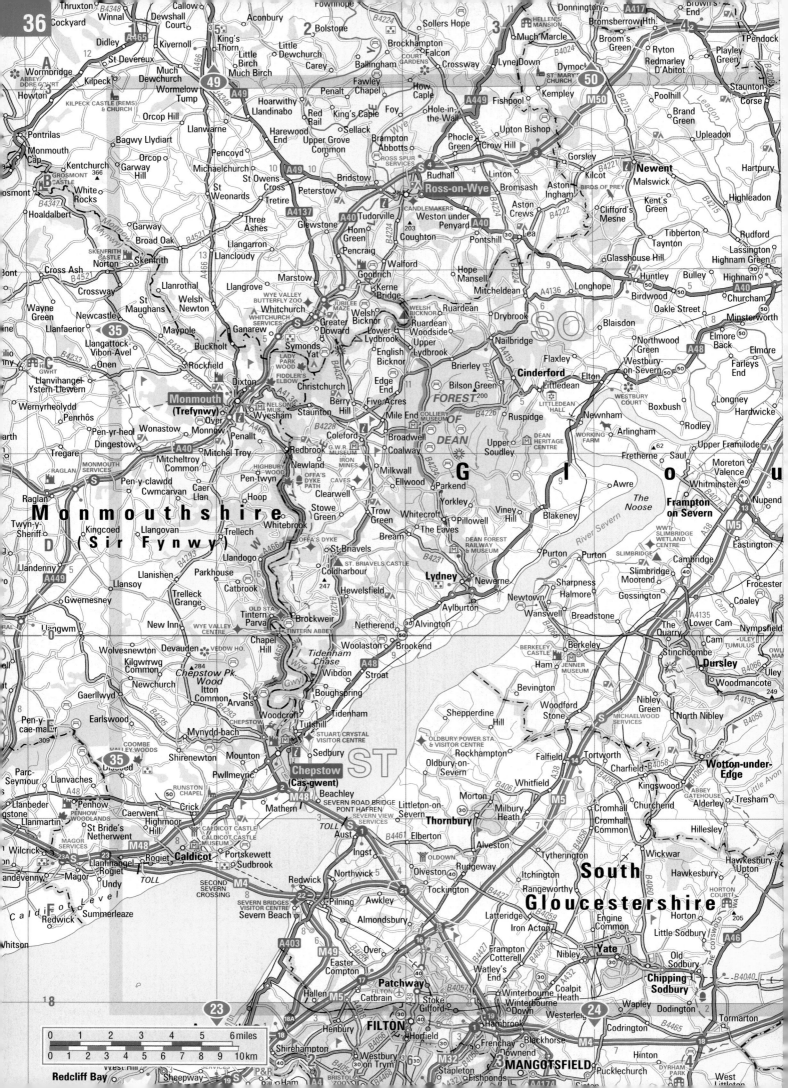

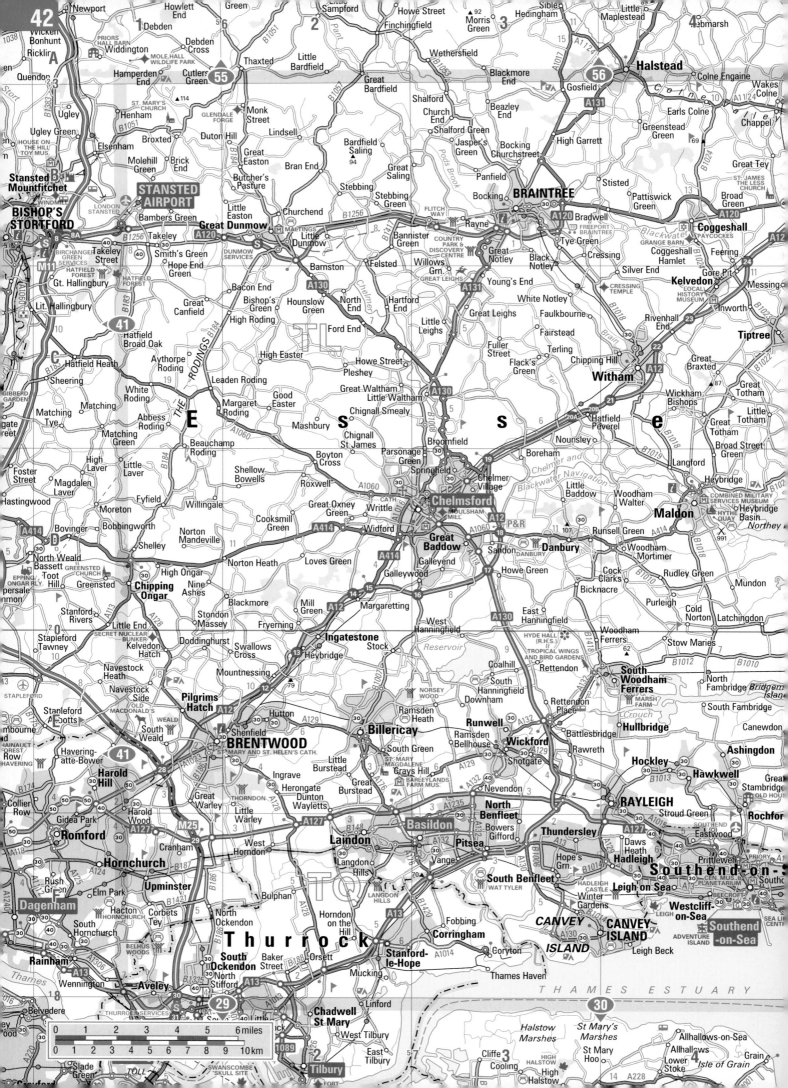

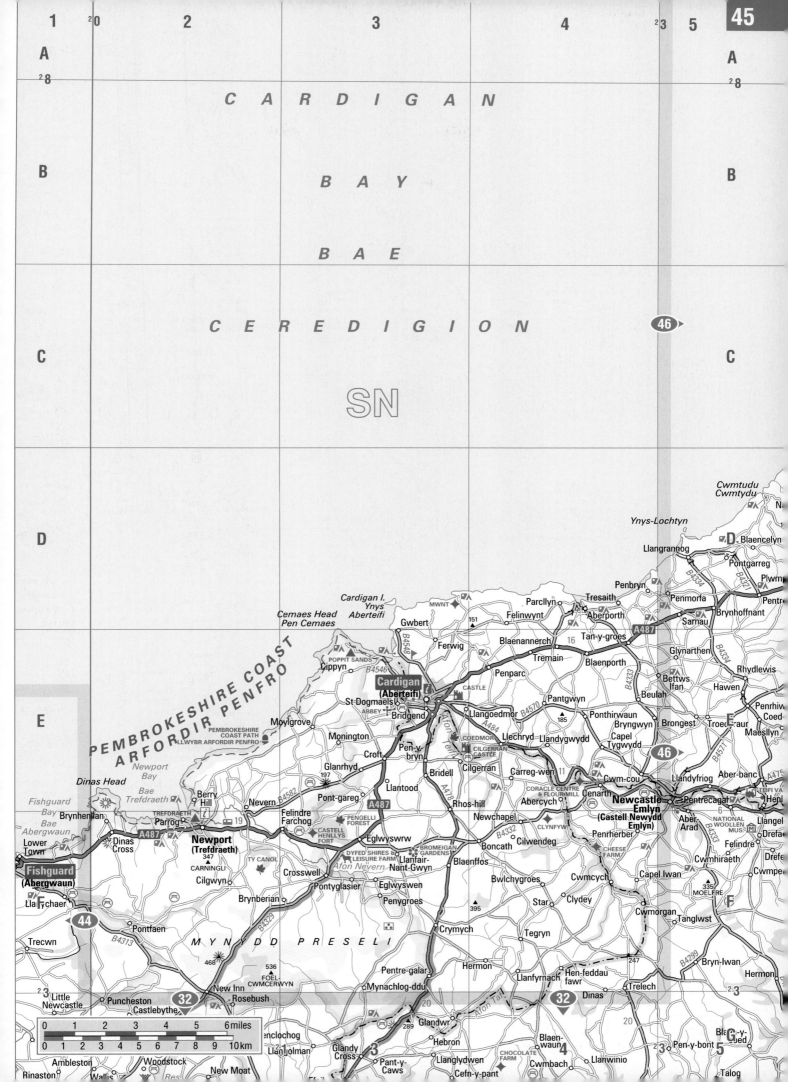

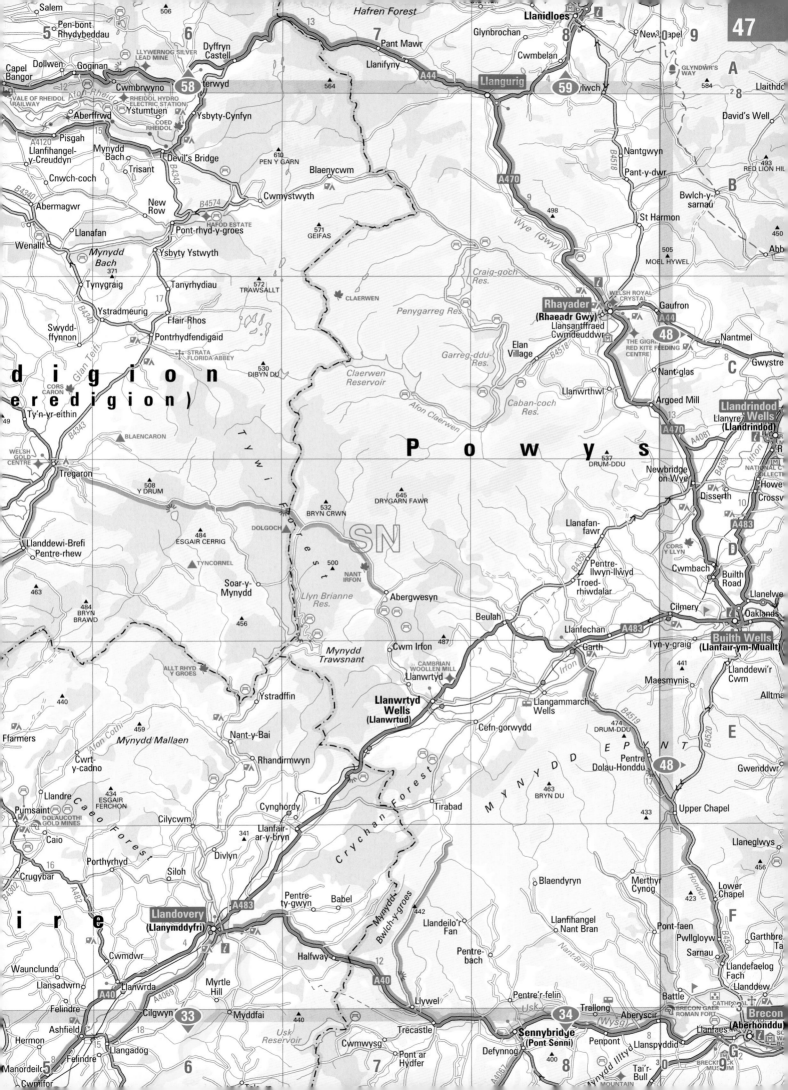

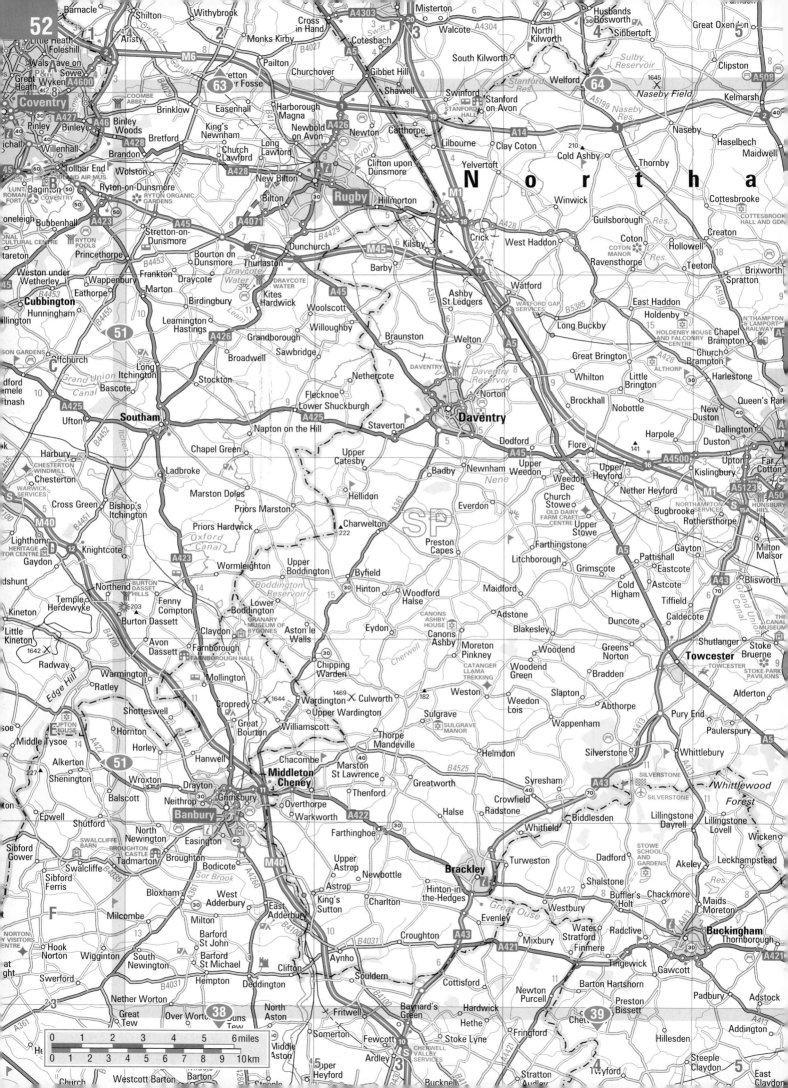

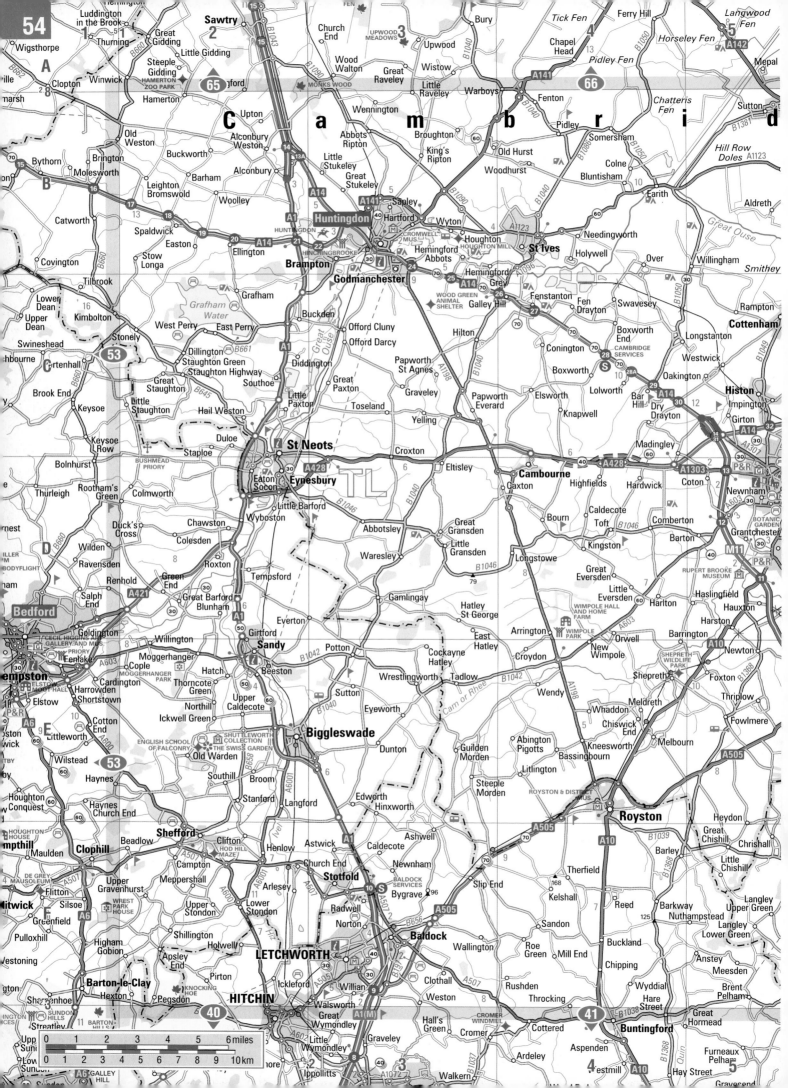

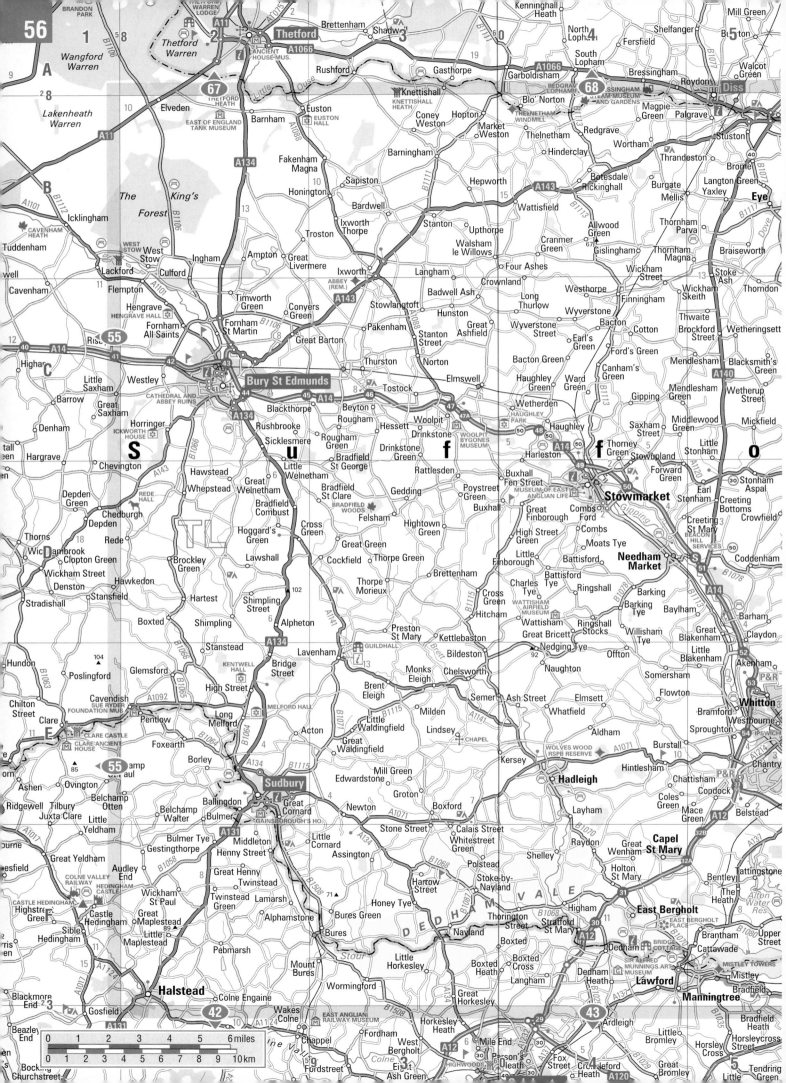

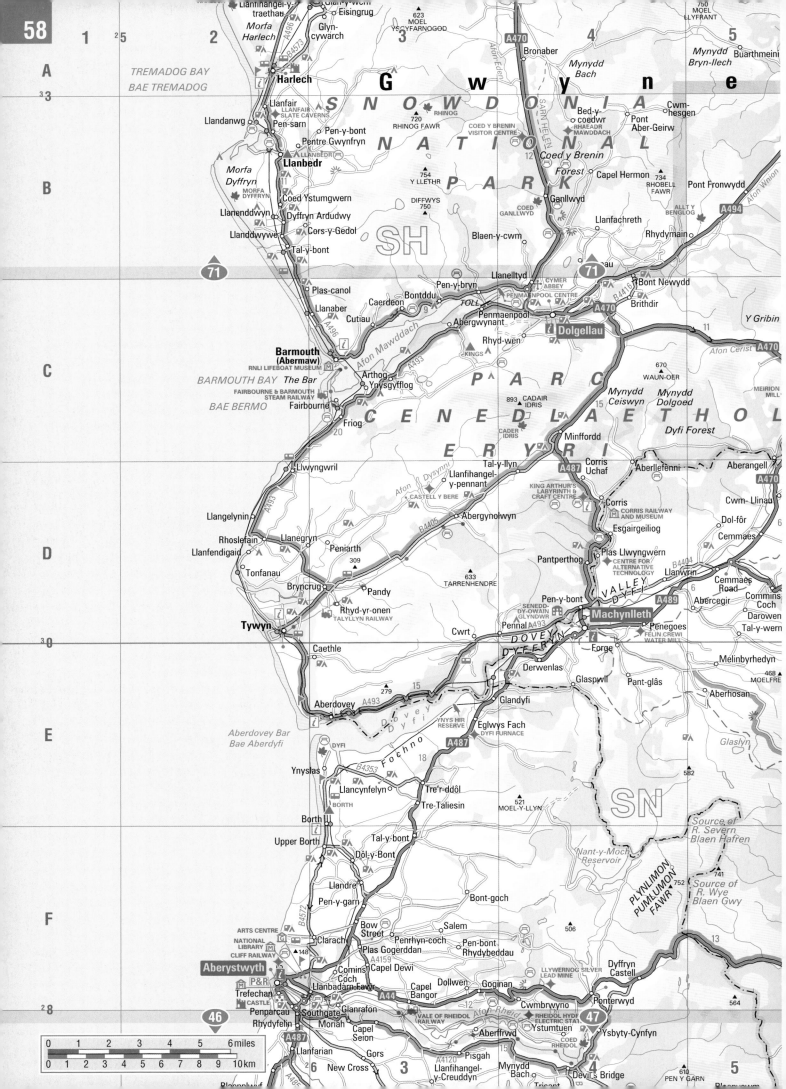

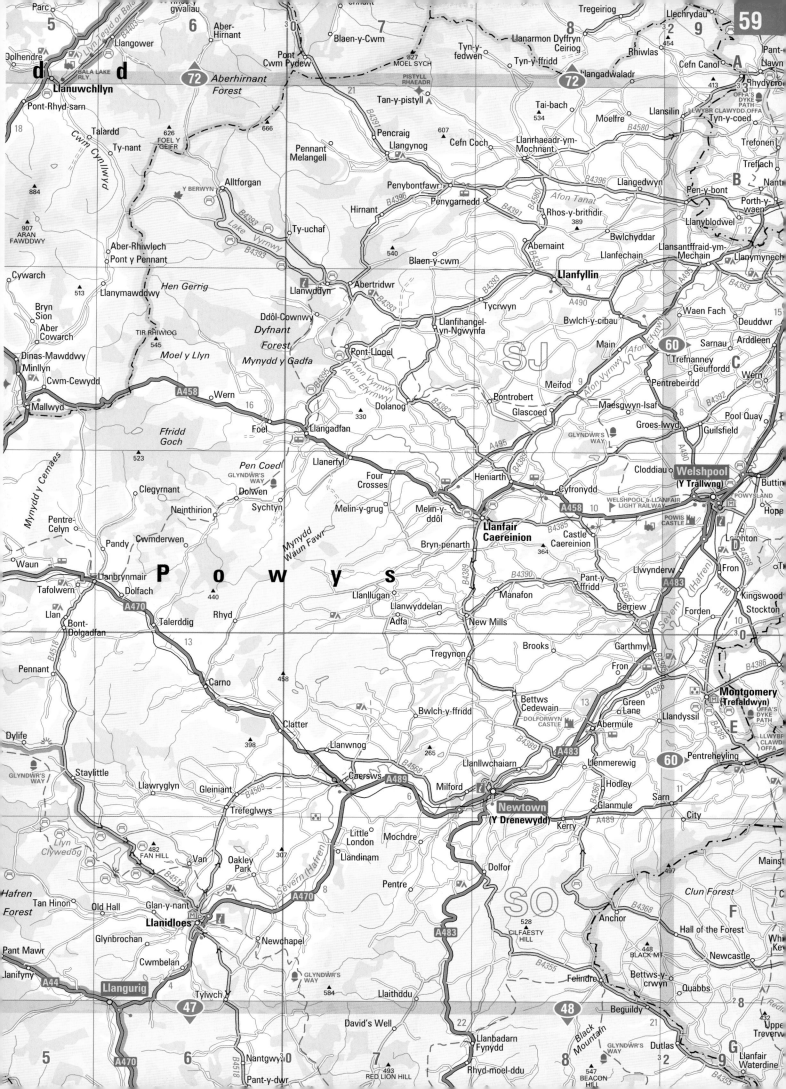

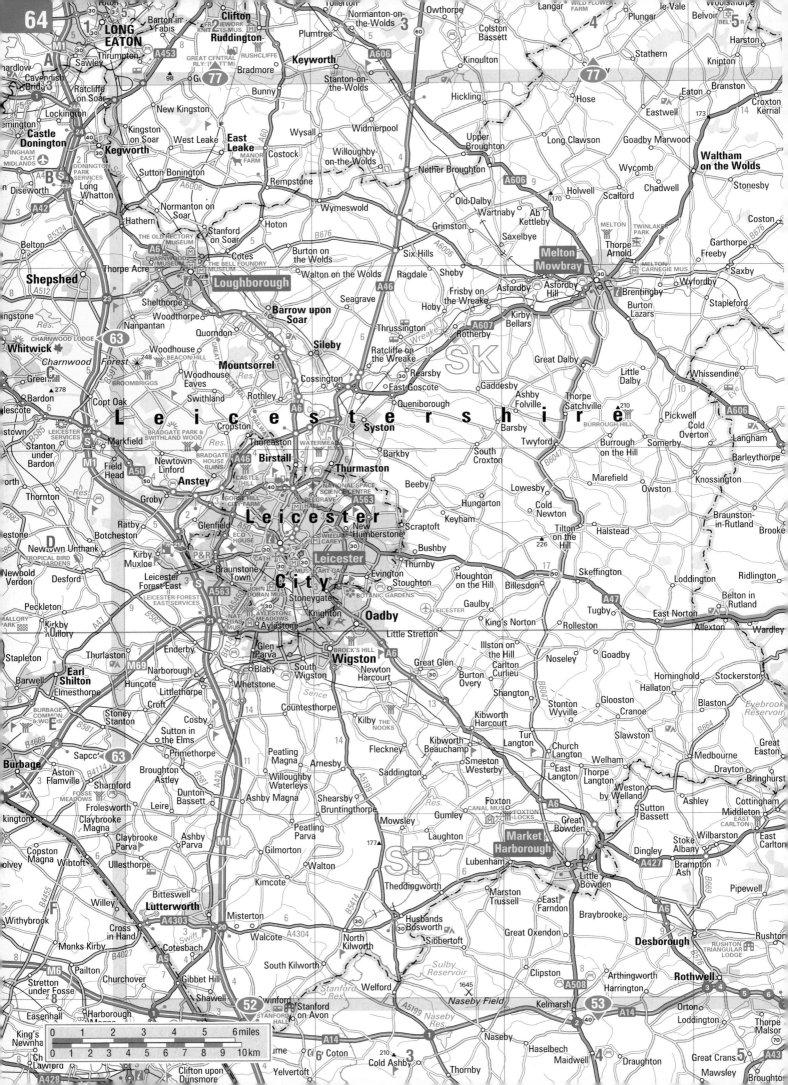

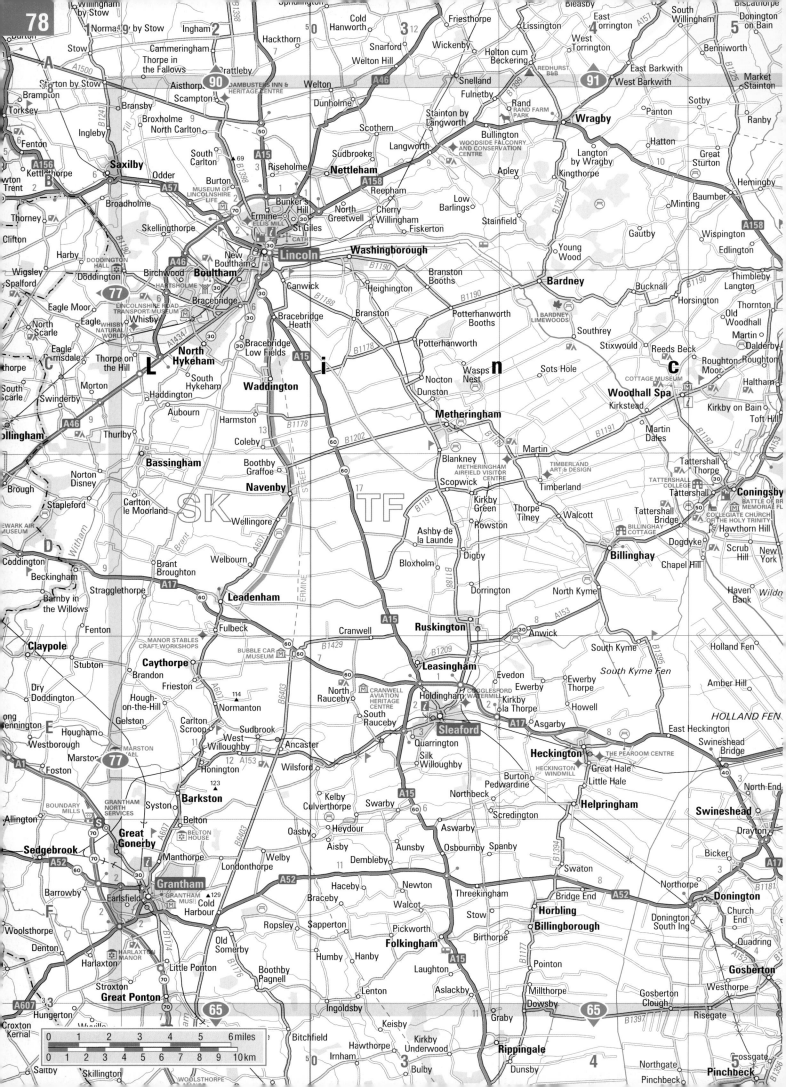

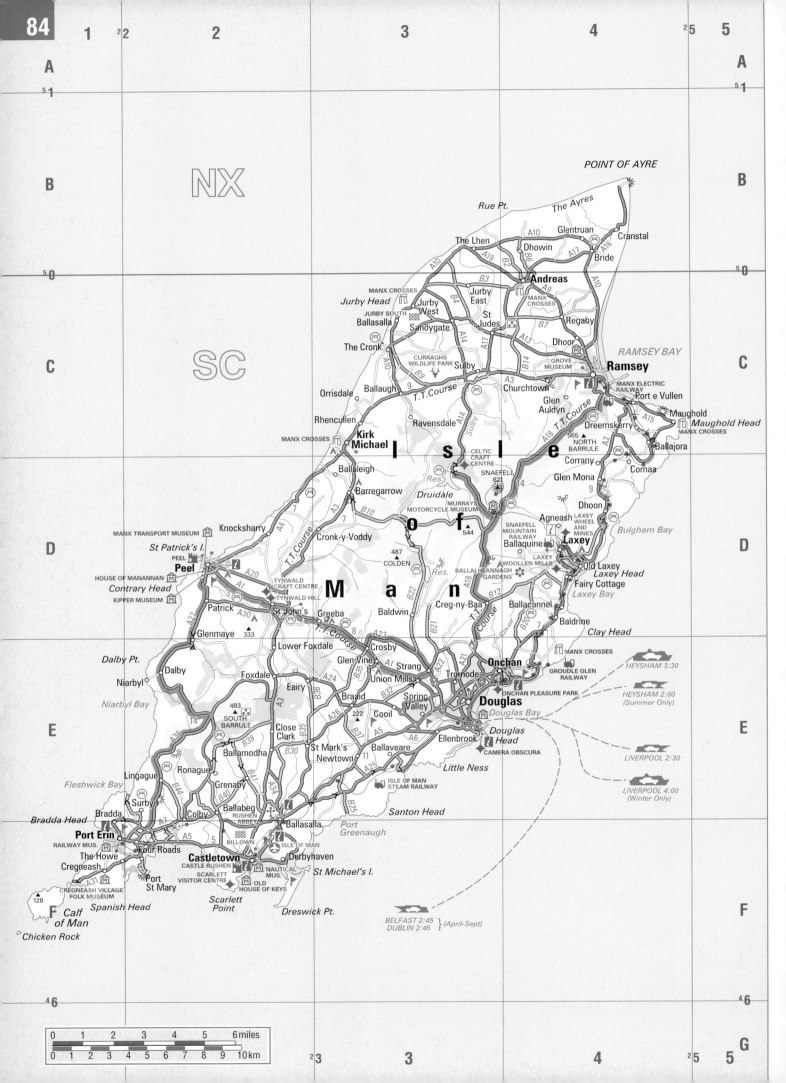

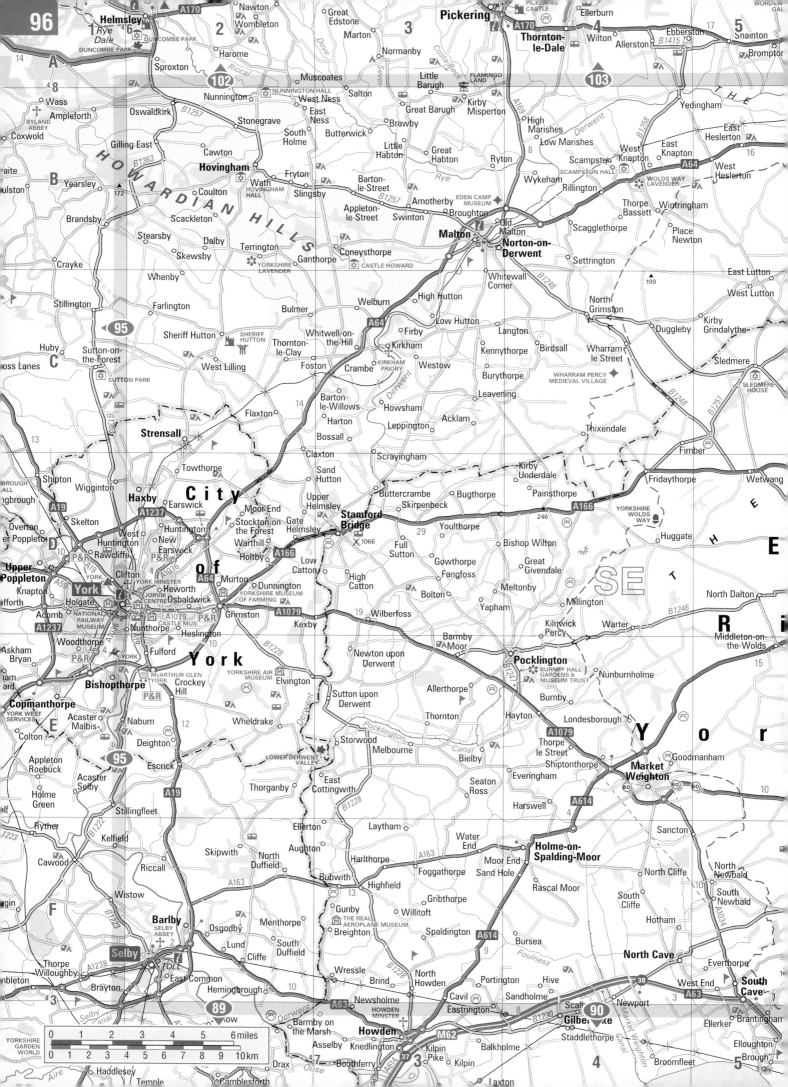

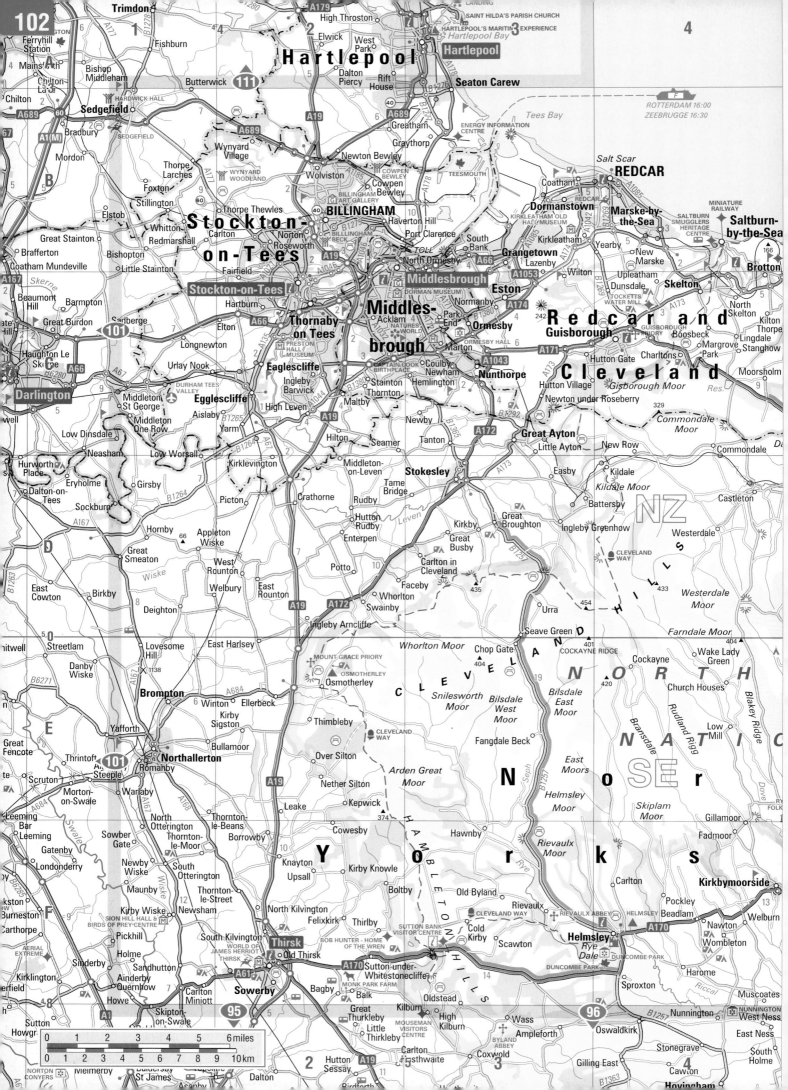

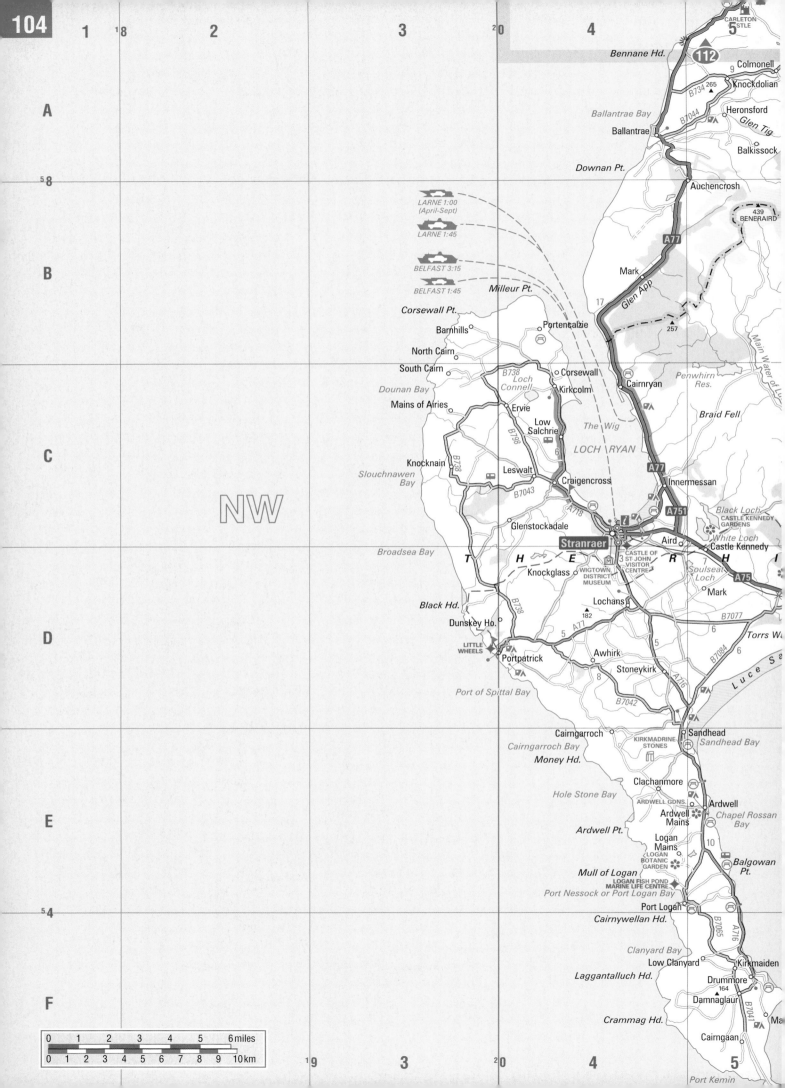

1 8 2 3 20 4 5

A

Bennane Hd.

CARLETON CSTLE

112

9 Colmonell

B734 265 ▲ Knockdolian

B7044 Heronsford

Ballantrae Bay Glen Tig

Ballantrae Balkissock

Downan Pt.

58

Auchencrosh

LARNE 1:00 (April–Sept)

LARNE 1:45

439 BENERAIRD

A77

B

BELFAST 3:15

BELFAST 1:45 Milleur Pt.

Mark

Corsewall Pt.

17 Glen App

257

Barnhills Portencalzie

North Cairn

Penwhirn Res.

South Cairn Corsewall

B738 Loch Connell

Cairnryan

Braid Fell

Dounan Bay Kirkcolm

Mains of Airies Ervie

The Wig

B798 Low Salchrie

LOCH RYAN

C

Slouchnawen Bay

Knocknain

B738

Leswalt

6

Craigencross

Innermessan

B7043

B7077

NW

A718

A751

Glenstockadale

Black Loch

CASTLE KENNEDY GARDENS

i

White Loch

Stranraer

Aird

Castle Kennedy

Broadsea Bay

T H E E CASTLE OF ST JOHN VISITOR CENTRE R H I

Knockglass

WIGTOWN DISTRICT MUSEUM

7 Soulseat Loch

A75

Black Hd.

Lochans

Mark

Dunskey Ho.

182

B7077

D

LITTLE WHEELS

A77

5

Torrs W

Portpatrick

Awhirk

8

B7084

6 Luce Sa

Port of Spittal Bay

Stoneykirk

A716

B7042

Cairngarroch

Sandhead

KIRKMADRINE STONES

Sandhead Bay

Cairngarroch Bay

Money Hd.

Clachanmore

Hole Stone Bay

ARDWELL GDNS.

Ardwell

Ardwell Pt.

Ardwell Mains

Chapel Rossan Bay

E

Logan Mains

LOGAN BOTANIC GARDEN

10 Balgowan Pt.

Mull of Logan

LOGAN FISH POND MARINE LIFE CENTRE

Port Nessock or Port Logan Bay

Port Logan

54 Cairnywellan Hd.

B7065 A716

Clanyard Bay

Low Clanyard

Kirkmaiden

Laggantalluch Hd.

Drummore

164

F

Damnaglaur

B7041 Ma

Crammag Hd.

Cairngaan

0 1 2 3 4 5 6 miles

0 1 2 3 4 5 6 7 8 9 10km

19 3 20 4 5

Port Kemin

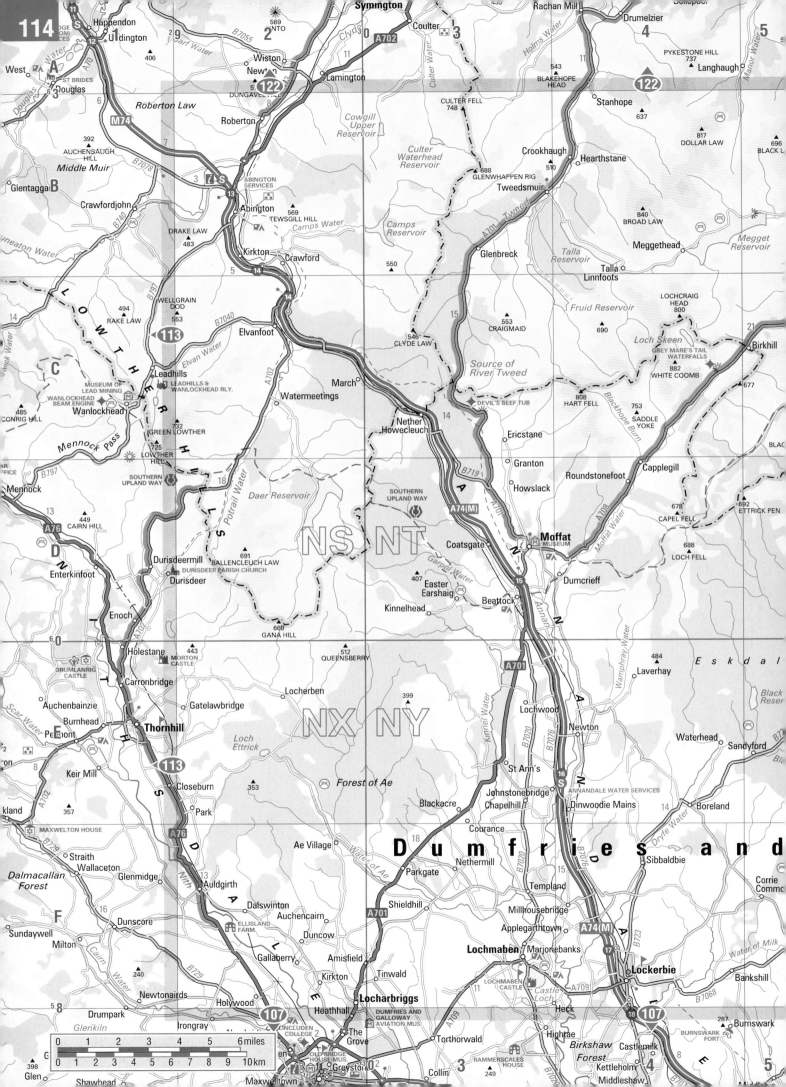

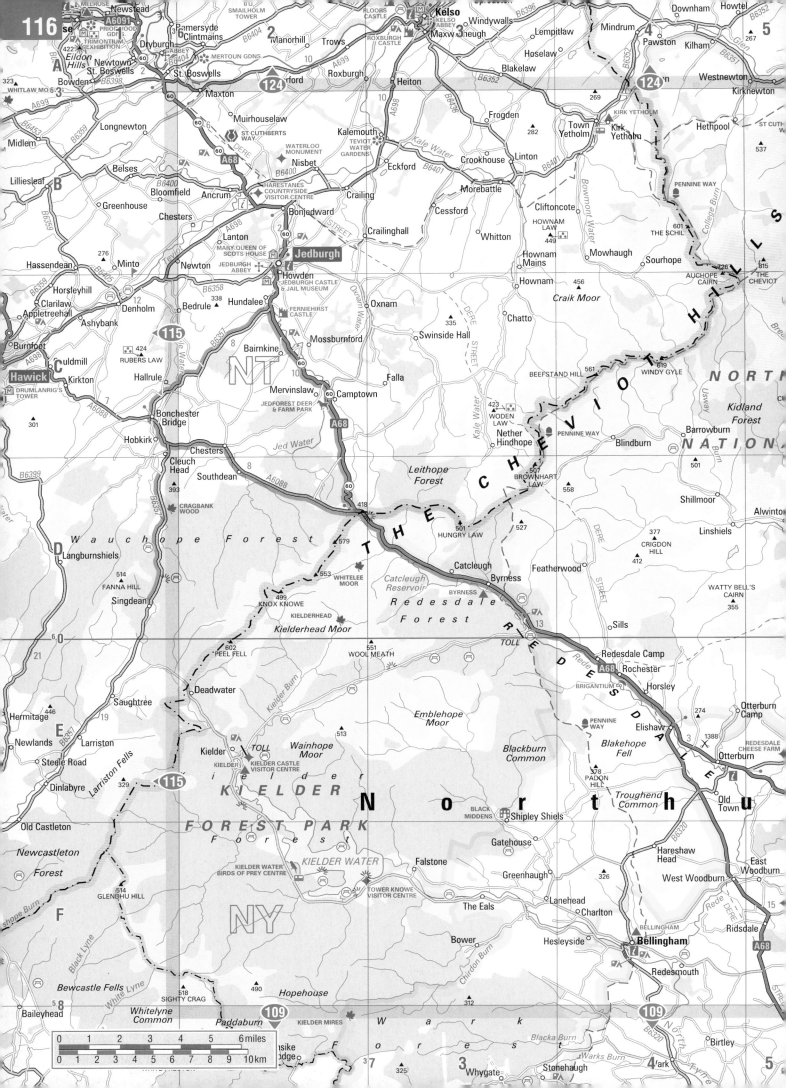

1   5   2   3   4   5

A

Carraig Mhór
Ardtalla
Claggain Bay
Kintour
Ardmore Pt.
KILDALTON CHURCH AND CROSSES
5
Eilean Craobhach
Eilean a'Chuirn
Eilean Bhride
◄126

B

Ardpatrick Ho.
Ptachoillan
Ardpatrick Pt.
Eilean Tràighe
Ronachan Pt.
A83
Clachan
Loch Ciaran
Balochroy
128
Loch Garasdale
Crossaig Glen
Crossa
269 CRUACH NAM FIADH
B842
Cour Ba
Cour
13
CRUACH MHIC GOUGAN 248
Rhunahaorine
241 BEINN BHREAC
Grogport
322 CNOC NAN CRAOBH
Beacharr
CRUACH MHIC-AN T-SAOIR 364
354 CRUACH NAN GABHAR
Brackley
Muasdale
Clachaig Water

Eilean Garbh
West Tarbert Bay
East Tarbert Bay
Tarbert
Druimyeon More
100
Gigha Island
Ardminish
Ardminish Bay
ACHAMORE GARDENS
0:20
Tayinloan
Gigalum Island
Cara Island
Killean
SOUND OF GIGHA

C

Glenacardoch Pt.
Belloch
Amod
A83
Glenbarr
CLAN MACALISTER CENTRE
Barr Water
426 BEINN BHREAC
Bridgend
Torrisdale-Square
Cleongart
19
454 BEINN AN TUIRC
Bellochantuy Bay
Bellochantuy
Killocraw
Saddell Glen
Saddell
SADDELL ABBEY
341 A'CHRUACH
Lussa Loch
14
Saddell Bay
Carradale
Port Righ
Carradale Pt.
Carradale Bay

D

NR
Tangy Loch
397 SGREADAN HILL
Ugadale
Skeroblingarry
Westport
Kilchenzie
Peninver
B842
Black Bay
A83
Glenlussa Water
Ardnacross Bay
Kilmichael
West Darlochan
Low Smerby
CAMPBELTOWN HERITAGE CENTRE
Machrihanish Bay
CAMPBELTOWN
Machrihanish
Trodigal
Campbeltown
Island Davaar
DAVAAR ISLAND CAVE PAINTING
Campbeltown Loch

E

Earadale Pt.
Drumlemble
B843
Stewarton
Kilkerran
Kildalloig
Knocknaha
352 BEINN GHUILEAN
Achinhoan Hd.
385 THE SLATE
B842
Woodbank
10
446 CNOC MOY
Rubh'a'Mharaiche
Feochaig
277 CNOC ODHAR
Conie Glen
Keprigan
Johnston's Pt.
6
Glen Breackerie
North Carrine
Macharioch
Polliwilline Bay
Strone Glen
428
Southend
Carskiey
Brunerican Bay
Cove Pt.
Port Mean
Sheep I.

F

MULL OF KINTYRE
Rubha Chlachan
123
Sanda Island

KILBRANNAN
KINTYRE
NR
ECHANNEL NORTH

0 1 2 3 4 5 6 miles
0 1 2 3 4 5 6 7 8 9 10 km

6

1   3   4   5

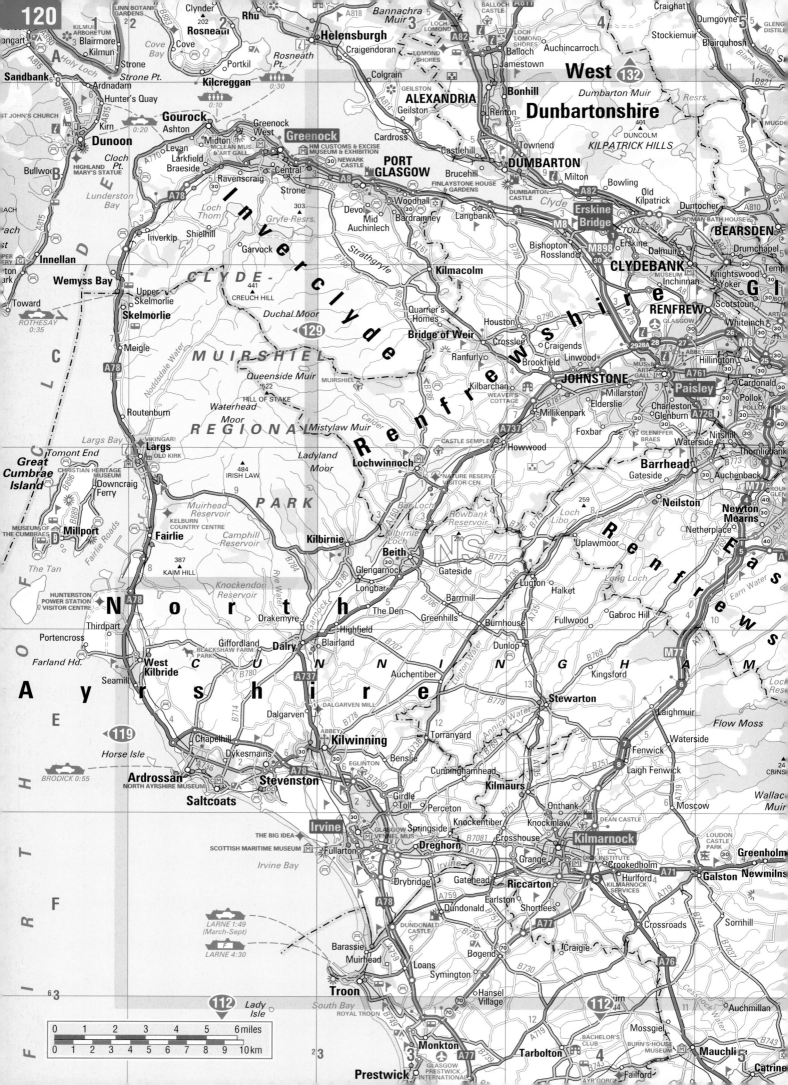

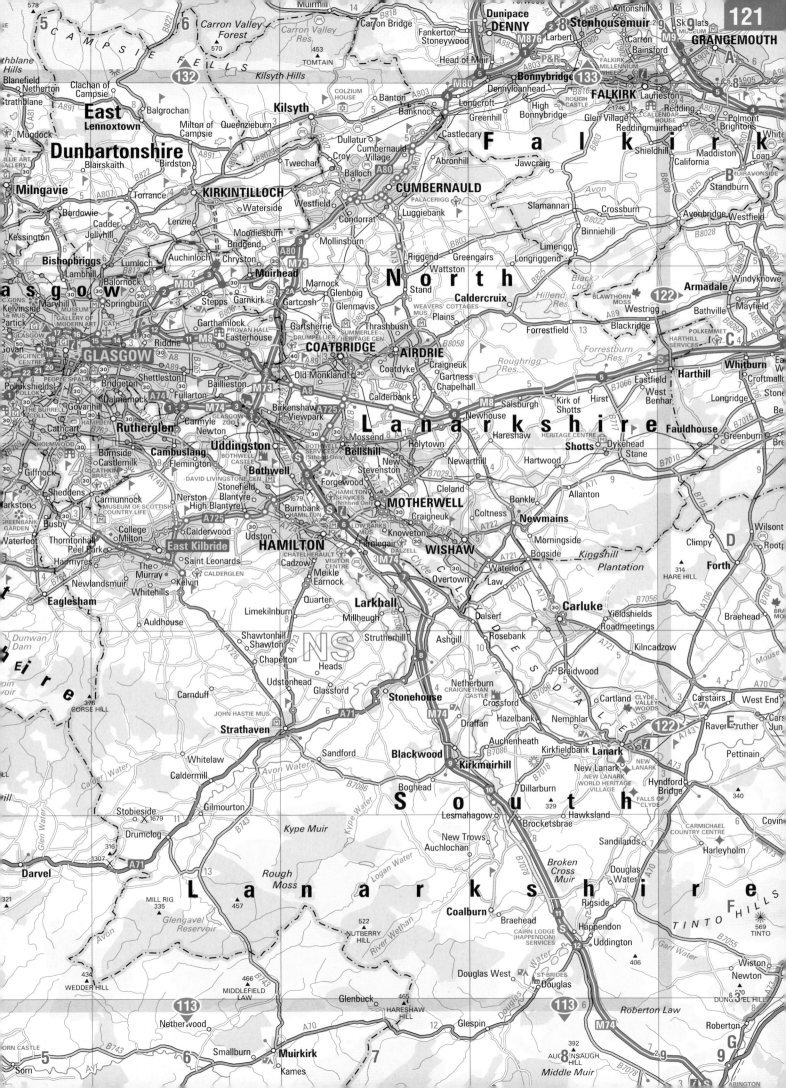

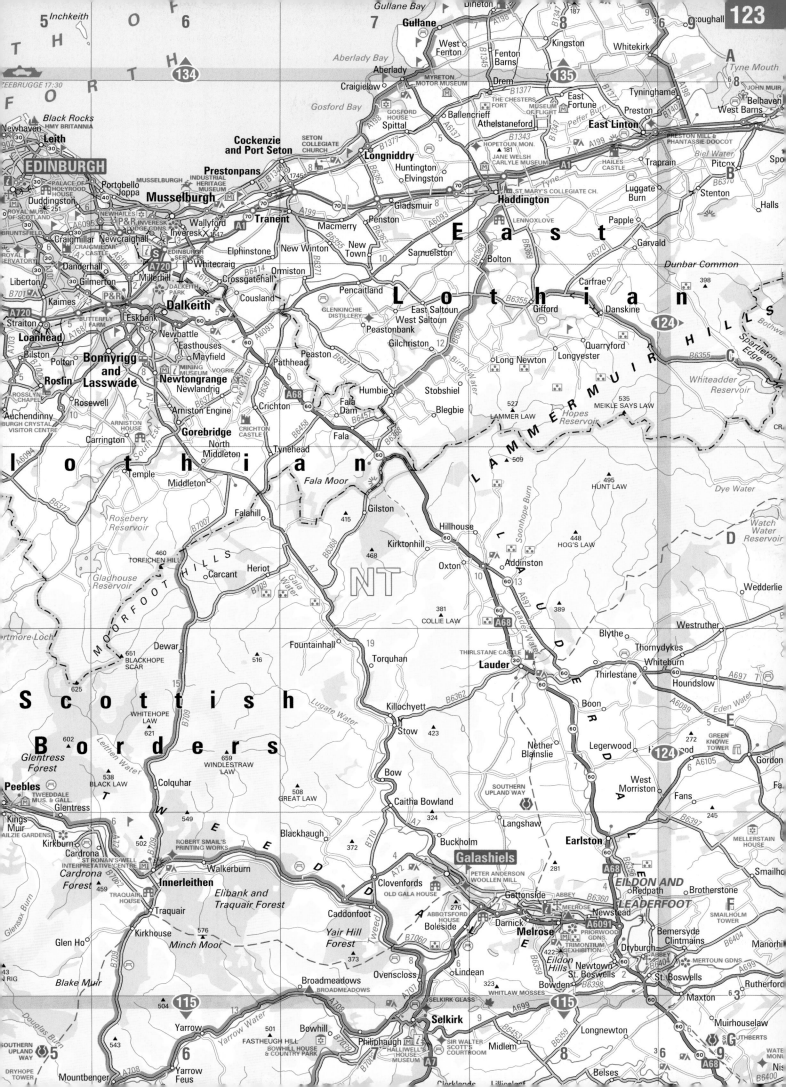

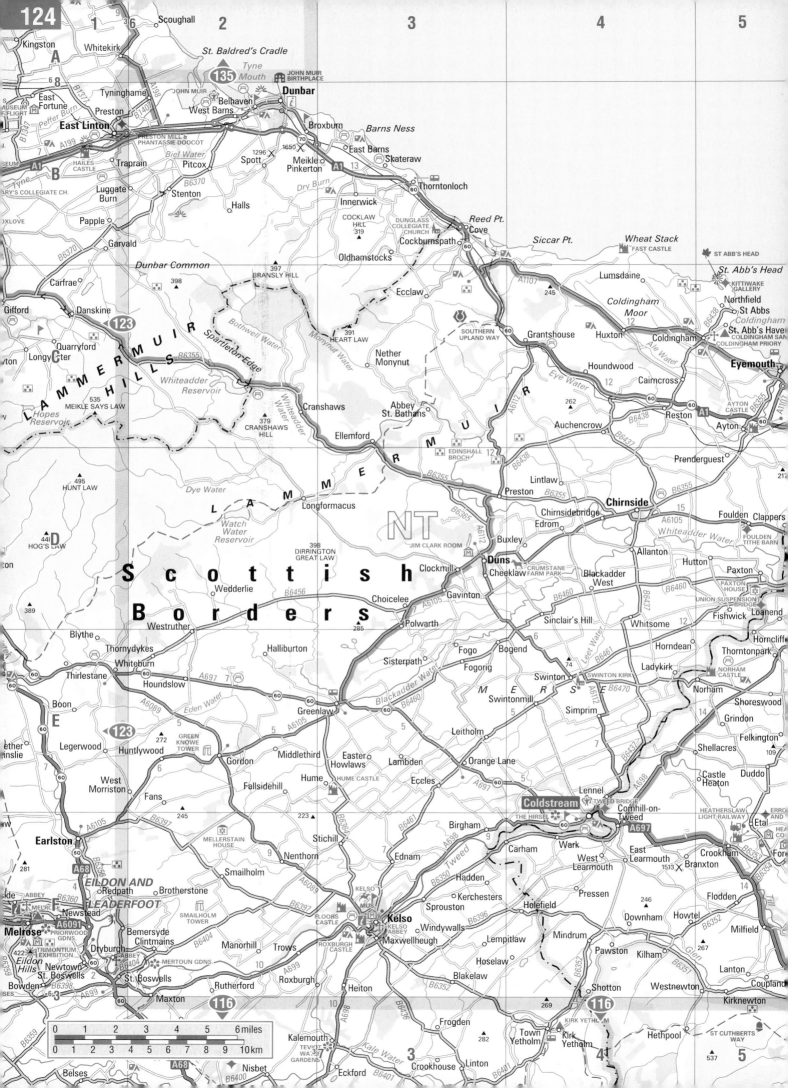

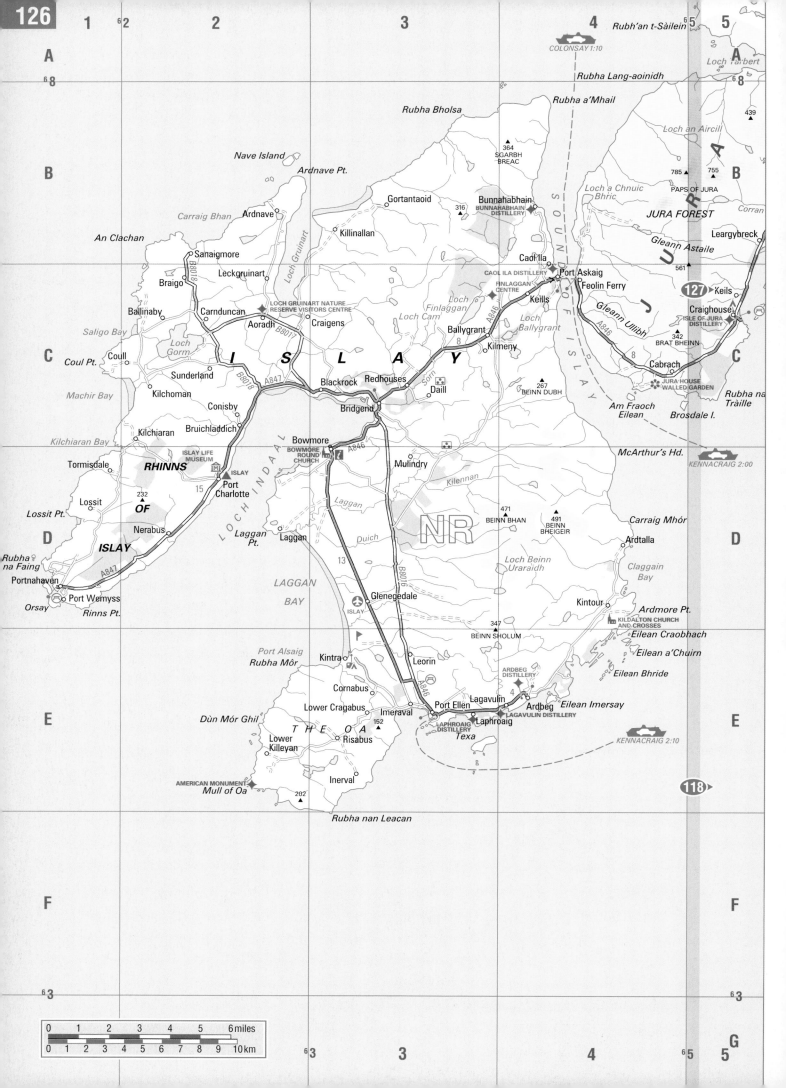

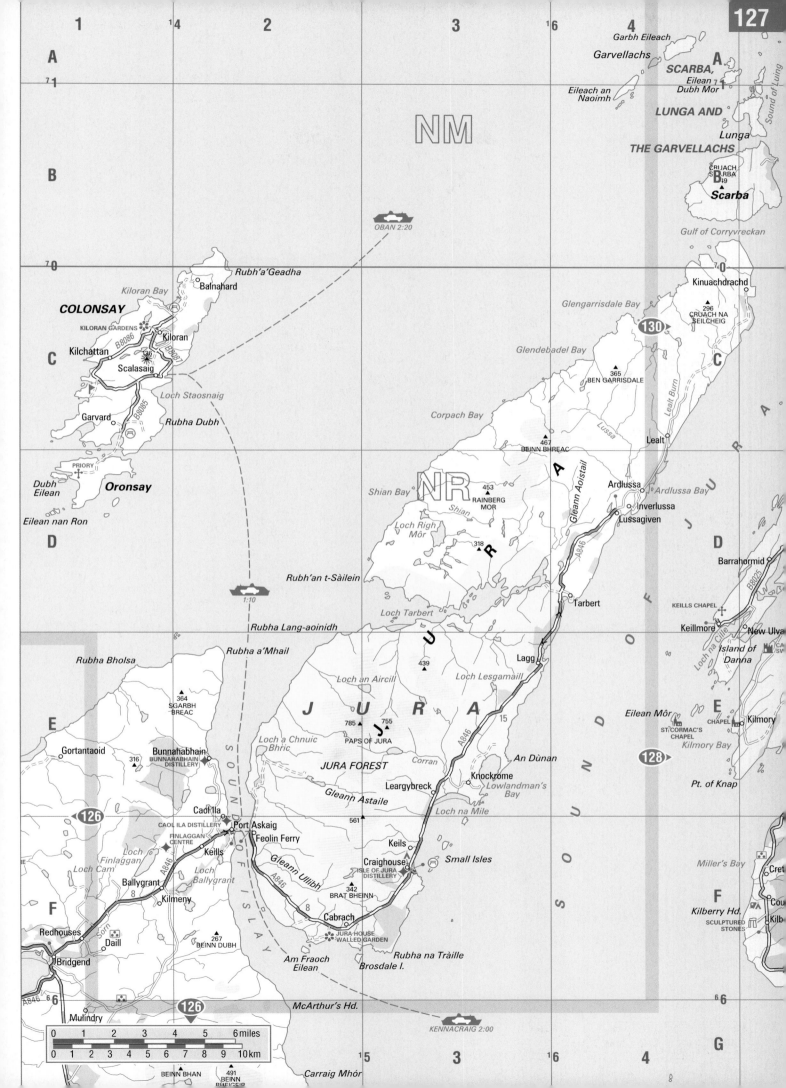

1 | 4 | **2** | 6 | **3** | 6 | **4**

A

1 A

B

Garbh Eileach
Garvellachs

SCARBA,
Eileach an
Naoimh
Eileach an
Naoimh

LUNGA AND

Lunga

THE GARVELLACHS

CRUACH
SCARBA
B 19

Scarba

Gulf of Corryvreckan

NM

70

Kinuachdrachd

Glengarrisdale Bay

296
CRUACH NA
SEILCHEIG

130

Glendebadel Bay

Rubh'a'Geadha
Balnahard

Kiloran Bay
COLONSAY

KILORAN GARDENS

Kiloran

Kilchattan

136

Scalasaig

B8086
B8087

B8085

Loch Staosnaig

Garvard

Rubha Dubh

PRIORY

Oronsay

Dubh
Eilean

Eilean nan Ron

C

BEN GARRISDALE
365

Corpach Bay

467
BEINN BHREAC

NR

Shian Bay

453
RAINBERG
MOR

Shian

Loch Righ
Mòr

318

Lealt

A

Gleann Aoistail

Ardlussa
Ardlussa Bay

Inverlussa
Lussagiven

Lussa

A846

Lealt Burn

R

D

Barrahormid

B8025

Rubh'an t-Sàilein

Rubha Lang-aoinidh

Rubha a'Mhail

Loch Tarbert

Tarbert

KEILLS CHAPEL

Keillmore

Loch na Cille

New Ulva

CA
SV

Island of
Danna

U

439

J U R A

Rubha Bholsa

364
SGARBH
BREAC

Loch an Aircill

Loch Lesgamaill

Lagg

15

Eilean Mòr

ST CORMAC'S
CHAPEL

CHAPEL

Kilmory

Kilmory Bay

Pt. of Knap

128

E

Gortantaoid

316

Bunnahabhain
BUNNAHABHAIN
DISTILLERY

Loch a Chnuic
Bhric

785
755
PAPS OF JURA

J

Corran

JURA FOREST

An Dùnan

Lowlandman's
Bay

Miller's Bay

Cret

126

Caol Ila
CAOL ILA DISTILLERY

FINLAGGAN
CENTRE

Keills

Loch
Finlaggan
Loch Cam'

Ballygrant

8

Kilmeny

Port Askaig

Feolin Ferry

Gleann Astaile

Leargybreck

Knockrome

Keils

Craighouse
ISLE OF JURA
DISTILLERY

Small Isles

561

Loch na Mile

F

Redhouses

Daill

Sorn

Bridgend

A846

267
BEINN DUBH

Loch
Ballygrant

Gleann Ullibh

A846

8

Cabrach

342
BRAT BHEINN

JURA HOUSE
WALLED GARDEN

Am Fraoch
Eilean

Brosdale I.

Rubha na Tràille

Kilberry Hd.

SCULPTURED
STONES

Kilb

Cou

G

Mulindry

A846

6

126

McArthur's Hd.

KENNACRAIG 2:00

OBAN 2:20

1:10

0   1   2   3   4   5   6 miles
0 1 2 3 4 5 6 7 8 9 10km

BEINN BHAN

491
BEINN
BHEIGEIR

Carraig Mhòr

SOUND OF ISLAY

SOUND OF JURA

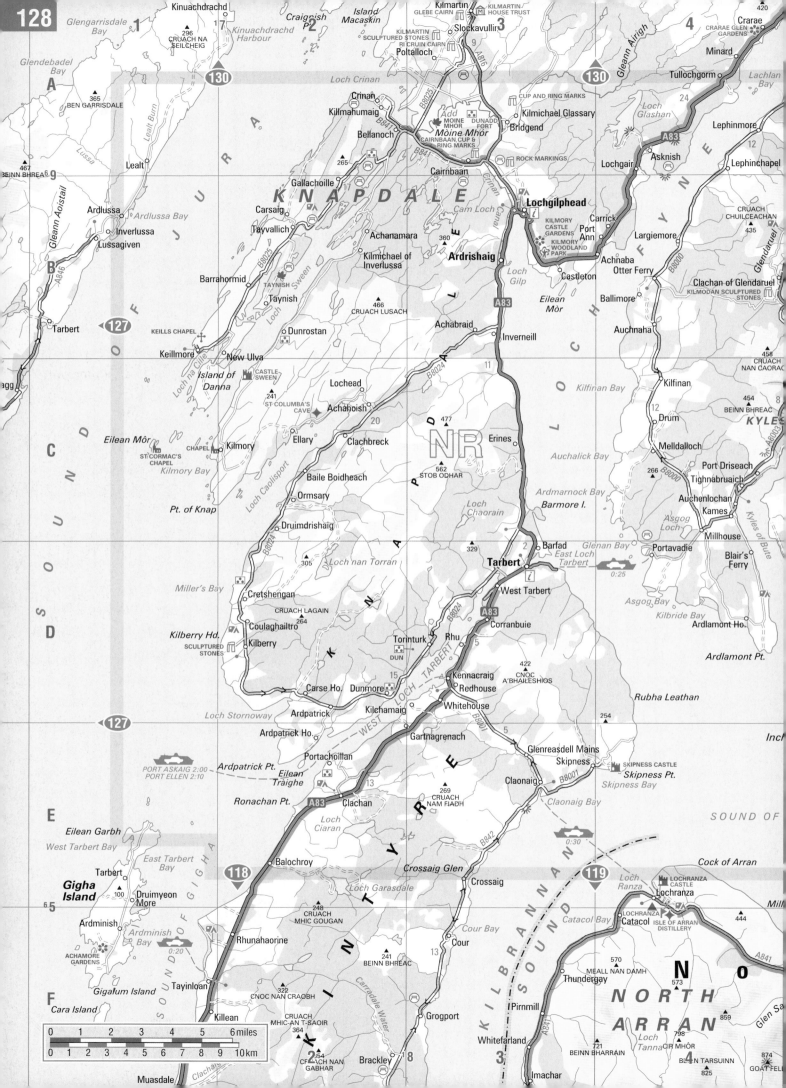

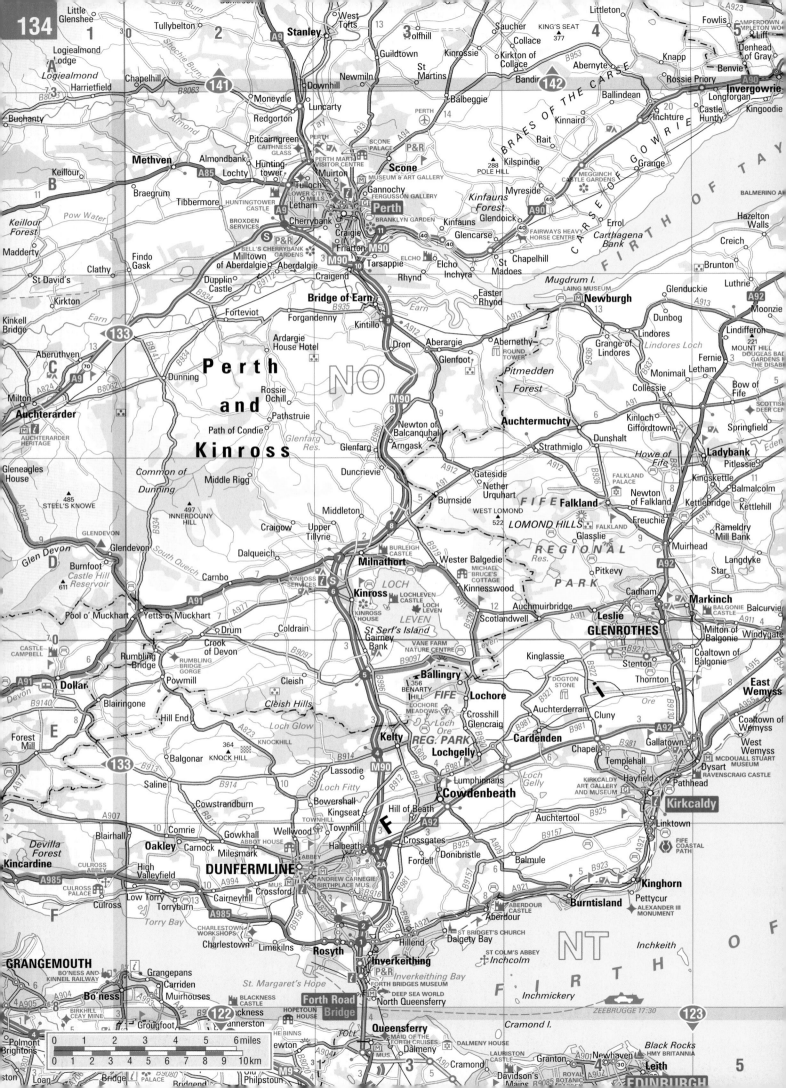

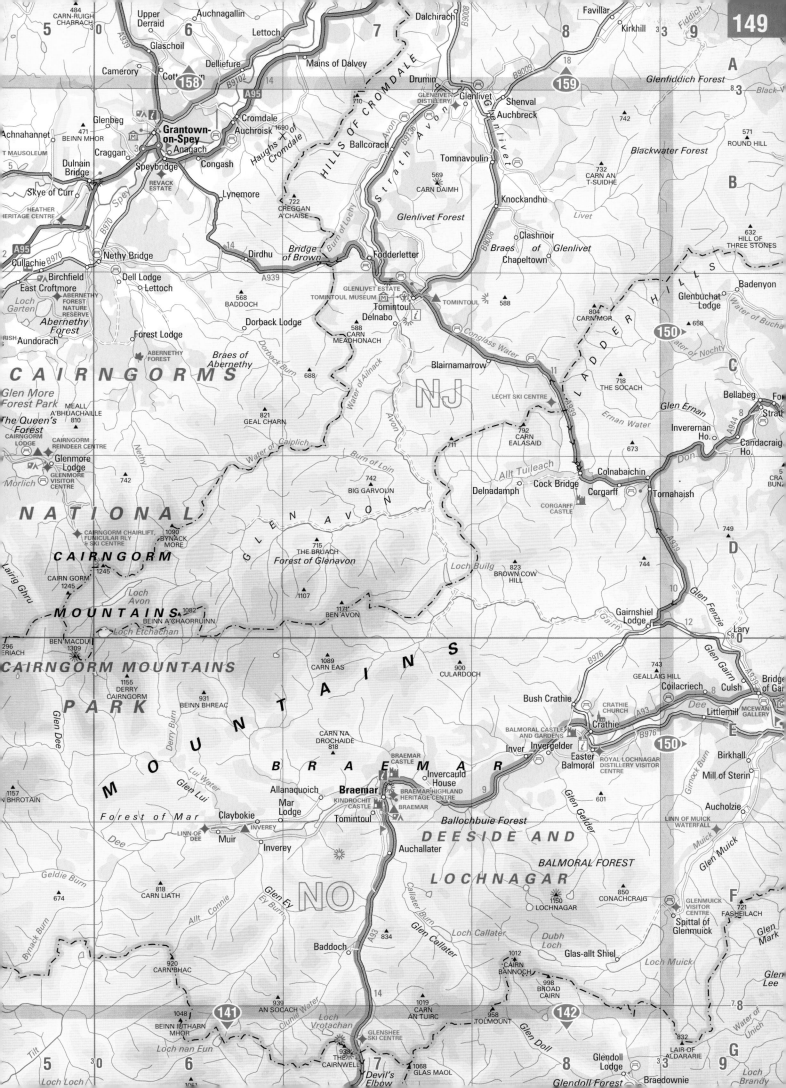

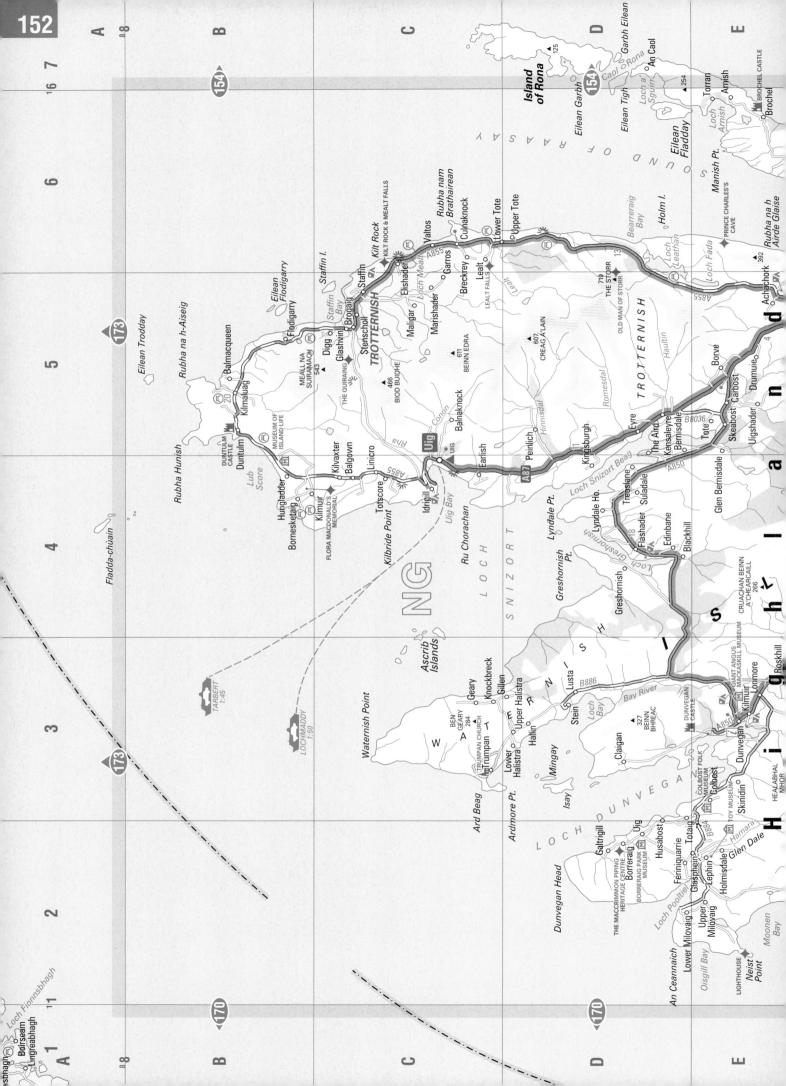

Island of Rona

Garbh Eilean
An Caol
Eilean Tigh
Eilean Fladday
Brochel Castle
Brochel
Torran
Arnish
Manish Pt.
PRINCE CHARLES'S CAVE
Rubha na h Airde Glaise
Achachork

Kilt Rock
KILT ROCK & MEALT FALLS
Staffin
Staffin I.
Staffin Bay
Eilean Flodigarry
Balmacqueen
Rubha na h-Aiseig
Eilean Trodday
Kilmaluag
Flodigarry
Digg
Glashvin
Stenscholl
Brogaig
TROTTERNISH

Valtos
Garros
Maligar
Marishader
Breckrey
Lealt
LEALT FALLS
Culnaknock
Lower Tote
Upper Tote
Rubha nam Brathairean

THE STORR
719
OLD MAN OF STORR
CREAG A'LAIN
607
BEINN EDRA
611

Loch Mealt
Loch Fada
Loch Leathan
Bearreraig Bay
Holm I.

MEALL NA SURAMACH
543
MUSEUM OF ISLAND LIFE
THE QUIRAING
BIOD BUIDHE
466

Rubha Hunish
Lub Score
DUNTULM CASTLE
Duntulm
Kilvaxter
Balgown
Linicro
Hungladder
Kilmuir
Bornesketaig
FLORA MACDONALD'S MEMORIAL
Kilbride Point
Totscore
Idrigill
A855

Uig Bay
Ru Chorachan
Loch Conon
Rha
Uig
Earlish
Peinlich
Balnaknock
A87

Kingsburgh
Romesdal
Hinnisdal
Haultin
TROTTERNISH
Eyre
Borve
Drumuie
Skeabost
Carbost
Uigshader
A855

NG

Ascrib Islands
Loch Snizort
Loch Snizort Beag
Lyndale Pt.
Greshornish Pt.
Lyndale Ho.
Treaslane
Suladale
The Aird
Kensaleyre
Bernisdale
Tote
B8036
Glen Bernisdale

Waternish Point
Ardmore Pt.
Ard Beag
Geary
Knockbreck
Gillen
Upper Halistra
Lower Halistra
Hallin
BEN GEARY
284
TRUMPAN CHURCH
Trumpan
W A T E R N I S H
Lusta
Stein
Loch Bay
Mingay
Isay
Claigan
BEINN BHREAC
327
Bay River
B886
Greshornish
Edinbane
Blackhill
Flashader
Loch Greshornish

CRUACHAN BEINN A'CHEARCAILL
266
DUNVEGAN CASTLE
GIANT ANGUS MACASKILL MUSEUM
Kilmuir
Lonmore
Roskhill
Dunvegan
COLBOST FOLK MUSEUM
Colbost
TOY MUSEUM
Skinidin
HEALABHAL MHOR
A850

W a t e r n i s h
Loch Dunvegan
Dunvegan Head

THE MACCRIMMON PIPING HERITAGE CENTRE
Galtrigill
BORRERAIG PARK MUSEUM
Borreraig
Uig
Husabost
Totaig
Feriniquarrie
Glasphein
Lephin
B884
Harmara
Glen Dale
Holmisdale
Skinidin

An Ceannaich
Lower Milovaig
Upper Milovaig
Loch Pooltiel
Oisgill Bay
LIGHTHOUSE
Neist Point
Moonen Bay

TARBERT 1:45
LOCHMADDY 1:50

Fladda-chùain

Loch Fionnsbhagh
Bòrseam
Lingreabhagh

SOUND OF RAASAY

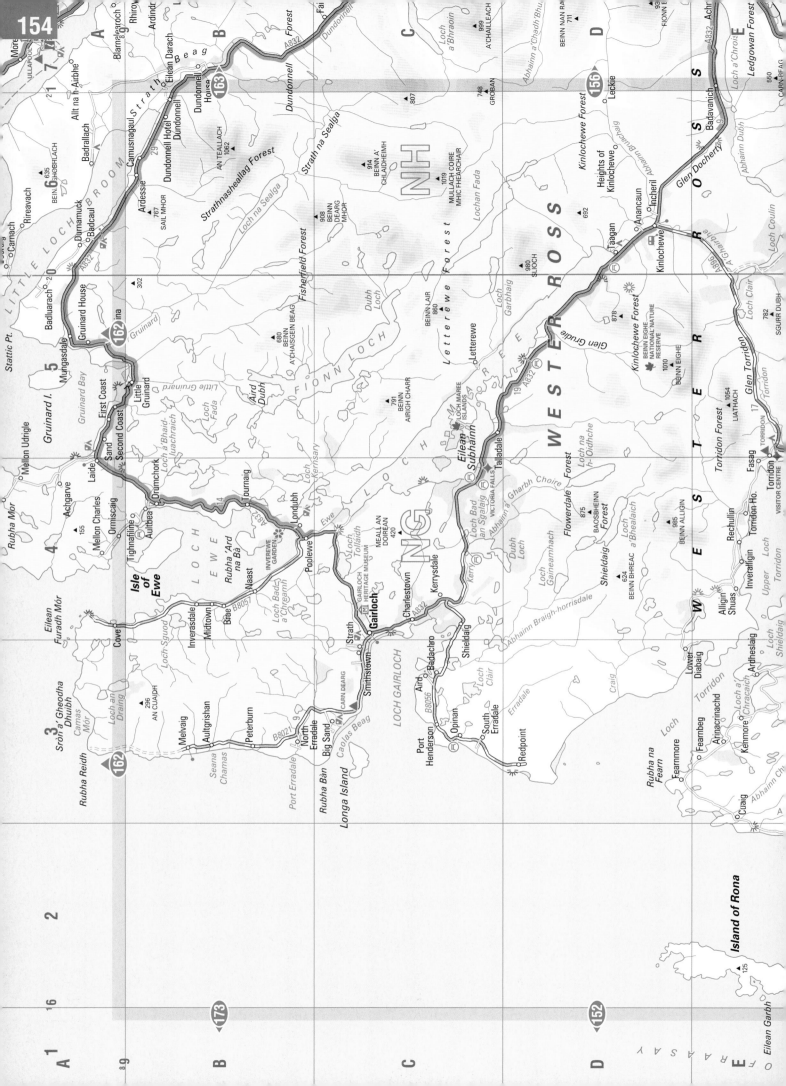

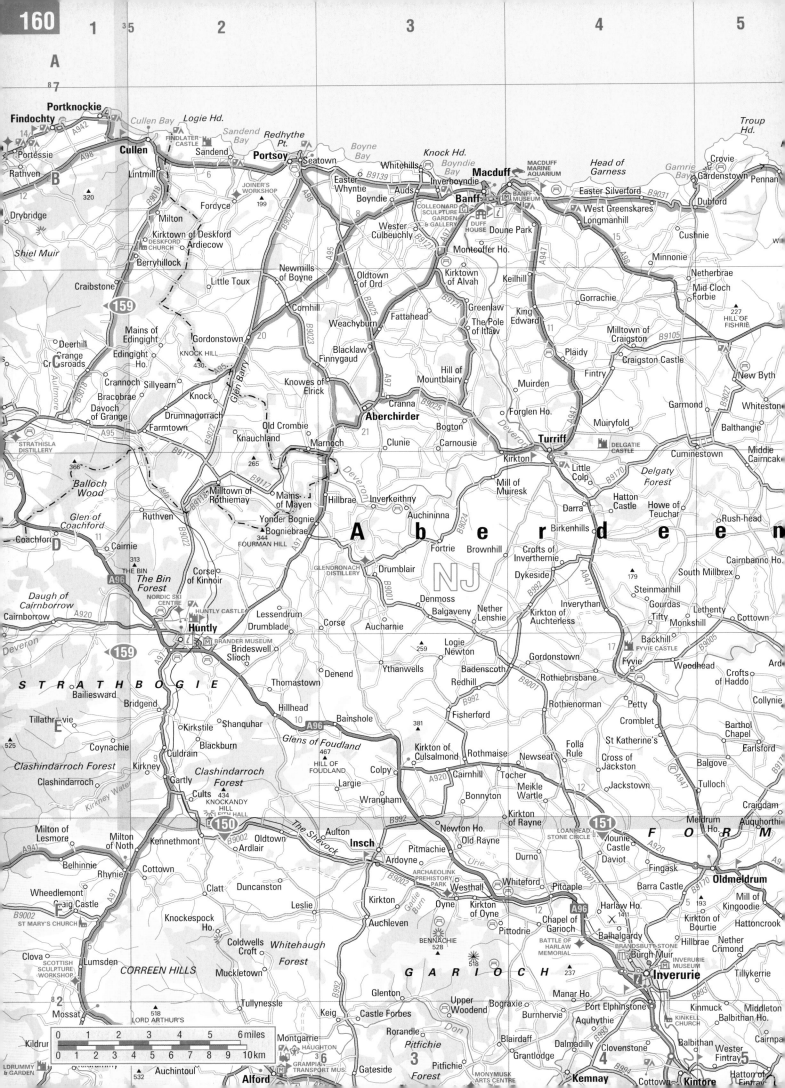

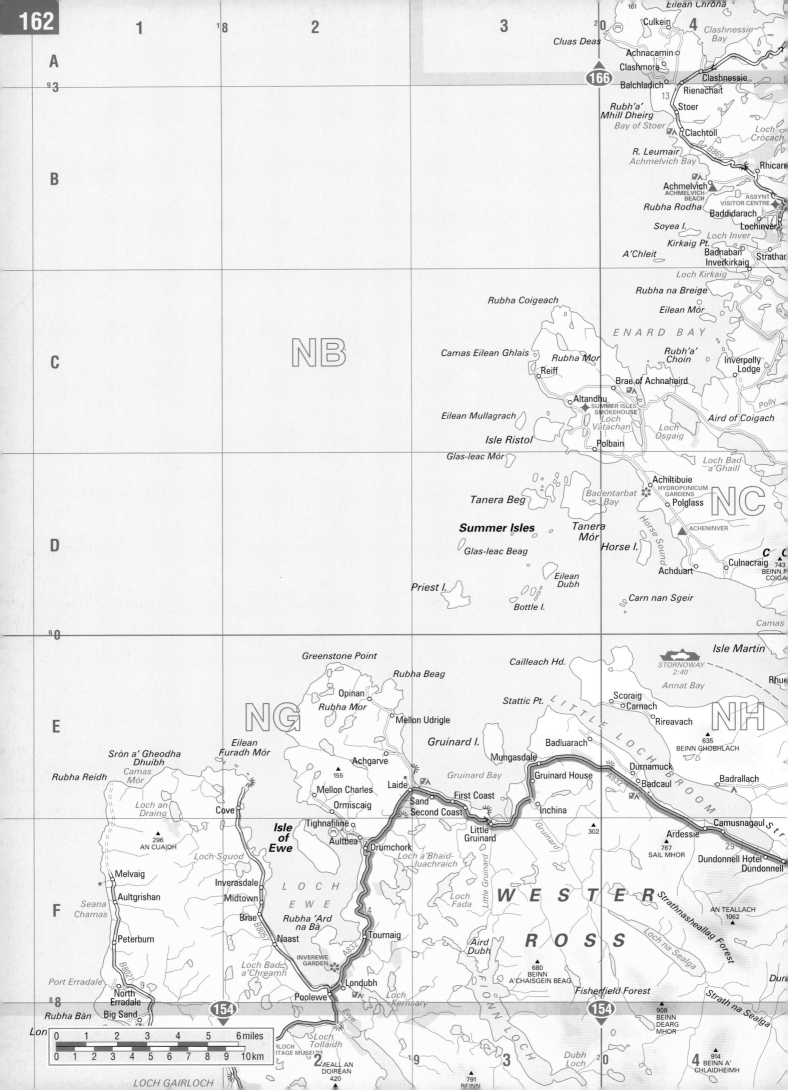

CAPE WRATH

Kearvaig

371
SGRIBHIS-
BHEINN

Geodha Ruadh na Fola

Inshore

Bay of Keisgaig

Loch
Keisgaig

Geodha Ruadh

457
FASHVEN

Loch Airigh
na Beinne

Am Balg

423
BEINN DEARG

Sandwood
Loch

Rubh'an Fhir Léithe

485
CREAG
RIABHACH

Grud

Loch na
Gàinimh

332
GHLAS
BHEINN

Sheigra

Strath Shinary

Balchrick

A838

Dròman

Oldshore Beg

521
FARRMHEALL

19

Eilean Roin Mor

Oldshoremore

NC

Loch Clash

Kinlochbervie

Gualin Ho.

B801

Badcall

Loch Inchard

Achriesgill

Bagh Loch an Roin

Achlyness

L. na Claise
Carnaich

Loch Dughaill

A838

Ceathramh Garbh

Rhiconich

Ardmore Pt.

GANU MOR
908

Rubha Ruadh

Ardmore

Foinaven

Fanagmore

Loch Laxford

NORTH-WEST SUTHERLAND

Tarbet

Loch a'Garbh-
bhaid Mór

Handa Island

Foindle

Loch an Eas
Uaine

A894

Sound of Handa

Laxford Bridge

Loch nam
Brac

787
ARKLE

Scourie Bay

Laxford

Scourie More

A838

Lochstack Lodge

Rubh'Aird an t-Sionnaich

Scourie

Gorm Loch

Loch Stack

719
BEN STACK

Upper Badcall

Lower Badcall

BEINN AUSKAIRD
386

Strath Stack

Eil. a'Bhreitheimh

18

Achfary

332

LOCH
A'MHUILINN

R E A Y   F O R E S

Rubha a'Mhucard

Loch
Crocach

Lochmore Lodge

Meall Mór

A894

Loch More

Calbha
Mór

Loch na Creige
Duibhe

Eddrachillis Bay

Calbha
Beag

Duartmore
Forest

Loch an Leathaid
Bhúain

Point of Stoer

Oldany
Island

Loch a'Chairn Bhàin

547

Aultanrynie

Cirean Geardail

R. nan Còsan

Kylestrome

Glendhu   Forest

161

Eilean Chrona

Culkein
Drumbeg

Loch Nedd

Kylesku

Kinloch

Cluas Deas

Oldany

B869

Loch Glendhu

Gleann   Dubh

Culkein

Clashnessie
Bay

Drumbeg

8

Unapool

530
BEINN AIRD
DA LOCH

566

Achnacarnin

Nedd

Gleann Leireag

Loch Glencoul

Clashmore

Loch
Poll

Newton

162

Balchladich

Clashnessie

163

792
BEINN LEOID

Rienachait

13

Stoer

Loch an
Leòthaid

808
QUINAG

A837

Glen Coul

A894

Loch
an Eircill

R. Leumair

Loch
Cròcach

Loch
Beannach

Lochassynt Lodge

EAS COUL AULIN
WATERFALL

776

Achmelvich Bay

B869

Rhicarn

BEINN UIDHE
740

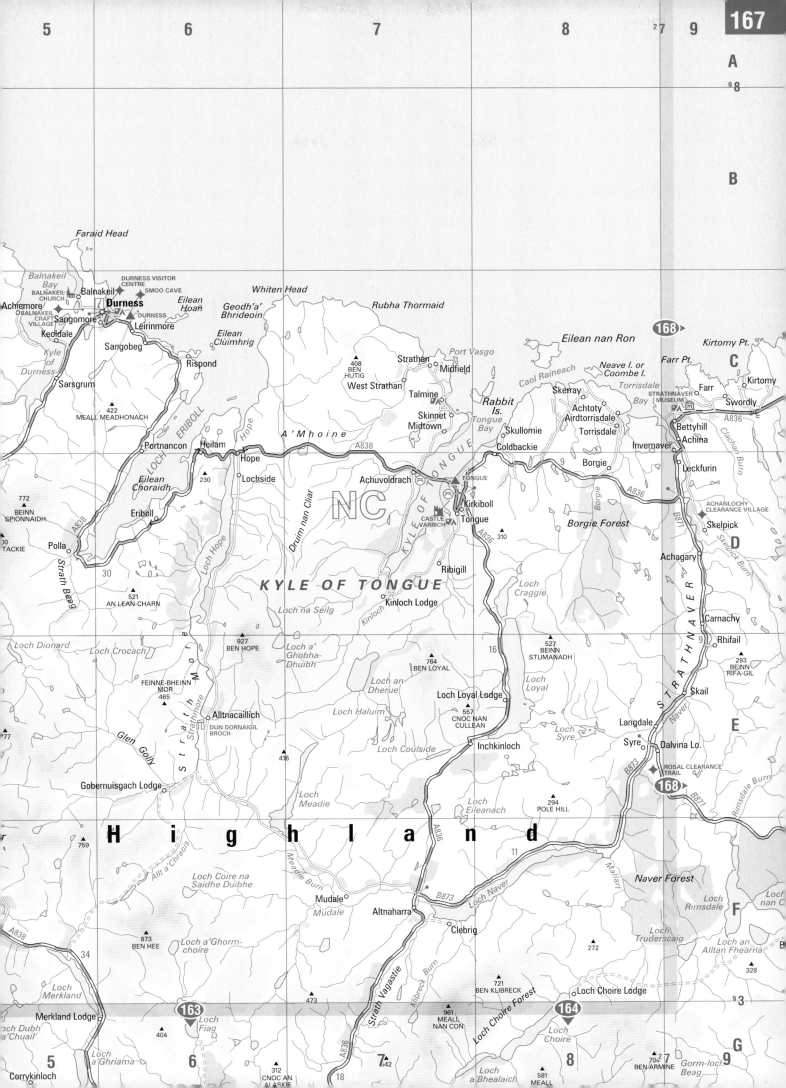

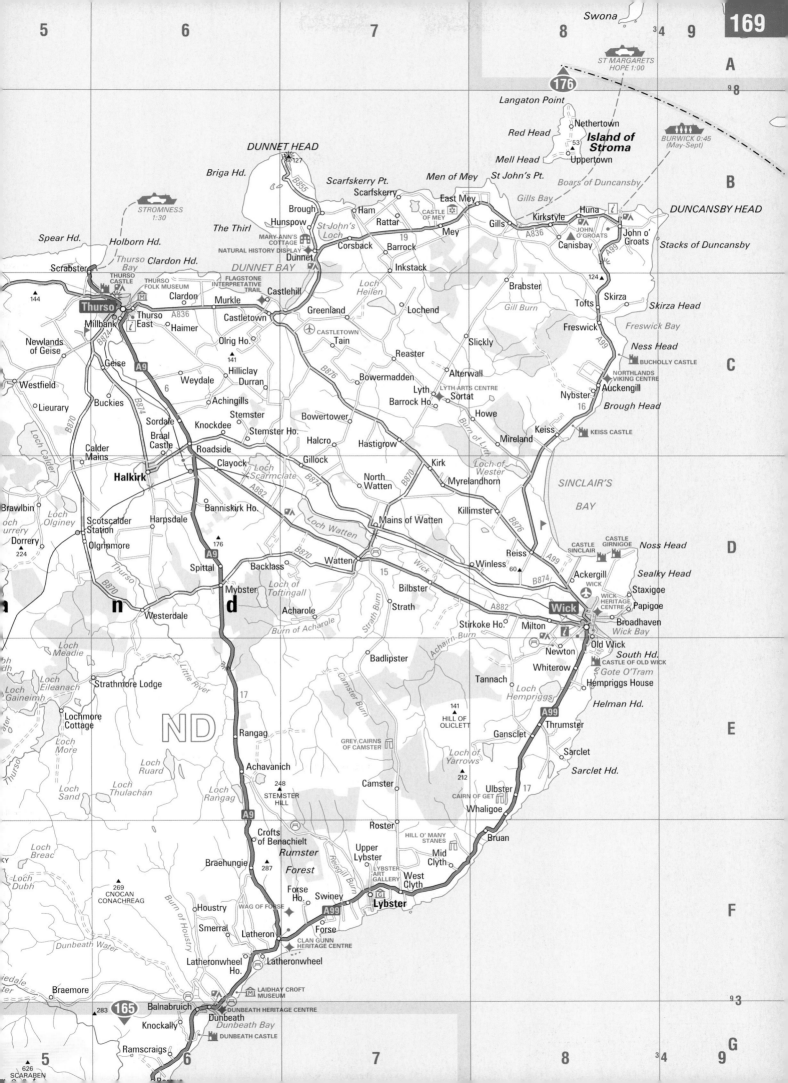

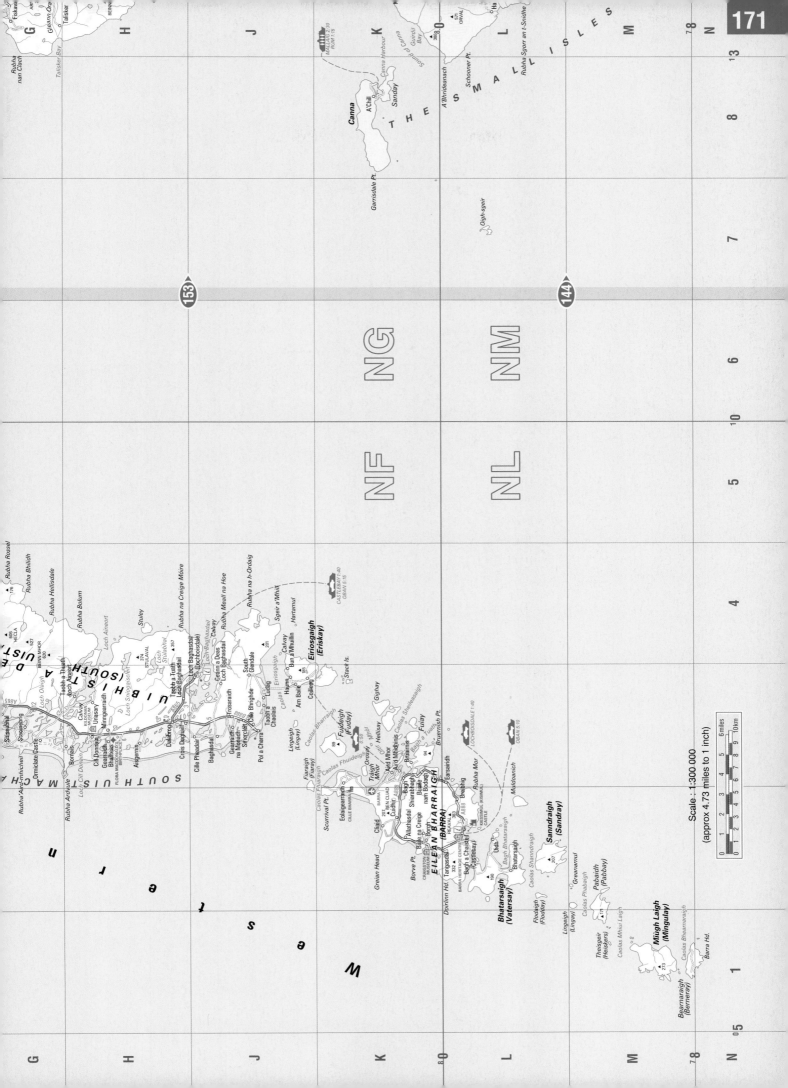

THE SMALL ISLES

Canna
Sound of Canna
Canna Harbour
A'Chill
Sanday
Garrisdale Pt.
Schooner Pt.
A'Bhrideanach
Rubha Sgor an t-Snidhe

MALLAIG 2:30
RUM 1:15

Oigh-sgeir

NG

NM

NF

NL

Rubha Rossel
Rubha Bhilidh
Rubha Hellisdale
Rubha Bolum
Rubha na Creige Mòire
Rubha Meall na Hoe
Rubha na h-Ordaig

BEINN MHOR 620
606 HECLA
427

Loch Aineort
Stuley
Loch Snigasclett
STULAVAL 374
Loch Stùlabhal
357
Loch Baghasdail (Lochboisdale)
Loch-Baghasdail
Ceann a Deas
Loch Baghasdail
Calvay
Calvay
Sgeir a'Mhuil
Hartamul
201

Caolas Eriosgaigh
Bun a'Mhuillin
Eirìosgaigh (Eriskay)

CASTLEBAY 1:40
OBAN 5:15

Taobh a Tuath Loch Aineort
UIBHIST A DEAS
SOUTH UIST
Taobh a Deas Loch Baghasdail
Calvay
South Glendale
Cille Bhrìghde
Taobh a Chaolais
Ludag
Haunn
Am Bail'
Coileag
Stack Is.

Cille Pheadair
Baghasdail
Gearraidh na Mònadh
Pol a Charra
Trosaraidh
Sheaclett

Loch Ollghaigh
Dalabrog

Cnoic Dagraidh
Lingeigh (Lingay)

SOUTH UIST MACHAIR

Rubha Ardvule

Flora Macdonald's Birthplace

Fiaraigh (Faray)
Caolas Fhudeigh
Caolas Fhudeigh
Fuideigh (Fuday)
150

Orosaigh
Hellisay
Gighay

Oronsay
Aird Mhidhinis
Bruairnis
Caolas Shellasaigh
94
Bruernish Pt.

Scurrival Pt.
Tràigh Mhòr
BARRA
Ard Mhor
Brèibhig
Fulay

LOCHBOISDALE 1:40
OBAN 5:10

Eolaigearraidh
CILLE BHARRA
Cuidhir
Bàgh Shiarabhagh
Bàgh nam Bodach
Earsairidh

Cliaid
BEN CLIAD 207
A888
Buaile
Rubha Mor
Muldoanich

Greian Head
Borve Pt.
Bàgh a' Chaisteil (Castlebay)
EILEAN BHARRAIGH (BARRA)
HEAVAL 383
KISIMUL CASTLE
Didi
Bagh Bhatarsaigh

Allathasdal
Baile na Creige
Bòrgh
332

BARRA HERITAGE CENTRE
Bhatarsaigh

CRAIGSTON MUSEUM
KIESSIMUL (KISIMUL) CASTLE

Doirlinn Hd. (Tangasdal)
190
Caolas Shanndraigh
Sanndraigh (Sandray)
207

Bhatarsaigh (Vatersay)
Flodaigh (Flodday)
Lingeigh (Lingay)
Caolas Phabaigh
Pabaidh (Pabbay)
Greanamul

Theisgeir (Heisters)
Caolas Mhiu Laigh

Miughlaigh (Mingulay)
273
Caolas Bheannraigh
Barra Hd.

Bearnaraigh (Bernaray)

Scale : 1:300 000
(approx 4.73 miles to 1 inch)

N
M
W
e
s
t
e
r
n

I
s
l
e
s

Rubha nan Clach
Talisker Bay
Talisker
Fiskavaig
Gleann Oraid
Talisker

Rubha Ardvule

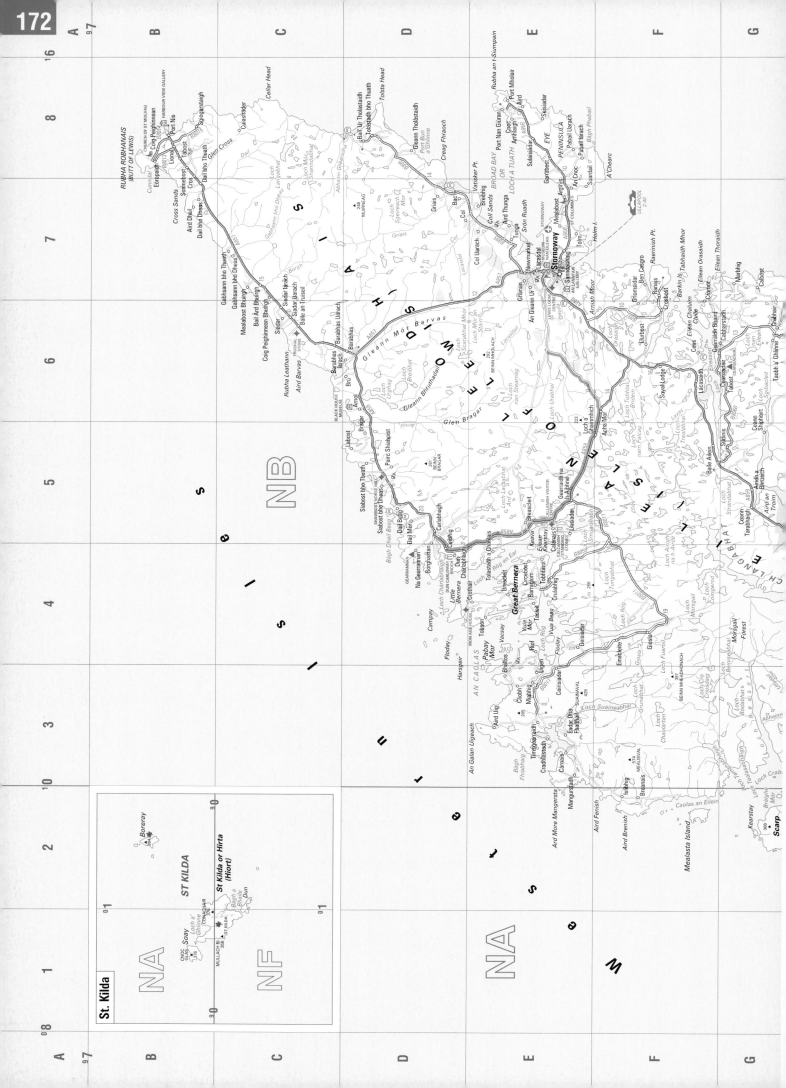

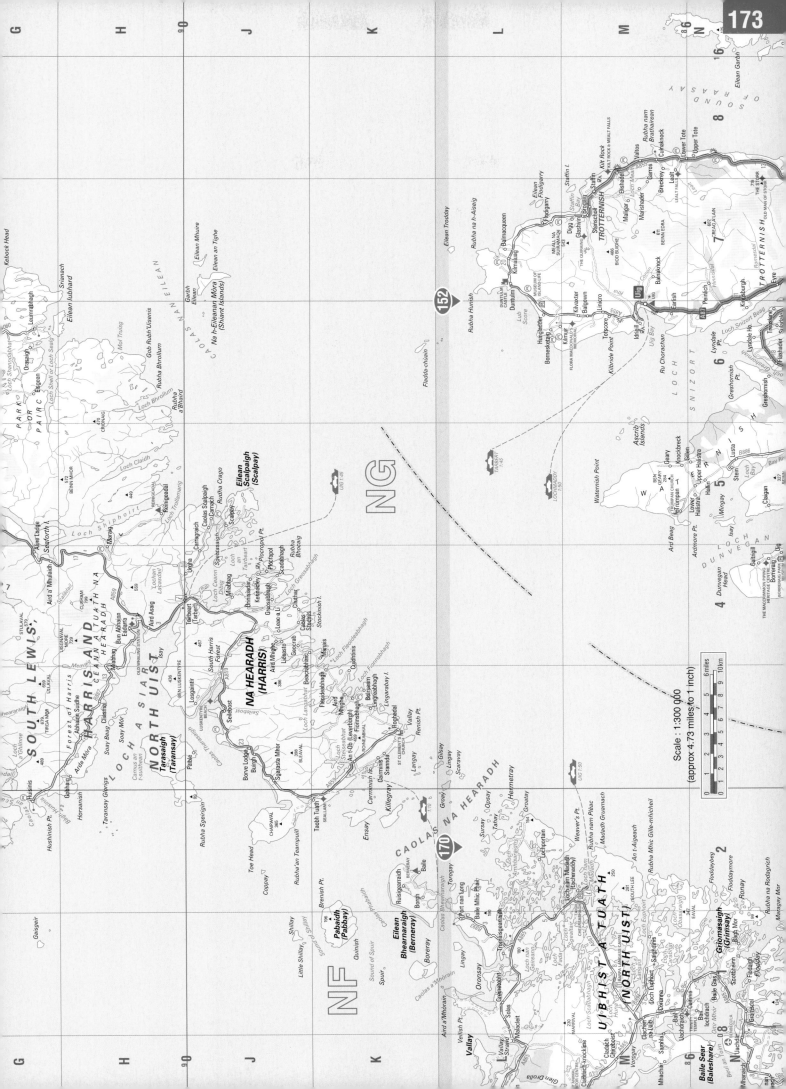

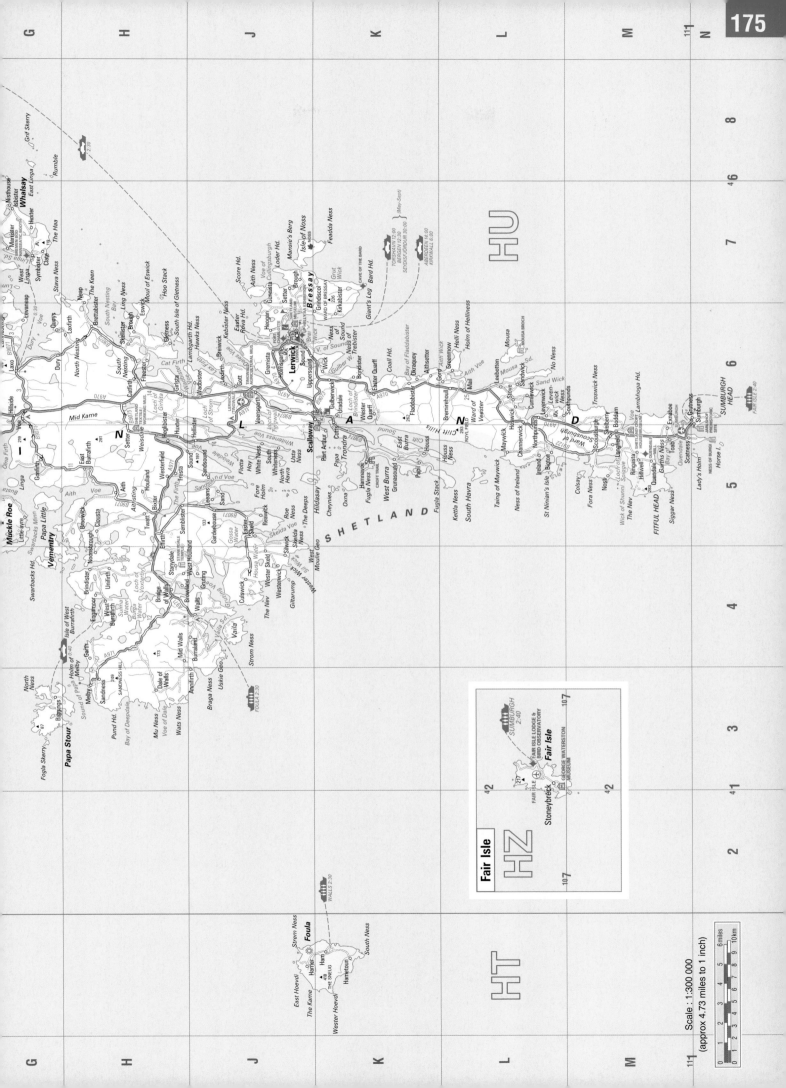

G H J K L M N

SHETLAND

HU

Fair Isle

HZ

HT

Scale : 1:300 000
(approx 4.73 miles to 1 inch)

0 1 2 3 4 5 6miles
0 1 2 3 4 5 6 7 8 9 10km

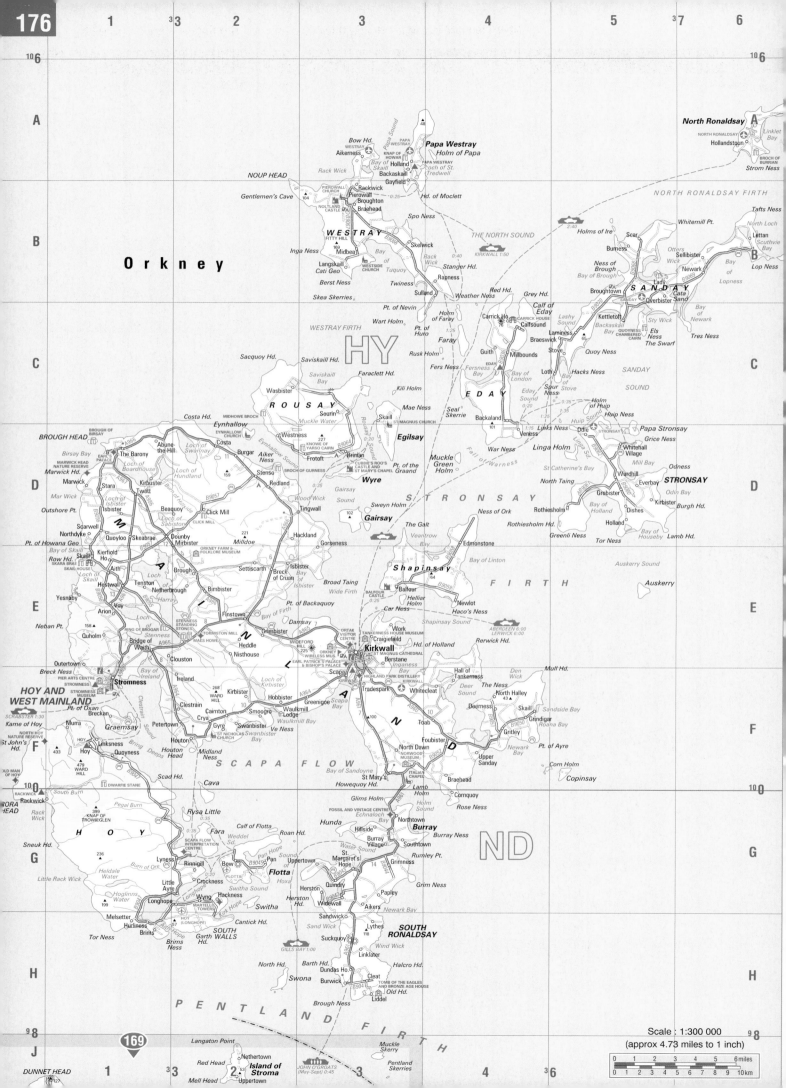

Aberdeen

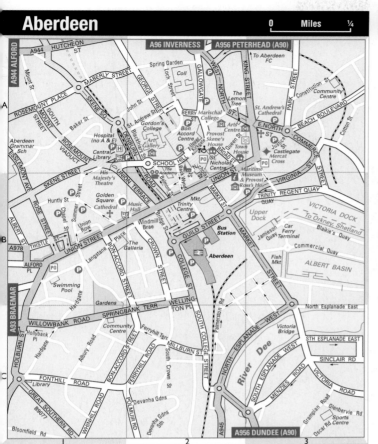

Bath

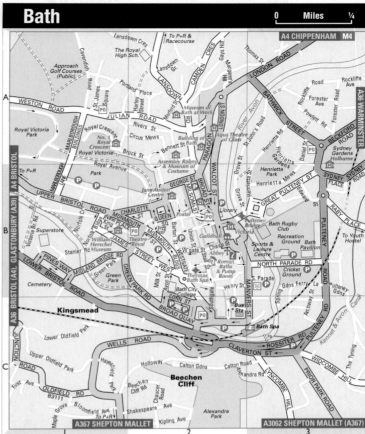

Birmingham

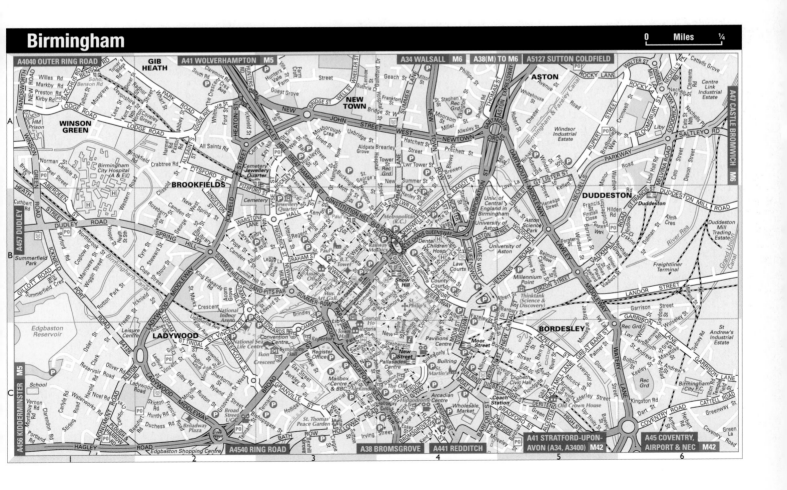

Blackpool

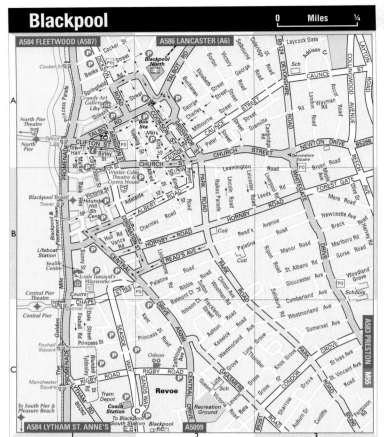

Bournemouth

Bradford

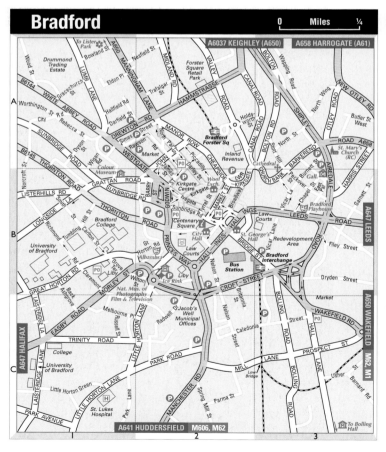

Brighton

Bristol

0   Miles   ¼

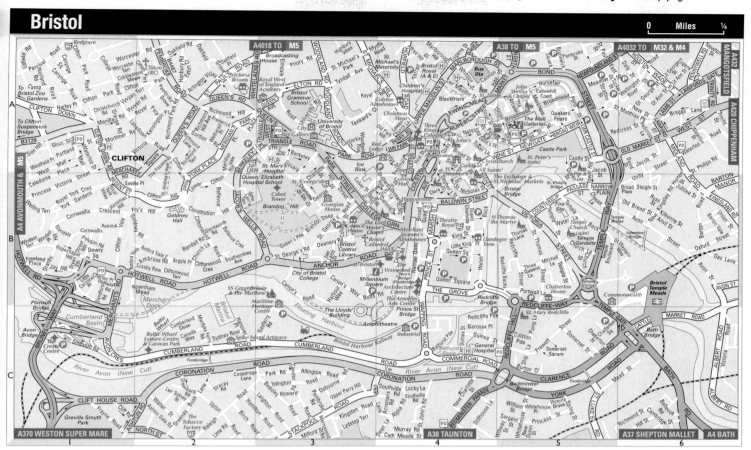

Cambridge

0   Miles   ¼

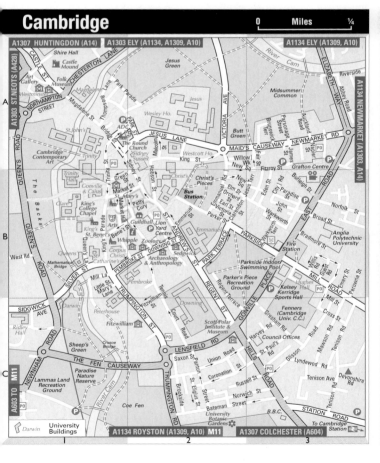

Canterbury

0   Miles   ¼

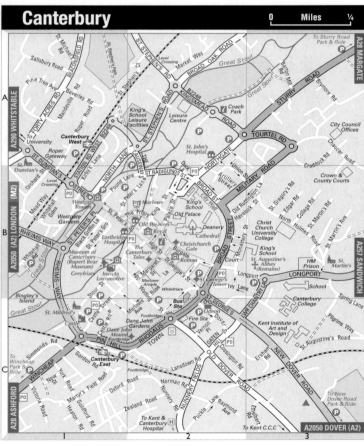

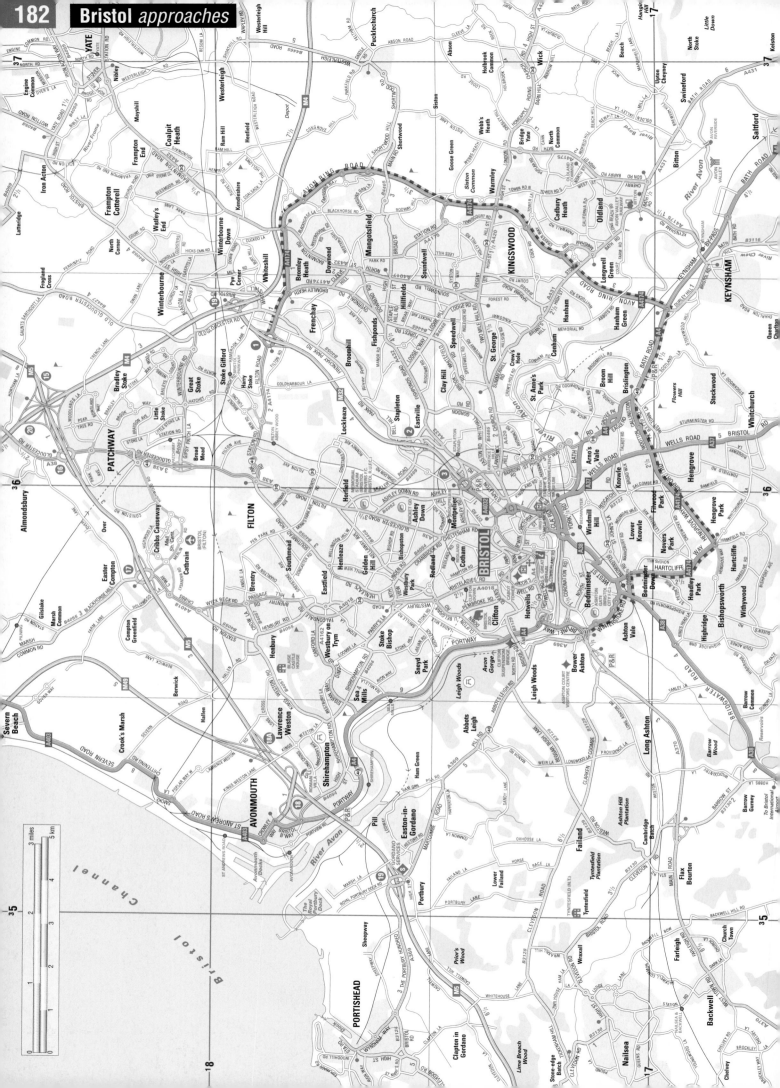

Cardiff / Caerdydd

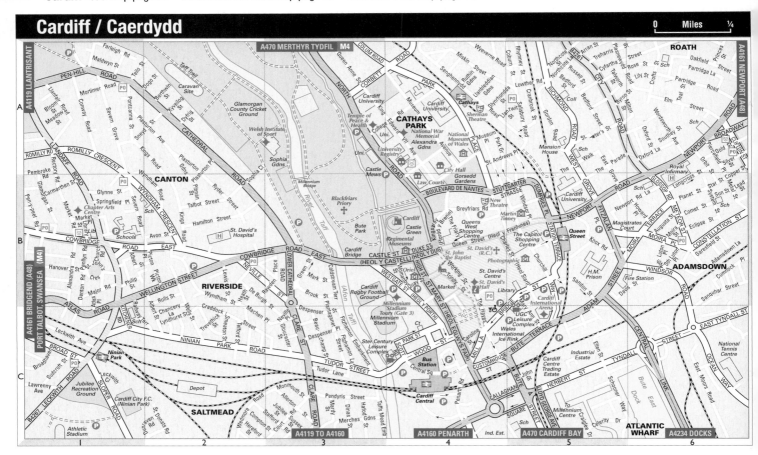

Cheltenham

Chester

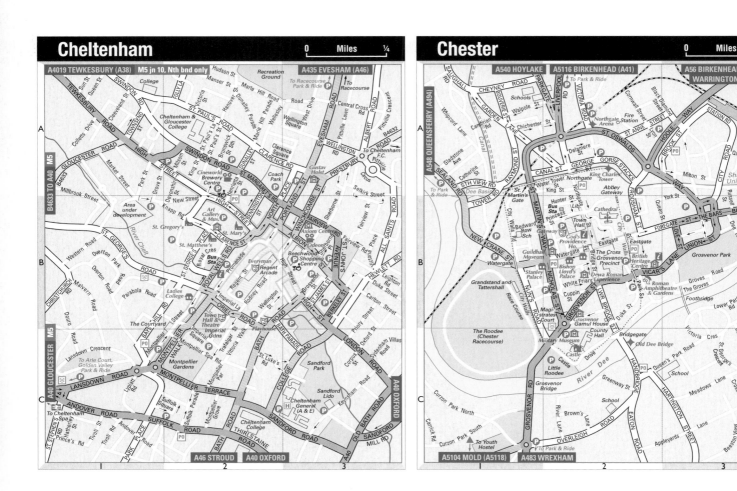

Colchester road map page 43 • **Coventry** road map page 51 • **Derby** road map page 76 • **Durham** road map page 111

185

Colchester

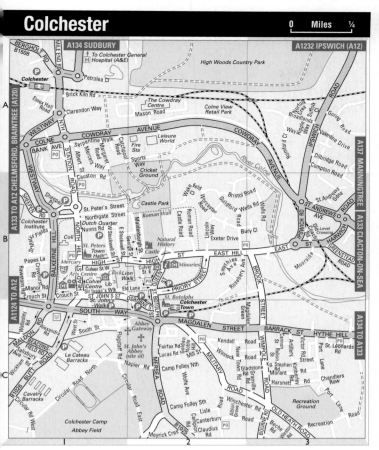

Coventry

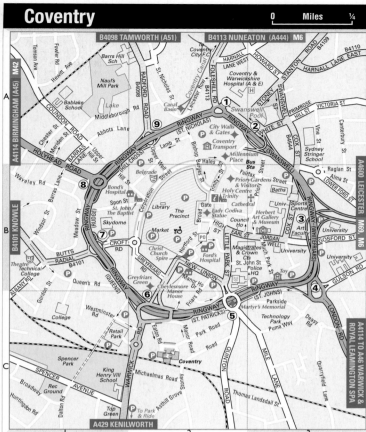

Derby

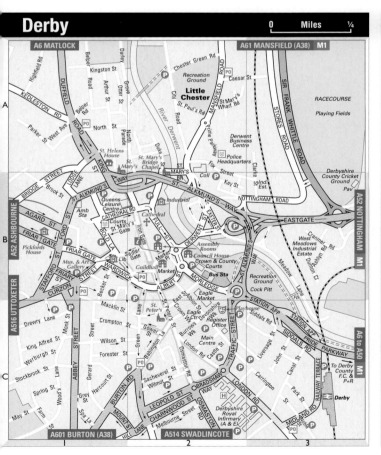

Durham

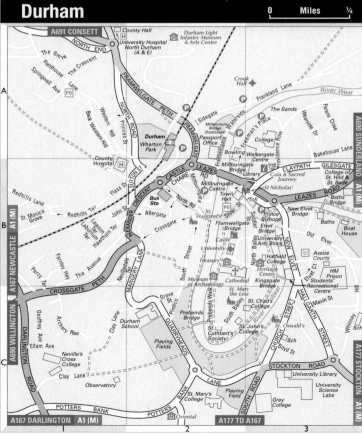

Edinburgh

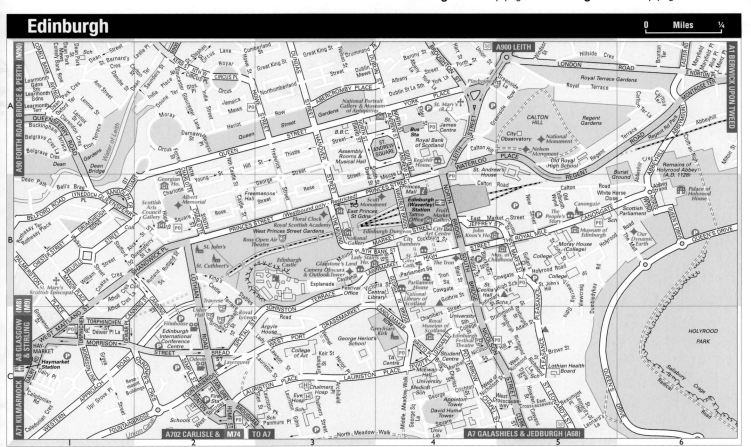

Glasgow

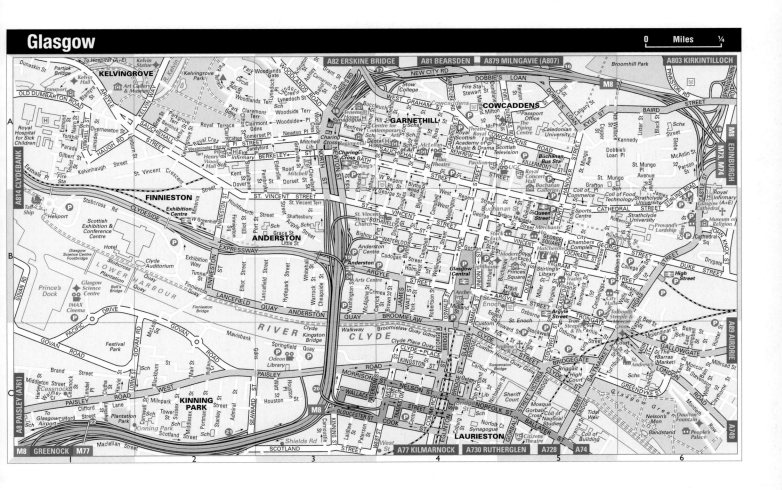

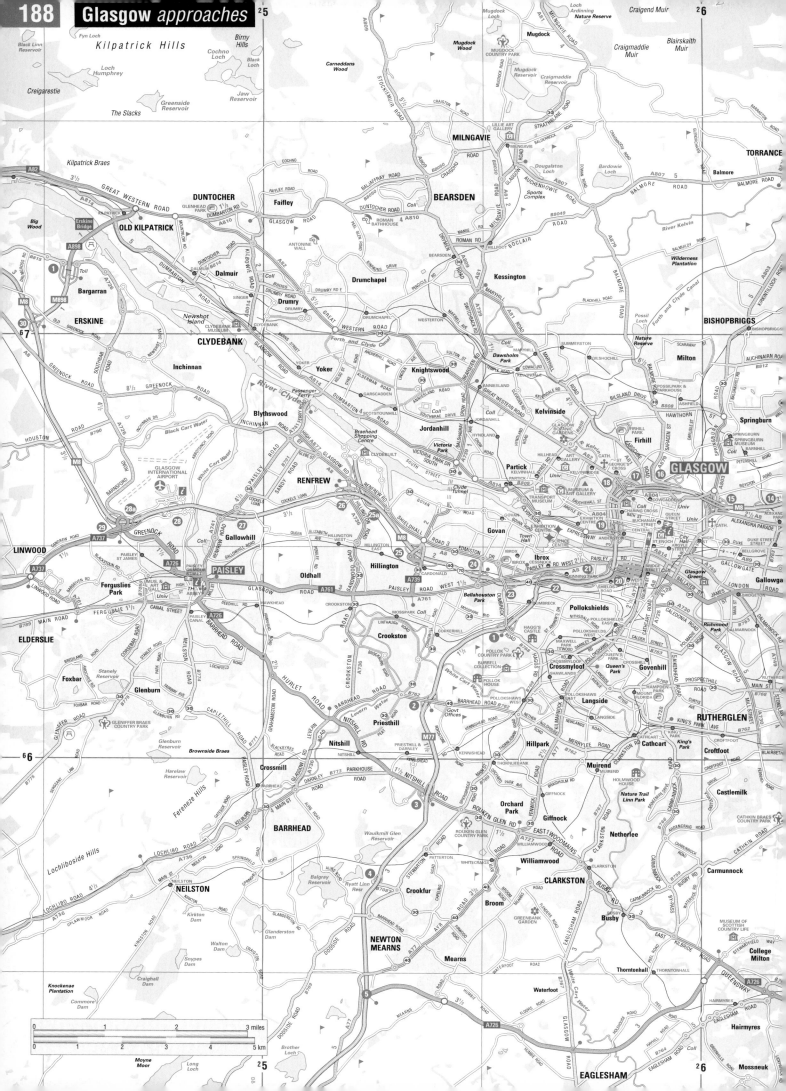

190

Exeter road map page 10 • **Gloucester** road map page 37 • **Hull** road map page 90 • **Ipswich** road map page 57

Exeter

0 Miles ¼

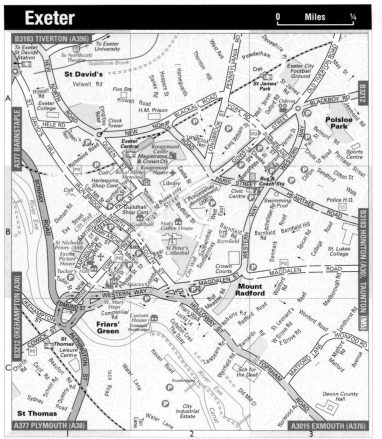

Gloucester

0 Miles ¼

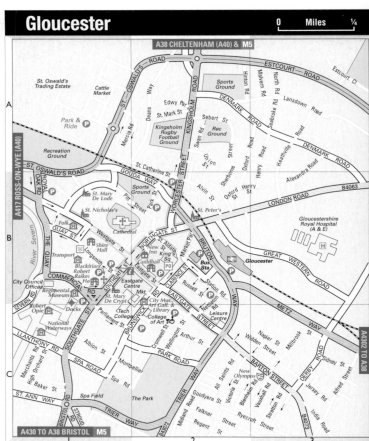

Hull

0 Miles ¼

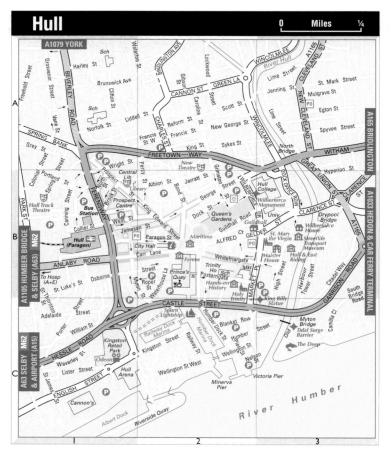

Ipswich

0 Miles ¼

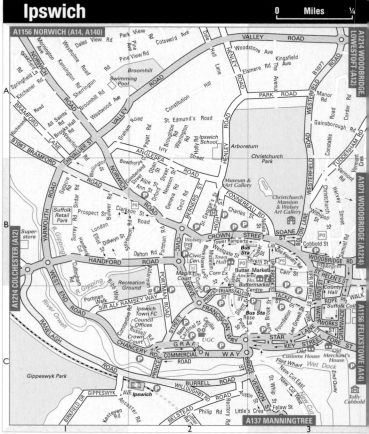

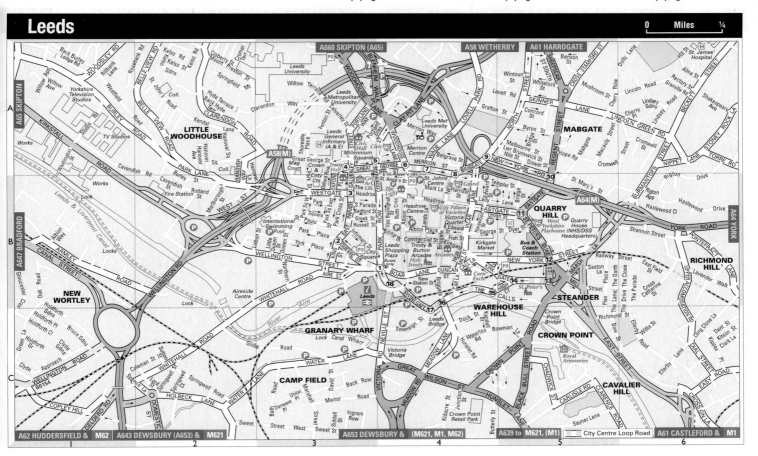

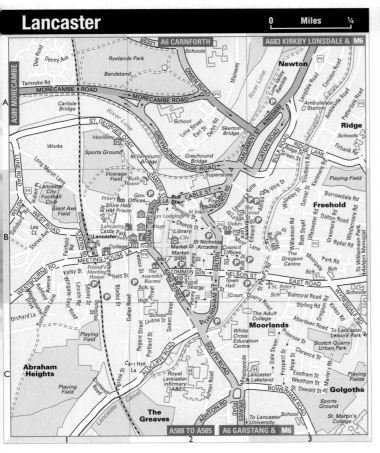

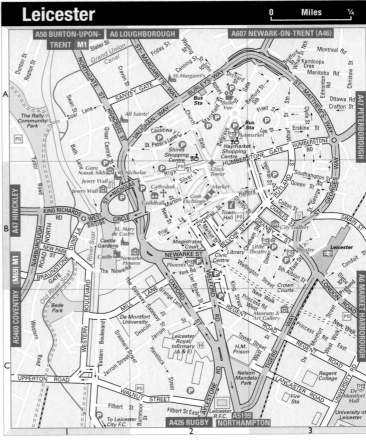

Liverpool

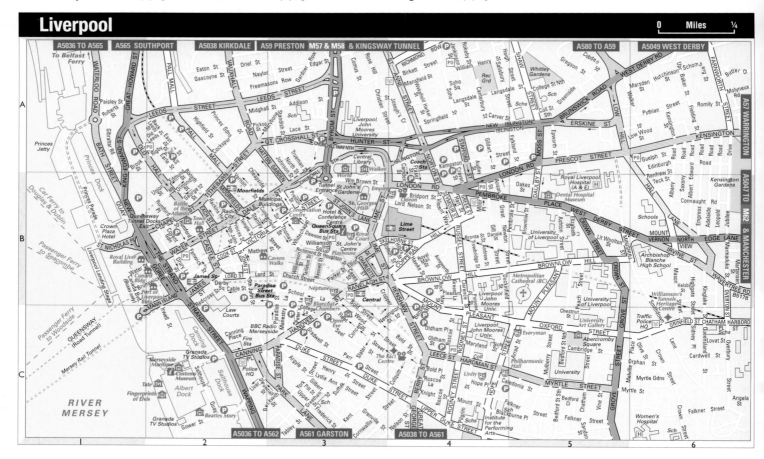

Lincoln

Middlesbrough

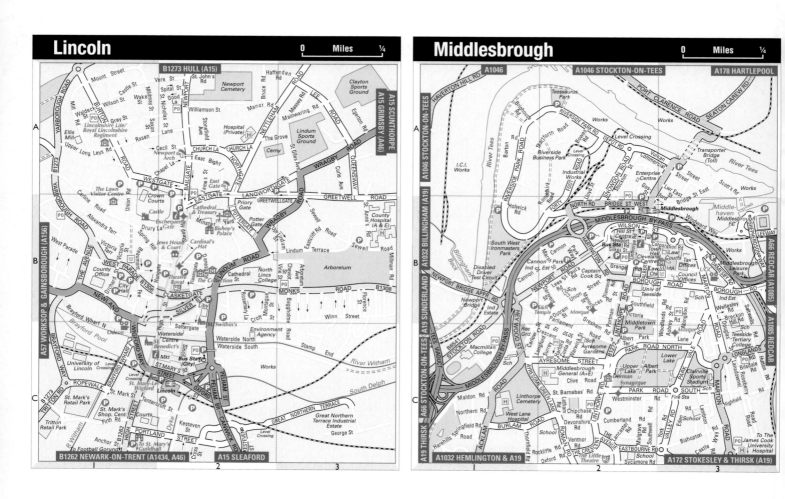

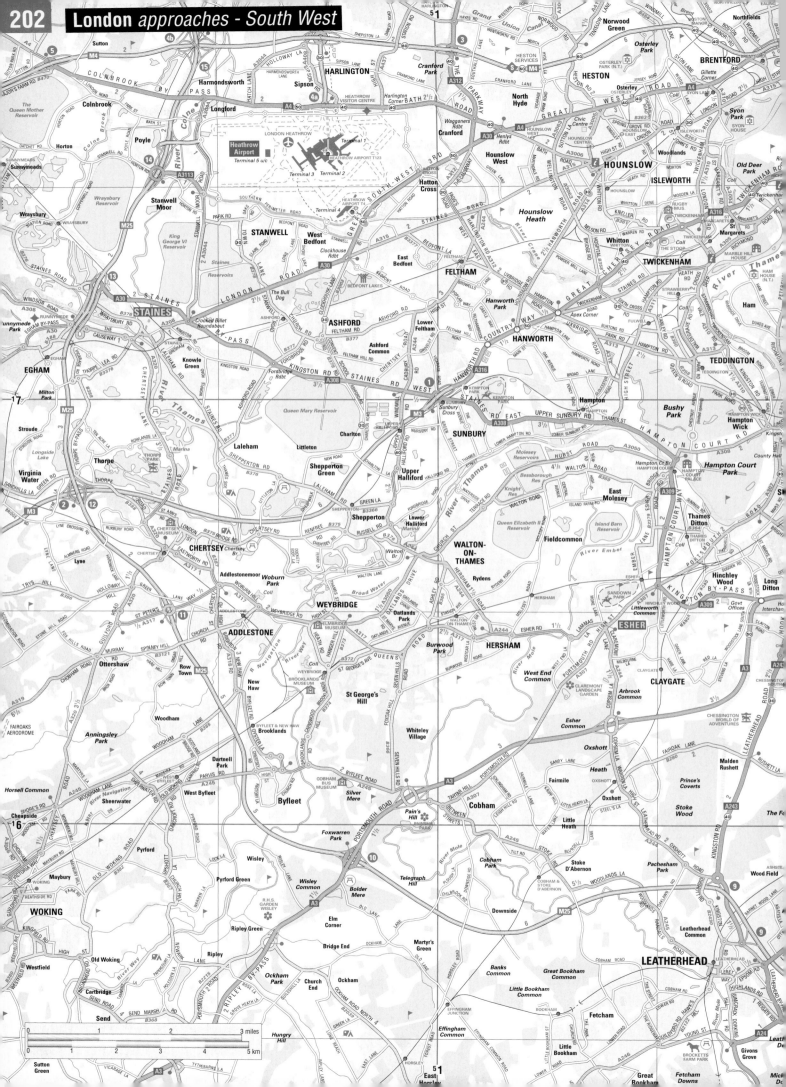

Manchester

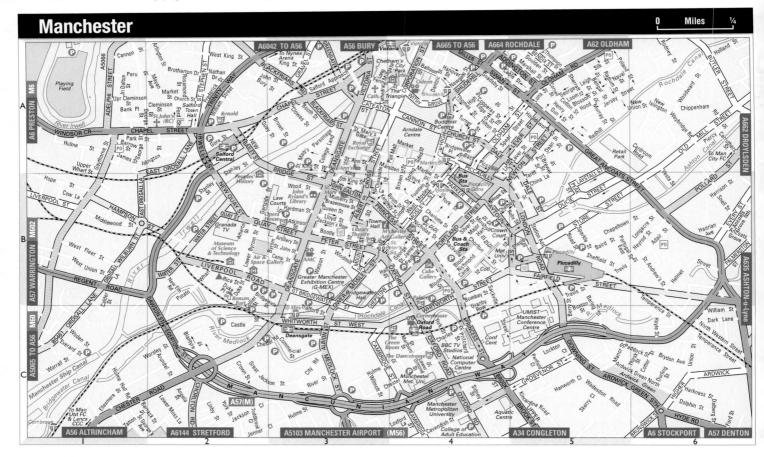

Milton Keynes

Northampton

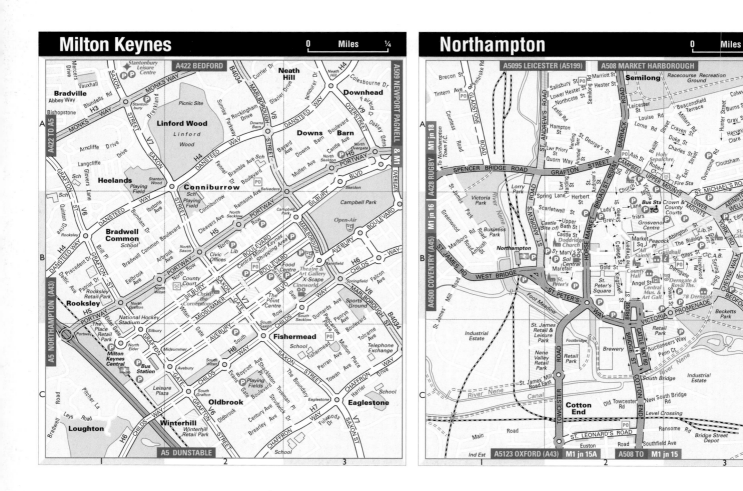

Newcastle upon Tyne

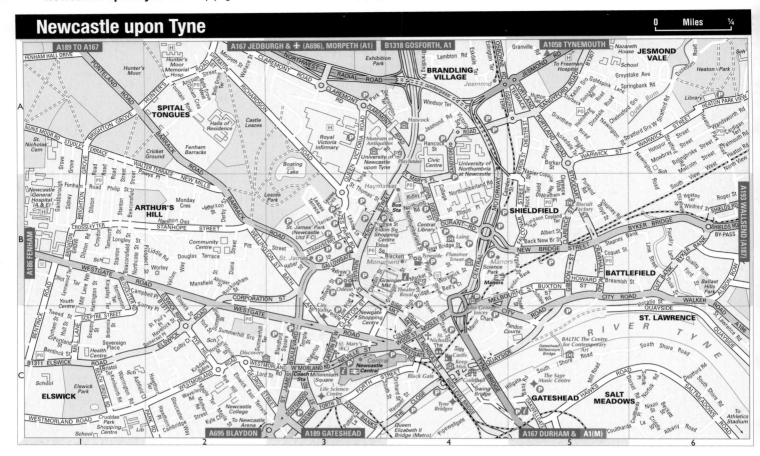

Norwich

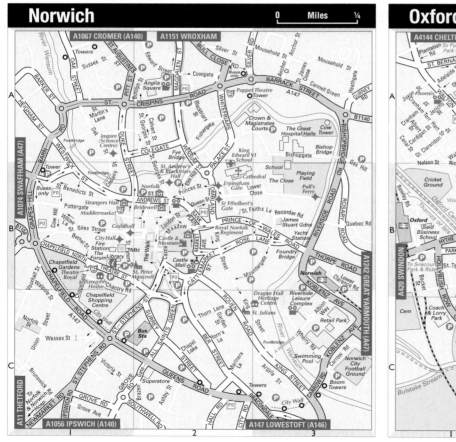

Oxford

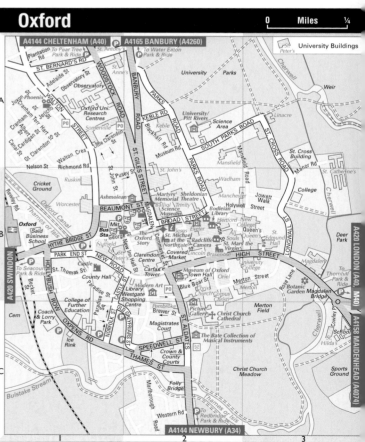

210

Nottingham road map page 77 • **Plymouth** road map page 6 • **Portsmouth** road map page 15 • **Preston** road map page 86

Nottingham

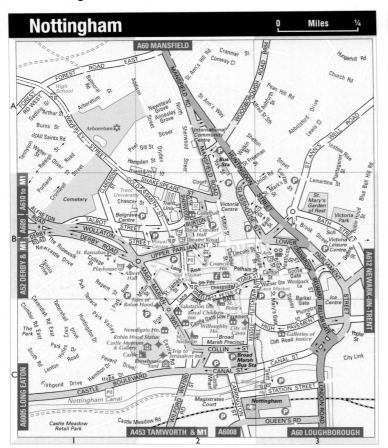

Plymouth

Portsmouth

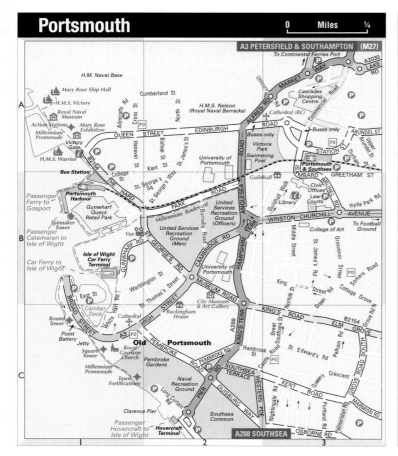

Preston

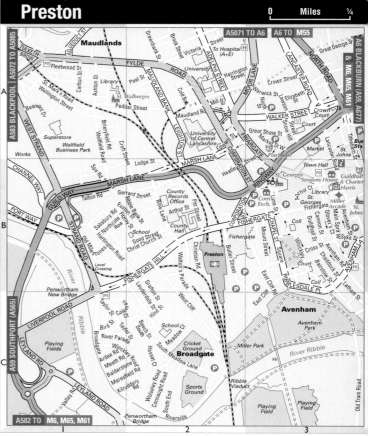

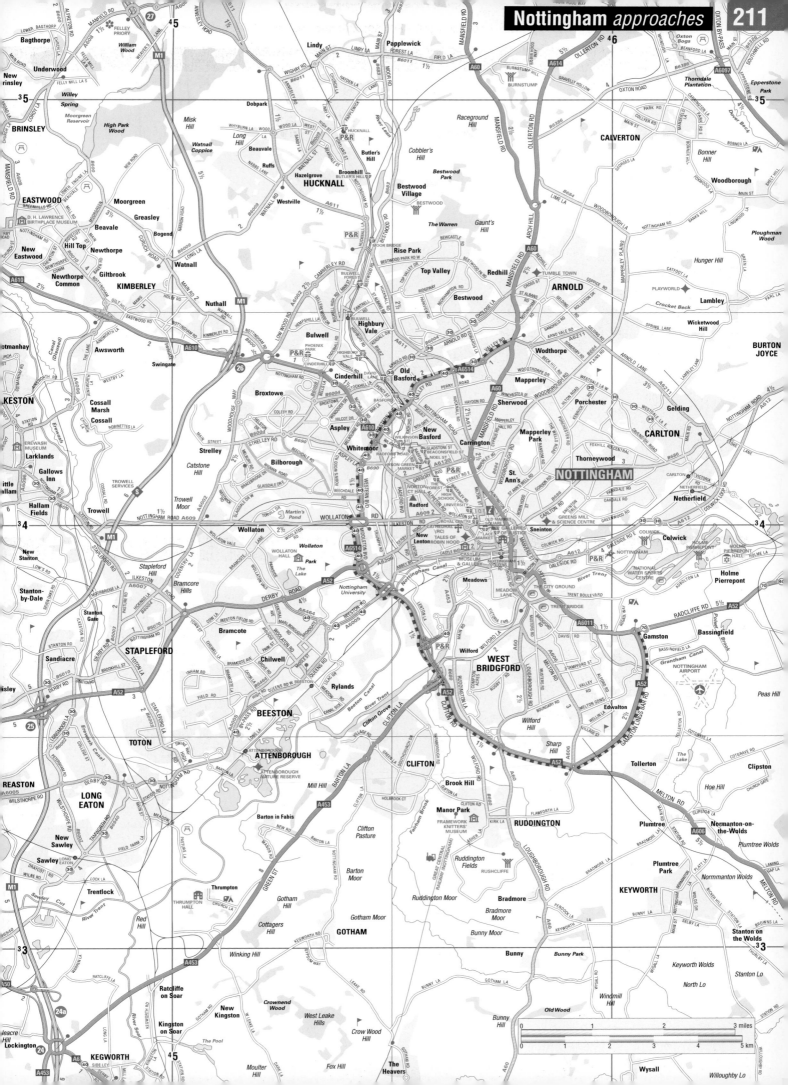

Reading

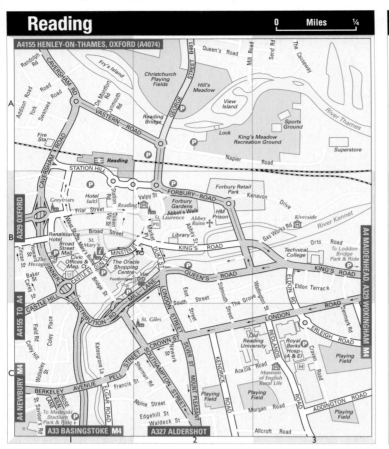

Salisbury

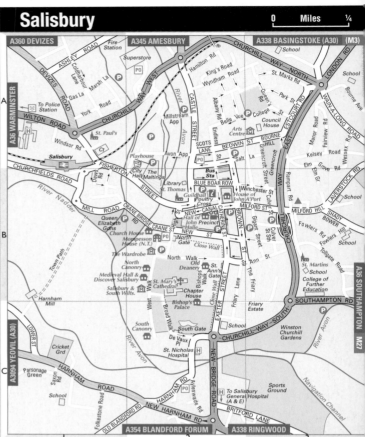

Sheffield

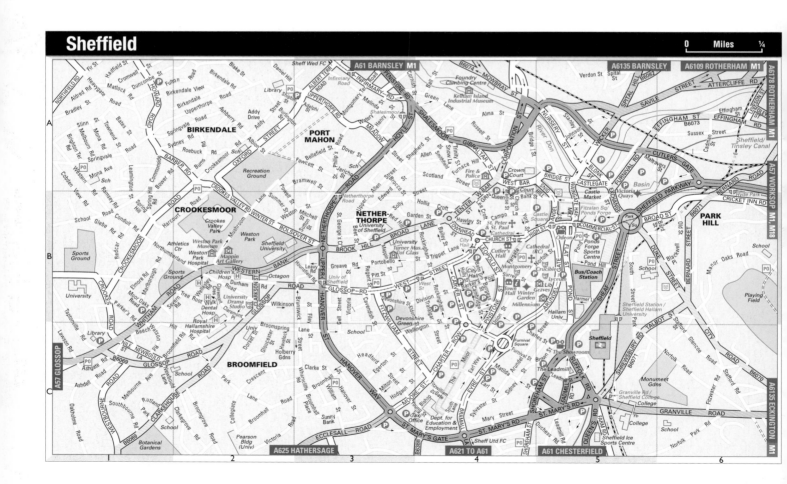

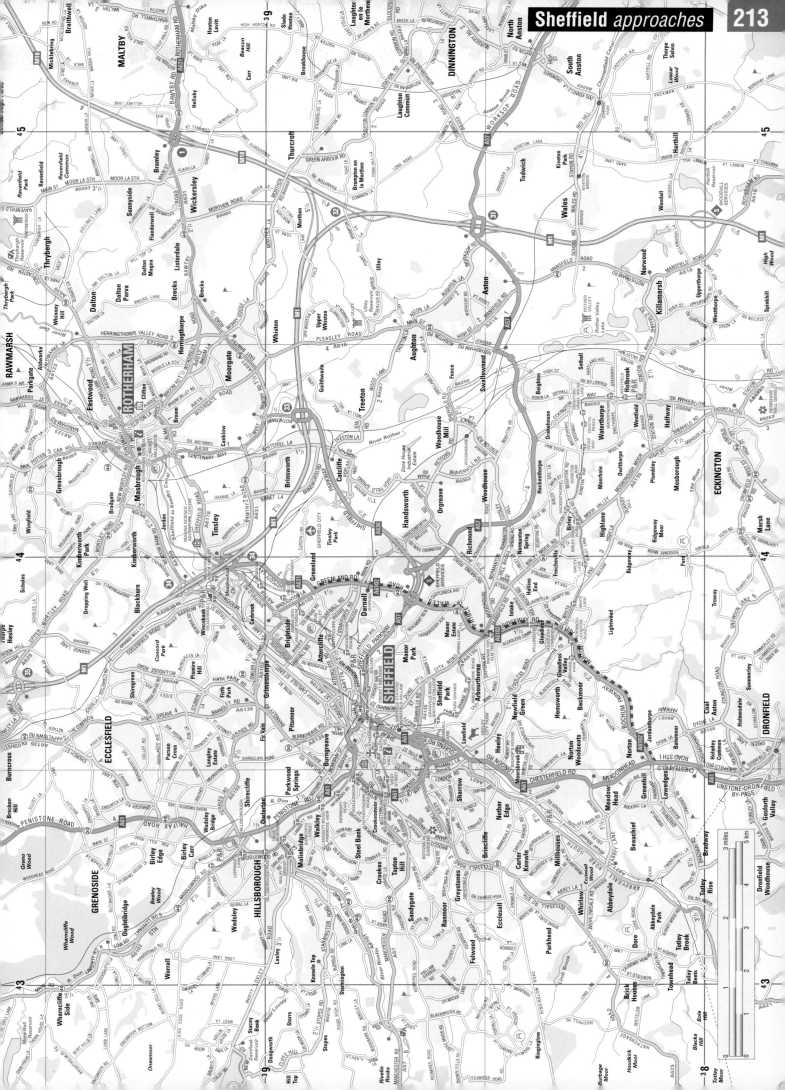

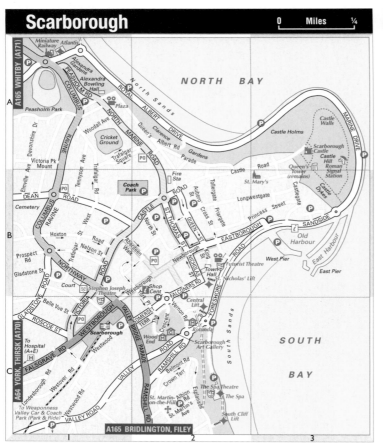

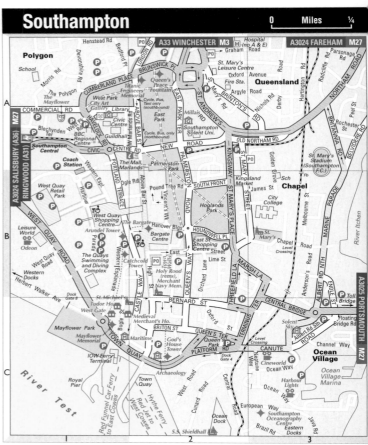

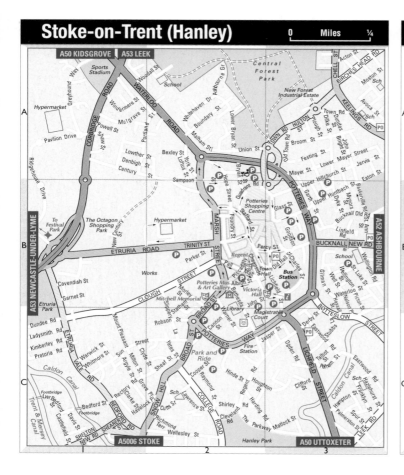

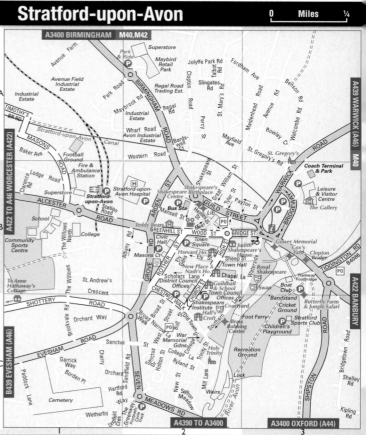

Sunderland road map page 111 • **Swansea** road map page 33 • **Telford** road map page 61 • **Torquay** road map page 7

215

Sunderland

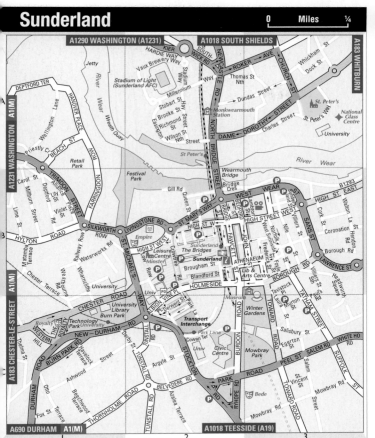

Swansea / Abertawe

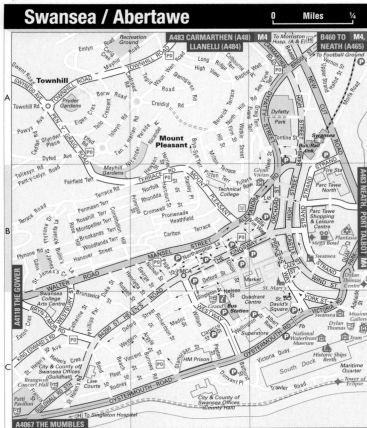

Telford

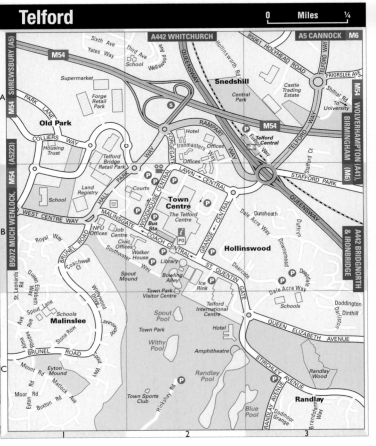

Torquay

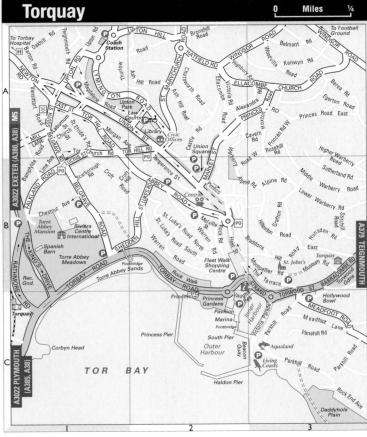

216

Winchester road map page 15 • **Windsor** road map page 27 • **Worcester** road map page 50 • **York** road map page 95

Winchester

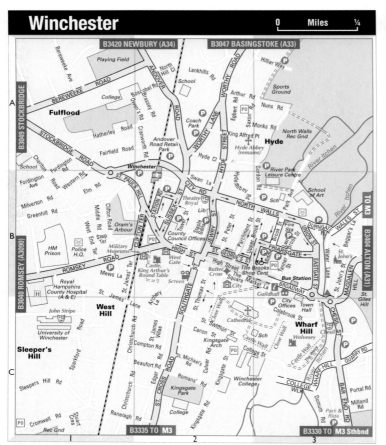

Windsor

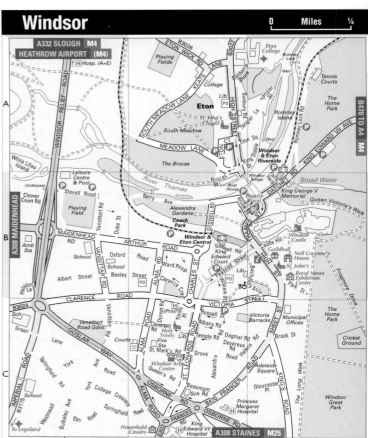

Worcester

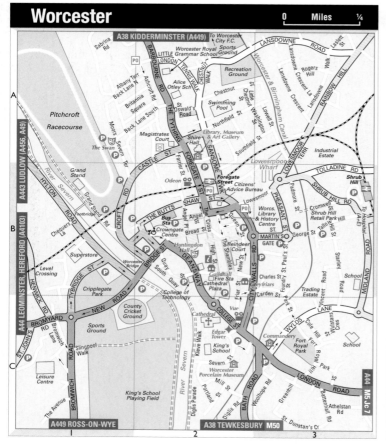

York

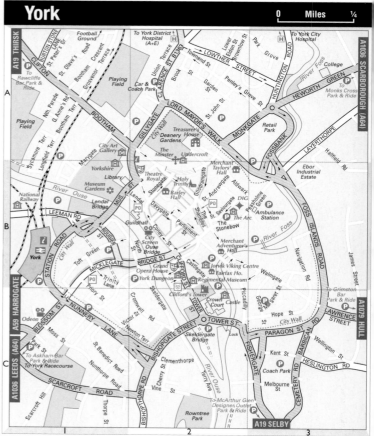

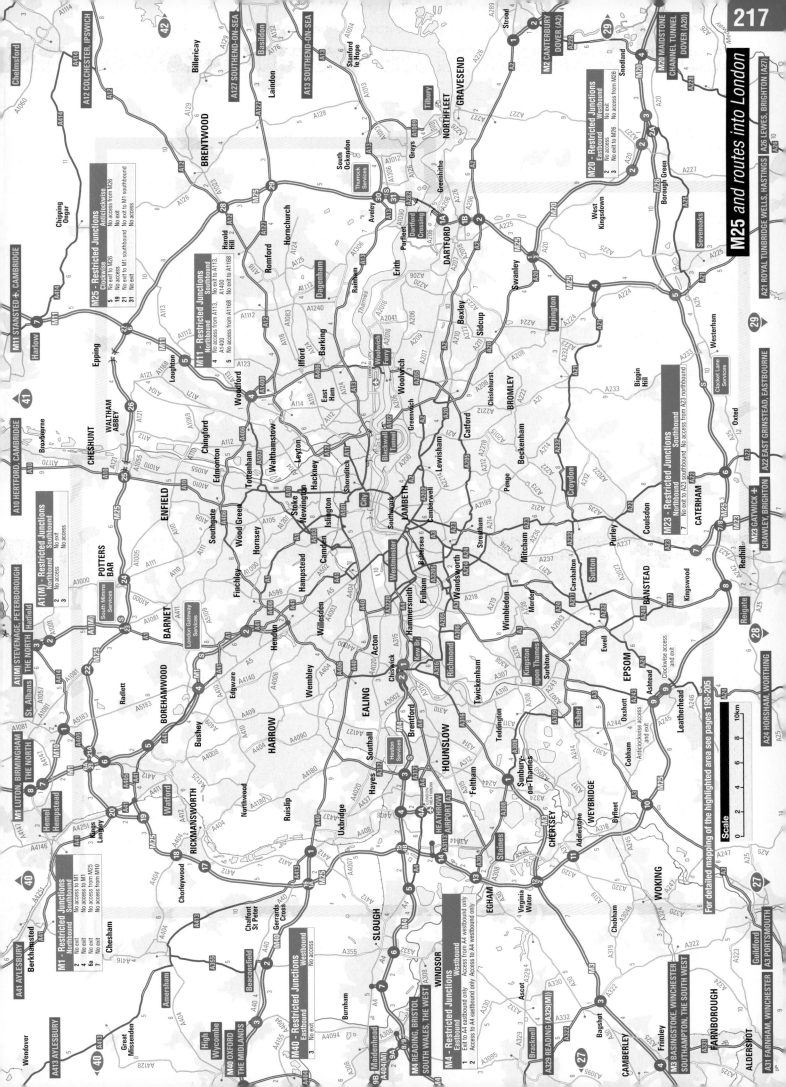

M25 *and routes into London*

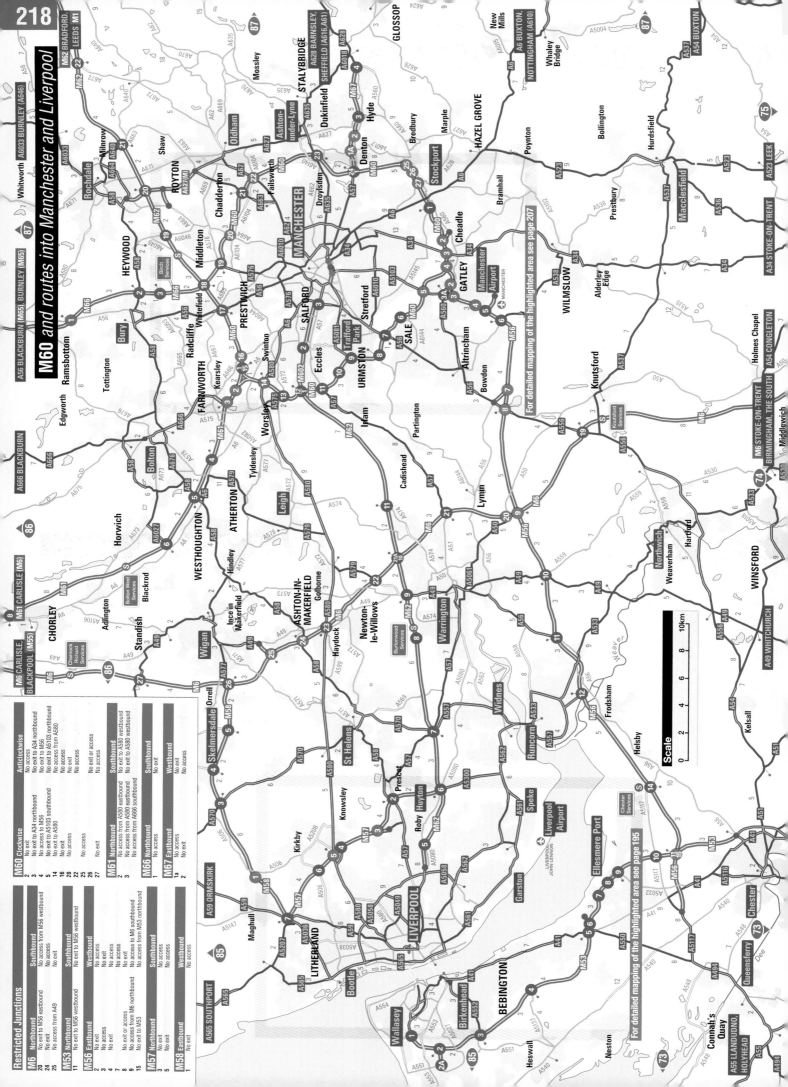

Heathrow Airport (London)

0　Miles　¼

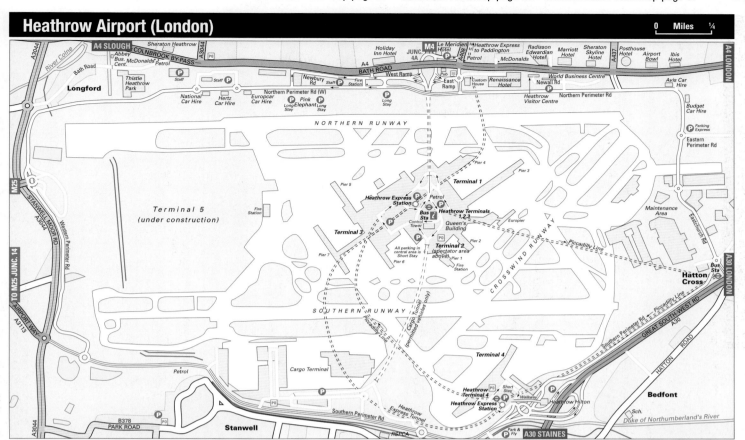

Gatwick Airport (London)

0　Miles　¼

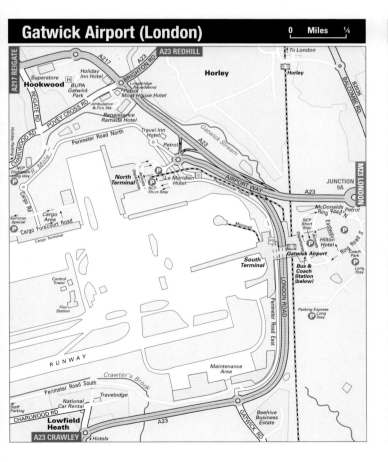

Manchester Airport

0　Miles　¼

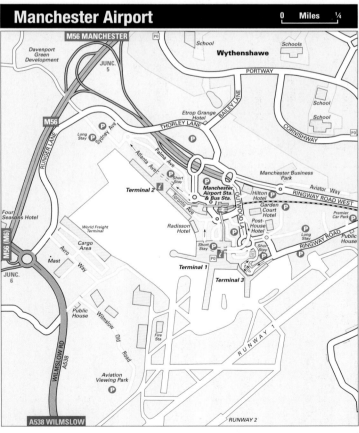

Port of Dover

0 — Miles — ¼

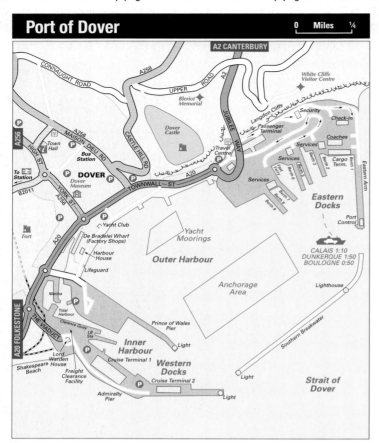

Port of Felixstowe

0 — Miles — ¼

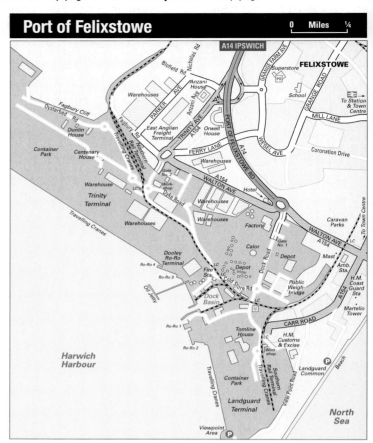

Portsmouth-Continental Ferry Port

0 — Miles — ¼

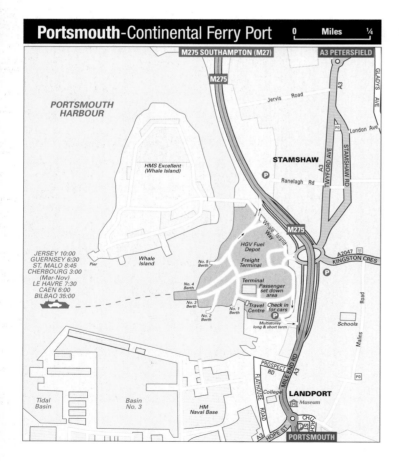

Port of Southampton

0 — Miles — 1

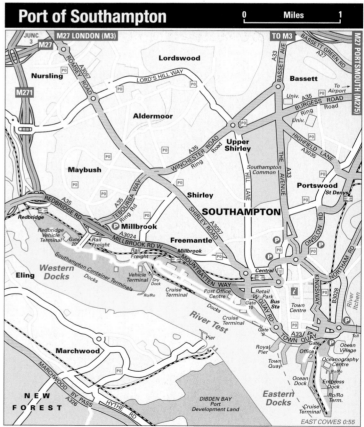

Boulogne

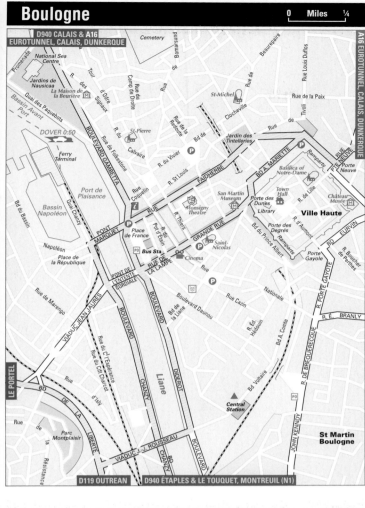

Calais

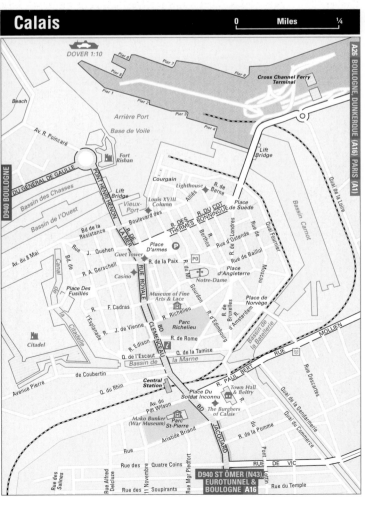

Boulogne and Calais *approaches*

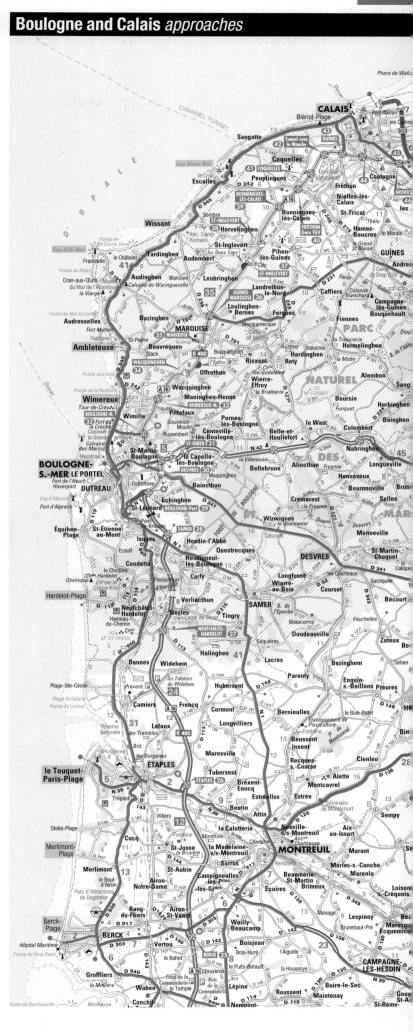

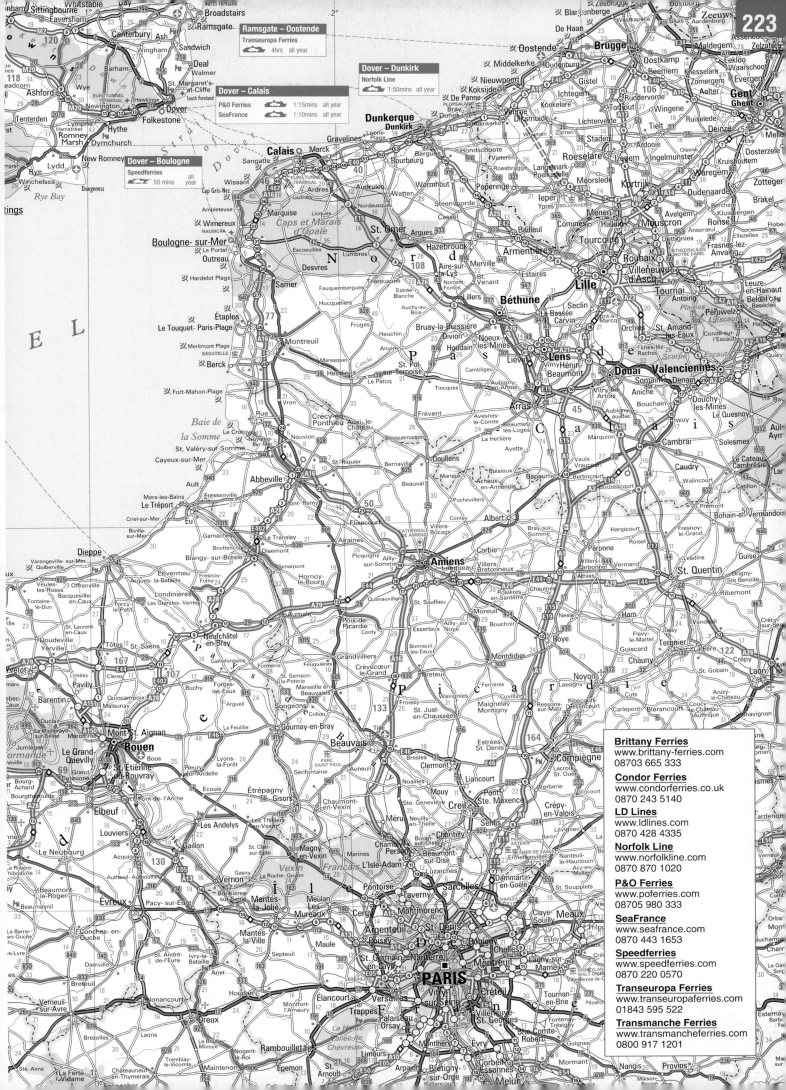

Index to road maps of Britain

How to use the index

Example

Trudoxhill Som **24** E2

— grid square
— page number
— county or unitary authority

Places of special interest are highlighted in *magenta*

Abbreviations used in the index

Aberdeen	**Aberdeen City**	Cumb	**Cumbria**
Aberds	**Aberdeenshire**	Darl	**Darlington**
Ald	**Alderney**	Denb	**Denbighshire**
Anglesey	**Isle of Anglesey**	Derby	**City of Derby**
Angus	**Angus**	Derbys	**Derbyshire**
Argyll	**Argyll and Bute**	Devon	**Devon**
Bath	**Bath and North East**	Dorset	**Dorset**
	Somerset	Dumfries	**Dumfries and Galloway**
Beds	**Bedfordshire**	Dundee	**Dundee City**
Bl Gwent	**Blaenau Gwent**	Durham	**Durham**
Blkburn	**Blackburn with Darwen**	E Ayrs	**East Ayrshire**
Blkpool	**Blackpool**	E Loth	**East Lothian**
Bmouth	**Bournemouth**	E Renf	**East Renfrewshire**
Borders	**Scottish Borders**	E Sus	**East Sussex**
Brack	**Bracknell**	E Yorks	**East Riding of Yorkshire**
Bridgend	**Bridgend**	Edin	**City of Edinburgh**
Brighton	**City of Brighton and Hove**	Essex	**Essex**
Bristol	**City and County of Bristol**	Falk	**Falkirk**
Bucks	**Buckinghamshire**	Fife	**Fife**
Caerph	**Caerphilly**	Flint	**Flintshire**
Cambs	**Cambridgeshire**	Glasgow	**City of Glasgow**
Cardiff	**Cardiff**	Glos	**Gloucestershire**
Carms	**Carmarthenshire**	Gtr Man	**Greater Manchester**
Ceredig	**Ceredigion**	Guern	**Guernsey**
Ches	**Cheshire**	Gwyn	**Gwynedd**
Clack	**Clackmannanshire**	Halton	**Halton**
Conwy	**Conwy**	Hants	**Hampshire**
Corn	**Cornwall**		

Hereford	**Herefordshire**	Reading	**Reading**
Herts	**Hertfordshire**	Redcar	**Redcar and Cleveland**
Highld	**Highland**	Renfs	**Renfrewshire**
Hrtlpl	**Hartlepool**	Rhondda	**Rhondda Cynon Taff**
Hull	**Hull**	Rutland	**Rutland**
I o M	**Isle of Man**	S Ayrs	**South Ayrshire**
I o W	**Isle of Wight**	S Glos	**South Gloucestershire**
Invclyd	**Inverclyde**	S Lnrk	**South Lanarkshire**
Jersey	**Jersey**	S Yorks	**South Yorkshire**
Kent	**Kent**	Scilly	**Scilly**
Lancs	**Lancashire**	Shetland	**Shetland**
Leicester	**City of Leicester**	Shrops	**Shropshire**
Leics	**Leicestershire**	Slough	**Slough**
Lincs	**Lincolnshire**	Som	**Somerset**
London	**Greater London**	Soton	**Southampton**
Luton	**Luton**	Staffs	**Staffordshire**
M Keynes	**Milton Keynes**	Sthend	**Southend-on-Sea**
M Tydf	**Merthyr Tydfil**	Stir	**Stirling**
M'bro	**Middlesbrough**	Stockton	**Stockton-on-Tees**
Medway	**Medway**	Stoke	**Stoke-on-Trent**
Mers	**Merseyside**	Suff	**Suffolk**
Midloth	**Midlothian**	Sur	**Surrey**
Mon	**Monmouthshire**	Swansea	**Swansea**
Moray	**Moray**	Swindon	**Swindon**
N Ayrs	**North Ayrshire**	T & W	**Tyne and Wear**
N Lincs	**North Lincolnshire**	Telford	**Telford and Wrekin**
N Lnrk	**North Lanarkshire**	Thurrock	**Thurrock**
N Som	**North Somerset**	Torbay	**Torbay**
N Yorks	**North Yorkshire**	Torf	**Torfaen**
NE Lincs	**North East Lincolnshire**	V Glam	**The Vale of Glamorgan**
Neath	**Neath Port Talbot**	W Berks	**West Berkshire**
Newport	**City and County of Newport**	W Dunb	**West Dunbartonshire**
Norf	**Norfolk**	W Isles	**Western Isles**
Northants	**Northamptonshire**	W Loth	**West Lothian**
Northumb	**Northumberland**	W Mid	**West Midlands**
Nottingham	**City of Nottingham**	W Sus	**West Sussex**
Notts	**Nottinghamshire**	W Yorks	**West Yorkshire**
Orkney	**Orkney**	Warks	**Warwickshire**
Oxon	**Oxfordshire**	Warr	**Warrington**
P'boro	**Peterborough**	Wilts	**Wiltshire**
Pembs	**Pembrokeshire**	Windsor	**Windsor and Maidenhead**
Perth	**Perth and Kinross**	Wokingham	**Wokingham**
Plym	**Plymouth**	Worcs	**Worcestershire**
Poole	**Poole**	Wrex	**Wrexham**
Powys	**Powys**	York	**City of York**
Ptsmth	**Portsmouth**		

Alne N Yorks 95 C7
Alness Highld 157 C7
Alnham Northumb 117 C5
Alnmouth Northumb 117 C8
Alnwick Northumb 117 C7
Alperton London 40 F4
Alphamstone Essex 56 F2
Alpheton Suff 56 D2
Alphington Devon 10 E4
Alport Derbys 76 C2
Alpraham Ches 74 D2
Alresford Essex 43 B6
Alrewas Staffs 63 C5
Alsager Ches 74 D4
Alsagers Bank Staffs 74 E5
Alsop en le Dale Derbys 75 D8
Alston Cumb 109 E7
Alston Devon 11 D8
Alstone Glos 50 F4
Alstonefield Staffs 75 D8
Alswear Devon 10 B2
Altandhu Highld 162 C3
Altanduin Highld 165 B5
Altarnun Corn 8 F4
Altass Highld 164 D1
Alterwall Highld 169 C7
Altham Lancs 93 F7
Althorne Essex 43 E5
Althorp House, Great Brington Northants 52 C4
Althorpe N Lincs 90 D2
Alticry Dumfries 105 D6
Altnabreac Station Highld 168 E5
Altnacealgach Hotel Highld 163 C6
Altnacraig Argyll 130 C4
Altnafeadh Highld 139 D6
Altnaharra Highld 167 F7
Altofts W Yorks 88 B4
Alton Derbys 76 C3
Alton Hants 26 F5
Alton Staffs 75 E7
Alton Pancras Dorset 12 D5
Alton Priors Wilts 25 C6
Alton Towers Staffs 75 E7
Altrincham Gtr Man 87 F5
Altrua Highld 146 F5
Altskeith Stirl 132 D3
Altyre Ho. Moray 158 D4
Alva Clack 133 E7
Alvanley Ches 73 B8
Alvaston Derby 76 F3
Alvechurch Worcs 50 B5
Alvecote Warks 63 D6
Alvediston Wilts 13 B7
Alveley Shrops 61 F7
Alverdiscott Devon 9 B7
Alverstoke Hants 15 E7
Alverstone I o W 15 F6
Alverton Notts 77 E7
Alves Moray 158 C5
Alvescot Oxon 38 D2
Alveston S Glos 36 F3
Alveston Warks 51 D7
Alvie Highld 148 D4
Alvingham Lincs 91 E7
Alvington Glos 36 D3
Alwalton Cambs 65 E8
Alweston Dorset 12 C4
Alwinton Northumb 116 D5
Alwoodley W Yorks 95 E5
Alyth Perth 142 E2
Am Baile W Isles 171 J3
Am Buth Argyll 130 C4
Amatnatua Highld 164 E1
Amber Hill Lincs 78 E5
Ambergate Derbys 76 D3
Amberley Glos 37 D5
Amberley W Sus 16 C4
Amble Northumb 117 D8
Amblecote W Mid 62 F2
Ambler Thorn W Yorks 87 B8
Ambleside Cumb 99 D5
Ambleston Pembs 44 C5
Ambrosden Oxon 39 C6
Amcotts N Lincs 90 C2
American Air Museum, Duxford Cambs 55 E5
Amersham Bucks 40 E2
Amerton Working Farm, Stowe-by-Chartley Staffs 62 B3
Amesbury Wilts 25 E6
Amington Staffs 63 D6
Amisfield Dumfries 114 F2
Amlwch Anglesey 82 B4
Amlwch Port Anglesey 82 B4
Ammanford = Rhydaman Carms 33 C7
Amod Argyll 118 C4
Amotherby N Yorks 96 B3
Ampfield Hants 14 B5
Ampleforth N Yorks 95 B8
Ampney Crucis Glos 37 D7
Ampney St Mary Glos 37 D7
Ampney St Peter Glos 37 D7
Amport Hants 25 E7
Ampthill Beds 53 F8
Ampton Suff 56 B2
Amroth Pembs 32 D2
Amulree Perth 141 F5
An Caol Highld 155 E2
An Cnoc W Isles 172 E7
An Gleann Ur W Isles 172 E7
An t-Ob = Leverburgh W Isles 173 K3
Anagach Highld 149 B6
Anaheilt Highld 138 C2
Anancaun Highld 154 D6
Ancaster Lincs 78 E2
Anchor Shrops 59 F8
Anchorsholme Blkpool 92 E3
Ancroft Northumb 125 E5
Ancrum Borders 116 B2
Anderby Lincs 79 B8
Anderson Dorset 13 E6
Anderton Ches 74 B3
Andover Hants 25 E8
Andover Down Hants 25 E8
Andoversford Glos 37 C7
Andreas I o M 84 C4
Anfield Mers 85 E4
Angersleigh Som 11 C6
Angle Pembs 44 E3
Angmering W Sus 16 D4
Angram N Yorks 95 E8
Angram N Yorks 100 E3
Anie Stirl 132 C4
Ankerville Highld 158 B2
Anlaby E Yorks 90 B4
Anmer Norf 80 E3
Anna Valley Hants 25 E8
Annan Dumfries 107 C8
Annat Argyll 131 C6
Annat Highld 155 E4
Annbank S Ayrs 112 B4
Anne Hathaway's Cottage, Stratford-upon-Avon Warks 51 D6
Annesley Notts 76 D5
Annesley Woodhouse Notts 76 D4
Annfield Plain Durham 110 D4
Annifirth Shetland 175 J3
Annitsford T & W 111 B5
Annscroft Shrops 60 D4
Ansdell Lancs 85 B4
Ansford Som 23 F8
Ansley Warks 63 E6
Anslow Staffs 63 B6
Anslow Gate Staffs 63 B5
Anstey Herts 54 F5
Anstey Leics 64 D2
Anstruther Easter Fife 135 D7
Anstruther Wester Fife 135 D7
Ansty Hants 26 E5
Ansty Warks 63 F7
Ansty Wilts 13 B7
Ansty W Sus 17 B6
Anthill Common Hants 15 C7
Anthorn Cumb 107 D8
Antingham Norf 81 D8
Anton's Gowt Lincs 79 E5
Antonshill Falk 133 F7
Antony Corn 5 D8
Anwick Lincs 78 D4
Anwoth Dumfries 106 D2
Aoradh Argyll 126 C2
Apes Hall Cambs 67 E5
Apethorpe Northants 65 E7
Apeton Staffs 62 C2
Apley Lincs 78 B4
Apperknowle Derbys 76 B3
Apperley Glos 37 B5
Apperley Bridge W Yorks 94 F4
Appersett N Yorks 100 E3
Appin Argyll 138 E3
Appin House Argyll 138 E3
Appleby N Lincs 90 C3
Appleby-in-Westmorland Cumb 100 B1
Appleby Magna Leics 63 D7
Appleby Parva Leics 63 D7
Applecross Highld 155 F3
Applecross Ho. Highld 155 F3
Appledore Devon 20 F3
Appledore Devon 11 C5
Appledore Kent 19 C6
Appledore Heath Kent 19 B6
Appleford Oxon 39 E5
Applegarthtown Dumfries 114 F4
Appleshaw Hants 25 E8
Applethwaite Cumb 98 B4
Appleton Halton 86 F3
Appleton Oxon 38 D4
Appleton-le-Moors N Yorks 103 F5
Appleton-le-Street N Yorks 96 B3
Appleton Roebuck N Yorks 95 E8
Appleton Thorn Warr 86 F4
Appleton Wiske N Yorks 102 D1
Appletreehall Borders 115 C8
Appletreewick N Yorks 94 C3
Appley Som 11 B5
Appley Bridge Lancs 86 D3
Apse Heath I o W 15 F6
Apsley End Beds 54 F2
Apuldram W Sus 16 D2
Aquhythie Aberds 151 C6
Arabella Highld 158 B2
Arbeadie Aberds 151 E5
Arbeia Roman Fort and Museum T & W 111 C6
Arberth = Narberth Pembs 32 C2
Arbirlot Angus 143 E6
Arboll Highld 165 F5
Arborfield Wokingham 27 C5
Arborfield Cross Wokingham 27 C5
Arborfield Garrison Wokingham 27 C5
Arbour-thorne S Yorks 88 F4
Arbroath Angus 143 E6
Arbuthnott Aberds 143 B7
Archiestown Moray 159 E6
Arclid Ches 74 C4
Ard-dhubh Highld 155 F3
Ardachu Highld 164 D3
Ardalanish Argyll 136 G4
Ardanaiseig Argyll 131 C6
Ardaneaskan Highld 155 G4
Ardanstur Argyll 130 D4
Ardargie House Hotel Perth 134 C2
Ardarroch Highld 155 G4
Ardbeg Argyll 126 E4
Ardbeg Argyll 129 B6
Ardbeg Distillery, Port Ellen Argyll 126 E4
Ardcharnich Highld 163 F5
Ardchiavaig Argyll 136 G4
Ardchullarie More Stirl 132 C4
Ardchyle Stirl 132 B4
Arddleen Powys 60 C2
Ardechvie Highld 146 E4
Ardeley Herts 41 B6
Ardelve Highld 155 H4
Arden Argyll 132 F2
Ardens Grafton Warks 51 D6
Ardentinny Argyll 129 B6
Ardentraive Argyll 129 C5
Ardeonaig Stirl 140 F3
Ardersier Highld 157 D8
Ardessie Highld 162 F4
Ardfern Argyll 130 E4
Ardgartan Argyll 131 E8
Ardgay Highld 164 E2
Ardgour Highld 138 C4
Ardheslaig Highld 154 E3
Ardiecow Moray 160 B2
Ardindrean Highld 163 F5
Ardingly W Sus 17 B7
Ardington Oxon 38 F4
Ardlair Aberds 150 B4
Ardlamont Ho. Argyll 128 D4
Ardleigh Essex 43 B6
Ardler Perth 142 E2
Ardley Oxon 39 B5
Ardlui Argyll 132 C2
Ardlussa Argyll 127 D4
Ardmair Highld 163 E5
Ardmay Argyll 131 E8
Ardminish Argyll 118 B3
Ardmolich Highld 145 F7
Ardmore Argyll 130 C3
Ardmore Highld 166 D4
Ardmore Highld 164 F4
Ardnacross Argyll 137 D6
Ardnadam Argyll 129 C6
Ardnagrask Highld 157 E6
Ardnarff Highld 155 G4
Ardnastang Highld 138 C2
Ardnave Argyll 126 B2
Ardno Argyll 131 E7
Ardo Aberds 160 E5
Ardo Ho. Aberds 151 B8
Ardoch Perth 141 F7
Ardochy House Highld 146 D5
Ardoyne Aberds 151 B5
Ardpatrick Argyll 128 D2
Ardpatrick Ho. Argyll 128 E2
Ardpeaton Argyll 129 B7
Ardrishaig Argyll 128 B3
Ardross Fife 135 D7
Ardross Highld 157 B7
Ardross Castle Highld 157 B7
Ardrossan N Ayrs 120 E2
Ardshealach Highld 137 B7
Ardsley S Yorks 88 D4
Ardslignish Highld 137 B6
Ardtalla Argyll 126 D4
Ardtalnaig Perth 140 F4
Ardtoe Highld 145 F6
Ardtrostan Perth 133 B5
Arduaine Argyll 130 D3
Ardullie Highld 157 C6
Ardvasar Highld 145 C6
Ardvorlich Perth 132 B5
Ardwell Dumfries 104 E5
Ardwell Mains Dumfries 104 E5
Ardwick Gtr Man 87 E6
Areley Kings Worcs 50 B3
Arford Hants 27 F6
Argoed Caerph 35 E5
Argoed Mill Powys 47 C8
Argyll & Sutherland Highlanders Museum (See Stirling Castle) Stirl 133 E6
Arichamish Argyll 130 E5
Arichastlich Argyll 131 B8
Aridhglas Argyll 136 F4
Arileod Argyll 136 C2
Arinacrinachd Highld 154 E3
Arinagour Argyll 136 C3
Arion Orkney 176 E1
Arisaig Highld 145 E6
Ariundle Highld 138 C2
Arkendale N Yorks 95 C6
Arkesden Essex 55 F5
Arkholme Lancs 93 B5
Arkle Town N Yorks 101 D5
Arkleton Dumfries 115 E6
Arkley London 41 E5
Arksey S Yorks 89 D6
Arkwright Town Derbys 76 B4
Arle Glos 37 B6
Arlecdon Cumb 98 C2
Arlesey Beds 54 F2
Arleston Telford 61 C6
Arley Ches 86 F4
Arlingham Glos 36 C4
Arlington Devon 20 E5
Arlington E Sus 18 E2
Arlington Glos 37 D8
Arlington Court Devon 20 E5
Armadale Highld 168 C2
Armadale W Loth 122 C2
Armadale Castle Highld 145 C6
Armathwaite Cumb 108 E5
Arminghall Norf 69 D5
Armitage Staffs 62 C4
Armley W Yorks 95 F5
Armscote Warks 51 E7
Armthorpe S Yorks 89 D7
Arnabost Argyll 136 C3
Arncliffe N Yorks 94 B2
Arncroach Fife 135 D7
Arne Dorset 13 F7
Arnesby Leics 64 E3
Arngask Perth 134 C3
Arnisdale Highld 145 B8
Arnish Highld 152 E6
Arniston Engine Midloth 123 C6
Arnol W Isles 172 D6
Arnold E Yorks 97 E7
Arnold Notts 77 E5
Arnolfini Gallery Bristol 23 B7
Arnprior Stirl 132 E5
Arnside Cumb 92 B4
Aros Mains Argyll 137 D6
Arowry Wrex 73 F8
Arpafeelie Highld 157 D7
Arrad Foot Cumb 99 F5
Arram E Yorks 97 E6
Arrathorne N Yorks 101 E7
Arreton I o W 15 F6
Arrington Cambs 54 D4
Arrivain Argyll 131 B8
Arrochar Argyll 131 E8
Arrow Warks 51 D5
Arthington W Yorks 95 E5
Arthingworth Northants 64 F4
Arthog Gwyn 58 C3
Arthrath Aberds 161 E6
Arthurstone Perth 142 E2
Artrochie Aberds 161 E7
Arundel W Sus 16 D4
Arundel Castle W Sus 16 D4
Aryhoulan Highld 138 C4
Asby Cumb 98 B2
Ascog Argyll 129 D6
Ascot Windsor 27 C7
Ascot Racecourse Windsor 27 C7
Ascott Warks 51 F8
Ascott-under-Wychwood Oxon 38 C3
Asenby N Yorks 95 B6
Asfordby Leics 64 C4
Asfordby Hill Leics 64 C4
Asgarby Lincs 78 E4
Asgarby Lincs 79 C6
Ash Kent 29 C6
Ash Kent 31 D6
Ash Som 12 B2
Ash Sur 27 D6
Ash Bullayne Devon 10 D2
Ash Green Warks 63 F7
Ash Magna Shrops 74 F2
Ash Mill Devon 10 B2
Ash Priors Som 11 B6
Ash Street Suff 56 E4
Ash Thomas Devon 10 C5
Ash Vale Sur 27 D6
Ashampstead W Berks 26 B3
Ashbocking Suff 57 D5
Ashbourne Derbys 75 E8
Ashbrittle Som 11 B5
Ashburton Devon 7 C5
Ashbury Devon 9 E7
Ashbury Oxon 38 F2
Ashby N Lincs 90 D3
Ashby by Partney Lincs 79 C7
Ashby cum Fenby NE Lincs 91 D6
Ashby de la Launde Lincs 78 D3
Ashby-de-la-Zouch Leics 63 C7
Ashby Folville Leics 64 C4
Ashby Magna Leics 64 E2
Ashby Parva Leics 64 F2
Ashby Puerorum Lincs 79 B6
Ashby St Ledgers Northants 52 C3
Ashby St Mary Norf 69 D6
Ashchurch Glos 50 F4
Ashcombe Devon 7 B7
Ashcott Som 23 F6
Ashdon Essex 55 E6
Ashe Hants 26 E3
Asheldham Essex 43 D5
Ashen Essex 55 E8
Ashendon Bucks 39 C7
Ashfield Carms 33 B7
Ashfield Stirl 133 D6
Ashfield Suff 57 C6
Ashfield Green Suff 57 B6
Ashfold Crossways W Sus 17 B6
Ashford Devon 20 F4
Ashford Hants 14 C2
Ashford Kent 30 E4
Ashford Sur 27 B8
Ashford Bowdler Shrops 49 B7
Ashford Carbonell Shrops 49 B7
Ashford Hill Hants 26 C3
Ashford in the Water Derbys 75 C8
Ashgill S Lnrk 121 E7
Ashill Devon 11 C5
Ashill Norf 67 D8
Ashill Som 11 C8
Ashingdon Essex 42 E4
Ashington Northumb 117 F8
Ashington Som 12 B3
Ashington W Sus 16 C5
Ashintully Castle Perth 141 C8
Ashkirk Borders 115 B7
Ashlett Hants 15 D5
Ashleworth Glos 37 B5
Ashley Cambs 55 C7
Ashley Ches 87 F5
Ashley Devon 9 C8
Ashley Dorset 14 D2
Ashley Glos 37 E6
Ashley Hants 14 E3
Ashley Hants 25 F8
Ashley Northants 64 E4
Ashley Staffs 74 F4
Ashley Green Bucks 40 D2
Ashley Heath Dorset 14 D2
Ashley Heath Staffs 74 F4
Ashmanhaugh Norf 69 B6
Ashmansworth Hants 26 D2
Ashmansworthy Devon 8 C5
Ashmore Dorset 13 C7
Ashorne Warks 51 D8
Ashover Derbys 76 C3
Ashow Warks 51 B8
Ashprington Devon 7 D6
Ashreigney Devon 9 C8
Ashtead Sur 28 D2
Ashton Ches 74 C2
Ashton Corn 2 D5
Ashton Hants 15 C6
Ashton Hereford 49 C7
Ashton Invclyd 129 C7
Ashton Northants 53 E5
Ashton Northants 65 F7
Ashton Common Wilts 24 D3
Ashton-In-Makerfield Gtr Man 86 E3
Ashton Keynes Wilts 37 E7
Ashton under Hill Worcs 50 F4
Ashton-under-Lyne Gtr Man 87 E7
Ashton upon Mersey Gtr Man 87 E5
Ashurst Hants 14 C4
Ashurst Kent 18 B2
Ashurst W Sus 17 C5
Ashurstwood W Sus 28 F5
Ashwater Devon 9 E5
Ashwell Herts 54 F3
Ashwell Rutland 65 C5
Ashwell Som 11 C8
Ashwellthorpe Norf 68 E4
Ashwick Som 23 E8
Ashwicken Norf 67 C7
Ashybank Borders 115 C8
Askam in Furness Cumb 92 B2
Askern S Yorks 89 C6
Askerswell Dorset 12 E3
Askett Bucks 39 D8
Askham Cumb 99 B7
Askham Notts 77 B7
Askham Bryan York 95 E8
Askham Richard York 95 E8
Asknish Argyll 128 A4
Askrigg N Yorks 100 E4
Askwith N Yorks 94 E4
Aslackby Lincs 78 F3
Aslacton Norf 68 E4
Aslockton Notts 77 F7
Asloun Aberds 150 C4
Aspatria Cumb 107 E8
Aspenden Herts 41 B6
Asperton Lincs 79 F5
Aspley Guise Beds 53 F7
Aspley Heath Beds 53 F7
Aspull Gtr Man 86 D4
Asselby E Yorks 89 B8
Asserby Lincs 79 B7
Assington Suff 56 F3
Assynt Ho. Highld 157 C6
Astbury Ches 74 C5
Astcote Northants 52 D4
Asterley Shrops 60 D3
Asterton Shrops 60 E3
Asthall Oxon 38 C2
Asthall Leigh Oxon 38 C3
Astley Shrops 60 C5
Astley Warks 63 F7
Astley Worcs 50 C2
Astley Abbotts Shrops 61 E7
Astley Bridge Gtr Man 86 C5
Astley Cross Worcs 50 C3
Astley Green Gtr Man 86 E5
Aston Ches 74 E3
Aston Ches 74 B2
Aston Derbys 88 F2
Aston Hereford 49 B6
Aston Herts 41 B5
Aston Oxon 38 D3
Aston Shrops 60 B5
Aston Staffs 74 E4
Aston S Yorks 89 F5
Aston Telford 61 D6
Aston W Mid 62 F4
Aston Wokingham 39 F7
Aston Abbotts Bucks 39 B8
Aston Botterell Shrops 61 F6
Aston-By-Stone Staffs 75 F6
Aston Cantlow Warks 51 D6
Aston Clinton Bucks 40 C1
Aston Crews Hereford 36 B3
Aston Cross Glos 50 F4
Aston End Herts 41 B5
Aston Eyre Shrops 61 E6
Aston Fields Worcs 50 C4
Aston Flamville Leics 63 E8
Aston Ingham Hereford 36 B3
Aston juxta Mondrum Ches 74 D3
Aston le Walls Northants 52 D2
Aston Magna Glos 51 F6
Aston Munslow Shrops 60 F5
Aston on Clun Shrops 60 F3
Aston-on-Trent Derbys 63 B8
Aston Rogers Shrops 60 D3
Aston Rowant Oxon 39 E7
Aston Sandford Bucks 39 D7
Aston Somerville Worcs 50 F5
Aston Subedge Glos 51 E6
Aston Tirrold Oxon 39 F5
Aston Upthorpe Oxon 39 F5
Astrop Northants 52 F3
Astwick Beds 54 F3
Astwood M Keynes 53 E7
Astwood Worcs 50 D3
Astwood Bank Worcs 50 C5
Aswarby Lincs 78 F3
Aswardby Lincs 79 B6
Atch Lench Worcs 50 D5
Atcham Shrops 60 D5
Athelhampton Dorset 13 E5
Athelington Suff 57 B6
Athelney Som 11 B8
Athelstaneford E Loth 123 B8
Atherington Devon 9 B7
Atherstone Warks 63 E7
Atherstone on Stour Warks 51 D7
Atherton Gtr Man 86 D4
Atley Hill N Yorks 101 D7
Atlow Derbys 76 E2
Attadale Highld 155 G5
Attadale Ho. Highld 155 G5
Attenborough Notts 76 F5
Atterby Lincs 90 E3
Attercliffe S Yorks 88 F4
Attleborough Norf 68 E3
Attleborough Warks 63 E7
Attlebridge Norf 68 C4
Atwick E Yorks 97 D7
Atworth Wilts 24 C3
Aubourn Lincs 78 C2
Auchagallon N Ayrs 119 C5
Auchallater Aberds 149 F7
Aucharnie Aberds 160 D3
Auchattie Aberds 151 E5
Auchavan Angus 142 C1
Auchbreck Moray 149 B8
Auchenback E Renf 120 D5
Auchenbainzie Dumfries 113 E8
Auchenblae Aberds 143 B7
Auchenbrack Dumfries 113 E7
Auchenbreck Argyll 129 B5
Auchencairn Dumfries 106 D4
Auchencairn Dumfries 114 F2
Auchencairn N Ayrs 119 D7
Auchencrosh S Ayrs 104 B5
Auchencrow Borders 124 C4
Auchendinny Midloth 123 C5
Auchengray S Lnrk 122 D2
Auchenhalrig Moray 159 C7
Auchenheath S Lnrk 121 E8
Auchenlochan Argyll 128 C4
Auchenmalg Dumfries 105 D6
Auchensoul S Ayrs 112 E2
Auchentiber N Ayrs 120 E3
Auchertyre Highld 155 H4
Auchgourish Highld 148 C5
Auchincarroch W Dunb 132 F3
Auchindrain Argyll 131 E6
Auchindrean Highld 163 F5
Auchininna Aberds 160 D3
Auchinleck E Ayrs 113 B5
Auchinloch N Lnrk 121 B6
Auchinroath Moray 159 D6
Auchintoul Aberds 150 C4
Auchiries Aberds 161 E7
Auchlee Aberds 151 E7
Auchleven Aberds 150 B5
Auchlochan S Lnrk 121 F8
Auchlossan Aberds 150 D4
Auchlunies Aberds 151 E7
Auchlyne Stirl 132 B4
Auchmacoy Aberds 161 E6
Auchmair Moray 150 B2
Auchmantle Dumfries 105 C5
Auchmillan E Ayrs 112 B5
Auchmithie Angus 143 E6
Auchmuirbridge Fife 134 D4
Auchmull Angus 143 B5
Auchnacree Angus 142 C4
Auchnagallin Highld 158 F4
Auchnagatt Aberds 161 D6
Auchnaha Argyll 128 B4
Auchnashelloch Perth 133 C6
Aucholzie Aberds 150 E2
Auchrannie Angus 142 D2
Auchroisk Highld 149 B6
Auchronie Angus 150 F3
Auchterarder Perth 133 C8
Auchteraw Highld 147 D6
Auchterderran Fife 134 E4
Auchterhouse Angus 142 F3
Auchtermuchty Fife 134 C4
Auchterneed Highld 157 D5
Auchtertool Fife 134 E4
Auchtertyre Moray 159 D5
Auchtubh Stirl 132 B4
Auckengill Highld 169 C8
Auckley S Yorks 89 D7
Audenshaw Gtr Man 87 E7
Audlem Ches 74 E3
Audley Staffs 74 D4
Audley End Essex 56 F2
Audley End House Essex 55 F6
Auds Aberds 160 B3
Aughton E Yorks 96 F3
Aughton Lancs 85 D4
Aughton Lancs 93 C5
Aughton S Yorks 89 F5
Aughton Wilts 25 D7
Aughton Park Lancs 86 D2
Auldearn Highld 158 D3
Aulden Hereford 49 D6
Auldgirth Dumfries 114 F2
Auldhame E Loth 135 F7
Auldhouse S Lnrk 121 D6
Ault a'chruinn Highld 146 B2
Aultanrynie Highld 166 F5
Aultbea Highld 162 F2
Aultdearg Highld 156 C3
Aultgrishan Highld 154 B3
Aultguish Inn Highld 156 B4
Aultibea Highld 165 B7
Aultiphurst Highld 168 C3
Aultmore Moray 159 D8
Aultnagoire Highld 147 B8
Aultnamain Inn Highld 164 F3
Aultnaslat Highld 146 D4
Aulton Aberds 150 B5
Aundorach Highld 149 C5
Aunsby Lincs 78 F3
Auquhorthies Aberds 151 B7
Aust S Glos 36 F2
Austendike Lincs 66 B2
Austerfield S Yorks 89 E7
Austrey Warks 63 D6
Austwick N Yorks 93 C7
Authorpe Lincs 91 F8
Authorpe Row Lincs 79 B8
Avebury Wilts 25 C6
Aveley Thurrock 42 F1
Avening Glos 37 E5
Averham Notts 77 D7
Aveton Gifford Devon 6 E4
Avielochan Highld 148 C5
Aviemore Highld 148 C4
Avington Hants 26 F3
Avington W Berks 25 C8
Avoch Highld 157 D8
Avon Hants 14 E2
Avon Dassett Warks 52 E2
Avonbridge Falk 122 B2
Avonmouth Bristol 23 B7
Avonwick Devon 6 D5
Awbridge Hants 14 B4
Awhirk Dumfries 104 D4
Awkley S Glos 36 F2
Awliscombe Devon 11 D6
Awre Glos 36 D4
Awsworth Notts 76 E4
Axbridge Som 23 D6
Axford Hants 26 E4
Axford Wilts 25 B7
Axminster Devon 11 E7
Axmouth Devon 11 E7
Axton Flint 85 F2
Aycliff Kent 31 E7
Aycliffe Durham 101 B7
Aydon Northumb 110 C3
Aylburton Glos 36 D3
Ayle Northumb 109 E7
Aylesbeare Devon 10 E5
Aylesbury Bucks 39 C8
Aylesby NE Lincs 91 D6
Aylesford Kent 29 D8
Aylesham Kent 31 D6
Aylestone Leicester 64 D2
Aylmerton Norf 81 D7
Aylsham Norf 81 E7
Aylton Hereford 49 F8
Aymestrey Hereford 49 C6
Aynho Northants 52 F3
Ayot St Lawrence Herts 40 C4
Ayot St Peter Herts 41 C5
Ayr S Ayrs 112 B3
Ayr Racecourse S Ayrs 112 B3
Aysgarth N Yorks 101 F5
Ayside Cumb 99 F5
Ayston Rutland 65 D5
Aythorpe Roding Essex 42 C1
Ayton Borders 124 C5
Aywick Shetland 174 E7
Azerley N Yorks 95 B5

B

Babbacombe Torbay 7 C7
Babbinswood Shrops 73 F7
Babcary Som 12 B3
Babel Carms 47 F7
Babell Flint 73 B5
Babraham Cambs 55 D6
Babworth Notts 89 F7
Bac W Isles 172 D7
Bachau Anglesey 82 C4
Back of Keppoch Highld 145 E6
Back Rogerton E Ayrs 113 B5
Backaland Orkney 176 C4
Backaskaill Orkney 176 A3
Backbarrow Cumb 99 F5
Backe Carms 32 C3
Backfolds Aberds 161 C7
Backford Ches 73 B8
Backford Cross Ches 73 B7
Backhill Aberds 160 E4
Backhill Aberds 161 E7
Backhill of Clackriach Aberds 161 D6
Backhill of Fortree Aberds 161 D6
Backhill of Trustach Aberds 150 E5
Backies Highld 165 D5
Backlass Highld 169 D7
Backwell N Som 23 C6
Backworth T & W 111 B6
Bacon End Essex 42 C2
Baconsthorpe Norf 81 D7
Bacton Hereford 49 F5
Bacton Norf 81 D9
Bacton Suff 56 C4
Bacton Green Suff 56 C4
Bacup Lancs 87 B6
Badachro Highld 154 C3
Badanloch Lodge Highld 168 F2
Badavanich Highld 156 D2
Badbury Swindon 38 F1
Badby Northants 52 D3
Badcall Highld 166 D4
Badcaul Highld 162 E4
Baddeley Green Stoke 75 D6
Baddesley Clinton Warks 51 B7
Baddesley Clinton Hall Warks 51 B7
Baddesley Ensor Warks 63 E6
Baddidarach Highld 162 B4
Baddoch Aberds 149 F7
Baddock Highld 157 D8
Badenscoth Aberds 160 E4
Badenyon Aberds 150 C2
Badger Shrops 61 E7
Badger's Mount Kent 29 C5
Badgeworth Glos 37 C6
Badgworth Som 23 D5
Badicaul Highld 155 H3
Badingham Suff 57 C7
Badlesmere Kent 30 D4
Badlipster Highld 169 E7
Badluarach Highld 162 E3
Badminton S Glos 37 F5
Badnaban Highld 162 B4
Badninish Highld 164 E4
Badrallach Highld 162 E4
Badsey Worcs 51 E5
Badshot Lea Sur 27 E6
Badsworth W Yorks 89 C5
Badwell Ash Suff 56 C3
Bae Colwyn = Colwyn Bay Conwy 83 D8
Bag Enderby Lincs 79 B6
Bagby N Yorks 102 F2
Bagendon Glos 37 D7
Bagh a Chaisteil = Castlebay W Isles 171 L2
Bagh Mor W Isles 170 E4
Bagh Shiarabhagh W Isles 171 K3
Baghasdal W Isles 171 J3
Bagillt Flint 73 B6
Baginton Warks 51 B8
Baglan Neath 33 E8
Bagley Shrops 60 B4
Bagnall Staffs 75 D6
Bagnor W Berks 26 C2
Bagshot Sur 27 C7
Bagshot Wilts 25 C8
Bagthorpe Norf 80 D3
Bagthorpe Notts 76 D4
Bagworth Leics 63 D8
Bagwy Llydiart Hereford 35 B8
Bail Àrd Bhuirgh W Isles 172 C7
Bail Uachdraich W Isles 170 D4
Baildon W Yorks 94 F4
Baile W Isles 173 K2
Baile a Mhanaich W Isles 170 E3
Baile Ailein W Isles 172 F5
Baile an Truiseil W Isles 172 C6
Baile Boidheach Argyll 128 C2
Baile Glas W Isles 170 E4
Baile Mhartainn W Isles 170 C3
Baile Mhic Phail W Isles 170 C4
Baile Mor Argyll 136 F3
Baile Mor W Isles 170 D3
Baile na Creige W Isles 171 K2
Baile nan Cailleach W Isles 170 E3
Baile Raghaill W Isles 170 C3
Bailebeag Highld 147 C8
Baileyhead Cumb 108 B5
Bailiesward Aberds 159 F8
Baillieston Glasgow 121 C6
Bail'lochdrach W Isles 170 E4
Bail'Ur Tholastaidh W Isles 172 D8
Bainbridge N Yorks 100 E4
Bainsford Falk 133 F7
Bainshole Aberds 160 E3
Bainton E Yorks 97 D5
Bainton P'boro 65 D7
Bairnkine Borders 116 C2
Baker Street Thurrock 42 F2
Baker's End Herts 41 C6
Bakewell Derbys 76 C2
Bala = Y Bala Gwyn 72 F3
Balachuirn Highld 153 E6
Balavil Highld 148 D3
Balbeg Highld 147 B7
Balbeg Highld 157 F5
Balbeggie Perth 134 B3
Balbithan Aberds 151 C6
Balbithan Ho. Aberds 151 C7
Balblair Highld 157 C8
Balblair Highld 164 E2
Balby S Yorks 89 D6
Balchladich Highld 166 F2
Balchraggan Highld 157 F6
Balchraggan Highld 157 E6
Balchrick Highld 166 D3
Balchrystie Fife 135 D6
Balcladaich Highld 147 B5
Balcombe W Sus 28 F4
Balcombe Lane W Sus 28 F4
Balcomie Fife 135 C8
Balcurvie Fife 134 D5
Baldersby N Yorks 95 B6
Baldersby St James N Yorks 95 B6
Balderstone Lancs 93 F6
Balderton Ches 73 C7
Balderton Notts 77 D8
Baldhu Corn 3 B6
Baldinnie Fife 135 C6
Baldock Herts 54 F3
Baldovie Dundee 142 F4
Baldrine I o M 84 D4
Baldslow E Sus 18 D4
Baldwin I o M 84 D3
Baldwinholme Cumb 108 D3
Baldwin's Gate Staffs 74 E4
Bale Norf 81 D6
Balearn Aberds 161 C7
Balemartine Argyll 136 F1
Balephuil Argyll 136 F1
Balerno Edin 122 C4
Balevullin Argyll 136 F1

Bilting Kent 30 E4
Bilton E Yorks 97 F7
Bilton Northumb 117 C8
Bilton Warks 52 B2
Bilton in Ainsty N Yorks 95 E7
Bimbister Orkney 176 E2
Binbrook Lincs 91 E6
Binchester Blocks Durham 110 F5
Bincombe Dorset 12 F4
Bindal Highld 165 F6
Binegar Som 23 E8
Binfield Brack 27 B6
Binfield Heath Oxon 26 B5
Bingfield Northumb 110 B2
Bingham Notts 77 F7
Bingley W Yorks 94 F4
Bings Heath Shrops 60 C5
Binham Norf 81 D5
Binley Hants 26 D2
Binley W Mid 51 B8
Binley Woods Warks 51 B8
Binniehill Falk 121 B8
Binsoe N Yorks 94 B5
Binstead I o W 15 E6
Binsted Hants 27 E5
Binton Warks 51 D6
Bintree Norf 81 E6
Binweston Shrops 60 D3
Birch Essex 43 C5
Birch Gtr Man 87 D6
Birch Green Essex 43 C5
Birch Heath Ches 74 C2
Birch Hill Ches 74 B2
Birch Vale Derbys 87 F8
Bircham Newton Norf 80 D3
Bircham Tofts Norf 80 D3
Birchanger Essex 41 B8
Birchencliffe W Yorks 88 C2
Bircher Hereford 49 C6
Birchfield Highld 149 B5
Birchgrove Cardiff 22 B3
Birchgrove Swansea 33 E8
Birchington Kent 31 C6
Birchmoor Warks 63 D6
Birchover Derbys 76 C2
Birchwood Lincs 78 C2
Birchwood Warr 86 E4
Bircotes Notts 89 E7
Birdbrook Essex 55 E8
Birdforth N Yorks 95 B7
Birdham W Sus 16 E2
Birdholme Derbys 76 C3
Birdingbury Warks 52 C2
Birdland Park, Bourton-on-the-Water Glos 38 B1
Birdlip Glos 37 C6
Birds Edge W Yorks 88 D3
Birdsall N Yorks 96 C4
Birdsgreen Shrops 61 F7
Birdsmoor Gate Dorset 11 D8
Birdston E Dunb 121 B6
Birdwell S Yorks 88 D4
Birdwood Glos 36 C4
Birgham Borders 124 F3
Birkby N Yorks 101 D8
Birkdale Mers 85 C4
Birkenhead Mers 85 F4
Birkenhills Aberds 160 D4
Birkenshaw N Lnrk 121 C6
Birkenshaw W Yorks 88 B3
Birkhall Aberds 150 E2
Birkhill Angus 142 F3
Birkhill Dumfries 114 C5
Birkholme Lincs 65 B6
Birkin N Yorks 89 B6
Birley Hereford 49 D6
Birling Kent 29 C7
Birling Northumb 117 D8
Birling Gap E Sus 18 F2
Birlingham Worcs 50 E4
Birmingham W Mid 62 F4
Birmingham Botanical Gardens W Mid 62 F4
Birmingham International Airport W Mid 63 F5
Birmingham Museum and Art Gallery W Mid 62 F4
Birmingham Museum of Science and Technology W Mid 62 F4
Birnam Perth 141 E7
Birse Aberds 150 E4
Birsemore Aberds 150 E4
Birstall Leics 64 D2
Birstall W Yorks 88 B3
Birstwith N Yorks 94 D5
Birthorpe Lincs 78 F4
Birtley Hereford 49 C5
Birtley Northumb 109 B8
Birtley T & W 111 D5
Birts Street Worcs 50 F2
Bisbrooke Rutland 65 E5
Biscathorpe Lincs 91 F6
Biscot Luton 40 B3
Bish Mill Devon 10 B2
Bisham Windsor 39 F8
Bishampton Worcs 50 D4
Bishop Auckland Durham 101 B7
Bishop Burton E Yorks 97 F5
Bishop Middleham Durham 111 F6
Bishop Monkton N Yorks 95 C6
Bishop Norton Lincs 90 E3
Bishop Sutton Bath 23 D7
Bishop Thornton N Yorks 95 C5
Bishop Wilton E Yorks 96 D3
Bishopbridge Lincs 90 E4
Bishopbriggs E Dunb 121 C6
Bishopmill Moray 159 C6
Bishops Cannings Wilts 24 C5
Bishop's Castle Shrops 60 F3
Bishop's Caundle Dorset 12 C4
Bishop's Cleeve Glos 37 B6
Bishops Frome Hereford 49 E8
Bishop's Green Essex 42 C2
Bishop's Hull Som 11 B7
Bishop's Itchington Warks 51 D8
Bishops Lydeard Som 11 B6
Bishops Nympton Devon 10 B2
Bishop's Offley Staffs 61 B7
Bishop's Stortford Herts 41 B7
Bishop's Sutton Hants 26 F4
Bishop's Tachbrook Warks 51 C8
Bishops Tawton Devon 20 F4
Bishop's Waltham Hants 15 C6
Bishop's Wood Staffs 62 D2
Bishopsbourne Kent 31 D5
Bishopsteignton Devon 7 B7
Bishopstoke Hants 15 C5
Bishopston Swansea 33 F6
Bishopstone Bucks 39 C8
Bishopstone E Sus 17 D8
Bishopstone Hereford 49 E6
Bishopstone Swindon 38 F2
Bishopstone Wilts 13 B8
Bishopstrow Wilts 24 E3
Bishopswood Som 11 C7
Bishopsworth Bristol 23 C7
Bishopthorpe York 95 E8
Bishopton Darl 102 B1
Bishopton Dumfries 105 E8
Bishopton N Yorks 95 B6
Bishopton Renfs 120 B4
Bishopton Warks 51 D6
Bishton Newport 35 F7
Bisley Glos 37 D6
Bisley Sur 27 D7
Bispham Blkpool 92 E3
Bispham Green Lancs 86 C2
Bissoe Corn 3 B6
Bisterne Close Hants 14 D3
Bitchfield Lincs 65 B6
Bittadon Devon 20 E4
Bittaford Devon 6 D4
Bittering Norf 68 C2
Bitterley Shrops 49 B7
Bitterne Soton 15 C5
Bitteswell Leics 64 F2
Bitton S Glos 23 C8
Bix Oxon 39 F7
Bixter Shetland 175 H5
Blaby Leics 64 E2
Black Bourton Oxon 38 D2
Black Callerton T & W 110 C4
Black Clauchrie S Ayrs 112 F2
Black Corries Lodge Highld 139 D6
Black Crofts Argyll 130 B5
Black Dog Devon 10 D3
Black Heddon Northumb 110 B3
Black Lane Gtr Man 87 D5
Black Marsh Shrops 60 E3
Black Mount Argyll 139 E6
Black Notley Essex 42 B3
Black Pill Swansea 33 E7
Black Tar Pembs 44 E4
Black Torrington Devon 9 D6
Blackacre Dumfries 114 E3
Blackadder West Borders 124 D4
Blackawton Devon 7 D6
Blackborough Devon 11 D5
Blackborough End Norf 67 C6
Blackboys E Sus 18 C2
Blackbrook Derbys 76 E3
Blackbrook Mers 86 E3
Blackbrook Staffs 74 F4
Blackburn Aberds 160 E2
Blackburn Aberds 151 C7
Blackburn Blkburn 86 B4
Blackburn W Loth 122 C2
Blackcraig Dumfries 113 F7
Blackden Heath Ches 74 B4
Blackdog Aberds 151 C8
Blackfell T & W 111 D5
Blackfield Hants 14 D5
Blackford Cumb 108 C3
Blackford Perth 133 D7
Blackford Som 23 E6
Blackford Som 12 B4
Blackfordby Leics 63 C7
Blackgang I o W 15 G5
Blackgang Chine Fantasy I o W 15 G5
Blackhall Colliery Durham 111 F7
Blackhall Mill T & W 110 D4
Blackhall Rocks Durham 111 F7
Blackham E Sus 29 F5
Blackhaugh Borders 123 F7
Blackheath Essex 43 B6
Blackheath Suff 57 B8
Blackheath Sur 27 E8
Blackheath W Mid 62 F3
Blackhill Aberds 161 D7
Blackhill Aberds 161 C7
Blackhill Highld 152 D4
Blackhills Highld 158 D3
Blackhills Moray 159 D6
Blackhorse S Glos 23 B8
Blackland Wilts 24 C5
Blacklaw Aberds 160 C3
Blackley Gtr Man 87 D6
Blacklunans Perth 142 C1
Blackmill Bridgend 34 F3
Blackmoor Hants 27 F5
Blackmoor Gate Devon 21 E5
Blackmore Essex 42 D2
Blackmore End Essex 55 F8
Blackmore End Herts 40 C4
Blackness Falk 122 B3
Blacknest Hants 27 E5
Blacko Lancs 93 E8
Blackpool Blkpool 92 F3
Blackpool Devon 7 E6
Blackpool Pembs 32 C1
Blackpool Airport Lancs 92 F3
Blackpool Gate Cumb 108 B5
Blackpool Pleasure Beach Blkpool 92 F3
Blackpool Sea Life Centre Blkpool 92 F3
Blackpool Tower Blkpool 92 F3
Blackpool Zoo Park Blkpool 92 F3
Blackridge W Loth 121 C8
Blackrock Argyll 126 C3
Blackrock Mon 35 C6
Blackrod Gtr Man 86 C4
Blackshaw Dumfries 107 C7
Blackshaw Head W Yorks 87 B7
Blacksmith's Green Suff 56 C5
Blackstone W Sus 17 C6
Blackthorn Oxon 39 C6
Blackthorpe Suff 56 C3
Blacktoft E Yorks 90 B2
Blacktop Aberdeen 151 D7
Blacktown Newport 35 F6
Blackwall Tunnel London 41 F6
Blackwater Corn 3 B6
Blackwater Hants 27 D6
Blackwater I o W 15 F6
Blackwaterfoot N Ayrs 119 D5
Blackwell Darl 101 C7
Blackwell Derbys 75 B8
Blackwell Derbys 76 D4
Blackwell Warks 51 E7
Blackwell Worcs 50 B4
Blackwell W Sus 28 F4
Blackwood S Lnrk 121 E7
Blackwood = Coed Duon Caerph 35 E5
Blackwood Hill Staffs 75 D6
Blacon Ches 73 C7
Bladnoch Dumfries 105 D8
Bladon Oxon 38 C4
Blaen-gwynfi Neath 34 E2
Blaen-waun Carms 32 B3
Blaen-y-coed Carms 32 B4
Blaen-y-Cwm Denb 72 F4
Blaen-y-cwm Gwyn 71 E8
Blaen-y-cwm Powys 59 B7
Blaenannerch Ceredig 45 E4
Blaenau Ffestiniog Gwyn 71 C8
Blaenavon Torf 35 D6
Blaencelyn Ceredig 46 D2
Blaendyryn Powys 47 F8
Blaenffos Pembs 45 F3
Blaengarw Bridgend 34 E3
Blaengwrach Neath 34 D2
Blaenpennal Ceredig 46 C5
Blaenplwyf Ceredig 46 B4
Blaenporth Ceredig 45 E4
Blaenrhondda Rhondda 34 D3
Blaenycwm Ceredig 47 B7
Blagdon N Som 23 D7
Blagdon Torbay 7 C6
Blagdon Hill Som 11 C7
Blagill Cumb 109 E7
Blaguegate Lancs 86 D2
Blaich Highld 138 B4
Blain Highld 137 B7
Blaina Bl Gwent 35 D6
Blair Atholl Perth 141 C5
Blair Castle, Blair Atholl Perth 141 C5
Blair Drummond Stirl 133 E6
Blair Drummond Safari Park, Dunblane Stirl 133 E6
Blairbeg N Ayrs 119 C7
Blairdaff Aberds 151 C5
Blairglas Argyll 129 B8
Blairgowrie Perth 142 E1
Blairhall Fife 134 F2
Blairingone Perth 133 E8
Blairland N Ayrs 120 E3
Blairlogie Stirl 133 E7
Blairlomond Argyll 131 F7
Blairmore Argyll 129 B6
Blairnamarrow Moray 149 C8
Blairquhosh Stirl 132 F4
Blair's Ferry Argyll 128 D4
Blairskaith E Dunb 121 B5
Blaisdon Glos 36 C4
Blakebrook Worcs 50 B3
Blakedown Worcs 50 B3
Blakelaw Borders 124 F3
Blakeley Staffs 62 E2
Blakeley Lane Staffs 75 E6
Blakemere Hereford 49 E5
Blakeney Glos 36 D3
Blakeney Norf 81 C6
Blakeney Point NNR Norf 81 C6
Blakenhall Ches 74 E4
Blakenhall W Mid 62 E3
Blakeshall Worcs 62 F2
Blakesley Northants 52 D4
Blanchland Northumb 110 D2
Bland Hill N Yorks 94 D5
Blandford Forum Dorset 13 D6
Blandford St Mary Dorset 13 D6
Blanefield Stirl 121 B5
Blankney Lincs 78 C3
Blantyre S Lnrk 121 D6
Blar a'Chaorainn Highld 139 C5
Blaran Argyll 130 D4
Blarghour Argyll 131 D5
Blarmachfoldach Highld 138 C4
Blarnalearoch Highld 163 E5
Blashford Hants 14 D2
Blaston Leics 64 E5
Blatherwycke Northants 65 E6
Blawith Cumb 98 F4
Blaxhall Suff 57 D7
Blaxton S Yorks 89 D7
Blaydon T & W 110 C4
Bleadon N Som 22 D5
Bleak Hey Nook Gtr Man 87 D8
Blean Kent 30 C5
Bleasby Lincs 90 F5
Bleasby Notts 77 E7
Bleasdale Lancs 93 E5
Bleatarn Cumb 100 C2
Blebocraigs Fife 135 C6
Bleddfa Powys 48 C4
Bledington Glos 38 B2
Bledlow Bucks 39 D7
Bledlow Ridge Bucks 39 E7
Blegbie E Loth 123 C7
Blencarn Cumb 109 F6
Blencogo Cumb 107 E8
Blendworth Hants 15 C8
Blenheim Palace, Woodstock Oxon 38 C4
Blenheim Park Norf 80 D4
Blennerhasset Cumb 107 E8
Blervie Castle Moray 158 D4
Bletchingdon Oxon 39 C5
Bletchingley Sur 28 D4
Bletchley M Keynes 53 F6
Bletchley Shrops 74 F3
Bletherston Pembs 32 B1
Bletsoe Beds 53 D8
Blewbury Oxon 39 F5
Blickling Norf 81 E7
Blickling Hall, Aylsham Norf 81 E7
Blidworth Notts 77 D5
Blindburn Northumb 116 C4
Blindcrake Cumb 107 F8
Blindley Heath Sur 28 E4
Blisland Corn 5 B6
Bliss Gate Worcs 50 B2
Blissford Hants 14 C2
Blisworth Northants 52 D5
Blithbury Staffs 62 B4
Blitterlees Cumb 107 D8
Blockley Glos 51 F6
Blofield Norf 69 D6
Blofield Heath Norf 69 C6
Blo'Norton Norf 56 B4
Bloomfield Borders 115 B8
Blore Staffs 75 E8
Blount's Green Staffs 75 F7
Blowick Mers 85 C4
Bloxham Oxon 52 F2
Bloxholm Lincs 78 D3
Bloxwich W Mid 62 D3
Bloxworth Dorset 13 E6
Blubberhouses N Yorks 94 D4
Blue Anchor Som 22 E2
Blue Anchor Swansea 33 E6
Blue Planet Aquarium Ches 73 B8
Blue Row Essex 43 C6
Blundeston Suff 69 E8
Blunham Beds 54 D2
Blunsdon St Andrew Swindon 37 F8
Bluntington Worcs 50 B3
Bluntisham Cambs 54 B4
Blunts Corn 5 C8
Blyborough Lincs 90 E3
Blyford Suff 57 B8
Blymhill Staffs 62 C2
Blyth Notts 89 F7
Blyth Northumb 117 F9
Blyth Bridge Borders 122 E4
Blythburgh Suff 57 B8
Blythe Borders 123 E8
Blythe Bridge Staffs 75 E6
Blyton Lincs 90 E2
Boarhills Fife 135 C7
Boarhunt Hants 15 D7
Boars Head Gtr Man 86 D3
Boars Hill Oxon 38 D4
Boarshead E Sus 18 B2
Boarstall Bucks 39 C6
Boasley Cross Devon 9 E6
Boat of Garten Highld 148 C5
Boath Highld 157 B6
Bobbing Kent 30 C2
Bobbington Staffs 62 E2
Bobbingworth Essex 41 D8
Bocaddon Corn 5 D6
Bochastle Stirl 132 D5
Bocking Essex 42 B3
Bocking Churchstreet Essex 42 B3
Boddam Aberds 161 D8
Boddam Shetland 175 M5
Boddington Glos 37 B5
Bodedern Anglesey 82 C3
Bodelwyddan Denb 72 B4
Bodenham Hereford 49 D7
Bodenham Wilts 14 B2
Bodenham Arboretum and Earth Centre Worcs 62 F2
Bodenham Moor Hereford 49 D7
Bodermid Gwyn 70 E2
Bodewryd Anglesey 82 B3
Bodfari Denb 72 B4
Bodffordd Anglesey 82 D4
Bodham Norf 81 C7
Bodiam E Sus 18 C4
Bodiam Castle E Sus 18 C4
Bodicote Oxon 52 F2
Bodieve Corn 4 B4
Bodinnick Corn 5 D6
Bodle Street Green E Sus 18 D3
Bodmin Corn 5 C5
Bodnant Garden, Colwyn Bay Conwy 83 D8
Bodney Norf 67 E8
Bodorgan Anglesey 82 E3
Bodsham Kent 30 E5
Boduan Gwyn 70 D4
Bodymoor Heath Warks 63 E5
Bogallan Highld 157 D7
Bogbrae Aberds 161 E7
Bogend Borders 124 E3
Bogend S Ayrs 120 F3
Boghall W Loth 122 C2
Boghead S Lnrk 121 E7
Bogmoor Moray 159 C7
Bogniebrae Aberds 160 D2
Bognor Regis W Sus 16 E3
Bograxie Aberds 151 C6
Bogside N Lnrk 121 D8
Bogton Aberds 160 C3
Bogue Dumfries 113 F6
Bohenie Highld 147 F5
Bohortha Corn 3 C7
Bohuntine Highld 147 F5
Boirseam W Isles 173 K3
Bojewyan Corn 2 C2
Bolam Durham 101 B6
Bolam Northumb 117 F6
Bolberry Devon 6 F4
Bold Heath Mers 86 F3
Boldon T & W 111 C6
Boldon Colliery T & W 111 C6
Boldre Hants 14 E4
Boldron Durham 101 C5
Bole Notts 89 F8
Bolehill Derbys 76 D2
Boleside Borders 123 F7
Bolham Devon 10 C4
Bolham Water Devon 11 C6
Bolingey Corn 4 D2
Bollington Ches 75 B6
Bollington Cross Ches 75 B6
Bolney W Sus 17 B6
Bolnhurst Beds 53 D8
Bolshan Angus 143 D6
Bolsover Derbys 76 B4
Bolsterstone S Yorks 88 E3
Bolstone Hereford 49 F7
Boltby N Yorks 102 F2
Bolter End Bucks 39 E7
Bolton Cumb 99 B8
Bolton E Loth 123 B8
Bolton E Yorks 96 D3
Bolton Gtr Man 86 D5
Bolton Northumb 117 C7
Bolton Abbey N Yorks 94 D3
Bolton Abbey, Skipton N Yorks 94 D3
Bolton Bridge N Yorks 94 D3
Bolton-by-Bowland Lancs 93 E7
Bolton Castle, Leyburn N Yorks 101 E5
Bolton le Sands Lancs 92 C4
Bolton Low Houses Cumb 108 E2
Bolton-on-Swale N Yorks 101 E7
Bolton Percy N Yorks 95 E8
Bolton Town End Lancs 92 C4
Bolton upon Dearne S Yorks 89 D5
Boltonfellend Cumb 108 C4
Boltongate Cumb 108 E2
Bolventor Corn 5 B6
Bomere Heath Shrops 60 C4
Bon-y-maen Swansea 33 E7
Bonar Bridge Highld 164 E3
Bonawe Argyll 131 B6
Bonby N Lincs 90 C4
Boncath Pembs 45 F4
Bonchester Bridge Borders 115 C8
Bonchurch I o W 15 G6
Bondleigh Devon 9 D8
Bonehill Devon 6 B5
Bonehill Staffs 63 D5
Bo'ness Falk 133 F8
Bonhill W Dunb 120 B3
Boningale Shrops 62 D2
Bonjedward Borders 116 B2
Bonkle N Lnrk 121 D8
Bonnavoulin Highld 137 C6
Bonnington Edin 122 C4
Bonnington Kent 19 B7
Bonnybank Fife 135 D5
Bonnybridge Falk 133 F7
Bonnykelly Aberds 161 C5
Bonnyrigg and Lasswade Midloth 123 C6
Bonnyton Aberds 160 E3
Bonnyton Angus 142 F3
Bonnyton Angus 143 D6
Bonsall Derbys 76 D2
Bonskeid House Perth 141 C5
Bont Mon 35 C7
Bont-Dolgadfan Powys 59 D5
Bont-goch Ceredig 58 F3
Bont-newydd Conwy 72 B4
Bont Newydd Gwyn 71 C8
Bont Newydd Gwyn 71 E8
Bontddu Gwyn 58 C3
Bonthorpe Lincs 79 B7
Bontnewydd Ceredig 46 C5
Bontnewydd Gwyn 82 F4
Bontuchel Denb 72 D4
Bonvilston V Glam 22 B2
Booker Bucks 39 E8
Boon Borders 123 E8
Boosbeck Redcar 102 C4
Boot Cumb 98 D3
Boot Street Suff 57 E6
Booth W Yorks 87 B8
Booth Wood W Yorks 87 C8
Boothby Graffoe Lincs 78 D2
Boothby Pagnell Lincs 78 F2
Boothen Stoke 75 E5
Boothferry E Yorks 89 B8
Boothville Northants 53 C5
Bootle Cumb 98 F3
Bootle Mers 85 E4
Booton Norf 81 E7
Boquhan Stirl 132 F4
Boraston Shrops 49 B8
Borden Kent 30 C2
Borden W Sus 16 B2
Bordley N Yorks 94 C2
Bordon Hants 27 F6
Bordon Camp Hants 27 F5
Boreham Essex 42 D3
Boreham Wilts 24 E3
Boreham Street E Sus 18 D3
Borehamwood Herts 40 E4
Boreland Dumfries 114 E4
Boreland Stirl 140 F2
Borgh W Isles 171 K2
Borgh W Isles 173 K2
Borghastan W Isles 172 D5
Borgie Highld 167 D8
Borgue Dumfries 106 E3
Borgue Highld 165 B8
Borley Essex 56 E2
Bornais W Isles 171 H3
Bornesketaig Highld 152 B4
Borness Dumfries 106 E3
Borough Green Kent 29 D7
Boroughbridge N Yorks 95 C6
Borras Head Wrex 73 D7
Borreraig Highld 152 D2
Borrobol Lodge Highld 165 B5
Borrowash Derbys 76 F4
Borrowby N Yorks 102 F2
Borrowdale Cumb 98 C4
Borrowfield Aberds 151 E7
Borth Ceredig 58 E3
Borth-y-Gest Gwyn 71 D6
Borthwickbrae Borders 115 C7
Borthwickshiels Borders 115 C7
Borve Highld 152 E5
Borve Lodge W Isles 173 J3
Borwick Lancs 92 B5
Bosavern Corn 2 C2
Bosbury Hereford 49 E8
Boscastle Corn 8 E3
Boscombe Bmouth 14 E2
Boscombe Wilts 25 F7
Boscoppa Corn 4 D5
Bosham W Sus 16 D2
Bosherston Pembs 44 F4
Boskenna Corn 2 D3
Bosley Ches 75 C6
Bossall N Yorks 96 C3
Bossiney Corn 8 F2
Bossingham Kent 31 E5
Bossington Som 21 E7
Bostock Green Ches 74 C3
Boston Lincs 79 E6
Boston Long Hedges Lincs 79 E6
Boston Spa W Yorks 95 E7
Boston West Lincs 79 E5
Boswinger Corn 3 B8
Botallack Corn 2 C2
Botany Bay London 41 E5
Botcherby Cumb 108 D4
Botcheston Leics 63 D8
Botesdale Suff 56 B4
Bothal Northumb 117 F8
Bothamsall Notts 77 B6
Bothel Cumb 107 F8
Bothenhampton Dorset 12 E2
Bothwell S Lnrk 121 D7
Botley Bucks 40 D2
Botley Hants 15 C6
Botley Oxon 38 D4
Botolph Claydon Bucks 39 B7
Botolphs W Sus 17 D5
Bottacks Highld 157 C5
Bottesford Leics 77 F8
Bottesford N Lincs 90 D2
Bottisham Cambs 55 C6
Bottlesford Wilts 25 D6
Bottom Boat W Yorks 88 B4
Bottom House Staffs 75 D7
Bottom of Hutton Lancs 86 B2
Bottom o'th'Moor Gtr Man 86 C4
Bottomcraig Fife 135 B5
Botusfleming Corn 6 C2
Botwnnog Gwyn 70 D3
Bough Beech Kent 29 E5
Boughrood Powys 48 F3
Boughspring Glos 36 E2
Boughton Norf 67 D6
Boughton Notts 77 C6
Boughton Northants 53 C5
Boughton Aluph Kent 30 E4
Boughton Lees Kent 30 E4
Boughton Malherbe Kent 30 E2
Boughton Monchelsea Kent 29 D8
Boughton Street Kent 30 D4
Boulby Redcar 103 C5
Boulden Shrops 60 F5
Boulmer Northumb 117 C8
Boulston Pembs 44 D4
Boultenstone Aberds 150 C3
Boultham Lincs 78 C2
Bourn Cambs 54 D4
Bourne Lincs 65 B7
Bourne End Beds 53 E7
Bourne End Bucks 40 F1
Bourne End Herts 40 D3
Bournemouth Bmouth 13 E8
Bournemouth International Airport Dorset 14 E2
Bournes Green Glos 37 D6
Bournes Green Sthend 43 F5
Bournheath Worcs 50 B4
Bournmoor Durham 111 D6
Bournville W Mid 62 F4
Bourton Dorset 24 F2
Bourton N Som 23 C5
Bourton Oxon 38 F2
Bourton Shrops 61 E5
Bourton on Dunsmore Warks 52 B2
Bourton on the Hill Glos 51 F6
Bourton-on-the-Water Glos 38 B1
Bousd Argyll 136 B3
Boustead Hill Cumb 108 D2
Bouth Cumb 99 F5
Bouthwaite N Yorks 94 B4
Boveney Bucks 27 B7
Boverton V Glam 21 C8
Bovey Tracey Devon 7 B6
Bovingdon Herts 40 D3
Bovingdon Green Bucks 39 F8
Bovingdon Green Herts 40 D3
Bovinger Essex 41 D8
Bovington Camp Dorset 13 F6
Bow Borders 123 E7
Bow Devon 10 D2
Bow Orkney 176 G2
Bow Brickhill M Keynes 53 F7
Bow of Fife Fife 134 C5
Bow Street Ceredig 58 F3
Bowbank Durham 100 B4
Bowburn Durham 111 F6
Bowcombe I o W 15 F5
Bowd Devon 11 E6
Bowden Borders 123 F8
Bowden Devon 7 E6
Bowden Hill Wilts 24 C4
Bowderdale Cumb 100 D1
Bowdon Gtr Man 87 F5
Bower Northumb 116 F3
Bower Hinton Som 12 C2
Bowerchalke Wilts 13 B8
Bowerhill Wilts 24 C4
Bowermadden Highld 169 C7
Bowers Gifford Essex 42 F3
Bowershall Fife 134 E2
Bowertower Highld 169 C7
Bowes Durham 100 C4
Bowgreave Lancs 92 E4
Bowgreen Gtr Man 87 F5
Bowhill Borders 115 B7
Bowhouse Dumfries 107 C7
Bowland Bridge Cumb 99 F6
Bowley Hereford 49 D7
Bowlhead Green Sur 27 F7
Bowling W Dunb 120 B4
Bowling W Yorks 94 F4
Bowling Bank Wrex 73 E7
Bowling Green Worcs 50 D3
Bowmanstead Cumb 99 E5
Bowmore Argyll 126 D3
Bowness-on-Solway Cumb 108 C2
Bowness-on-Windermere Cumb 99 E6
Bowood House and Gardens, Calne Wilts 24 C4
Bowsden Northumb 125 E5
Bowside Lodge Highld 168 C3
Bowston Cumb 99 E6
Bowthorpe Norf 68 D4
Box Glos 37 D5
Box Wilts 24 C3
Box End Beds 53 E8
Boxbush Glos 36 C4
Boxford Suff 56 E3
Boxford W Berks 26 B2
Boxgrove W Sus 16 D3
Boxley Kent 29 D8
Boxmoor Herts 40 D3
Boxted Essex 56 F4
Boxted Suff 56 D2
Boxted Cross Essex 56 F4
Boxted Heath Essex 56 F4
Boxworth Cambs 54 C4
Boxworth End Cambs 54 C4
Boyden Gate Kent 31 C6
Boylestone Derbys 75 F8
Boyndie Aberds 160 B3
Boynton E Yorks 97 C7
Boysack Angus 143 E6
Boyton Corn 8 E5
Boyton Suff 57 E7
Boyton Wilts 24 F4
Boyton Cross Essex 42 D2
Boyton End Suff 55 E8
Bozeat Northants 53 D7
Braaid I o M 84 E3
Braal Castle Highld 169 C6
Brabling Green Suff 57 C6
Brabourne Kent 30 E4
Brabourne Lees Kent 30 E4
Brabster Highld 169 C8
Bracadale Highld 153 F4
Bracara Highld 145 D7
Braceborough Lincs 65 C7
Bracebridge Lincs 78 C2
Bracebridge Heath Lincs 78 C2
Bracebridge Low Fields Lincs 78 C2
Braceby Lincs 78 F3
Bracewell Lancs 93 E8
Brackenfield Derbys 76 D3
Brackenthwaite Cumb 108 E2
Brackenthwaite N Yorks 95 D5
Bracklesham W Sus 16 E2
Brackletter Highld 146 F4
Brackley Argyll 118 B4
Brackley Northants 52 F3
Brackloch Highld 163 B5
Bracknell Brack 27 C6
Braco Perth 133 D7
Bracobrae Moray 160 C2
Bracon Ash Norf 68 E4
Bracorina Highld 145 D7
Bradbourne Derbys 76 D2
Bradbury Durham 101 B8
Bradda I o M 84 F1
Bradden Northants 52 E4
Braddock Corn 5 C6
Bradeley Stoke 75 D5
Bradenham Bucks 39 E8
Bradenham Norf 68 D2
Bradenstoke Wilts 24 B5
Bradfield Essex 56 F5
Bradfield Norf 81 D8
Bradfield W Berks 26 B4
Bradfield Combust Suff 56 D2
Bradfield Green Ches 74 D3
Bradfield Heath Essex 43 B7
Bradfield St Clare Suff 56 D3
Bradfield St George Suff 56 C3
Bradford Corn 5 B6
Bradford Derbys 76 C2
Bradford Devon 9 D6
Bradford Northumb 125 F7
Bradford W Yorks 94 F4
Bradford Abbas Dorset 12 C3
Bradford Cathedral W Yorks 94 F4
Bradford Industrial Museum W Yorks 94 F4
Bradford Leigh Wilts 24 C3
Bradford-on-Avon Wilts 24 C3
Bradford on Tone Som 11 B6
Bradford Peverell Dorset 12 E4
Brading I o W 15 F7
Bradley Derbys 76 E2
Bradley Hants 26 E4
Bradley NE Lincs 91 D6
Bradley Staffs 62 C2
Bradley W Mid 62 E3
Bradley W Yorks 88 B2
Bradley Green Worcs 50 C4
Bradley in the Moors Staffs 75 E7
Bradlow Hereford 50 F2
Bradmore Notts 77 F5
Bradmore W Mid 62 E2
Bradninch Devon 10 D5
Bradnop Staffs 75 D7
Bradpole Dorset 12 E2
Bradshaw Gtr Man 86 C5
Bradshaw W Yorks 87 C8
Bradstone Devon 9 F5
Bradwall Green Ches 74 C4
Bradway S Yorks 88 F4
Bradwell Derbys 88 F2
Bradwell Essex 42 B4
Bradwell M Keynes 53 F6
Bradwell Norf 69 D8
Bradwell Staffs 74 E5
Bradwell Grove Oxon 38 D2
Bradwell on Sea Essex 43 D6
Bradwell Waterside Essex 43 D5
Bradworthy Devon 8 C5
Bradworthy Cross Devon 8 C5
Brae Dumfries 107 B5
Brae Highld 154 B4
Brae Highld 163 D8
Brae Shetland 174 G5
Brae of Achnahaird Highld 162 C4
Brae Roy Lodge Highld 147 E6
Braeantra Highld 157 B6
Braedownie Angus 142 B2
Braefield Highld 156 F5
Braegrum Perth 134 B2
Braehead Dumfries 105 D8
Braehead Orkney 176 F4
Braehead Orkney 176 B3
Braehead S Lnrk 121 F8
Braehead S Lnrk 122 D2
Braehead of Lunan Angus 143 D6
Braehoulland Shetland 174 F4
Braehungie Highld 169 F6
Braelangwell Lodge Highld 164 E2
Braemar Aberds 149 E7
Braemore Highld 169 F5
Braemore Highld 156 B2
Braes of Enzie Moray 159 D7
Braeside Invclyd 129 C7
Braeswick Orkney 176 C5
Braewick Shetland 175 H5
Brafferton Darl 101 B7
Brafferton N Yorks 95 B7
Brafield-on-the-Green Northants 53 D6
Bragar W Isles 172 D5
Bragbury End Herts 41 B5
Bragleenmore Argyll 130 C5
Braichmelyn Gwyn 83 E6
Braid Edin 122 C5
Braides Lancs 92 D4
Braidley N Yorks 101 F5
Braidwood S Lnrk 121 E8

Braigo Argyll 126 C2
Brailsford Derbys 76 E2
Brainshaugh Northumb 117 D8
Braintree Essex 42 B3
Braiseworth Suff 56 B5
Braishfield Hants 14 B4
Braithwaite Cumb 98 B4
Braithwaite S Yorks 89 C7
Braithwaite W Yorks 94 E3
Braithwell S Yorks 89 E6
Bramber W Sus 17 C5
Bramcote Notts 76 F5
Bramcote Warks 63 F8
Bramdean Hants 15 B7
Bramerton Norf 69 D5
Bramfield Herts 41 C5
Bramfield Suff 57 B7
Bramford Suff 56 E5
Bramhall Gtr Man 87 F6
Bramham W Yorks 95 E7
Bramhope W Yorks 95 E5
Bramley Hants 26 D4
Bramley Sur 27 E8
Bramley S Yorks 89 E5
Bramley W Yorks 94 F5
Bramling Kent 31 D6
Brampford Speke Devon 10 E4
Brampton Cambs 54 B3
Brampton Cumb 100 B1
Brampton Cumb 108 C5
Brampton Derbys 76 B3
Brampton Hereford 49 F6
Brampton Lincs 77 B8
Brampton Norf 81 E8
Brampton Suff 69 F7
Brampton S Yorks 88 D5
Brampton Abbotts Hereford 36 B3
Brampton Ash Northants 64 F4
Brampton Bryan Hereford 49 B5
Brampton en le Morthen S Yorks 89 F5
Bramshall Staffs 75 F7
Bramshaw Hants 14 C3
Bramshill Hants 26 C5
Bramshott Hants 27 F6
Bran End Essex 42 B2
Branault Highld 137 B6
Brancaster Norf 80 C3
Brancaster Staithe Norf 80 C3
Brancepeth Durham 110 F5
Branch End Northumb 110 C3
Branchill Moray 158 D4
Brand Green Glos 36 B4
Branderburgh Moray 159 B6
Brandesburton E Yorks 97 E7
Brandeston Suff 57 C6
Brandhill Shrops 49 B6
Brandis Corner Devon 9 D6
Brandiston Norf 81 E7
Brandon Durham 110 F5
Brandon Lincs 78 E2
Brandon Northumb 117 C6
Brandon Suff 67 F7
Brandon Warks 52 B2
Brandon Bank Norf 67 F6
Brandon Creek Norf 67 E6
Brandon Parva Norf 68 D3
Brands Hatch Motor Racing Circuit Kent 29 C6
Brandsby N Yorks 95 B8
Brandy Wharf Lincs 90 E4
Brane Corn 2 D3
Branksome Poole 13 E8
Branksome Park Poole 13 E8
Bransby Lincs 77 B8
Branscombe Devon 11 F6
Bransford Worcs 50 D2
Bransgore Hants 14 E2
Branshill Clack 133 E7
Bransholme Hull 97 F7
Branson's Cross Worcs 51 B5
Branston Leics 64 B5
Branston Lincs 78 C3
Branston Staffs 63 B6
Branston Booths Lincs 78 C3
Branstone I o W 15 F6
Bransty Cumb 98 C1
Brant Broughton Lincs 78 D2
Brantham Suff 56 F5
Branthwaite Cumb 98 B2
Branthwaite Cumb 108 F2
Brantingham E Yorks 90 B3
Branton Northumb 117 C6
Branton S Yorks 89 D7
Branxholm Park Borders 115 C7
Branxholme Borders 115 C7
Branxton Northumb 124 F4
Brassey Green Ches 74 C2
Brassington Derbys 76 D2
Brasted Kent 29 D5
Brasted Chart Kent 29 D5
Brathens Aberds 151 E5
Bratoft Lincs 79 C7
Brattleby Lincs 90 F3
Bratton Telford 61 C6
Bratton Wilts 24 D4
Bratton Clovelly Devon 9 E6
Bratton Fleming Devon 20 F5
Bratton Seymour Som 12 B4
Braughing Herts 41 B6
Braunston Northants 52 C3
Braunston-in-Rutland Rutland 64 D5
Braunstone Town Leics 64 D2
Braunton Devon 20 F3
Brawby N Yorks 96 B3
Brawl Highld 168 C3
Brawlbin Highld 169 D5
Bray Windsor 27 B7
Bray Shop Corn 5 B8
Bray Wick Windsor 27 B6
Braybrooke Northants 64 F4
Braye Ald 16
Brayford Devon 21 F5
Braystones Cumb 98 D2
Braythorn N Yorks 94 E5
Brayton N Yorks 95 F9
Brazacott Corn 8 E4
Breach Kent 30 C2
Breachacha Castle Argyll 136 C2
Breachwood Green Herts 40 B4
Breacleit W Isles 172 E4
Breaden Heath Shrops 73 F8
Breadsall Derbys 76 F3
Breadstone Glos 36 D4
Breage Corn 2 D5
Breakachy Highld 157 E5
Bream Glos 36 D3
Breamore Hants 14 C2
Brean Som 22 D4
Breanais W Isles 172 F2
Brearton N Yorks 95 C6
Breascleit W Isles 172 E5
Breaston Derbys 76 F4
Brechfa Carms 46 F4
Brechin Angus 143 C5
Breck of Cruan Orkney 176 E2
Breckan Orkney 176 F1
Breckrey Highld 152 C6
Brecon = Aberhonddu Powys 34 B4
Brecon Beacons Mountain Centre Powys 34 B3
Bredbury Gtr Man 87 E7
Brede E Sus 18 D5
Bredenbury Hereford 49 D8
Bredfield Suff 57 D6
Bredgar Kent 30 C2
Bredhurst Kent 29 C8
Bredicot Worcs 50 D4
Bredon Worcs 50 F4
Bredon's Norton Worcs 50 F4
Bredwardine Hereford 48 E5
Breedon on the Hill Leics 63 B8
Breibhig W Isles 171 L2
Breibhig W Isles 172 E7
Breich W Loth 122 C2
Breightmet Gtr Man 86 D5
Breighton E Yorks 96 F3
Breinton Hereford 49 F6
Breinton Common Hereford 49 E6
Breiwick Shetland 175 J6
Bremhill Wilts 24 B4
Bremirehoull Shetland 175 L6
Brenchley Kent 29 E7
Brendon Devon 21 E6
Brenkley T & W 110 B5
Brent Eleigh Suff 56 E3
Brent Knoll Som 22 D5
Brent Pelham Herts 54 F5
Brentford London 28 B2
Brentingby Leics 64 C4
Brentwood Essex 42 E1
Brenzett Kent 19 C7
Brereton Staffs 62 C4
Brereton Green Ches 74 C4
Brereton Heath Ches 74 C5
Bressingham Norf 68 F3
Bretby Derbys 63 B6
Bretford Warks 52 B2
Bretforton Worcs 51 E5
Bretherdale Head Cumb 99 D7
Bretherton Lancs 86 B2
Brettabister Shetland 175 H6
Brettenham Norf 68 F2
Brettenham Suff 56 D3
Bretton Derbys 76 B2
Bretton Flint 73 C7
Brewer Street Sur 28 D4
Brewlands Bridge Angus 142 C1
Brewood Staffs 62 D2
Briach Moray 158 D4
Briants Puddle Dorset 13 E6
Brick End Essex 42 B1
Brickendon Herts 41 D6
Bricket Wood Herts 40 D4
Bricklehampton Worcs 50 E4
Bride I o M 84 B4
Bridekirk Cumb 107 F8
Bridell Pembs 45 E3
Bridestowe Devon 9 F7
Brideswell Aberds 160 E2
Bridford Devon 10 F3
Bridfordmills Devon 10 F3
Bridge Kent 31 D5
Bridge End Lincs 78 F4
Bridge Green Essex 55 F5
Bridge Hewick N Yorks 95 B6
Bridge of Alford Aberds 150 C4
Bridge of Allan Stirl 133 E6
Bridge of Avon Moray 159 F5
Bridge of Awe Argyll 131 C6
Bridge of Balgie Perth 140 E2
Bridge of Cally Perth 141 D8
Bridge of Canny Aberds 151 E5
Bridge of Craigisla Angus 142 D2
Bridge of Dee Dumfries 106 D4
Bridge of Don Aberdeen 151 C8
Bridge of Dun Angus 143 D6
Bridge of Dye Aberds 151 F5
Bridge of Earn Perth 134 C3
Bridge of Ericht Perth 140 D2
Bridge of Feugh Aberds 151 E6
Bridge of Forss Highld 168 C5
Bridge of Gairn Aberds 150 E2
Bridge of Gaur Perth 140 D2
Bridge of Muchalls Aberds 151 E7
Bridge of Oich Highld 147 D6
Bridge of Orchy Argyll 131 B8
Bridge of Waith Orkney 176 E1
Bridge of Walls Shetland 175 H4
Bridge of Weir Renfs 120 C3
Bridge Sollers Hereford 49 E6
Bridge Street Suff 56 E2
Bridge Trafford Ches 73 B8
Bridge Yate S Glos 23 B8
Bridgefoot Angus 142 F3
Bridgefoot Cumb 98 B2
Bridgehampton Som 12 B3
Bridgehill Durham 110 D3
Bridgemary Hants 15 D6
Bridgemont Derbys 87 F8
Bridgend Aberds 160 E2
Bridgend Aberds 150 C4
Bridgend Angus 143 C5
Bridgend Argyll 128 A3
Bridgend Argyll 126 C3
Bridgend Argyll 118 C4
Bridgend Cumb 99 C5
Bridgend Fife 135 C5
Bridgend Moray 159 F7
Bridgend N Lnrk 121 B6
Bridgend Pembs 45 E3
Bridgend W Loth 122 B3
Bridgend = Pen-y-bont ar Ogwr Bridgend 21 B8
Bridgend of Lintrathen Angus 142 D2
Bridgerule Devon 8 D4
Bridges Shrops 60 E3
Bridgeton Glasgow 121 C6
Bridgetown Corn 8 F5
Bridgetown Som 21 F8
Bridgham Norf 68 F2
Bridgnorth Shrops 61 E7
Bridgnorth Cliff Railway Shrops 61 E7
Bridgtown Staffs 62 D3
Bridgwater Som 22 F5
Bridlington E Yorks 97 C7
Bridport Dorset 12 E2
Bridstow Hereford 36 B2
Brierfield Lancs 93 F8
Brierley Glos 36 C3
Brierley Hereford 49 D6
Brierley S Yorks 88 C5
Brierley Hill W Mid 62 F3
Briery Hill Bl Gwent 35 D5
Brig o'Turk Stirl 132 D4
Brigg N Lincs 90 D4
Briggswath N Yorks 103 D6
Brigham Cumb 107 F7
Brigham E Yorks 97 D6
Brighouse W Yorks 88 B2
Brighstone I o W 14 F5
Brightgate Derbys 76 D2
Brighthampton Oxon 38 D3
Brightling E Sus 18 C3
Brightlingsea Essex 43 C6
Brighton Brighton 17 D7
Brighton Corn 4 D4
Brighton Hill Hants 26 E4
Brighton Museum and Art Gallery Brighton 17 D7
Brighton Racecourse Brighton 17 D7
Brighton Sea Life Centre Brighton 17 D7
Brightons Falk 122 B2
Brightwalton W Berks 26 B2
Brightwell Suff 57 E6
Brightwell Baldwin Oxon 39 E6
Brightwell cum Sotwell Oxon 39 E5
Brignall Durham 101 C5
Brigsley NE Lincs 91 D6
Brigsteer Cumb 99 F6
Brigstock Northants 65 F6
Brill Bucks 39 C6
Brilley Hereford 48 E4
Brimaston Pembs 44 C4
Brimfield Hereford 49 C7
Brimington Derbys 76 B4
Brimley Devon 7 B5
Brimpsfield Glos 37 C6
Brimpton W Berks 26 C3
Brims Orkney 176 H1
Brimscombe Glos 37 D5
Brimstage Mers 85 F4
Brinacory Highld 145 D7
Brind E Yorks 96 F3
Brindister Shetland 175 H4
Brindister Shetland 175 K6
Brindle Lancs 86 B4
Brindley Ford Staffs 75 D5
Brineton Staffs 62 C2
Bringhurst Leics 64 E5
Brington Cambs 53 B8
Brinian Orkney 176 D3
Briningham Norf 81 D6
Brinkhill Lincs 79 B6
Brinkley Cambs 55 D7
Brinklow Warks 52 B2
Brinkworth Wilts 37 F7
Brinmore Highld 148 B2
Brinscall Lancs 86 B4
Brinsea N Som 23 C6
Brinsley Notts 76 E4
Brinsop Hereford 49 E6
Brinsworth S Yorks 88 F5
Brinton Norf 81 D6
Brisco Cumb 108 D4
Brisley Norf 81 E5
Brislington Bristol 23 B8
Bristol Bristol 23 B7
Bristol City Museum and Art Gallery Bristol 23 B7
Bristol International Airport N Som 23 C7
Bristol Zoo Bristol 23 B7
Briston Norf 81 D6
Britannia Lancs 87 B6
Britford Wilts 14 B2
Brithdir Gwyn 58 C4
British Legion Village Kent 29 D8
British Museum London 41 F5
Briton Ferry Neath 33 E8
Britwell Salome Oxon 39 E6
Brixham Torbay 7 D7
Brixton Devon 6 D3
Brixton London 28 B4
Brixton Deverill Wilts 24 F3
Brixworth Northants 52 B5
Brize Norton Oxon 38 D3
Broad Blunsdon Swindon 38 E1
Broad Campden Glos 51 F6
Broad Chalke Wilts 13 B8
Broad Green Beds 53 E7
Broad Green Essex 42 B4
Broad Green Worcs 50 D2
Broad Haven Pembs 44 D3
Broad Heath Worcs 49 C8
Broad Hill Cambs 55 B6
Broad Hinton Wilts 25 B6
Broad Laying Hants 26 C2
Broad Marston Worcs 51 E6
Broad Oak Carms 33 B6
Broad Oak Cumb 98 E3
Broad Oak Dorset 12 E2
Broad Oak Dorset 13 C5
Broad Oak E Sus 18 D5
Broad Oak E Sus 18 C3
Broad Oak Hereford 36 B1
Broad Oak Mers 86 E3
Broad Street Kent 30 D2
Broad Street Green Essex 42 D4
Broad Town Wilts 25 B5
Broadbottom Gtr Man 87 E7
Broadbridge W Sus 16 D2
Broadbridge Heath W Sus 28 F2
Broadclyst Devon 10 E4
Broadfield Gtr Man 87 C6
Broadfield Lancs 86 B3
Broadfield Pembs 32 D2
Broadfield W Sus 28 F3
Broadford Highld 155 H2
Broadford Bridge W Sus 16 B4
Broadhaugh Borders 115 D7
Broadhaven Highld 169 D8
Broadheath Gtr Man 87 F5
Broadhembury Devon 11 D6
Broadhempston Devon 7 C6
Broadholme Derbys 76 E3
Broadholme Lincs 77 B8
Broadland Row E Sus 18 D5
Broadlay Carms 32 D4
Broadley Lancs 87 C6
Broadley Moray 159 C7
Broadley Common Essex 41 D7
Broadmayne Dorset 12 F5
Broadmeadows Borders 123 F7
Broadmere Hants 26 E4
Broadmoor Pembs 32 D1
Broadoak Kent 31 C5
Broadrashes Moray 159 D8
Broadsea Aberds 161 B6
Broadstairs Kent 31 C7
Broadstone Poole 13 E8
Broadstone Shrops 60 F5
Broadtown Lane Wilts 25 B5
Broadview Gardens, Hadlow Kent 29 E7
Broadwas Worcs 50 D2
Broadwater Herts 41 B5
Broadwater W Sus 17 D5
Broadway Carms 32 D3
Broadway Pembs 44 D3
Broadway Som 11 C8
Broadway Suff 57 B7
Broadway Worcs 51 F5
Broadwell Glos 38 B2
Broadwell Glos 36 C2
Broadwell Oxon 38 D2
Broadwell Warks 52 C2
Broadwell House Northumb 110 D2
Broadwey Dorset 12 F4
Broadwindsor Dorset 12 D2
Broadwood Kelly Devon 9 D8
Broadwoodwidger Devon 9 F6
Brobury Hereford 48 E5
Brochel Highld 152 E6
Brochloch Dumfries 113 E5
Brochroy Argyll 131 B6
Brockamin Worcs 50 D2
Brockbridge Hants 15 C7
Brockdam Northumb 117 B7
Brockdish Norf 57 B6
Brockenhurst Hants 14 D4
Brocketsbrae S Lnrk 121 F8
Brockford Street Suff 56 C5
Brockhall Northants 52 C4
Brockham Sur 28 E2
Brockhampton Glos 37 B7
Brockhampton Hereford 49 F7
Brockhole -National Park Visitor Centre, Windermere Cumb 99 D5
Brockholes W Yorks 88 C2
Brockhurst Derbys 76 C3
Brockhurst Hants 15 D7
Brocklebank Cumb 108 E3
Brocklesby Lincs 90 C5
Brockley N Som 23 C6
Brockley Green Suff 56 D2
Brockleymoor Cumb 108 F4
Brockton Shrops 60 F3
Brockton Shrops 61 E5
Brockton Shrops 60 D3
Brockton Shrops 61 D7
Brockton Telford 61 C7
Brockweir Glos 36 D2
Brockwood Hants 15 B7
Brockworth Glos 37 C5
Brocton Staffs 62 C3
Brodick N Ayrs 119 C7
Brodick Castle N Ayrs 119 C7
Brodsworth S Yorks 89 D6
Brogaig Highld 152 C5
Brogborough Beds 53 F7
Broken Cross Ches 74 B3
Broken Cross Ches 75 B5
Brokenborough Wilts 37 F6
Bromborough Mers 85 F4
Brome Suff 56 B5
Brome Street Suff 57 B5
Bromeswell Suff 57 D7
Bromfield Cumb 107 E8
Bromfield Shrops 49 B6
Bromham Beds 53 D8
Bromham Wilts 24 C4
Bromley London 28 C5
Bromley W Mid 62 F3
Bromley Common London 28 C5
Bromley Green Kent 19 B6
Brompton Medway 29 C8
Brompton N Yorks 102 E1
Brompton N Yorks 103 F7
Brompton-on-Swale N Yorks 101 E7
Brompton Ralph Som 22 F2
Brompton Regis Som 21 F8
Bromsash Hereford 36 B3
Bromsberrow Heath Glos 50 F2
Bromsgrove Worcs 50 B4
Bromyard Hereford 49 D8
Bromyard Downs Hereford 49 D8
Bronaber Gwyn 71 D8
Brongest Ceredig 46 E2
Bronington Wrex 73 F8
Bronllys Powys 48 F3
Bronnant Ceredig 46 C5
Bronte Parsonage Museum, Keighley W Yorks 94 F3
Bronwydd Arms Carms 33 B5
Bronydd Powys 48 E4
Bronygarth Shrops 73 F6
Brook Carms 32 D3
Brook Hants 14 C3
Brook Hants 14 B4
Brook I o W 14 F4
Brook Kent 30 E4
Brook Sur 27 F7
Brook Sur 27 E8
Brook End Beds 53 C8
Brook Hill Hants 14 C3
Brook Street Kent 29 E6
Brook Street Kent 19 B6
Brook Street W Sus 17 B7
Brooke Norf 69 E5
Brooke Rutland 64 D5
Brookenby Lincs 91 E6
Brookend Glos 36 E2
Brookfield Renfs 120 C4
Brookhouse Lancs 92 C5
Brookhouse Green Ches 74 C5
Brookland Kent 19 C6
Brooklands Dumfries 106 B5
Brooklands Gtr Man 87 E5
Brooklands Shrops 74 E2
Brookmans Park Herts 41 D5
Brooks Powys 59 E8
Brooks Green W Sus 16 B5
Brookthorpe Glos 37 C5
Brookville Norf 67 E7
Brookwood Sur 27 D7
Broom Beds 54 E2
Broom S Yorks 88 E5
Broom Warks 51 D5
Broom Worcs 50 B4
Broom Green Norf 81 E5
Broom Hill Dorset 13 D8
Broome Norf 69 E6
Broome Shrops 60 F4
Broome Park Northumb 117 C7
Broomedge Warr 86 F5
Broomer's Corner W Sus 16 B5
Broomfield Aberds 161 E6
Broomfield Essex 42 C3
Broomfield Kent 30 D2
Broomfield Kent 31 C5
Broomfield Som 22 F4
Broomfleet E Yorks 90 B2
Broomhall Ches 74 E3
Broomhall Windsor 27 C7
Broomhaugh Northumb 110 C3
Broomhill Norf 67 D6
Broomhill Northumb 117 D8
Broomhill S Yorks 88 D5
Broomholm Norf 81 D9
Broomley Northumb 110 C3
Broompark Durham 110 E5
Broom's Green Hereford 50 F2
Broomy Lodge Hants 14 C3
Brora Highld 165 D6
Broseley Shrops 61 D6
Brotherhouse Bar Lincs 66 C2
Brotherstone Borders 124 F2
Brothertoft Lincs 79 E5
Brotherton N Yorks 89 B5
Brotton Redcar 102 C4
Broubster Highld 168 C5
Brough Cumb 100 C2
Brough Derbys 88 F2
Brough E Yorks 90 B3
Brough Highld 169 B7
Brough Notts 77 D8
Brough Orkney 176 E2
Brough Shetland 174 F6
Brough Shetland 174 G7
Brough Shetland 174 F7
Brough Shetland 175 J7
Brough Shetland 175 H6
Brough Lodge Shetland 174 D7
Brough Sowerby Cumb 100 C2
Broughall Shrops 74 E2
Broughton Borders 122 F4
Broughton Cambs 54 B3
Broughton Flint 73 C7
Broughton Hants 25 F8
Broughton Lancs 92 F5
Broughton M Keynes 53 E6
Broughton N Lincs 90 D3
Broughton Northants 53 B6
Broughton N Yorks 94 D2
Broughton N Yorks 96 B3
Broughton Orkney 176 B3
Broughton Oxon 52 F2
Broughton V Glam 21 B8
Broughton Astley Leics 64 E2
Broughton Beck Cumb 98 F4
Broughton Common Wilts 24 C3
Broughton Gifford Wilts 24 C3
Broughton Hackett Worcs 50 D4
Broughton in Furness Cumb 98 F4
Broughton Mills Cumb 98 E4
Broughton Moor Cumb 107 F7
Broughton Park Gtr Man 87 D6
Broughton Poggs Oxon 38 D2
Broughtown Orkney 176 B5
Broughty Ferry Dundee 142 F4
Browhouses Dumfries 108 C2
Browland Shetland 175 H4
Brown Candover Hants 26 F3
Brown Edge Lancs 85 C4
Brown Edge Staffs 75 D6
Brown Heath Ches 73 C8
Brownhill Aberds 161 D5
Brownhill Aberds 160 D3
Brownhill Blkburn 93 F6
Brownhill Shrops 60 B4
Brownhills Fife 135 C7
Brownhills W Mid 62 D4
Brownlow Ches 74 C5
Brownlow Heath Ches 74 C5
Brownmuir Aberds 143 B7
Brown's End Glos 50 F2
Brownshill Glos 37 D5
Brownston Devon 6 D4
Brownyside Northumb 117 B7
Broxa N Yorks 103 E7
Broxbourne Herts 41 D6
Broxburn E Loth 124 B2
Broxburn W Loth 122 B3
Broxholme Lincs 78 B2
Broxted Essex 42 B1
Broxton Ches 73 D8
Broxwood Hereford 49 D5
Broyle Side E Sus 17 C8
Brù W Isles 172 D6
Bruairnis W Isles 171 K3
Bruan Highld 169 F8
Bruar Lodge Perth 141 B5
Brucehill W Dunb 120 B3
Bruera Ches 73 C8
Bruern Abbey Oxon 38 B2
Bruichladdich Argyll 126 C2
Bruisyard Suff 57 C7
Brumby N Lincs 90 D2
Brund Staffs 75 C8
Brundall Norf 69 D6
Brundish Suff 57 C6
Brundish Street Suff 57 B6
Brunery Highld 145 F7
Brunshaw Lancs 93 F8
Brunswick Village T & W 110 B5
Bruntcliffe W Yorks 88 B3
Bruntingthorpe Leics 64 E3
Brunton Fife 134 B5
Brunton Northumb 117 B8
Brunton Wilts 25 D7
Brushford Devon 9 D8
Brushford Som 10 B4
Bruton Som 23 F8
Bryanston Dorset 13 D6
Brydekirk Dumfries 107 B8
Bryher Scilly 2 E3
Brymbo Wrex 73 D6
Brympton Som 12 C3
Bryn Carms 33 D6
Bryn Gtr Man 86 D3
Bryn Neath 34 E2
Bryn Shrops 60 F2
Bryn-coch Neath 33 E8
Bryn Du Anglesey 82 D3
Bryn Gates Gtr Man 86 D3
Bryn-glas Conwy 83 E8
Bryn Golau Rhondda 34 F3
Bryn-Iwan Carms 46 F2
Bryn-mawr Gwyn 70 D3
Bryn-nantllech Conwy 72 C3
Bryn-penarth Powys 59 D8
Bryn Rhyd-yr-Arian Conwy 72 C3
Bryn Saith Marchog Denb 72 D4
Bryn Sion Gwyn 59 C5
Bryn-y-gwenin Mon 35 C7
Bryn-y-maen Conwy 83 D8
Bryn-yr-eryr Gwyn 70 C4
Brynamman Carms 33 C8
Brynberian Pembs 45 F3
Brynbryddan Neath 34 E1
Brynbuga = Usk Mon 35 D7
Bryncae Rhondda 34 F3
Bryncethin Bridgend 34 F3
Bryncir Gwyn 71 C5
Bryncroes Gwyn 70 D3
Bryncrug Gwyn 58 D3
Bryneglwys Denb 72 E5
Brynford Flint 73 B5
Bryngwran Anglesey 82 D3
Bryngwyn Ceredig 45 E4
Bryngwyn Mon 35 D7
Bryngwyn Powys 48 E3
Brynhenllan Pembs 45 F2
Brynhoffnant Ceredig 46 D2
Brynithel Bl Gwent 35 D6
Brynmawr Bl Gwent 35 C5
Brynmenyn Bridgend 34 F3
Brynmill Swansea 33 E7
Brynna Rhondda 34 F3
Brynrefail Anglesey 82 C4
Brynrefail Gwyn 83 E5
Brynsadler Rhondda 34 F4
Brynsiencyn Anglesey 82 E4
Brynteg Anglesey 82 C4
Brynteg Ceredig 46 E3
Buaile nam Bodach W Isles 171 K3
Bualintur Highld 153 G5
Buarthmeini Gwyn 72 F2
Bubbenhall Warks 51 B8
Bubwith E Yorks 96 F3
Buccleuch Borders 115 C6
Buchanhaven Aberds 161 D8
Buchanty Perth 133 B8
Buchlyvie Stirl 132 E4
Buckabank Cumb 108 E3
Buckden Cambs 54 C2
Buckden N Yorks 94 B2
Buckenham Norf 69 D6
Buckerell Devon 11 D6
Buckfast Devon 6 C5
Buckfast Abbey, Buckfastleigh Devon 6 C5
Buckfastleigh Devon 6 C5
Buckhaven Fife 135 E5
Buckholm Borders 123 F7
Buckholt Mon 36 C2
Buckhorn Weston Dorset 13 B5
Buckhurst Hill Essex 41 E7
Buckie Moray 159 C8
Buckies Highld 169 C6
Buckingham Bucks 52 F4
Buckingham Palace London 28 B3
Buckland Bucks 40 C1
Buckland Devon 6 E4
Buckland Glos 51 F5
Buckland Hants 14 E4
Buckland Herts 54 F4
Buckland Kent 31 E7
Buckland Oxon 38 E3
Buckland Sur 28 D3
Buckland Abbey Devon 6 C2
Buckland Brewer Devon 9 B6
Buckland Common Bucks 40 D2
Buckland Dinham Som 24 D2
Buckland Filleigh Devon 9 D6
Buckland in the Moor Devon 6 B5
Buckland Monachorum Devon 6 C2
Buckland Newton Dorset 12 D4
Buckland St Mary Som 11 C7
Bucklebury W Berks 26 B3
Bucklegate Lincs 79 F6
Bucklerheads Angus 142 F4
Bucklers Hard Hants 14 E5
Bucklesham Suff 57 E6
Buckley = Bwcle Flint 73 C6
Bucklow Hill Ches 86 F5
Buckminster Leics 65 B5
Bucknall Lincs 78 C4
Bucknall Stoke 75 E6
Bucknell Oxon 39 B5
Bucknell Shrops 49 B5
Buckpool Moray 159 C8
Buck's Cross Devon 8 B5
Bucks Green W Sus 27 F8
Bucks Horn Oak Hants 27 E6
Buck's Mills Devon 9 B5
Bucksburn Aberdeen 151 D7
Buckskin Hants 26 D4
Buckton E Yorks 97 B7
Buckton Hereford 49 B5
Buckton Northumb 125 F6
Buckworth Cambs 54 B2
Budbrooke Warks 51 C7
Budby Notts 77 C6
Budd's Titson Corn 8 D4
Bude Corn 8 D4
Budlake Devon 10 E4
Budle Northumb 125 F7
Budleigh Salterton Devon 11 F5
Budock Water Corn 3 C6
Buerton Ches 74 E3
Buffler's Holt Bucks 52 F4
Bugbrooke Northants 52 D4
Buglawton Ches 75 C5
Bugle Corn 4 D5
Bugley Wilts 24 E3
Bugthorpe E Yorks 96 D3
Buildwas Shrops 61 D6
Builth Road Powys 48 D2
Builth Wells = Llanfair-ym-Muallt Powys 48 D2
Buirgh W Isles 173 J3
Bulby Lincs 65 B7
Bulcote Notts 77 E6
Buldoo Highld 168 C4
Bulford Wilts 25 E6
Bulford Camp Wilts 25 E6
Bulkeley Ches 74 D2
Bulkington Warks 63 F7
Bulkington Wilts 24 D4
Bulkworthy Devon 9 C5
Bull Hill Hants 14 E4
Bullamoor N Yorks 102 E1
Bullbridge Derbys 76 D3
Bullbrook Brack 27 C6
Bulley Glos 36 C4
Bullgill Cumb 107 F7
Bullington Hants 26 E2
Bullington Lincs 78 B3
Bull's Green Herts 41 C5
Bullwood Argyll 129 C6
Bulmer Essex 56 E2
Bulmer N Yorks 96 C2
Bulmer Tye Essex 56 F2
Bulphan Thurrock 42 F2
Bulverhythe E Sus 18 E4
Bulwark Aberds 161 D6
Bulwell Nottingham 76 E5
Bulwick Northants 65 E6
Bumble's Green Essex 41 D7
Bun Abhainn Eadarra W Isles 173 H4
Bun a'Mhuillin W Isles 171 J3
Bun Loyne Highld 146 D5
Bunacaimb Highld 145 E6
Bunarkaig Highld 146 F4
Bunbury Ches 74 D2
Bunbury Heath Ches 74 D2
Bunchrew Highld 157 E7
Bundalloch Highld 155 H4
Buness Shetland 174 C8
Bunessan Argyll 136 F4
Bungay Suff 69 F6
Bunker's Hill Lincs 78 B2
Bunker's Hill Lincs 79 D5
Bunkers Hill Oxon 38 C4
Bunloit Highld 147 B8
Bunnahabhain Argyll 126 B4
Bunny Notts 64 B2
Buntait Highld 156 F4
Buntingford Herts 41 B6
Bunwell Norf 68 E4
Burbage Derbys 75 B7
Burbage Leics 63 E8
Burbage Wilts 25 C7
Burchett's Green Windsor 39 F8
Burcombe Wilts 25 F5
Burcot Oxon 39 E5
Burcott Bucks 40 B1
Burdon T & W 111 D6
Bures Suff 56 F3
Bures Green Suff 56 F3
Burford Ches 74 D3
Burford Oxon 38 C2
Burford Shrops 49 C7
Burg Argyll 136 D4
Burgar Orkney 176 D2
Burgate Hants 14 C2
Burgate Suff 56 B4
Burgess Hill W Sus 17 C7
Burgh Suff 57 D6
Burgh-by-Sands Cumb 108 D3
Burgh Castle Norf 69 D7
Burgh Heath Sur 28 D3
Burgh le Marsh Lincs 79 C8
Burgh Muir Aberds 151 B6
Burgh next Aylsham Norf 81 E8
Burgh on Bain Lincs 91 F6
Burgh St Margaret Norf 69 C7
Burgh St Peter Norf 69 E7
Burghclere Hants 26 C2
Burghead Moray 158 C5
Burghfield W Berks 26 C4
Burghfield Common W Berks 26 C4
Burghfield Hill W Berks 26 C4
Burghill Hereford 49 E6
Burghwallis S Yorks 89 C6
Burham Kent 29 C8
Buriton Hants 15 B8
Burland Ches 74 D3
Burlawn Corn 4 B4
Burleigh Brack 27 C6
Burlescombe Devon 11 C5
Burleston Dorset 13 E5
Burley Hants 14 D3
Burley Rutland 65 C5
Burley W Yorks 95 F5
Burley Gate Hereford 49 E7
Burley in Wharfedale W Yorks 94 E4
Burley Lodge Hants 14 D3
Burley Street Hants 14 D3
Burleydam Ches 74 E3
Burlingjobb Powys 48 D4
Burlow E Sus 18 D2
Burlton Shrops 60 B4
Burmarsh Kent 19 B7
Burmington Warks 51 F7
Burn N Yorks 89 B6
Burn of Cambus Stirl 133 D6
Burnaston Derbys 76 F2
Burnbank S Lnrk 121 D7
Burnby E Yorks 96 E4
Burncross S Yorks 88 E4
Burneside Cumb 99 E7
Burness Orkney 176 B5
Burneston N Yorks 101 F8
Burnett Bath 23 C8
Burnfoot Borders 115 C7
Burnfoot Borders 115 C8
Burnfoot E Ayrs 112 D4
Burnfoot Perth 133 D8

Burnham Bucks 40 F2
Burnham N Lincs 90 C4
Burnham Deepdale Norf 80 C4
Burnham Green Herts 41 C5
Burnham Market Norf 80 C4
Burnham Norton Norf 80 C4
Burnham-on-Crouch Essex 43 E5
Burnham-on-Sea Som 22 E5
Burnham Overy Staithe Norf 80 C4
Burnham Overy Town Norf 80 C4
Burnham Thorpe Norf 80 C4
Burnhead Dumfries 113 E8
Burnhead S Ayrs 112 D2
Burnhervie Aberds 151 C6
Burnhill Green Staffs 61 D7
Burnhope Durham 110 E4
Burnhouse N Ayrs 120 D3
Burniston N Yorks 103 E8
Burnlee W Yorks 88 D2
Burnley Lancs 93 F8
Burnley Lane Lancs 93 F8
Burnmouth Borders 125 C5
Burnopfield Durham 110 D4
Burnsall N Yorks 94 C3
Burnside Angus 143 D5
Burnside E Ayrs 113 C5
Burnside Fife 134 D3
Burnside Shetland 174 F4
Burnside S Lnrk 121 C6
Burnside W Loth 122 B3
Burnside of Duntrune Angus 142 F4
Burnswark Dumfries 107 B8
Burnt Heath Derbys 76 B2
Burnt Houses Durham 101 B6
Burnt Yates N Yorks 95 C5
Burntcommon Sur 27 D8
Burnthouse Corn 3 C6
Burntisland Fife 134 F4
Burnton E Ayrs 112 D4
Burntwood Staffs 62 D4
Burnwynd Edin 122 C4
Burpham Sur 27 D8
Burpham W Sus 16 D4
Burradon Northumb 117 D5
Burradon T & W 111 B5
Burrafirth Shetland 174 B8
Burraland Shetland 174 F5
Burraland Shetland 175 J4
Burras Corn 3 C5
Burravoe Shetland 174 G5
Burravoe Shetland 174 F7
Burray Village Orkney 176 G3
Burrells Cumb 100 C1
Burrelton Perth 142 F2
Burridge Devon 20 F4
Burridge Hants 15 C6
Burrill N Yorks 101 F7
Burringham N Lincs 90 D2
Burrington Devon 9 C8
Burrington Hereford 49 B6
Burrington N Som 23 D6
Burrough Green Cambs 55 D7
Burrough on the Hill Leics 64 C4
Burrow-bridge Som 11 B8
Burrowhill Sur 27 C7
Burry Swansea 33 E5
Burry Green Swansea 33 E5
Burry Port = Porth Tywyn Carms 33 D5
Burscough Lancs 86 C2
Burscough Bridge Lancs 86 C2
Bursea E Yorks 96 F4
Burshill E Yorks 97 E6
Bursledon Hants 15 D5
Burslem Stoke 75 E5
Burstall Suff 56 E4
Burstock Dorset 12 D2
Burston Norf 68 F4
Burston Staffs 75 F6
Burstow Sur 28 E4
Burstwick E Yorks 91 B6
Burtersett N Yorks 100 F3
Burtle Som 23 E5
Burton Ches 73 B7
Burton Ches 74 C2
Burton Dorset 14 E2
Burton Lincs 78 B2
Burton Northumb 125 F7
Burton Pembs 44 E4
Burton Som 22 E3
Burton Wilts 24 B3
Burton Agnes E Yorks 97 C7
Burton Bradstock Dorset 12 F2
Burton Dassett Warks 51 D8
Burton Fleming E Yorks 97 B6
Burton Green W Mid 51 B7
Burton Green Wrex 73 D7
Burton Hastings Warks 63 E8
Burton-in-Kendal Cumb 92 B5
Burton in Lonsdale N Yorks 93 B6
Burton Joyce Notts 77 E6
Burton Latimer Northants 53 B7
Burton Lazars Leics 64 C4
Burton-le-Coggles Lincs 65 B6
Burton Leonard N Yorks 95 C6
Burton on the Wolds Leics 64 B2
Burton Overy Leics 64 E3
Burton Pedwardine Lincs 78 E4
Burton Pidsea E Yorks 97 F8
Burton Salmon N Yorks 89 B5
Burton Stather N Lincs 90 C2
Burton upon Stather N Lincs 90 C2
Burton upon Trent Staffs 63 B6
Burtonwood Warr 86 E3
Burwardsley Ches 74 D2
Burwarton Shrops 61 F6
Burwash E Sus 18 C3
Burwash Common E Sus 18 C3
Burwash Weald E Sus 18 C3
Burwell Cambs 55 C6
Burwell Lincs 79 B6
Burwen Anglesey 82 B4
Burwick Orkney 176 H3
Bury Cambs 66 F2
Bury Gtr Man 87 C6
Bury Som 10 B4
Bury W Sus 16 C4
Bury Green Herts 41 B7
Bury St Edmunds Suff 56 C2
Burythorpe N Yorks 96 C3
Busby E Renf 121 D5
Buscot Oxon 38 E2
Bush Bank Hereford 49 D6
Bush Crathie Aberds 149 E8
Bush Green Norf 68 F5
Bushbury W Mid 62 D3
Bushby Leics 64 D3
Bushey Herts 40 E4
Bushey Heath Herts 40 E4
Bushley Worcs 50 F3
Bushton Wilts 25 B5
Buslingthorpe Lincs 90 F4
Busta Shetland 174 G5
Butcher's Cross E Sus 18 C2
Butcher's Pasture Essex 42 B2
Butcombe N Som 23 C7
Butetown Cardiff 22 B3
Butleigh Som 23 F7
Butleigh Wootton Som 23 F7
Butler's Cross Bucks 39 D8
Butler's End Warks 63 F6
Butlers Marston Warks 51 E8
Butley Suff 57 D7
Butley High Corner Suff 57 E7
Butt Green Ches 74 D3
Butterburn Cumb 109 B6
Buttercrambe N Yorks 96 D3
Butterknowle Durham 101 B6
Butterleigh Devon 10 D4
Buttermere Cumb 98 C3
Buttermere Wilts 25 C8
Buttershaw W Yorks 88 B2
Butterstone Perth 141 E7
Butterton Staffs 75 D7
Butterwick Durham 102 B1
Butterwick Lincs 79 E6
Butterwick N Yorks 96 B3
Butterwick N Yorks 97 B5
Buttington Powys 60 D2
Buttonoak Shrops 50 B2
Butt's Green Hants 14 B4
Buttsash Hants 14 D5
Buxhall Suff 56 D4
Buxhall Fen Street Suff 56 D4
Buxley Borders 124 D4
Buxted E Sus 17 B8
Buxton Derbys 75 B7
Buxton Norf 81 E8
Buxworth Derbys 87 F8
Bwcle = Buckley Flint 73 C6
Bwlch Powys 35 B5
Bwlch-Llan Ceredig 46 D4
Bwlch-y-cibau Powys 59 C8
Bwlch-y-fadfa Ceredig 46 E3
Bwlch-y-ffridd Powys 59 E7
Bwlch-y-sarnau Powys 48 B2
Bwlchgwyn Wrex 73 D6
Bwlchnewydd Carms 32 B4
Bwlchtocyn Gwyn 70 E4
Bwlchyddar Powys 59 B8
Bwlchygroes Pembs 45 F4
Byermoor T & W 110 D4
Byers Green Durham 110 F5
Byfield Northants 52 D3
Byfleet Sur 27 C8
Byford Hereford 49 E5
Bygrave Herts 54 F3
Byker T & W 111 C5
Bylchau Conwy 72 C3
Byley Ches 74 C4
Bynea Carms 33 E6
Byrness Northumb 116 D3
Bythorn Cambs 53 B8
Byton Hereford 49 C5
Byworth W Sus 16 B3

C

Cabharstadh W Isles 172 F6
Cablea Perth 141 F6
Cabourne Lincs 90 D5
Cabrach Argyll 127 F2
Cabrach Moray 150 B2
Cabrich Highld 157 E6
Cabus Lancs 92 E4
Cackle Street E Sus 17 B8
Cadbury Devon 10 D4
Cadbury Barton Devon 9 C8
Cadbury World, Bournville W Mid 62 F4
Cadder E Dunb 121 B6
Caddington Beds 40 C3
Caddonfoot Borders 123 F7
Cade Street E Sus 18 C3
Cadeby Leics 63 D8
Cadeby S Yorks 89 D6
Cadeleigh Devon 10 D4
Cadgwith Corn 3 E6
Cadham Fife 134 D4
Cadishead Gtr Man 86 E5
Cadle Swansea 33 E7
Cadley Lancs 92 F5
Cadley Wilts 25 D7
Cadley Wilts 25 C7
Cadmore End Bucks 39 E7
Cadnam Hants 14 C3
Cadney N Lincs 90 D4
Cadole Flint 73 C6
Cadoxton V Glam 22 C3
Cadoxton-Juxta-Neath Neath 34 E1
Cadshaw Blkburn 86 C5
Cadwell Park Motor Racing Circuit Lincs 91 F6
Cadzow S Lnrk 121 D7
Caeathro Gwyn 82 E4
Caehopkin Powys 34 C2
Caenby Lincs 90 F4
Caenby Corner Lincs 90 F3
Cae'r-bryn Carms 33 C6
Caer Llan Mon 36 D1
Caerau Bridgend 34 E2
Caerau Cardiff 22 B3
Caerdeon Gwyn 58 C3
Caerdydd = Cardiff Cardiff 22 B3
Caerfarchell Pembs 44 C2
Caerffili = Caerphilly Caerph 35 F5
Caerfyrddin = Carmarthen Carms 33 B5
Caergeiliog Anglesey 82 D3
Caergwrle Flint 73 D7
Caergybi = Holyhead Anglesey 82 C2
Caerleon = Caerllion Newport 35 E7
Caerllion = Caerleon Newport 35 E7
Caernarfon Gwyn 82 E4
Caernarfon Castle Gwyn 82 E4
Caerphilly = Caerffili Caerph 35 F5
Caersws Powys 59 E7
Caerwedros Ceredig 46 D2
Caerwent Mon 36 E1
Caerwych Gwyn 71 D7
Caerwys Flint 72 B5
Caethle Gwyn 58 E3
Caim Anglesey 83 C6
Caio Carms 47 F5
Cairinis W Isles 170 D4
Cairisiadar W Isles 172 E3
Cairminis W Isles 173 K3
Cairnbaan Argyll 128 A3
Cairnbanno Ho. Aberds 160 D5
Cairnborrow Aberds 159 E8
Cairnbrogie Aberds 151 B7
Cairnbulg Castle Aberds 161 B7
Cairncross Angus 142 B4
Cairncross Borders 124 C4
Cairndow Argyll 131 D7
Cairness Aberds 161 B7
Cairneyhill Fife 134 F2
Cairnfield Ho. Moray 159 C8
Cairngaan Dumfries 104 F5
Cairngarroch Dumfries 104 E4
Cairnhill Aberds 160 E3
Cairnie Aberds 159 E8
Cairnie Aberds 151 D7
Cairnorrie Aberds 161 D5
Cairnpark Aberds 151 C7
Cairnryan Dumfries 104 C4
Cairnton Orkney 176 F2
Caister-on-Sea Norf 69 C8
Caistor Lincs 90 D5
Caistor St Edmund Norf 68 D5
Caistron Northumb 117 D5
Caitha Bowland Borders 123 E7
Caithness Glass, Perth Perth 134 B2
Calais Street Suff 56 F3
Calanais W Isles 172 E5
Calbost W Isles 172 G7
Calbourne I o W 14 F5
Calceby Lincs 79 B6
Calcot Row W Berks 26 B4
Calcott Kent 31 C5
Caldback Shetland 174 C8
Caldbeck Cumb 108 F3
Caldbergh N Yorks 101 F5
Caldecote Cambs 54 D4
Caldecote Cambs 65 F8
Caldecote Herts 54 F3
Caldecote Northants 52 D4
Caldecott Northants 53 C7
Caldecott Oxon 38 E4
Caldecott Rutland 65 E5
Calder Bridge Cumb 98 D2
Calder Hall Cumb 98 D2
Calder Mains Highld 169 D5
Calder Vale Lancs 92 E5
Calderbank N Lnrk 121 C7
Calderbrook Gtr Man 87 C7
Caldercruix N Lnrk 121 C8
Caldermill S Lnrk 121 E6
Calderwood S Lnrk 121 D6
Caldhame Angus 142 E4
Caldicot Mon 36 F1
Caldwell Derbys 63 C6
Caldwell N Yorks 101 C6
Caldy Mers 85 F3
Caledrhydiau Ceredig 46 D3
Calfsound Orkney 176 C4
Calgary Argyll 136 C4
Califer Moray 158 D4
California Falk 122 B2
California Norf 69 C8
Calke Derbys 63 B7
Callakille Highld 155 E2
Callaly Northumb 117 D6
Callander Stirl 132 D5
Callaughton Shrops 61 E6
Callestick Corn 4 D2
Calligarry Highld 145 C6
Callington Corn 5 C8
Callow Hereford 49 F6
Callow End Worcs 50 E3
Callow Hill Wilts 37 F7
Callow Hill Worcs 50 B2
Callows Grave Worcs 49 C7
Calmore Hants 14 C4
Calmsden Glos 37 D7
Calne Wilts 24 B5
Calow Derbys 76 B4
Calshot Hants 15 D5
Calstock Corn 6 C2
Calstone Wellington Wilts 24 C5
Calthorpe Norf 81 D7
Calthwaite Cumb 108 E4
Calton N Yorks 94 D2
Calton Staffs 75 D8
Calveley Ches 74 D2
Calver Derbys 76 B2
Calver Hill Hereford 49 E5
Calverhall Shrops 74 F3
Calverleigh Devon 10 C4
Calverley W Yorks 94 F5
Calvert Bucks 39 B6
Calverton M Keynes 53 F5
Calverton Notts 77 E6
Calvine Perth 141 C5
Calvo Cumb 107 D8
Cam Glos 36 E4
Camas-luinie Highld 146 B2
Camasnacroise Highld 138 D2
Camastianavaig Highld 153 F6
Camasunary Highld 153 H6
Camault Muir Highld 157 E6
Camb Shetland 174 D7
Camber E Sus 19 D6
Camberley Sur 27 C6
Camberwell London 28 B4
Camblesforth N Yorks 89 B7
Cambo Northumb 117 F6
Cambois Northumb 117 F9
Camborne Corn 3 B5
Cambourne Cambs 54 D4
Cambridge Cambs 55 D5
Cambridge Glos 36 D4
Cambridge Airport Cambs 55 D5
Cambridge Town Sthend 43 F5
Cambus Clack 133 E7
Cambusavie Farm Highld 164 E4
Cambusbarron Stirl 133 E6
Cambuskenneth Stirl 133 E7
Cambuslang S Lnrk 121 C6
Cambusmore Lodge Highld 164 E4
Camden London 41 F5
Camelford Corn 8 F3
Camelot Theme Park, Chorley Lancs 86 C3
Camelsdale W Sus 27 F6
Camerory Highld 158 F4
Camer's Green Worcs 50 F2
Camerton Bath 23 D8
Camerton Cumb 107 F7
Camerton E Yorks 91 B6
Camghouran Perth 140 D2
Cammachmore Aberds 151 E8
Cammeringham Lincs 90 F3
Camore Highld 164 E4
Camp Hill Warks 63 E7
Campbeltown Argyll 118 D4
Campbeltown Airport Argyll 118 D3
Camperdown T & W 111 B5
Campmuir Perth 142 F2
Campsall S Yorks 89 C6
Campsey Ash Suff 57 D7
Campton Beds 54 F2
Camptown Borders 116 C2
Camrose Pembs 44 C4
Camserney Perth 141 E5
Camster Highld 169 E7
Camuschoirk Highld 138 C1
Camuscross Highld 145 B6
Camusnagaul Highld 138 B4
Camusnagaul Highld 162 F4
Camusrory Highld 145 D8
Camusteel Highld 155 F3
Camusterrach Highld 155 F3
Camusvrachan Perth 140 E3
Canada Hants 14 C3
Canadia E Sus 18 D4
Canal Side S Yorks 89 C7
Candacraig Ho. Aberds 150 C2
Candlesby Lincs 79 C7
Candy Mill S Lnrk 122 E3
Cane End Oxon 26 B4
Canewdon Essex 42 E4
Canford Bottom Dorset 13 D8
Canford Cliffs Poole 13 F8
Canford Magna Poole 13 E8
Canham's Green Suff 56 C4
Canholes Derbys 75 B7
Canisbay Highld 169 B8
Cann Dorset 13 B6
Cann Common Dorset 13 B6
Cannard's Grave Som 23 E8
Cannich Highld 156 F4
Cannington Som 22 F4
Cannock Staffs 62 D3
Cannock Wood Staffs 62 C4
Canon Bridge Hereford 49 E6
Canon Frome Hereford 49 E8
Canon Pyon Hereford 49 E6
Canonbie Dumfries 108 B3
Canons Ashby Northants 52 D3
Canonstown Corn 2 C4
Canterbury Kent 30 D5
Canterbury Cathedral Kent 30 D5
Canterbury Tales Kent 30 D5
Cantley Norf 69 D6
Cantley S Yorks 89 D7
Cantlop Shrops 60 D5
Canton Cardiff 22 B3
Cantraybruich Highld 157 E8
Cantraydoune Highld 157 E8
Cantraywood Highld 157 E8
Cantsfield Lancs 93 B6
Canvey Island Essex 42 F3
Canwick Lincs 78 C2
Canworthy Water Corn 8 E4
Caol Highld 139 B5
Caol Ila Argyll 126 B4
Caolas Argyll 136 F2
Caolas Scalpaigh W Isles 173 J5
Caolas Stocinis W Isles 173 J4
Capel Sur 28 E2
Capel Bangor Ceredig 58 F3
Capel Betws Lleucu Ceredig 46 D5
Capel Carmel Gwyn 70 E2
Capel Coch Anglesey 82 C4
Capel Curig Conwy 83 F7
Capel Cynon Ceredig 46 E2
Capel Dewi Ceredig 46 E3
Capel Dewi Ceredig 58 F3
Capel Dewi Carms 33 B5
Capel Garmon Conwy 83 F8
Capel-gwyn Anglesey 82 D3
Capel Gwyn Carms 33 B5
Capel Gwynfe Carms 33 B8
Capel Hendre Carms 33 C6
Capel Hermon Gwyn 71 E8
Capel Isaac Carms 33 B6
Capel Iwan Carms 45 F4
Capel le Ferne Kent 31 F6
Capel Llanilltern Cardiff 34 F4
Capel Mawr Anglesey 82 D4
Capel St Andrew Suff 57 E7
Capel St Mary Suff 56 F4
Capel Seion Ceredig 46 B5
Capel Tygwydd Ceredig 45 E4
Capel Uchaf Gwyn 70 C5
Capel-y-graig Gwyn 82 E5
Capelulo Conwy 83 D7
Capenhurst Ches 73 B7
Capernwray Lancs 92 B5
Capheaton Northumb 117 F6
Cappercleuch Borders 115 B5
Capplegill Dumfries 114 D4
Capton Devon 7 D6
Caputh Perth 141 F7
Car Colston Notts 77 E7
Carbis Bay Corn 2 C4
Carbost Highld 153 F4
Carbost Highld 152 E5
Carbrook S Yorks 88 F4
Carbrooke Norf 68 D2
Carburton Notts 77 B6
Carcant Borders 123 D6
Carcary Angus 143 D6
Carclaze Corn 4 D5
Carcroft S Yorks 89 C6
Cardenden Fife 134 E4
Cardeston Shrops 60 C3
Cardiff = Caerdydd Cardiff 22 B3
Cardiff Bay Barrage Cardiff 22 B3
Cardiff Castle Cardiff 22 B3
Cardiff International Airport V Glam 22 C2
Cardigan = Aberteifi Ceredig 45 E3
Cardington Beds 53 E8
Cardington Shrops 60 E5
Cardinham Corn 5 C6
Cardonald Glasgow 120 C5
Cardow Moray 159 E5
Cardrona Borders 123 F6
Cardross Argyll 120 B3
Cardurnock Cumb 107 D8
Careby Lincs 65 C7
Careston Castle Angus 143 D5
Carew Pembs 32 D1
Carew Cheriton Pembs 32 D1
Carew Newton Pembs 32 D1
Carey Hereford 49 F7
Carfrae E Loth 123 C8
Cargenbridge Dumfries 107 B6
Cargill Perth 142 F1
Cargo Cumb 108 D3
Cargreen Corn 6 C2
Carham Northumb 124 F4
Carhampton Som 22 E2
Carharrack Corn 3 B6
Carie Perth 140 F3
Carie Perth 140 D3
Carines Corn 4 D2
Carisbrooke I o W 15 F5
Carisbrooke Castle I o W 15 F5
Cark Cumb 92 B3
Carlabhagh W Isles 172 D5
Carland Cross Corn 4 D3
Carlby Lincs 65 C7
Carlecotes S Yorks 88 D2
Carlesmoor N Yorks 94 B4
Carleton Cumb 99 B7
Carleton Cumb 108 D4
Carleton Lancs 92 F3
Carleton N Yorks 94 E2
Carleton Forehoe Norf 68 D3
Carleton Rode Norf 68 E4
Carlin How Redcar 103 C5
Carlingcott Bath 23 D8
Carlisle Cumb 108 D4
Carlisle Airport Cumb 108 C4
Carlisle Cathedral Cumb 108 D3
Carlisle Racecourse Cumb 108 D3
Carlops Borders 122 D4
Carlton Beds 53 D7
Carlton Cambs 55 D7
Carlton Leics 63 D7
Carlton Notts 77 E6
Carlton N Yorks 102 F4
Carlton N Yorks 89 B7
Carlton N Yorks 101 F5
Carlton N Yorks 101 C6
Carlton Stockton 102 B1
Carlton Suff 57 C7
Carlton S Yorks 88 C4
Carlton W Yorks 88 B4
Carlton Colville Suff 69 F8
Carlton Curlieu Leics 64 E3
Carlton Husthwaite N Yorks 95 B7
Carlton in Cleveland N Yorks 102 D3
Carlton in Lindrick Notts 89 F6
Carlton le Moorland Lincs 78 D2
Carlton Miniott N Yorks 102 F1
Carlton on Trent Notts 77 C7
Carlton Scroop Lincs 78 E2
Carluke S Lnrk 121 D8
Carmarthen = Caerfyrddin Carms 33 B5
Carmel Anglesey 82 C3
Carmel Carms 33 C6
Carmel Flint 73 B5
Carmel Guern 16
Carmel Gwyn 82 F4
Carmont Aberds 151 F7
Carmunnock Glasgow 121 D6
Carmyle Glasgow 121 C6
Carmyllie Angus 143 E5
Carn-gorm Highld 146 B2
Carnaby E Yorks 97 C7
Carnach Highld 162 E4
Carnach Highld 146 B3
Carnach W Isles 173 J5
Carnachy Highld 168 D2
Càrnais W Isles 172 E3
Carnbee Fife 135 D7
Carnbo Perth 134 D2
Carnbrea Corn 3 B5
Carnduff S Lnrk 121 E6
Carnduncan Argyll 126 C2
Carne Corn 3 C8
Carnforth Lancs 92 B4
Carnhedryn Pembs 44 C3
Carnhell Green Corn 2 C5
Carnkie Corn 3 C6
Carnkie Corn 3 C5
Carno Powys 59 E6
Carnoch Highld 156 F4
Carnoch Highld 156 D3
Carnock Fife 134 F2
Carnon Downs Corn 3 B6
Carnousie Aberds 160 C3
Carnoustie Angus 143 F5
Carnwath S Lnrk 122 E2
Carnyorth Corn 2 C2
Carperby N Yorks 101 F5
Carpley Green N Yorks 100 F4
Carr S Yorks 89 E6
Carr Hill T & W 111 C5
Carradale Argyll 118 C5
Carragraich W Isles 173 J4
Carrbridge Highld 148 B5
Carrefour Selous Jersey 17
Carreg-wen Pembs 45 E4
Carreglefn Anglesey 82 C3
Carrick Argyll 128 B4
Carrick Fife 135 B6
Carrick Castle Argyll 129 A6
Carrick Ho. Orkney 176 C4
Carriden Falk 134 F2
Carrington Gtr Man 86 E5
Carrington Lincs 79 D6
Carrington Midloth 123 C6
Carrog Conwy 71 C8
Carrog Denb 72 E5
Carron Falk 133 F7
Carron Moray 159 E6
Carron Bridge N Lnrk 133 F6
Carronbridge Dumfries 113 E8
Carrshield Northumb 109 E8
Carrutherstown Dumfries 107 B8
Carrville Durham 111 E6
Carsaig Argyll 137 F6
Carsaig Argyll 128 B2
Carscreugh Dumfries 105 D6
Carse Gray Angus 142 D4
Carse Ho. Argyll 128 D2
Carsegowan Dumfries 105 D8
Carseriggan Dumfries 105 C7
Carsethorn Dumfries 107 D6
Carshalton London 28 C3
Carsington Derbys 76 D2
Carskiey Argyll 118 F3
Carsluith Dumfries 105 D8
Carsphairn Dumfries 113 E5
Carstairs S Lnrk 122 E2
Carstairs Junction S Lnrk 122 E2
Carswell Marsh Oxon 38 E3
Carter's Clay Hants 14 B4
Carterton Oxon 38 D2
Carterway Heads Northumb 110 D3
Carthew Corn 4 D5
Carthorpe N Yorks 101 F8
Cartington Northumb 117 D6
Cartland S Lnrk 121 E8
Cartmel Cumb 92 B3
Cartmel Fell Cumb 99 F6
Cartmel Racecourse Cumb 92 B3
Carway Carms 33 D5
Cary Fitzpaine Som 12 B3
Cas-gwent = Chepstow Mon 36 E2
Cascob Powys 48 C4
Cashlie Perth 140 E1
Cashmere Visitor Centre, Elgin Moray 159 E6
Cashmoor Dorset 13 C7
Casnewydd = Newport Newport 35 F7
Cassey Compton Glos 37 C7
Cassington Oxon 38 C4
Cassop Durham 111 F6
Castell Denb 72 C5
Castell Coch Cardiff 35 F5
Castell-Howell Ceredig 46 E3
Castell-Nedd = Neath Neath 33 E8
Castell Newydd Emlyn = Newcastle Emlyn Carms 46 E2
Castell-y-bwch Torf 35 E6
Castellau Rhondda 34 F4
Casterton Cumb 93 B6
Castle Acre Norf 67 C8
Castle Ashby Northants 53 D6
Castle Bolton N Yorks 101 E5
Castle Bromwich W Mid 62 F5
Castle Bytham Lincs 65 C6
Castle Caereinion Powys 59 D8
Castle Camps Cambs 55 E7
Castle Carrock Cumb 108 D5
Castle Cary Som 23 F8
Castle Combe Wilts 24 B3
Castle Combe Motor Racing Circuit Wilts 24 B3
Castle Donington Leics 63 B8
Castle Douglas Dumfries 106 C4
Castle Drogo, Exeter Devon 10 E2
Castle Eaton Swindon 37 E8
Castle Eden Durham 111 F7
Castle Forbes Aberds 150 C5
Castle Frome Hereford 49 E8
Castle Green Sur 27 C7
Castle Gresley Derbys 63 C6
Castle Heaton Northumb 124 E5
Castle Hedingham Essex 55 F8
Castle Hill Kent 29 E7
Castle Howard, Malton N Yorks 96 B3
Castle Huntly Perth 134 B5
Castle Kennedy Dumfries 104 D5
Castle O'er Dumfries 115 E5
Castle Pulverbatch Shrops 60 D4
Castle Rising Norf 67 B6
Castle Stuart Highld 157 E8
Castlebay = Bagh a Chaisteil W Isles 171 L2
Castlebythe Pembs 32 B1
Castlecary N Lnrk 121 B7
Castlecraig Highld 158 C2
Castlefairn Dumfries 113 F7
Castleford W Yorks 88 B5
Castlehill Borders 122 F5
Castlehill Highld 169 C6
Castlehill W Dunb 120 B3
Castlemaddy Dumfries 113 F5
Castlemartin Pembs 44 F4
Castlemilk Dumfries 107 B8
Castlemilk Glasgow 121 D6
Castlemorris Pembs 44 B4
Castlemorton Worcs 50 F2
Castleside Durham 110 E3
Castlethorpe M Keynes 53 E6
Castleton Angus 142 E3
Castleton Argyll 128 B3
Castleton Derbys 88 F2
Castleton Gtr Man 87 C6
Castleton Newport 35 F6
Castleton N Yorks 102 D4
Castletown Ches 73 D8
Castletown Highld 169 C6
Castletown Highld 157 E8
Castletown I o M 84 F2
Castletown T & W 111 D6
Castleweary Borders 115 D7
Castley N Yorks 95 E5
Caston Norf 68 E2
Castor P'boro 65 E8
Catacol N Ayrs 119 B6
Catbrain S Glos 36 F2
Catbrook Mon 36 D2
Catchall Corn 2 D3
Catchems Corner W Mid 51 B7
Catchgate Durham 110 D4
Catcleugh Northumb 116 D3
Catcliffe S Yorks 88 F5
Catcott Som 23 F5
Caterham Sur 28 D4
Catfield Norf 69 B6
Catfirth Shetland 175 H6
Catford London 28 B4
Catforth Lancs 92 F4
Cathays Cardiff 22 B3
Cathcart Glasgow 121 C5
Cathedine Powys 35 B5
Catherington Hants 15 C7
Catherton Shrops 49 B8
Catlodge Highld 148 E2
Catlowdy Cumb 108 B4
Catmore W Berks 38 F4
Caton Lancs 92 C5
Caton Green Lancs 92 C5
Catrine E Ayrs 113 B5
Cat's Ash Newport 35 E7
Catsfield E Sus 18 D4
Catshill Worcs 50 B4
Cattal N Yorks 95 D7
Cattawade Suff 56 F5
Catterall Lancs 92 E4
Catterick N Yorks 101 E7
Catterick Bridge N Yorks 101 E7
Catterick Garrison N Yorks 101 E6
Catterick Racecourse N Yorks 101 E7
Catterlen Cumb 108 F4
Catterline Aberds 143 B8
Catterton N Yorks 95 E8
Catthorpe Leics 52 B3
Cattistock Dorset 12 E3
Catton Northumb 109 D8
Catton N Yorks 95 B6
Catwick E Yorks 97 E7
Catworth Cambs 53 B8
Caudlesprings Norf 68 D2
Caudwell's Mill, Matlock Derbys 76 C2
Caulcott Oxon 39 B5
Cauldcots Angus 143 E6
Cauldhame Stirl 132 E5
Cauldmill Borders 115 C8
Cauldon Staffs 75 E7
Caulkerbush Dumfries 107 D6
Caulside Dumfries 115 F7
Caunsall Worcs 62 F2
Caunton Notts 77 D7
Causeway End Dumfries 105 C8
Causeway Foot W Yorks 94 F3
Causeway-head Stirl 133 E6
Causewayend S Lnrk 122 F3
Causewayhead Cumb 107 D8
Causey Park Bridge Northumb 117 E7
Causeyend Aberds 151 C8
Cautley Cumb 100 E1
Cavendish Suff 56 E2
Cavendish Bridge Leics 63 B8
Cavenham Suff 55 C8
Caversfield Oxon 39 B5
Caversham Reading 26 B5
Caverswall Staffs 75 E6
Cavil E Yorks 96 F3
Cawdor Highld 158 D2
Cawdor Castle and Gardens Highld 158 E2
Cawkwell Lincs 79 B5
Cawood N Yorks 95 F8
Cawsand Corn 6 D2
Cawston Norf 81 E7
Cawthorne S Yorks 88 D3
Cawthorpe Lincs 65 B7
Cawton N Yorks 96 B2
Caxton Cambs 54 D4
Caynham Shrops 49 B7
Caythorpe Lincs 78 E2
Caythorpe Notts 77 E6
Cayton N Yorks 103 F8
Ceann a Bhaigh W Isles 170 D3
Ceann a Deas Loch Baghasdail W Isles 171 J3
Ceann Shiphoirt W Isles 172 G5
Ceann Tarabhaigh W Isles 172 G5
Ceannacroc Lodge Highld 146 C5
Cearsiadair W Isles 172 F6
Cefn Berain Conwy 72 C3
Cefn-brith Conwy 72 D3
Cefn Canol Powys 73 F6
Cefn-coch Conwy 83 E8
Cefn Coch Powys 59 B8
Cefn-coed-y-cymmer M Tydf 34 D4
Cefn Cribbwr Bridgend 34 F2
Cefn Cross Bridgend 34 F2
Cefn-ddwysarn Gwyn 72 F3
Cefn Einion Shrops 60 F2
Cefn-gorwydd Powys 47 E8
Cefn-mawr Wrex 73 E6
Cefn-y-bedd Flint 73 D7
Cefn-y-pant Carms 32 B2
Cefneithin Carms 33 C6
Cei-bach Ceredig 46 D3
Ceinewydd = New Quay Ceredig 46 D2
Ceint Anglesey 82 D4
Cellan Ceredig 46 E5
Cellarhead Staffs 75 E6
Cemaes Anglesey 82 B3
Cemmaes Powys 58 D5
Cemmaes Road Powys 58 D5
Cenarth Carms 45 E4
Cenin Gwyn 71 C5
Central Invclyd 129 C7
Ceos W Isles 172 F6
Ceres Fife 135 C6
Cerne Abbas Dorset 12 D4
Cerney Wick Glos 37 E7
Cerrigceinwen Anglesey 82 D4
Cerrigydrudion Conwy 72 E3
Cessford Borders 116 B3
Ceunant Gwyn 82 E5
Chaceley Glos 50 F3
Chacewater Corn 3 B6
Chackmore Bucks 52 F4
Chacombe Northants 52 E2
Chad Valley W Mid 62 F4
Chadderton Gtr Man 87 D7
Chadderton Fold Gtr Man 87 D6
Chaddesden Derby 76 F3
Chaddesley Corbett Worcs 50 B3
Chaddleworth W Berks 26 B2
Chadlington Oxon 38 B3
Chadshunt Warks 51 D8
Chadwell Leics 64 B4
Chadwell St Mary Thurrock 29 B7

Chadwick End W Mid 51 B7
Chadwick Green Mers 86 E3
Chaffcombe Som 11 C8
Chagford Devon 10 F2
Chailey E Sus 17 C7
Chain Bridge Lincs 79 E6
Chainbridge Cambs 66 D4
Chainhurst Kent 29 E8
Chalbury Dorset 13 D8
Chalbury Common Dorset 13 D8
Chaldon Sur 28 D4
Chaldon Herring Dorset 13 F5
Chale I o W 15 G5
Chale Green I o W 15 G5
Chalfont Common Bucks 40 E3
Chalfont St Giles Bucks 40 E2
Chalfont St Peter Bucks 40 E3
Chalford Glos 37 D5
Chalgrove Oxon 39 E6
Chalk Kent 29 B7
Challacombe Devon 21 E5
Challoch Dumfries 105 C7
Challock Kent 30 D4
Chalton Beds 40 B3
Chalton Hants 15 C8
Chalvington E Sus 18 E2
Chancery Ceredig 46 B4
Chandler's Ford Hants 14 B5
Channel Tunnel Kent 19 B8
Channerwick Shetland 175 L6
Chantry Som 24 E2
Chantry Suff 56 E5
Chapel Fife 134 E4
Chapel Allerton Som 23 D6
Chapel Allerton W Yorks 95 F6
Chapel Amble Corn 4 B4
Chapel Brampton Northants 52 C5
Chapel Chorlton Staffs 74 F5
Chapel-en-le-Frith Derbys 87 F8
Chapel End Warks 63 E7
Chapel Green Warks 63 F6
Chapel Green Warks 52 C2
Chapel Haddlesey N Yorks 89 B6
Chapel Head Cambs 66 F3
Chapel Hill Aberds 161 E7
Chapel Hill Lincs 78 D5
Chapel Hill Mon 36 E2
Chapel Hill N Yorks 95 E6
Chapel Lawn Shrops 48 B5
Chapel-le-Dale N Yorks 93 B7
Chapel Milton Derbys 87 F8
Chapel of Garioch Aberds 151 B6
Chapel Row W Berks 26 C3
Chapel St Leonards Lincs 79 B8
Chapel Stile Cumb 99 D5
Chapelgate Lincs 66 B4
Chapelhall N Lnrk 121 C7
Chapelhill Dumfries 114 E3
Chapelhill Highld 158 B2
Chapelhill N Ayrs 120 E2
Chapelhill Perth 134 B4
Chapelhill Perth 141 F7
Chapelknowe Dumfries 108 B3
Chapelton Angus 143 E6
Chapelton Devon 9 B7
Chapelton Highld 148 C5
Chapelton S Lnrk 121 E6
Chapeltown Blkburn 86 C5
Chapeltown Moray 149 B8
Chapeltown S Yorks 88 E4
Chapmans Well Devon 9 E5
Chapmanslade Wilts 24 E3
Chapmore End Herts 41 C6
Chappel Essex 42 B4
Chard Som 11 D8
Chardstock Devon 11 D8
Charfield S Glos 36 E4
Charford Worcs 50 C4
Charing Kent 30 E3
Charing Cross Dorset 14 C2
Charing Heath Kent 30 E3
Charingworth Glos 51 F7
Charlbury Oxon 38 C3
Charlcombe Bath 24 C2
Charlecote Warks 51 D7
Charlecote Park, Wellesbourne Warks 51 D7
Charles Devon 21 F5
Charles Manning's Amusement Park, Felixstowe Suff 57 F6
Charles Tye Suff 56 D4
Charlesfield Dumfries 107 C8
Charleston Angus 142 E3
Charleston Renfs 120 C4
Charlestown Aberdeen 151 D8
Charlestown Corn 4 D5
Charlestown Derbys 87 E8
Charlestown Dorset 12 G4
Charlestown Fife 134 F2
Charlestown Gtr Man 87 D6
Charlestown Highld 157 E7
Charlestown Highld 154 C4
Charlestown W Yorks 87 B7
Charlestown of Aberlour Moray 159 E6
Charlesworth Derbys 87 E8
Charleton Devon 7 E5
Charlton London 28 B5
Charlton Hants 25 E8
Charlton Herts 40 B4
Charlton Northants 52 F3
Charlton Northumb 116 F4
Charlton Som 23 D8
Charlton Telford 61 C5
Charlton Wilts 13 B7
Charlton Wilts 25 D6
Charlton Wilts 37 F6
Charlton Worcs 50 E5
Charlton W Sus 16 C2
Charlton Abbots Glos 37 B7
Charlton Adam Som 12 B3
Charlton-All-Saints Wilts 14 B2
Charlton Down Dorset 12 E4
Charlton Horethorne Som 12 B4
Charlton Kings Glos 37 B6
Charlton Mackerell Som 12 B3
Charlton Marshall Dorset 13 D6
Charlton Musgrove Som 12 B5
Charlton on Otmoor Oxon 39 C5
Charltons Redcar 102 C4
Charlwood Sur 28 E3
Charlynch Som 22 F4
Charminster Dorset 12 E4
Charmouth Dorset 11 E8
Charndon Bucks 39 B6
Charney Bassett Oxon 38 E3
Charnock Richard Lancs 86 C3
Charsfield Suff 57 D6
Chart Corner Kent 29 D8
Chart Sutton Kent 30 E2
Charter Alley Hants 26 D3
Charterhouse Som 23 D6
Charterville Allotments Oxon 38 C3
Chartham Kent 30 D5
Chartham Hatch Kent 30 D5
Chartridge Bucks 40 D2
Chartwell, Westerham Kent 29 D5
Charvil Wokingham 27 B5
Charwelton Northants 52 D3
Chasetown Staffs 62 D4
Chastleton Oxon 38 B2
Chasty Devon 8 D5
Chatburn Lancs 93 E7
Chatcull Staffs 74 F4
Chatham Medway 29 C8
Chathill Northumb 117 B7
Chatsworth, Bakewell Derbys 76 B2
Chattenden Medway 29 B8
Chatteris Cambs 66 F3
Chattisham Suff 56 E4
Chatto Borders 116 C3
Chatton Northumb 117 B6
Chawleigh Devon 10 C2
Chawley Oxon 38 D4
Chawston Beds 54 D2
Chawton Hants 26 F5
Cheadle Gtr Man 87 F6
Cheadle Staffs 75 E7
Cheadle Heath Gtr Man 87 F6
Cheadle Hulme Gtr Man 87 F6
Cheam London 28 C3
Cheapside Sur 27 D8
Chearsley Bucks 39 C7
Chebsey Staffs 62 B2
Checkendon Oxon 39 F6
Checkley Ches 74 E4
Checkley Hereford 49 F7
Checkley Staffs 75 F7
Chedburgh Suff 55 D8
Cheddar Som 23 D6
Cheddar Showcaves and Gorge Som 23 D6
Cheddington Bucks 40 C2
Cheddleton Staffs 75 D6
Cheddon Fitzpaine Som 11 B7
Chedglow Wilts 37 E6
Chedgrave Norf 69 E6
Chedington Dorset 12 D2
Chediston Suff 57 B7
Chedworth Glos 37 C7
Chedworth Roman Villa Glos 37 C7
Chedzoy Som 22 F5
Cheeklaw Borders 124 D3
Cheeseman's Green Kent 19 B7
Cheglinch Devon 20 E4
Cheldon Devon 10 C2
Chelford Ches 74 B5
Chell Heath Stoke 75 D5
Chellaston Derby 76 F3
Chellington Beds 53 D7
Chelmarsh Shrops 61 F7
Chelmer Village Essex 42 D3
Chelmondiston Suff 57 F6
Chelmorton Derbys 75 C8
Chelmsford Essex 42 D3
Chelsea London 28 B3
Chelsfield London 29 C5
Chelsworth Suff 56 E3
Cheltenham Glos 37 B6
Cheltenham Racecourse Glos 37 B6
Chelveston Northants 53 C7
Chelvey N Som 23 C6
Chelwood Bath 23 C8
Chelwood Common E Sus 17 B8
Chelwood Gate E Sus 17 B8
Chelworth Wilts 37 E6
Chelworth Green Wilts 37 E7
Chemistry Shrops 74 E2
Chenies Bucks 40 E3
Cheny Longville Shrops 60 F4
Chepstow = Cas-gwent Mon 36 E2
Chepstow Racecourse Mon 36 E2
Chequerfield W Yorks 89 B5
Cherhill Wilts 24 B5
Cherington Glos 37 E6
Cherington Warks 51 F7
Cheriton Devon 21 E6
Cheriton Hants 15 B6
Cheriton Kent 19 B8
Cheriton Swansea 33 E5
Cheriton Bishop Devon 10 E2
Cheriton Fitzpaine Devon 10 D3
Cheriton or Stackpole Elidor Pembs 44 F4
Cherrington Telford 61 B6
Cherry Burton E Yorks 97 E5
Cherry Hinton Cambs 55 D5
Cherry Orchard Worcs 50 D3
Cherry Willingham Lincs 78 B3
Cherrybank Perth 134 B3
Chertsey Sur 27 C8
Cheselbourne Dorset 13 E5
Chesham Bucks 40 D2
Chesham Bois Bucks 40 E2
Cheshire Candle Workshops, Burwardsley Ches 74 D2
Cheshunt Herts 41 D6
Cheslyn Hay Staffs 62 D3
Chessington London 28 C2
Chessington World of Adventures London 28 C2
Chester Ches 73 C8
Chester Cathedral Ches 73 C7
Chester-Le-Street Durham 111 D5
Chester Moor Durham 111 E5
Chester Racecourse Ches 73 C7
Chester Zoo Ches 73 B8
Chesterblade Som 23 E8
Chesterfield Derbys 76 B3
Chesters Borders 116 C2
Chesters Borders 116 B2
Chesters Roman Fort Northumb 110 B2
Chesterton Cambs 65 E8
Chesterton Cambs 55 C5
Chesterton Glos 37 D7
Chesterton Oxon 39 B5
Chesterton Shrops 61 E7
Chesterton Staffs 74 E5
Chesterton Warks 51 D8
Chesterwood Northumb 109 C8
Chestfield Kent 30 C5
Cheston Devon 6 D4
Cheswardine Shrops 61 B7
Cheswick Northumb 125 E6
Chetnole Dorset 12 D4
Chettiscombe Devon 10 C4
Chettisham Cambs 66 F5
Chettle Dorset 13 C7
Chetton Shrops 61 E6
Chetwode Bucks 39 B6
Chetwynd Aston Telford 61 C7
Cheveley Cambs 55 C7
Chevening Kent 29 D5
Chevington Suff 55 D8
Chevithorne Devon 10 C4
Chew Magna Bath 23 C7
Chew Stoke Bath 23 C7
Chewton Keynsham Bath 23 C8
Chewton Mendip Som 23 D7
Chicheley M Keynes 53 E7
Chichester W Sus 16 D2
Chichester Cathedral W Sus 16 D2
Chickerell Dorset 12 F4
Chicklade Wilts 24 F4
Chicksgrove Wilts 24 F4
Chidden Hants 15 C7
Chiddingfold Sur 27 F7
Chiddingly E Sus 18 D2
Chiddingstone Kent 29 E5
Chiddingstone Causeway Kent 29 E6
Chiddingstone Hoath Kent 29 E5
Chideock Dorset 12 E2
Chidham W Sus 15 D8
Chidswell W Yorks 88 B3
Chieveley W Berks 26 B2
Chignall St James Essex 42 D2
Chignall Smealy Essex 42 C2
Chigwell Essex 41 E7
Chigwell Row Essex 41 E7
Chilbolton Hants 25 F8
Chilcomb Hants 15 B6
Chilcombe Dorset 12 E3
Chilcompton Som 23 D8
Chilcote Leics 63 C6
Child Okeford Dorset 13 C6
Childer Thornton Ches 73 B7
Childrey Oxon 38 F3
Child's Ercall Shrops 61 B6
Childswickham Worcs 51 F5
Childwall Mers 86 F2
Childwick Green Herts 40 C4
Chilfrome Dorset 12 E3
Chilgrove W Sus 16 C2
Chilham Kent 30 D4
Chilhampton Wilts 25 F5
Chilla Devon 9 D6
Chillaton Devon 9 F6
Chillenden Kent 31 D6
Chillerton I o W 15 F5
Chillesford Suff 57 D7
Chillingham Northumb 117 B6
Chillington Devon 7 E5
Chillington Som 11 C8
Chilmark Wilts 24 F4
Chilson Oxon 38 C3
Chilsworthy Corn 6 B2
Chilsworthy Devon 8 D5
Chilthorne Domer Som 12 C3
Chiltington E Sus 17 C7
Chilton Bucks 39 C6
Chilton Durham 101 B7
Chilton Oxon 38 F4
Chilton Cantelo Som 12 B3
Chilton Foliat Wilts 25 B8
Chilton Lane Durham 111 F6
Chilton Polden Som 23 F5
Chilton Street Suff 55 E8
Chilton Trinity Som 22 F4
Chilvers Coton Warks 63 E7
Chilwell Notts 76 F5
Chilworth Hants 14 C5
Chilworth Sur 27 E8
Chimney Oxon 38 D3
Chineham Hants 26 D4
Chingford London 41 E6
Chinley Derbys 87 F8
Chinley Head Derbys 87 F8
Chinnor Oxon 39 D7
Chipnall Shrops 74 F4
Chippenhall Green Suff 57 B6
Chippenham Cambs 55 C7
Chippenham Wilts 24 B4
Chipperfield Herts 40 D3
Chipping Herts 54 F4
Chipping Lancs 93 E6
Chipping Campden Glos 51 F6
Chipping Hill Essex 42 C4
Chipping Norton Oxon 38 B3
Chipping Ongar Essex 42 D1
Chipping Sodbury S Glos 36 F4
Chipping Warden Northants 52 E2
Chipstable Som 10 B5
Chipstead Kent 29 D5
Chipstead Sur 28 D3
Chirbury Shrops 60 E2
Chirk = Y Waun Wrex 73 F6
Chirk Bank Shrops 73 F6
Chirk Castle Wrex 73 F6
Chirmorrie S Ayrs 105 B6
Chirnside Borders 124 D4
Chirnsidebridge Borders 124 D4
Chirton Wilts 25 D5
Chisbury Wilts 25 C7
Chiselborough Som 12 C2
Chiseldon Swindon 25 B6
Chiserley W Yorks 87 B8
Chislehampton Oxon 39 E5
Chislehurst London 28 B5
Chislet Kent 31 C6
Chiswell Green Herts 40 D4
Chiswick London 28 B3
Chiswick End Cambs 54 E4
Chisworth Derbys 87 E7
Chithurst W Sus 16 B2
Chittering Cambs 55 B5
Chitterne Wilts 24 E4
Chittlehamholt Devon 9 B8
Chittlehampton Devon 9 B8
Chittoe Wilts 24 C4
Chivenor Devon 20 F4
Chobham Sur 27 C7
Choicelee Borders 124 D3
Cholderton Wilts 25 E7
Cholesbury Bucks 40 D2
Chollerford Northumb 110 B2
Chollerton Northumb 110 B2
Cholmondeston Ches 74 C3
Cholsey Oxon 39 F5
Cholstrey Hereford 49 D6
Chop Gate N Yorks 102 E3
Choppington Northumb 117 F8
Chopwell T & W 110 D4
Chorley Ches 74 D2
Chorley Lancs 86 C3
Chorley Shrops 61 F6
Chorley Staffs 62 C4
Chorleywood Herts 40 E3
Chorlton cum Hardy Gtr Man 87 E6
Chorlton Lane Ches 73 E8
Choulton Shrops 60 F3
Chowdene T & W 111 D5
Chowley Ches 73 D8
Chrishall Essex 54 F5
Christ Church Oxford Oxon 39 D5
Christchurch Cambs 66 E4
Christchurch Dorset 14 E2
Christchurch Glos 36 C2
Christchurch Newport 35 F7
Christchurch Priory Dorset 14 E2
Christian Malford Wilts 24 B4
Christleton Ches 73 C8
Christmas Common Oxon 39 E7
Christon N Som 23 D5
Christon Bank Northumb 117 B8
Christow Devon 10 F3
Chryston N Lnrk 121 B6
Chudleigh Devon 7 B6
Chudleigh Knighton Devon 7 B6
Chulmleigh Devon 9 C8
Chunal Derbys 87 E8
Church Lancs 86 B5
Church Aston Telford 61 C7
Church Brampton Northants 52 C5
Church Broughton Derbys 76 F2
Church Crookham Hants 27 D6
Church Eaton Staffs 62 C2
Church End Beds 40 B2
Church End Beds 54 F2
Church End Beds 53 F7
Church End Cambs 66 F2
Church End Cambs 66 D3
Church End E Yorks 97 D6
Church End Essex 55 E6
Church End Essex 42 B3
Church End Hants 26 D4
Church End Lincs 78 F5
Church End Warks 63 E6
Church End Warks 63 E6
Church End Wilts 24 B5
Church Enstone Oxon 38 B3
Church Fenton N Yorks 95 F8
Church Green Devon 11 E6
Church Green Norf 68 E3
Church Gresley Derbys 63 C6
Church Hanborough Oxon 38 C4
Church Hill Ches 74 C3
Church Houses N Yorks 102 E4
Church Knowle Dorset 13 F7
Church Laneham Notts 77 B8
Church Langton Leics 64 E4
Church Lawford Warks 52 B2
Church Lawton Ches 74 D5
Church Leigh Staffs 75 F7
Church Lench Worcs 50 D5
Church Mayfield Staffs 75 E8
Church Minshull Ches 74 C3
Church Norton W Sus 16 E2
Church Preen Shrops 60 E5
Church Pulverbatch Shrops 60 D4
Church Stoke Powys 60 E2
Church Stowe Northants 52 D4
Church Street Kent 29 B8
Church Stretton Shrops 60 E4
Church Town N Lincs 89 D8
Church Town Sur 28 D4
Church Village Rhondda 34 F4
Church Warsop Notts 77 C5
Churcham Glos 36 C4
Churchbank Shrops 48 B4
Churchbridge Staffs 62 D3
Churchdown Glos 37 C5
Churchend Essex 42 B2
Churchend Essex 43 E6
Churchend S Glos 36 E4
Churchfield W Mid 62 E4
Churchgate Street Essex 41 C7
Churchill Devon 20 E4
Churchill Devon 11 D8
Churchill N Som 23 D6
Churchill Oxon 38 B2
Churchill Worcs 50 B3
Churchill Worcs 50 D4
Churchinford Som 11 C7
Churchover Warks 64 F2
Churchstanton Som 11 C6
Churchstow Devon 6 E5
Churchtown Derbys 76 C2
Churchtown I o M 84 C4
Churchtown Lancs 92 E4
Churchtown Mers 85 C4
Churnsike Lodge Northumb 109 B6
Churston Ferrers Torbay 7 D7
Churt Sur 27 F6
Churton Ches 73 D8
Churwell W Yorks 88 B3
Chute Standen Wilts 25 D8
Chwilog Gwyn 70 D5
Chyandour Corn 2 C3
Cilan Uchaf Gwyn 70 E3
Cilcain Flint 73 C5
Cilcennin Ceredig 46 C4
Cilfor Gwyn 71 D7
Cilfrew Neath 34 D1
Cilfynydd Rhondda 34 E4
Cilgerran Pembs 45 E3
Cilgwyn Carms 33 B8
Cilgwyn Gwyn 82 F4
Cilgwyn Pembs 45 F2
Ciliau Aeron Ceredig 46 D3
Cill Donnain W Isles 171 H3
Cille Bhrighde W Isles 171 J3
Cille Pheadair W Isles 171 J3
Cilmery Powys 48 D2
Cilsan Carms 33 B6
Ciltalgarth Gwyn 72 E2
Cilwendeg Pembs 45 F4
Cilybebyll Neath 33 D8
Cilycwm Carms 47 F6
Cimla Neath 34 E1
Cinderford Glos 36 C3
Cippyn Pembs 45 E3
Circebost W Isles 172 E4
Cirencester Glos 37 D7
Ciribhig W Isles 172 D4
City Powys 60 F2
City Dulas Anglesey 82 C4
City of London = London, City of London 41 F6
Clachaig Argyll 129 B6
Clachan Argyll 128 E2
Clachan Argyll 130 D3
Clachan Argyll 138 E2
Clachan Argyll 131 D7
Clachan Highld 153 F6
Clachan W Isles 170 F3
Clachan na Luib W Isles 170 D4
Clachan of Campsie E Dunb 121 B6
Clachan of Glendaruel Argyll 128 B4
Clachan-Seil Argyll 130 D3
Clachan Strachur Argyll 131 E6
Clachaneasy Dumfries 105 B7
Clachanmore Dumfries 104 E4
Clachbreck Argyll 128 C2
Clachnabrain Angus 142 C3
Clachtoll Highld 162 B4
Clackmannan Clack 133 E8
Clacton-on-Sea Essex 43 C7
Cladach Chireboist W Isles 170 D3
Claddach-knockline W Isles 170 D3
Cladich Argyll 131 C6
Claggan Highld 137 D7
Claggan Highld 139 B5
Claigan Highld 152 D3
Claines Worcs 50 D3
Clandown Bath 23 D8
Clanfield Hants 15 C7
Clanfield Oxon 38 D2
Clanville Hants 25 E8
Claonaig Argyll 128 E3
Claonel Highld 164 D2
Clap Hill Kent 19 B7
Clapgate Dorset 13 D8
Clapgate Herts 41 B7
Clapham Beds 53 D8
Clapham London 28 B3
Clapham N Yorks 93 C7
Clapham W Sus 16 D4
Clappers Borders 124 D5
Clappersgate Cumb 99 D5
Clapton Som 12 D2
Clapton-in-Gordano N Som 23 B6
Clapton-on-the-Hill Glos 38 C1
Clapworthy Devon 9 B8
Clara Vale T & W 110 C4
Clarach Ceredig 58 F3
Clarbeston Pembs 32 B1
Clarbeston Road Pembs 32 B1
Clarborough Notts 89 F8
Clardon Highld 169 C6
Clare Suff 55 E8
Clarebrand Dumfries 106 C4
Claremont Landscape Garden, Esher Sur 28 C2
Clarencefield Dumfries 107 C7
Clarilaw Borders 115 C8
Clark's Green Sur 28 F2
Clarkston E Renf 121 D5
Clashandorran Highld 157 E6
Clashcoig Highld 164 E3
Clashindarroch Aberds 159 F8
Clashmore Highld 166 F2
Clashmore Highld 164 F4
Clashnessie Highld 166 F2
Clashnoir Moray 149 B8
Clate Shetland 175 G7
Clathy Perth 133 C8
Clatt Aberds 150 B4
Clatter Powys 59 E6
Clatterford I o W 15 F5
Clatterin Bridge Aberds 143 B6
Clatworthy Som 22 F2
Claughton Lancs 92 E5
Claughton Lancs 93 C5
Claughton Mers 85 F4
Claverdon Warks 51 C6
Claverham N Som 23 C6
Clavering Essex 55 F5
Claverley Shrops 61 E7
Claverton Bath 24 C2
Clawdd-newydd Denb 72 D4
Clawthorpe Cumb 92 B5
Clawton Devon 9 E5
Claxby Lincs 90 E5
Claxby Lincs 79 B7
Claxton Norf 69 D6
Claxton N Yorks 96 C2
Clay Common Suff 69 F7
Clay Coton Northants 52 B3
Clay Cross Derbys 76 C3
Clay Hill W Berks 26 B3
Clay Lake Lincs 66 B2
Claybokie Aberds 149 E6
Claybrooke Magna Leics 63 F8
Claybrooke Parva Leics 63 F8
Claydon Oxon 52 D2
Claydon Suff 56 D5
Claygate Dumfries 108 B3
Claygate Kent 29 E8
Claygate Sur 28 C2
Claygate Cross Kent 29 D7
Clayhanger Devon 10 B5
Clayhanger W Mid 62 D4
Clayhidon Devon 11 C6
Clayhill E Sus 18 C5
Clayhill Hants 14 D4
Clayock Highld 169 D6
Claypole Lincs 77 E8
Clayton Staffs 75 E5
Clayton S Yorks 89 D5
Clayton W Sus 17 C6
Clayton W Yorks 94 F4
Clayton Green Lancs 86 B3
Clayton-le-Moors Lancs 93 F7
Clayton-le-Woods Lancs 86 B3
Clayton West W Yorks 88 C3
Clayworth Notts 89 F8
Cleadale Highld 144 E4
Cleadon T & W 111 C6
Clearbrook Devon 6 C3
Clearwell Glos 36 D2
Cleasby N Yorks 101 C7
Cleat Orkney 176 H3
Cleatlam Durham 101 C6
Cleator Cumb 98 C2
Cleator Moor Cumb 98 C2
Clebrig Highld 167 F7
Cleckheaton W Yorks 88 B2
Clee St Margaret Shrops 61 F5
Cleedownton Shrops 61 F5
Cleehill Shrops 49 B7
Cleethorpes NE Lincs 91 D7
Cleeton St Mary Shrops 49 B8
Cleeve N Som 23 C6
Cleeve Hill Glos 37 B6
Cleeve Prior Worcs 51 E5
Clegyrnant Powys 59 D6
Clehonger Hereford 49 F6
Cleish Perth 134 E2
Cleland N Lnrk 121 D8
Clench Common Wilts 25 C6
Clenchwarton Norf 67 B5
Clent Worcs 50 B4
Cleobury Mortimer Shrops 49 B8
Cleobury North Shrops 61 F6
Cleongart Argyll 118 C3
Clephanton Highld 158 D2
Clerklands Borders 115 B8
Clestrain Orkney 176 F2
Cleuch Head Borders 115 C8
Cleughbrae Dumfries 107 B7
Clevancy Wilts 25 B5
Clevedon N Som 23 B6
Cleveley Oxon 38 B3
Cleveleys Lancs 92 E3
Cleverton Wilts 37 F6
Clevis Bridgend 21 B7
Clewer Som 23 D6
Cley next the Sea Norf 81 C6
Cliaid W Isles 171 K2
Cliasmol W Isles 173 H3
Cliburn Cumb 99 B7
Click Mill Orkney 176 D2
Cliddesden Hants 26 E4
Cliff End E Sus 19 D5
Cliffburn Angus 143 E6
Cliffe Medway 29 B8
Cliffe N Yorks 96 F2
Cliffe Woods Medway 29 B8
Clifford Hereford 48 E4
Clifford W Yorks 95 E7
Clifford Chambers Warks 51 D6
Clifford's Mesne Glos 36 B4
Cliffsend Kent 31 C7
Clifton Beds 54 F2
Clifton Bristol 23 B7
Clifton Cumb 99 B7
Clifton Derbys 75 E8
Clifton Lancs 92 F4
Clifton Nottingham 77 F5
Clifton Northumb 117 F8
Clifton N Yorks 94 E4
Clifton Oxon 52 F2
Clifton Stirl 139 F7
Clifton S Yorks 89 E6
Clifton Worcs 50 E3
Clifton York 95 D8
Clifton Campville Staffs 63 C6
Clifton Green Gtr Man 87 D5
Clifton Hampden Oxon 39 E5
Clifton Reynes M Keynes 53 D7
Clifton upon Dunsmore Warks 52 B3
Clifton upon Teme Worcs 50 C2
Cliftoncote Borders 116 B4
Cliftonville Kent 31 B7
Climaen gwyn Neath 33 D8
Climping W Sus 16 D4
Climpy S Lnrk 122 D2
Clink Som 24 E2
Clint N Yorks 95 D5
Clint Green Norf 68 C3
Clintmains Borders 124 F2
Cliobh W Isles 172 E3
Clippesby Norf 69 C7
Clipsham Rutland 65 C6
Clipston Northants 64 F4
Clipstone Notts 77 C5
Clitheroe Lancs 93 E7
Cliuthar W Isles 173 J4
Clive Shrops 60 B5
Clivocast Shetland 174 C8
Clixby Lincs 90 D5
Clocaenog Denb 72 D4
Clochan Moray 159 C8
Clock Face Mers 86 E3
Clockmill Borders 124 D3
Cloddiau Powys 60 D2
Clodock Hereford 35 B7
Clola Aberds 161 D7
Clophill Beds 53 F8
Clopton Northants 65 F7
Clopton Suff 57 D6
Clopton Corner Suff 57 D6
Clopton Green Suff 55 D8
Close Clark I o M 84 E2
Closeburn Dumfries 113 E8
Closworth Som 12 C3
Clothall Herts 54 F3
Clotton Ches 74 C2
Clough Foot W Yorks 87 B7
Cloughton N Yorks 103 E8
Cloughton Newlands N Yorks 103 E8
Clousta Shetland 175 H5
Clouston Orkney 176 E1
Clova Aberds 150 B3
Clova Angus 142 B3
Clove Lodge Durham 100 C4
Clovelly Devon 8 B5
Clovelly Village Devon 8 B5
Clovenfords Borders 123 F7
Clovenstone Aberds 151 C6
Clovullin Highld 138 C4
Clow Bridge Lancs 87 B6
Clowne Derbys 76 B4
Clows Top Worcs 50 B2
Cloy Wrex 73 E7
Cluanie Inn Highld 146 C3
Cluanie Lodge Highld 146 C3
Clun Shrops 60 F3
Clunbury Shrops 60 F3
Clunderwen Carms 32 C2
Clune Highld 148 B3
Clunes Highld 146 F5
Clungunford Shrops 49 B5
Clunie Aberds 160 C3
Clunie Perth 141 E8
Clunton Shrops 60 F3
Cluny Fife 134 E4
Cluny Castle Highld 148 E2
Clutton Bath 23 D8
Clutton Ches 73 D8
Clwt-grugoer Conwy 72 C3
Clwt-y-bont Gwyn 83 E5
Clydach Mon 35 C6
Clydach Swansea 33 D7
Clydach Vale Rhondda 34 E3
Clydebank W Dunb 120 B4
Clydey Pembs 45 F4
Clyffe Pypard Wilts 25 B5
Clynder Argyll 129 B7
Clyne Neath 34 D2
Clynelish Highld 165 D5
Clynnog-fawr Gwyn 82 F4
Clyro Powys 48 E4
Clyst Honiton Devon 10 E4
Clyst Hydon Devon 10 D5
Clyst St George Devon 10 F4
Clyst St Lawrence Devon 10 D5
Clyst St Mary Devon 10 E4
Cnoc Amhlaigh W Isles 172 E8
Cnwch-coch Ceredig 47 B5
Coachford Aberds 159 E8
Coad's Green Corn 5 B7
Coal Aston Derbys 76 B3
Coalbrookdale Telford 61 D6
Coalbrookvale Bl Gwent 35 D5
Coalburn S Lnrk 121 F8
Coalburns T & W 110 C4
Coalcleugh Northumb 109 E8
Coaley Glos 36 D4
Coalhall E Ayrs 112 C4
Coalhill Essex 42 E3
Coalpit Heath S Glos 36 F3
Coalport Telford 61 D6
Coalsnaughton Clack 133 E8
Coaltown of Balgonie Fife 134 E4
Coaltown of Wemyss Fife 134 E5
Coalville Leics 63 C8
Coalway Glos 36 C2
Coat Som 12 B2
Coatbridge N Lnrk 121 C7
Coatdyke N Lnrk 121 C7
Coate Swindon 38 F1
Coate Wilts 24 C5
Coates Cambs 66 E3
Coates Glos 37 D6
Coates Lancs 93 E8
Coates Notts 90 F2
Coates W Sus 16 C3
Coatham Redcar 102 B3
Coatham Mundeville Darl 101 B7
Coatsgate Dumfries 114 D3
Cobbaton Devon 9 B8
Cobbler's Green Norf 69 E5
Coberley Glos 37 C6
Cobham Kent 29 C7
Cobham Sur 28 C2
Cobholm Island Norf 69 D8
Cobleland Stirl 132 E4
Cobnash Hereford 49 C6
Coburty Aberds 161 B6
Cock Bank Wrex 73 E7
Cock Bridge Aberds 149 D8
Cock Clarks Essex 42 D4
Cockayne N Yorks 102 E4
Cockayne Hatley Cambs 54 E3
Cockburnspath Borders 124 B3
Cockenzie and Port Seton E Loth 123 B7
Cockerham Lancs 92 D4
Cockermouth Cumb 107 F8
Cockernhoe Green Herts 40 B4
Cockfield Durham 101 B6
Cockfield Suff 56 D3
Cockfosters London 41 E5
Cocking W Sus 16 C2
Cockington Torbay 7 C6
Cocklake Som 23 E6
Cockley Beck Cumb 98 D4
Cockley Cley Norf 67 D7
Cockshutt Shrops 60 B4
Cockthorpe Norf 81 C5
Cockwood Devon 10 F4
Cockyard Hereford 49 F6
Codda Corn 5 B6
Coddenham Suff 56 D5
Coddington Ches 73 D8
Coddington Hereford 50 E2
Coddington Notts 77 D8
Codford St Mary Wilts 24 F4
Codford St Peter Wilts 24 F4
Codicote Herts 41 C5
Codmore Hill W Sus 16 B4
Codnor Derbys 76 E4
Codrington S Glos 24 B2
Codsall Staffs 62 D2
Codsall Wood Staffs 62 D2
Coed Duon = Blackwood Caerph 35 E5
Coed Mawr Gwyn 83 D5
Coed Morgan Mon 35 C7
Coed-Talon Flint 73 D6
Coed-y-bryn Ceredig 46 E2
Coed-y-paen Mon 35 E7
Coed-yr-ynys Powys 35 B5

Crossmoor Lancs 92 F4
Crossroads Aberds 151 E6
Crossroads E Ayrs 120 F4
Crossway Hereford 49 F8
Crossway Mon 35 C8
Crossway Powys 48 D2
Crossway Green Worcs 50 C3
Crossways Dorset 13 F5
Crosswell Pembs 45 F3
Crosswood Ceredig 47 B5
Crosthwaite Cumb 99 E6
Croston Lancs 86 C2
Crostwick Norf 69 C5
Crostwight Norf 69 B6
Crothair W Isles 172 E4
Crouch Kent 29 D7
Crouch Hill Dorset 12 C5
Crouch House Green Kent 28 E5
Croucheston Wilts 13 B8
Croughton Northants 52 F3
Crovie Aberds 160 B5
Crow Edge S Yorks 88 D2
Crow Hill Hereford 36 B3
Crowan Corn 2 C5
Crowborough E Sus 18 B2
Crowcombe Som 22 F3
Crowdecote Derbys 75 C8
Crowden Derbys 87 E8
Crowell Oxon 39 E7
Crowfield Northants 52 E4
Crowfield Suff 56 D5
Crowhurst E Sus 18 D4
Crowhurst Sur 28 E4
Crowhurst Lane End Sur 28 E4
Crowland Lincs 66 C2
Crowlas Corn 2 C4
Crowle N Lincs 89 C8
Crowle Worcs 50 D4
Crowmarsh Gifford Oxon 39 F6
Crown Corner Suff 57 B6
Crownhill Plym 6 D2
Crownland Suff 56 C4
Crownthorpe Norf 68 D3
Crowntown Corn 2 C5
Crows-an-wra Corn 2 D2
Crowshill Norf 68 D2
Crowsnest Shrops 60 D3
Crowthorne Brack 27 C6
Crowton Ches 74 B2
Croxall Staffs 63 C5
Croxby Lincs 91 E5
Croxdale Durham 111 F5
Croxden Staffs 75 F7
Croxley Green Herts 40 E3
Croxton Cambs 54 C3
Croxton N Lincs 90 C4
Croxton Norf 67 F8
Croxton Staffs 74 F4
Croxton Kerrial Leics 64 B5
Croxtonbank Staffs 74 F4
Croy Highld 157 E8
Croy N Lnrk 119 B7
Croyde Devon 20 F3
Croydon Cambs 54 E4
Croydon London 28 C4
Crubenmore Lodge Highld 148 E2
Cruckmeole Shrops 60 D4
Cruckton Shrops 60 C4
Cruden Bay Aberds 161 E7
Crudgington Telford 61 C6
Crudwell Wilts 37 E6
Crug Powys 48 B3
Crugmeer Corn 4 B4
Crugybar Carms 47 F5
Crulabhig W Isles 172 E4
Crumlin = Crymlyn Caerph 35 E6
Crumpsall Gtr Man 87 D6
Crundale Kent 30 E4
Crundale Pembs 44 D4
Cruwys Morchard Devon 10 C3
Crux Easton Hants 26 D2
Crwbin Carms 33 C5
Crya Orkney 176 F2
Cryers Hill Bucks 40 E1
Crymlyn Gwyn 83 D6
Crymlyn = Crumlin Caerph 35 E6
Crymych Pembs 45 F3
Crynant Neath 34 D1
Crynfryn Ceredig 46 C4
Crystal Palace National Sports Centre London 28 B4
Cuaig Highld 154 E3
Cuan Argyll 130 D3
Cubbington Warks 51 C8
Cubeck N Yorks 100 F4
Cubert Corn 4 D2
Cubley S Yorks 88 D3
Cubley Common Derbys 75 F8
Cublington Bucks 39 B8
Cublington Hereford 49 F6
Cuckfield W Sus 17 B7
Cucklington Som 13 B5
Cuckney Notts 77 B5
Cuckoo Hill Notts 89 E8
Cuddesdon Oxon 39 D6
Cuddington Bucks 39 C7
Cuddington Ches 74 B3
Cuddington Heath Ches 73 E8
Cuddy Hill Lancs 92 F4
Cudham London 28 D5
Cudliptown Devon 6 B3
Cudworth Som 11 C8
Cudworth S Yorks 88 D4
Cuffley Herts 41 D6
Cuiashader W Isles 172 C8
Cuidhir W Isles 171 K2
Cuidhtinis W Isles 173 K3
Culbo Highld 157 C7
Culbokie Highld 157 D7
Culburnie Highld 157 E5
Culcabock Highld 157 E7
Culcairn Highld 157 C7
Culcharry Highld 158 D2
Culcheth Warr 86 E4
Culdrain Aberds 160 E2
Culduie Highld 155 F3
Culford Suff 56 B2
Culgaith Cumb 99 B8
Culham Oxon 39 E5
Culkein Highld 166 F2
Culkein Drumbeg Highld 166 F3
Culkerton Glos 37 E6
Cullachie Highld 149 B5
Cullen Moray 160 B2
Cullercoats T & W 111 B6
Cullicudden Highld 157 C7
Cullingworth W Yorks 94 F3
Cullipool Argyll 130 D3
Cullivoe Shetland 174 C7
Culloch Perth 133 C6
Culloden Highld 157 E8
Culloden Battlefield, Inverness Highld 157 E8
Cullompton Devon 10 D5
Culmaily Highld 165 E5
Culmazie Dumfries 105 D7
Culmington Shrops 60 F4
Culmstock Devon 11 C6
Culnacraig Highld 162 D4
Culnaknock Highld 152 C6
Culpho Suff 57 E6
Culrain Highld 164 E2
Culross Fife 133 F8
Culroy S Ayrs 112 C3
Culsh Aberds 161 D5
Culsh Aberds 150 E2
Culshabbin Dumfries 105 D7
Culswick Shetland 175 J4
Cultercullen Aberds 151 B8
Cults Aberdeen 151 D7
Cults Aberds 160 E2
Cults Dumfries 105 E8
Culverstone Green Kent 29 C7
Culverthorpe Lincs 78 E3
Culworth Northants 52 E3
Culzean Castle, Maybole S Ayrs 112 D2
Culzie Lodge Highld 157 B6
Cumbernauld N Lnrk 121 B7
Cumbernauld Village N Lnrk 121 B7
Cumberworth Lincs 79 B8
Cuminestown Aberds 160 C5
Cumlewick Shetland 175 L6
Cummersdale Cumb 108 D3
Cummertrees Dumfries 107 C8
Cummingston Moray 158 C5
Cumnock E Ayrs 113 B5
Cumnor Oxon 38 D4
Cumrew Cumb 108 D5
Cumwhinton Cumb 108 D4
Cumwhitton Cumb 108 D5
Cundall N Yorks 95 B7
Cunninghamhead N Ayrs 120 E3
Cunnister Shetland 174 D7
Cupar Fife 135 C5
Cupar Muir Fife 135 C5
Cupernham Hants 14 B4
Curbar Derbys 76 B2
Curbridge Hants 15 C6
Curbridge Oxon 38 D3
Curdridge Hants 15 C6
Curdworth Warks 63 E5
Curland Som 11 C7
Curlew Green Suff 57 C7
Currarie S Ayrs 112 E1
Curridge W Berks 26 B2
Currie Edin 122 C4
Curry Mallet Som 11 B8
Curry Rivel Som 11 B8
Curtisden Green Kent 29 E8
Curtisknowle Devon 6 D5
Cury Corn 3 D5
Cushnie Aberds 160 B4
Cushuish Som 22 F3
Cusop Hereford 48 E4
Cutcloy Dumfries 105 F8
Cutcombe Som 21 F8
Cutgate Gtr Man 87 C6
Cutiau Gwyn 58 C3
Cutlers Green Essex 55 F6
Cutnall Green Worcs 50 C3
Cutsdean Glos 51 F5
Cutthorpe Derbys 76 B3
Cutts Shetland 175 K6
Cutty Sark, Greenwich London 28 B4
Cuxham Oxon 39 E6
Cuxton Medway 29 C8
Cuxwold Lincs 91 D5
Cwm Bl Gwent 35 D5
Cwm Denb 72 B4
Cwm Swansea 33 E7
Cwm-byr Carms 46 F5
Cwm-Cewydd Gwyn 59 C5
Cwm-cou Ceredig 45 E4
Cwm-Dulais Swansea 33 D7
Cwm-felin-fach Caerph 35 E5
Cwm Ffrwd-oer Torf 35 D6
Cwm-hesgen Gwyn 71 E8
Cwm-hwnt Rhondda 34 D3
Cwm Irfon Powys 47 E7
Cwm-Llinau Powys 58 D5
Cwm-mawr Carms 33 C6
Cwm-parc Rhondda 34 E3
Cwm Penmachno Conwy 71 C8
Cwm-y-glo Carms 33 C6
Cwm-y-glo Gwyn 82 E5
Cwmafan Neath 34 E1
Cwmaman Rhondda 34 E4
Cwmann Carms 46 E4
Cwmavon Torf 35 D6
Cwmbach Carms 32 B3
Cwmbach Carms 33 D5
Cwmbach Powys 48 D2
Cwmbach Powys 48 F3
Cwmbâch Rhondda 34 D4
Cwmbelan Powys 59 F6
Cwmbran = Cwmbrân Torf 35 E6
Cwmbrân = Cwmbran Torf 35 E6
Cwmbrwyno Ceredig 58 F4
Cwmcarn Caerph 35 E6
Cwmcarvan Mon 36 D1
Cwmcych Pembs 45 F4
Cwmdare Rhondda 34 D3
Cwmderwen Powys 59 D6
Cwmdu Carms 46 F5
Cwmdu Powys 35 B5
Cwmdu Swansea 33 E7
Cwmduad Carms 46 F2
Cwmdwr Carms 47 F6
Cwmfelin Bridgend 34 F2
Cwmfelin M Tydf 34 D4
Cwmfelin Boeth Carms 32 C2
Cwmfelin Mynach Carms 32 B3
Cwmffrwd Carms 33 C5
Cwmgiedd Powys 34 C1
Cwmgors Neath 33 C8
Cwmgwili Carms 33 C6
Cwmgwrach Neath 34 D2
Cwmhiraeth Carms 46 F2
Cwmifor Carms 33 B7
Cwmisfael Carms 33 C5
Cwmllynfell Neath 33 C8
Cwmorgan Carms 45 F4
Cwmpengraig Carms 46 F2
Cwmrhos Powys 35 B5
Cwmsychpant Ceredig 46 E3
Cwmtillery Bl Gwent 35 D6
Cwmwysg Powys 34 B2
Cwmyoy Mon 35 B6
Cwmystwyth Ceredig 47 B6
Cwrt Gwyn 58 D3
Cwrt-newydd Ceredig 46 E3
Cwrt-y-cadno Carms 47 E5
Cwrt-y-gollen Powys 35 C6
Cydweli = Kidwelly Carms 33 D5
Cyffordd Llandudno = Llandudno Junction Conwy 83 D7
Cyffylliog Denb 72 D4
Cyfronydd Powys 59 D8
Cymer Neath 34 E2
Cyncoed Cardiff 35 F5
Cynghordy Carms 47 E7
Cynheidre Carms 33 D5
Cynwyd Denb 72 E4
Cynwyl Elfed Carms 32 B4
Cywarch Gwyn 59 C5

D

Dacre Cumb 99 B6
Dacre N Yorks 94 C4
Dacre Banks N Yorks 94 C4
Daddry Shield Durham 109 F8
Dadford Bucks 52 F4
Dadlington Leics 63 E8
Dafarn Faig Gwyn 71 C5
Dafen Carms 33 D6
Daffy Green Norf 68 D2
Dagenham London 41 F7
Daglingworth Glos 37 D6
Dagnall Bucks 40 C2
Dail Beag W Isles 172 D5
Dail bho Dheas W Isles 172 B7
Dail bho Thuath W Isles 172 B7
Dail Mor W Isles 172 D5
Daill Argyll 126 C3
Dailly S Ayrs 112 D2
Dairsie or Osnaburgh Fife 135 C6
Daisy Hill Gtr Man 86 D4
Dalabrog W Isles 171 H3
Dalavich Argyll 131 D5
Dalbeattie Dumfries 106 C5
Dalblair E Ayrs 113 C6
Dalbog Angus 143 B5
Dalbury Derbys 76 F2
Dalby I o M 84 E2
Dalby N Yorks 96 B2
Dalchalloch Perth 140 C4
Dalchalm Highld 165 D6
Dalchenna Argyll 131 E6
Dalchirach Moray 159 F5
Dalchork Highld 164 C2
Dalchreichart Highld 147 C5
Dalchruin Perth 133 C6
Dalderby Lincs 78 C5
Dale Pembs 44 E3
Dale Abbey Derbys 76 F4
Dale Head Cumb 99 C6
Dale of Walls Shetland 175 H3
Dalelia Highld 137 B8
Daless Highld 158 F2
Dalfaber Highld 148 C5
Dalgarven N Ayrs 120 E2
Dalgety Bay Fife 134 F3
Dalginross Perth 133 B6
Dalguise Perth 141 E6
Dalhalvaig Highld 168 D3
Dalham Suff 55 C8
Dalinlongart Argyll 129 B6
Dalkeith Midloth 123 C6
Dallam Warr 86 E3
Dallas Moray 158 D5
Dalleagles E Ayrs 113 C5
Dallinghoo Suff 57 D6
Dallington E Sus 18 D3
Dallington Northants 52 C5
Dallow N Yorks 94 B4
Dalmadilly Aberds 151 C6
Dalmally Argyll 131 C7
Dalmarnock Glasgow 121 C6
Dalmary Stirl 132 E4
Dalmellington E Ayrs 112 D4
Dalmeny Edin 122 B4
Dalmigavie Highld 148 C3
Dalmigavie Lodge Highld 148 B3
Dalmore Highld 157 C7
Dalmuir W Dunb 120 B4
Dalnabreck Highld 137 B7
Dalnacardoch Lodge Perth 140 B4
Dalnacroich Highld 156 D4
Dalnaglar Castle Perth 141 C8
Dalnahaitnach Highld 148 B4
Dalnaspidal Lodge Perth 140 B3
Dalnavaid Perth 141 C7
Dalnavie Highld 157 B7
Dalnawillan Lodge Highld 168 E5
Dalness Highld 139 D5
Dalnessie Highld 164 C3
Dalqueich Perth 134 D2
Dalreavoch Highld 164 D4
Dalry N Ayrs 120 E2
Dalrymple E Ayrs 112 C3
Dalserf S Lnrk 121 D8
Dalston Cumb 108 D3
Dalswinton Dumfries 114 F2
Dalton Dumfries 107 B8
Dalton Lancs 86 D2
Dalton Northumb 110 D2
Dalton Northumb 110 B4
Dalton N Yorks 95 B7
Dalton N Yorks 101 D6
Dalton S Yorks 89 E5
Dalton-in-Furness Cumb 92 B2
Dalton-le-Dale Durham 111 E7
Dalton-on-Tees N Yorks 101 D7
Dalton Piercy Hrtlpl 111 F7
Dalveich Stirl 132 B5
Dalvina Lodge Highld 167 E8
Dalwhinnie Highld 148 F2
Dalwood Devon 11 D7
Dalwyne S Ayrs 112 E3
Dam Green Norf 68 F3
Dam Side Lancs 92 E4
Damerham Hants 14 C2
Damgate Norf 69 D7
Damnaglaur Dumfries 104 F5
Damside Borders 122 E4
Danbury Essex 42 D3
Danby N Yorks 103 D5
Danby Wiske N Yorks 101 E8
Dandaleith Moray 159 E6
Danderhall Midloth 123 C6
Dane End Herts 41 B6
Danebridge Ches 75 C6
Danehill E Sus 17 B8
Danemoor Green Norf 68 D3
Danesford Shrops 61 E7
Daneshill Hants 26 D4
Dangerous Corner Lancs 86 C3
Danskine E Loth 123 C8
Darcy Lever Gtr Man 86 D5
Darenth Kent 29 B6
Daresbury Halton 86 F3
Darfield S Yorks 88 D5
Darfoulds Notts 77 B5
Dargate Kent 30 C4
Darite Corn 5 C7
Darlaston W Mid 62 E3
Darley N Yorks 94 D5
Darley Bridge Derbys 76 C2
Darley Head N Yorks 94 D4
Darley Moor Motor Racing Circuit Derbys 75 E8
Darlingscott Warks 51 E7
Darlington Darl 101 C7
Darliston Shrops 74 F2
Darlton Notts 77 B7
Darnall S Yorks 88 F4
Darnick Borders 123 F8
Darowen Powys 58 D5
Darra Aberds 160 D4
Darracott Devon 20 F3
Darras Hall Northumb 110 B4
Darrington W Yorks 89 B5
Darsham Suff 57 C8
Dartford Kent 29 B6
Dartford Crossing Kent 29 B6
Dartington Devon 7 C5
Dartington Cider Press Centre Devon 7 C5
Dartington Crystal Devon 9 C6
Dartmeet Devon 6 B4
Dartmouth Devon 7 D6
Darton S Yorks 88 D4
Darvel E Ayrs 121 F5
Darwell Hole E Sus 18 D3
Darwen Blkburn 86 B4
Datchet Windsor 27 B7
Datchworth Herts 41 C5
Datchworth Green Herts 41 C5
Daubhill Gtr Man 86 D5
Daugh of Kinermony Moray 159 E6
Dauntsey Wilts 37 F6
Dava Moray 158 F4
Davenham Ches 74 B3
Davenport Green Ches 74 B5
Daventry Northants 52 C3
David's Well Powys 48 B2
Davidson's Mains Edin 122 B5
Davidstow Corn 8 F3
Davington Dumfries 115 D5
Daviot Aberds 151 B6
Daviot Highld 157 F8
Davoch of Grange Moray 159 D8
Davyhulme Gtr Man 87 E5
Dawley Telford 61 D6
Dawlish Devon 7 B7
Dawlish Warren Devon 7 B7
Dawn Conwy 83 D8
Daws Heath Essex 42 F4
Daw's House Corn 8 F5
Dawsmere Lincs 79 F7
Dayhills Staffs 75 F6
Daylesford Glos 38 B2
Ddôl-Cownwy Powys 59 C7
Ddrydwy Anglesey 82 D3
Deadwater Northumb 116 E2
Deaf Hill Durham 111 F6
Deal Kent 31 D7
Deal Hall Essex 43 E6
Dean Cumb 98 B2
Dean Devon 6 C5
Dean Devon 20 E4
Dean Dorset 13 C7
Dean Hants 15 C6
Dean Som 23 E8
Dean Prior Devon 6 C5
Dean Row Ches 87 F6
Deanburnhaugh Borders 115 C6
Deane Gtr Man 86 D4
Deane Hants 26 D3
Deanich Lodge Highld 163 F7
Deanland Dorset 13 C7
Deans W Loth 122 C3
Deanscales Cumb 98 B2
Deanshanger Northants 53 F5
Deanston Stirl 133 D6
Dearham Cumb 107 F7
Debach Suff 57 D6
Debden Essex 41 E7
Debden Essex 55 F6
Debden Cross Essex 55 F6
Debenham Suff 57 C5
Dechmont W Loth 122 B3
Deddington Oxon 52 F2
Dedham Essex 56 F4
Dedham Heath Essex 56 F4
Deebank Aberds 151 E5
Deene Northants 65 E6
Deenethorpe Northants 65 E6
Deep Sea World, North Queensferry Fife 134 F3
Deepcar S Yorks 88 E3
Deepcut Sur 27 D7
Deepdale Cumb 100 F2
Deeping Gate Lincs 65 D8
Deeping St James Lincs 65 D8
Deeping St Nicholas Lincs 66 C2
Deerhill Moray 159 D8
Deerhurst Glos 37 B5
Deerness Orkney 176 F4
Defford Worcs 50 E4
Defynnog Powys 34 B3
Deganwy Conwy 83 D7
Deighton N Yorks 102 D1
Deighton W Yorks 88 C2
Deighton York 96 E2
Deiniolen Gwyn 83 E5
Delabole Corn 8 F2
Delamere Ches 74 C2
Delfrigs Aberds 151 B8
Dell Lodge Highld 149 C6
Delliefure Highld 158 F4
Delnabo Moray 149 C7
Delnadamph Aberds 149 D8
Delph Gtr Man 87 D7
Delves Durham 110 E4
Delvine Perth 141 E8
Dembleby Lincs 78 F3
Denaby Main S Yorks 89 E5
Denbigh = Dinbych Denb 72 C4
Denbury Devon 7 C6
Denby Derbys 76 E3
Denby Dale W Yorks 88 D3
Denchworth Oxon 38 E3
Dendron Cumb 92 B2
Denel End Beds 53 F8
Denend Aberds 160 E3
Denford Northants 53 B7
Dengie Essex 43 D5
Denham Bucks 40 F3
Denham Suff 55 C8
Denham Suff 57 B5
Denham Green Bucks 40 F3
Denham Street Suff 57 B5
Denhead Aberds 161 C6
Denhead Fife 135 C6
Denhead of Arbilot Angus 143 E5
Denhead of Gray Dundee 142 F3
Denholm Borders 115 C8
Denholme W Yorks 94 F3
Denholme Clough W Yorks 94 F3
Denio Gwyn 70 D4
Denmead Hants 15 C7
Denmore Aberdeen 151 C8
Denmoss Aberds 160 D3
Dennington Suff 57 C6
Denny Falk 133 F7
Denny Lodge Hants 14 D4
Dennyloanhead Falk 133 F7
Denshaw Gtr Man 87 C7
Denside Aberds 151 E7
Densole Kent 31 E6
Denston Suff 55 D8
Denstone Staffs 75 E8
Dent Cumb 100 F2
Denton Cambs 65 F8
Denton Darl 101 C7
Denton E Sus 17 D8
Denton Gtr Man 87 E7
Denton Kent 31 E6
Denton Lincs 77 F8
Denton Norf 69 F5
Denton Northants 53 D6
Denton N Yorks 94 E4
Denton Oxon 39 D5
Denton's Green Mers 86 E2
Denver Norf 67 D6
Denwick Northumb 117 C8
Deopham Norf 68 D3
Deopham Green Norf 68 E3
Depden Suff 55 D8
Depden Green Suff 55 D8
Deptford London 28 B4
Deptford Wilts 24 F5
Derby Derby 76 F3
Derbyhaven I o M 84 F2
Dereham Norf 68 C2
Deri Caerph 35 D5
Derril Devon 8 D5
Derringstone Kent 31 E6
Derrington Staffs 62 B2
Derriton Devon 8 D5
Derry Hill Wilts 24 B4
Derryguaig Argyll 137 E5
Derrythorpe N Lincs 90 D2
Dersingham Norf 80 D2
Dervaig Argyll 137 C5
Derwen Denb 72 D4
Derwenlas Powys 58 E4
Desborough Northants 64 F5
Desford Leics 63 D8
Detchant Northumb 125 F6
Detling Kent 29 D8
Deuddwr Powys 60 C2
Devauden Mon 36 E1
Devil's Bridge Ceredig 47 B6
Devizes Wilts 24 C5
Devol Invclyd 120 B3
Devon & Exeter Racecourse Devon 10 F4
Devonport Plym 6 D2
Devonside Clack 133 E8
Devoran Corn 3 C6
Dewar Borders 123 E6
Dewlish Dorset 13 E5
Dewsbury W Yorks 88 B3
Dewsbury Moor W Yorks 88 B3
Dewshall Court Hereford 49 F6
Dhoon I o M 84 D4
Dhoor I o M 84 C4
Dhowin I o M 84 B4
Dial Post W Sus 17 C5
Dibden Hants 14 D5
Dibden Purlieu Hants 14 D5
Dickleburgh Norf 68 F4
Didbrook Glos 51 F5
Didcot Oxon 39 F5
Diddington Cambs 54 C2
Diddlebury Shrops 60 F5
Didley Hereford 49 F6
Didling W Sus 16 C2
Didmarton Glos 37 F5
Didsbury Gtr Man 87 E6
Didworthy Devon 6 C4
Digby Lincs 78 D3
Digg Highld 152 C5
Diggerland, Cullompton Devon 10 D5
Diggerland, Langley Park Durham 110 E5
Diggle Gtr Man 87 D8
Digmoor Lancs 86 D2
Digswell Park Herts 41 C5
Dihewyd Ceredig 46 D3
Dilham Norf 69 B6
Dilhorne Staffs 75 E6
Dillarburn S Lnrk 121 E8
Dillington Cambs 54 C2
Dilston Northumb 110 C2
Dilton Marsh Wilts 24 E3
Dilwyn Hereford 49 D6
Dinas Carms 45 F4
Dinas Gwyn 70 D3
Dinas Cross Pembs 45 F2
Dinas Dinlle Gwyn 82 F4
Dinas-Mawddwy Gwyn 59 C5
Dinas Powys V Glam 22 B3
Dinbych = Denbigh Denb 72 C4
Dinbych-y-Pysgod = Tenby Pembs 32 D2
Dinder Som 23 E7
Dinedor Hereford 49 F7
Dingestow Mon 36 C1
Dingle Mers 85 F4
Dingleden Kent 18 B5
Dingley Northants 64 F4
Dingwall Highld 157 D6
Dinlabyre Borders 115 E8
Dinmael Conwy 72 E4
Dinnet Aberds 150 E3
Dinnington Som 12 C2
Dinnington S Yorks 89 F6
Dinnington T & W 110 B5
Dinorwic Gwyn 83 E5
Dinton Bucks 39 C7
Dinton Wilts 24 F5
Dinwoodie Mains Dumfries 114 E4
Dinworthy Devon 8 C5
Dippen N Ayrs 119 D7
Dippenhall Sur 27 E6
Dipple Moray 159 D7
Dipple S Ayrs 112 D2
Diptford Devon 6 D5
Dipton Durham 110 D4
Dirdhu Highld 149 B6
Dirleton E Loth 135 F7
Dirt Pot Northumb 109 E8
Discoed Powys 48 C4
Discovery Point Dundee 135 B6
Diseworth Leics 63 B8
Dishes Orkney 176 D5
Dishforth N Yorks 95 B6
Disley Ches 87 F7
Diss Norf 56 B5
Disserth Powys 48 D2
Distington Cumb 98 B2
Ditchampton Wilts 25 F5
Ditcheat Som 23 F8
Ditchingham Norf 69 E6
Ditchling E Sus 17 C7
Ditherington Shrops 60 C5
Dittisham Devon 7 D6
Ditton Halton 86 F2
Ditton Kent 29 D8
Ditton Green Cambs 55 D7
Ditton Priors Shrops 61 F6
Divach Highld 147 B7
Divlyn Carms 47 F6
Dixton Glos 50 F4
Dixton Mon 36 C2
Dobcross Gtr Man 87 D7
Dobwalls Corn 5 C7
Doc Penfro = Pembroke Dock Pembs 44 E4
Doccombe Devon 10 F2
Dochfour Ho. Highld 157 F7
Dochgarroch Highld 157 E7
Docking Norf 80 D3
Docklow Hereford 49 D7
Dockray Cumb 99 B5
Dockroyd W Yorks 94 F3
Dodburn Borders 115 D7
Doddinghurst Essex 42 E1
Doddington Cambs 66 E3
Doddington Kent 30 D3
Doddington Lincs 78 B2
Doddington Northumb 125 F5
Doddington Shrops 49 B8
Doddiscombsleigh Devon 10 F3
Dodford Northants 52 C4
Dodford Worcs 50 B4
Dodington S Glos 24 A2
Dodleston Ches 73 C7
Dods Leigh Staffs 75 F7
Dodworth S Yorks 88 D4
Doe Green Warr 86 F3
Doe Lea Derbys 76 C4
Dog Village Devon 10 E4
Dogdyke Lincs 78 D5
Dogmersfield Hants 27 D5
Dogridge Wilts 37 F7
Dogsthorpe P'boro 65 D8
Dol-fôr Powys 58 D5
Dôl-y-Bont Ceredig 58 F3
Dol-y-cannau Powys 48 E4
Dolanog Powys 59 C7
Dolau Powys 48 C3
Dolau Rhondda 34 F3
Dolbenmaen Gwyn 71 C6
Dolfach Powys 59 D6
Dolfor Powys 59 F8
Dolgarrog Conwy 83 E7
Dolgellau Gwyn 58 C4
Dolgran Carms 46 F3
Dolhendre Gwyn 72 F2
Doll Highld 165 D5
Dollar Clack 133 E8
Dolley Green Powys 48 C4
Dollwen Ceredig 58 F3
Dolphin Flint 73 B5
Dolphinholme Lancs 92 D5
Dolphinton S Lnrk 122 E4
Dolton Devon 9 C7
Dolwen Conwy 83 D8
Dolwen Powys 59 D6
Dolwyd Conwy 83 D8
Dolwyddelan Conwy 83 F7
Dolyhir Powys 48 D4
Doncaster S Yorks 89 D6
Doncaster Racecourse S Yorks 89 D7
Dones Green Ches 74 B3
Donhead St Andrew Wilts 13 B7
Donhead St Mary Wilts 13 B7
Donibristle Fife 134 F3
Donington Lincs 78 F5
Donington on Bain Lincs 91 F6
Donington Park Motor Racing Circuit Leics 63 B8
Donington South Ing Lincs 78 F5
Donisthorpe Leics 63 C7
Donkey Town Sur 27 C7
Donnington Glos 38 B1
Donnington Hereford 50 F2
Donnington Shrops 61 D5
Donnington Telford 61 C7
Donnington W Berks 26 C2
Donnington W Sus 16 D2
Donnington Wood Telford 61 C7
Donyatt Som 11 C8
Doonfoot S Ayrs 112 C3
Dorback Lodge Highld 149 C6
Dorchester Dorset 12 E4
Dorchester Oxon 39 E5
Dorchester Abbey, Wallingford Oxon 39 E5
Dordon Warks 63 D6
Dore S Yorks 88 F4
Dores Highld 157 F6
Dorking Sur 28 E2
Dormansland Sur 28 E5
Dormanstown Redcar 102 B3
Dormington Hereford 49 E7
Dormston Worcs 50 D4
Dornal S Ayrs 105 B6
Dorney Bucks 27 B7
Dornie Highld 155 H4
Dornoch Highld 164 F4
Dornock Dumfries 108 C2
Dorrery Highld 169 D5
Dorridge W Mid 51 B6
Dorrington Lincs 78 D3
Dorrington Shrops 60 D4
Dorsington Warks 51 E6
Dorstone Hereford 48 E5
Dorton Bucks 39 C6
Dorusduain Highld 146 B2
Dosthill Staffs 63 E6
Dottery Dorset 12 E2
Doublebois Corn 5 C6
Dougarie N Ayrs 119 C5
Doughton Glos 37 E5
Douglas I o M 84 E3
Douglas S Lnrk 121 F8
Douglas & Angus Dundee 142 F4
Douglas Water S Lnrk 121 F8
Douglas West S Lnrk 121 F8
Douglastown Angus 142 E4
Doulting Som 23 E8
Dounby Orkney 176 D1
Doune Highld 163 D8
Doune Stirl 133 D6
Doune Park Aberds 160 B4
Douneside Aberds 150 D3
Dounie Highld 164 E3
Dounreay Highld 168 C4
Dousland Devon 6 C3
Dovaston Shrops 60 B3
Dove Cottage and Wordsworth Museum Cumb 99 D5
Dove Holes Derbys 75 B7
Dovenby Cumb 107 F7
Dover Kent 31 E7
Dover Castle Kent 31 E7
Dovercourt Essex 57 F6
Doverdale Worcs 50 C3
Doveridge Derbys 75 F8
Doversgreen Sur 28 E3
Dowally Perth 141 E7
Dowbridge Lancs 92 F4
Dowdeswell Glos 37 C6
Dowlais M Tydf 34 D4
Dowland Devon 9 C7
Dowlish Wake Som 11 C8
Down Ampney Glos 37 E8
Down Hatherley Glos 37 B5
Down St Mary Devon 10 D2
Down Thomas Devon 6 D3
Downcraig Ferry N Ayrs 129 E6
Downderry Corn 5 D8
Downe London 28 C5
Downend I o W 15 F6
Downend S Glos 23 B8
Downend W Berks 26 B2
Downfield Dundee 142 F3
Downgate Corn 5 B8
Downham Essex 42 E3
Downham Lancs 93 E7
Downham Northumb 124 F4
Downham Market Norf 67 D6
Downhead Som 23 E8
Downhill Perth 141 F7
Downhill T & W 111 D6
Downholland Cross Lancs 85 D4
Downholme N Yorks 101 E6
Downies Aberds 151 E8
Downley Bucks 39 E8
Downside Som 23 E8
Downside Sur 28 D2
Downton Hants 14 E3
Downton Wilts 14 B2
Downton on the Rock Hereford 49 B6
Dowsby Lincs 65 B8
Dowsdale Lincs 66 C2
Dowthwaitehead Cumb 99 B5
Doxey Staffs 62 B3
Doxford Northumb 117 B7
Doxford Park T & W 111 D6
Doynton S Glos 24 B2
Draffan S Lnrk 121 E7
Dragonby N Lincs 90 C3
Drakeland Corner Devon 6 D3
Drakemyre N Ayrs 120 D2
Drake's Broughton Worcs 50 E4
Drakes Cross Worcs 51 B5
Drakewalls Corn 6 B2
Draughton Northants 53 B5
Draughton N Yorks 94 D3
Drax N Yorks 89 B7
Draycote Warks 52 B2
Draycott Derbys 76 F4
Draycott Glos 51 F6
Draycott Som 23 D6
Draycott in the Clay Staffs 63 B5
Draycott in the Moors Staffs 75 E6
Drayford Devon 10 C2
Drayton Leics 64 E5
Drayton Lincs 78 F5
Drayton Norf 68 C4
Drayton Oxon 52 E2
Drayton Oxon 38 E4
Drayton Ptsmth 15 D7
Drayton Som 12 B2
Drayton Worcs 50 B4
Drayton Bassett Staffs 63 D5
Drayton Beauchamp Bucks 40 C2
Drayton Manor Park, Tamworth Staffs 63 D5
Drayton Parslow Bucks 39 B8
Drayton St Leonard Oxon 39 E5
Dre-fach Ceredig 46 E4
Dre-fach Carms 33 C7
Dreamland Theme Park, Margate Kent 31 B7
Drebley N Yorks 94 D3
Dreemskerry I o M 84 C4
Dreenhill Pembs 44 D4

Drefach Carms 46 F2
Drefach Carms 33 C6
Drefelin Carms 46 F2
Dreghorn N Ayrs 120 F3
Drellingore Kent 31 E6
Drem E Loth 123 B8
Dresden Stoke 75 E6
Dreumasdal W Isles 170 G3
Drewsteignton Devon 10 E2
Driby Lincs 79 B6
Driffield E Yorks 97 D6
Driffield Glos 37 E7
Drigg Cumb 98 E2
Drighlington W Yorks 88 B3
Drimnin Highld 137 C6
Drimpton Dorset 12 D2
Drimsynie Argyll 131 E7
Drinisiadar W Isles 173 J4
Drinkstone Suff 56 C3
Drinkstone Green Suff 56 C3
Drishaig Argyll 131 D7
Drissaig Argyll 130 D5
Drochil Borders 122 E4
Drointon Staffs 62 B4
Droitwich Spa Worcs 50 C3
Droman Highld 166 D3
Dron Perth 134 C3
Dronfield Derbys 76 B3
Dronfield Woodhouse Derbys 76 B3
Drongan E Ayrs 112 C4
Dronley Angus 142 F3
Droxford Hants 15 C7
Droylsden Gtr Man 87 E7
Druid Denb 72 E4
Druidston Pembs 44 D3
Druimarbin Highld 138 B4
Druimavuic Argyll 138 E4
Druimdrishaig Argyll 128 C2
Druimindarroch Highld 145 E6
Druimyeon More Argyll 118 A3
Drum Argyll 128 C4
Drum Perth 134 D2
Drumbeg Highld 166 F3
Drumblade Aberds 160 D2
Drumblair Aberds 160 D3
Drumbuie Dumfries 113 F5
Drumbuie Highld 155 G3
Drumburgh Cumb 108 D2
Drumburn Dumfries 107 C6
Drumchapel Glasgow 120 B5
Drumchardine Highld 157 E6
Drumchork Highld 162 F2
Drumclog S Lnrk 121 F6
Drumderfit Highld 157 D7
Drumeldrie Fife 135 D6
Drumelzier Borders 122 F4
Drumfearn Highld 145 B6
Drumgask Highld 148 E2
Drumgley Angus 142 D4
Drumguish Highld 148 E3
Drumin Moray 159 F5
Drumlasie Aberds 150 D5
Drumlemble Argyll 118 E3
Drumligair Aberds 151 C8
Drumlithie Aberds 151 F6
Drummoddie Dumfries 105 E7
Drummond Highld 157 C7
Drummore Dumfries 104 F5
Drummuir Moray 159 E7
Drummuir Castle Moray 159 E7
Drumnadrochit Highld 147 B8
Drumnagorrach Moray 160 C2
Drumoak Aberds 151 E6
Drumpark Dumfries 107 A5
Drumphail Dumfries 105 C6
Drumrash Dumfries 106 B3
Drumrunie Highld 163 D5
Drums Aberds 151 B8
Drumsallie Highld 138 B3
Drumstinchall Dumfries 107 D5
Drumsturdy Angus 142 F4
Drumtochty Castle Aberds 143 B6
Drumtroddan Dumfries 105 E7
Drumuie Highld 152 E5
Drumuillie Highld 148 B5
Drumvaich Stirl 133 D5
Drumwhindle Aberds 161 E6
Drunkendub Angus 143 E6
Drury Flint 73 C6
Drury Square Norf 68 C2
Drusillas Park, Polegate E Sus 18 E2
Dry Doddington Lincs 77 E8
Dry Drayton Cambs 54 C4
Drybeck Cumb 100 C1
Drybridge Moray 159 C8
Drybridge N Ayrs 120 F3
Drybrook Glos 36 C3
Dryburgh Borders 123 F8
Dryhope Borders 115 B5
Drylaw Edin 122 B5
Drym Corn 2 C5
Drymen Stirl 132 F3
Drymuir Aberds 161 D6
Drynoch Highld 153 F5
Dryslwyn Carms 33 B6
Dryton Shrops 61 D5
Dubford Aberds 160 B5
Dubton Angus 143 D5
Duchally Highld 163 C7
Duchlage Argyll 129 B8
Duck Corner Suff 57 E7
Duckington Ches 73 D8
Ducklington Oxon 38 D3
Duckmanton Derbys 76 B4
Duck's Cross Beds 54 D2
Duddenhoe End Essex 55 F5
Duddingston Edin 123 B5
Duddington Northants 65 D6
Duddleswell E Sus 17 B8
Duddo Northumb 124 E5
Duddon Ches 74 C2
Duddon Bridge Cumb 98 F4
Dudleston Shrops 73 F7
Dudleston Heath Shrops 73 F7
Dudley T & W 111 B5
Dudley W Mid 62 E3
Dudley Port W Mid 62 E3
Dudley Zoological Gardens W Mid 62 E3
Duffield Derbys 76 E3
Duffryn Newport 35 F6
Duffryn Neath 34 E2
Dufftown Moray 159 F7
Duffus Moray 159 C5
Dufton Cumb 100 B1
Duggleby N Yorks 96 C4
Duirinish Highld 155 G3
Duisdalemore Highld 145 B7
Duisky Highld 138 B4
Dukestown Bl Gwent 35 C5
Dukinfield Gtr Man 87 E7
Dulas Anglesey 82 C4
Dulcote Som 23 E7
Dulford Devon 11 D5
Dull Perth 141 E5
Dullatur N Lnrk 121 B7
Dullingham Cambs 55 D7
Dulnain Bridge Highld 149 B5
Duloe Beds 54 C2
Duloe Corn 5 D7
Dulsie Highld 158 E3
Dulverton Som 10 B4
Dulwich London 28 B4
Dumbarton W Dunb 120 B3
Dumbleton Glos 50 F5
Dumcrieff Dumfries 114 D4
Dumfries Dumfries 107 B6
Dumgoyne Stirl 132 F4
Dummer Hants 26 E3
Dumpford W Sus 16 B2
Dumpton Kent 31 C7
Dun Angus 143 D6
Dun Charlabhaigh W Isles 172 D4
Dunain Ho. Highld 157 E7
Dunalastair Perth 140 D4
Dunan Highld 153 G6
Dunans Argyll 129 A5
Dunball Som 22 E5
Dunbar E Loth 124 B2
Dunbeath Highld 165 B8
Dunbeg Argyll 130 B4
Dunblane Stirl 133 D6
Dunbog Fife 134 C4
Duncanston Aberds 150 B4
Duncanston Highld 157 D6
Dunchurch Warks 52 B2
Duncote Northants 52 D4
Duncow Dumfries 114 F2
Duncraggan Stirl 132 D4
Duncrievie Perth 134 D3
Duncton W Sus 16 C3
Dundas Ho. Orkney 176 H3
Dundee Dundee 142 F4
Dundee Airport Dundee 135 B5
Dundeugh Dumfries 113 F5
Dundon Som 23 F6
Dundonald S Ayrs 120 F3
Dundonnell Highld 162 F4
Dundonnell Hotel Highld 162 F4
Dundonnell House Highld 163 F5
Dundraw Cumb 108 E2
Dundreggan Highld 147 C6
Dundreggan Lodge Highld 147 C6
Dundrennan Dumfries 106 E4
Dundry N Som 23 C7
Dunecht Aberds 151 D6
Dunfermline Fife 134 F2
Dunfield Glos 37 E8
Dunford Bridge S Yorks 88 D2
Dungworth S Yorks 88 F3
Dunham Notts 77 B8
Dunham Massey Gtr Man 86 F5
Dunham-on-the-Hill Ches 73 B8
Dunham Town Gtr Man 86 F5
Dunhampton Worcs 50 C3
Dunholme Lincs 78 B3
Dunino Fife 135 C7
Dunipace Falk 133 F7
Dunira Perth 133 B6
Dunkeld Perth 141 E7
Dunkerton Bath 24 D2
Dunkeswell Devon 11 D6
Dunkeswick N Yorks 95 E6
Dunkirk Kent 30 D4
Dunkirk Norf 81 E8
Dunk's Green Kent 29 D7
Dunlappie Angus 143 C5
Dunley Hants 26 D2
Dunley Worcs 50 C2
Dunlichity Lodge Highld 157 F7
Dunlop E Ayrs 120 E4
Dunmaglass Lodge Highld 147 B8
Dunmore Argyll 128 D2
Dunmore Falk 133 F7
Dunnet Highld 169 B7
Dunnichen Angus 143 E5
Dunninald Angus 143 D7
Dunning Perth 134 C2
Dunnington E Yorks 97 D7
Dunnington Warks 51 D5
Dunnington York 96 D2
Dunnockshaw Lancs 87 B6
Dunollie Argyll 130 B4
Dunoon Argyll 129 C6
Dunragit Dumfries 105 D5
Dunrobin Castle Museum & Gardens Highld 165 D5
Dunrostan Argyll 128 B2
Duns Borders 124 D3
Duns Tew Oxon 38 B4
Dunsby Lincs 65 B8
Dunscore Dumfries 113 F8
Dunscroft S Yorks 89 D7
Dunsdale Redcar 102 C4
Dunsden Green Oxon 26 B5
Dunsfold Sur 27 F8
Dunsford Devon 10 F3
Dunshalt Fife 134 C4
Dunshillock Aberds 161 D6
Dunskey Ho. Dumfries 104 D4
Dunsley N Yorks 103 C6
Dunsmore Bucks 40 D1
Dunsop Bridge Lancs 93 D6
Dunstable Beds 40 B3
Dunstall Staffs 63 B5
Dunstall Common Worcs 50 E3
Dunstall Green Suff 55 C8
Dunstan Northumb 117 C8
Dunstan Steads Northumb 117 B8
Dunster Som 21 E8
Dunster Castle, Minehead Som 21 E8
Dunston Lincs 78 C3
Dunston Norf 68 D5
Dunston Staffs 62 C3
Dunston T & W 110 C5
Dunsville S Yorks 89 D7
Dunswell E Yorks 97 F6
Dunsyre S Lnrk 122 E3
Dunterton Devon 5 B8
Duntisbourne Abbots Glos 37 D6
Duntisbourne Leer Glos 37 D6
Duntisbourne Rouse Glos 37 D6
Duntish Dorset 12 D4
Duntocher W Dunb 120 B4
Dunton Beds 54 E3
Dunton Bucks 39 B8
Dunton Norf 80 D4
Dunton Bassett Leics 64 E2
Dunton Green Kent 29 D6
Dunton Wayletts Essex 42 E2
Duntulm Highld 152 B5
Dunure S Ayrs 112 C2
Dunvant Swansea 33 E6
Dunvegan Highld 152 E3
Dunvegan Castle Highld 152 E3
Dunwich Suff 57 B8
Dunwood Staffs 75 D6
Dupplin Castle Perth 134 C2
Durdar Cumb 108 D4
Durgates E Sus 18 B3
Durham Durham 111 E5
Durham Cathedral Durham 111 E5
Durham Tees Valley Airport Stockton 102 C1
Durisdeer Dumfries 113 D8
Durisdeermill Dumfries 113 D8
Durkar W Yorks 88 C4
Durleigh Som 22 F4
Durley Hants 15 C6
Durley Wilts 25 C7
Durnamuck Highld 162 E4
Durness Highld 167 C6
Durno Aberds 151 B6
Duror Highld 138 D3
Durran Argyll 131 E5
Durran Highld 169 C6
Durrington Wilts 25 E6
Durrington W Sus 16 D5
Dursley Glos 36 E4
Durston Som 11 B7
Durweston Dorset 13 D6
Dury Shetland 175 G6
Duston Northants 52 C5
Duthil Highld 148 B5
Dutlas Powys 48 B4
Duton Hill Essex 42 B2
Dutson Corn 8 F5
Dutton Ches 74 B2
Duxford Cambs 55 E5
Duxford Oxon 38 E3
Duxford Airfield (Imperial War Museum), Sawston Cambs 55 E5
Dwygyfylchi Conwy 83 D7
Dwyran Anglesey 82 E4
Dyce Aberdeen 151 C7
Dye House Northumb 110 D2
Dyffryn Bridgend 34 E2
Dyffryn Carms 32 B4
Dyffryn Pembs 44 B4
Dyffryn Ardudwy Gwyn 71 E6
Dyffryn Castell Ceredig 58 F4
Dyffryn Ceidrych Carms 33 B8
Dyffryn Cellwen Neath 34 D2
Dyke Lincs 65 B8
Dyke Moray 158 D3
Dykehead Angus 142 C3
Dykehead N Lnrk 121 D8
Dykehead Stirl 132 E4
Dykelands Aberds 143 C7
Dykends Angus 142 D2
Dykeside Aberds 160 D4
Dykesmains N Ayrs 120 E2
Dylife Powys 59 E5
Dymchurch Kent 19 C7
Dymock Glos 50 F2
Dyrham S Glos 24 B2
Dyrham Park S Glos 24 B2
Dysart Fife 134 E5
Dyserth Denb 72 B4

E

Eachwick Northumb 110 B4
Eadar Dha Fhadhail W Isles 172 E3
Eagland Hill Lancs 92 E4
Eagle Lincs 77 C8
Eagle Barnsdale Lincs 77 C8
Eagle Moor Lincs 77 C8
Eaglescliffe Stockton 102 C2
Eaglesfield Cumb 98 B2
Eaglesfield Dumfries 108 B2
Eaglesham E Renf 121 D5
Eaglethorpe Northants 65 E7
Eairy I o M 84 E2
Eakley Lanes M Keynes 53 D6
Eakring Notts 77 C6
Ealand N Lincs 89 C8
Ealing London 40 F4
Eals Northumb 109 D6
Eamont Bridge Cumb 99 B7
Earby Lancs 94 E2
Earcroft Blkburn 86 B4
Eardington Shrops 61 E7
Eardisland Hereford 49 D6
Eardisley Hereford 48 E5
Eardiston Shrops 60 B3
Eardiston Worcs 49 C8
Earith Cambs 54 B4
Earl Shilton Leics 63 E8
Earl Soham Suff 57 C6
Earl Sterndale Derbys 75 C7
Earl Stonham Suff 56 D5
Earle Northumb 117 B5
Earley Wokingham 27 B5
Earlham Norf 68 D5
Earlish Highld 152 C4
Earls Barton Northants 53 C6
Earls Colne Essex 42 B4
Earl's Croome Worcs 50 E3
Earl's Green Suff 56 C4
Earlsdon W Mid 51 B8
Earlsferry Fife 135 E6
Earlsfield Lincs 78 F2
Earlsford Aberds 160 E5
Earlsheaton W Yorks 88 B3
Earlsmill Moray 158 D3
Earlston Borders 123 F8
Earlston E Ayrs 120 F4
Earlswood Mon 36 E1
Earlswood Sur 28 E3
Earlswood Warks 51 B6
Earnley W Sus 16 E2
Earsairidh W Isles 171 L3
Earsdon T & W 111 B6
Earsham Norf 69 F6
Earswick York 96 D2
Eartham W Sus 16 D3
Easby N Yorks 102 D3
Easby N Yorks 101 D6
Easdale Argyll 130 D3
Easebourne W Sus 16 B2
Easenhall Warks 52 B2
Eashing Sur 27 E7
Easington Bucks 39 C6
Easington Durham 111 E7
Easington E Yorks 91 C7
Easington Northumb 125 F7
Easington Oxon 52 F2
Easington Oxon 39 E6
Easington Redcar 103 C5
Easington Colliery Durham 111 E7
Easington Lane T & W 111 E6
Easingwold N Yorks 95 C8
Easole Street Kent 31 D6
Eassie Angus 142 E3
East Aberthaw V Glam 22 C2
East Adderbury Oxon 52 F2
East Allington Devon 7 E5
East Anstey Devon 10 B3
East Appleton N Yorks 101 E7
East Ardsley W Yorks 88 B4
East Ashling W Sus 16 D2
East Auchronie Aberds 151 D7
East Ayton N Yorks 103 F7
East Bank Bl Gwent 35 D6
East Barkwith Lincs 91 F5
East Barming Kent 29 D8
East Barnby N Yorks 103 C6
East Barnet London 41 E5
East Barns E Loth 124 B3
East Barsham Norf 80 D5
East Beckham Norf 81 D7
East Bedfont London 27 B8
East Bergholt Suff 56 F4
East Bilney Norf 68 C2
East Blatchington E Sus 17 D8
East Boldre Hants 14 D4
East Brent Som 22 D5
East Bridgford Notts 77 E6
East Buckland Devon 21 F5
East Budleigh Devon 11 F5
East Burrafirth Shetland 175 H5
East Burton Dorset 13 F6
East Butsfield Durham 110 E4
East Butterwick N Lincs 90 D2
East Cairnbeg Aberds 143 B7
East Calder W Loth 122 C3
East Carleton Norf 68 D4
East Carlton Northants 64 F5
East Carlton W Yorks 94 E5
East Chaldon Dorset 13 F5
East Challow Oxon 38 F3
East Chiltington E Sus 17 C7
East Chinnock Som 12 C2
East Chisenbury Wilts 25 D6
East Clandon Sur 27 D8
East Claydon Bucks 39 B7
East Clyne Highld 165 D6
East Coker Som 12 C3
East Combe Som 22 F3
East Common N Yorks 96 F2
East Compton Som 23 E8
East Cottingwith E Yorks 96 E3
East Cowes I o W 15 E6
East Cowick E Yorks 89 B7
East Cowton N Yorks 101 D8
East Cramlington Northumb 111 B5
East Cranmore Som 23 E8
East Creech Dorset 13 F7
East Croachy Highld 148 B2
East Croftmore Highld 149 C5
East Curthwaite Cumb 108 E3
East Dean E Sus 18 F2
East Dean Hants 14 B3
East Dean W Sus 16 C3
East Down Devon 20 E5
East Drayton Notts 77 B7
East Ella Hull 90 B4
East End Dorset 13 E7
East End E Yorks 91 B6
East End Hants 14 E4
East End Hants 15 B7
East End Hants 26 C2
East End Herts 41 B7
East End Kent 18 B5
East End N Som 23 B6
East End Oxon 38 C3
East Farleigh Kent 29 D8
East Farndon Northants 64 F4
East Ferry Lincs 90 E2
East Fortune E Loth 123 B8
East Garston W Berks 25 B8
East Ginge Oxon 38 F4
East Goscote Leics 64 C3
East Grafton Wilts 25 C7
East Grimstead Wilts 14 B3
East Grinstead W Sus 28 F4
East Guldeford E Sus 19 C6
East Haddon Northants 52 C4
East Hagbourne Oxon 39 F5
East Halton N Lincs 90 C5
East Ham London 41 F7
East Hanney Oxon 38 E4
East Hanningfield Essex 42 D3
East Hardwick W Yorks 89 C5
East Harling Norf 68 F2
East Harlsey N Yorks 102 E2
East Harnham Wilts 14 B2
East Harptree Bath 23 D7
East Hartford Northumb 111 B5
East Harting W Sus 15 C8
East Hatley Cambs 54 D3
East Hauxwell N Yorks 101 E6
East Haven Angus 143 F5
East Heckington Lincs 78 E4
East Hedleyhope Durham 110 E4
East Hendred Oxon 38 F4
East Herrington T & W 111 D6
East Heslerton N Yorks 96 B5
East Hoathly E Sus 18 D2
East Horrington Som 23 E7
East Horsley Sur 27 D8
East Horton Northumb 125 F6
East Huntspill Som 22 E5
East Hyde Beds 40 C4
East Ilkerton Devon 21 E6
East Ilsley W Berks 38 F4
East Keal Lincs 79 C6
East Kennett Wilts 25 C6
East Keswick W Yorks 95 E6
East Kilbride S Lnrk 121 D6
East Kirkby Lincs 79 C6
East Knapton N Yorks 96 B4
East Knighton Dorset 13 F6
East Knoyle Wilts 24 F3
East Kyloe Northumb 125 F6
East Lambrook Som 12 C2
East Lamington Highld 157 B8
East Langdon Kent 31 E7
East Langton Leics 64 E4
East Langwell Highld 164 D4
East Lavant W Sus 16 D2
East Lavington W Sus 16 C3
East Layton N Yorks 101 D6
East Leake Notts 64 B2
East Learmouth Northumb 124 F4
East Leigh Devon 9 D8
East Lexham Norf 67 C8
East Lilburn Northumb 117 B6
East Linton E Loth 123 B8
East Liss Hants 15 B8
East Looe Corn 5 D7
East Lound N Lincs 89 E8
East Lulworth Dorset 13 F6
East Lutton N Yorks 96 C5
East Lydford Som 23 F7
East Mains Aberds 151 E5
East Malling Kent 29 D8
East March Angus 142 F4
East Marden W Sus 16 C2
East Markham Notts 77 B7
East Marton N Yorks 94 D2
East Meon Hants 15 B7
East Mere Devon 10 C4
East Mersea Essex 43 C6
East Mey Highld 169 B8
East Molesey Sur 28 C2
East Morden Dorset 13 E7
East Morton W Yorks 94 E3
East Ness N Yorks 96 B2
East Newton E Yorks 97 F8
East Norton Leics 64 D4
East Nynehead Som 11 B6
East Oakley Hants 26 D3
East Ogwell Devon 7 B6
East Orchard Dorset 13 C6
East Ord Northumb 125 D5
East Panson Devon 9 E5
East Peckham Kent 29 E7
East Pennard Som 23 F7
East Perry Cambs 54 C2
East Portlemouth Devon 6 F5
East Prawle Devon 7 F5
East Preston W Sus 16 D4
East Putford Devon 9 C5
East Quantoxhead Som 22 E3
East Rainton T & W 111 E6
East Ravendale NE Lincs 91 E6
East Raynham Norf 80 E4
East Rhidorroch Lodge Highld 163 E6
East Rigton W Yorks 95 E6
East Rounton N Yorks 102 D2
East Row N Yorks 103 C6
East Rudham Norf 80 E4
East Runton Norf 81 C7
East Ruston Norf 69 B6
East Saltoun E Loth 123 C7
East Sleekburn Northumb 117 F8
East Somerton Norf 69 C7
East Stockwith Lincs 89 E8
East Stoke Dorset 13 F6
East Stoke Notts 77 E7
East Stour Dorset 13 B6
East Stourmouth Kent 31 C6
East Stowford Devon 9 B8
East Stratton Hants 26 F3
East Studdal Kent 31 E7
East Suisnish Highld 153 F6
East Taphouse Corn 5 C6
East-the-Water Devon 9 B6
East Thirston Northumb 117 E7
East Tilbury Thurrock 29 B7
East Tisted Hants 26 F5
East Torrington Lincs 90 F5
East Tuddenham Norf 68 C3
East Tytherley Hants 14 B3
East Tytherton Wilts 24 B4
East Village Devon 10 D3
East Wall Shrops 60 E5
East Walton Norf 67 C7
East Wellow Hants 14 B4
East Wemyss Fife 134 E5
East Whitburn W Loth 122 C2
East Williamston Pembs 32 D1
East Winch Norf 67 C6
East Winterslow Wilts 25 F7
East Wittering W Sus 15 E8
East Witton N Yorks 101 F6
East Woodburn Northumb 116 F5
East Woodhay Hants 26 C2
East Worldham Hants 26 F5
East Worlington Devon 10 C2
East Worthing W Sus 17 D5
Eastbourne E Sus 18 F3
Eastbridge Suff 57 C8
Eastburn W Yorks 94 E3
Eastbury Herts 40 E3
Eastbury W Berks 25 B8
Eastby N Yorks 94 D3
Eastchurch Kent 30 B3
Eastcombe Glos 37 D5
Eastcote London 40 F4
Eastcote Northants 52 D4
Eastcote W Mid 51 B6
Eastcott Corn 8 C4
Eastcott Wilts 24 D5
Eastcourt Wilts 37 E6
Eastcourt Wilts 25 C7
Easter Ardross Highld 157 B7
Easter Balmoral Aberds 149 E8
Easter Boleskine Highld 147 B8
Easter Compton S Glos 36 F2
Easter Cringate Stirl 133 F6
Easter Davoch Aberds 150 D3
Easter Earshaig Dumfries 114 D3
Easter Fearn Highld 164 F3
Easter Galcantray Highld 158 E2
Easter Howgate Midloth 122 C5
Easter Howlaws Borders 124 E3
Easter Kinkell Highld 157 D6
Easter Lednathie Angus 142 C3
Easter Milton Highld 158 D3
Easter Moniack Highld 157 E6
Easter Ord Aberds 151 D7
Easter Quarff Shetland 175 K6
Easter Rhynd Perth 134 C3
Easter Row Stirl 133 E6
Easter Silverford Aberds 160 B4
Easter Skeld Shetland 175 J5
Easter Whyntie Aberds 160 B3
Eastergate W Sus 16 D3
Easterhouse Glasgow 121 C6
Eastern Green W Mid 63 F6
Easterton Wilts 24 D5
Eastertown Som 22 D5
Eastertown of Auchleuchries Aberds 161 E7
Eastfield N Lnrk 121 C8
Eastfield N Yorks 103 F8
Eastfield Hall Northumb 117 D8
Eastgate Durham 110 F2
Eastgate Norf 81 E7
Eastham Mers 85 F4
Eastham Ferry Mers 85 F4
Easthampstead Brack 27 C6
Eastheath Wokingham 27 C6
Easthope Shrops 61 E5
Easthorpe Essex 43 B5
Easthorpe Leics 77 F8
Easthorpe Notts 77 D7
Easthouses Midloth 123 C6
Eastington Devon 10 D2
Eastington Glos 36 D4
Eastington Glos 37 C8
Eastleach Martin Glos 38 D2
Eastleach Turville Glos 38 D1
Eastleigh Devon 9 B6
Eastleigh Hants 14 C5
Eastling Kent 30 D3
Eastmoor Derbys 76 B3
Eastmoor Norf 67 D7
Eastney Ptsmth 15 E7
Eastnor Hereford 50 F2
Eastoft N Lincs 90 C2
Eastoke Hants 15 E8
Easton Cambs 54 B2
Easton Cumb 108 D2
Easton Cumb 108 B4
Easton Devon 10 F2
Easton Dorset 12 G4
Easton Hants 26 F3
Easton Lincs 65 B6
Easton Norf 68 C4
Easton Som 23 E7
Easton Suff 57 D6
Easton Wilts 24 B3
Easton Grey Wilts 37 F5
Easton-in-Gordano N Som 23 B7
Easton Maudit Northants 53 D6
Easton on the Hill Northants 65 D7
Easton Royal Wilts 25 C7
Eastpark Dumfries 107 C7
Eastrea Cambs 66 E2
Eastriggs Dumfries 108 C2
Eastrington E Yorks 89 B8
Eastry Kent 31 D7
Eastville Bristol 23 B8
Eastville Lincs 79 D7
Eastwell Leics 64 B4
Eastwick Herts 41 C7
Eastwick Shetland 174 F5
Eastwood Notts 76 E4
Eastwood Sthend 42 F4
Eastwood W Yorks 87 B7
Eathorpe Warks 51 C8
Eaton Ches 74 C2
Eaton Ches 75 C5
Eaton Leics 64 B4
Eaton Norf 68 D5
Eaton Notts 77 B7
Eaton Oxon 38 D4
Eaton Shrops 60 F3
Eaton Shrops 60 F5
Eaton Bishop Hereford 49 F6
Eaton Bray Beds 40 B2
Eaton Constantine Shrops 61 D5
Eaton Green Beds 40 B2
Eaton Hastings Oxon 38 E2
Eaton on Tern Shrops 61 B6
Eaton Socon Cambs 54 D2
Eavestone N Yorks 94 C5
Ebberston N Yorks 103 F6
Ebbesbourne Wake Wilts 13 B7
Ebbw Vale = Glyn Ebwy Bl Gwent 35 D5
Ebchester Durham 110 D4
Ebford Devon 10 F4
Ebley Glos 37 D5
Ebnal Ches 73 E8
Ebrington Glos 51 E6
Ecchinswell Hants 26 D2
Ecclaw Borders 124 C3
Ecclefechan Dumfries 107 B8
Eccles Borders 124 E3
Eccles Gtr Man 87 E5
Eccles Kent 29 C8
Eccles on Sea Norf 69 B7
Eccles Road Norf 68 E3
Ecclesall S Yorks 88 F4
Ecclesfield S Yorks 88 E4
Ecclesgreig Aberds 143 C7
Eccleshall Staffs 62 B2
Eccleshill W Yorks 94 F4
Ecclesmachan W Loth 122 B3
Eccleston Ches 73 C8
Eccleston Lancs 86 C3
Eccleston Mers 86 E2
Eccleston Park Mers 86 E2
Eccup W Yorks 95 E5
Echt Aberds 151 D6
Eckford Borders 116 B3
Eckington Derbys 76 B4
Eckington Worcs 50 E4
Ecton Northants 53 C6
Edale Derbys 88 F2
Edburton W Sus 17 C6
Edderside Cumb 107 E7
Edderton Highld 164 F4
Eddistone Devon 8 B4
Eddleston Borders 122 E5
Eden Camp Museum, Malton N Yorks 96 B3
Eden Park London 28 C4
Edenbridge Kent 28 E5
Edenfield Lancs 87 C5
Edenhall Cumb 109 F5
Edenham Lincs 65 B7
Edensor Derbys 76 C2
Edentaggart Argyll 129 A8
Edenthorpe S Yorks 89 D7
Edentown Cumb 108 D3
Ederline Argyll 130 E4
Edern Gwyn 70 D3
Edgarley Som 23 F7
Edgbaston W Mid 62 F4
Edgcott Bucks 39 B6
Edgcott Som 21 F7
Edge Shrops 60 D3
Edge End Glos 36 C2
Edge Green Ches 73 D8
Edge Hill Mers 85 F4
Edgebolton Shrops 61 B5
Edgefield Norf 81 D6
Edgefield Street Norf 81 D6
Edgeside Lancs 87 B6
Edgeworth Glos 37 D6
Edgmond Telford 61 C7
Edgmond Marsh Telford 61 B7
Edgton Shrops 60 F3
Edgware London 40 E4
Edgworth Blkburn 86 C5
Edinample Stirl 132 B4
Edinbane Highld 152 D4
Edinburgh Edin 123 B5
Edinburgh Airport Edin 122 B4
Edinburgh Castle Edin 123 B5
Edinburgh Crystal Visitor Centre, Penicuik Midloth 122 C5
Edinburgh Zoo Edin 122 B5
Edingale Staffs 63 C6
Edingight Ho. Moray 160 C2
Edingley Notts 77 D6
Edingthorpe Norf 69 A6
Edingthorpe Green Norf 69 A6
Edington Som 23 F5
Edington Wilts 24 D4
Edintore Moray 159 E8
Edith Weston Rutland 65 D6
Edithmead Som 22 E5
Edlesborough Bucks 40 C2
Edlingham Northumb 117 D7
Edlington Lincs 78 B5
Edmondsham Dorset 13 C8
Edmondsley Durham 110 E5
Edmondthorpe Leics 65 C5
Edmonstone Orkney 176 D4
Edmonton London 41 E6
Edmundbyers Durham 110 D3
Ednam Borders 124 F3
Ednaston Derbys 76 E2
Edradynate Perth 141 D5
Edrom Borders 124 D4
Edstaston Shrops 74 F2
Edstone Warks 51 C6
Edvin Loach Hereford 49 D8
Edwalton Notts 77 F5
Edwardstone Suff 56 E3
Edwinsford Carms 46 F5
Edwinstowe Notts 77 C6
Edworth Beds 54 E3
Edwyn Ralph Hereford 49 D8
Edzell Angus 143 C5
Efail Isaf Rhondda 34 F4
Efailnewydd Gwyn 70 D4
Efailwen Carms 32 B2
Efenechtyd Denb 72 D5
Effingham Sur 28 D2
Effirth Shetland 175 H5
Efford Devon 10 D3
Egdon Worcs 50 D4
Egerton Gtr Man 86 C5
Egerton Kent 30 E3
Egerton Forstal Kent 30 E2
Eggborough N Yorks 89 B6
Eggbuckland Plym 6 D3
Eggington Beds 40 B2
Egginton Derbys 63 B6
Egglescliffe Stockton 102 C2
Eggleston Durham 100 B4
Egham Sur 27 B8
Egleton Rutland 65 D5
Eglingham Northumb 117 C7
Egloshayle Corn 4 B5
Egloskerry Corn 8 F4
Eglwys-Brewis V Glam 22 C2
Eglwys Cross Wrex 73 E8
Eglwys Fach Ceredig 58 E3
Eglwysbach Conwy 83 D8
Eglwyswen Pembs 45 F3
Eglwyswrw Pembs 45 F3
Egmanton Notts 77 C7
Egremont Cumb 98 C2
Egremont Mers 85 E4
Egton N Yorks 103 D6
Egton Bridge N Yorks 103 D6
Eight Ash Green Essex 43 B5
Eignaig Highld 138 E1
Eil Highld 148 C4
Eilanreach Highld 145 B8
Eilean Darach Highld 163 F5
Eileanach Lodge Highld 157 C6
Einacleite W Isles 172 F4
Eisgean W Isles 173 G6
Eisingrug Gwyn 71 D7
Elan Village Powys 47 C8
Elberton S Glos 36 F3
Elburton Plym 6 D3
Elcho Perth 134 B3
Elcombe Swindon 37 F8
Eldernell Cambs 66 E3
Eldersfield Worcs 50 F3
Elderslie Renfs 120 C4
Eldon Durham 101 B7
Eldrick S Ayrs 112 F2
Eldroth N Yorks 93 C7
Eldwick W Yorks 94 E4
Elfhowe Cumb 99 E6
Elford Northumb 125 F7
Elford Staffs 63 C5
Elgin Moray 159 C6
Elgol Highld 153 H6
Elham Kent 31 E5
Elie Fife 135 D6
Elim Anglesey 82 C3
Eling Hants 14 C4
Elishader Highld 152 C6
Elishaw Northumb 116 E4
Elkesley Notts 77 B6
Elkstone Glos 37 C6
Ellan Highld 148 B4

Elland W Yorks 88 B2
Ellary Argyll 128 C2
Ellastone Staffs 75 E8
Ellemford Borders 124 C3
Ellenbrook I o M 84 E3
Ellenhall Staffs 62 B2
Ellen's Green Sur 27 F8
Ellerbeck N Yorks 102 E2
Ellerburn N Yorks 103 F6
Ellerby N Yorks 103 C5
Ellerdine Heath Telford 61 B6
Ellerhayes Devon 10 D4
Elleric Argyll 138 E4
Ellerker E Yorks 90 B3
Ellerton E Yorks 96 F3
Ellerton Shrops 61 B7
Ellesborough Bucks 39 D8
Ellesmere Shrops 73 F8
Ellesmere Port Ches 73 B8
Ellingham Norf 69 E6
Ellingham Northumb 117 B7
Ellingstring N Yorks 101 F6
Ellington Cambs 54 B2
Ellington Northumb 117 E8
Elliot Angus 143 F6
Ellisfield Hants 26 E4
Ellistown Leics 63 C8
Ellon Aberds 161 E6
Ellonby Cumb 108 F4
Ellough Suff 69 F7
Elloughton E Yorks 90 B3
Ellwood Glos 36 D2
Elm Cambs 66 D4
Elm Hill Dorset 13 B6
Elm Park London 41 F8
Elmbridge Worcs 50 C4
Elmdon Essex 55 F5
Elmdon W Mid 63 F5
Elmdon Heath W Mid 63 F5
Elmers End London 28 C4
Elmesthorpe Leics 63 E8
Elmfield I o W 15 E7
Elmhurst Staffs 62 C5
Elmley Castle Worcs 50 E4
Elmley Lovett Worcs 50 C3
Elmore Glos 36 C4
Elmore Back Glos 36 C4
Elmscott Devon 8 B4
Elmsett Suff 56 E4
Elmstead Market Essex 43 B6
Elmsted Kent 30 E5
Elmstone Kent 31 C6
Elmstone Hardwicke Glos 37 B6
Elmswell E Yorks 97 D5
Elmswell Suff 56 C3
Elmton Derbys 76 B5
Elphin Highld 163 C6
Elphinstone E Loth 123 B6
Elrick Aberds 151 D7
Elrig Dumfries 105 E7
Elsdon Northumb 117 E5
Elsecar S Yorks 88 E4
Elsenham Essex 41 B8
Elsfield Oxon 39 C5
Elsham N Lincs 90 C4
Elsing Norf 68 C3
Elslack N Yorks 94 E2
Elson Shrops 73 F7
Elsrickle S Lnrk 122 E3
Elstead Sur 27 E7
Elsted W Sus 16 C2
Elsthorpe Lincs 65 B7
Elstob Durham 101 B8
Elston Notts 77 E7
Elston Wilts 25 E5
Elstone Devon 9 C8
Elstow Beds 53 E8
Elstree Herts 40 E4
Elstronwick E Yorks 97 F8
Elswick Lancs 92 F4
Elsworth Cambs 54 C4
Elterwater Cumb 99 D5
Eltham London 28 B5
Eltisley Cambs 54 D3
Elton Cambs 65 E7
Elton Ches 73 B8
Elton Derbys 76 C2
Elton Glos 36 C4
Elton Hereford 49 B6
Elton Notts 77 F7
Elton Stockton 102 C2
Elton Green Ches 73 B8
Elvanfoot S Lnrk 114 C2
Elvaston Derbys 76 F4
Elveden Suff 56 B2
Elvingston E Loth 123 B7
Elvington Kent 31 D6
Elvington York 96 E2
Elwick Hrtlpl 111 F7
Elwick Northumb 125 F7
Elworth Ches 74 C4
Elworthy Som 22 F2
Ely Cambs 66 F5
Ely Cardiff 22 B3
Ely Cathedral and Museum Cambs 66 F5
Emberton M Keynes 53 E6
Embleton Cumb 107 F8
Embleton Northumb 117 B8
Embo Highld 165 E5
Embo Street Highld 165 E5
Emborough Som 23 D8
Embsay N Yorks 94 D3
Emery Down Hants 14 D3
Emley W Yorks 88 C3
Emmbrook Wokingham 27 C5
Emmer Green Reading 26 B5
Emmington Oxon 39 D7
Emneth Norf 66 D4
Emneth Hungate Norf 66 D5
Empingham Rutland 65 D6
Empshott Hants 27 F5
Emstrey Shrops 60 C5
Emsworth Hants 15 D8
Enborne W Berks 26 C2
Enchmarsh Shrops 60 E5
Enderby Leics 64 E2
Endmoor Cumb 99 F7
Endon Staffs 75 D6
Endon Bank Staffs 75 D6
Enfield London 41 E6
Enfield Wash London 41 E6
Enford Wilts 25 D6
Engamoor Shetland 175 H4
Engine Common S Glos 36 F3
Englefield W Berks 26 B4
Englefield Green Sur 27 B7
Englesea-brook Ches 74 D4
English Bicknor Glos 36 C2
English Frankton Shrops 60 B4
Englishcombe Bath 24 C2
Enham Alamein Hants 25 E8
Enmore Som 22 F4
Ennerdale Bridge Cumb 98 C2
Enoch Dumfries 113 D8
Enochdhu Perth 141 C7
Ensay Argyll 136 D4
Ensbury Bmouth 13 E8
Ensdon Shrops 60 C4
Ensis Devon 9 B7
Enstone Oxon 38 B3
Enterkinfoot Dumfries 113 D8
Enterpen N Yorks 102 D2
Enville Staffs 62 F2
Eolaigearraidh W Isles 171 K3
Eorabus Argyll 136 F4
Eòropaidh W Isles 172 B8
Epperstone Notts 77 E6
Epping Essex 41 D7
Epping Green Essex 41 D7
Epping Green Herts 41 D5
Epping Upland Essex 41 D7
Eppleby N Yorks 101 C6
Eppleworth E Yorks 97 F6
Epsom Sur 28 C3
Epsom Racecourse Sur 28 D3
Epwell Oxon 51 E8
Epworth N Lincs 89 D8
Epworth Turbary N Lincs 89 D8
Erbistock Wrex 73 E7
Erbusaig Highld 155 H3
Erchless Castle Highld 156 E5
Erddig Wrex 73 E7
Erdington W Mid 62 E5
Eredine Argyll 131 E5
Eriboll Highld 167 D6
Ericstane Dumfries 114 C3
Eridge Green E Sus 18 B2
Erines Argyll 128 C3
Eriswell Suff 55 B8
Erith London 29 B6
Erlestoke Wilts 24 D4
Ermine Lincs 78 B2
Ermington Devon 6 D4
Erpingham Norf 81 D7
Errogie Highld 147 B8
Errol Perth 134 B4
Erskine Renfs 120 B4
Erskine Bridge Renfs 120 B4
Ervie Dumfries 104 C4
Erwarton Suff 57 F6
Erwood Powys 48 E2
Eryholme N Yorks 101 D8
Eryrys Denb 73 D6
Escomb Durham 101 B6
Escrick N Yorks 96 E2
Esgairdawe Carms 46 E5
Esgairgeiliog Powys 58 D4
Esh Durham 110 E4
Esh Winning Durham 110 E4
Esher Sur 28 C2
Esholt W Yorks 94 E4
Eshott Northumb 117 E8
Eshton N Yorks 94 D2
Esk Valley N Yorks 103 D6
Eskadale Highld 157 F5
Eskbank Midloth 123 C6
Eskdale Green Cumb 98 D3
Eskdalemuir Dumfries 115 E5
Eske E Yorks 97 E6
Eskham Lincs 91 E7
Esprick Lancs 92 F4
Essendine Rutland 65 C7
Essendon Herts 41 D5
Essich Highld 157 F7
Essington Staffs 62 D3
Esslemont Aberds 151 B8
Eston Redcar 102 C3
Eswick Shetland 175 H6
Etal Northumb 124 F5
Etchilhampton Wilts 24 C5
Etchingham E Sus 18 C4
Etchinghill Kent 19 B8
Etchinghill Staffs 62 C4
Ethie Castle Angus 143 E6
Ethie Mains Angus 143 E6
Etling Green Norf 68 C3
Eton Windsor 27 B7
Eton Wick Windsor 27 B7
Etteridge Highld 148 E2
Ettersgill Durham 100 B3
Ettingshall W Mid 62 E3
Ettington Warks 51 E7
Etton E Yorks 97 E5
Etton P'boro 65 D8
Ettrick Borders 115 C5
Ettrickbridge Borders 115 B6
Ettrickhill Borders 115 C5
Etwall Derbys 76 F2
Eureka!, Halifax W Yorks 87 B8
Euston Suff 56 B2
Euximoor Drove Cambs 66 E4
Euxton Lancs 86 C3
Evanstown Bridgend 34 F3
Evanton Highld 157 C7
Evedon Lincs 78 E3
Evelix Highld 164 E4
Evenjobb Powys 48 C4
Evenley Northants 52 F3
Evenlode Glos 38 B2
Evenwood Durham 101 B6
Evenwood Gate Durham 101 B6
Everbay Orkney 176 D5
Evercreech Som 23 F8
Everdon Northants 52 D3
Everingham E Yorks 96 E4
Everleigh Wilts 25 D7
Everley N Yorks 103 F7
Eversholt Beds 53 F7
Evershot Dorset 12 D3
Eversley Hants 27 C5
Eversley Cross Hants 27 C5
Everthorpe E Yorks 96 F5
Everton Beds 54 D3
Everton Hants 14 E3
Everton Mers 85 E4
Everton Notts 89 E7
Evertown Dumfries 108 B3
Evesbatch Hereford 49 E8
Evesham Worcs 50 E5
Evington Leicester 64 D3
Ewden Village S Yorks 88 E3
Ewell Sur 28 C3
Ewell Minnis Kent 31 E6
Ewelme Oxon 39 E6
Ewen Glos 37 E7
Ewenny V Glam 21 B8
Ewerby Lincs 78 E4
Ewerby Thorpe Lincs 78 E4
Ewes Dumfries 115 E6
Ewesley Northumb 117 E6
Ewhurst Sur 27 E8
Ewhurst Green E Sus 18 C4
Ewhurst Green Sur 27 F8
Ewloe Flint 73 C7
Ewloe Green Flint 73 C6
Ewood Blkburn 86 B4
Eworthy Devon 9 E6
Ewshot Hants 27 E6
Ewyas Harold Hereford 35 B7
Exbourne Devon 9 D8
Exbury Hants 14 E5
Exbury Gardens, Fawley Hants 14 D5
Exebridge Som 10 B4
Exelby N Yorks 101 F7
Exeter Devon 10 E4
Exeter Cathedral Devon 10 E4
Exeter International Airport Devon 10 E4
Exford Som 21 F7
Exhall Warks 51 D6
Exley Head W Yorks 94 F3
Exminster Devon 10 F4
Exmouth Devon 10 F5
Exnaboe Shetland 175 M5
Exning Suff 55 C7
Explosion, Gosport Hants 15 D7
Exton Devon 10 F4
Exton Hants 15 B7
Exton Rutland 65 C6
Exton Som 21 F8
Exwick Devon 10 E4
Eyam Derbys 76 B2
Eydon Northants 52 D3
Eye Hereford 49 C6
Eye P'boro 66 D2
Eye Suff 56 B5
Eye Green P'boro 66 D2
Eyemouth Borders 124 C5
Eyeworth Beds 54 E3
Eyhorne Street Kent 30 D2
Eyke Suff 57 D7
Eynesbury Cambs 54 D2
Eynort Highld 153 G4
Eynsford Kent 29 C6
Eynsham Oxon 38 D4
Eype Dorset 12 E2
Eyre Highld 152 D5
Eyre Highld 153 F6
Eythorne Kent 31 E6
Eyton Hereford 49 C6
Eyton Shrops 60 F3
Eyton Wrex 73 E7
Eyton upon the Weald Moors Telford 61 C6

F

Faccombe Hants 25 D8
Faceby N Yorks 102 D2
Facit Lancs 87 C6
Faddiley Ches 74 D2
Fadmoor N Yorks 102 F4
Faerdre Swansea 33 D7
Failand N Som 23 B7
Failford S Ayrs 112 B4
Failsworth Gtr Man 87 D6
Fain Highld 156 B2
Fair Green Norf 67 C6
Fair Hill Cumb 108 F5
Fair Oak Hants 15 C5
Fair Oak Green Hants 26 C4
Fairbourne Gwyn 58 C3
Fairburn N Yorks 89 B5
Fairfield Derbys 75 B7
Fairfield Stockton 102 C2
Fairfield Worcs 50 E5
Fairfield Worcs 50 B4
Fairford Glos 38 D1
Fairhaven Lancs 85 B4
Fairlie N Ayrs 129 E7
Fairlight E Sus 19 D5
Fairlight Cove E Sus 19 D5
Fairmile Devon 11 E5
Fairmilehead Edin 122 C5
Fairoak Staffs 74 F4
Fairseat Kent 29 C7
Fairstead Essex 42 C3
Fairstead Norf 67 C6
Fairwarp E Sus 17 B8
Fairy Cottage I o M 84 D4
Fairy Cross Devon 9 B6
Fakenham Norf 80 E5
Fakenham Magna Suff 56 B3
Fakenham Racecourse Norf 80 E5
Fala Midloth 123 C7
Fala Dam Midloth 123 C7
Falahill Borders 123 D6
Falcon Hereford 49 F8
Faldingworth Lincs 90 F4
Falfield S Glos 36 E3
Falkenham Suff 57 F6
Falkirk Falk 121 B8
Falkland Fife 134 D4
Falkland Palace Fife 134 D4
Falla Borders 116 C3
Fallgate Derbys 76 C3
Fallin Stirl 133 E7
Fallowfield Gtr Man 87 E6
Fallsidehill Borders 124 E2
Falmer E Sus 17 D7
Falmouth Corn 3 C7
Falsgrave N Yorks 103 F8
Falstone Northumb 116 F3
Fanagmore Highld 166 E3
Fangdale Beck N Yorks 102 E3
Fangfoss E Yorks 96 D3
Fankerton Falk 133 F6
Fanmore Argyll 137 D5
Fannich Lodge Highld 156 C3
Fans Borders 124 E2
Far Bank S Yorks 89 C7
Far Bletchley M Keynes 53 F6
Far Cotton Northants 52 D5
Far Forest Worcs 50 B2
Far Laund Derbys 76 E3
Far Sawrey Cumb 99 E5
Farcet Cambs 66 E2
Farden Shrops 49 B7
Fareham Hants 15 D6
Farewell Staffs 62 C4
Farforth Lincs 79 B6
Faringdon Oxon 38 E2
Farington Lancs 86 B3
Farlam Cumb 109 D5
Farlary Highld 164 D4
Farleigh N Som 23 C6
Farleigh Sur 28 C4
Farleigh Hungerford Som 24 D3
Farleigh Wallop Hants 26 E4
Farlesthorpe Lincs 79 B7
Farleton Cumb 99 F7
Farleton Lancs 93 C5
Farley Shrops 60 D3
Farley Staffs 75 E7
Farley Wilts 14 B3
Farley Green Sur 27 E8
Farley Hill Luton 40 B3
Farley Hill Wokingham 26 C5
Farleys End Glos 36 C4
Farlington N Yorks 96 C2
Farlow Shrops 61 F6
Farmborough Bath 23 C8
Farmcote Glos 37 B7
Farmcote Shrops 61 E7
Farmington Glos 37 C8
Farmoor Oxon 38 D4
Farmtown Moray 160 C2
Farnborough London 28 C5
Farnborough Hants 27 D6
Farnborough Warks 52 E2
Farnborough W Berks 38 F4
Farnborough Green Hants 27 D6
Farncombe Sur 27 E7
Farndish Beds 53 C7
Farndon Ches 73 D8
Farndon Notts 77 D7
Farnell Angus 143 D6
Farnham Dorset 13 C7
Farnham Essex 41 B7
Farnham N Yorks 95 C6
Farnham Suff 57 C7
Farnham Sur 27 E6
Farnham Common Bucks 40 F2
Farnham Green Essex 41 B7
Farnham Royal Bucks 40 F2
Farnhill N Yorks 94 E3
Farningham Kent 29 C6
Farnley N Yorks 94 E5
Farnley W Yorks 95 F5
Farnley Tyas W Yorks 88 C2
Farnsfield Notts 77 D6
Farnworth Gtr Man 86 D5
Farnworth Halton 86 F3
Farr Highld 157 F7
Farr Highld 148 D4
Farr Highld 168 C2
Farr House Highld 157 F7
Farringdon Devon 10 E5
Farrington Gurney Bath 23 D8
Farsley W Yorks 94 F5
Farthinghoe Northants 52 F3
Farthingloe Kent 31 E6
Farthingstone Northants 52 D4
Fartown W Yorks 88 C2
Farway Devon 11 E6
Fasag Highld 154 E4
Fascadale Highld 137 A6
Faslane Port Argyll 129 B7
Fasnacloich Argyll 138 E4
Fasnakyle Ho. Highld 147 B6
Fassfern Highld 138 B4
Fatfield T & W 111 D6
Fattahead Aberds 160 C3
Faugh Cumb 108 D5
Fauldhouse W Loth 122 C2
Faulkbourne Essex 42 C3
Faulkland Som 24 D2
Fauls Shrops 74 F2
Faversham Kent 30 C4
Favillar Moray 159 F6
Fawdington N Yorks 95 B7
Fawfieldhead Staffs 75 C7
Fawkham Green Kent 29 C6
Fawler Oxon 38 C3
Fawley Bucks 39 F7
Fawley Hants 15 D5
Fawley W Berks 38 F3
Fawley Chapel Hereford 36 B2
Faxfleet E Yorks 90 B2
Faygate W Sus 28 F3
Fazakerley Mers 85 E4
Fazeley Staffs 63 D6
Fearby N Yorks 101 F6
Fearn Highld 158 B2
Fearn Lodge Highld 164 F3
Fearn Station Highld 158 B2
Fearnan Perth 140 E4
Fearnbeg Highld 154 E3
Fearnhead Warr 86 E4
Fearnmore Highld 154 D3
Featherstone Staffs 62 D3
Featherstone W Yorks 88 B5
Featherwood Northumb 116 D4
Feckenham Worcs 50 C5
Feering Essex 42 B4
Feetham N Yorks 100 E4
Feizor N Yorks 93 C7
Felbridge Sur 28 F4
Felbrigg Norf 81 D8
Felcourt Sur 28 E4
Felden Herts 40 D3
Felin-Crai Powys 34 B2
Felindre Ceredig 46 D4
Felindre Carms 33 B6
Felindre Carms 47 F5
Felindre Carms 33 B8
Felindre Carms 46 F2
Felindre Powys 59 F8
Felindre Swansea 33 D7
Felindre Farchog Pembs 45 F3
Felinfach Ceredig 46 D4
Felinfach Powys 48 F2
Felinfoel Carms 33 D6
Felingwm isaf Carms 33 B6
Felingwm uchaf Carms 33 B6
Felinwynt Ceredig 45 D4
Felixkirk N Yorks 102 F2
Felixstowe Suff 57 F6
Felixstowe Ferry Suff 57 F7
Felkington Northumb 124 E5
Felkirk W Yorks 88 C4
Fell Side Cumb 108 F3
Felling T & W 111 C5
Felmersham Beds 53 D7
Felmingham Norf 81 E8
Felpham W Sus 16 E3
Felsham Suff 56 D3
Felsted Essex 42 B2
Feltham London 28 B2
Felthorpe Norf 68 C4
Felton Hereford 49 E7
Felton Northumb 117 D7
Felton N Som 23 C7
Felton Butler Shrops 60 C3
Feltwell Norf 67 E7
Fen Ditton Cambs 55 C5
Fen Drayton Cambs 54 C4
Fen End W Mid 51 B7
Fen Side Lincs 79 D6
Fenay Bridge W Yorks 88 C2
Fence Lancs 93 F8
Fence Houses T & W 111 D6
Fengate Norf 81 E7
Fengate P'boro 66 E2
Fenham Northumb 125 E6
Fenhouses Lincs 79 E5
Feniscliffe Blkburn 86 B4
Feniscowles Blkburn 86 B4
Feniton Devon 11 E6
Fenlake Beds 53 E8
Fenny Bentley Derbys 75 D8
Fenny Bridges Devon 11 E6
Fenny Compton Warks 52 D2
Fenny Drayton Leics 63 E7
Fenny Stratford M Keynes 53 F6
Fenrother Northumb 117 E7
Fenstanton Cambs 54 C4
Fenton Cambs 54 B4
Fenton Lincs 77 D8
Fenton Lincs 77 B8
Fenton Stoke 75 E5
Fenton Barns E Loth 135 F7
Fenton Town Northumb 125 F5
Fenwick E Ayrs 120 E4
Fenwick Northumb 110 B3
Fenwick Northumb 125 E6
Fenwick S Yorks 89 C6
Feochaig Argyll 118 E4
Feock Corn 3 C7
Feolin Ferry Argyll 127 F2
Ferens Art Gallery, Hull Hull 90 B4
Ferindonald Highld 145 C6
Feriniquarrie Highld 152 D2
Ferlochan Argyll 138 E3
Fern Angus 142 C4
Ferndale Rhondda 34 E4
Ferndown Dorset 13 D8
Ferness Highld 158 E3
Ferney Green Cumb 99 E6
Fernham Oxon 38 E2
Fernhill Heath Worcs 50 D3
Fernhurst W Sus 16 B2
Fernie Fife 134 C5
Ferniegair S Lnrk 121 D7
Fernilea Highld 153 F4
Fernilee Derbys 75 B7
Ferrensby N Yorks 95 C6
Ferring W Sus 16 D4
Ferry Hill Cambs 66 F3
Ferry Point Highld 164 F4
Ferrybridge W Yorks 89 B5
Ferryden Angus 143 D7
Ferryhill Aberdeen 151 D8
Ferryhill Durham 111 F5
Ferryhill Station Durham 111 F6
Ferryside Carms 32 C4
Fersfield Norf 68 F3
Fersit Highld 139 B7
Ferwig Ceredig 45 E3
Feshiebridge Highld 148 D4
Festival Park Visitor Centre, Ebbw Vale Bl Gwent 35 D5
Fetcham Sur 28 D2
Fetlar Airport Shetland 174 D8
Fetterangus Aberds 161 C6
Fettercairn Aberds 143 B6
Fettes Highld 157 D6
Fewcott Oxon 39 B5
Fewston N Yorks 94 D4
Ffair-Rhos Ceredig 47 C6
Ffairfach Carms 33 B7
Ffaldybrenin Carms 46 E5
Ffarmers Carms 47 E5
Ffawyddog Powys 35 C6
Ffestiniog Railway, Porthmadog Gwyn 71 C7
Fforest Carms 33 D6
Fforest-fâch Swansea 33 E7
Ffos-y-ffin Ceredig 46 C3
Ffostrasol Ceredig 46 E2
Ffridd-Uchaf Gwyn 83 F5
Ffrith Flint 73 D6
Ffrwd Gwyn 82 F4
Ffynnon ddrain Carms 33 B5
Ffynnon-oer Ceredig 46 D4
Ffynnongroyw Flint 85 F2
Fidden Argyll 136 F4
Fiddes Aberds 151 F7
Fiddington Glos 50 F4
Fiddington Som 22 E4
Fiddleford Dorset 13 C6
Fiddlers Hamlet Essex 41 D7
Field Staffs 75 F7
Field Broughton Cumb 99 F5
Field Dalling Norf 81 D6
Field Head Leics 63 D8
Fifehead Magdalen Dorset 13 B5
Fifehead Neville Dorset 13 C5
Fifield Oxon 38 C2
Fifield Wilts 25 D6
Fifield Windsor 27 B7
Fifield Bavant Wilts 13 B8
Figheldean Wilts 25 E6
Filands Wilts 37 F6
Filby Norf 69 C7
Filey N Yorks 97 A7
Filgrave M Keynes 53 E6
Filkins Oxon 38 D2
Filleigh Devon 9 B8
Filleigh Devon 10 C2
Fillingham Lincs 90 F3
Fillongley Warks 63 F6
Filton S Glos 23 B8
Fimber E Yorks 96 C4
Finavon Angus 142 D4
Finchairn Argyll 130 E5
Fincham Norf 67 D6
Finchampstead Wokingham 27 C5
Finchdean Hants 15 C8
Finchingfield Essex 55 F7
Finchley London 41 E5
Findern Derbys 76 F3
Findhorn Moray 158 C4
Findhorn Bridge Highld 148 B4
Findo Gask Perth 134 B2
Findochty Moray 159 C8
Findon Aberds 151 E8
Findon W Sus 16 D5
Findon Mains Highld 157 C7
Findrack Ho. Aberds 150 D5
Finedon Northants 53 B7
Fingal Street Suff 57 C6
Fingask Aberds 151 B6
Fingerpost Worcs 50 B2
Fingest Bucks 39 E7
Finghall N Yorks 101 F6
Fingland Cumb 108 D2
Fingland Dumfries 113 C7
Finglesham Kent 31 D7
Fingringhoe Essex 43 B6
Finlarig Stirl 140 F2
Finmere Oxon 52 F4
Finnart Perth 140 D2
Finningham Suff 56 C4
Finningley S Yorks 89 E7
Finnygaud Aberds 160 C2
Finsbury London 41 F6
Finstall Worcs 50 C4
Finsthwaite Cumb 99 F5
Finstock Oxon 38 C3
Finstown Orkney 176 E2
Fintry Aberds 160 C4
Fintry Dundee 142 F4
Fintry Stirl 132 F5
Finzean Aberds 150 E5
Fionnphort Argyll 136 F4
Fionnsbhagh W Isles 173 K3
Fir Tree Durham 110 F4
Firbeck S Yorks 89 F6
Firby N Yorks 101 F7
Firby N Yorks 96 C3
Firgrove Gtr Man 87 C7
Firsby Lincs 79 C7
Firsdown Wilts 25 F7
First Coast Highld 162 E3
Fishbourne I o W 15 E6
Fishbourne W Sus 16 D2
Fishbourne Palace W Sus 16 D2
Fishburn Durham 111 F6
Fishcross Clack 133 E7
Fisher Place Cumb 99 C5
Fisherford Aberds 160 E3
Fisher's Pond Hants 15 B5
Fisherstreet W Sus 27 F7
Fisherton Highld 157 D8
Fisherton S Ayrs 112 C2
Fishguard = Abergwaun Pembs 44 B4
Fishlake S Yorks 89 C7
Fishleigh Barton Devon 9 B7
Fishponds Bristol 23 B8
Fishpool Glos 36 B3
Fishtoft Lincs 79 E6
Fishtoft Drove Lincs 79 E6
Fishtown of Usan Angus 143 D7
Fishwick Borders 124 D5
Fiskavaig Highld 153 F4
Fiskerton Lincs 78 B3
Fiskerton Notts 77 D7
Fitling E Yorks 97 F8
Fittleton Wilts 25 E6
Fittleworth W Sus 16 C4
Fitton End Cambs 66 C4
Fitz Shrops 60 C4
Fitzhead Som 11 B6
Fitzwilliam W Yorks 88 C5
Fitzwilliam Museum, Cambridge Cambs 55 D5
Fiunary Highld 137 D7
Five Acres Glos 36 C2
Five Ashes E Sus 18 C2
Five Oak Green Kent 29 E7
Five Oaks Jersey 17
Five Oaks W Sus 16 B4
Five Roads Carms 33 D5
Fivecrosses Ches 74 B2
Fivehead Som 11 B8
Flack's Green Essex 42 C3
Flackwell Heath Bucks 40 F1
Fladbury Worcs 50 E4
Fladdabister Shetland 175 K6
Flagg Derbys 75 C8
Flambards Experience, Helston Corn 3 D5
Flamborough E Yorks 97 B8
Flamingo Land, Pickering N Yorks 96 B3
Flamstead Herts 40 C3
Flamstead End Herts 41 D6
Flansham W Sus 16 D3
Flanshaw W Yorks 88 B4
Flasby N Yorks 94 D2
Flash Staffs 75 C7
Flashader Highld 152 D4
Flask Inn N Yorks 103 D7
Flaunden Herts 40 D3
Flawborough Notts 77 E7
Flawith N Yorks 95 C7
Flax Bourton N Som 23 C7
Flaxby N Yorks 95 D6
Flaxholme Derbys 76 E3
Flaxley Glos 36 C3
Flaxpool Som 22 F3
Flaxton N Yorks 96 C2
Fleckney Leics 64 E3
Flecknoe Warks 52 C3
Fledborough Notts 77 B8
Fleet Hants 27 D6
Fleet Hants 15 D8
Fleet Lincs 66 B3
Fleet Air Arm Museum, Yeovil Som 12 B3
Fleet Hargate Lincs 66 B3
Fleetham Northumb 117 B7
Fleetlands Hants 15 D6
Fleetville Herts 40 D4
Fleetwood Lancs 92 E3
Flemingston V Glam 22 B2
Flemington S Lnrk 121 D6
Flempton Suff 56 C2
Fleoideabhagh W Isles 173 K3
Fletchertown Cumb 108 E2
Fletching E Sus 17 B8
Flexbury Corn 8 D4
Flexford Sur 27 E7
Flimby Cumb 107 F7
Flimwell E Sus 18 B4
Flint = Y Fflint Flint 73 B6
Flint Mountain Flint 73 B6
Flintham Notts 77 E7
Flinton E Yorks 97 F8
Flintsham Hereford 48 D5
Flitcham Norf 80 E3
Flitton Beds 53 F8
Flitwick Beds 53 F8
Flixborough N Lincs 90 C2
Flixborough Stather N Lincs 90 C2
Flixton Gtr Man 86 E5
Flixton N Yorks 97 B6
Flixton Suff 69 F6
Flockton W Yorks 88 C3
Flodaigh W Isles 170 E4
Flodden Northumb 124 F5
Flodigarry Highld 152 B5
Flood's Ferry Cambs 66 E3
Flookburgh Cumb 92 B3
Florden Norf 68 E4
Flore Northants 52 C4
Flotterton Northumb 117 D5
Flowton Suff 56 E4
Flush House W Yorks 88 D2
Flushing Aberds 161 D7
Flushing Corn 3 C7
Flyford Flavell Worcs 50 D4
Foals Green Suff 57 B6
Fobbing Thurrock 42 F3
Fochabers Moray 159 D7
Fochriw Caerph 35 D5
Fockerby N Lincs 90 C2
Fodderletter Moray 149 B7
Fodderty Highld 157 D6
Foel Powys 59 C6
Foel-gastell Carms 33 C6
Foffarty Angus 142 E4
Foggathorpe E Yorks 96 F3
Fogo Borders 124 E3
Fogorig Borders 124 E3
Foindle Highld 166 E3
Folda Angus 142 C1
Fole Staffs 75 F7
Foleshill W Mid 63 F7
Folke Dorset 12 C4
Folkestone Kent 31 F6
Folkestone Racecourse Kent 19 B8
Folkingham Lincs 78 F3
Folkington E Sus 18 E2
Folksworth Cambs 65 F8
Folkton N Yorks 97 B6
Folla Rule Aberds 160 E4
Follifoot N Yorks 95 D6
Folly Gate Devon 9 E7
Fonthill Bishop Wilts 24 F4
Fonthill Gifford Wilts 24 F4
Fontmell Magna Dorset 13 C6
Fontwell W Sus 16 D3
Fontwell Park Racecourse W Sus 16 D3
Foolow Derbys 75 B8
Foots Cray London 29 B5
Forbestown Aberds 150 C2
Force Mills Cumb 99 E5
Forcett N Yorks 101 C6
Ford Argyll 130 E4
Ford Bucks 39 D7
Ford Devon 9 B6
Ford Glos 37 B7
Ford Northumb 124 F5
Ford Shrops 60 C4
Ford Staffs 75 D7
Ford Wilts 24 B3
Ford W Sus 16 D3
Ford End Essex 42 C2
Ford Street Som 11 C6
Fordcombe Kent 29 E6
Fordell Fife 134 F3
Forden Powys 60 D2
Forder Green Devon 7 C5
Fordham Cambs 55 B7
Fordham Essex 43 B5
Fordham Norf 67 E6
Fordhouses W Mid 62 D3
Fordingbridge Hants 14 C2
Fordon E Yorks 97 B6
Fordoun Aberds 143 B7
Ford's Green Suff 56 C4
Fordstreet Essex 43 B5
Fordwells Oxon 38 C3
Fordwich Kent 31 D5
Fordyce Aberds 160 B2
Forebridge Staffs 62 B3
Forest Durham 109 F8
Forest Becks Lancs 93 D7
Forest Gate London 41 F7
Forest Green Sur 28 E2
Forest Hall Cumb 99 D7
Forest Head Cumb 109 D5
Forest Hill Oxon 39 D5
Forest Lane Head N Yorks 95 D6
Forest Lodge Argyll 139 E6
Forest Lodge Highld 149 C6
Forest Lodge Perth 141 B6
Forest Mill Clack 133 E8
Forest Row E Sus 28 F5
Forest Town Notts 77 C5
Forestburn Gate Northumb 117 E6
Foresterseat Moray 159 D5
Forestside W Sus 15 C8
Forfar Angus 142 D4
Forgandenny Perth 134 C2
Forge Powys 58 E4
Forge Side Torf 35 D6
Forgewood N Lnrk 121 D7
Forgie Moray 159 D7
Forglen Ho. Aberds 160 C3
Formby Mers 85 D4
Forncett End Norf 68 E4
Forncett St Mary Norf 68 E4
Forncett St Peter Norf 68 E4
Forneth Perth 141 E7
Fornham All Saints Suff 56 C2
Fornham St Martin Suff 56 C2
Forres Moray 158 D4
Forrest Lodge Dumfries 113 F5
Forrestfield N Lnrk 121 C8
Forsbrook Staffs 75 E6
Forse Highld 169 F7
Forse Ho. Highld 169 F7
Forsinain Highld 168 E4
Forsinard Highld 168 E3
Forsinard Station Highld 168 E3
Forston Dorset 12 E4
Fort Augustus Highld 147 D6
Fort George Guern 16
Fort George Highld 157 D8
Fort Victoria Country Park & Marine Aquarium I o W 14 F4
Fort William Highld 139 B5
Forteviot Perth 134 C2
Forth S Lnrk 122 D2
Forth Road Bridge Fife 122 B4
Forthampton Glos 50 F3
Fortingall Perth 140 E4
Forton Hants 26 E2
Forton Lancs 92 D4
Forton Shrops 60 C4
Forton Som 11 D8
Forton Staffs 61 B7
Forton Heath Shrops 60 C4
Fortrie Aberds 160 D3
Fortrose Highld 157 D8
Fortuneswell Dorset 12 G4
Forty Green Bucks 40 E2

Forty Hill London 41 E6
Forward Green Suff 56 D4
Fosbury Wilts 25 D8
Fosdyke Lincs 79 F6
Foss Perth 140 D4
Foss Cross Glos 37 D7
Fossebridge Glos 37 C7
Foster Street Essex 41 D7
Fosterhouses S Yorks 89 C7
Foston Derbys 75 F8
Foston Lincs 77 E8
Foston N Yorks 96 C2
Foston on the Wolds E Yorks 97 D7
Fotherby Lincs 91 E7
Fotheringhay Northants 65 E7
Foubister Orkney 176 F4
Foul Mile E Sus 18 D3
Foulby W Yorks 88 C4
Foulden Borders 124 D5
Foulden Norf 67 E7
Foulis Castle Highld 157 C6
Foulridge Lancs 93 E8
Foulsham Norf 81 E6
Fountainhall Borders 123 E7
Fountains Abbey, Ripon N Yorks 95 C5
Four Ashes Staffs 62 F2
Four Ashes Suff 56 B4
Four Crosses Powys 59 D7
Four Crosses Powys 60 C2
Four Crosses Wrex 73 D6
Four Elms Kent 29 E5
Four Forks Som 22 F4
Four Gotes Cambs 66 C4
Four Lane Ends Ches 74 C2
Four Lanes Corn 3 C5
Four Marks Hants 26 F4
Four Mile Bridge Anglesey 82 D2
Four Oaks E Sus 19 C5
Four Oaks W Mid 63 F6
Four Oaks W Mid 62 E5
Four Roads Carms 33 D5
Four Roads I o M 84 F2
Four Throws Kent 18 C4
Fourlane Ends Derbys 76 D3
Fourlanes End Ches 74 D5
Fourpenny Highld 165 E5
Fourstones Northumb 109 C8
Fovant Wilts 13 B8
Foveran Aberds 151 B8
Fowey Corn 5 D6
Fowley Common Warr 86 E4
Fowlis Angus 142 F3
Fowlis Wester Perth 133 B8
Fowlmere Cambs 54 E5
Fownhope Hereford 49 F7
Fox Corner Sur 27 D7
Fox Lane Hants 27 D6
Fox Street Essex 43 B6
Foxbar Renfs 120 C4
Foxcombe Hill Oxon 38 D4
Foxdale I o M 84 E2
Foxearth Essex 56 E2
Foxfield Cumb 98 F4
Foxham Wilts 24 B4
Foxhole Corn 4 D4
Foxhole Swansea 33 E7
Foxholes N Yorks 97 B6
Foxhunt Green E Sus 18 D2
Foxley Norf 81 E6
Foxley Wilts 37 F5
Foxt Staffs 75 E7
Foxton Cambs 54 E5
Foxton Durham 102 B1
Foxton Leics 64 E4
Foxton Canal Locks Leics 64 F3
Foxup N Yorks 93 B8
Foxwist Green Ches 74 C3
Foxwood Shrops 49 B8
Foy Hereford 36 B2
Foyers Highld 147 B7
Fraddam Corn 2 C4
Fraddon Corn 4 D4
Fradley Staffs 63 C5
Fradswell Staffs 75 F6
Fraisthorpe E Yorks 97 C7
Framfield E Sus 17 B8
Framingham Earl Norf 69 D5
Framingham Pigot Norf 69 D5
Framlingham Suff 57 C6
Framlington Castle Suff 57 C6
Frampton Dorset 12 E4
Frampton Lincs 79 F6
Frampton Cotterell S Glos 36 F3
Frampton Mansell Glos 37 D6
Frampton on Severn Glos 36 D4
Frampton West End Lincs 79 E5
Framsden Suff 57 D5
Framwellgate Moor Durham 111 E5
Franche Worcs 50 B3
Frankby Mers 85 F3
Frankley Worcs 62 F3
Frank's Bridge Powys 48 D3
Frankton Warks 52 B2
Frant E Sus 18 B2
Fraserburgh Aberds 161 B6
Frating Green Essex 43 B6
Fratton Ptsmth 15 E7
Freathy Corn 5 D8
Freckenham Suff 55 B7
Freckleton Lancs 86 B2
Freeby Leics 64 B5
Freehay Staffs 75 E7
Freeland Oxon 38 C4
Freeport Hornsea Outlet Village E Yorks 97 E7
Freester Shetland 175 H6
Freethorpe Norf 69 D7
Freiston Lincs 79 E6
Fremington Devon 20 F4
Fremington N Yorks 101 E5
Frenchay S Glos 23 B8
Frenchbeer Devon 9 F8
Frenich Stirl 132 D3
Frensham Sur 27 E6
Fresgoe Highld 168 C4
Freshfield Mers 85 D3
Freshford Bath 24 C2
Freshwater I o W 14 F4
Freshwater Bay I o W 14 F4
Freshwater East Pembs 32 E1
Fressingfield Suff 57 B6
Freston Suff 57 F5
Freswick Highld 169 C8
Fretherne Glos 36 D4
Frettenham Norf 68 C5
Freuchie Fife 134 D4
Freuchies Angus 142 C2
Freystrop Pembs 44 D4
Friar's Gate E Sus 29 F5
Friarton Perth 134 B3
Friday Bridge Cambs 66 D4
Friday Street E Sus 18 E3
Fridaythorpe E Yorks 96 D4
Friern Barnet London 41 E5
Friesland Argyll 136 C2
Friesthorpe Lincs 90 F4
Frieston Lincs 78 E2
Frieth Bucks 39 E7
Frilford Oxon 38 E4
Frilsham W Berks 26 B3
Frimley Sur 27 D6
Frimley Green Sur 27 D6
Frindsbury Medway 29 B8
Fring Norf 80 D3
Fringford Oxon 39 B6
Frinsted Kent 30 D2
Frinton-on-Sea Essex 43 B8
Friockheim Angus 143 E5
Friog Gwyn 58 C3
Frisby on the Wreake Leics 64 C3
Friskney Lincs 79 D7
Friskney Eaudike Lincs 79 D7
Friskney Tofts Lincs 79 D7
Friston E Sus 18 F2
Friston Suff 57 C8
Fritchley Derbys 76 D3
Frith Bank Lincs 79 E6
Frith Common Worcs 49 C8
Fritham Hants 14 C3
Frithelstock Devon 9 C6
Frithelstock Stone Devon 9 C6
Frithville Lincs 79 D6
Frittenden Kent 30 E2
Frittiscombe Devon 7 E6
Fritton Norf 68 E5
Fritton Norf 69 D7
Fritwell Oxon 39 B5
Frizinghall W Yorks 94 F4
Frizington Cumb 98 C2
Frocester Glos 36 D4
Frodesley Shrops 60 D5
Frodingham N Lincs 90 C2
Frodsham Ches 74 B2
Frogden Borders 116 B3
Froggatt Derbys 76 B2
Froghall Staffs 75 E7
Frogmore Devon 7 E5
Frogmore Hants 27 D6
Frognall Lincs 65 C8
Frogshail Norf 81 D8
Frolesworth Leics 64 E2
Frome Som 24 E2
Frome St Quintin Dorset 12 D3
Fromes Hill Hereford 49 E8
Fron Denb 72 C4
Fron Gwyn 82 F5
Fron Gwyn 70 D4
Fron Powys 48 C2
Fron Powys 60 D2
Fron Powys 59 E8
Froncysyllte Wrex 73 E6
Frongoch Gwyn 72 F3
Frostenden Suff 69 F7
Frosterley Durham 110 F3
Frotoft Orkney 176 D3
Froxfield Wilts 25 C7
Froxfield Green Hants 15 B8
Froyle Hants 27 E5
Fryerning Essex 42 D2
Fryton N Yorks 96 B2
Fulbeck Lincs 78 D2
Fulbourn Cambs 55 D6
Fulbrook Oxon 38 C2
Fulford Som 11 B7
Fulford Staffs 75 F6
Fulford York 96 E2
Fulham London 28 B3
Fulking W Sus 17 C6
Full Sutton E Yorks 96 D3
Fullarton Glasgow 121 C6
Fullarton N Ayrs 120 F3
Fuller Street Essex 42 C3
Fuller's Moor Ches 73 D8
Fullerton Hants 25 F8
Fulletby Lincs 79 B5
Fullwood E Ayrs 120 D4
Fulmer Bucks 40 F2
Fulmodestone Norf 81 D5
Fulnetby Lincs 78 B3
Fulstow Lincs 91 E7
Fulwell T & W 111 D6
Fulwood Lancs 92 F5
Fulwood S Yorks 88 F4
Fundenhall Norf 68 E4
Fundenhall Street Norf 68 E4
Funtington W Sus 15 D8
Funtley Hants 15 D6
Funtullich Perth 133 B6
Funzie Shetland 174 D8
Furley Devon 11 D7
Furnace Argyll 131 E6
Furnace Carms 33 D6
Furnace End Warks 63 E6
Furneaux Pelham Herts 41 B7
Furness Vale Derbys 87 F8
Furze Platt Windsor 40 F1
Furzehill Devon 21 E6
Fyfett Som 11 C7
Fyfield Essex 42 D1
Fyfield Glos 38 D2
Fyfield Hants 25 E7
Fyfield Oxon 38 E4
Fyfield Wilts 25 C6
Fylingthorpe N Yorks 103 D7
Fyvie Aberds 160 E4

G

Gabhsann bho Dheas W Isles 172 C7
Gabhsann bho Thuath W Isles 172 C7
Gablon Highld 164 E4
Gabroc Hill E Ayrs 120 D4
Gaddesby Leics 64 C3
Gadebridge Herts 40 D3
Gaer Powys 35 B5
Gaerllwyd Mon 35 E8
Gaerwen Anglesey 82 D4
Gagingwell Oxon 38 B4
Gaick Lodge Highld 148 F3
Gailey Staffs 62 C3
Gainford Durham 101 C6
Gainsborough Lincs 90 E2
Gainsborough Suff 57 E5
Gainsford End Essex 55 F8
Gairloch Highld 154 C4
Gairlochy Highld 146 F4
Gairney Bank Perth 134 E3
Gairnshiel Lodge Aberds 149 D8
Gaisgill Cumb 99 D8
Gaitsgill Cumb 108 E3
Galashiels Borders 123 F7
Galgate Lancs 92 D4
Galhampton Som 12 B4
Gallaberry Dumfries 114 F2
Gallachoille Argyll 128 B2
Gallanach Argyll 130 C4
Gallanach Argyll 136 B3
Gallantry Bank Ches 74 D2
Gallatown Fife 134 E4
Galley Common Warks 63 E7
Galley Hill Cambs 54 C4
Galleyend Essex 42 D3
Galleywood Essex 42 D3
Gallin Perth 140 E2
Gallowfauld Angus 142 E4
Gallows Green Staffs 75 E7
Galltair Highld 155 H4
Galmisdale Highld 144 E4
Galmpton Devon 6 E4
Galmpton Torbay 7 D6
Galphay N Yorks 95 B5
Galston E Ayrs 120 F5
Galtrigill Highld 152 D2
Gamblesby Cumb 109 F6
Gamesley Derbys 87 E8
Gamlingay Cambs 54 D3
Gammersgill N Yorks 101 F5
Gamston Notts 77 B7
Ganarew Hereford 36 C2
Ganavan Argyll 130 B4
Gang Corn 5 C8
Ganllwyd Gwyn 71 E8
Gannochy Angus 143 B5
Gannochy Perth 134 B3
Gansclet Highld 169 E8
Ganstead E Yorks 97 F7
Ganthorpe N Yorks 96 B2
Ganton N Yorks 97 B5
Garbat Highld 156 C5
Garbhallt Argyll 131 F6
Garboldisham Norf 68 F3
Garden City Flint 73 C7
Garden Village Wrex 73 D7
Garden Village W Yorks 95 F7
Gardenstown Aberds 160 B4
Garderhouse Shetland 175 J5
Gardham E Yorks 97 E5
Gardin Shetland 174 G6
Gare Hill Som 24 E2
Garelochhead Argyll 129 A7
Garford Oxon 38 E4
Garforth W Yorks 95 F7
Gargrave N Yorks 94 D2
Gargunnock Stirl 133 E6
Garlic Street Norf 68 F5
Garlieston Dumfries 105 E8
Garlinge Green Kent 30 D5
Garlogie Aberds 151 D6
Garmond Aberds 160 C5
Garmony Argyll 137 D7
Garmouth Moray 159 C7
Garn-yr-erw Torf 35 C6
Garnant Carms 33 C7
Garndiffaith Torf 35 D6
Garndolbenmaen Gwyn 71 C5
Garnedd Conwy 83 F7
Garnett Bridge Cumb 99 E7
Garnfadryn Gwyn 70 D3
Garnkirk N Lnrk 121 C6
Garnlydan Bl Gwent 35 C5
Garnswllt Swansea 33 D7
Garrabost W Isles 172 E8
Garraron Argyll 130 E4
Garras Corn 3 D6
Garreg Gwyn 71 C7
Garrick Perth 133 C7
Garrigill Cumb 109 E7
Garriston N Yorks 101 E6
Garroch Dumfries 113 F5
Garrogie Lodge Highld 147 C8
Garros Highld 152 C5
Garrow Perth 141 E5
Garryhorn Dumfries 113 E5
Garsdale Cumb 100 F2
Garsdale Head Cumb 100 E2
Garsdon Wilts 37 F6
Garshall Green Staffs 75 F6
Garsington Oxon 39 D5
Garstang Lancs 92 E4
Garston Mers 86 F2
Garswood Mers 86 E3
Gartcosh N Lnrk 121 C6
Garth Bridgend 34 E2
Garth Gwyn 83 D5
Garth Powys 47 E8
Garth Shetland 175 H4
Garth Wrex 73 E6
Garth Row Cumb 99 E7
Garthamlock Glasgow 121 C6
Garthbrengy Powys 48 F2
Garthdee Aberdeen 151 D8
Gartheli Ceredig 46 D4
Garthmyl Powys 59 E8
Garthorpe Leics 64 B5
Garthorpe N Lincs 90 C2
Gartly Aberds 160 E2
Gartmore Stirl 132 E4
Gartnagrenach Argyll 128 E2
Gartness N Lnrk 121 C7
Gartness Stirl 132 F4
Gartocharn W Dunb 132 F3
Garton E Yorks 97 F8
Garton-on-the-Wolds E Yorks 97 D5
Gartsherrie N Lnrk 121 C7
Gartymore Highld 165 C7
Garvald E Loth 123 B8
Garvamore Highld 147 E8
Garvard Argyll 127 C1
Garvault Hotel Highld 168 F2
Garve Highld 156 C4
Garvestone Norf 68 D3
Garvock Aberds 143 B7
Garvock Invclyd 129 C7
Garway Hereford 36 B1
Garway Hill Hereford 35 B8
Gaskan Highld 138 B1
Gastard Wilts 24 C3
Gasthorpe Norf 68 F2
Gatcombe I o W 15 F5
Gate Burton Lincs 90 F2
Gate Helmsley N Yorks 96 D2
Gateacre Mers 86 F2
Gatebeck Cumb 99 F7
Gateford Notts 89 F6
Gateforth N Yorks 89 B6
Gatehead E Ayrs 120 F3
Gatehouse Northumb 116 F3
Gatehouse of Fleet Dumfries 106 D3
Gatelawbridge Dumfries 114 E2
Gateley Norf 81 E5
Gatenby N Yorks 101 F8
Gateshead T & W 111 C5
Gateshead International Stadium T & W 111 C5
Gatesheath Ches 73 C8
Gateside Aberds 150 C5
Gateside Angus 142 E4
Gateside E Renf 120 D4
Gateside Fife 134 D3
Gateside N Ayrs 120 D3
Gathurst Gtr Man 86 D3
Gatley Gtr Man 87 F6
Gattonside Borders 123 F8
Gaufron Powys 47 C8
Gaulby Leics 64 D3
Gauldry Fife 135 B5
Gaunt's Common Dorset 13 D8
Gautby Lincs 78 B4
Gavinton Borders 124 D3
Gawber S Yorks 88 D4
Gawcott Bucks 52 F4
Gawsworth Ches 75 C5
Gawthorpe W Yorks 88 B3
Gawthrop Cumb 100 F1
Gawthwaite Cumb 98 F4
Gay Street W Sus 16 B4
Gaydon Warks 51 D8
Gayfield Orkney 176 A3
Gayhurst M Keynes 53 E6
Gayle N Yorks 100 F3
Gayles N Yorks 101 D6
Gayton Mers 85 F3
Gayton Norf 67 C7
Gayton Northants 52 D5
Gayton Staffs 62 B3
Gayton le Marsh Lincs 91 F8
Gayton le Wold Lincs 91 F6
Gayton Thorpe Norf 67 C7
Gaywood Norf 67 B6
Gazeley Suff 55 C8
Geanies House Highld 158 B2
Gearraidh Bhailteas W Isles 171 H3
Gearraidh Bhaird W Isles 172 F6
Gearraidh na h-Aibhne W Isles 172 E5
Gearraidh na Monadh W Isles 171 J3
Geary Highld 152 C3
Geddes House Highld 158 D2
Gedding Suff 56 D3
Geddington Northants 65 F5
Gedintailor Highld 153 F6
Gedling Notts 77 E6
Gedney Lincs 66 B4
Gedney Broadgate Lincs 66 B4
Gedney Drove End Lincs 66 B4
Gedney Dyke Lincs 66 B4
Gedney Hill Lincs 66 C3
Gee Cross Gtr Man 87 E7
Geilston Argyll 120 B3
Geirinis W Isles 170 F3
Geise Highld 169 C6
Geisiadar W Isles 172 E4
Geldeston Norf 69 E6
Gell Conwy 83 E8
Gelli Pembs 32 C1
Gelli Rhondda 34 E3
Gellideg M Tydf 34 D4
Gellifor Denb 72 C5
Gelligaer Caerph 35 E5
Gellilydan Gwyn 71 D7
Gellinudd Neath 33 D8
Gellyburn Perth 141 F7
Gellywen Carms 32 B3
Gelston Dumfries 106 D4
Gelston Lincs 78 E2
Gembling E Yorks 97 D7
Gentleshaw Staffs 62 C4
Geocrab W Isles 173 J4
George Green Bucks 40 F3
George Nympton Devon 10 B2
Georgefield Dumfries 115 E5
Georgeham Devon 20 F3
Georgetown Bl Gwent 35 D5
Gerlan Gwyn 83 E6
Germansweek Devon 9 E6
Germoe Corn 2 D4
Gerrans Corn 3 C7
Gerrards Cross Bucks 40 F3
Gestingthorpe Essex 56 F2
Geuffordd Powys 60 C2
Gib Hill Ches 74 B3
Gibbet Hill Warks 64 F2
Gibbshill Dumfries 106 B4
Gidea Park London 41 F8
Gidleigh Devon 9 F8
Giffnock E Renf 121 D5
Gifford E Loth 123 C8
Giffordland N Ayrs 120 E2
Giffordtown Fife 134 C4
Giggleswick N Yorks 93 C8
Gilberdyke E Yorks 90 B2
Gilchriston E Loth 123 C7
Gilcrux Cumb 107 F8
Gildersome W Yorks 88 B3
Gildingwells S Yorks 89 F6
Gileston V Glam 22 C2
Gilfach Caerph 35 E5
Gilfach Goch Rhondda 34 F3
Gilfachrheda Ceredig 46 D3
Gillamoor N Yorks 102 F4
Gillar's Green Mers 86 E2
Gillen Highld 152 D3
Gilling East N Yorks 96 B2
Gilling West N Yorks 101 D6
Gillingham Dorset 13 B6
Gillingham Medway 29 C8
Gillingham Norf 69 E7
Gillock Highld 169 D7
Gillow Heath Staffs 75 D5
Gills Highld 169 B8
Gill's Green Kent 18 B4
Gilmanscleuch Borders 115 B6
Gilmerton Edin 123 C5
Gilmerton Perth 133 B7
Gilmonby Durham 100 C4
Gilmorton Leics 64 F2
Gilmourton S Lnrk 121 E6
Gilsland Cumb 109 C6
Gilsland Spa Cumb 109 C6
Gilston Borders 123 D7
Gilston Herts 41 C7
Gilwern Mon 35 C6
Gimingham Norf 81 D8
Giosla W Isles 172 F4
Gipping Suff 56 C4
Gipsey Bridge Lincs 79 E5
Girdle Toll N Ayrs 120 E3
Girlsta Shetland 175 H6
Girsby N Yorks 102 D1
Girtford Beds 54 D2
Girthon Dumfries 106 D3
Girton Cambs 54 C5
Girton Notts 77 C8
Girvan S Ayrs 112 E1
Gisburn Lancs 93 E8
Gisleham Suff 69 F8
Gislingham Suff 56 B4
Gissing Norf 68 F4
Gittisham Devon 11 E6
Gladestry Powys 48 D4
Gladsmuir E Loth 123 B7
Glais Swansea 33 D8
Glaisdale N Yorks 103 D5
Glame Highld 153 E6
Glamis Angus 142 E3
Glamis Castle Angus 142 E3
Glan Adda Gwyn 83 D5
Glan-Conwy Conwy 83 F8
Glan Conwy Conwy 83 D8
Glan-Duar Carms 46 E4
Glan-Dwyfach Gwyn 71 C5
Glan Gors Anglesey 82 D4
Glan-rhyd Gwyn 82 F4
Glan-traeth Anglesey 82 D2
Glan-y-don Flint 73 B5
Glan-y-nant Powys 59 F6
Glan-y-wern Gwyn 71 D7
Glan-yr-afon Anglesey 83 C6
Glan-yr-afon Gwyn 72 E3
Glan-yr-afon Gwyn 72 E4
Glanaman Carms 33 C7
Glandford Norf 81 C6
Glandwr Pembs 32 B2
Glandy Cross Carms 32 B2
Glandyfi Ceredig 58 E3
Glangrwyney Powys 35 C6
Glanmule Powys 59 E8
Glanrafon Ceredig 58 F3
Glanrhyd Gwyn 70 D3
Glanrhyd Pembs 45 E3
Glanton Northumb 117 C6
Glanton Pike Northumb 117 C6
Glanvilles Wootton Dorset 12 D4
Glapthorn Northants 65 E7
Glapwell Derbys 76 C4
Glas-allt Shiel Aberds 149 F8
Glasbury Powys 48 F3
Glaschoil Highld 158 F4
Glascoed Denb 72 B3
Glascoed Mon 35 D7
Glascoed Powys 59 C8
Glascorrie Aberds 150 E2
Glascote Staffs 63 D6
Glascwm Powys 48 D3
Glasdrum Argyll 138 E4
Glasfryn Conwy 72 D3
Glasgow Glasgow 121 C5
Glasgow Airport Renfs 120 C4
Glasgow Art Gallery & Museum Glasgow 121 C5
Glasgow Botanic Gardens Glasgow 121 C5
Glasgow Cathedral Glasgow 121 C6
Glasgow Prestwick International Airport S Ayrs 112 B3
Glashvin Highld 152 C5
Glasinfryn Gwyn 83 E5
Glasnacardoch Highld 145 D6
Glasnakille Highld 153 H6
Glasphein Highld 152 E2
Glaspwll Powys 58 E4
Glassburn Highld 156 F4
Glasserton Dumfries 105 F8
Glassford S Lnrk 121 E7
Glasshouse Hill Glos 36 B4
Glasshouses N Yorks 94 C4
Glasslie Fife 134 D4
Glasson Cumb 108 C2
Glasson Lancs 92 D4
Glassonby Cumb 109 F5
Glasterlaw Angus 143 D5
Glaston Rutland 65 D5
Glastonbury Som 23 F7
Glastonbury Abbey Som 23 F6
Glatton Cambs 65 F8
Glazebrook Warr 86 E4
Glazebury Warr 86 E4
Glazeley Shrops 61 F7
Gleadless S Yorks 88 F4
Gleadsmoss Ches 74 C5
Gleann Tholàstaidh W Isles 172 D8
Gleaston Cumb 92 B2
Gleiniant Powys 59 E6
Glemsford Suff 56 E2
Glen Dumfries 106 D2
Glen Dumfries 106 B5
Glen Auldyn I o M 84 C4
Glen Bernisdale Highld 152 E5
Glen Ho. Borders 123 F5
Glen Mona I o M 84 D4
Glen Nevis House Highld 139 B5
Glen Parva Leics 64 E2
Glen Sluain Argyll 131 F6
Glen Tanar House Aberds 150 E3
Glen Trool Lodge Dumfries 112 F4
Glen Village Falk 121 B8
Glen Vine I o M 84 E3
Glenamachrie Argyll 130 C5
Glenbarr Argyll 118 C3
Glenbeg Highld 137 B6
Glenbeg Highld 149 B6
Glenbervie Aberds 151 F6
Glenboig N Lnrk 121 C7
Glenborrodale Highld 137 B7
Glenbranter Argyll 131 F7
Glenbreck Borders 114 B3
Glenbrein Lodge Highld 147 C7
Glenbrittle House Highld 153 G5
Glenbuchat Lodge Aberds 150 C2
Glenbuck E Ayrs 113 B7
Glenburn Renfs 120 C4
Glencalvie Lodge Highld 164 F1
Glencanisp Lodge Highld 163 B5
Glencaple Dumfries 107 C6
Glencarron Lodge Highld 155 E6
Glencarse Perth 134 B3
Glencassley Castle Highld 163 D8
Glenceitlein Highld 139 E5
Glencoe Highld 138 D4
Glencraig Fife 134 E3
Glencripesdale Highld 137 C7
Glencrosh Dumfries 113 F7
Glendavan Ho. Aberds 150 D3
Glendevon Perth 133 D8
Glendoe Lodge Highld 147 D7
Glendoebeg Highld 147 D7
Glendoick Perth 134 B4
Glendoll Lodge Angus 142 B2
Glendoune S Ayrs 112 E1
Glenduckie Fife 134 C4
Glendye Lodge Aberds 150 F5
Gleneagles Hotel Perth 133 C8
Gleneagles House Perth 133 D8
Glenegedale Argyll 126 D3
Glenelg Highld 145 B8
Glenernie Moray 158 E4
Glenfarg Perth 134 C3
Glenfarquhar Lodge Aberds 151 F6
Glenferness House Highld 158 E3
Glenfeshie Lodge Highld 148 E4
Glenfiddich Distillery, Dufftown Moray 159 E7
Glenfield Leics 64 D2
Glenfinnan Highld 145 E8
Glenfoot Perth 134 C3
Glenfyne Lodge Argyll 131 D8
Glengap Dumfries 106 D3
Glengarnock N Ayrs 120 D3
Glengorm Castle Argyll 137 C5
Glengrasco Highld 153 E5
Glenhead Farm Angus 142 C2
Glenhoul Dumfries 113 F6
Glenhurich Highld 138 C2
Glenkerry Borders 115 C5
Glenkiln Dumfries 106 B5
Glenkindie Aberds 150 C3
Glenlatterach Moray 159 D5
Glenlee Dumfries 113 F6
Glenlichorn Perth 133 C6
Glenlivet Moray 149 B7
Glenlochsie Perth 141 B7
Glenloig N Ayrs 119 C6
Glenluce Dumfries 105 D6
Glenmallan Argyll 131 F8
Glenmarksie Highld 156 D4
Glenmassan Argyll 129 B6
Glenmavis N Lnrk 121 C7
Glenmaye I o M 84 E2
Glenmidge Dumfries 113 F8
Glenmore Argyll 130 D4
Glenmore Highld 153 E5
Glenmore Lodge Highld 149 D5
Glenmoy Angus 142 C4
Glenogil Angus 142 C4
Glenprosen Lodge Angus 142 C2
Glenprosen Village Angus 142 C3
Glenquiech Angus 142 C4
Glenreasdell Mains Argyll 128 E3
Glenree N Ayrs 119 D6
Glenridding Cumb 99 C5
Glenrossal Highld 164 D1
Glenrothes Fife 134 D4
Glensanda Highld 138 E2
Glensaugh Aberds 143 B6
Glenshero Lodge Highld 147 E8
Glenstockadale Dumfries 104 C4
Glenstriven Argyll 129 C5
Glentaggart S Lnrk 113 B8
Glentham Lincs 90 E4
Glentirranmuir Stirl 133 E5
Glenton Aberds 150 B5
Glentress Borders 123 F5
Glentromie Lodge Highld 148 E3
Glentrool Village Dumfries 105 B7
Glentruan I o M 84 B4
Glentruim House Highld 148 E2
Glenturret Distillery, Crieff Perth 133 B7
Glentworth Lincs 90 F3
Glenuig Highld 145 F6
Glenurquhart Highld 157 C8
Glespin S Lnrk 113 B8
Gletness Shetland 175 H6
Glewstone Hereford 36 B2
Glinton P'boro 65 D8
Glooston Leics 64 E4
Glororum Northumb 125 F7
Glossop Derbys 87 E8
Gloster Hill Northumb 117 D8
Gloucester Glos 37 C5
Gloucester Cathedral Glos 37 C5
Gloucestershire Airport Glos 37 B5
Gloup Shetland 174 C7
Glusburn N Yorks 94 E3
Glutt Lodge Highld 168 F4
Glutton Bridge Derbys 75 C7
Glympton Oxon 38 B4
Glyn-Ceiriog Wrex 73 F6
Glyn-cywarch Gwyn 71 D7
Glyn Ebwy = Ebbw Vale Bl Gwent 35 D5
Glyn-neath = Glynedd Neath 34 D2
Glynarthen Ceredig 46 E2
Glynbrochan Powys 59 F6
Glyncoch Rhondda 34 E4
Glyncorrwg Neath 34 E2
Glynde E Sus 17 D8
Glyndebourne E Sus 17 C8
Glyndyfrdwy Denb 72 E5
Glynedd = Glyn-neath Neath 34 D2
Glynogwr Bridgend 34 F3
Glyntaff Rhondda 34 F4
Glyntawe Powys 34 C2
Gnosall Staffs 62 B2
Gnosall Heath Staffs 62 B2
Goadby Leics 64 E4
Goadby Marwood Leics 64 B4
Goat Lees Kent 30 E4
Goatacre Wilts 24 B5
Goathill Dorset 12 C4
Goathland N Yorks 103 D6
Goathurst Som 22 F4
Gobernuisgach Lodge Highld 167 E6
Gobhaig W Isles 173 H3
Gobowen Shrops 73 F7
Godalming Sur 27 E7
Godley Gtr Man 87 E7
Godmanchester Cambs 54 B3
Godmanstone Dorset 12 E4
Godmersham Kent 30 D4
Godney Som 23 E6
Godolphin Cross Corn 2 C5
Godre'r-graig Neath 34 D1
Godshill Hants 14 C2
Godshill I o W 15 F6
Godstone Sur 28 D4
Godstone Farm Sur 28 D4
Godwinscroft Hants 14 E2
Goetre Mon 35 D7
Goferydd Anglesey 82 C2
Goff's Oak Herts 41 D6
Gogar Edin 122 B4
Goginan Ceredig 58 F3
Golan Gwyn 71 C6
Golant Corn 5 D6
Golberdon Corn 5 B8
Golborne Gtr Man 86 E4
Golcar W Yorks 88 C2
Gold Hill Norf 66 E5
Goldcliff Newport 35 F7
Golden Cross E Sus 18 D2
Golden Green Kent 29 E7
Golden Grove Carms 33 C6
Golden Hill Hants 14 E3
Golden Pot Hants 26 E5
Golden Valley Glos 37 B6
Goldenhill Stoke 75 D5
Golders Green London 41 F5
Goldhanger Essex 43 D5
Golding Shrops 60 D5
Goldington Beds 53 D8
Goldsborough N Yorks 95 D6
Goldsborough N Yorks 103 C6
Goldsithney Corn 2 C4
Goldsworthy Devon 9 B5
Goldthorpe S Yorks 89 D5
Gollanfield Highld 158 D2
Golspie Highld 165 D5
Golval Highld 168 C3
Gomeldon Wilts 25 F6
Gomersal W Yorks 88 B3
Gomshall Sur 27 E8
Gonalston Notts 77 E6
Gonfirth Shetland 175 G5
Good Easter Essex 42 C2
Gooderstone Norf 67 D7
Goodleigh Devon 20 F5
Goodmanham E Yorks 96 E4
Goodnestone Kent 30 C4
Goodnestone Kent 31 D6
Goodrich Hereford 36 C2
Goodrington Torbay 7 D6
Goodshaw Lancs 87 B6
Goodwick = Wdig Pembs 44 B4
Goodwood Racecourse W Sus 16 C2
Goodworth Clatford Hants 25 E8
Goole E Yorks 89 B8
Goonbell Corn 3 B6
Goonhavern Corn 4 D2
Goose Eye W Yorks 94 E3
Goose Green Gtr Man 86 D3
Goose Green Norf 68 F4
Goose Green W Sus 16 C5
Gooseham Corn 8 C4
Goosey Oxon 38 E3
Goosnargh Lancs 93 F5
Goostrey Ches 74 B4
Gorcott Hill Warks 51 C5
Gord Shetland 175 L6
Gordon Borders 124 E2
Gordonbush Highld 165 D5
Gordonsburgh Moray 159 C8
Gordonstoun Moray 159 C5
Gordonstown Aberds 160 C2
Gordonstown Aberds 160 E4
Gore Kent 31 D7
Gore Cross Wilts 24 D5
Gore Pit Essex 42 C4
Gorebridge Midloth 123 C6
Gorefield Cambs 66 C4
Gorey Jersey 17
Gorgie Edin 122 B5
Goring Oxon 39 F6
Goring-by-Sea W Sus 16 D5
Goring Heath Oxon 26 B4
Gorleston-on-Sea Norf 69 D8
Gornalwood W Mid 62 E3
Gorrachie Aberds 160 C4
Gorran Churchtown Corn 3 B8
Gorran Haven Corn 3 B9
Gorrenberry Borders 115 E7
Gors Ceredig 46 B5
Gorse Hill Swindon 38 F1
Gorsedd Flint 73 B5
Gorseinon Swansea 33 E6
Gorseness Orkney 176 E3
Gorsgoch Ceredig 46 D3
Gorslas Carms 33 C6
Gorsley Glos 36 B3
Gorstan Highld 156 C4
Gorstanvorran Highld 138 B2
Gorsteyhill Staffs 74 D4
Gorsty Hill Staffs 62 B5
Gortantaoid Argyll 126 B3
Gorton Gtr Man 87 E6
Gosbeck Suff 57 D5
Gosberton Lincs 78 F5
Gosberton Clough Lincs 65 B8
Gosfield Essex 42 B3
Gosford Hereford 49 C7
Gosforth Cumb 98 D2
Gosforth T & W 110 C5
Gosmore Herts 40 B4
Gosport Hants 15 E7
Gossabrough Shetland 174 E7
Gossington Glos 36 D4
Goswick Northumb 125 E6
Gotham Notts 76 F5
Gotherington Glos 37 B6
Gott Shetland 175 J6
Goudhurst Kent 18 B4
Goulceby Lincs 79 B5

Isham Northants 53 B6
Islay Airport Argyll 126 D3
Isle Abbotts Som 11 B8
Isle Brewers Som 11 B8
Isle of Man Airport I o M 84 F2
Isle of Man Steam Railway I o M 84 F1
Isle of Whithorn Dumfries 105 F8
Isleham Cambs 55 B7
Isleornsay Highld 145 B7
Islesburgh Shetland 174 G5
Islesteps Dumfries 107 B6
Isleworth London 28 B2
Isley Walton Leics 63 B8
Islibhig W Isles 172 F2
Islington London 41 F6
Islip Northants 53 B7
Islip Oxon 39 C5
Istead Rise Kent 29 C7
Isycoed Wrex 73 D8
Itchen Soton 14 C5
Itchen Abbas Hants 26 F3
Itchen Stoke Hants 26 F3
Itchingfield W Sus 16 B5
Itchington S Glos 36 F3
Itteringham Norf 81 D7
Itton Devon 9 E8
Itton Common Mon 36 E1
Ivegill Cumb 108 E4
Iver Bucks 40 F3
Iver Heath Bucks 40 F3
Iveston Durham 110 D4
Ivinghoe Bucks 40 C2
Ivinghoe Aston Bucks 40 C2
Ivington Hereford 49 D6
Ivington Green Hereford 49 D6
Ivy Chimneys Essex 41 D7
Ivy Cross Dorset 13 B6
Ivy Hatch Kent 29 D6
Ivybridge Devon 6 D4
Ivychurch Kent 19 C7
Iwade Kent 30 C3
Iwerne Courtney or Shroton Dorset 13 C6
Iwerne Minster Dorset 13 C6
Ixworth Suff 56 B3
Ixworth Thorpe Suff 56 B3

J

Jack Hill N Yorks 94 D5
Jack in the Green Devon 10 E5
Jacksdale Notts 76 D4
Jackstown Aberds 160 E4
Jacobstow Corn 8 E3
Jacobstowe Devon 9 D7
Jameston Pembs 32 E1
Jamestown Dumfries 115 E6
Jamestown Highld 157 D5
Jamestown W Dunb 132 F2
Jarlshof Prehistoric Site Shetland 175 M5
Jarrow T & W 111 C6
Jarvis Brook E Sus 18 C2
Jasper's Green Essex 42 B3
Java Argyll 130 B3
Jawcraig Falk 121 B8
Jaywick Essex 43 C7
Jealott's Hill Brack 27 B6
Jedburgh Borders 116 B2
Jeffreyston Pembs 32 D1
Jellyhill E Dunb 121 B6
Jemimaville Highld 157 C8
Jersey Airport Jersey 17
Jersey Farm Herts 40 D4
Jersey Zoo & Wildlife Park Jersey 17
Jesmond T & W 111 C5
Jevington E Sus 18 E2
Jockey End Herts 40 C3
Jodrell Bank Visitor Centre, Holmes Chapel Ches 74 B4
John o'Groats Highld 169 B8
Johnby Cumb 108 F4
John's Cross E Sus 18 C4
Johnshaven Aberds 143 C7
Johnston Pembs 44 D4
Johnstone Renfs 120 C4
Johnstonebridge Dumfries 114 E3
Johnstown Carms 33 C5
Johnstown Wrex 73 E7
Joppa Edin 123 B6
Joppa S Ayrs 112 C4
Jordans Bucks 40 E2
Jordanthorpe S Yorks 88 F4
Jorvik Centre York 96 D2
Judges Lodging, Presteigne Powys 48 C5
Jump S Yorks 88 D4
Jumpers Green Dorset 14 E2
Juniper Green Edin 122 C4
Jurby East I o M 84 C3
Jurby South Motor Racing Circuit I o M 84 C3
Jurby West I o M 84 C3

K

Kaber Cumb 100 C2
Kaimend S Lnrk 122 E2
Kaimes Edin 123 C5
Kalemouth Borders 116 B3
Kames Argyll 128 C4
Kames Argyll 130 D4
Kames E Ayrs 113 B6
Kea Corn 3 B7
Keadby N Lincs 90 C2
Keal Cotes Lincs 79 C6
Kearsley Gtr Man 87 D5
Kearstwick Cumb 99 F8
Kearton N Yorks 100 E4
Kearvaig Highld 166 B4
Keasden N Yorks 93 C7
Keckwick Halton 86 F3
Keddington Lincs 91 F7
Kedington Suff 55 E8
Kedleston Derbys 76 E3
Kedleston Hall Derbys 76 E3
Keelby Lincs 91 C5
Keele Staffs 74 E5
Keeley Green Beds 53 E8
Keeston Pembs 44 D4
Keevil Wilts 24 D4
Kegworth Leics 63 B8
Kehelland Corn 2 B5
Keig Aberds 150 C5
Keighley W Yorks 94 E3
Keighley and Worth Valley Railway W Yorks 94 F3
Keil Highld 138 D3
Keilarsbrae Clack 133 E7
Keilhill Aberds 160 C4
Keillmore Argyll 128 B1
Keillor Perth 142 E2
Keillour Perth 133 B8
Keills Argyll 126 C4
Keils Argyll 127 F3
Keinton Mandeville Som 23 F7
Keir Mill Dumfries 113 E8
Keisby Lincs 65 B7
Keiss Highld 169 C8
Keith Moray 159 D8
Keith Inch Aberds 161 D8
Keithock Angus 143 C6
Kelbrook Lancs 94 E2
Kelby Lincs 78 E3
Keld Cumb 99 C7
Keld N Yorks 100 D3
Keldholme N Yorks 103 F5
Kelfield N Lincs 90 D2
Kelfield N Yorks 95 F8
Kelham Notts 77 D7
Kellan Argyll 137 D6
Kellas Angus 142 F4
Kellas Moray 159 D5
Kellaton Devon 7 F6
Kelleth Cumb 100 D1
Kelleythorpe E Yorks 97 D5
Kelling Norf 81 C6
Kellingley N Yorks 89 B6
Kellington N Yorks 89 B6
Kelloe Durham 111 F6
Kelloholm Dumfries 113 C7
Kelly Devon 9 F5
Kelly Bray Corn 5 B8
Kelmarsh Northants 52 B5
Kelmscot Oxon 38 E2
Kelsale Suff 57 C7
Kelsall Ches 74 C2
Kelsall Hill Ches 74 C2
Kelshall Herts 54 F4
Kelsick Cumb 107 D8
Kelso Borders 124 F3
Kelso Racecourse Borders 124 F3
Kelstedge Derbys 76 C3
Kelstern Lincs 91 E6
Kelston Bath 24 C2
Keltneyburn Perth 140 E4
Kelton Dumfries 107 B6
Kelty Fife 134 E3
Kelvedon Essex 42 C4
Kelvedon Hatch Essex 42 E1
Kelvin S Lnrk 121 D6
Kelvinside Glasgow 121 C5
Kelynack Corn 2 C2
Kemback Fife 135 C6
Kemberton Shrops 61 D7
Kemble Glos 37 E6
Kemerton Worcs 50 F4
Kemeys Commander Mon 35 D7
Kemnay Aberds 151 C6
Kemp Town Brighton 17 D7
Kempley Glos 36 B3
Kemps Green Warks 51 B6
Kempsey Worcs 50 E3
Kempsford Glos 38 E1
Kempshott Hants 26 D4
Kempston Beds 53 E8
Kempston Hardwick Beds 53 E8
Kempton Shrops 60 F3
Kempton Park Racecourse Sur 28 B2
Kemsing Kent 29 D6
Kemsley Kent 30 C3
Kenardington Kent 19 B6
Kenchester Hereford 49 E6
Kencot Oxon 38 D2
Kendal Cumb 99 E7
Kendoon Dumfries 113 F6
Kendray S Yorks 88 D4
Kenfig Bridgend 34 F2
Kenfig Hill Bridgend 34 F2
Kenilworth Warks 51 B7
Kenilworth Castle Warks 51 B7
Kenknock Stirl 140 F1
Kenley London 28 D4
Kenley Shrops 61 D5
Kenmore Highld 154 E3
Kenmore Perth 140 E4
Kenn Devon 10 F4
Kenn N Som 23 C6
Kennacley W Isles 173 J4
Kennacraig Argyll 128 D3
Kennerleigh Devon 10 D3
Kennet Clack 133 E8
Kennethmont Aberds 150 B4
Kennett Cambs 55 C7
Kennford Devon 10 F4
Kenninghall Norf 68 F3
Kenninghall Heath Norf 68 F3
Kennington Kent 30 E4
Kennington Oxon 39 D5
Kennoway Fife 135 D5
Kenny Hill Suff 55 B7
Kennythorpe N Yorks 96 C3
Kenovay Argyll 136 F1
Kensaleyre Highld 152 D5
Kensington London 28 B3
Kensworth Beds 40 C3
Kensworth Common Beds 40 C3
Kent International Airport Kent 31 C7
Kent Street E Sus 18 D4
Kent Street Kent 29 D7
Kent Street W Sus 17 B6
Kentallen Highld 138 D4
Kentchurch Hereford 35 B8
Kentford Suff 55 C8
Kentisbeare Devon 11 D5
Kentisbury Devon 20 E5
Kentisbury Ford Devon 20 E5
Kentmere Cumb 99 D6
Kenton Devon 10 F4
Kenton Suff 57 C5
Kenton T & W 110 C5
Kenton Bankfoot T & W 110 C5
Kentra Highld 137 B7
Kents Bank Cumb 92 B3
Kent's Green Glos 36 B4
Kent's Oak Hants 14 B4
Kenwick Shrops 73 F8
Kenwyn Corn 3 B7
Keoldale Highld 167 C5
Keppanach Highld 138 C4
Keppoch Highld 146 B2
Keprigan Argyll 118 E3
Kepwick N Yorks 102 E2
Kerchesters Borders 124 F3
Keresley W Mid 63 F7
Kernborough Devon 7 E5
Kerne Bridge Hereford 36 C2
Kerris Corn 2 D3
Kerry Powys 59 F8
Kerrycroy Argyll 129 D6
Kerry's Gate Hereford 49 F5
Kerrysdale Highld 154 C4
Kersall Notts 77 C7
Kersey Suff 56 E4
Kershopefoot Cumb 115 F7
Kersoe Worcs 50 F4
Kerswell Devon 11 D5
Kerswell Green Worcs 50 E3
Kesgrave Suff 57 E6
Kessingland Suff 69 F8
Kessingland Beach Suff 69 F8
Kessington E Dunb 121 B5
Kestle Corn 3 B8
Kestle Mill Corn 4 D3
Keston London 28 C5
Keswick Cumb 98 B4
Keswick Norf 68 D5
Keswick Norf 81 D9
Ketley Telford 61 C6
Ketley Bank Telford 61 C6
Ketsby Lincs 79 B6
Kettering Northants 53 B6
Ketteringham Norf 68 D4
Kettins Perth 142 F2
Kettlebaston Suff 56 D3
Kettlebridge Fife 134 D5
Kettleburgh Suff 57 C6
Kettlehill Fife 134 D5
Kettleholm Dumfries 107 B8
Kettleness N Yorks 103 C6
Kettleshume Ches 75 B6
Kettlesing Bottom N Yorks 94 D5
Kettlesing Head N Yorks 94 D5
Kettlestone Norf 81 D5
Kettlethorpe Lincs 77 B8
Kettletoft Orkney 176 C5
Kettlewell N Yorks 94 B2
Ketton Rutland 65 D6
Kew London 28 B2
Kew Br. London 28 B2
Kew Gardens London 28 B2
Kewstoke N Som 22 C5
Kexbrough S Yorks 88 D4
Kexby Lincs 90 F2
Kexby York 96 D3
Key Green Ches 75 C5
Keyham Leics 64 D3
Keyhaven Hants 14 E4
Keyingham E Yorks 91 B6
Keymer W Sus 17 C7
Keynsham Bath 23 C8
Keysoe Beds 53 C8
Keysoe Row Beds 53 C8
Keyston Cambs 53 B8
Keyworth Notts 77 F6
Kibblesworth T & W 110 D5
Kibworth Beauchamp Leics 64 E3
Kibworth Harcourt Leics 64 E3
Kidbrooke London 28 B5
Kiddemore Green Staffs 62 D2
Kidderminster Worcs 50 B3
Kiddington Oxon 38 B4
Kidlington Oxon 38 C4
Kidmore End Oxon 26 B4
Kidsgrove Staffs 74 D5
Kidstones N Yorks 100 F4
Kidwelly = Cydweli Carms 33 D5
Kiel Crofts Argyll 130 B5
Kielder Northumb 116 E2
Kielder Castle Visitor Centre Northumb 116 E2
Kierfiold Ho. Orkney 176 E1
Kilbagie Clack 133 F8
Kilbarchan Renfs 120 C4
Kilbeg Highld 145 C6
Kilberry Argyll 128 D2
Kilbirnie N Ayrs 120 D3
Kilbride Argyll 130 C4
Kilbride Argyll 130 C5
Kilbride Highld 153 G6
Kilburn Angus 142 C3
Kilburn Derbys 76 E3
Kilburn London 41 F5
Kilburn N Yorks 95 B8
Kilby Leics 64 E3
Kilchamaig Argyll 128 D3
Kilchattan Argyll 127 C1
Kilchattan Bay Argyll 129 E6
Kilchenzie Argyll 118 D3
Kilcheran Argyll 130 B4
Kilchiaran Argyll 126 C2
Kilchoan Argyll 130 D3
Kilchoan Highld 137 B5
Kilchoman Argyll 126 C2
Kilchrenan Argyll 131 C6
Kilconquhar Fife 135 D6
Kilcot Glos 36 B3
Kilcoy Highld 157 D6
Kilcreggan Argyll 129 B7
Kildale N Yorks 102 D4
Kildalloig Argyll 118 E4
Kildary Highld 157 B8
Kildermorie Lodge Highld 157 B6
Kildonan N Ayrs 119 D7
Kildonan Lodge Highld 165 B6
Kildonnan Highld 144 E4
Kildrummy Aberds 150 C3
Kildwick N Yorks 94 E3
Kilfinan Argyll 128 C4
Kilfinnan Highld 147 E5
Kilgetty Pembs 32 D2
Kilgwrrwg Common Mon 36 E1
Kilham E Yorks 97 C6
Kilham Northumb 124 F4
Kilkenneth Argyll 136 F1
Kilkerran Argyll 118 E4
Kilkhampton Corn 8 C4
Killamarsh Derbys 89 F5
Killay Swansea 33 E7
Killbeg Argyll 137 D7
Killean Argyll 118 B3
Killearn Stirl 132 F4
Killen Highld 157 D7
Killerby Darl 101 C6
Killerton House, Exeter Devon 10 D4
Killichonan Perth 140 D2
Killiechonate Highld 146 F5
Killiechronan Argyll 137 D6
Killiecrankie Perth 141 C6
Killiemor Argyll 137 E5
Killiemore House Argyll 137 F5
Killilan Highld 155 G5
Killimster Highld 169 D8
Killin Stirl 140 F2
Killin Lodge Highld 147 D8
Killinallan Argyll 126 B3
Killinghall N Yorks 95 D5
Killington Cumb 99 F8
Killingworth T & W 111 B5
Killmahumaig Argyll 128 A2
Killochyett Borders 123 E7
Killocraw Argyll 118 C3
Killundine Highld 137 D6
Kilmacolm Invclyd 120 C3
Kilmaha Argyll 130 E5
Kilmahog Stirl 132 D5
Kilmalieu Highld 138 D2
Kilmaluag Highld 152 B5
Kilmany Fife 135 B5
Kilmarie Highld 153 H6
Kilmarnock E Ayrs 120 F4
Kilmaron Castle Fife 135 C5
Kilmartin Argyll 130 F4
Kilmaurs E Ayrs 120 E4
Kilmelford Argyll 130 D4
Kilmeny Argyll 126 C3
Kilmersdon Som 23 D8
Kilmeston Hants 15 B6
Kilmichael Argyll 118 D3
Kilmichael Glassary Argyll 128 A3
Kilmichael of Inverlussa Argyll 128 B2
Kilmington Devon 11 E7
Kilmington Wilts 24 F2
Kilmonivaig Highld 146 F4
Kilmorack Highld 157 E5
Kilmore Argyll 130 C4
Kilmore Highld 145 C6
Kilmory Argyll 128 C2
Kilmory Highld 137 A6
Kilmory Highld 144 C3
Kilmory N Ayrs 119 D6
Kilmuir Highld 152 E3
Kilmuir Highld 157 E7
Kilmuir Highld 157 B8
Kilmuir Highld 152 B4
Kilmun Argyll 129 B6
Kilmun Argyll 130 D5
Kiln Pit Hill Northumb 110 D3
Kilncadzow S Lnrk 121 E8
Kilndown Kent 18 B4
Kilnhurst S Yorks 89 E5
Kilninian Argyll 136 D4
Kilninver Argyll 130 C4
Kilnsea E Yorks 91 C8
Kilnsey N Yorks 94 C2
Kilnwick E Yorks 97 E5
Kilnwick Percy E Yorks 96 D4
Kiloran Argyll 127 C1
Kilpatrick N Ayrs 119 D6
Kilpeck Hereford 49 F6
Kilphedir Highld 165 C6
Kilpin E Yorks 89 B8
Kilpin Pike E Yorks 89 B8
Kilrenny Fife 135 D7
Kilsby Northants 52 B3
Kilspindie Perth 134 B4
Kilsyth N Lnrk 121 B7
Kiltarlity Highld 157 E6
Kilton Notts 77 B5
Kilton Som 22 E3
Kilton Thorpe Redcar 102 C4
Kilvaxter Highld 152 C4
Kilve Som 22 E3
Kilvington Notts 77 E7
Kilwinning N Ayrs 120 E3
Kimber worth S Yorks 88 E5
Kimberley Norf 68 D3
Kimberley Notts 76 E5
Kimble Wick Bucks 39 D8
Kimblesworth Durham 111 E5
Kimbolton Cambs 53 C8
Kimbolton Hereford 49 C7
Kimcote Leics 64 F2
Kimmeridge Dorset 13 G7
Kimmerston Northumb 125 F5
Kimpton Hants 25 E7
Kimpton Herts 40 C4
Kinbrace Highld 168 F3
Kinbuck Stirl 133 D6
Kincaple Fife 135 C6
Kincardine Fife 133 F8
Kincardine Highld 164 F3
Kincardine Bridge Fife 133 F8
Kincardine O'Neil Aberds 150 E4
Kinclaven Perth 142 F1
Kincorth Aberdeen 151 D8
Kincorth Ho. Moray 158 C4
Kincraig Highld 148 D4
Kincraigie Perth 141 E6
Kindallachan Perth 141 E6
Kinderland, Scarborough N Yorks 103 E8
Kineton Glos 37 B7
Kineton Warks 51 D8
Kinfauns Perth 134 B3
King Edward Aberds 160 C4
King Sterndale Derbys 75 B7
Kingairloch Highld 138 D2
Kingarth Argyll 129 E5
Kingcoed Mon 35 D8
Kingerby Lincs 90 E4
Kingham Oxon 38 B2
Kingholm Quay Dumfries 107 B6
Kinghorn Fife 134 F4
Kingie Highld 146 D4
Kinglassie Fife 134 E4
Kingoodie Perth 134 B5
King's Acre Hereford 49 E6
King's Bromley Staffs 62 C5
King's Caple Hereford 36 B2
King's Cliffe Northants 65 E7
Kings College Chapel, Cambridge Cambs 54 D5
King's Coughton Warks 51 D5
King's Heath W Mid 62 F4
Kings Hedges Cambs 55 C5
Kings Langley Herts 40 D3
King's Lynn Norf 67 B6
King's Meaburn Cumb 99 B8
King's Mills Wrex 73 E7
Kings Muir Borders 123 F5
King's Newnham Warks 52 B2
King's Newton Derbys 63 B7
King's Norton Leics 64 D3
King's Norton W Mid 51 B5
King's Nympton Devon 9 C8
King's Pyon Hereford 49 D6
King's Ripton Cambs 54 B3
King's Somborne Hants 25 F8
King's Stag Dorset 12 C5
King's Stanley Glos 37 D5
King's Sutton Northants 52 F2
King's Thorn Hereford 49 F7
King's Walden Herts 40 B4
Kings Worthy Hants 26 F2
Kingsand Corn 6 D2
Kingsbarns Fife 135 C7
Kingsbridge Devon 6 E5
Kingsbridge Som 21 F8
Kingsburgh Highld 152 D4
Kingsbury London 41 F5
Kingsbury Warks 63 E6
Kingsbury Episcopi Som 12 B2
Kingsclere Hants 26 D3
Kingscote Glos 37 E5
Kingscott Devon 9 C7
Kingscross N Ayrs 119 D7
Kingsdon Som 12 B3
Kingsdown Kent 31 E7
Kingseat Fife 134 E3
Kingsey Bucks 39 D7
Kingsfold W Sus 28 F2
Kingsford E Ayrs 120 E4
Kingsford Worcs 62 F2
Kingsforth N Lincs 90 C4
Kingsgate Kent 31 B7
Kingsheanton Devon 20 F4
Kingshouse Hotel Highld 139 D6
Kingside Hill Cumb 107 D8
Kingskerswell Devon 7 C6
Kingskettle Fife 134 D5
Kingsland Anglesey 82 C2
Kingsland Hereford 49 C6
Kingsley Ches 74 B2
Kingsley Hants 27 F5
Kingsley Staffs 75 E7
Kingsley Green W Sus 27 F6
Kingsley Holt Staffs 75 E7
Kingsley Park Northants 53 C5
Kingsmuir Angus 142 E4
Kingsmuir Fife 135 D7
Kingsnorth Kent 19 B7
Kingstanding W Mid 62 E4
Kingsteignton Devon 7 B6
Kingsthorpe Northants 53 C5
Kingston Cambs 54 D4
Kingston Devon 6 E4
Kingston Dorset 13 D5
Kingston Dorset 13 G7
Kingston E Loth 135 F7
Kingston Hants 14 D2
Kingston I o W 15 F5
Kingston Kent 31 D5
Kingston Moray 159 C7
Kingston Bagpuize Oxon 38 E4
Kingston Blount Oxon 39 E7
Kingston by Sea W Sus 17 D6
Kingston Deverill Wilts 24 F3
Kingston Gorse W Sus 16 D4
Kingston Lacy, Wimborne Minster Dorset 13 D7
Kingston Lisle Oxon 38 F3
Kingston Maurward Dorset 12 E5
Kingston near Lewes E Sus 17 D7
Kingston on Soar Notts 64 B2
Kingston Russell Dorset 12 E3
Kingston St Mary Som 11 B7
Kingston Seymour N Som 23 C6
Kingston Upon Hull Hull 90 B4
Kingston upon Thames London 28 C2
Kingston Vale London 28 B3
Kingstone Hereford 49 F6
Kingstone Som 11 C8
Kingstone Staffs 62 B4
Kingstown Cumb 108 D3
Kingswear Devon 7 D6
Kingswells Aberdeen 151 D7
Kingswinford W Mid 62 F2
Kingswood Bucks 39 C6
Kingswood Glos 36 E4
Kingswood Hereford 48 D4
Kingswood Kent 30 D2
Kingswood Powys 60 D2
Kingswood S Glos 23 B8
Kingswood Sur 28 D3
Kingswood Warks 51 B6
Kingthorpe Lincs 78 B4
Kington Hereford 48 D4
Kington Worcs 50 D4
Kington Langley Wilts 24 B4
Kington Magna Dorset 13 B5
Kington St Michael Wilts 24 B4
Kingussie Highld 148 D3
Kingweston Som 23 F7
Kininvie Ho. Moray 159 E7
Kinkell Bridge Perth 133 C8
Kinknockie Aberds 161 D7
Kinlet Shrops 61 F7
Kinloch Fife 134 C4
Kinloch Highld 144 D3
Kinloch Highld 166 F5
Kinloch Highld 145 B6
Kinloch Perth 141 E8
Kinloch Perth 142 E2
Kinloch Hourn Highld 146 D2
Kinloch Laggan Highld 147 F8
Kinloch Lodge Highld 167 D7
Kinloch Rannoch Perth 140 D3
Kinlochan Highld 138 C2
Kinlochard Stirl 132 D3
Kinlochbeoraid Highld 145 E8
Kinlochbervie Highld 166 D4
Kinlocheil Highld 138 B3
Kinlochewe Highld 154 D6
Kinlochleven Highld 139 C5
Kinlochmoidart Highld 145 F7
Kinlochmorar Highld 145 D8
Kinlochmore Highld 139 C5
Kinlochspelve Argyll 130 C2
Kinloid Highld 145 E6
Kinloss Moray 158 C4
Kinmel Bay Conwy 72 A3
Kinmuck Aberds 151 C7
Kinmundy Aberds 151 C7
Kinnadie Aberds 161 D6
Kinnaird Perth 134 B4
Kinnaird Castle Angus 143 D6
Kinneff Aberds 143 B8
Kinnelhead Dumfries 114 D3
Kinnell Angus 143 D6
Kinnerley Shrops 60 B3
Kinnersley Hereford 48 E5
Kinnersley Worcs 50 E3
Kinnerton Powys 48 C4
Kinnesswood Perth 134 D3
Kinninvie Durham 101 B5
Kinnordy Angus 142 D3
Kinoulton Notts 77 F6
Kinross Perth 134 D3
Kinrossie Perth 142 F1
Kinsbourne Green Herts 40 C4
Kinsey Heath Ches 74 E3
Kinsham Hereford 49 C5
Kinsham Worcs 50 F4
Kinsley W Yorks 88 C5
Kinson Bmouth 13 E8
Kintbury W Berks 25 C8
Kintessack Moray 158 C3
Kintillo Perth 134 C3
Kintocher Aberds 150 D4
Kinton Hereford 49 B6
Kinton Shrops 60 C3
Kintore Aberds 151 C6
Kintour Argyll 126 D4
Kintra Argyll 136 F4
Kintra Argyll 126 E3
Kintraw Argyll 130 E4
Kinuachdrachd Argyll 130 F3
Kinveachy Highld 148 C5
Kinver Staffs 62 F2
Kippax W Yorks 95 F7
Kippen Stirl 133 E5
Kippford or Scaur Dumfries 106 D5
Kirbister Orkney 176 F2
Kirbister Orkney 176 D5
Kirbuster Orkney 176 D1
Kirby Bedon Norf 69 D5
Kirby Bellars Leics 64 C4
Kirby Cane Norf 69 E6
Kirby Cross Essex 43 B8
Kirby Grindalythe N Yorks 96 C5
Kirby Hill N Yorks 95 C6
Kirby Hill N Yorks 101 D6
Kirby Knowle N Yorks 102 F2
Kirby-le-Soken Essex 43 B8
Kirby Misperton N Yorks 96 B3
Kirby Muxloe Leics 64 D2
Kirby Row Norf 69 E6
Kirby Sigston N Yorks 102 E2
Kirby Underdale E Yorks 96 D4
Kirby Wiske N Yorks 102 F1
Kirdford W Sus 16 B4
Kirk Highld 169 D7
Kirk Bramwith S Yorks 89 C7
Kirk Deighton N Yorks 95 D6
Kirk Ella E Yorks 90 B4
Kirk Hallam Derbys 76 E4
Kirk Hammerton N Yorks 95 D7
Kirk Ireton Derbys 76 D2
Kirk Langley Derbys 76 F2
Kirk Merrington Durham 111 F5
Kirk Michael I o M 84 C3
Kirk of Shotts N Lnrk 121 C8
Kirk Sandall S Yorks 89 D7
Kirk Smeaton N Yorks 89 C6
Kirk Yetholm Borders 116 B4
Kirkabister Shetland 175 K6
Kirkandrews Dumfries 106 E3
Kirkandrews upon Eden Cumb 108 D3
Kirkbampton Cumb 108 D3
Kirkbean Dumfries 107 D6
Kirkbride Cumb 108 D2
Kirkbuddo Angus 143 E5
Kirkburn Borders 123 F5
Kirkburn E Yorks 97 D5
Kirkburton W Yorks 88 C2
Kirkby Lincs 90 E4
Kirkby Mers 86 E2
Kirkby N Yorks 102 D3
Kirkby Fleetham N Yorks 101 E7
Kirkby Green Lincs 78 D3
Kirkby In Ashfield Notts 76 D5
Kirkby-in-Furness Cumb 98 F4
Kirkby la Thorpe Lincs 78 E4
Kirkby Lonsdale Cumb 93 B6
Kirkby Malham N Yorks 93 C8
Kirkby Mallory Leics 63 D8
Kirkby Malzeard N Yorks 94 B5
Kirkby Mills N Yorks 103 F5
Kirkby on Bain Lincs 78 C5
Kirkby Overblow N Yorks 95 E6
Kirkby Stephen Cumb 100 D2
Kirkby Thore Cumb 99 B8
Kirkby Underwood Lincs 65 B7
Kirkby Wharfe N Yorks 95 E8
Kirkbymoorside N Yorks 102 F4
Kirkcaldy Fife 134 E4
Kirkcambeck Cumb 108 C5
Kirkcarswell Dumfries 106 E4
Kirkcolm Dumfries 104 C4
Kirkconnel Dumfries 113 C7
Kirkconnell Dumfries 107 C6
Kirkcowan Dumfries 105 C7
Kirkcudbright Dumfries 106 D3
Kirkdale Mers 85 E4
Kirkfieldbank S Lnrk 121 E8
Kirkgunzeon Dumfries 107 C5
Kirkham Lancs 92 F4
Kirkham N Yorks 96 C3
Kirkhamgate W Yorks 88 B3
Kirkharle Northumb 117 F6
Kirkheaton Northumb 110 B3
Kirkheaton W Yorks 88 C2
Kirkhill Angus 143 C6
Kirkhill Highld 157 E6
Kirkhill Midloth 122 C5
Kirkhill Moray 159 F6
Kirkhope Borders 115 B6
Kirkhouse Borders 123 F6
Kirkiboll Highld 167 D7
Kirkibost Highld 153 H6
Kirkinch Angus 142 E3
Kirkinner Dumfries 105 D8
Kirkintilloch E Dunb 121 B6
Kirkland Cumb 98 C2
Kirkland Cumb 109 F6
Kirkland Dumfries 113 E8
Kirkland Dumfries 113 C7
Kirkleatham Redcar 102 B3
Kirklevington Stockton 102 D2
Kirkley Suff 69 E8
Kirklington Notts 77 D6
Kirklington N Yorks 101 F8
Kirklinton Cumb 108 C4
Kirkliston Edin 122 B4
Kirkmaiden Dumfries 104 F5
Kirkmichael Perth 141 D7
Kirkmichael S Ayrs 112 D3
Kirkmuirhill S Lnrk 121 E7
Kirknewton Northumb 124 F5
Kirknewton W Loth 122 C4
Kirkney Aberds 160 E2
Kirkoswald Cumb 109 E5
Kirkoswald S Ayrs 112 D2
Kirkpatrick Durham Dumfries 106 B4
Kirkpatrick-Fleming Dumfries 108 B2
Kirksanton Cumb 98 F3
Kirkstall W Yorks 95 F5
Kirkstead Lincs 78 C4
Kirkstile Aberds 160 E2
Kirkstyle Highld 169 B8
Kirkton Aberds 150 B5
Kirkton Aberds 160 D3
Kirkton Angus 142 E4
Kirkton Angus 142 F4
Kirkton Borders 115 C8
Kirkton Dumfries 114 F2
Kirkton Fife 135 B5
Kirkton Highld 155 H4
Kirkton Highld 155 F5
Kirkton Highld 164 E4
Kirkton Highld 157 D8
Kirkton Perth 133 C8
Kirkton S Lnrk 114 B2
Kirkton Stirl 132 D4
Kirkton Manor Borders 122 F5
Kirkton of Airlie Angus 142 D3
Kirkton of Auchterhouse Angus 142 F3
Kirkton of Auchterless Aberds 160 D4
Kirkton of Barevan Highld 158 E2
Kirkton of Bourtie Aberds 151 B7
Kirkton of Collace Perth 142 F1
Kirkton of Craig Angus 143 D7
Kirkton of Culsalmond Aberds 160 E3
Kirkton of Durris Aberds 151 E6
Kirkton of Glenbuchat Aberds 150 C2
Kirkton of Glenisla Angus 142 C2
Kirkton of Kingoldrum Angus 142 D3
Kirkton of Largo Fife 135 D6
Kirkton of Lethendy Perth 141 E8
Kirkton of Logie Buchan Aberds 151 B8
Kirkton of Maryculter Aberds 151 E7
Kirkton of Menmuir Angus 143 C5
Kirkton of Monikie Angus 142 F4
Kirkton of Oyne Aberds 151 B5
Kirkton of Rayne Aberds 160 F3
Kirkton of Skene Aberds 151 D7
Kirkton of Tough Aberds 150 C5
Kirktonhill Borders 123 D7
Kirktown Aberds 161 C7
Kirktown of Alvah Aberds 160 B3
Kirktown of Deskford Moray 160 B2
Kirktown of Fetteresso Aberds 151 F7
Kirktown of Mortlach Moray 159 F7
Kirktown of Slains Aberds 161 F7
Kirkurd Borders 122 E4
Kirkwall Orkney 176 E3
Kirkwall Airport Orkney 176 F3
Kirkwhelpington Northumb 117 F5
Kirmington N Lincs 90 C5
Kirmond le Mire Lincs 91 E5
Kirn Argyll 129 C6
Kirriemuir Angus 142 D3
Kirstead Green Norf 69 E5
Kirtlebridge Dumfries 108 B2
Kirtleton Dumfries 115 F5
Kirtling Cambs 55 D7
Kirtling Green Cambs 55 D7
Kirtlington Oxon 38 C4
Kirtomy Highld 168 C2
Kirton Lincs 79 F6
Kirton Notts 77 C6
Kirton Suff 57 F6
Kirton End Lincs 79 E5
Kirton Holme Lincs 79 E5
Kirton in Lindsey N Lincs 90 E3
Kislingbury Northants 52 D4
Kites Hardwick Warks 52 C2
Kittisford Som 11 B5
Kittle Swansea 33 F6
Kitt's Green W Mid 63 F5
Kitt's Moss Gtr Man 87 F6
Kittybrewster Aberdeen 151 D8
Kitwood Hants 26 F4
Kivernoll Hereford 49 F6
Kiveton Park S Yorks 89 F5
Knaith Lincs 90 F2
Knaith Park Lincs 90 F2
Knap Corner Dorset 13 B6
Knaphill Sur 27 D7
Knapp Perth 142 F2
Knapp Som 11 B8
Knapthorpe Notts 77 D7
Knapton Norf 81 D9
Knapton York 95 D8
Knapton Green Hereford 49 D6
Knapwell Cambs 54 C4

Loughborough Leics 64 C2
Loughor Swansea 33 E6
Loughton Essex 41 E7
Loughton M Keynes 53 F6
Loughton Shrops 61 F6
Louis Tussaud's Waxworks Blkpool 92 F3
Lound Lincs 65 C7
Lound Notts 89 F7
Lound Suff 69 E8
Lount Leics 63 C7
Louth Lincs 91 F7
Love Clough Lancs 87 B6
Lovedean Hants 15 C7
Lover Wilts 14 B3
Loversall S Yorks 89 E6
Loves Green Essex 42 D2
Lovesome Hill N Yorks 102 E1
Loveston Pembs 32 D1
Lovington Som 23 F7
Low Ackworth W Yorks 89 C5
Low Barlings Lincs 78 B3
Low Bentham N Yorks 93 C6
Low Bradfield S Yorks 88 E3
Low Bradley N Yorks 94 E3
Low Braithwaite Cumb 108 E4
Low Brunton Northumb 110 B2
Low Burnham N Lincs 89 D8
Low Burton N Yorks 101 F7
Low Buston Northumb 117 D8
Low Catton E Yorks 96 D3
Low Clanyard Dumfries 104 F5
Low Coniscliffe Darl 101 C7
Low Crosby Cumb 108 D4
Low Dalby N Yorks 103 F6
Low Dinsdale Darl 101 C8
Low Ellington N Yorks 101 F7
Low Etherley Durham 101 B6
Low Fell T & W 111 D5
Low Fulney Lincs 66 B2
Low Garth N Yorks 103 D5
Low Gate Northumb 110 C2
Low Grantley N Yorks 94 B5
Low Habberley Worcs 50 B3
Low Ham Som 12 B2
Low Hesket Cumb 108 E4
Low Hesleyhurst Northumb 117 E6
Low Hutton N Yorks 96 C3
Low Laithe N Yorks 94 C4
Low Leighton Derbys 87 F8
Low Lorton Cumb 98 B3
Low Marishes N Yorks 96 B4
Low Marnham Notts 77 C8
Low Mill N Yorks 102 E4
Low Moor Lancs 93 E7
Low Moor W Yorks 88 B2
Low Moorsley T & W 111 E6
Low Newton Cumb 99 F6
Low Newton-by-the-Sea Northumb 117 B8
Low Row Cumb 108 F3
Low Row Cumb 109 C5
Low Row N Yorks 100 E4
Low Salchrie Dumfries 104 C4
Low Smerby Argyll 118 D4
Low Torry Fife 134 F2
Low Worsall N Yorks 102 D1
Low Wray Cumb 99 D5
Lowbridge House Cumb 99 D7
Lowca Cumb 98 B1
Lowdham Notts 77 E6
Lowe Shrops 74 F2
Lowe Hill Staffs 75 D6
Lower Aisholt Som 22 F4
Lower Arncott Oxon 39 C6
Lower Ashton Devon 10 F3
Lower Assendon Oxon 39 F7
Lower Badcall Highld 166 E3
Lower Bartle Lancs 92 F4
Lower Basildon W Berks 26 B4
Lower Beeding W Sus 17 B6
Lower Benefield Northants 65 F6
Lower Boddington Northants 52 D2
Lower Brailes Warks 51 F8
Lower Breakish Highld 155 H2
Lower Broadheath Worcs 50 D3
Lower Bullingham Hereford 49 F7
Lower Cam Glos 36 D4
Lower Chapel Powys 48 F2
Lower Chute Wilts 25 D8
Lower Cragabus Argyll 126 E3
Lower Crossings Derbys 87 F8
Lower Cumberworth W Yorks 88 D3
Lower Cwm-twrch Powys 34 C1
Lower Darwen Blkburn 86 B4
Lower Dean Beds 53 C8
Lower Diabaig Highld 154 D3
Lower Dicker E Sus 18 D2
Lower Dinchope Shrops 60 F4
Lower Down Shrops 60 F3
Lower Drift Corn 2 D3
Lower Dunsforth N Yorks 95 C7
Lower Egleton Hereford 49 E8
Lower Elkstone Staffs 75 D7
Lower End Beds 40 B2
Lower Everleigh Wilts 25 D6
Lower Farringdon Hants 26 F5
Lower Foxdale I o M 84 E2
Lower Frankton Shrops 73 F7
Lower Froyle Hants 27 E5
Lower Gledfield Highld 164 E2
Lower Green Norf 81 D5
Lower Hacheston Suff 57 D7
Lower Halistra Highld 152 D3
Lower Halstow Kent 30 C2
Lower Hardres Kent 31 D5
Lower Hawthwaite Cumb 98 F4
Lower Heath Ches 75 C5
Lower Hempriggs Moray 158 C5
Lower Hergest Hereford 48 D4
Lower Heyford Oxon 38 B4
Lower Higham Kent 29 B8
Lower Holbrook Suff 57 F5
Lower Hordley Shrops 60 B3
Lower Horsebridge E Sus 18 D2
Lower Killeyan Argyll 126 E2
Lower Kingswood Sur 28 D3
Lower Kinnerton Ches 73 C7
Lower Langford N Som 23 C6
Lower Largo Fife 135 D6
Lower Leigh Staffs 75 F7
Lower Lemington Glos 51 F7
Lower Lenie Highld 147 B8
Lower Lydbrook Glos 36 C2
Lower Lye Hereford 49 C6
Lower Machen Newport 35 F6
Lower Maes-coed Hereford 48 F5
Lower Mayland Essex 43 D5
Lower Midway Derbys 63 B7
Lower Milovaig Highld 152 D2
Lower Moor Worcs 50 E4
Lower Nazeing Essex 41 D6
Lower Netchwood Shrops 61 E6
Lower Ollach Highld 153 F6
Lower Penarth V Glam 22 B3
Lower Penn Staffs 62 E2
Lower Pennington Hants 14 E4
Lower Peover Ches 74 B4
Lower Pexhill Ches 75 B5
Lower Place Gtr Man 87 C7
Lower Quinton Warks 51 E6
Lower Rochford Worcs 49 C8
Lower Seagry Wilts 37 F6
Lower Shelton Beds 53 E7
Lower Shiplake Oxon 27 B5
Lower Shuckburgh Warks 52 C2
Lower Slaughter Glos 38 B1
Lower Stanton St Quintin Wilts 37 F6
Lower Stoke Medway 30 B2
Lower Stondon Beds 54 F2
Lower Stow Bedon Norf 68 E2
Lower Street Norf 81 D8
Lower Street Norf 69 C6
Lower Strensham Worcs 50 E4
Lower Stretton Warr 86 F4
Lower Sundon Beds 40 B3
Lower Swanwick Hants 15 D5
Lower Swell Glos 38 B1
Lower Tean Staffs 75 F7
Lower Thurlton Norf 69 E7
Lower Tote Highld 152 C6
Lower Town Pembs 44 B4
Lower Tysoe Warks 51 E8
Lower Upham Hants 15 C6
Lower Vexford Som 22 F3
Lower Weare Som 23 D6
Lower Welson Hereford 48 D4
Lower Whitley Ches 74 B3
Lower Wield Hants 26 E4
Lower Winchendon Bucks 39 C7
Lower Withington Ches 74 C5
Lower Woodend Bucks 39 F8
Lower Woodford Wilts 25 F6
Lower Wyche Worcs 50 E2
Lowesby Leics 64 D4
Lowestoft Suff 69 E8
Loweswater Cumb 98 B3
Lowford Hants 15 C5
Lowgill Cumb 99 E8
Lowgill Lancs 93 C6
Lowick Northants 65 F6
Lowick Northumb 125 F6
Lowick Bridge Cumb 98 F4
Lowick Green Cumb 98 F4
Lowlands Torf 35 E6
Lowmoor Row Cumb 99 B8
Lownie Moor Angus 142 E4
Lowsonford Warks 51 C6
Lowther Cumb 99 B7
Lowthorpe E Yorks 97 C6
Lowton Gtr Man 86 E4
Lowton Common Gtr Man 86 E4
Loxbeare Devon 10 C4
Loxhill Sur 27 F8
Loxhore Devon 20 F5
Loxley Warks 51 D7
Loxton N Som 23 D5
Loxwood W Sus 27 F8
Lubcroy Highld 163 D7
Lubenham Leics 64 F4
Luccombe Som 21 E8
Luccombe Village I o W 15 G6
Lucker Northumb 125 F7
Luckett Corn 5 B8
Luckington Wilts 37 F5
Lucklawhill Fife 135 B6
Luckwell Bridge Som 21 F8
Lucton Hereford 49 C6
Ludag W Isles 171 J3
Ludborough Lincs 91 E6
Ludchurch Pembs 32 C2
Luddenden W Yorks 87 B8
Luddenden Foot W Yorks 87 B8
Luddesdown Kent 29 C7
Luddington N Lincs 90 C2
Luddington Warks 51 D6
Luddington in the Brook Northants 65 F8
Lude House Perth 141 C5
Ludford Lincs 91 F6
Ludford Shrops 49 B7
Ludgershall Bucks 39 C6
Ludgershall Wilts 25 D7
Ludgvan Corn 2 C4
Ludham Norf 69 C6
Ludlow Shrops 49 B7
Ludlow Racecourse Shrops 49 B6
Ludwell Wilts 13 B7
Ludworth Durham 111 E6
Luffincott Devon 8 E5
Lugar E Ayrs 113 B5
Lugg Green Hereford 49 C6
Luggate Burn E Loth 124 B2
Luggiebank N Lnrk 121 B7
Lugton E Ayrs 120 D4
Lugwardine Hereford 49 E7
Luib Highld 153 G6
Lulham Hereford 49 E6
Lullenden Sur 28 E5
Lullington Derbys 63 C6
Lullington Som 24 D2
Lulsgate Bottom N Som 23 C7
Lulsley Worcs 50 D2
Lulworth Castle Dorset 13 F6
Lumb W Yorks 87 B8
Lumby N Yorks 95 F7
Lumloch E Dunb 121 C6
Lumphanan Aberds 150 D4
Lumphinnans Fife 134 E3
Lumsdaine Borders 124 C4
Lumsden Aberds 150 B3
Lunan Angus 143 D6
Lunanhead Angus 142 D4
Luncarty Perth 134 B2
Lund E Yorks 97 E5
Lund N Yorks 96 F2
Lund Shetland 174 C7
Lunderton Aberds 161 D8
Lundie Angus 142 F2
Lundie Highld 146 C4
Lundin Links Fife 135 D6
Lunga Argyll 130 E3
Lunna Shetland 174 G6
Lunning Shetland 174 G7
Lunnon Swansea 33 F6
Lunsford's Cross E Sus 18 D4
Lunt Mers 85 D4
Luntley Hereford 49 D5
Luppitt Devon 11 D6
Lupset W Yorks 88 C4
Lupton Cumb 99 F7
Lurgashall W Sus 16 B3
Lusby Lincs 79 C6
Luson Devon 6 E4
Luss Argyll 132 E2
Lussagiven Argyll 127 D4
Lusta Highld 152 D3
Lustleigh Devon 10 F2
Luston Hereford 49 C6
Luthermuir Aberds 143 C6
Luthrie Fife 134 C5
Luton Devon 7 B7
Luton Luton 40 B3
Luton Medway 29 C8
Lutterworth Leics 64 F2
Lutton Devon 6 D3
Lutton Lincs 66 B4
Lutton Northants 65 F8
Lutworthy Devon 10 C2
Luxborough Som 21 F8
Luxulyan Corn 5 D5
Lybster Highld 169 F7
Lydbury North Shrops 60 F3
Lydcott Devon 21 F5
Lydd Kent 19 C7
Lydd on Sea Kent 19 C7
Lydden Kent 31 E6
Lydden Motor Racing Circuit Kent 31 E6
Lyddington Rutland 65 E5
Lyde Green Hants 26 D5
Lydeard St Lawrence Som 22 F3
Lydford Devon 9 F7
Lydford-on-Fosse Som 23 F7
Lydgate W Yorks 87 B7
Lydham Shrops 60 E3
Lydiard Green Wilts 37 F7
Lydiard Millicent Wilts 37 F7
Lydiate Mers 85 D4
Lydlinch Dorset 12 C5
Lydney Glos 36 D3
Lydstep Pembs 32 E1
Lye W Mid 62 F3
Lye Green Bucks 40 D2
Lye Green E Sus 18 B2
Lyford Oxon 38 E3
Lymbridge Green Kent 30 E5
Lyme Park, Disley Ches 87 F7
Lyme Regis Dorset 11 E8
Lyminge Kent 31 E5
Lymington Hants 14 E4
Lyminster W Sus 16 D4
Lymm Warr 86 F4
Lymore Hants 14 E3
Lympne Kent 19 B8
Lympsham Som 22 D5
Lympstone Devon 10 F4
Lynchat Highld 148 D3
Lyndale Ho. Highld 152 D4
Lyndhurst Hants 14 D4
Lyndon Rutland 65 D6
Lyne Sur 27 C8
Lyne Down Hereford 49 F8
Lyne of Gorthleck Highld 147 B8
Lyne of Skene Aberds 151 C6
Lyneal Shrops 73 F8
Lyneham Oxon 38 B2
Lyneham Wilts 24 B5
Lynemore Highld 149 B6
Lynemouth Northumb 117 E8
Lyness Orkney 176 G2
Lyng Norf 68 C3
Lyng Som 11 B8
Lynmouth Devon 21 E6
Lynsted Kent 30 C3
Lynton Devon 21 E6
Lynton & Lynmouth Cliff Railway Devon 21 E6
Lyon's Gate Dorset 12 D4
Lyonshall Hereford 48 D5
Lytchett Matravers Dorset 13 E7
Lytchett Minster Dorset 13 E7
Lyth Highld 169 C7
Lytham Lancs 85 B4
Lytham St Anne's Lancs 85 B4
Lythe N Yorks 103 C6
Lythes Orkney 176 H3

M

Mabe Burnthouse Corn 3 C6
Mabie Dumfries 107 B6
Mablethorpe Lincs 91 F9
Macclesfield Ches 75 B6
Macclesfield Forest Ches 75 B6
Macduff Aberds 160 B4
Mace Green Suff 56 E5
Macharioch Argyll 118 F4
Machen Caerph 35 F6
Machrihanish Argyll 118 D3
Machynlleth Powys 58 D4
Machynys Carms 33 E6
Mackerel's Common W Sus 16 B4
Mackworth Derbys 76 F3
Macmerry E Loth 123 B7
Madame Tussaud's London 41 F5
Madderty Perth 133 B8
Maddiston Falk 122 B2
Madehurst W Sus 16 C3
Madeley Staffs 74 E4
Madeley Telford 61 D6
Madeley Heath Staffs 74 E4
Madeley Park Staffs 74 E4
Madingley Cambs 54 C4
Madley Hereford 49 F6
Madresfield Worcs 50 E3
Madron Corn 2 C3
Maen-y-groes Ceredig 46 D2
Maenaddwyn Anglesey 82 C4
Maenclochog Pembs 32 B1
Maendy V Glam 22 B2
Maentwrog Gwyn 71 C7
Maer Staffs 74 F4
Maerdy Conwy 72 E4
Maerdy Rhondda 34 E3
Maes-Treylow Powys 48 C4
Maesbrook Shrops 60 B2
Maesbury Shrops 60 B3
Maesbury Marsh Shrops 60 B3
Maesgwyn-Isaf Powys 59 C8
Maesgwynne Carms 32 B3
Maeshafn Denb 73 C6
Maesllyn Ceredig 46 E2
Maesmynis Powys 48 E2
Maesteg Bridgend 34 E2
Maestir Ceredig 46 D4
Maesy cwmmer Caerph 35 E5
Maesybont Carms 33 C6
Maesycrugiau Carms 46 E3
Maesymeillion Ceredig 46 E3
Magdalen Laver Essex 41 D8
Maggieknockater Moray 159 E7
Magham Down E Sus 18 D3
Maghull Mers 85 D4
Magna Science Adventure Centre, Rotherham S Yorks 88 E5
Magor Mon 35 F8
Magpie Green Suff 56 B4
Maiden Bradley Wilts 24 F3
Maiden Law Durham 110 E4
Maiden Newton Dorset 12 E3
Maiden Wells Pembs 44 F4
Maidencombe Torbay 7 C7
Maidenhall Suff 57 E5
Maidenhead Windsor 40 F1
Maidens S Ayrs 112 D2
Maiden's Green Brack 27 B6
Maidensgrave Suff 57 E6
Maidenwell Corn 5 B6
Maidenwell Lincs 79 B6
Maidford Northants 52 D4
Maids Moreton Bucks 52 F5
Maidstone Kent 29 D8
Maidwell Northants 52 B5
Mail Shetland 175 L6
Main Powys 59 C8
Maindee Newport 35 F7
Mains of Airies Dumfries 104 C3
Mains of Allardice Aberds 143 B8
Mains of Annochie Aberds 161 D6
Mains of Ardestie Angus 143 F5
Mains of Balhall Angus 143 C5
Mains of Ballindarg Angus 142 D4
Mains of Balnakettle Aberds 143 B6
Mains of Birness Aberds 161 E6
Mains of Burgie Moray 158 D4
Mains of Clunas Highld 158 E2
Mains of Crichie Aberds 161 D6
Mains of Dalvey Highld 158 F5
Mains of Dellavaird Aberds 151 F6
Mains of Drum Aberds 151 E7
Mains of Edingight Moray 160 C2
Mains of Fedderate Aberds 161 D5
Mains of Inkhorn Aberds 161 E6
Mains of Mayen Moray 160 D2
Mains of Melgund Angus 143 D5
Mains of Thornton Aberds 143 B6
Mains of Watten Highld 169 D7
Mainsforth Durham 111 F6
Mainsriddle Dumfries 107 D6
Mainstone Shrops 60 F2
Maisemore Glos 37 B5
Malacleit W Isles 170 C3
Malborough Devon 6 F5
Malcoff Derbys 87 F8
Maldon Essex 42 D4
Malham N Yorks 94 C2
Maligar Highld 152 C5
Mallaig Highld 145 D6
Malleny Mills Edin 122 C4
Malling Stirl 132 D4
Mallory Park Motor Racing Circuit Leics 63 D8
Malltraeth Anglesey 82 E4
Mallwyd Gwyn 59 C5
Malmesbury Wilts 37 F6
Malmsmead Devon 21 E6
Malpas Ches 73 E8
Malpas Corn 3 B7
Malpas Newport 35 E7
Malswick Glos 36 B4
Maltby Stockton 102 C2
Maltby S Yorks 89 E6
Maltby le Marsh Lincs 91 F8
Malting Green Essex 43 B5
Maltman's Hill Kent 30 E3
Malton N Yorks 96 B3
Malvern Link Worcs 50 E2
Malvern Wells Worcs 50 E2
Mamble Worcs 49 B8
Man-moel Caerph 35 D5
Manaccan Corn 3 D6
Manafon Powys 59 D8
Manais W Isles 173 K4
Manar Ho. Aberds 151 B6
Manaton Devon 10 F2
Manby Lincs 91 F7
Mancetter Warks 63 E7
Manchester Gtr Man 87 E6
Manchester Airport Gtr Man 87 F6
Manchester National Velodrome Gtr Man 87 E6
Mancot Flint 73 C7
Mandally Highld 147 D5
Manea Cambs 66 F4
Manfield N Yorks 101 C7
Mangaster Shetland 174 F5
Mangotsfield S Glos 23 B8
Mangurstadh W Isles 172 E3
Mankinholes W Yorks 87 B7
Manley Ches 74 B2
Mannal Argyll 136 F1
Mannerston W Loth 122 B3
Manningford Bohune Wilts 25 D6
Manningford Bruce Wilts 25 D6
Manningham W Yorks 94 F4
Mannings Heath W Sus 17 B6
Mannington Dorset 13 D8
Manningtree Essex 56 F4
Mannofield Aberdeen 151 D8
Manor Estate S Yorks 88 F4
Manor Park London 41 F7
Manorbier Pembs 32 E1
Manordeilo Carms 33 B7
Manorhill Borders 124 F2
Manorowen Pembs 44 B4
Mansel Lacy Hereford 49 E6
Manselfield Swansea 33 F6
Mansell Gamage Hereford 49 E5
Mansergh Cumb 99 F8
Mansfield E Ayrs 113 C6
Mansfield Notts 76 C5
Mansfield Woodhouse Notts 76 C5
Mansriggs Cumb 98 F4
Manston Dorset 13 C6
Manston Kent 31 C7
Manston W Yorks 95 F6
Manswood Dorset 13 D7
Manthorpe Lincs 65 C7
Manthorpe Lincs 78 F2
Manton N Lincs 90 D3
Manton Notts 77 B5
Manton Rutland 65 D5
Manton Wilts 25 C6
Manuden Essex 41 B7
Manx Electric Railway I o M 84 C4
Maperton Som 12 B4
Maple Cross Herts 40 E3
Maplebeck Notts 77 C7
Mapledurham Oxon 26 B4
Mapledurwell Hants 26 D4
Maplehurst W Sus 17 B5
Maplescombe Kent 29 C6
Mapleton Derbys 75 E8
Mapperley Derbys 76 E4
Mapperley Park Nottingham 77 E5
Mapperton Dorset 12 E3
Mappleborough Green Warks 51 C5
Mappleton E Yorks 97 E8
Mappowder Dorset 12 D5
Mar Lodge Aberds 149 E6
Maraig W Isles 173 H4
Marazanvose Corn 4 D3
Marazion Corn 2 C4
Marbhig W Isles 172 G7
Marbury Ches 74 E2
March Cambs 66 E4
March S Lnrk 114 C2
Marcham Oxon 38 E4
Marchamley Shrops 61 B5
Marchington Staffs 75 F8
Marchington Woodlands Staffs 62 B5
Marchroes Gwyn 70 E4
Marchwiel Wrex 73 E7
Marchwood Hants 14 C4
Marcross V Glam 21 C8
Marden Hereford 49 E7
Marden Kent 29 E8
Marden T & W 111 B6
Marden Wilts 25 D5
Marden Beech Kent 29 E8
Marden Thorn Kent 29 E8
Mardy Mon 35 C7
Marefield Leics 64 D4
Mareham le Fen Lincs 79 C5
Mareham on the Hill Lincs 79 C5
Marehay Derbys 76 E3
Marehill W Sus 16 C4
Maresfield E Sus 17 B8
Marfleet Hull 90 B5
Marford Wrex 73 D7
Margam Neath 34 F1
Margaret Marsh Dorset 13 C6
Margaret Roding Essex 42 C1
Margaretting Essex 42 D2
Margate Kent 31 B7
Margnaheglish N Ayrs 119 C7
Margrove Park Redcar 102 C4
Marham Norf 67 C7
Marhamchurch Corn 8 D4
Marholm P'boro 65 D8
Mariandyrys Anglesey 83 C6
Marianglas Anglesey 82 C5
Mariansleigh Devon 10 B2
Marionburgh Aberds 151 D6
Marishader Highld 152 C5
Maritime and Industrial Museum Swansea 33 E7
Marjoriebanks Dumfries 114 F3
Mark Dumfries 104 D5
Mark S Ayrs 104 B4
Mark Som 23 E5
Mark Causeway Som 23 E5
Mark Cross E Sus 17 C8
Mark Cross E Sus 18 B2
Markbeech Kent 29 E5
Markby Lincs 79 B7
Market Bosworth Leics 63 D8
Market Deeping Lincs 65 D8
Market Drayton Shrops 74 F3
Market Harborough Leics 64 F4
Market Lavington Wilts 24 D5
Market Overton Rutland 65 C5
Market Rasen Lincs 90 F5
Market Rasen Racecourse Lincs 90 F5
Market Stainton Lincs 78 B5
Market Warsop Notts 77 C5
Market Weighton E Yorks 96 E4
Market Weston Suff 56 B3
Markethill Perth 142 F2
Markfield Leics 63 C8
Markham Caerph 35 D5
Markham Moor Notts 77 B7
Markinch Fife 134 D4
Markington N Yorks 95 C5
Marks Tey Essex 43 B5
Marksbury Bath 23 C8
Markyate Herts 40 C3
Marland Gtr Man 87 C6
Marlborough Wilts 25 C6
Marlbrook Hereford 49 D7
Marlbrook Worcs 50 B4
Marlcliff Warks 51 D5
Marldon Devon 7 C6
Marlesford Suff 57 D7
Marley Green Ches 74 E2
Marley Hill T & W 110 D5
Marley Mount Hants 14 E3
Marlingford Norf 68 D4
Marloes Pembs 44 E2
Marlow Bucks 39 F8
Marlow Hereford 49 B6
Marlow Bottom Bucks 40 F1
Marlpit Hill Kent 28 E5
Marlpool Derbys 76 E4
Marnhull Dorset 13 C5
Marnoch Aberds 160 C2
Marnock N Lnrk 121 C7
Marple Gtr Man 87 F7
Marple Bridge Gtr Man 87 F7
Marr S Yorks 89 D6
Marrel Highld 165 C7
Marrick N Yorks 101 E5
Marrister Shetland 175 G7
Marros Carms 32 D3
Marsden T & W 111 C6
Marsden W Yorks 87 C8
Marsett N Yorks 100 F4
Marsh Devon 11 C7
Marsh W Yorks 94 F3
Marsh Baldon Oxon 39 E5
Marsh Gibbon Bucks 39 B6
Marsh Green Devon 10 E5
Marsh Green Kent 28 E5
Marsh Green Staffs 75 D5
Marsh Lane Derbys 76 B4
Marsh Street Som 21 E8
Marshall's Heath Herts 40 C4
Marshalsea Dorset 11 D8
Marshalswick Herts 40 D4
Marsham Norf 81 E7
Marshaw Lancs 93 D5
Marshborough Kent 31 D7
Marshbrook Shrops 60 F4
Marshchapel Lincs 91 E7
Marshfield Newport 35 F6
Marshfield S Glos 24 B2
Marshgate Corn 8 E3
Marshland St James Norf 66 D5
Marshside Mers 85 C4
Marshwood Dorset 11 E8
Marske N Yorks 101 D6
Marske-by-the-Sea Redcar 102 B4
Marston Ches 74 B3
Marston Hereford 49 D5
Marston Lincs 77 E8
Marston Oxon 39 D5
Marston Staffs 62 C2
Marston Staffs 62 B3
Marston Warks 63 E6
Marston Wilts 24 D4
Marston Doles Warks 52 D2
Marston Green W Mid 63 F5
Marston Magna Som 12 B3
Marston Meysey Wilts 37 E8
Marston Montgomery Derbys 75 F8
Marston Moretaine Beds 53 E7
Marston on Dove Derbys 63 B6
Marston St Lawrence Northants 52 E3
Marston Stannett Hereford 49 D7
Marston Trussell Northants 64 F3
Marstow Hereford 36 C2
Marsworth Bucks 40 C2
Marten Wilts 25 D7
Marthall Ches 74 B5
Martham Norf 69 C7
Martin Hants 13 C8
Martin Kent 31 E7
Martin Lincs 78 D4
Martin Lincs 78 C5
Martin Dales Lincs 78 C4
Martin Drove End Hants 13 B8
Martin Hussingtree Worcs 50 C3
Martin Mill Kent 31 E7
Martinhoe Devon 21 E5
Martinhoe Cross Devon 21 E5
Martinscroft Warr 86 F4
Martinstown Dorset 12 F4
Martlesham Suff 57 E6
Martlesham Heath Suff 57 E6
Martletwy Pembs 32 C1
Martley Worcs 50 D2
Martock Som 12 C2
Marton Ches 75 C5
Marton E Yorks 97 F7
Marton Lincs 90 F2
Marton M'bro 102 C3
Marton N Yorks 95 C7
Marton N Yorks 103 F5
Marton Shrops 60 D2
Marton Shrops 60 B4
Marton Warks 52 C2
Marton-le-Moor N Yorks 95 B6
Martyr Worthy Hants 26 F3
Martyr's Green Sur 27 D8
Marwell Zoo, Bishop's Waltham Hants 15 B6
Marwick Orkney 176 D1
Marwood Devon 20 F4
Mary Arden's House, Stratford-upon-Avon Warks 51 D6
Mary Rose Ptsmth 15 D7
Mary Tavy Devon 6 B3
Marybank Highld 157 D5
Maryburgh Highld 157 D6
Maryhill Glasgow 121 C5
Marykirk Aberds 143 C6
Marylebone Gtr Man 86 D3
Marypark Moray 159 F5
Maryport Cumb 107 F7
Maryport Dumfries 104 F5
Maryton Angus 143 D6
Marywell Aberds 150 E4
Marywell Aberds 151 E8
Marywell Angus 143 E6
Masham N Yorks 101 F7
Mashbury Essex 42 C2
Masongill N Yorks 93 B6
Masonhill S Ayrs 112 B3
Mastin Moor Derbys 76 B4
Mastrick Aberdeen 151 D7
Matching Essex 41 C8
Matching Green Essex 41 C8
Matching Tye Essex 41 C8
Matfen Northumb 110 B3
Matfield Kent 29 E7
Mathern Mon 36 E2
Mathon Hereford 50 E2
Mathry Pembs 44 B3
Matlaske Norf 81 D7
Matlock Derbys 76 C2
Matlock Bath Derbys 76 D2
Matson Glos 37 C5
Matterdale End Cumb 99 B5
Mattersey Notts 89 F7
Mattersey Thorpe Notts 89 F7
Mattingley Hants 26 D5
Mattishall Norf 68 C3
Mattishall Burgh Norf 68 C3
Mauchline E Ayrs 112 B4
Maud Aberds 161 D6
Maugersbury Glos 38 B2
Maughold I o M 84 C4
Mauld Highld 156 F5
Maulden Beds 53 F8
Maulds Meaburn Cumb 99 C8
Maunby N Yorks 102 F1
Maund Bryan Hereford 49 D7
Maundown Som 11 B5
Mautby Norf 69 C7
Mavis Enderby Lincs 79 C6
Maw Green Ches 74 D4
Mawbray Cumb 107 E7
Mawdesley Lancs 86 C2
Mawdlam Bridgend 34 F2
Mawgan Corn 3 D6
Mawla Corn 3 B6
Mawnan Corn 3 D6
Mawnan Smith Corn 3 D6
Mawsley Northants 53 B6
Maxey P'boro 65 D8
Maxstoke Warks 63 F6
Maxton Borders 124 F2
Maxton Kent 31 E7
Maxwellheugh Borders 124 F3
Maxwelltown Dumfries 107 B6
Maxworthy Corn 8 E4
May Bank Staffs 75 E5
Mayals Swansea 33 E7
Maybole S Ayrs 112 D3
Mayfield E Sus 18 C2
Mayfield Midloth 123 C6
Mayfield Staffs 75 E8
Mayfield W Loth 122 C2
Mayford Sur 27 D7
Mayland Essex 43 D5
Maynard's Green E Sus 18 D2
Maypole Mon 36 C1
Maypole Scilly 2 E4
Maypole Green Essex 43 B5
Maypole Green Norf 69 E7
Maypole Green Suff 57 C6
Maywick Shetland 175 L5
Meadle Bucks 39 D8
Meadowtown Shrops 60 D3
Meaford Staffs 75 F5
Meal Bank Cumb 99 E7
Mealabost W Isles 172 E7
Mealabost Bhuirgh W Isles 172 C7
Mealsgate Cumb 108 E2
Meanwood W Yorks 95 F5
Mearbeck N Yorks 93 C8
Meare Som 23 E6
Meare Green Som 11 B8
Mears Ashby Northants 53 C6
Measham Leics 63 C7
Meath Green Sur 28 E3
Meathop Cumb 99 F6
Meaux E Yorks 97 F6
Meavy Devon 6 C3
Medbourne Leics 64 E4
Medburn Northumb 110 B4
Meddon Devon 8 C4
Meden Vale Notts 77 C5
Medlam Lincs 79 D6
Medmenham Bucks 39 F8
Medomsley Durham 110 D4
Medstead Hants 26 F4
Meer End W Mid 51 B7
Meerbrook Staffs 75 C6
Meers Bridge Lincs 91 F8
Meesden Herts 54 F5
Meeth Devon 9 D7
Meggethead Borders 114 B4
Meidrim Carms 32 B3
Meifod Denb 72 D4
Meifod Powys 59 C8
Meigle N Ayrs 129 D6
Meigle Perth 142 E2
Meikle Earnock S Lnrk 121 D7
Meikle Ferry Highld 164 F4
Meikle Forter Angus 142 C1
Meikle Gluich Highld 164 F3
Meikle Pinkerton E Loth 124 B3
Meikle Strath Aberds 143 B6
Meikle Tarty Aberds 151 B8
Meikle Wartle Aberds 160 E4
Meikleour Perth 142 F1
Meinciau Carms 33 C5
Meir Stoke 75 E6
Meir Heath Staffs 75 E6
Melbourn Cambs 54 E4
Melbourne Derbys 63 B7
Melbourne E Yorks 96 E3
Melbourne S Lnrk 122 E3
Melbury Abbas Dorset 13 B6
Melbury Bubb Dorset 12 D3
Melbury Osmond Dorset 12 D3
Melbury Sampford Dorset 12 D3
Melby Shetland 175 H3
Melchbourne Beds 53 C8
Melcombe Bingham Dorset 13 D5
Melcombe Regis Dorset 12 F4
Meldon Devon 9 E7
Meldon Northumb 117 F7
Meldreth Cambs 54 E4

Meldrum Ho. Aberds 151 B7
Melfort Argyll 130 D4
Melgarve Highld 147 E7
Meliden Denb 72 A4
Melin-y-coed Conwy 83 E8
Melin-y-ddôl Powys 59 D7
Melin-y-grug Powys 59 D7
Melin-y-Wig Denb 72 E4
Melinbyrhedyn Powys 58 E5
Melincourt Neath 34 D2
Melkinthorpe Cumb 99 B7
Melkridge Northumb 109 C7
Melksham Wilts 24 C4
Melldalloch Argyll 128 C4
Melling Lancs 93 B5
Melling Mers 85 D4
Melling Mount Mers 86 D2
Mellis Suff 56 B5
Mellon Charles Highld 162 E2
Mellon Udrigle Highld 162 E2
Mellor Gtr Man 87 F7
Mellor Lancs 93 F6
Mellor Brook Lancs 93 F6
Mells Som 24 E2
Melmerby Cumb 109 F6
Melmerby N Yorks 95 B6
Melmerby N Yorks 101 F5
Melplash Dorset 12 E2
Melrose Borders 123 F8
Melsetter Orkney 176 H1
Melsonby N Yorks 101 D6
Meltham W Yorks 88 C2
Melton Suff 57 D6
Melton Constable Norf 81 D6
Melton Mowbray Leics 64 C4
Melton Ross N Lincs 90 C4
Meltonby E Yorks 96 D3
Melvaig Highld 154 B3
Melverley Shrops 60 C3
Melverley Green Shrops 60 C3
Melvich Highld 168 C3
Membury Devon 11 D7
Memsie Aberds 161 B6
Memus Angus 142 D4
Menabilly Corn 5 D5
Menai Bridge = Porthaethwy Anglesey 83 D5
Mendham Suff 69 F5
Mendlesham Suff 56 C5
Mendlesham Green Suff 56 C4
Menheniot Corn 5 C7
Mennock Dumfries 113 D8
Menston W Yorks 94 E4
Menstrie Clack 133 E7
Menthorpe N Yorks 96 F2
Mentmore Bucks 40 C2
Meoble Highld 145 E7
Meole Brace Shrops 60 C4
Meols Mers 85 E3
Meonstoke Hants 15 C7
Meopham Kent 29 C7
Meopham Station Kent 29 C7
Mepal Cambs 66 F4
Meppershall Beds 54 F2
Merbach Hereford 48 E5
Mere Ches 86 F5
Mere Wilts 24 F3
Mere Brow Lancs 86 C2
Mere Green W Mid 62 E5
Mereclough Lancs 93 F8
Mereside Blkpool 92 F3
Mereworth Kent 29 D7
Mergie Aberds 151 F6
Meriden W Mid 63 F6
Merkadale Highld 153 F4
Merkland Dumfries 106 B4
Merkland S Ayrs 112 E2
Merkland Lodge Highld 163 B8
Merley Poole 13 E8
Merlin's Bridge Pembs 44 D4
Merrington Shrops 60 B4
Merrion Pembs 44 F4
Merriott Som 12 C2
Merrivale Devon 6 B3
Merrow Sur 27 D8
Merrymeet Corn 5 C7
Merseyside Maritime Museum Mers 85 F4
Mersham Kent 19 B7
Merstham Sur 28 D3
Merston W Sus 16 D2
Merstone I o W 15 F6
Merther Corn 3 B7
Merthyr Carms 32 B4
Merthyr Cynog Powys 47 F8
Merthyr-Dyfan V Glam 22 C3
Merthyr Mawr Bridgend 21 B7
Merthyr Tudful = Merthyr Tydfil M Tydf 34 D4
Merthyr Tydfil = Merthyr Tudful M Tydf 34 D4
Merthyr Vale M Tydf 34 E4
Merton Devon 9 C7
Merton London 28 B3
Merton Norf 68 E2
Merton Oxon 39 C5
Mervinslaw Borders 116 C2
Meshaw Devon 10 C2
Messing Essex 42 C4
Messingham N Lincs 90 D2
Metfield Suff 69 F5
Metheringham Lincs 78 C3
Methil Fife 135 E5
Methlem Gwyn 70 D2
Methley W Yorks 88 B4
Methlick Aberds 161 E5
Methven Perth 134 B2
Methwold Norf 67 E7
Methwold Hythe Norf 67 E7
Metroland, Gateshead T & W 110 C5
Mettingham Suff 69 F6
Mevagissey Corn 3 B9
Mewith Head N Yorks 93 C7
Mexborough S Yorks 89 D5
Mey Highld 169 B7
Meysey Hampton Glos 37 E8
Miabhag W Isles 173 J4
Miabhag W Isles 173 H3
Miabhig W Isles 172 E3
Michaelchurch Hereford 36 B2
Michaelchurch Escley Hereford 48 F5
Michaelchurch on Arrow Powys 48 D4
Michaelston-le-Pit V Glam 22 B3
Michaelston-y-Fedw Newport 35 F6
Michaelstow Corn 5 B5
Michealston-super-Ely Cardiff 22 B3
Micheldever Hants 26 F3
Michelmersh Hants 14 B4
Mickfield Suff 56 C5
Mickle Trafford Ches 73 C8
Micklebring S Yorks 89 E6
Mickleby N Yorks 103 C6
Mickleham Sur 28 D2
Mickleover Derby 76 F3
Micklethwaite W Yorks 94 E4
Mickleton Durham 100 B4
Mickleton Glos 51 E6
Mickletown W Yorks 88 B4
Mickley N Yorks 95 B5
Mickley Square Northumb 110 C3
Mid Ardlaw Aberds 161 B6
Mid Auchinlech Invclyd 120 B3
Mid Beltie Aberds 150 D5
Mid Calder W Loth 122 C3
Mid Cloch Forbie Aberds 160 C4
Mid Clyth Highld 169 F7
Mid-Hants Railway (Watercress Line), New Alresford Hants 26 F3
Mid Lavant W Sus 16 D2
Mid Main Highld 156 F5
Mid Urchany Highld 158 E2
Mid Walls Shetland 175 H4
Mid Yell Shetland 174 D7
Midbea Orkney 176 B3
Middle Assendon Oxon 39 F7
Middle Aston Oxon 38 B4
Middle Barton Oxon 38 B4
Middle Cairncake Aberds 160 D5
Middle Claydon Bucks 39 B7
Middle Drums Angus 143 D5
Middle Handley Derbys 76 B4
Middle Littleton Worcs 51 E5
Middle Maes-coed Hereford 48 F5
Middle Mill Pembs 44 C3
Middle Rasen Lincs 90 F4
Middle Rigg Perth 134 D2
Middle Tysoe Warks 51 E8
Middle Wallop Hants 25 F7
Middle Winterslow Wilts 25 F7
Middle Woodford Wilts 25 F6
Middlebie Dumfries 108 B2
Middleforth Green Lancs 86 B3
Middleham N Yorks 101 F6
Middlehope Shrops 60 F4
Middlemarsh Dorset 12 D4
Middlemuir Aberds 151 B8
Middlesbrough M'bro 102 B2
Middleshaw Cumb 99 F7
Middleshaw Dumfries 107 B8
Middlesmoor N Yorks 94 B3
Middlestone Durham 111 F5
Middlestone Moor Durham 110 F5
Middlestown W Yorks 88 C3
Middlethird Borders 124 E2
Middleton Aberds 151 C7
Middleton Argyll 136 F1
Middleton Cumb 99 F8
Middleton Derbys 76 D2
Middleton Derbys 75 C8
Middleton Essex 56 F2
Middleton Gtr Man 87 D6
Middleton Hants 26 E2
Middleton Hereford 49 C7
Middleton Lancs 92 D4
Middleton Midloth 123 D6
Middleton Norf 67 C6
Middleton Northants 64 F5
Middleton Northumb 117 F6
Middleton Northumb 125 F7
Middleton N Yorks 103 F5
Middleton Perth 134 D3
Middleton Perth 141 E8
Middleton Shrops 49 B7
Middleton Shrops 60 E2
Middleton Shrops 60 B3
Middleton Suff 57 C8
Middleton Swansea 33 F5
Middleton Warks 63 E5
Middleton W Yorks 88 B3
Middleton W Yorks 94 E4
Middleton Cheney Northants 52 E2
Middleton Green Staffs 75 F6
Middleton Hall Northumb 117 B5
Middleton-in-Teesdale Durham 100 B4
Middleton Moor Suff 57 C8
Middleton-on-Leven N Yorks 102 D2
Middleton-on-Sea W Sus 16 D3
Middleton on the Hill Hereford 49 C7
Middleton-on-the-Wolds E Yorks 96 E5
Middleton One Row Darl 102 C1
Middleton Priors Shrops 61 E6
Middleton Quernham N Yorks 95 B6
Middleton Railway, Hunslet W Yorks 88 B4
Middleton St George Darl 101 C8
Middleton Scriven Shrops 61 F6
Middleton Stoney Oxon 39 B5
Middleton Tyas N Yorks 101 D7
Middletown Cumb 98 D1
Middletown Powys 60 C3
Middlewich Ches 74 C3
Middlewood Green Suff 56 C4
Middlezoy Som 23 F5
Middridge Durham 101 B7
Midfield Highld 167 C7
Midge Hall Lancs 86 B3
Midgeholme Cumb 109 D6
Midgham W Berks 26 C3
Midgley W Yorks 87 B8
Midgley W Yorks 88 C3
Midhopestones S Yorks 88 E3
Midhurst W Sus 16 B2
Midlem Borders 115 B8
Midmar Aberds 151 D5
Midsomer Norton Bath 23 D8
Midton Invclyd 129 C7
Midtown Highld 167 C7
Midtown Highld 154 B4
Midtown of Buchromb Moray 159 E7
Midville Lincs 79 D6
Midway Ches 87 F7
Migdale Highld 164 E3
Migvie Aberds 150 D3
Milarrochy Stirl 132 E3
Milborne Port Som 12 C4
Milborne St Andrew Dorset 13 E6
Milborne Wick Som 12 B4
Milbourne Northumb 110 B4
Milburn Cumb 100 B1
Milbury Heath S Glos 36 E3
Milcombe Oxon 52 F2
Milden Suff 56 E3
Mildenhall Suff 55 B8
Mildenhall Wilts 25 C7
Mile Cross Norf 68 C5
Mile Elm Wilts 24 C4
Mile End Essex 43 B5
Mile End Glos 36 C2
Mile Oak Brighton 17 D6
Milebrook Powys 48 B5
Milebush Kent 29 E8
Mileham Norf 68 C2
Milesmark Fife 134 F2
Milestones, Basingstoke Hants 26 D4
Milfield Northumb 124 F5
Milford Derbys 76 E3
Milford Devon 8 B4
Milford Powys 59 E7
Milford Staffs 62 B3
Milford Sur 27 E7
Milford Wilts 14 B2
Milford Haven = Aberdaugleddau Pembs 44 E4
Milford on Sea Hants 14 E3
Milkwall Glos 36 D2
Milkwell Wilts 13 B7
Mill Bank W Yorks 87 B8
Mill Common Suff 69 F7
Mill End Bucks 39 F7
Mill End Herts 54 F4
Mill Green Essex 42 D2
Mill Green Norf 68 F4
Mill Green Suff 56 E3
Mill Hill London 41 E5
Mill Lane Hants 27 D5
Mill of Kingoodie Aberds 151 B7
Mill of Muiresk Aberds 160 D3
Mill of Sterin Aberds 150 E2
Mill of Uras Aberds 151 F7
Mill Place N Lincs 90 D3
Mill Side Cumb 99 F6
Mill Street Norf 68 C3
Milland W Sus 16 B2
Millarston Renfs 120 C4
Millbank Aberds 161 D8
Millbank Highld 169 C6
Millbeck Cumb 98 B4
Millbounds Orkney 176 C4
Millbreck Aberds 161 D7
Millbridge Sur 27 E6
Millbrook Beds 53 F8
Millbrook Corn 6 D2
Millbrook Soton 14 C4
Millburn S Ayrs 112 B4
Millcombe Devon 7 E6
Millcorner E Sus 18 C5
Milldale Staffs 75 D8
Millden Lodge Angus 143 B5
Milldens Angus 143 D5
Millennium Stadium Cardiff 22 B3
Millerhill Midloth 123 C6
Miller's Dale Derbys 75 B8
Miller's Green Derbys 76 D2
Millgreen Shrops 61 B6
Millhalf Hereford 48 E4
Millhayes Devon 11 D7
Millhead Lancs 92 B4
Millheugh S Lnrk 121 D7
Millholme Cumb 99 E7
Millhouse Argyll 128 C4
Millhouse Cumb 108 F3
Millhouse Green S Yorks 88 D3
Millhousebridge Dumfries 114 F4
Millhouses S Yorks 88 F4
Millikenpark Renfs 120 C4
Millin Cross Pembs 44 D4
Millington E Yorks 96 D4
Millmeece Staffs 74 F5
Millom Cumb 98 F3
Millook Corn 8 E3
Millpool Corn 5 B6
Millport N Ayrs 129 E6
Millquarter Dumfries 113 F6
Millthorpe Lincs 78 F4
Millthrop Cumb 100 E1
Milltimber Aberdeen 151 D7
Milltown Corn 5 D6
Milltown Derbys 76 C3
Milltown Devon 20 F4
Milltown Dumfries 108 B3
Milltown of Aberdalgie Perth 134 B2
Milltown of Auchindoun Moray 159 E7
Milltown of Craigston Aberds 160 C4
Milltown of Edinvillie Moray 159 E6
Milltown of Kildrummy Aberds 150 C3
Milltown of Rothiemay Moray 160 D2
Milltown of Towie Aberds 150 C3
Milnathort Perth 134 D3
Milner's Heath Ches 73 C8
Milngavie E Dunb 121 B5
Milnrow Gtr Man 87 C7
Milnshaw Lancs 87 B5
Milnthorpe Cumb 99 F6
Milo Carms 33 C6
Milson Shrops 49 B8
Milstead Kent 30 D3
Milston Wilts 25 E6
Milton Angus 142 E3
Milton Cambs 55 C5
Milton Cumb 109 C5
Milton Derbys 63 B7
Milton Dumfries 105 D6
Milton Dumfries 106 B5
Milton Dumfries 113 F8
Milton Highld 156 D4
Milton Highld 157 F5
Milton Highld 157 E6
Milton Highld 169 D8
Milton Highld 157 B8
Milton Moray 160 B2
Milton Notts 77 B7
Milton N Som 22 C5
Milton Oxon 52 F2
Milton Oxon 38 E4
Milton Pembs 32 D1
Milton Perth 133 C8
Milton Ptsmth 15 E7
Milton Stirl 132 D4
Milton Stoke 75 D6
Milton W Dunb 120 B4
Milton Abbas Dorset 13 D6
Milton Abbot Devon 6 B2
Milton Bridge Midloth 122 C5
Milton Bryan Beds 53 F7
Milton Clevedon Som 23 F8
Milton Coldwells Aberds 161 E6
Milton Combe Devon 6 C2
Milton Damerel Devon 9 C5
Milton End Glos 37 D8
Milton Ernest Beds 53 D8
Milton Green Ches 73 D8
Milton Hill Oxon 38 E4
Milton Keynes M Keynes 53 F6
Milton Keynes Village M Keynes 53 F6
Milton Lilbourne Wilts 25 C6
Milton Malsor Northants 52 D5
Milton Morenish Perth 140 F3
Milton of Auchinhove Aberds 150 D4
Milton of Balgonie Fife 134 D5
Milton of Buchanan Stirl 132 E3
Milton of Campfield Aberds 150 D5
Milton of Campsie E Dunb 121 B6
Milton of Corsindae Aberds 151 D5
Milton of Cushnie Aberds 150 C4
Milton of Dalcapon Perth 141 D6
Milton of Edradour Perth 141 D6
Milton of Gollanfield Highld 157 D8
Milton of Lesmore Aberds 150 B3
Milton of Logie Aberds 150 D3
Milton of Murtle Aberdeen 151 D7
Milton of Noth Aberds 150 B4
Milton of Tullich Aberds 150 E2
Milton on Stour Dorset 13 B5
Milton Regis Kent 30 C3
Milton under Wychwood Oxon 38 C2
Miltonduff Moray 159 C5
Miltonhill Moray 158 C4
Miltonise Dumfries 105 B5
Milverton Som 11 B6
Milverton Warks 51 C8
Milwich Staffs 75 F6
Minard Argyll 131 F5
Minchinhampton Glos 37 D5
Mindrum Northumb 124 F4
Minehead Som 21 E8
Minera Wrex 73 D6
Minesmere RSPB Nature Reserve Suff 57 C8
Minety Wilts 37 E7
Minffordd Gwyn 71 D6
Minffordd Gwyn 58 C4
Minffordd Gwyn 83 D5
Miningsby Lincs 79 C6
Minions Corn 5 B7
Minishant S Ayrs 112 C3
Minllyn Gwyn 59 C5
Minnes Aberds 151 B8
Minngearraidh W Isles 171 H3
Minnigaff Dumfries 105 C8
Minnonie Aberds 160 B4
Minskip N Yorks 95 C6
Minstead Hants 14 C3
Minsted W Sus 16 B2
Minster Kent 30 B3
Minster Kent 31 C7
Minster Lovell Oxon 38 C3
Minsterley Shrops 60 D3
Minsterworth Glos 36 C4
Minterne Magna Dorset 12 D4
Minting Lincs 78 B4
Mintlaw Aberds 161 D7
Minto Borders 115 B8
Minton Shrops 60 E4
Minwear Pembs 32 C1
Minworth W Mid 63 E5
Mirbister Orkney 176 D2
Mirehouse Cumb 98 C1
Mireland Highld 169 C8
Mirfield W Yorks 88 C3
Miserden Glos 37 D6
Miskin Rhondda 34 F4
Misson Notts 89 E7
Misterton Leics 64 F2
Misterton Notts 89 E8
Misterton Som 12 D2
Mistley Essex 56 F5
Mitcham London 28 C3
Mitchel Troy Mon 36 C1
Mitcheldean Glos 36 C3
Mitchell Corn 4 D3
Mitcheltroy Common Mon 36 D1
Mitford Northumb 117 F7
Mithian Corn 4 D2
Mitton Staffs 62 C2
Mixbury Oxon 52 F4
Moat Cumb 108 B4
Moats Tye Suff 56 D4
Mobberley Ches 74 B4
Mobberley Staffs 75 E7
Moccas Hereford 49 E5
Mochdre Conwy 83 D8
Mochdre Powys 59 F7
Mochrum Dumfries 105 E7
Mockbeggar Hants 14 D2
Mockerkin Cumb 98 B2
Modbury Devon 6 D4
Moddershall Staffs 75 F6
Model Village, Babbacombe Devon 7 C7
Moelfre Anglesey 82 C5
Moelfre Powys 59 B8
Moffat Dumfries 114 D3
Moggerhanger Beds 54 E2
Moira Leics 63 C7
Mol-chlach Highld 153 H5
Molash Kent 30 D4
Mold = Yr Wyddgrug Flint 73 C6
Moldgreen W Yorks 88 C2
Molehill Green Essex 42 B1
Molescroft E Yorks 97 E6
Molesden Northumb 117 F7
Molesworth Cambs 53 B8
Moll Highld 153 F6
Molland Devon 10 B3
Mollington Ches 73 B7
Mollington Oxon 52 E2
Mollinsburn N Lnrk 121 B7
Monachty Ceredig 46 C4
Monachylemore Stirl 132 C3
Monar Lodge Highld 156 E3
Monaughty Powys 48 C4
Monboddo House Aberds 143 B7
Mondynes Aberds 143 B7
Monevechadan Argyll 131 E7
Monewden Suff 57 D6
Moneydie Perth 134 B2
Moniaive Dumfries 113 E7
Monifieth Angus 142 F4
Monikie Angus 142 F4
Monimail Fife 134 C4
Monington Pembs 45 E3
Monk Bretton S Yorks 88 D4
Monk Fryston N Yorks 89 B6
Monk Sherborne Hants 26 D4
Monk Soham Suff 57 C6
Monk Street Essex 42 B2
Monken Hadley London 41 E5
Monkhopton Shrops 61 E6
Monkland Hereford 49 D6
Monkleigh Devon 9 B6
Monknash V Glam 21 B8
Monkokehampton Devon 9 D7
Monks Eleigh Suff 56 E3
Monk's Gate W Sus 17 B6
Monks Heath Ches 74 B5
Monks Kirby Warks 63 F8
Monks Risborough Bucks 39 D8
Monkseaton T & W 111 B6
Monkshill Aberds 160 D4
Monksilver Som 22 F2
Monkspath W Mid 51 B6
Monkswood Mon 35 D7
Monkton Devon 11 D6
Monkton Kent 31 C6
Monkton Pembs 44 E4
Monkton S Ayrs 112 B3
Monkton Combe Bath 24 C2
Monkton Deverill Wilts 24 F3
Monkton Farleigh Wilts 24 C3
Monkton Heathfield Som 11 B7
Monkton Up Wimborne Dorset 13 C8
Monkwearmouth T & W 111 D6
Monkwood Hants 26 F4
Monmouth = Trefynwy Mon 36 C2
Monmouth Cap Mon 35 B7
Monnington on Wye Hereford 49 E5
Monreith Dumfries 105 E7
Monreith Mains Dumfries 105 E7
Mont Saint Guern 16
Montacute Som 12 C2
Montacute House Som 12 C3
Montcoffer Ho. Aberds 160 B3
Montford Argyll 129 D6
Montford Shrops 60 C4
Montford Bridge Shrops 60 C4
Montgarrie Aberds 150 C4
Montgomery = Trefaldwyn Powys 60 E2
Montrave Fife 135 D5
Montrose Angus 143 D7
Montsale Essex 43 E6
Monxton Hants 25 E8
Monyash Derbys 75 C8
Monymusk Aberds 151 C5
Monzie Perth 133 B7
Monzie Castle Perth 133 B7
Moodiesburn N Lnrk 121 B6
Moonzie Fife 134 C5
Moor Allerton W Yorks 95 F5
Moor Crichel Dorset 13 D7
Moor End E Yorks 96 F4
Moor End York 96 D2
Moor Monkton N Yorks 95 D8
Moor of Granary Moray 158 D4
Moor of Ravenstone Dumfries 105 E7
Moor Row Cumb 98 C2
Moor Street Kent 30 C2
Moorby Lincs 79 C5
Moordown Bmouth 13 E8
Moore Halton 86 F3
Moorend Glos 36 D4
Moorends S Yorks 89 C7
Moorgate S Yorks 88 E5
Moorgreen Notts 76 E4
Moorhall Derbys 76 B3
Moorhampton Hereford 49 E5
Moorhead W Yorks 94 F4
Moorhouse Cumb 108 D3
Moorhouse Notts 77 C7
Moorlinch Som 23 F5
Moorsholm Redcar 102 C4
Moorside Gtr Man 87 D7
Moorthorpe W Yorks 89 C5
Moortown Hants 14 D2
Moortown I o W 14 F5
Moortown Lincs 90 E4
Morangie Highld 164 F4
Morar Highld 145 D6
Morborne Cambs 65 E8
Morchard Bishop Devon 10 D2
Morcombelake Dorset 12 E2
Morcott Rutland 65 D6
Morda Shrops 60 B2
Morden Dorset 13 E7
Morden London 28 C3
Mordiford Hereford 49 F7
Mordon Durham 101 B8
More Shrops 60 E3
Morebath Devon 10 B4
Morebattle Borders 116 B3
Morecambe Lancs 92 C4
Morefield Highld 163 E5
Moreleigh Devon 7 D5
Morenish Perth 140 F2
Moresby Cumb 98 B1
Moresby Parks Cumb 98 C1
Morestead Hants 15 B6
Moreton Dorset 13 F6
Moreton Essex 41 D8
Moreton Mers 85 E3
Moreton Oxon 39 D6
Moreton Staffs 61 C7
Moreton Corbet Shrops 61 B5
Moreton-in-Marsh Glos 51 F7
Moreton Jeffries Hereford 49 E8
Moreton Morrell Warks 51 D8
Moreton on Lugg Hereford 49 E7
Moreton Pinkney Northants 52 E3
Moreton Say Shrops 74 F3
Moreton Valence Glos 36 D4
Moretonhampstead Devon 10 F2
Morfa Carms 33 C6
Morfa Carms 33 E6
Morfa Bach Carms 32 C4
Morfa Bychan Gwyn 71 D6
Morfa Dinlle Gwyn 82 F4
Morfa Glas Neath 34 D2
Morfa Nefyn Gwyn 70 C3
Morfydd Denb 72 E5
Morgan's Vale Wilts 14 B2
Moriah Ceredig 46 B5
Morland Cumb 99 B7
Morley Derbys 76 E3
Morley Durham 101 B6
Morley W Yorks 88 B3
Morley Green Ches 87 F6
Morley St Botolph Norf 68 E3
Morningside Edin 122 B5
Morningside N Lnrk 121 D8
Morningthorpe Norf 68 E5
Morpeth Northumb 117 F8
Morphie Aberds 143 C7
Morrey Staffs 62 C5
Morris Green Essex 55 F8
Morriston Swansea 33 E7
Morston Norf 81 C6
Mortehoe Devon 20 E3
Mortimer W Berks 26 C4
Mortimer West End Hants 26 C4
Mortimer's Cross Hereford 49 C6
Mortlake London 28 B3
Morton Cumb 108 D3
Morton Derbys 76 C4
Morton Lincs 65 B7
Morton Lincs 90 E2
Morton Lincs 77 C8
Morton Norf 68 C4
Morton Notts 77 D7
Morton Shrops 60 B2
Morton S Glos 36 E3
Morton Bagot Warks 51 C6
Morton-on-Swale N Yorks 101 E8
Morvah Corn 2 C3
Morval Corn 5 D7
Morvich Highld 146 B2
Morvich Highld 164 D4
Morville Shrops 61 E6
Morville Heath Shrops 61 E6
Morwenstow Corn 8 C4
Mosborough S Yorks 88 F5
Moscow E Ayrs 120 E4
Mosedale Cumb 108 F3
Moseley W Mid 62 F4
Moseley W Mid 62 E3
Moseley Worcs 50 D3
Mosquito Aircraft Museum, London Colney Herts 40 D4
Moss Argyll 136 F1
Moss Highld 137 B7
Moss S Yorks 89 C6
Moss Wrex 73 D7
Moss Bank Mers 86 E3
Moss Edge Lancs 92 E4
Moss End Brack 27 B6
Moss of Barmuckity Moray 159 C6
Moss Pit Staffs 62 B3
Moss-side Highld 158 D2
Moss Side Lancs 92 F3
Mossat Aberds 150 C3
Mossbank Shetland 174 F6
Mossbay Cumb 98 B1
Mossblown S Ayrs 112 B4
Mossbrow Gtr Man 86 F5
Mossburnford Borders 116 C2
Mossdale Dumfries 106 B3
Mossend N Lnrk 121 C7
Mosser Cumb 98 B3
Mossfield Highld 157 B7
Mossgiel E Ayrs 112 B4
Mosside Angus 142 D4
Mossley Ches 75 C5
Mossley Gtr Man 87 D7
Mossley Hill Mers 85 F4
Mosstodloch Moray 159 D7
Mosston Angus 143 E5
Mossy Lea Lancs 86 C3
Mosterton Dorset 12 D2
Moston Gtr Man 87 D6
Moston Shrops 61 B5
Moston Green Ches 74 C4
Mostyn Flint 85 F2
Mostyn Quay Flint 85 E2
Motcombe Dorset 13 B6
Mothecombe Devon 6 E4
Motherby Cumb 99 B6
Motherwell N Lnrk 121 D7
Mottingham London 28 B5
Mottisfont Hants 14 B4
Mottisfont Abbey Garden Hants 14 B4
Mottistone I o W 14 F5
Mottram in Longdendale Gtr Man 87 E7
Mottram St Andrew Ches 75 B5
Mouilpied Guern 16
Mouldsworth Ches 74 B2
Moulin Perth 141 D6
Moulsecoomb Brighton 17 D7
Moulsford Oxon 39 F5
Moulsoe M Keynes 53 E7
Moulton Ches 74 C3
Moulton Lincs 66 B3
Moulton Northants 53 C5
Moulton N Yorks 101 D7
Moulton Suff 55 C7
Moulton V Glam 22 B2
Moulton Chapel Lincs 66 C2
Moulton Eaugate Lincs 66 C3
Moulton St Mary Norf 69 D6
Moulton Seas End Lincs 66 B3
Mounie Castle Aberds 151 B6
Mount Corn 4 D2
Mount Corn 5 C6
Mount Highld 158 E3
Mount Bures Essex 56 F3
Mount Canisp Highld 157 B8
Mount Hawke Corn 3 B6
Mount Pleasant Ches 74 D5
Mount Pleasant Derbys 76 E3
Mount Pleasant Derbys 63 C6
Mount Pleasant Flint 73 B6
Mount Pleasant Hants 14 E3
Mount Pleasant W Yorks 88 B3
Mount Sorrel Wilts 13 B8
Mount Tabor W Yorks 87 B8
Mountain W Yorks 94 F3
Mountain Ash = Aberpennar Rhondda 34 E4
Mountain Cross Borders 122 E4
Mountain Water Pembs 44 C4
Mountbenger Borders 115 B6
Mountfield E Sus 18 C4
Mountgerald Highld 157 C6
Mountjoy Corn 4 C3
Mountnessing Essex 42 E2
Mounton Mon 36 E2
Mountsorrel Leics 64 C2
Mousehole Corn 2 D3
Mousen Northumb 125 F7
Mouswald Dumfries 107 B7
Mow Cop Ches 75 D5
Mowhaugh Borders 116 B4
Mowsley Leics 64 F3
Moxley W Mid 62 E3
Moy Highld 147 F7
Moy Highld 157 F8
Moy Hall Highld 157 F8
Moy Ho. Moray 158 C4
Moy Lodge Highld 147 F7
Moyles Court Hants 14 D2
Moylgrove Pembs 45 E3
Muasdale Argyll 118 B3
Much Birch Hereford 49 F7
Much Cowarne Hereford 49 E8
Much Dewchurch Hereford 49 F6
Much Hadham Herts 41 C7
Much Hoole Lancs 86 B2
Much Marcle Hereford 49 F8
Much Wenlock Shrops 61 D6
Muchalls Aberds 151 E8
Muchelney Som 12 B2
Muchlarnick Corn 5 D7
Muchrachd Highld 156 F3
Muckernich Highld 157 D6
Mucking Thurrock 42 F2
Muckleford Dorset 12 E4
Mucklestone Staffs 74 F4
Muckleton Shrops 61 B5
Muckletown Aberds 150 B4
Muckley Corner Staffs 62 D4
Muckton Lincs 91 F7
Mudale Highld 167 F7
Muddiford Devon 20 F4
Mudeford Dorset 14 E2
Mudford Som 12 C3
Mudgley Som 23 E6
Mugdock Stirl 121 B5
Mugeary Highld 153 F5
Mugginton Derbys 76 E2
Muggleswick Durham 110 E3
Muie Highld 164 D3
Muir Aberds 149 F6
Muir of Fairburn Highld 157 D5
Muir of Fowlis Aberds 150 C4
Muir of Ord Highld 157 D6
Muir of Pert Angus 142 F4
Muirden Aberds 160 C4
Muirdrum Angus 143 F5
Muirhead Angus 142 F3
Muirhead Fife 134 D4
Muirhead N Lnrk 121 C6
Muirhead S Ayrs 120 F3
Muirhouselaw Borders 116 B2
Muirhouses Falk 134 F2
Muirkirk E Ayrs 113 B6
Muirmill Stirl 133 F6
Muirshearlich Highld 146 F4
Muirskie Aberds 151 E7
Muirtack Aberds 161 E6
Muirton Highld 157 C8
Muirton Perth 134 B3
Muirton Perth 133 C8
Muirton Mains Highld 157 D5
Muirton of Ardblair Perth 142 E1
Muirton of Ballochy Angus 143 C6
Muiryfold Aberds 160 C4
Muker N Yorks 100 E4
Mulbarton Norf 68 D4
Mulben Moray 159 D7
Mulindry Argyll 126 D3
Mullardoch House Highld 156 F3
Mullion Corn 3 E5
Mullion Cove Corn 3 E5
Mumby Lincs 79 B8
Muncaster Owl Trust World HQ Cumb 98 E3
Munderfield Row Hereford 49 D8
Munderfield Stocks Hereford 49 D8
Mundesley Norf 81 D9
Mundford Norf 67 E8
Mundham Norf 69 E6
Mundon Essex 42 D4
Mundurno Aberdeen 151 C8
Munerigie Highld 147 D5
Muness Shetland 174 C8
Mungasdale Highld 162 E3
Mungrisdale Cumb 108 F3
Munlochy Highld 157 D7
Munsley Hereford 49 E8
Munslow Shrops 60 F5
Murchington Devon 9 F8
Murcott Oxon 39 C5
Murkle Highld 169 C6
Murlaggan Highld 146 E3
Murlaggan Highld 147 F6

North End Lincs 78 E5
North End N Som 23 C6
North End Ptsmth 15 D7
North End Som 11 B7
North End W Sus 16 C4
North Erradale Highld 154 B3
North Fambridge Essex 42 E4
North Fearns Highld 153 F6
North Featherstone W Yorks 88 B5
North Ferriby E Yorks 90 B3
North Frodingham E Yorks 97 D7
North Gluss Shetland 174 F5
North Gorley Hants 14 C2
North Green Norf 68 F5
North Green Suff 57 C7
North Greetwell Lincs 78 B3
North Grimston N Yorks 96 C4
North Halley Orkney 176 F4
North Halling Medway 29 C8
North Hayling Hants 15 D8
North Hazelrigg Northumb 125 F6
North Heasley Devon 21 F6
North Heath W Sus 16 B4
North Hill Cambs 55 B5
North Hill Corn 5 B7
North Hinksey Oxon 38 D4
North Holmwood Sur 28 E2
North Howden E Yorks 96 F3
North Huish Devon 6 D5
North Hykeham Lincs 78 C2
North Johnston Pembs 44 D4
North Kelsey Lincs 90 D4
North Kelsey Moor Lincs 90 D4
North Kessock Highld 157 E7
North Killingholme N Lincs 90 C5
North Kilvington N Yorks 102 F2
North Kilworth Leics 64 F3
North Kirkton Aberds 161 C8
North Kiscadale N Ayrs 119 D7
North Kyme Lincs 78 D4
North Lancing W Sus 17 D5
North Lee Bucks 39 D8
North Leigh Oxon 38 C3
North Leverton with Habblesthorpe Notts 89 F8
North Littleton Worcs 51 E5
North Lopham Norf 68 F3
North Luffenham Rutland 65 D6
North Marden W Sus 16 C2
North Marston Bucks 39 B7
North Middleton Midloth 123 D6
North Middleton Northumb 117 B6
North Molton Devon 10 B2
North Moreton Oxon 39 F5
North Mundham W Sus 16 D2
North Muskham Notts 77 D7
North Newbald E Yorks 96 F5
North Newington Oxon 52 F2
North Newnton Wilts 25 D6
North Newton Som 22 F4
North Nibley Glos 36 E4
North Norfolk Railway, Sheringham Norf 81 C7
North Oakley Hants 26 D3
North Ockendon London 42 F1
North Ormesby M'bro 102 B3
North Ormsby Lincs 91 E6
North Otterington N Yorks 102 F1
North Owersby Lincs 90 E4
North Perrott Som 12 D2
North Petherton Som 22 F4
North Petherwin Corn 8 F4
North Pickenham Norf 67 D8
North Piddle Worcs 50 D4
North Poorton Dorset 12 E3
North Port Argyll 131 C6
North Queensferry Fife 134 F3
North Radworthy Devon 21 F6
North Rauceby Lincs 78 E3
North Reston Lincs 91 F7
North Rigton N Yorks 95 E5
North Rode Ches 75 C5
North Roe Shetland 174 E5
North Ronaldsay Airport Orkney 176 A6
North Runcton Norf 67 C6
North Sandwick Shetland 174 D7
North Scale Cumb 92 C1
North Scarle Lincs 77 C8
North Seaton Northumb 117 F8
North Shian Argyll 138 E3
North Shields T & W 111 C6
North Shoebury Sthend 43 F5
North Shore Blkpool 92 F3
North Side Cumb 98 B2
North Side P'boro 66 E2
North Skelton Redcar 102 C4
North Somercotes Lincs 91 E8
North Stainley N Yorks 95 B5
North Stainmore Cumb 100 C3
North Stifford Thurrock 42 F2
North Stoke Bath 24 C2
North Stoke Oxon 39 F6
North Stoke W Sus 16 C4
North Street Hants 26 F4
North Street Kent 30 D4
North Street Medway 30 B2
North Street W Berks 26 B4
North Sunderland Northumb 125 F8
North Tamerton Corn 8 E5
North Tawton Devon 9 D8
North Thoresby Lincs 91 E6
North Tidworth Wilts 25 E7
North Togston Northumb 117 D8
North Tuddenham Norf 68 C3
North Walbottle T & W 110 C4
North Walsham Norf 81 D8
North Waltham Hants 26 E3
North Warnborough Hants 26 D5
North Water Bridge Angus 143 C6
North Watten Highld 169 D7
North Weald Bassett Essex 41 D7
North Wheatley Notts 89 F8
North Whilborough Devon 7 C6
North Wick Bath 23 C7
North Willingham Lincs 91 F5
North Wingfield Derbys 76 C4
North Witham Lincs 65 B6
North Woolwich London 28 B5
North Wootton Dorset 12 C4
North Wootton Norf 67 B6
North Wootton Som 23 E7
North Wraxall Wilts 24 B3
North Wroughton Swindon 38 F1
North Yorkshire Moors Railway, Pickering N Yorks 103 F6
Northacre Norf 68 E2
Northallerton N Yorks 102 E1
Northam Devon 9 B6
Northam Soton 14 C5
Northampton Northants 53 C5
Northaw Herts 41 D5
Northbeck Lincs 78 E3
Northborough P'boro 65 D8
Northbourne Kent 31 D7
Northbridge Street E Sus 18 C4
Northchapel W Sus 16 B3
Northchurch Herts 40 D2
Northcott Devon 8 E5
Northdown Kent 31 B7
Northdyke Orkney 176 D1
Northend Bath 24 C2
Northend Bucks 39 E7
Northend Warks 51 D8
Northenden Gtr Man 87 E6
Northfield Aberdeen 151 D8
Northfield Borders 124 C5
Northfield E Yorks 90 B4
Northfield W Mid 50 B5
Northfields Lincs 65 D7
Northfleet Kent 29 B7
Northgate Lincs 65 B8
Northhouse Borders 115 D7
Northiam E Sus 18 C5
Northill Beds 54 E2
Northington Hants 26 F3
Northlands Lincs 79 D6
Northlea Durham 111 D7
Northleach Glos 37 C8
Northleigh Devon 11 E6
Northlew Devon 9 E7
Northmoor Oxon 38 D4
Northmoor Green or Moorland Som 22 F5
Northmuir Angus 142 D3
Northney Hants 15 D8
Northolt London 40 F4
Northop Flint 73 C6
Northop Hall Flint 73 C6
Northorpe Lincs 65 C7
Northorpe Lincs 78 F5
Northorpe Lincs 90 E2
Northover Som 12 B3
Northover Som 23 F6
Northowram W Yorks 88 B2
Northport Dorset 13 F7
Northpunds Shetland 175 L6
Northrepps Norf 81 D8
Northtown Orkney 176 G3
Northumbria Craft Centre, Morpeth Northumb 117 F7
Northway Glos 50 F4
Northwich Ches 74 B3
Northwick S Glos 36 F2
Northwold Norf 67 E7
Northwood Derbys 76 C2
Northwood London 40 E3
Northwood I o W 15 E5
Northwood Kent 31 C7
Northwood Shrops 73 F8
Northwood Green Glos 36 C4
Norton E Sus 17 D8
Norton Glos 37 B5
Norton Halton 86 F3
Norton Herts 54 F3
Norton I o W 14 F4
Norton Mon 35 C8
Norton Notts 77 B5
Norton Northants 52 C4
Norton Powys 48 C5
Norton Shrops 60 F4
Norton Shrops 61 D5
Norton Shrops 61 D7
Norton Stockton 102 B2
Norton Suff 56 C3
Norton S Yorks 89 C6
Norton Wilts 37 F5
Norton Worcs 50 D3
Norton Worcs 50 E5
Norton W Sus 16 E2
Norton W Sus 16 D3
Norton Bavant Wilts 24 E4
Norton Bridge Staffs 75 F5
Norton Canes Staffs 62 D4
Norton Canon Hereford 49 E5
Norton Corner Norf 81 E6
Norton Disney Lincs 77 D8
Norton East Staffs 62 D4
Norton Ferris Wilts 24 F2
Norton Fitzwarren Som 11 B6
Norton Green I o W 14 F4
Norton Hawkfield Bath 23 C7
Norton Heath Essex 42 D2
Norton in Hales Shrops 74 F4
Norton-in-the-Moors Stoke 75 D5
Norton-Juxta-Twycross Leics 63 D7
Norton-le-Clay N Yorks 95 B7
Norton Lindsey Warks 51 C7
Norton Malreward Bath 23 C8
Norton Mandeville Essex 42 D1
Norton-on-Derwent N Yorks 96 B3
Norton St Philip Som 24 D2
Norton sub Hamdon Som 12 C2
Norton Woodseats S Yorks 88 F4
Norwell Notts 77 C7
Norwell Woodhouse Notts 77 C7
Norwich Norf 68 D5
Norwich Castle Museum Norf 68 D5
Norwich Cathedral Norf 68 D5
Norwich International Airport Norf 68 C5
Norwick Shetland 174 B8
Norwood Derbys 89 F5
Norwood Hill Sur 28 E3
Norwoodside Cambs 66 E4
Noseley Leics 64 E4
Noss Shetland 175 M5
Noss Mayo Devon 6 E3
Nosterfield N Yorks 101 F7
Nostie Highld 155 H4
Notgrove Glos 37 B8
Nothe Fort, Weymouth Dorset 12 G4
Nottage Bridgend 21 B7
Nottingham Nottingham 77 F5
Nottingham Castle Museum Nottingham 77 E5
Nottingham East Midlands Airport Leics 63 B8
Nottingham Racecourse Nottingham 77 F6
Nottington Dorset 12 F4
Notton Wilts 24 C4
Notton W Yorks 88 C4
Nounsley Essex 42 C3
Noutard's Green Worcs 50 C2
Novar House Highld 157 C7
Nox Shrops 60 C4
Nuffield Oxon 39 F6
Nun Hills Lancs 87 B6
Nun Monkton N Yorks 95 D8
Nunburnholme E Yorks 96 E4
Nuncargate Notts 76 D5
Nuneaton Warks 63 E7
Nuneham Courtenay Oxon 39 E5
Nunney Som 24 E2
Nunnington N Yorks 96 B2
Nunnykirk Northumb 117 E6
Nunsthorpe NE Lincs 91 D6
Nunthorpe M'bro 102 C3
Nunthorpe York 96 D2
Nunton Wilts 14 B2
Nunwick N Yorks 95 B6
Nupend Glos 36 D4
Nursling Hants 14 C4
Nursted Hants 15 B8
Nutbourne W Sus 16 C4
Nutbourne W Sus 15 D8
Nutfield Sur 28 D4
Nuthall Notts 76 E5
Nuthampstead Herts 54 F5
Nuthurst W Sus 17 B5
Nutley E Sus 17 B8
Nutley Hants 26 E4
Nutwell S Yorks 89 D7
Nybster Highld 169 C8
Nyetimber W Sus 16 E2
Nyewood W Sus 16 B2
Nymans Gardens, Crawley W Sus 17 B6
Nymet Rowland Devon 10 D2
Nymet Tracey Devon 10 D2
Nympsfield Glos 37 D5
Nynehead Som 11 B6
Nyton W Sus 16 D3

O

Oad Street Kent 30 C2
Oadby Leics 64 D3
Oak Cross Devon 9 E7
Oakamoor Staffs 75 E7
Oakbank W Loth 122 C3
Oakdale Caerph 35 E5
Oake Som 11 B6
Oaken Staffs 62 D2
Oakenclough Lancs 92 E5
Oakengates Telford 61 C7
Oakenholt Flint 73 B6
Oakenshaw Durham 110 F5
Oakenshaw W Yorks 88 B2
Oakerthorpe Derbys 76 D3
Oakes W Yorks 88 C2
Oakfield Torf 35 E7
Oakford Ceredig 46 D3
Oakford Devon 10 B4
Oakfordbridge Devon 10 B4
Oakgrove Ches 75 C6
Oakham Rutland 65 D5
Oakhanger Hants 27 F5
Oakhill Som 23 E8
Oakhurst Kent 29 D6
Oakington Cambs 54 C5
Oaklands Herts 41 C5
Oaklands Powys 48 D2
Oakle Street Glos 36 C4
Oakley Beds 53 D8
Oakley Bucks 39 C6
Oakley Fife 134 F2
Oakley Hants 26 D3
Oakley Oxon 39 D7
Oakley Poole 13 E8
Oakley Suff 57 B5
Oakley Green Windsor 27 B7
Oakley Park Powys 59 F6
Oakmere Ches 74 C2
Oakridge Glos 37 D6
Oakridge Hants 26 D4
Oaks Shrops 60 D4
Oaks Green Derbys 75 F8
Oaksey Wilts 37 E6
Oakthorpe Leics 63 C7
Oakwood Adventure Park, Narberth Pembs 32 C1
Oakwoodhill Sur 28 F2
Oakworth W Yorks 94 F3
Oape Highld 163 D8
Oare Kent 30 C4
Oare Som 21 E7
Oare W Berks 26 B3
Oare Wilts 25 C6
Oasby Lincs 78 F3
Oathlaw Angus 142 D4
Oatlands N Yorks 95 D6
Oban Argyll 130 C4
Oban Highld 145 E8
Oborne Dorset 12 C4
Obthorpe Lincs 65 C7
Occlestone Green Ches 74 C3
Occold Suff 57 B5
Ochiltree E Ayrs 112 B5
Ochtermuthill Perth 133 C7
Ochtertyre Perth 133 B7
Ockbrook Derbys 76 F4
Ockham Sur 27 D8
Ockle Highld 137 A6
Ockley Sur 28 F2
Ocle Pychard Hereford 49 E7
Octon E Yorks 97 C6
Octon Cross Roads E Yorks 97 C6
Odcombe Som 12 C3
Odd Down Bath 24 C2
Oddendale Cumb 99 C7
Odder Lincs 78 B2
Oddingley Worcs 50 D4
Oddington Glos 38 B2
Oddington Oxon 39 C5
Odell Beds 53 D7
Odie Orkney 176 D5
Odiham Hants 26 D5
Odstock Wilts 14 B2
Odstone Leics 63 D7
Offchurch Warks 51 C8
Offenham Worcs 51 E5
Offham E Sus 17 C7
Offham Kent 29 D7
Offham W Sus 16 D4
Offord Cluny Cambs 54 C3
Offord Darcy Cambs 54 C3
Offton Suff 56 E4
Offwell Devon 11 E6
Ogbourne Maizey Wilts 25 B6
Ogbourne St Andrew Wilts 25 B6
Ogbourne St George Wilts 25 B7
Ogil Angus 142 C4
Ogle Northumb 110 B4
Ogmore V Glam 21 B7
Ogmore-by-Sea V Glam 21 B7
Ogmore Vale Bridgend 34 E3
Okeford Fitzpaine Dorset 13 C6
Okehampton Devon 9 E7
Okehampton Camp Devon 9 E7
Okraquoy Shetland 175 K6
Old Northants 53 B5
Old Aberdeen Aberdeen 151 D8
Old Alresford Hants 26 F3
Old Arley Warks 63 E6
Old Basford Nottingham 76 E5
Old Basing Hants 26 D4
Old Bewick Northumb 117 B6
Old Blacksmith's Shop Centre, Gretna Green Dumfries 108 C3
Old Bolingbroke Lincs 79 C6
Old Bramhope W Yorks 94 E5
Old Brampton Derbys 76 B3
Old Bridge of Tilt Perth 141 C5
Old Bridge of Urr Dumfries 106 C4
Old Buckenham Norf 68 E3
Old Burghclere Hants 26 D2
Old Byland N Yorks 102 F3
Old Cassop Durham 111 F6
Old Castleton Borders 115 E8
Old Catton Norf 68 C5
Old Clee NE Lincs 91 D6
Old Cleeve Som 22 E2
Old Clipstone Notts 77 C6
Old Colwyn Conwy 83 D8
Old Coulsdon London 28 D4
Old Crombie Aberds 160 C2
Old Dailly S Ayrs 112 E2
Old Dalby Leics 64 B3
Old Deer Aberds 161 D6
Old Denaby S Yorks 89 E5
Old Edlington S Yorks 89 E6
Old Eldon Durham 101 B7
Old Ellerby E Yorks 97 F7
Old Felixstowe Suff 57 F7
Old Fletton P'boro 65 E8
Old Glossop Derbys 87 E8
Old Goole E Yorks 89 B8
Old Hall Powys 59 F6
Old Heath Essex 43 B6
Old Heathfield E Sus 18 C2
Old Hill W Mid 62 F3
Old House, Rochford Essex 42 E4
Old Hunstanton Norf 80 C2
Old Hurst Cambs 54 B3
Old Hutton Cumb 99 F7
Old Kea Corn 3 B7
Old Kilpatrick W Dunb 120 B4
Old Kinnernie Aberds 151 D6
Old Knebworth Herts 41 B5
Old Langho Lancs 93 F7
Old Laxey I o M 84 D4
Old Leake Lincs 79 D7
Old Malton N Yorks 96 B3
Old Micklefield W Yorks 95 F7
Old Milton Hants 14 E3
Old Milverton Warks 51 C7
Old Monkland N Lnrk 121 C7
Old Netley Hants 15 D5
Old Philpstoun W Loth 122 B3
Old Quarrington Durham 111 F6
Old Radnor Powys 48 D4
Old Rattray Aberds 161 C7
Old Rayne Aberds 151 B5
Old Romney Kent 19 C7
Old Sarum, Salisbury Wilts 25 F6
Old Sodbury S Glos 36 F4
Old Somerby Lincs 78 F2
Old Stratford Northants 53 E5
Old Thirsk N Yorks 102 F2
Old Town Cumb 108 E4
Old Town Cumb 99 F7
Old Town Northumb 116 E4
Old Town Scilly 2 E4
Old Trafford Gtr Man 87 E6
Old Tupton Derbys 76 C3
Old Warden Beds 54 E2
Old Weston Cambs 53 B8
Old Whittington Derbys 76 B3
Old Wick Highld 169 D8
Old Windsor Windsor 27 B8
Old Wives Lees Kent 30 D4
Old Woking Sur 27 D8
Old Woodhall Lincs 78 C5
Oldany Highld 166 F3
Oldberrow Warks 51 C6
Oldborough Devon 10 D2
Oldbury Shrops 61 E7
Oldbury Warks 63 E7
Oldbury W Mid 62 F3
Oldbury-on-Severn S Glos 36 E3
Oldbury on the Hill Glos 37 F5
Oldcastle Bridgend 21 B8
Oldcastle Mon 35 B7
Oldcotes Notts 89 F6
Oldfallow Staffs 62 C3
Oldfield Worcs 50 C3
Oldford Som 24 D2
Oldham Gtr Man 87 D7
Oldhamstocks E Loth 124 B3
Oldland S Glos 23 B8
Oldmeldrum Aberds 151 B7
Oldshore Beg Highld 166 D3
Oldshoremore Highld 166 D4
Oldstead N Yorks 102 F3
Oldtown Aberds 150 B4
Oldtown of Ord Aberds 160 C3
Oldway Swansea 33 F6
Oldways End Devon 10 B3
Oldwhat Aberds 161 C5
Olgrinmore Highld 169 D5
Oliver's Battery Hants 15 B5
Ollaberry Shetland 174 E5
Ollerton Ches 74 B4
Ollerton Notts 77 C6
Ollerton Shrops 61 B6
Olmarch Ceredig 46 D5
Olney M Keynes 53 D6
Olrig Ho. Highld 169 C6
Olton W Mid 62 F5
Olveston S Glos 36 F3
Olwen Ceredig 46 E4
Ombersley Worcs 50 C3
Ompton Notts 77 C6
Onchan I o M 84 E3
Onecote Staffs 75 D7
Onen Mon 35 C8
Ongar Hill Norf 67 B5
Ongar Street Hereford 49 C5
Onibury Shrops 49 B6
Onich Highld 138 C4
Onllwyn Neath 34 C2
Onneley Staffs 74 E4
Onslow Village Sur 27 E7
Onthank E Ayrs 120 E4
Openwoodgate Derbys 76 E3
Opinan Highld 162 E2
Opinan Highld 154 C3
Orange Lane Borders 124 E3
Orange Row Norf 66 B5
Orasaigh W Isles 173 G6
Orbliston Moray 159 D7
Orbost Highld 153 E3
Orby Lincs 79 C7
Orchard Hill Devon 9 B6
Orchard Portman Som 11 B7
Orcheston Wilts 25 E5
Orcop Hereford 36 B1
Orcop Hill Hereford 36 B1
Ord Highld 145 B6
Ordhead Aberds 151 C5
Ordie Aberds 150 D3
Ordiequish Moray 159 D7
Ordsall Notts 89 F7
Ore E Sus 18 D5
Oreton Shrops 61 F6
Orford Suff 57 E8
Orford Warr 86 E4
Orgreave Staffs 63 C5
Orlestone Kent 19 B6
Orleton Hereford 49 C6
Orleton Worcs 49 C8
Orlingbury Northants 53 B6
Ormesby Redcar 102 C3
Ormesby St Margaret Norf 69 C7
Ormesby St Michael Norf 69 C7
Ormiclate Castle W Isles 171 G3
Ormiscaig Highld 162 E2
Ormiston E Loth 123 C7
Ormsaigbeg Highld 137 B5
Ormsaigmore Highld 137 B5
Ormsary Argyll 128 C2
Ormsgill Cumb 92 B1
Ormskirk Lancs 86 D2
Orpington London 29 C5
Orrell Gtr Man 86 D3
Orrell Mers 85 E4
Orrisdale I o M 84 C3
Orroland Dumfries 106 E4
Orsett Thurrock 42 F2
Orslow Staffs 62 C2
Orston Notts 77 E7
Orthwaite Cumb 108 F2
Ortner Lancs 92 D5
Orton Cumb 99 D8
Orton Northants 53 B6
Orton Longueville P'boro 65 E8
Orton-on-the-Hill Leics 63 D7
Orton Waterville P'boro 65 E8
Orwell Cambs 54 D4
Osbaldeston Lancs 93 F6
Osbaldwick York 96 D2
Osbaston Shrops 60 B3
Osborne House I o W 15 E6
Osbournby Lincs 78 F3
Oscroft Ches 74 C2
Ose Highld 153 E4
Osgathorpe Leics 63 C8
Osgodby Lincs 90 E4
Osgodby N Yorks 96 F2
Osgodby N Yorks 103 F8
Oskaig Highld 153 F6
Oskamull Argyll 137 D5
Osmaston Derby 76 F3
Osmaston Derbys 76 E2
Osmington Dorset 12 F5
Osmington Mills Dorset 12 F5
Osmotherley N Yorks 102 E2
Ospisdale Highld 164 F4
Ospringe Kent 30 C4
Ossett W Yorks 88 B3
Ossington Notts 77 C7
Ostend Essex 43 E5
Oswaldkirk N Yorks 96 B2
Oswaldtwistle Lancs 86 B5
Oswestry Shrops 60 B2
Otford Kent 29 D6
Otham Kent 29 D8
Othery Som 23 F5
Otley Suff 57 D6
Otley W Yorks 94 E5
Otter Ferry Argyll 128 B4
Otterbourne Hants 15 B5
Otterburn Northumb 116 E4
Otterburn N Yorks 93 D8
Otterburn Camp Northumb 116 E4
Otterham Corn 8 E3
Otterhampton Som 22 E4
Ottershaw Sur 27 C8
Otterswick Shetland 174 E7
Otterton Devon 11 F5
Ottery St Mary Devon 11 E6
Ottinge Kent 31 E5
Ottringham E Yorks 91 B6
Oughterby Cumb 108 D2
Oughtershaw N Yorks 100 F3
Oughterside Cumb 107 E8
Oughtibridge S Yorks 88 E4
Oughtrington Warr 86 F4
Oulston N Yorks 95 B8
Oulton Cumb 108 D2
Oulton Norf 81 E7
Oulton Staffs 75 F6
Oulton Suff 69 E8
Oulton W Yorks 88 B4
Oulton Broad Suff 69 E8
Oulton Park Motor Racing Circuit Ches 74 C2
Oulton Street Norf 81 E7
Oundle Northants 65 F7
Ousby Cumb 109 F6
Ousdale Highld 165 B7
Ousden Suff 55 D8
Ousefleet E Yorks 90 B2
Ouston Durham 111 D5
Ouston Northumb 110 B3
Out Newton E Yorks 91 B7
Out Rawcliffe Lancs 92 E4
Outertown Orkney 176 E1
Outgate Cumb 99 E5
Outhgill Cumb 100 D2
Outlane W Yorks 87 C8
Outwell Norf 66 D5
Outwick Hants 14 C2
Outwood Sur 28 E4
Outwood W Yorks 88 B4
Outwoods Staffs 61 C7
Ovenden W Yorks 87 B8
Ovenscloss Borders 123 F7
Over Cambs 54 B4
Over Ches 74 C3
Over S Glos 36 F2
Over Compton Dorset 12 C3
Over Green W Mid 63 E5
Over Haddon Derbys 76 C2
Over Hulton Gtr Man 86 D4
Over Kellet Lancs 92 B5
Over Kiddington Oxon 38 B4
Over Knutsford Ches 74 B4
Over Monnow Mon 36 C2
Over Norton Oxon 38 B3
Over Peover Ches 74 B4
Over Silton N Yorks 102 E2
Over Stowey Som 22 F3
Over Stratton Som 12 C2
Over Tabley Ches 86 F5
Over Wallop Hants 25 F7
Over Whitacre Warks 63 E6
Over Worton Oxon 38 B4
Overbister Orkney 176 B5
Overbury Worcs 50 F4
Overcombe Dorset 12 F4
Overgreen Derbys 76 B3
Overleigh Som 23 F6
Overley Green Warks 51 D5
Overpool Ches 73 B7
Overscaig Hotel Highld 163 B8
Overseal Derbys 63 C6
Oversland Kent 30 D4
Overstone Northants 53 C6
Overstrand Norf 81 C8
Overthorpe Northants 52 E2
Overton Aberdeen 151 C7
Overton Ches 74 B2
Overton Dumfries 107 C6
Overton Hants 26 E3
Overton Lancs 92 D4
Overton N Yorks 95 D8
Overton Shrops 49 B7
Overton Swansea 33 F5
Overton W Yorks 88 C3
Overton = Owrtyn Wrex 73 E7
Overton Bridge Wrex 73 E7
Overtown N Lnrk 121 D8
Oving Bucks 39 B7
Oving W Sus 16 D3
Ovingdean Brighton 17 D7
Ovingham Northumb 110 C3
Ovington Durham 101 C6
Ovington Essex 55 E8
Ovington Hants 26 F3
Ovington Norf 68 D2
Ovington Northumb 110 C3
Ower Hants 14 C4
Owermoigne Dorset 13 F5
Owlbury Shrops 60 E3
Owler Bar Derbys 76 B2
Owlerton S Yorks 88 F4
Owl's Green Suff 57 C6
Owlswick Bucks 39 D7
Owmby Lincs 90 D4
Owmby-by-Spital Lincs 90 F4
Owrtyn = Overton Wrex 73 E7
Owslebury Hants 15 B6
Owston Leics 64 D4
Owston S Yorks 89 C6
Owston Ferry N Lincs 90 D2
Owstwick E Yorks 97 F8
Owthorne E Yorks 91 B7
Owthorpe Notts 77 F6
Oxborough Norf 67 D7
Oxburgh Hall Norf 67 D7
Oxcombe Lincs 79 B6
Oxen Park Cumb 99 F5
Oxenholme Cumb 99 F7
Oxenhope W Yorks 94 F3
Oxenton Glos 50 F4
Oxenwood Wilts 25 D8
Oxford Oxon 39 D5
Oxford University Botanic Garden Oxon 39 D5
Oxhey Herts 40 E4
Oxhill Warks 51 E8
Oxley W Mid 62 D3
Oxley Green Essex 43 C5
Oxley's Green E Sus 18 C3
Oxnam Borders 116 C2
Oxshott Sur 28 C2
Oxspring S Yorks 88 D3
Oxted Sur 28 D4
Oxton Borders 123 D7
Oxton Notts 77 D6
Oxwich Swansea 33 F5
Oxwick Norf 80 E5
Oykel Bridge Highld 163 D7
Oyne Aberds 151 B5

P

Pabail Iarach W Isles 172 E8
Pabail Uarach W Isles 172 E8
Pace Gate N Yorks 94 D4
Packington Leics 63 C7
Padanaram Angus 142 D4
Padbury Bucks 52 F5
Paddington London 41 F5
Paddlesworth Kent 19 B8
Paddock Wood Kent 29 E7
Paddockhaugh Moray 159 D6
Paddockhole Dumfries 115 F5
Padfield Derbys 87 E8
Padiham Lancs 93 F7
Padog Conwy 83 F8
Padside N Yorks 94 D4
Padstow Corn 4 B4
Padworth W Berks 26 C4
Page Bank Durham 110 F5
Pagelsham Eastend Essex 43 E5
Pagham W Sus 16 E2
Paglesham Churchend Essex 43 E5
Paibeil W Isles 170 D3
Paible W Isles 173 J3
Paignton Torbay 7 C6
Paignton & Dartmouth Steam Railway Devon 7 C6
Paignton Zoo Torbay 7 D6
Pailton Warks 63 F8
Painscastle Powys 48 E3
Painshawfield Northumb 110 C3
Painsthorpe E Yorks 96 D4
Painswick Glos 37 D5
Pairc Shiaboist W Isles 172 D5
Paisley Renfs 120 C4
Pakefield Suff 69 E8
Pakenham Suff 56 C3
Palace House, Beaulieu Hants 14 D4
Palace of Holyroodhouse Edin 123 B5
Pale Gwyn 72 F3
Palestine Hants 25 E7
Paley Street Windsor 27 B6
Palfrey W Mid 62 E4
Palgowan Dumfries 112 F3
Palgrave Suff 56 B5
Pallion T & W 111 D6
Palmarsh Kent 19 B8
Palnackie Dumfries 106 D5
Palnure Dumfries 105 C8
Palterton Derbys 76 C4
Pamber End Hants 26 D4
Pamber Green Hants 26 D4
Pamber Heath Hants 26 C4
Pamphill Dorset 13 D7
Pampisford Cambs 55 E5
Pan Orkney 176 G2
Panbride Angus 143 F5
Pancrasweek Devon 8 D4
Pandy Gwyn 58 D3
Pandy Mon 35 B7
Pandy Powys 59 D6
Pandy Wrex 73 F5
Pandy Tudur Conwy 83 E8
Panfield Essex 42 B3
Pangbourne W Berks 26 B4
Pannal N Yorks 95 D6
Panshanger Herts 41 C5
Pant Shrops 60 B2
Pant-glas Carms 33 B6
Pant-glas Gwyn 71 C5
Pant-glâs Powys 58 E4
Pant-glas Shrops 73 F6
Pant Mawr Powys 59 F5
Pant-teg Carms 33 B5
Pant-y-Caws Carms 32 B2
Pant-y-dwr Powys 47 B8
Pant-y-ffridd Powys 59 D8
Pant-y-Wacco Flint 72 B5
Pant-yr-awel Bridgend 34 F3
Pantgwyn Ceredig 45 E4
Pantgwyn Carms 33 B6
Pantlasau Swansea 33 E7
Panton Lincs 78 B4
Pantperthog Gwyn 58 D4
Pantyffynnon Carms 33 C7
Pantymwyn Flint 73 C5
Panxworth Norf 69 C6
Papa Westray Airport Orkney 176 A3
Papcastle Cumb 107 F8
Papigoe Highld 169 D8
Papil Shetland 175 K5
Papley Orkney 176 G3
Papple E Loth 123 B8
Papplewick Notts 76 D5
Papworth Everard Cambs 54 C3
Papworth St Agnes Cambs 54 C3
Par Corn 5 D5
Paradise Wildlife Park, Broxbourne Herts 41 D6
Parbold Lancs 86 C2
Parbrook Som 23 F7
Parbrook W Sus 16 B4
Parc Gwyn 72 F2
Parc-Seymour Newport 35 E8
Parc-y-rhôs Carms 46 E4
Parcllyn Ceredig 45 D4
Pardshaw Cumb 98 B2
Parham Suff 57 C7
Park Dumfries 114 E2
Park Corner Oxon 39 F6
Park Corner Windsor 40 F1
Park End M'bro 102 C3
Park End Northumb 109 B8
Park Gate Hants 15 D6
Park Hill Notts 77 D6
Park Hill N Yorks 95 C6
Park Rose Pottery and Leisure Park, Bridlington E Yorks 97 C7
Park Street W Sus 28 F2
Parkend Glos 36 D3
Parkeston Essex 57 F6
Parkgate Ches 73 B6
Parkgate Dumfries 114 F3
Parkgate Kent 19 B5
Parkgate Sur 28 E3
Parkham Devon 9 B5
Parkham Ash Devon 9 B5
Parkhill Ho. Aberds 151 C7
Parkhouse Mon 36 D1
Parkhouse Green Derbys 76 C4
Parkhurst I o W 15 E5
Parkmill Swansea 33 F6
Parkneuk Aberds 143 B7

Predannack Wollas Corn 3 E5
Prees Shrops 74 F2
Prees Green Shrops 74 F2
Prees Heath Shrops 74 F2
Prees Higher Heath Shrops 74 F2
Prees Lower Heath Shrops 74 F2
Preesall Lancs 92 E3
Preesgweene Shrops 73 F6
Prenderguest Borders 124 D5
Prendwick Northumb 117 C6
Prengwyn Ceredig 46 E3
Prenteg Gwyn 71 C6
Prenton Mers 85 F4
Prescot Mers 86 E2
Prescott Shrops 60 B4
Pressen Northumb 124 F4
Prestatyn Denb 72 A4
Prestbury Ches 75 B6
Prestbury Glos 37 B6
Presteigne = Llanandras Powys 48 C5
Presthope Shrops 61 E5
Prestleigh Som 23 E8
Preston Borders 124 D3
Preston Brighton 17 D7
Preston Devon 7 B6
Preston Dorset 12 F5
Preston E Loth 123 B8
Preston E Yorks 97 F7
Preston Glos 37 D7
Preston Glos 49 F8
Preston Herts 40 B4
Preston Kent 30 C4
Preston Kent 31 C6
Preston Lancs 86 B3
Preston Northumb 117 B7
Preston Rutland 65 D5
Preston Shrops 60 C5
Preston Wilts 24 B5
Preston Wilts 25 B7
Preston Bagot Warks 51 C6
Preston Bissett Bucks 39 B6
Preston Bowyer Som 11 B6
Preston Brockhurst Shrops 60 B5
Preston Brook Halton 86 F3
Preston Candover Hants 26 E4
Preston Capes Northants 52 D3
Preston Crowmarsh Oxon 39 E6
Preston Gubbals Shrops 60 C4
Preston Hall Museum, Stockton-on-Tees Stockton 102 C2
Preston on Stour Warks 51 E7
Preston on the Hill Halton 86 F3
Preston on Wye Hereford 49 E5
Preston Plucknett Som 12 C3
Preston St Mary Suff 56 D3
Preston-under-Scar N Yorks 101 E5
Preston upon the Weald Moors Telford 61 C6
Preston Wynne Hereford 49 E7
Prestonmill Dumfries 107 D6
Prestonpans E Loth 123 B6
Prestwich Gtr Man 87 D6
Prestwick Northumb 110 B4
Prestwick S Ayrs 112 B3
Prestwood Bucks 40 D1
Price Town Bridgend 34 E3
Prickwillow Cambs 67 F5
Priddy Som 23 D7
Priest Hutton Lancs 92 B5
Priest Weston Shrops 60 E2
Priesthaugh Borders 115 D7
Primethorpe Leics 64 E2
Primrose Green Norf 68 C3
Primrose Valley N Yorks 97 B7
Primrosehill Herts 40 D3
Princes Gate Pembs 32 C2
Princes Risborough Bucks 39 D8
Princethorpe Warks 52 B2
Princetown Caerph 35 C5
Princetown Devon 6 B3
Prinknash Abbey, Gloucester Glos 37 C5
Prion Denb 72 C4
Prior Muir Fife 135 C7
Prior Park Northumb 125 D5
Priors Frome Hereford 49 F7
Priors Hardwick Warks 52 D2
Priors Marston Warks 52 D2
Priorslee Telford 61 C7
Priory Church, Lancaster Lancs 92 C4
Priory Wood Hereford 48 E4
Priston Bath 23 C8
Pristow Green Norf 68 F4
Prittlewell Sthend 42 F4
Privett Hants 15 B7
Prixford Devon 20 F4
Probus Corn 3 B7
Proncy Highld 164 E4
Prospect Cumb 107 E8
Prudhoe Northumb 110 C3
Ptarmigan Lodge Stirl 132 D2
Pubil Perth 140 E1
Puckeridge Herts 41 B6
Puckington Som 11 C8
Pucklechurch S Glos 23 B8
Pucknall Hants 14 B4
Puckrup Glos 50 F3
Puddinglake Ches 74 C4
Puddington Ches 73 B7
Puddington Devon 10 C3
Puddledock Norf 68 E3
Puddletown Dorset 13 E5
Pudleston Hereford 49 D7
Pudsey W Yorks 94 F5
Pulborough W Sus 16 C4
Puleston Telford 61 B7
Pulford Ches 73 D7
Pulham Dorset 12 D5
Pulham Market Norf 68 F4
Pulham St Mary Norf 68 F5
Pulloxhill Beds 53 F8
Pumpherston W Loth 122 C3
Pumsaint Carms 47 E5
Puncheston Pembs 32 B1
Puncknowle Dorset 12 F3
Punnett's Town E Sus 18 C3
Purbrook Hants 15 D7
Purewell Dorset 14 E2
Purfleet Thurrock 29 B6
Puriton Som 22 E5
Purleigh Essex 42 D4
Purley London 28 C4
Purley W Berks 26 B4
Purlogue Shrops 48 B4
Purls Bridge Cambs 66 F4
Purse Caundle Dorset 12 C4
Purslow Shrops 60 F3
Purston Jaglin W Yorks 88 C5
Purton Glos 36 D3
Purton Glos 36 D3
Purton Wilts 37 F7
Purton Stoke Wilts 37 E7
Pury End Northants 52 E5
Pusey Oxon 38 E3
Putley Hereford 49 F8
Putney London 28 B3
Putsborough Devon 20 E3
Puttenham Herts 40 C1
Puttenham Sur 27 E7
Puxton N Som 23 C6
Pwll Carms 33 D5
Pwll-glas Denb 72 D5
Pwll-trap Carms 32 C3
Pwll-y-glaw Neath 34 E1
Pwllcrochan Pembs 44 E4
Pwllgloyw Powys 48 F2
Pwllheli Gwyn 70 D4
Pwllmeyric Mon 36 E2
Pye Corner Newport 35 F7
Pye Green Staffs 62 C3
Pyecombe W Sus 17 C6
Pyewipe NE Lincs 91 C6
Pyle I o W 15 G5
Pyle = Y Pîl Bridgend 34 F2
Pylle Som 23 F8
Pymoor Cambs 66 F4
Pyrford Sur 27 D8
Pyrton Oxon 39 E6
Pytchley Northants 53 B6
Pyworthy Devon 8 D5

Q

Quabbs Shrops 60 F2
Quadring Lincs 78 F5
Quainton Bucks 39 C7
Quarley Hants 25 E7
Quarndon Derbys 76 E3
Quarrier's Homes Invclyd 120 C3
Quarrington Lincs 78 E3
Quarrington Hill Durham 111 F6
Quarry Bank W Mid 62 F3
Quarry Bank Mill, Wilmslow Ches 87 F6
Quarryford E Loth 123 C8
Quarryhill Highld 164 F4
Quarrywood Moray 159 C5
Quarter S Lnrk 121 D7
Quatford Shrops 61 E7
Quatt Shrops 61 F7
Quebec Durham 110 E4
Quedgeley Glos 37 C5
Queen Adelaide Cambs 67 F5
Queen Camel Som 12 B3
Queen Charlton Bath 23 C8
Queen Dart Devon 10 C3
Queen Oak Dorset 24 F2
Queen Street Kent 29 E7
Queen Street Wilts 37 F7
Queenborough Kent 30 B3
Queenhill Worcs 50 F3
Queen's Head Shrops 60 B3
Queen's Park Beds 53 E8
Queen's Park Northants 53 C5
Queen's View Centre, Loch Tummel Perth 141 D5
Queensbury W Yorks 94 F4
Queensferry Edin 122 B4
Queensferry Flint 73 C7
Queenstown Blkpool 92 F3
Queenzieburn N Lnrk 121 B6
Quemerford Wilts 24 C5
Quendale Shetland 175 M5
Quendon Essex 55 F6
Queniborough Leics 64 C3
Quenington Glos 37 D8
Quernmore Lancs 92 D5
Quethiock Corn 5 C8
Quholm Orkney 176 E1
Quicks Green W Berks 26 B3
Quidenham Norf 68 F3
Quidhampton Hants 26 D3
Quidhampton Wilts 25 F6
Quilquox Aberds 161 E6
Quina Brook Shrops 74 F2
Quindry Orkney 176 G3
Quinton Northants 53 D5
Quinton W Mid 62 F3
Quintrell Downs Corn 4 C3
Quixhill Staffs 75 E8
Quoditch Devon 9 E6
Quoig Perth 133 B7
Quorndon Leics 64 C2
Quothquan S Lnrk 122 F2
Quoyloo Orkney 176 D1
Quoyness Orkney 176 F1
Quoys Shetland 174 B8
Quoys Shetland 175 G6

R

Raasay Ho. Highld 153 F6
Rabbit's Cross Kent 29 E8
Raby Mers 73 B7
Rachan Mill Borders 122 F4
Rachub Gwyn 83 E6
Rackenford Devon 10 C3
Rackham W Sus 16 C4
Rackheath Norf 69 C5
Racks Dumfries 107 B7
Rackwick Orkney 176 G1
Rackwick Orkney 176 B3
Radbourne Derbys 76 F2
Radcliffe Gtr Man 87 D5
Radcliffe Northumb 117 D8
Radcliffe on Trent Notts 77 F6
Radclive Bucks 52 F4
Radcot Oxon 38 E2
Raddery Highld 157 D8
Radernie Fife 135 D6
Radford Semele Warks 51 C8
Radipole Dorset 12 F4
Radlett Herts 40 E4
Radley Oxon 39 E5
Radmanthwaite Notts 76 C5
Radmoor Shrops 61 B6
Radmore Green Ches 74 D2
Radnage Bucks 39 E7
Radstock Bath 23 D8
Radstone Northants 52 E3
Radway Warks 51 E8
Radway Green Ches 74 D4
Radwell Beds 53 D8
Radwell Herts 54 F3
Radwinter Essex 55 F7
Radyr Cardiff 35 F5
RAF Museum, Cosford Shrops 61 D7
RAF Museum, Hendon London 41 F5
Rafford Moray 158 D4
Ragdale Leics 64 C3
Raglan Mon 35 D8
Ragley Hall Warks 51 D5
Ragnall Notts 77 B8
Rahane Argyll 129 B7
Rainford Mers 86 D2
Rainford Junction Mers 86 D2
Rainham London 41 F8
Rainham Medway 30 C2
Rainhill Mers 86 E2
Rainhill Stoops Mers 86 E3
Rainow Ches 75 B6
Rainton N Yorks 95 B6
Rainworth Notts 77 D5
Raisbeck Cumb 99 D8
Raise Cumb 109 E7
Rait Perth 134 B4
Raithby Lincs 91 F7
Raithby Lincs 79 C6
Rake W Sus 16 B2
Rakewood Gtr Man 87 C7
Ram Carms 46 E4
Ram Lane Kent 30 E3
Ramasaig Highld 153 E2
Rame Corn 3 C6
Rame Corn 6 E2
Rameldry Mill Bank Fife 134 D5
Ramnageo Shetland 174 C8
Rampisham Dorset 12 D3
Rampside Cumb 92 C2
Rampton Cambs 54 C5
Rampton Notts 77 B7
Ramsbottom Gtr Man 87 C5
Ramsbury Wilts 25 B7
Ramscraigs Highld 165 B8
Ramsdean Hants 15 B8
Ramsdell Hants 26 D3
Ramsden Oxon 38 C3
Ramsden Bellhouse Essex 42 E3
Ramsden Heath Essex 42 E3
Ramsey Cambs 66 F2
Ramsey Essex 57 F6
Ramsey I o M 84 C4
Ramsey Forty Foot Cambs 66 F3
Ramsey Heights Cambs 66 F2
Ramsey Island Essex 43 D5
Ramsey Mereside Cambs 66 F2
Ramsey St Mary's Cambs 66 F2
Ramseycleuch Borders 115 C5
Ramsgate Kent 31 C7
Ramsgill N Yorks 94 B4
Ramshorn Staffs 75 E7
Ramsnest Common Sur 27 F7
Ranais W Isles 172 F7
Ranby Lincs 78 B5
Ranby Notts 89 F7
Rand Lincs 78 B4
Randwick Glos 37 D5
Ranfurly Renfs 120 C3
Rangag Highld 169 E6
Rangemore Staffs 63 B5
Rangeworthy S Glos 36 F3
Rankinston E Ayrs 112 C4
Ranmoor S Yorks 88 F4
Ranmore Common Sur 28 D2
Rannerdale Cumb 98 C3
Rannoch Station Perth 139 D8
Ranochan Highld 145 E8
Ranskill Notts 89 F7
Ranton Staffs 62 B2
Ranworth Norf 69 C6
Raploch Stirl 133 E6
Rapness Orkney 176 B4
Rascal Moor E Yorks 96 F4
Rascarrel Dumfries 106 E4
Rashiereive Aberds 151 B8
Raskelf N Yorks 95 B7
Rassau Bl Gwent 35 C5
Rastrick W Yorks 88 B2
Ratagan Highld 146 C2
Ratby Leics 64 D2
Ratcliffe Culey Leics 63 E7
Ratcliffe on Soar Leics 63 B8
Ratcliffe on the Wreake Leics 64 C3
Rathen Aberds 161 B7
Rathillet Fife 135 B5
Rathmell N Yorks 93 D8
Ratho Edin 122 B4
Ratho Station Edin 122 B4
Rathven Moray 159 C8
Ratley Warks 51 E8
Ratlinghope Shrops 60 E4
Rattar Highld 169 B7
Ratten Row Lancs 92 E4
Rattery Devon 6 C5
Rattlesden Suff 56 D3
Rattray Perth 142 E1
Raughton Head Cumb 108 E3
Raunds Northants 53 B7
Ravenfield S Yorks 89 E5
Ravenglass Cumb 98 E2
Ravenglass and Eskdale Railway & Museum Cumb 98 E2
Raveningham Norf 69 E6
Ravenscar N Yorks 103 D7
Ravenscraig Invclyd 129 C7
Ravensdale I o M 84 C3
Ravensden Beds 53 D8
Ravenseat N Yorks 100 D3
Ravenshead Notts 77 D5
Ravensmoor Ches 74 D3
Ravensthorpe Northants 52 B4
Ravensthorpe W Yorks 88 B3
Ravenstone Leics 63 C8
Ravenstone M Keynes 53 D6
Ravenstonedale Cumb 100 D2
Ravenstown Cumb 92 B3
Ravenstruther S Lnrk 122 E2
Ravensworth N Yorks 101 D6
Raw N Yorks 103 D7
Rawcliffe E Yorks 89 B7
Rawcliffe York 95 D8
Rawcliffe Bridge E Yorks 89 B7
Rawdon W Yorks 94 F5
Rawmarsh S Yorks 88 E5
Rawreth Essex 42 E3
Rawridge Devon 11 D7
Rawtenstall Lancs 87 B6
Raxton Aberds 161 E5
Raydon Suff 56 F4
Raylees Northumb 117 E5
Rayleigh Essex 42 E4
Rayne Essex 42 B3
Rayners Lane London 40 F4
Raynes Park London 28 C3
Reach Cambs 55 C6
Read Lancs 93 F7
Reading Reading 26 B5
Reading Street Kent 19 B6
Reagill Cumb 99 C8
Rearquhar Highld 164 E4
Rearsby Leics 64 C3
Reaster Highld 169 C7
Reawick Shetland 175 J5
Reay Highld 168 C4
Rechullin Highld 154 E4
Reculver Kent 31 C6
Red Dial Cumb 108 E2
Red Hill Worcs 50 D3
Red House Glass Cone, Wordsley W Mid 62 F2
Red Houses Jersey 17
Red Lodge Suff 55 B7
Red Rail Hereford 36 B2
Red Rock Gtr Man 86 D3
Red Roses Carms 32 C3
Red Row Northumb 117 E8
Red Street Staffs 74 D5
Red Wharf Bay Anglesey 82 C5
Redberth Pembs 32 D1
Redbourn Herts 40 C4
Redbourne N Lincs 90 E3
Redbrook Glos 36 C2
Redbrook Wrex 74 E2
Redburn Highld 157 C6
Redburn Highld 158 E3
Redburn Northumb 109 C7
Redcar Redcar 102 B4
Redcar Racecourse Redcar 102 B4
Redcastle Angus 143 D6
Redcastle Highld 157 E6
Redcliff Bay N Som 23 B6
Redding Falk 122 B2
Reddingmuirhead Falk 122 B2
Reddish Gtr Man 87 E6
Redditch Worcs 50 C5
Rede Suff 56 D2
Redenhall Norf 69 F5
Redesdale Camp Northumb 116 E4
Redesmouth Northumb 116 F4
Redford Aberds 143 B7
Redford Angus 143 E5
Redford Durham 110 F3
Redfordgreen Borders 115 C6
Redgorton Perth 134 B2
Redgrave Suff 56 B4
Redhill Aberds 160 E3
Redhill Aberds 151 D6
Redhill N Som 23 C7
Redhill Sur 28 D3
Redhouse Argyll 128 D3
Redhouses Argyll 126 C3
Redisham Suff 69 F7
Redland Bristol 23 B7
Redland Orkney 176 D2
Redlingfield Suff 57 B5
Redlynch Som 23 F9
Redlynch Wilts 14 B3
Redmarley D'Abitot Glos 50 F2
Redmarshall Stockton 102 B1
Redmile Leics 77 F7
Redmire N Yorks 101 E5
Redmoor Corn 5 C5
Rednal Shrops 60 B3
Redpath Borders 123 F8
Redpoint Highld 154 D3
Redruth Corn 3 B5
Redvales Gtr Man 87 D6
Redwick Newport 35 F8
Redwick S Glos 36 F2
Redworth Darl 101 B7
Reed Herts 54 F4
Reedham Norf 69 D7
Reedness E Yorks 89 B8
Reeds Beck Lincs 78 C5
Reepham Lincs 78 B3
Reepham Norf 81 E6
Reeth N Yorks 101 E5
Regaby I o M 84 C4
Regoul Highld 158 D2
Reiff Highld 162 C3
Reigate Sur 28 D3
Reighton N Yorks 97 B7
Reighton Gap N Yorks 97 B7
Reinigeadal W Isles 173 H5
Reiss Highld 169 D8
Rejerrah Corn 4 D2
Releath Corn 3 C5
Relubbus Corn 2 C4
Relugas Moray 158 E3
Remenham Wokingham 39 F7
Remenham Hill Wokingham 39 F7
Remony Perth 140 E4
Rempstone Notts 64 B2
Rendcomb Glos 37 D7
Rendham Suff 57 C7
Rendlesham Suff 57 D7
Renfrew Renfs 120 C5
Renhold Beds 53 D8
Renishaw Derbys 76 B4
Rennington Northumb 117 C8
Renton W Dunb 120 B3
Renwick Cumb 109 E5
Repps Norf 69 C7
Repton Derbys 63 B7
Reraig Highld 155 H4
Rescobie Angus 143 D5
Resipole Highld 137 B8
Resolis Highld 157 C7
Resolven Neath 34 D2
Reston Borders 124 C4
Reswallie Angus 143 D5
Retew Corn 4 D4
Retford Notts 89 F8
Rettendon Essex 42 E3
Rettendon Place Essex 42 E3
Revesby Lincs 79 C5
Revesby Bridge Lincs 79 C6
Rew Street I o W 15 E5
Rewe Devon 10 E4
Reydon Suff 57 B8
Reydon Smear Suff 57 B8
Reymerston Norf 68 D3
Reynalton Pembs 32 D1
Reynoldston Swansea 33 E5
Rezare Corn 5 B8
Rhaeadr Gwy = Rhayader Powys 47 C8
Rhandirmwyn Carms 47 E6
Rhayader = Rhaeadr Gwy Powys 47 C8
Rhedyn Gwyn 70 D3
Rhemore Highld 137 C6
Rhencullen I o M 84 C3
Rhes-y-cae Flint 73 B5
Rhewl Denb 72 C5
Rhewl Denb 73 E5
Rhian Highld 164 C2
Rhicarn Highld 162 B4
Rhiconich Highld 166 D4
Rhicullen Highld 157 B7
Rhidorroch Ho. Highld 163 E5
Rhifail Highld 168 E2
Rhigos Rhondda 34 D3
Rhilochan Highld 164 D4
Rhiroy Highld 163 F5
Rhisga = Risca Caerph 35 E6
Rhiw Gwyn 70 E3
Rhiwabon = Ruabon Wrex 73 E7
Rhiwbina Cardiff 35 F5
Rhiwbryfdir Gwyn 71 C7
Rhiwderin Newport 35 F6
Rhiwlas Gwyn 83 E5
Rhiwlas Gwyn 72 F3
Rhiwlas Powys 73 F5
Rhodes Gtr Man 87 D6
Rhodes Minnis Kent 31 E5
Rhodesia Notts 77 B5
Rhodiad Pembs 44 C2
Rhondda Rhondda 34 E3
Rhonehouse or Kelton Hill Dumfries 106 D4
Rhoose = Y Rhws V Glam 22 C2
Rhôs Carms 46 F2
Rhôs Neath 33 D8
Rhos-fawr Gwyn 70 D4
Rhos-goch Powys 48 E3
Rhos-hill Pembs 45 E3
Rhos-on-Sea Conwy 83 C8
Rhos-y-brithdir Powys 59 B8
Rhos-y-garth Ceredig 46 B5
Rhos-y-gwaliau Gwyn 72 F3
Rhos-y-llan Gwyn 70 D3
Rhos-y-Madoc Wrex 73 E7
Rhos-y-meirch Powys 48 C4
Rhosaman Carms 33 C8
Rhosbeirio Anglesey 82 B3
Rhoscefnhir Anglesey 82 D5
Rhoscolyn Anglesey 82 D2
Rhoscrowther Pembs 44 E4
Rhosesmor Flint 73 C6
Rhosgadfan Gwyn 82 F5
Rhosgoch Anglesey 82 C4
Rhoshirwaun Gwyn 70 E2
Rhoslan Gwyn 71 C5
Rhoslefain Gwyn 58 D2
Rhosllanerchrugog Wrex 73 E6
Rhosmaen Carms 33 B7
Rhosmeirch Anglesey 82 D4
Rhosneigr Anglesey 82 D3
Rhosnesni Wrex 73 D7
Rhosrobin Wrex 73 D7
Rhossili Swansea 33 F5
Rhosson Pembs 44 C2
Rhostryfan Gwyn 82 F4
Rhostyllen Wrex 73 E7
Rhosybol Anglesey 82 C4
RHS Garden, Wisley Sur 27 D8
Rhu Argyll 128 D3
Rhu Argyll 129 B7
Rhuallt Denb 72 B4
Rhuddall Heath Ches 74 C2
Rhuddlan Ceredig 46 E3
Rhuddlan Denb 72 B4
Rhue Highld 162 E4
Rhulen Powys 48 E3
Rhunahaorine Argyll 118 B4
Rhuthun = Ruthin Denb 72 D5
Rhyd Gwyn 71 C7
Rhyd Powys 59 D6
Rhyd-Ddu Gwyn 83 F5
Rhyd-moel-ddu Powys 48 B2
Rhyd-Rosser Ceredig 46 C4
Rhyd-uchaf Gwyn 72 F3
Rhyd-wen Gwyn 58 C4
Rhyd-y-clafdy Gwyn 70 D4
Rhŷd-y-foel Conwy 72 B3
Rhyd-y-fro Neath 33 D8
Rhyd-y-gwin Swansea 33 D7
Rhyd-y-meirch Mon 35 D7
Rhyd-y-meudwy Denb 72 D5
Rhyd-y-pandy Swansea 33 D7
Rhyd-y-sarn Gwyn 71 C7
Rhyd-yr-onen Gwyn 58 D3
Rhydaman = Ammanford Carms 33 C7
Rhydargaeau Carms 33 B5
Rhydcymerau Carms 46 F4
Rhydd Worcs 50 E3
Rhydding Neath 33 E8
Rhydfudr Ceredig 46 C4
Rhydlewis Ceredig 46 E2
Rhydlios Gwyn 70 D2
Rhydlydan Conwy 83 F8
Rhydness Powys 48 E3
Rhydowen Ceredig 46 E3
Rhydspence Hereford 48 E4
Rhydtalog Flint 73 D6
Rhydwyn Anglesey 82 C3
Rhydycroesau Shrops 73 F6
Rhydyfelin Ceredig 46 B4
Rhydyfelin Rhondda 34 F4
Rhydymain Gwyn 58 B5
Rhydymwyn Flint 73 C6
Rhyl = Y Rhyl Denb 72 A4
Rhymney = Rhymni Caerph 35 D5
Rhymni = Rhymney Caerph 35 D5
Rhynd Fife 135 B6
Rhynd Perth 134 B3
Rhynie Aberds 150 B3
Rhynie Highld 158 B2
Ribbesford Worcs 50 B2
Ribblehead N Yorks 93 B7
Ribbleton Lancs 93 F5
Ribchester Lancs 93 F6
Ribigill Highld 167 D7
Riby Lincs 91 D5
Riby Cross Roads Lincs 91 D5
Riccall N Yorks 96 F2
Riccarton E Ayrs 120 F4
Richards Castle Hereford 49 C6
Richings Park Bucks 27 B8
Richmond London 28 B2
Richmond N Yorks 101 D6
Rickarton Aberds 151 F7
Rickinghall Suff 56 B4
Rickleton T & W 111 D5
Rickling Essex 55 F5
Rickmansworth Herts 40 E3
Riddings Cumb 108 B4
Riddings Derbys 76 D4
Riddlecombe Devon 9 C8
Riddlesden W Yorks 94 E3
Riddrie Glasgow 121 C6
Ridge Dorset 13 F7
Ridge Hants 14 C4
Ridge Wilts 24 F4
Ridge Green Sur 28 E4
Ridge Lane Warks 63 E6
Ridgebourne Powys 48 C2
Ridgehill N Som 23 C7
Ridgeway Cross Hereford 50 E2
Ridgewell Essex 55 E8
Ridgewood E Sus 17 C8
Ridgmont Beds 53 F7
Riding Mill Northumb 110 C3
Ridleywood Wrex 73 D8
Ridlington Norf 69 A6
Ridlington Rutland 64 D5
Ridsdale Northumb 116 F5
Riechip Perth 141 E7
Riemore Perth 141 E7
Rienachait Highld 166 F2
Rievaulx N Yorks 102 F3
Rievaulx Abbey N Yorks 102 F3
Rift House Hrtlpl 111 F7
Rigg Dumfries 108 C2
Riggend N Lnrk 121 B7
Rigsby Lincs 79 B7
Rigside S Lnrk 121 F8
Riley Green Lancs 86 B4
Rileyhill Staffs 62 C5
Rilla Mill Corn 5 B7
Rillington N Yorks 96 B4
Rimington Lancs 93 E8
Rimpton Som 12 B4
Rimswell E Yorks 91 B7
Rinaston Pembs 44 C4
Ringasta Shetland 175 M5
Ringford Dumfries 106 D3
Ringinglow S Yorks 88 F3
Ringland Norf 68 C4
Ringles Cross E Sus 17 B8
Ringmer E Sus 17 C8
Ringmore Devon 6 E4
Ringorm Moray 159 E6
Ring's End Cambs 66 D3
Ringsfield Suff 69 F7
Ringsfield Corner Suff 69 F7
Ringshall Herts 40 C2
Ringshall Suff 56 D4
Ringshall Stocks Suff 56 D4
Ringstead Norf 80 C3
Ringstead Northants 53 B7
Ringwood Hants 14 D2
Ringwould Kent 31 E7
Rinmore Aberds 150 C3
Rinnigill Orkney 176 G2
Rinsey Corn 2 D4
Riof W Isles 172 E4
Ripe E Sus 18 D2
Ripley Derbys 76 D3
Ripley Hants 14 E2
Ripley N Yorks 95 C5
Ripley Sur 27 D8
Riplingham E Yorks 97 F5
Ripon N Yorks 95 B6
Ripon Cathedral N Yorks 95 B6
Ripon Racecourse N Yorks 95 C6
Rippingale Lincs 65 B7
Ripple Kent 31 E7
Ripple Worcs 50 F3
Ripponden W Yorks 87 C8
Rireavach Highld 162 E4
Risabus Argyll 126 E3
Risbury Hereford 49 D7
Risby Suff 55 C8
Risca = Rhisga Caerph 35 E6
Rise E Yorks 97 E7
Riseden E Sus 18 B3
Risegate Lincs 66 B2
Riseholme Lincs 78 B2
Riseley Beds 53 C8
Riseley Wokingham 26 C5
Rishangles Suff 57 C5
Rishton Lancs 93 F7
Rishworth W Yorks 87 C8
Rising Bridge Lancs 87 B5
Risley Derbys 76 F4
Risley Warr 86 E4
Risplith N Yorks 94 C5
Rispond Highld 167 C6
Rivar Wilts 25 C8
Rivenhall End Essex 42 C4
River Bank Cambs 55 C6
Riverhead Kent 29 D6
Rivington Lancs 86 C4
Roa Island Cumb 92 C2
Roachill Devon 10 B3
Road Green Norf 69 E5
Roade Northants 53 D5
Roadhead Cumb 108 B5
Roadmeetings S Lnrk 121 E8
Roadside Highld 169 C6
Roadside of Catterline Aberds 143 B8
Roadside of Kinneff Aberds 143 B8
Roadwater Som 22 F2
Roag Highld 153 E3
Roath Cardiff 22 B3
Rob Roy and Trossachs Visitor Centre, Callander Stirl 132 D5
Robert Burns Centre, Dumfries Dumfries 107 B6
Roberton Borders 115 C7
Roberton S Lnrk 114 B2
Robertsbridge E Sus 18 C4
Roberttown W Yorks 88 B2
Robeston Cross Pembs 44 E3
Robeston Wathen Pembs 32 C1
Robin Hood W Yorks 88 B4
Robin Hood Doncaster Sheffield International Airport S Yorks 89 E7
Robin Hood's Bay N Yorks 103 D7
Roborough Devon 9 C7
Roborough Devon 6 C3
Roby Mers 86 E2
Roby Mill Lancs 86 D3
Rocester Staffs 75 F8
Roch Pembs 44 C3
Roch Gate Pembs 44 C3
Rochdale Gtr Man 87 C6
Roche Corn 4 C4
Rochester Medway 29 C8
Rochester Northumb 116 E4
Rochester Castle Medway 29 C8
Rochester Cathedral Medway 29 C8
Rochford Essex 42 E4
Rock Corn 4 B4
Rock Northumb 117 B8
Rock Worcs 50 B2
Rock W Sus 16 C5
Rock Ferry Mers 85 F4
Rockbeare Devon 10 E5
Rockbourne Hants 14 C2
Rockcliffe Cumb 108 C3
Rockcliffe Dumfries 107 D5
Rockfield Highld 165 F6
Rockfield Mon 36 C1
Rockford Hants 14 D2
Rockhampton S Glos 36 E3
Rockingham Northants 65 E5
Rockingham Motor Speedway Northants 65 E6
Rockland All Saints Norf 68 E2
Rockland St Mary Norf 69 D6
Rockland St Peter Norf 68 E2
Rockley Wilts 25 B6
Rockwell End Bucks 39 F7
Rockwell Green Som 11 B6
Rodborough Glos 37 D5
Rodbourne Swindon 37 F8
Rodbourne Wilts 37 F6
Rodbourne Cheney Swindon 37 F8
Rodd Hereford 48 C5
Roddam Northumb 117 B6
Rodden Dorset 12 F4
Rode Som 24 D3
Rode Heath Ches 74 D5
Rodeheath Ches 75 C5
Roden Telford 61 C5
Rodhuish Som 22 F2
Rodington Telford 61 C5
Rodley Glos 36 C4
Rodley W Yorks 94 F5
Rodmarton Glos 37 E6
Rodmell E Sus 17 D8
Rodmersham Kent 30 C3
Rodney Stoke Som 23 D6
Rodsley Derbys 76 E2
Rodway Som 22 F4
Rodwell Dorset 12 G4
Roe Green Herts 54 F4
Roecliffe N Yorks 95 C6
Roehampton London 28 B3
Roesound Shetland 174 G5
Roffey W Sus 28 F2
Rogart Highld 164 D4
Rogart Station Highld 164 D4
Rogate W Sus 16 B2
Rogerstone Newport 35 F6
Roghadal W Isles 173 K3
Rogiet Mon 36 F1
Rogue's Alley Cambs 66 D3
Roke Oxon 39 E6
Roker T & W 111 D7
Rollesby Norf 69 C7
Rolleston Leics 64 D4
Rolleston Notts 77 D7
Rolleston-on-Dove Staffs 63 B6
Rolston E Yorks 97 E8
Rolvenden Kent 18 B5
Rolvenden Layne Kent 19 B5
Romaldkirk Durham 100 B4
Roman Baths & Pump Room, Bath Bath 24 C2
Romanby N Yorks 102 E1
Romannobridge Borders 122 E4
Romansleigh Devon 10 B2
Romford London 41 F8
Romiley Gtr Man 87 E7
Romney, Hythe and Dymchurch Light Railway Kent 19 B8
Romsey Hants 14 B4
Romsey Town Cambs 55 D5
Romsley Shrops 61 F7
Romsley Worcs 50 B4
Ronague I o M 84 E2
Rookhope Durham 110 E2
Rookley I o W 15 F6
Rooks Bridge Som 23 D5
Roos E Yorks 97 F8
Roosebeck Cumb 92 C2
Rootham's Green Beds 54 D2
Rootpark S Lnrk 122 D2
Ropley Hants 26 F4
Ropley Dean Hants 26 F4
Ropsley Lincs 78 F2
Rora Aberds 161 C7
Rorandle Aberds 151 C5
Rorrington Shrops 60 D3
Roscroggan Corn 3 B5
Rose Corn 4 D2
Rose Ash Devon 10 B2
Rose Green W Sus 16 E3
Rose Grove Lancs 93 F8
Rose Hill E Sus 17 C8
Rose Hill Lancs 93 F8
Rose Hill Suff 57 E5
Roseacre Kent 29 D8
Roseacre Lancs 92 F4
Rosebank S Lnrk 121 E8
Rosebrough Northumb 117 B7
Rosebush Pembs 32 B1
Rosecare Corn 8 E3
Rosedale Abbey N Yorks 103 E5
Roseden Northumb 117 B6
Rosefield Highld 158 D2
Rosehall Highld 164 D1
Rosehaugh Mains Highld 157 D7
Rosehearty Aberds 161 B6
Rosehill Shrops 74 F3
Roseisle Moray 158 C5
Roselands E Sus 18 E3
Rosemarket Pembs 44 E4

South Wheatley Corn 8 E4
South Wheatley Notts 89 F8
South Whiteness Shetland 175 J5
South Widcombe Bath 23 D7
South Wigston Leics 64 E2
South Willingham Lincs 91 F5
South Wingfield Derbys 76 D3
South Witham Lincs 65 C6
South Wonston Hants 26 F2
South Woodham Ferrers Essex 42 E4
South Wootton Norf 67 B6
South Wraxall Wilts 24 C3
South Zeal Devon 9 E8
Southall London 40 F4
Southam Glos 37 B6
Southam Warks 52 C2
Southampton Soton 14 C5
Southampton International Airport Hants 15 C5
Southborough Kent 29 E6
Southbourne Bmouth 14 E2
Southbourne W Sus 15 D8
Southburgh Norf 68 D2
Southburn E Yorks 97 D5
Southchurch Sthend 43 F5
Southcott Wilts 25 D6
Southcourt Bucks 39 C8
Southdean Borders 116 D2
Southdene Mers 86 E2
Southease E Sus 17 D8
Southend Argyll 118 F3
Southend W Berks 26 B3
Southend Wilts 25 B6
Southend Airport Essex 42 F4
Southend-on-Sea Sthend 42 F4
Southend Sea Life Centre Essex 42 E4
Southernden Kent 30 E2
Southerndown V Glam 21 B7
Southerness Dumfries 107 D6
Southery Norf 67 E6
Southfield Northumb 111 B5
Southfleet Kent 29 B7
Southgate Ceredig 46 B4
Southgate London 41 E5
Southgate Norf 81 E7
Southgate Swansea 33 F6
Southill Beds 54 E2
Southleigh Devon 11 E7
Southminster Essex 43 E5
Southmoor Oxon 38 E3
Southoe Cambs 54 C2
Southolt Suff 57 C5
Southorpe P'boro 65 D7
Southowram W Yorks 88 B2
Southport Mers 85 C4
Southpunds Shetland 175 L6
Southrepps Norf 81 D8
Southrey Lincs 78 C4
Southrop Glos 38 D1
Southrope Hants 26 E4
Southsea Ptsmth 15 E7
Southstoke Bath 24 C2
Southtown Norf 69 D8
Southtown Orkney 176 G3
Southwaite Cumb 108 E4
Southwark London 28 B4
Southwater W Sus 17 B5
Southwater Street W Sus 17 B5
Southway Som 23 E7
Southwell Dorset 12 G4
Southwell Notts 77 D6
Southwell Minster Notts 77 D7
Southwell Racecourse Notts 77 D7
Southwick Hants 15 D7
Southwick Northants 65 E7
Southwick T & W 111 D6
Southwick Wilts 24 D3
Southwick W Sus 17 D6
Southwold Suff 57 B9
Southwood Norf 69 D6
Southwood Som 23 F7
Soval Lodge W Isles 172 F6
Sowber Gate N Yorks 102 F1
Sowerby N Yorks 102 F2
Sowerby W Yorks 87 B8
Sowerby Bridge W Yorks 87 B8
Sowerby Row Cumb 108 F3
Sowood W Yorks 87 C8
Sowton Devon 10 E4
Soyal Highld 164 E2
Spa Common Norf 81 D8
Spacey Houses N Yorks 95 D6
Spadeadam Farm Cumb 109 B5
Spalding Lincs 66 B2
Spaldington E Yorks 96 F3
Spaldwick Cambs 54 B2
Spalford Notts 77 C8
Spanby Lincs 78 F3
Sparham Norf 68 C3
Spark Bridge Cumb 99 F5
Sparkford Som 12 B4
Sparkhill W Mid 62 F4
Sparkwell Devon 6 D3
Sparrow Green Norf 68 C2
Sparrowpit Derbys 87 F8
Sparsholt Hants 26 F2
Sparsholt Oxon 38 F3
Spartylea Northumb 109 E8
Spaunton N Yorks 103 F5
Spaxton Som 23 F7
Spean Bridge Highld 146 F5
Spear Hill W Sus 16 C5
Speen Bucks 39 E8
Speen W Berks 26 C2
Speeton N Yorks 97 B7
Speke Mers 86 F2
Speke Hall Mers 86 F2
Speldhurst Kent 29 E6
Spellbrook Herts 41 C7
Spelsbury Oxon 38 B3
Spelter Bridgend 34 E2
Spencers Wood Wokingham 26 C5
Spennithorne N Yorks 101 F6
Spennymoor Durham 111 F5
Spetchley Worcs 50 D3
Spetisbury Dorset 13 D7
Spexhall Suff 69 F6
Spey Bay Moray 159 C7
Speybridge Highld 149 B6
Speyview Moray 159 E6
Spilsby Lincs 79 C7
Spindlestone Northumb 125 F7
Spinkhill Derbys 76 B4
Spinningdale Highld 164 F3
Spirit of the West, St Columb Major Corn 4 C4
Spirthill Wilts 24 B4
Spital Hill S Yorks 89 E7
Spital in the Street Lincs 90 F3
Spitfire and Hurricane Memorial, Manston Kent 31 C7
Spithurst E Sus 17 C8
Spittal Dumfries 105 D7
Spittal E Loth 123 B7
Spittal Highld 169 D6
Spittal Northumb 125 D6
Spittal Pembs 44 C4
Spittal Stirl 132 F4
Spittal of Glenmuick Aberds 150 F2
Spittal of Glenshee Perth 141 B8
Spittalfield Perth 141 E8
Spixworth Norf 68 C5
Splayne's Green E Sus 17 B8
Spofforth N Yorks 95 D6
Spon End W Mid 51 B8
Spon Green Flint 73 C6
Spondon Derby 76 F4
Spooner Row Norf 68 E3
Sporle Norf 67 C8
Spott E Loth 124 B2
Spratton Northants 52 B5
Spreakley Sur 27 E6
Spreyton Devon 9 E8
Spridlington Lincs 90 F4
Spring Vale S Yorks 88 D3
Spring Valley I o M 84 E3
Springburn Glasgow 121 C6
Springfield Dumfries 108 C3
Springfield Essex 42 D3
Springfield Fife 134 C5
Springfield Moray 158 D4
Springfield W Mid 62 F4
Springhill Staffs 62 D3
Springholm Dumfries 106 C5
Springkell Dumfries 108 B2
Springside N Ayrs 120 F3
Springthorpe Lincs 90 F2
Springwell T & W 111 D5
Sproatley E Yorks 97 F7
Sproston Green Ches 74 C4
Sprotbrough S Yorks 89 D6
Sproughton Suff 56 E5
Sprouston Borders 124 F3
Sprowston Norf 68 C5
Sproxton Leics 65 B5
Sproxton N Yorks 102 F4
Spurstow Ches 74 D2
Spynie Moray 159 C6
Squires Gate Blkpool 92 F3
Srannda W Isles 173 K3
Sronphadruig Lodge Perth 140 B4
SS Great Britain Bristol 23 B7
Stableford Shrops 61 E7
Stableford Staffs 74 F5
Stacey Bank S Yorks 88 E3
Stackhouse N Yorks 93 C8
Stackpole Pembs 44 F4
Staddiscombe Devon 6 D3
Staddlethorpe E Yorks 90 B2
Stadhampton Oxon 39 E6
Stadhlaigearraidh W Isles 170 G3
Staffield Cumb 108 E5
Staffin Highld 152 C5
Stafford Staffs 62 B3
Stagsden Beds 53 E7
Stainburn Cumb 98 B2
Stainburn N Yorks 94 E5
Stainby Lincs 65 B6
Staincross S Yorks 88 C4
Staindrop Durham 101 B6
Staines Sur 27 B8
Stainfield Lincs 65 B7
Stainfield Lincs 78 B4
Stainforth N Yorks 93 C8
Stainforth S Yorks 89 C7
Staining Lancs 92 F3
Stainland W Yorks 87 C8
Stainsacre N Yorks 103 D7
Stainsby Derbys 76 C4
Stainton Cumb 99 F7
Stainton Cumb 99 B6
Stainton Durham 101 C5
Stainton M'bro 102 C2
Stainton N Yorks 101 E6
Stainton S Yorks 89 E6
Stainton by Langworth Lincs 78 B3
Stainton le Vale Lincs 91 E5
Stainton with Adgarley Cumb 92 B2
Staintondale N Yorks 103 E7
Stair Cumb 98 B4
Stair E Ayrs 112 B4
Stairhaven Dumfries 105 D6
Staithes N Yorks 103 C5
Stake Pool Lancs 92 E4
Stakeford Northumb 117 F8
Stalbridge Dorset 12 C5
Stalbridge Weston Dorset 12 C5
Stalham Norf 69 B6
Stalham Green Norf 69 B6
Stalisfield Green Kent 30 D3
Stalling Busk N Yorks 100 F4
Stallingborough NE Lincs 91 C5
Stalmine Lancs 92 E3
Stalybridge Gtr Man 87 E7
Stambourne Essex 55 F8
Stambourne Green Essex 55 F8
Stamford Lincs 65 D7
Stamford Bridge Ches 73 C8
Stamford Bridge E Yorks 96 D3
Stamfordham Northumb 110 B3
Stanah Cumb 99 C5
Stanborough Herts 41 C5
Stanbridge Beds 40 B2
Stanbridge Dorset 13 D8
Stanbrook Worcs 50 E3
Stanbury W Yorks 94 F3
Stand Gtr Man 87 D5
Stand N Lnrk 121 C7
Standburn Falk 122 B2
Standeford Staffs 62 D3
Standen Kent 30 E2
Standen, East Grinstead W Sus 28 F4
Standford Hants 27 F6
Standingstone Cumb 107 F7
Standish Gtr Man 86 C3
Standlake Oxon 38 D3
Standon Hants 14 B5
Standon Herts 41 B6
Standon Staffs 74 F5
Stane N Lnrk 121 D8
Stanfield Norf 80 E5
Stanford Beds 54 E2
Stanford Kent 19 B8
Stanford Bishop Hereford 49 D8
Stanford Bridge Worcs 50 C2
Stanford Dingley W Berks 26 B3
Stanford in the Vale Oxon 38 E3
Stanford-le-Hope Thurrock 42 F2
Stanford on Avon Northants 52 B3
Stanford on Soar Notts 64 B2
Stanford on Teme Worcs 50 C2
Stanford Rivers Essex 41 D8
Stanfree Derbys 76 B4
Stanghow Redcar 102 C4
Stanground P'boro 66 E2
Stanhoe Norf 80 D4
Stanhope Borders 114 B4
Stanhope Durham 110 F2
Stanion Northants 65 F6
Stanley Derbys 76 E4
Stanley Durham 110 D4
Stanley Lancs 86 D2
Stanley Perth 141 F8
Stanley Staffs 75 D6
Stanley W Yorks 88 B4
Stanley Common Derbys 76 E4
Stanley Gate Lancs 86 D2
Stanley Hill Hereford 49 E8
Stanlow Ches 73 B8
Stanmer Brighton 17 D7
Stanmore London 40 E4
Stanmore Hants 15 B5
Stanmore W Berks 26 B2
Stannergate Dundee 142 F4
Stanningley W Yorks 94 F5
Stannington Northumb 110 B5
Stannington S Yorks 88 F4
Stansbatch Hereford 48 C5
Stansfield Suff 55 D8
Stanstead Suff 56 E2
Stanstead Abbotts Herts 41 C6
Stansted Kent 29 C7
Stansted Mountfitchet Essex 41 B8
Stanton Glos 51 F5
Stanton Mon 35 B7
Stanton Northumb 117 F7
Stanton Staffs 75 E8
Stanton Suff 56 B3
Stanton by Bridge Derbys 63 B7
Stanton-by-Dale Derbys 76 F4
Stanton Drew Bath 23 C7
Stanton Fitzwarren Swindon 38 E1
Stanton Harcourt Oxon 38 D4
Stanton Hill Notts 76 C4
Stanton in Peak Derbys 76 C2
Stanton Lacy Shrops 49 B6
Stanton Long Shrops 61 E5
Stanton-on-the-Wolds Notts 77 F6
Stanton Prior Bath 23 C8
Stanton St Bernard Wilts 25 C5
Stanton St John Oxon 39 D5
Stanton St Quintin Wilts 24 B4
Stanton Street Suff 56 C3
Stanton under Bardon Leics 63 C8
Stanton upon Hine Heath Shrops 61 B5
Stanton Wick Bath 23 C8
Stanwardine in the Fields Shrops 60 B4
Stanwardine in the Wood Shrops 60 B4
Stanway Essex 43 B5
Stanway Glos 51 F5
Stanway Green Suff 57 B6
Stanwell Sur 27 B8
Stanwell Moor Sur 27 B8
Stanwick Northants 53 B7
Stanwick-St-John N Yorks 101 C6
Stanwix Cumb 108 D4
Stanydale Shetland 175 H4
Staoinebrig W Isles 171 G3
Stape N Yorks 103 E5
Stapehill Dorset 13 D8
Stapeley Ches 74 E3
Stapeley Water Gardens, Nantwich Ches 74 D3
Stapenhill Staffs 63 B6
Staple Kent 31 D6
Staple Som 22 E3
Staple Cross E Sus 18 C4
Staple Fitzpaine Som 11 C7
Staplefield W Sus 17 B6
Stapleford Cambs 55 D5
Stapleford Herts 41 C6
Stapleford Leics 64 C5
Stapleford Lincs 77 D8
Stapleford Notts 76 F4
Stapleford Wilts 25 F5
Stapleford Abbotts Essex 41 E8
Stapleford Tawney Essex 41 E8
Staplegrove Som 11 B7
Staplehay Som 11 B7
Staplehurst Kent 29 E8
Staplers I o W 15 F6
Stapleton Bristol 23 B8
Stapleton Cumb 108 B5
Stapleton Hereford 48 C5
Stapleton Leics 63 E8
Stapleton N Yorks 101 C7
Stapleton Shrops 60 D4
Stapleton Som 12 B2
Stapley Som 11 C6
Staploe Beds 54 C2
Staplow Hereford 49 E8
Star Fife 134 D5
Star Pembs 45 F4
Star Som 23 D6
Stara Orkney 176 D1
Starbeck N Yorks 95 D6
Starbotton N Yorks 94 B2
Starcross Devon 10 F4
Stareton Warks 51 B8
Starkholmes Derbys 76 D3
Starlings Green Essex 55 F5
Starston Norf 68 F5
Startforth Durham 101 C5
Startley Wilts 37 F6
Stathe Som 11 B8
Stathern Leics 77 F7
Station Town Durham 111 F7
Staughton Green Cambs 54 C2
Staughton Highway Cambs 54 C2
Staunton Glos 36 C2
Staunton Glos 36 B4
Staunton in the Vale Notts 77 E8
Staunton on Arrow Hereford 49 C5
Staunton on Wye Hereford 49 E5
Staveley Cumb 99 F5
Staveley Cumb 99 E6
Staveley Derbys 76 B4
Staveley N Yorks 95 C6
Staverton Devon 7 C5
Staverton Glos 37 B5
Staverton Northants 52 C3
Staverton Wilts 24 C3
Staverton Bridge Glos 37 B5
Stawell Som 23 F5
Staxigoe Highld 169 D8
Staxton N Yorks 97 B6
Staylittle Powys 59 E5
Staynall Lancs 92 E3
Staythorpe Notts 77 D7
Stean N Yorks 94 B3
Stearsby N Yorks 96 B2
Steart Som 22 E4
Stebbing Essex 42 B2
Stebbing Green Essex 42 B2
Stedham W Sus 16 B2
Steele Road Borders 115 E8
Steen's Bridge Hereford 49 D7
Steep Hants 15 B8
Steep Marsh Hants 15 B8
Steeple Dorset 13 F7
Steeple Essex 43 D5
Steeple Ashton Wilts 24 D4
Steeple Aston Oxon 38 B4
Steeple Barton Oxon 38 B4
Steeple Bumpstead Essex 55 E7
Steeple Claydon Bucks 39 B6
Steeple Gidding Cambs 65 F8
Steeple Langford Wilts 24 F5
Steeple Morden Cambs 54 E3
Steeton W Yorks 94 E3
Stein Highld 152 D3
Steinmanhill Aberds 160 D4
Stelling Minnis Kent 30 E5
Stemster Highld 169 C6
Stemster Ho. Highld 169 C6
Stenalees Corn 4 D5
Stenhousemuir Falk 133 F7
Stenigot Lincs 91 F6
Stenness Shetland 174 F4
Stenscholl Highld 152 C5
Stenso Orkney 176 D2
Stenson Derbys 63 B7
Stenton E Loth 124 B2
Stenton Fife 134 E4
Stenwith Lincs 77 F8
Stepaside Pembs 32 D2
Stepping Hill Gtr Man 87 F7
Steppingley Beds 53 F8
Stepps N Lnrk 121 C6
Sterndale Moor Derbys 75 C8
Sternfield Suff 57 C7
Sterridge Devon 20 E4
Stert Wilts 24 D5
Stetchworth Cambs 55 D7
Stevenage Herts 41 B5
Stevenston N Ayrs 120 E2
Steventon Hants 26 E3
Steventon Oxon 38 E4
Stevington Beds 53 D7
Stewartby Beds 53 E8
Stewarton Argyll 118 E3
Stewarton E Ayrs 120 E4
Stewkley Bucks 40 B1
Stewton Lincs 91 F7
Steyne Cross I o W 15 F7
Steyning W Sus 17 C5
Steynton Pembs 44 E4
Stibb Corn 8 C4
Stibb Cross Devon 9 C6
Stibb Green Wilts 25 C7
Stibbard Norf 81 E5
Stibbington Cambs 65 E7
Stichill Borders 124 F3
Sticker Corn 4 D4
Stickford Lincs 79 D6
Sticklepath Devon 9 E8
Stickney Lincs 79 D6
Stiffkey Norf 81 C5
Stifford's Bridge Hereford 50 E2
Stillingfleet N Yorks 95 E8
Stillington N Yorks 95 C8
Stillington Stockton 102 B1
Stilton Cambs 65 F8
Stinchcombe Glos 36 E4
Stinsford Dorset 12 E5
Stirchley Telford 61 D7
Stirkoke Ho. Highld 169 D8
Stirling Aberds 161 D8
Stirling Stirl 133 E6
Stirling Castle Stirl 133 E6
Stisted Essex 42 B3
Stithians Corn 3 C6
Stittenham Highld 157 B7
Stivichall W Mid 51 B8
Stixwould Lincs 78 C4
Stoak Ches 73 B8
Stobieside S Lnrk 121 F6
Stobo Borders 122 F4
Stoborough Dorset 13 F7
Stoborough Green Dorset 13 F7
Stobshiel E Loth 123 C7
Stobswood Northumb 117 E8
Stock Essex 42 E2
Stock Green Worcs 50 D4
Stock Wood Worcs 50 D5
Stockbridge Hants 25 F8
Stockbury Kent 30 C2
Stockcross W Berks 26 C2
Stockdalewath Cumb 108 E3
Stockerston Leics 64 E5
Stockheath Hants 15 D8
Stockiemuir Stirl 132 F4
Stocking Pelham Herts 41 B7
Stockingford Warks 63 E7
Stockland Devon 11 D7
Stockland Bristol Som 22 E4
Stockleigh English Devon 10 D3
Stockleigh Pomeroy Devon 10 D3
Stockley Wilts 24 C5
Stocklinch Som 11 C8
Stockport Gtr Man 87 E6
Stocksbridge S Yorks 88 E3
Stocksfield Northumb 110 C3
Stockton Hereford 49 C7
Stockton Norf 69 E6
Stockton Shrops 60 D2
Stockton Shrops 61 E7
Stockton Warks 52 C2
Stockton Wilts 24 F4
Stockton Heath Warr 86 F4
Stockton-on-Tees Stockton 102 C2
Stockton on Teme Worcs 50 C2
Stockton on the Forest York 96 D2
Stockwood Park Museum, Luton Luton 40 C3
Stodmarsh Kent 31 C6
Stody Norf 81 D6
Stoer Highld 162 B4
Stoford Som 12 C3
Stoford Wilts 25 F5
Stogumber Som 22 F2
Stogursey Som 22 E4
Stoke Devon 8 B4
Stoke Hants 26 D2
Stoke Hants 15 D8
Stoke Medway 30 B2
Stoke Suff 57 E5
Stoke Abbott Dorset 12 D2
Stoke Albany Northants 64 F5
Stoke Ash Suff 56 B5
Stoke Bardolph Notts 77 E6
Stoke Bliss Worcs 49 C8
Stoke Bruerne Northants 52 E5
Stoke by Clare Suff 55 E8
Stoke-by-Nayland Suff 56 F3
Stoke Canon Devon 10 E4
Stoke Charity Hants 26 F2
Stoke Climsland Corn 5 B8
Stoke D'Abernon Sur 28 D2
Stoke Doyle Northants 65 F7
Stoke Dry Rutland 65 E5
Stoke Farthing Wilts 13 B8
Stoke Ferry Norf 67 E7
Stoke Fleming Devon 7 E6
Stoke Gabriel Devon 7 D6
Stoke Gifford S Glos 23 B8
Stoke Golding Leics 63 E7
Stoke Goldington M Keynes 53 E6
Stoke Green Bucks 40 F2
Stoke Hammond Bucks 40 B1
Stoke Heath Shrops 61 B6
Stoke Holy Cross Norf 68 D5
Stoke Lacy Hereford 49 E8
Stoke Lyne Oxon 39 B5
Stoke Mandeville Bucks 39 C8
Stoke Newington London 41 F6
Stoke on Tern Shrops 61 B6
Stoke-on-Trent Stoke 75 E5
Stoke Orchard Glos 37 B6
Stoke Poges Bucks 40 F2
Stoke Prior Hereford 49 D7
Stoke Prior Worcs 50 C4
Stoke Rivers Devon 20 F5
Stoke Rochford Lincs 65 B6
Stoke Row Oxon 39 F6
Stoke St Gregory Som 11 B8
Stoke St Mary Som 11 B7
Stoke St Michael Som 23 E8
Stoke St Milborough Shrops 61 F5
Stoke sub Hamdon Som 12 C2
Stoke Talmage Oxon 39 E6
Stoke Trister Som 12 B5
Stoke Wake Dorset 13 D5
Stokeford Dorset 13 F6
Stokeham Notts 77 B7
Stokeinteignhead Devon 7 B7
Stokenchurch Bucks 39 E7
Stokenham Devon 7 E6
Stokesay Shrops 60 F4
Stokesby Norf 69 C7
Stokesley N Yorks 102 D3
Stolford Som 22 E4
Ston Easton Som 23 D8
Stondon Massey Essex 42 D1
Stone Bucks 39 C7
Stone Glos 36 E3
Stone Kent 19 C6
Stone Kent 29 B6
Stone Staffs 75 F6
Stone S Yorks 89 F6
Stone Worcs 50 B3
Stone Allerton Som 23 D6
Stone Bridge Corner P'boro 66 D2
Stone Chair W Yorks 88 B2
Stone Cross E Sus 18 E3
Stone Cross Kent 31 D7
Stone-edge Batch N Som 23 B6
Stone House Cumb 100 F2
Stone Street Kent 29 D6
Stone Street Suff 56 F3
Stone Street Suff 69 F6
Stonebroom Derbys 76 D4
Stoneferry Hull 97 F7
Stonefield S Lnrk 121 D6
Stonegate E Sus 18 C3
Stonegate N Yorks 103 D5
Stonegrave N Yorks 96 B2
Stonehaugh Northumb 109 B7
Stonehaven Aberds 151 F7
Stonehenge, Amesbury Wilts 25 E6
Stonehouse Glos 37 D5
Stonehouse Northumb 109 D6
Stonehouse S Lnrk 121 E7
Stoneleigh Warks 51 B8
Stonely Cambs 54 C2
Stoner Hill Hants 15 B8
Stone's Green Essex 43 B7
Stonesby Leics 64 B5
Stonesfield Oxon 38 C3
Stonethwaite Cumb 98 C4
Stoney Cross Hants 14 C3
Stoney Middleton Derbys 76 B2
Stoney Stanton Leics 63 E8
Stoney Stoke Som 24 F2
Stoney Stratton Som 23 F8
Stoney Stretton Shrops 60 D3
Stoneybreck Shetland 175 L3
Stoneyburn W Loth 122 C2
Stoneygate Aberds 161 E7
Stoneygate Leicester 64 D3
Stoneyhills Essex 43 E5
Stoneykirk Dumfries 104 D4
Stoneywood Aberdeen 151 C7
Stoneywood Falk 133 F6
Stonganess Shetland 174 C7
Stonham Aspal Suff 56 D5
Stonnall Staffs 62 D4
Stonor Oxon 39 F7
Stonton Wyville Leics 64 E4
Stony Cross Hereford 50 E2
Stony Stratford M Keynes 53 E5
Stonyfield Highld 157 B7
Stoodleigh Devon 10 C4
Stopes S Yorks 88 F3
Stopham W Sus 16 C4
Stopsley Luton 40 B4
Stores Corner Suff 57 E7
Storeton Mers 85 F4
Stornoway W Isles 172 E7
Stornoway Airport W Isles 172 E7
Storridge Hereford 50 E2
Storrington W Sus 16 C4
Storrs Cumb 99 E5
Storth Cumb 99 F6
Storwood E Yorks 96 E3
Stotfield Moray 159 B6
Stotfold Beds 54 F3
Stottesdon Shrops 61 F6
Stoughton Leics 64 D3
Stoughton Sur 27 D7
Stoughton W Sus 16 C2
Stoul Highld 145 D7
Stoulton Worcs 50 E4
Stour Provost Dorset 13 B5
Stour Row Dorset 13 B6
Stourbridge W Mid 62 F3
Stourhead Garden Wilts 24 F2
Stourpaine Dorset 13 D6
Stourport on Severn Worcs 50 B3
Stourton Staffs 62 F2
Stourton Warks 51 F7
Stourton Wilts 24 F2
Stourton Caundle Dorset 12 C5
Stove Orkney 176 C5
Stove Shetland 175 L6
Stoven Suff 69 F7
Stow Borders 123 E7
Stow Lincs 90 F2
Stow Lincs 78 F3
Stow Bardolph Norf 67 D6
Stow Bedon Norf 68 E2
Stow cum Quy Cambs 55 C6
Stow Longa Cambs 54 B2
Stow Maries Essex 42 E4
Stow-on-the-Wold Glos 38 B1
Stowbridge Norf 67 D6
Stowe Shrops 48 B5
Stowe-by-Chartley Staffs 62 B4
Stowe Green Glos 36 D2
Stowe House and Gardens, Buckingham Bucks 52 F4
Stowell Som 12 B4
Stowford Devon 9 F6
Stowlangtoft Suff 56 C3
Stowmarket Suff 56 D4
Stowting Kent 30 E5
Stowupland Suff 56 D4
Straad Argyll 129 D5
Strachan Aberds 151 E5
Stradbroke Suff 57 B6
Stradishall Suff 55 D8
Stradsett Norf 67 D6
Stragglethorpe Lincs 78 D2
Straid S Ayrs 112 E1
Straith Dumfries 113 F8
Straiton Edin 123 C5
Straiton S Ayrs 112 D3
Straloch Aberds 151 B7
Straloch Perth 141 C7
Stramshall Staffs 75 F7
Strang I o M 84 E3
Stranraer Dumfries 104 C4
Stratfield Mortimer W Berks 26 C4
Stratfield Saye Hants 26 C4
Stratfield Turgis Hants 26 D4
Stratford London 41 F6
Stratford Racecourse Warks 51 D6
Stratford St Andrew Suff 57 C7
Stratford St Mary Suff 56 F4
Stratford Sub Castle Wilts 25 F6
Stratford Tony Wilts 13 B8
Stratford-upon-Avon Warks 51 D6
Strath Highld 169 D7
Strath Highld 154 C3
Strathan Highld 146 E2
Strathan Highld 167 C7
Strathan Highld 162 B4
Strathaven S Lnrk 121 E7
Strathblane Stirl 121 B5
Strathcanaird Highld 163 D5
Strathcarron Highld 155 F5
Strathcoil Argyll 130 B2
Strathdon Aberds 150 C2
Strathellie Aberds 161 B7
Strathkinness Fife 135 C6
Strathmashie House Highld 147 E8
Strathmiglo Fife 134 C4
Strathmore Lodge Highld 169 E6
Strathpeffer Highld 157 D5
Strathrannoch Highld 156 B4
Strathtay Perth 141 D6
Strathvaich Lodge Highld 156 B4
Strathwhillan N Ayrs 119 C7
Strathy Highld 168 C3
Strathyre Stirl 132 C4
Stratton Corn 8 D4
Stratton Dorset 12 E4
Stratton Glos 37 D7
Stratton Audley Oxon 39 B6
Stratton on the Fosse Som 23 D8
Stratton St Margaret Swindon 38 F1
Stratton St Michael Norf 68 E5
Stratton Strawless Norf 81 E8
Stravithie Fife 135 C7
Streat E Sus 17 C7
Streatham London 28 B4
Streatley Beds 40 B3
Streatley W Berks 39 F5
Street Lancs 92 D5
Street N Yorks 103 D5
Street Som 23 F6
Street Dinas Shrops 73 F7
Street End Kent 30 D5
Street End W Sus 16 E2
Street Gate T & W 110 D5
Street Lydan Wrex 73 F8
Streethay Staffs 62 C5
Streetlam N Yorks 101 E8
Streetly W Mid 62 E4
Streetly End Cambs 55 E7
Strefford Shrops 60 F4
Strelley Notts 76 E5
Strensall York 96 C2
Stretcholt Som 22 E4
Strete Devon 7 E6
Stretford Gtr Man 87 E6
Strethall Essex 55 F5
Stretham Cambs 55 B6
Strettington W Sus 16 D2
Stretton Ches 73 D8
Stretton Derbys 76 C3
Stretton Rutland 65 C6
Stretton Staffs 62 C2
Stretton Staffs 63 B6
Stretton Warr 86 F4
Stretton Grandison Hereford 49 E8
Stretton-on-Dunsmore Warks 52 B2
Stretton-on-Fosse Warks 51 F7
Stretton Sugwas Hereford 49 E6
Stretton under Fosse Warks 63 F8
Stretton Westwood Shrops 61 E5
Strichen Aberds 161 C6
Strines Gtr Man 87 F7
Stringston Som 22 E3
Strixton Northants 53 C7
Stroat Glos 36 E2
Stromeferry Highld 155 G4
Stromemore Highld 155 G4
Stromness Orkney 176 F1
Stronaba Highld 146 F5
Stronachlachar Stirl 132 C3
Stronchreggan Highld 138 B4
Stronchrubie Highld 163 C6
Strone Argyll 129 B6
Strone Highld 147 B8
Strone Highld 146 F4
Strone Invclyd 129 C7
Stronmilchan Argyll 131 C7
Stronsay Airport Orkney 176 D5
Strontian Highld 138 C2
Strood Medway 29 C8
Strood Green Sur 28 E3
Strood Green W Sus 16 B4
Strood Green W Sus 28 F2
Stroud Glos 37 D5
Stroud Hants 15 B8
Stroud Green Essex 42 E4
Stroxton Lincs 78 F2
Struan Highld 153 F4
Struan Perth 141 C5
Strubby Lincs 91 F8
Strumpshaw Norf 69 D6
Strutherhill S Lnrk 121 E7
Struy Highld 156 F4
Stryt-issa Wrex 73 E6
Stuartfield Aberds 161 D6
Stub Place Cumb 98 E2
Stubbington Hants 15 D6
Stubbins Lancs 87 C5
Stubbs Cross Kent 19 B6
Stubb's Green Norf 69 E5
Stubbs Green Norf 69 E6
Stubhampton Dorset 13 C7
Stubton Lincs 77 E8
Stuckgowan Argyll 132 D2
Stuckton Hants 14 C2
Stud Green Windsor 27 B6
Studham Beds 40 C3
Studland Dorset 13 F8
Studley Warks 51 C5
Studley Wilts 24 B4
Studley Roger N Yorks 95 B5
Stump Cross Essex 55 E6
Stuntney Cambs 55 B6
Sturbridge Staffs 74 F5
Sturmer Essex 55 E7
Sturminster Marshall Dorset 13 D7
Sturminster Newton Dorset 13 C5
Sturry Kent 31 C5
Sturton N Lincs 90 D3
Sturton by Stow Lincs 90 F2
Sturton le Steeple Notts 89 F8
Stuston Suff 56 B5
Stutton N Yorks 95 E7
Stutton Suff 57 F5
Styal Ches 87 F6
Styrrup Notts 89 E7
Suainebost W Isles 172 B8
Suardail W Isles 172 E7
Succoth Aberds 159 F8
Succoth Argyll 131 E8
Suckley Worcs 50 D2
Suckquoy Orkney 176 H3
Sudborough Northants 65 F6
Sudbourne Suff 57 D8
Sudbrook Lincs 78 E2
Sudbrook Mon 36 F2
Sudbrooke Lincs 78 B3
Sudbury Derbys 75 F8
Sudbury London 40 F4
Sudbury Suff 56 E2
Suddie Highld 157 D7
Sudeley Castle and Gardens Glos 37 B7
Sudgrove Glos 37 D6
Suffield Norf 81 D8
Suffield N Yorks 103 E7
Sugnall Staffs 74 F4
Suladale Highld 152 D4
Sulaisiadar W Isles 172 E8
Sulby I o M 84 C3
Sulgrave Northants 52 E3
Sulham W Berks 26 B4
Sulhamstead W Berks 26 C4
Sulland Orkney 176 B4
Sullington W Sus 16 C4
Sullom Shetland 174 F5
Sullom Voe Oil Terminal Shetland 174 F5

Sul – Thu 251

Sully V Glam 22 C3
Sumburgh Shetland 175 N6
Sumburgh Airport Shetland 175 M5
Summer Bridge N Yorks 94 C5
Summer-house Darl 101 C7
Summercourt Corn 4 D3
Summerfield Norf 80 D3
Summergangs Hull 97 F7
Summerleaze Mon 35 F8
Summerlee Heritage Centre, Coatbridge N Lnrk 121 C7
Summersdale W Sus 16 D2
Summerseat Gtr Man 87 C5
Summertown Oxon 39 D5
Summit Gtr Man 87 D7
Sunbury-on-Thames Sur 28 C2
Sundaywell Dumfries 113 F8
Sunderland Argyll 126 C2
Sunderland Cumb 107 F8
Sunderland T & W 111 D6
Sunderland Bridge Durham 111 F5
Sundhope Borders 115 B6
Sundon Park Luton 40 B3
Sundown Adventure Land, Rampton Notts 77 B7
Sundridge Kent 29 D5
Sunipol Argyll 136 C4
Sunk Island E Yorks 91 C6
Sunningdale Windsor 27 C7
Sunninghill Windsor 27 C7
Sunningwell Oxon 38 D4
Sunniside Durham 110 F4
Sunniside T & W 110 D5
Sunnyhurst Blkburn 86 B4
Sunnylaw Stirl 133 E6
Sunnyside W Sus 28 F4
Sunton Wilts 25 D7
Surbiton London 28 C2
Surby I o M 84 E2
Surfleet Lincs 66 B2
Surfleet Seas End Lincs 66 B2
Surlingham Norf 69 D6
Sustead Norf 81 D7
Susworth Lincs 90 D2
Sutcombe Devon 8 C5
Suton Norf 68 E3
Sutors of Cromarty Highld 158 C2
Sutterby Lincs 79 B6
Sutterton Lincs 79 F5
Sutton Beds 54 E3
Sutton Cambs 54 B5
Sutton London 28 C3
Sutton Kent 31 E7
Sutton Mers 86 E3
Sutton Norf 69 B6
Sutton Notts 77 F7
Sutton Notts 89 F7
Sutton N Yorks 89 B5
Sutton Oxon 38 D4
Sutton P'boro 65 E7
Sutton Shrops 61 F7
Sutton Shrops 74 F3
Sutton Som 23 F8
Sutton Staffs 61 B7
Sutton Suff 57 E7
Sutton Sur 27 E8
Sutton S Yorks 89 C6
Sutton W Sus 16 C3
Sutton at Hone Kent 29 B6
Sutton Bassett Northants 64 E4
Sutton Benger Wilts 24 B4
Sutton Bonington Notts 64 B2
Sutton Bridge Lincs 66 B4
Sutton Cheney Leics 63 D8
Sutton Coldfield W Mid 62 E5
Sutton Courtenay Oxon 39 E5
Sutton Crosses Lincs 66 B4
Sutton Grange N Yorks 95 B5
Sutton Green Sur 27 D8
Sutton Howgrave N Yorks 95 B6
Sutton In Ashfield Notts 76 D4
Sutton-in-Craven N Yorks 94 E3
Sutton in the Elms Leics 64 E2
Sutton Ings Hull 97 F7
Sutton Lane Ends Ches 75 B6
Sutton Leach Mers 86 E3
Sutton Maddock Shrops 61 D7
Sutton Mallet Som 23 F5
Sutton Mandeville Wilts 13 B7
Sutton Manor Mers 86 E3
Sutton Montis Som 12 B4
Sutton on Hull Hull 97 F7
Sutton on Sea Lincs 91 F9
Sutton-on-the-Forest N Yorks 95 C8
Sutton on the Hill Derbys 76 F2
Sutton on Trent Notts 77 C7
Sutton St Edmund Lincs 66 C3
Sutton St James Lincs 66 C3
Sutton St Nicholas Hereford 49 E7
Sutton Scarsdale Derbys 76 C4
Sutton Scotney Hants 26 F2
Sutton under Brailes Warks 51 F8
Sutton-under-Whitestonecliffe N Yorks 102 F2
Sutton upon Derwent E Yorks 96 E3
Sutton Valence Kent 30 E2
Sutton Veny Wilts 24 E3
Sutton Waldron Dorset 13 C6
Sutton Weaver Ches 74 B2
Sutton Wick Bath 23 D7
Swaby Lincs 79 B6
Swadlincote Derbys 63 C7
Swaffham Norf 67 D8
Swaffham Bulbeck Cambs 55 C6
Swaffham Prior Cambs 55 C6
Swafield Norf 81 D8
Swainby N Yorks 102 D2
Swainshill Hereford 49 E6
Swainsthorpe Norf 68 D5
Swainswick Bath 24 C2
Swalcliffe Oxon 51 F8
Swalecliffe Kent 30 C5
Swallow Lincs 91 D5
Swallowcliffe Wilts 13 B7
Swallowfield Wokingham 26 C5
Swallownest S Yorks 89 F5
Swallows Cross Essex 42 E2
Swan Green Ches 74 B4
Swan Green Suff 57 B6
Swanage Dorset 13 G8
Swanage Railway Dorset 13 G8
Swanbister Orkney 176 F2
Swanbourne Bucks 39 B8
Swanland E Yorks 90 B3
Swanley Kent 29 C6
Swanley Village Kent 29 C6
Swanmore Hants 15 C6
Swannery, Abbotsbury Dorset 12 F3
Swannington Leics 63 C8
Swannington Norf 68 C4
Swanscombe Kent 29 B7
Swansea = Abertawe Swansea 33 E7
Swanton Abbott Norf 81 E8
Swanton Morley Norf 68 C3
Swanton Novers Norf 81 D6
Swanton Street Kent 30 D2
Swanwick Derbys 76 D4
Swanwick Hants 15 D6
Swarby Lincs 78 E3
Swardeston Norf 68 D5
Swarister Shetland 174 E7
Swarkestone Derbys 63 B7
Swarland Northumb 117 D7
Swarland Estate Northumb 117 D7
Swarthmoor Cumb 92 B2
Swathwick Derbys 76 C3
Swaton Lincs 78 F4
Swavesey Cambs 54 C4
Sway Hants 14 E3
Swayfield Lincs 65 B6
Swaythling Soton 14 C5
Sweet Green Worcs 49 C8
Sweetham Devon 10 E3
Sweethouse Corn 5 C5
Sweffling Suff 57 C7
Swepstone Leics 63 C7
Swerford Oxon 51 F8
Swettenham Ches 74 C5
Swetton N Yorks 94 B4
Swffryd Bl Gwent 35 E6
Swiftsden E Sus 18 C4
Swilland Suff 57 D5
Swillington W Yorks 95 F6
Swimbridge Devon 9 B8
Swimbridge Newland Devon 20 F5
Swinbrook Oxon 38 C2
Swinderby Lincs 77 C8
Swindon Glos 37 B6
Swindon Staffs 62 E2
Swindon Swindon 38 F1
Swine E Yorks 97 F7
Swinefleet E Yorks 89 B8
Swineshead Beds 53 C8
Swineshead Lincs 78 E5
Swineshead Bridge Lincs 78 E5
Swiney Highld 169 F7
Swinford Leics 52 B3
Swinford Oxon 38 D4
Swingate Notts 76 E5
Swingfield Minnis Kent 31 E6
Swingfield St Kent 31 E6
Swinhoe Northumb 117 B8
Swinhope Lincs 91 E6
Swining Shetland 174 G6
Swinithwaite N Yorks 101 F5
Swinnow Moor W Yorks 94 F5
Swinscoe Staffs 75 E8
Swinside Hall Borders 116 C3
Swinstead Lincs 65 B7
Swinton Borders 124 E4
Swinton Gtr Man 87 D5
Swinton N Yorks 94 B5
Swinton N Yorks 96 B3
Swinton S Yorks 88 E5
Swintonmill Borders 124 E4
Swithland Leics 64 C2
Swordale Highld 157 C6
Swordland Highld 145 D7
Swordly Highld 168 C2
Sworton Heath Ches 86 F4
Swydd-ffynnon Ceredig 47 C5
Swynnerton Staffs 75 F5
Swyre Dorset 12 F3
Sychtyn Powys 59 D6
Syde Glos 37 C6
Sydenham London 28 B4
Sydenham Oxon 39 D7
Sydenham Damerel Devon 6 B2
Syderstone Norf 80 D4
Sydling St Nicholas Dorset 12 E4
Sydmonton Hants 26 D2
Syerston Notts 77 E7
Syke Gtr Man 87 C6
Sykehouse S Yorks 89 C7
Sykes Lancs 93 D6
Syleham Suff 57 B6
Sylen Carms 33 D6
Symbister Shetland 175 G7
Symington S Ayrs 120 F3
Symington S Lnrk 122 F2
Symonds Yat Hereford 36 C2
Symondsbury Dorset 12 E2
Synod Inn Ceredig 46 D3
Syon Park & House London 28 B2
Syre Highld 167 E8
Syreford Glos 37 B7
Syresham Northants 52 E4
Syston Leics 64 C3
Syston Lincs 78 E2
Sytchampton Worcs 50 C3
Sywell Northants 53 C6

T

Taagan Highld 154 D6
Tàbost W Isles 172 B8
Tabost W Isles 172 G6
Tackley Oxon 38 B4
Tacleit W Isles 172 E4
Tacolneston Norf 68 E4
Tadcaster N Yorks 95 E7
Taddington Derbys 75 B8
Taddiport Devon 9 C6
Tadley Hants 26 C4
Tadlow Beds 54 E3
Tadmarton Oxon 51 F8
Tadworth Sur 28 D3
Tafarn-y-gelyn Denb 73 C5
Tafarnau-bach Bl Gwent 35 C5
Taff's Well Rhondda 35 F5
Tafolwern Powys 59 D5
Tai Conwy 83 E7
Tai-bach Powys 59 B8
Tai-mawr Conwy 72 E3
Tai-Ucha Denb 72 D4
Taibach Neath 34 F1
Taigh a Ghearraidh W Isles 170 C3
Tain Highld 164 F4
Tain Highld 169 C7
Tainant Wrex 73 E6
Tainlon Gwyn 82 F4
Tai'r-Bull Powys 34 B3
Tairbeart = Tarbert W Isles 173 H4
Tairgwaith Neath 33 C8
Takeley Essex 42 B1
Takeley Street Essex 41 B8
Tal-sarn Ceredig 46 D4
Tal-y-bont Ceredig 58 F3
Tal-y-Bont Conwy 83 E7
Tal-y-bont Gwyn 83 D6
Tal-y-bont Gwyn 71 E6
Tal-y-cafn Conwy 83 D7
Tal-y-llyn Gwyn 58 D4
Tal-y-wern Powys 58 D5
Talachddu Powys 48 F2
Talacre Flint 85 F2
Talardd Gwyn 59 B5
Talaton Devon 11 E5
Talbenny Pembs 44 D3
Talbot Green Rhondda 34 F4
Talbot Village Poole 13 E8
Tale Devon 11 D5
Talerddig Powys 59 D6
Talgarreg Ceredig 46 D3
Talgarth Powys 48 F3
Talisker Highld 153 F4
Talke Staffs 74 D5
Talkin Cumb 109 D5
Talla Linnfoots Borders 114 B4
Talladale Highld 154 C5
Tallarn Green Wrex 73 E8
Tallentire Cumb 107 F8
Talley Carms 46 F5
Tallington Lincs 65 D7
Talmine Highld 167 C7
Talog Carms 32 B4
Talsarn Carms 34 B1
Talsarnau Gwyn 71 D7
Talskiddy Corn 4 C4
Talwrn Anglesey 82 D4
Talwrn Wrex 73 E6
Talybont-on-Usk Powys 35 B5
Talygarn Rhondda 34 F4
Talyllyn Powys 35 B5
Talysarn Gwyn 82 F4
Talywain Torf 35 D6
Tame Bridge N Yorks 102 D3
Tamerton Foliot Plym 6 C2
Tamworth Staffs 63 D6
Tan Hinon Powys 59 F5
Tan-lan Conwy 83 E7
Tan-lan Gwyn 71 C7
Tan-y-bwlch Gwyn 71 C7
Tan-y-fron Conwy 72 C3
Tan-y-graig Anglesey 82 D5
Tan-y-graig Gwyn 70 D4
Tan-y-groes Ceredig 45 E4
Tan-y-pistyll Powys 59 B7
Tan-yr-allt Gwyn 82 F4
Tandem W Yorks 88 C2
Tanden Kent 19 B6
Tandridge Sur 28 D4
Tanerdy Carms 33 B5
Tanfield Durham 110 D4
Tanfield Lea Durham 110 D4
Tangasdal W Isles 171 L2
Tangiers Pembs 44 D4
Tangley Hants 25 D8
Tanglwst Carms 46 F2
Tangmere W Sus 16 D3
Tangwick Shetland 174 F4
Tank Museum, Bovington Dorset 13 F6
Tankersley S Yorks 88 D4
Tankerton Kent 30 C5
Tannach Highld 169 E8
Tannachie Aberds 151 F6
Tannadice Angus 142 D4
Tannington Suff 57 C6
Tansley Derbys 76 D3
Tansley Knoll Derbys 76 C3
Tansor Northants 65 E7
Tantobie Durham 110 D4
Tanton N Yorks 102 C3
Tanworth-in-Arden Warks 51 B6
Tanygrisiau Gwyn 71 C7
Tanyrhydiau Ceredig 47 C6
Taobh a Chaolais W Isles 171 J3
Taobh a Thuath Loch Aineort W Isles 171 H3
Taobh a Tuath Loch Baghasdail W Isles 171 H3
Taobh a'Ghlinne W Isles 172 G6
Taobh Tuath W Isles 173 K2
Taplow Bucks 40 F2
Tapton Derbys 76 B3
Tarbat Ho. Highld 157 B8
Tarbert Argyll 127 D4
Tarbert Argyll 128 D3
Tarbert Argyll 118 A3
Tarbert = Tairbeart W Isles 173 H4
Tarbet Argyll 132 D2
Tarbet Highld 166 E3
Tarbet Highld 145 D7
Tarbock Green Mers 86 F2
Tarbolton S Ayrs 112 B4
Tarbrax S Lnrk 122 D3
Tardebigge Worcs 50 C5
Tarfside Angus 142 B4
Tarland Aberds 150 D3
Tarleton Lancs 86 B2
Tarlogie Highld 164 F4
Tarlscough Lancs 86 C2
Tarlton Glos 37 E6
Tarnbrook Lancs 93 D5
Tarporley Ches 74 C2
Tarr Som 22 F3
Tarrant Crawford Dorset 13 D7
Tarrant Gunville Dorset 13 C7
Tarrant Hinton Dorset 13 C7
Tarrant Keyneston Dorset 13 D7
Tarrant Launceston Dorset 13 D7
Tarrant Monkton Dorset 13 D7
Tarrant Rawston Dorset 13 D7
Tarrant Rushton Dorset 13 D7
Tarrel Highld 165 F5
Tarring Neville E Sus 17 D8
Tarrington Hereford 49 E8
Tarsappie Perth 134 B3
Tarskavaig Highld 145 C5
Tarves Aberds 161 E5
Tarvie Highld 156 D5
Tarvie Perth 141 C7
Tarvin Ches 73 C8
Tasburgh Norf 68 E5
Tasley Shrops 61 E6
Taston Oxon 38 B3
Tate Gallery London 28 B3
Tate Gallery, Albert Dock Mers 85 F4
Tate Modern London 28 B4
Tate St Ives Corn 2 B4
Tatenhill Staffs 63 B6
Tathall End M Keynes 53 E6
Tatham Lancs 93 C6
Tathwell Lincs 91 F7
Tatling End Bucks 40 F3
Tatsfield Sur 28 D5
Tattenhall Ches 73 D8
Tattenhoe M Keynes 53 F6
Tatterford Norf 80 E4
Tattersett Norf 80 D4
Tattershall Lincs 78 D5
Tattershall Bridge Lincs 78 D4
Tattershall Thorpe Lincs 78 D5
Tattingstone Suff 56 F5
Tatton House, Knutsford Ches 86 F5
Tatworth Som 11 D8
Taunton Som 11 B7
Taunton Racecourse Som 11 B7
Taverham Norf 68 C4
Tavernspite Pembs 32 C2
Tavistock Devon 6 B2
Taw Green Devon 9 E8
Tawstock Devon 9 B7
Taxal Derbys 75 B7
Tay Bridge Dundee 135 B6
Tayinloan Argyll 118 B3
Taymouth Castle Perth 140 E4
Taynish Argyll 128 B2
Taynton Glos 36 B4
Taynton Oxon 38 C2
Taynuilt Argyll 131 B6
Tayport Fife 135 B6
Tayvallich Argyll 128 B2
Tealby Lincs 91 E5
Tealing Angus 142 F4
Teangue Highld 145 C6
Teanna Mhachair W Isles 170 D3
Tebay Cumb 99 D8
Tebworth Beds 40 B2
Tedburn St Mary Devon 10 E3
Teddington Glos 50 F4
Teddington London 28 B2
Tedstone Delamere Hereford 49 D8
Tedstone Wafre Hereford 49 D8
Teeton Northants 52 B4
Teffont Evias Wilts 24 F4
Teffont Magna Wilts 24 F4
Tegryn Pembs 45 F4
Teigh Rutland 65 C5
Teigncombe Devon 9 F8
Teigngrace Devon 7 B6
Teignmouth Devon 7 B7
Telford Telford 61 D6
Telham E Sus 18 D4
Tellisford Som 24 D3
Telscombe E Sus 17 D8
Telscombe Cliffs E Sus 17 D7
Templand Dumfries 114 F3
Temple Corn 5 B6
Temple Glasgow 120 C5
Temple Midloth 123 D6
Temple Balsall W Mid 51 B7
Temple Bar Ceredig 46 D4
Temple Bar Carms 33 C6
Temple Cloud Bath 23 D8
Temple Combe Som 12 B5
Temple Ewell Kent 31 E6
Temple Grafton Warks 51 D6
Temple Guiting Glos 37 B7
Temple Herdewyke Warks 51 D8
Temple Hirst N Yorks 89 B7
Temple Normanton Derbys 76 C4
Temple Sowerby Cumb 99 B8
Templehall Fife 134 E4
Templeton Devon 10 C3
Templeton Pembs 32 C2
Templeton Bridge Devon 10 C3
Templetown Durham 110 D4
Tempsford Beds 54 D2
Ten Mile Bank Norf 67 E6
Tenbury Wells Worcs 49 C7
Tenby = Dinbych-y-Pysgod Pembs 32 D2
Tendring Essex 43 B7
Tendring Green Essex 43 B7
Tenston Orkney 176 E1
Tenterden Kent 19 B5
Terling Essex 42 C3
Ternhill Shrops 74 F3
Terregles Banks Dumfries 107 B6
Terrick Bucks 39 D8
Terrington N Yorks 96 B2
Terrington St Clement Norf 66 C5
Terrington St John Norf 66 C5
Teston Kent 29 D8
Testwood Hants 14 C4
Tetbury Glos 37 E5
Tetbury Upton Glos 37 E5
Tetchill Shrops 73 F7
Tetcott Devon 8 E5
Tetford Lincs 79 B6
Tetney Lincs 91 D7
Tetney Lock Lincs 91 D7
Tetsworth Oxon 39 D6
Tettenhall W Mid 62 E2
Teuchan Aberds 161 E7
Teversal Notts 76 C4
Teversham Cambs 55 D5
Teviothead Borders 115 D7
Tewel Aberds 151 F7
Tewin Herts 41 C5
Tewkesbury Glos 50 F3
Tewkesbury Abbey Glos 50 F3
Teynham Kent 30 C3
Thackthwaite Cumb 98 B3
Thainston Aberds 143 B6
Thakeham W Sus 16 C5
Thame Oxon 39 D7
Thames Ditton Sur 28 C2
Thames Haven Thurrock 42 F3
Thamesmead London 41 F7
Thanington Kent 30 D5
Thankerton S Lnrk 122 F2
Tharston Norf 68 E4
Thatcham W Berks 26 C3
Thatto Heath Mers 86 E3
Thaxted Essex 55 F7
The Aird Highld 152 D5
The All England Jumping Course, Hickstead W Sus 17 C6
The Arms Norf 67 E8
The Bage Hereford 48 E4
The Balloch Perth 133 C7
The Barony Orkney 176 D1
The Bluebell Railway, Sheffield Park E Sus 17 B8
The Bog Shrops 60 E3
The Bourne Sur 27 E6
The Braes Highld 153 F6
The Broad Hereford 49 C6
The Burrell Collection Glasgow 121 C5
The Butts Som 24 E2
The Camp Glos 37 D6
The Camp Herts 40 D4
The Chequer Wrex 73 E8
The City Bucks 39 E7
The Common Wilts 25 F7
The Craigs Highld 164 E1
The Cronk I o M 84 C3
The Dell Suff 69 E7
The Den N Ayrs 120 D3
The Dinosaur Museum, Dorchester Dorset 12 E4
The Eals Northumb 116 F3
The Eaves Glos 36 D3
The Flatt Cumb 109 B5
The Four Alls Shrops 74 F3
The Friars, Aylesford Kent 29 D8
The Garths Shetland 174 B8
The Green Cumb 98 F3
The Green Wilts 24 F3
The Grove Dumfries 107 B6
The Hall Shetland 174 D8
The Haven W Sus 27 F8
The Heath Norf 81 E7
The Heath Suff 56 F5
The Hill Cumb 98 F3
The Howe Cumb 99 F6
The Howe I o M 84 F1
The Hundred Hereford 49 C7
The Lee Bucks 40 D2
The Lhen I o M 84 B3
The Living RainForest W Berks 26 B3
The Long Man of Wilmington E Sus 18 E2
The Lost Gardens of Heligan, Mevagissey Corn 4 E4
The Lowry, Salford Gtr Man 87 E6
The Marsh Powys 60 E3
The Marsh Wilts 37 F7
The Middles Durham 110 D5
The Moor Kent 18 C4
The Moors Centre, Danby N Yorks 103 D5
The Mumbles = Y Mwmbwls Swansea 33 F7
The Murray S Lnrk 121 D6
The National Archives, Kew London 28 B3
The National Tramway Museum, Crich Derbys 76 D3
The Needles Old Battery I o W 14 F3
The Neuk Aberds 151 E6
The Oval Bath 24 C2
The Oval Cricket Ground London 28 B4
The Oxford Story, Oxford Oxon 39 D5
The Pole of Itlaw Aberds 160 C3
The Quarry Glos 36 E4
The Rhos Pembs 32 C1
The Rock Telford 61 D6
The Ryde Herts 41 D5
The Sands Sur 27 E6
The Stocks Kent 19 C6
The Tales of Robin Hood Nottingham 77 E5
The Throat Wokingham 27 C6
The Tutankhamun Exhibition, Dorchester Dorset 12 E4
The Vauld Hereford 49 E7
The Vyne Hants 26 D4
The World of Beatrix Potter, Bowness-on-Windermere Cumb 99 E6
The Wyke Shrops 61 D7
Theakston N Yorks 101 F8
Thealby N Lincs 90 C2
Theale Som 23 E6
Theale W Berks 26 B4
Thearne E Yorks 97 F6
Theberton Suff 57 C8
Theddingworth Leics 64 F3
Theddlethorpe All Saints Lincs 91 F8
Theddlethorpe St Helen Lincs 91 F8
Thelbridge Barton Devon 10 C2
Thelnetham Suff 56 B4
Thelveton Norf 68 F4
Thelwall Warr 86 F4
Themelthorpe Norf 81 E6
Thenford Northants 52 E3
Therfield Herts 54 F4
Thetford Lincs 65 C8
Thetford Norf 67 F8
Theydon Bois Essex 41 E7
Thickwood Wilts 24 B3
Thimbleby Lincs 78 C5
Thimbleby N Yorks 102 E2
Thingwall Mers 85 F3
Thirdpart N Ayrs 119 B8
Thirlby N Yorks 102 F2
Thirlestane Borders 123 E8
Thirn N Yorks 101 F7
Thirsk N Yorks 102 F2
Thirsk Racecourse N Yorks 102 F2
Thirtleby E Yorks 97 F7
Thistleton Lancs 92 F4
Thistleton Rutland 65 C6
Thistley Green Suff 55 B7
Thixendale N Yorks 96 C4
Thockrington Northumb 110 B2
Tholomas Drove Cambs 66 D3
Tholthorpe N Yorks 95 C7
Thomas Chapel Pembs 32 D2
Thomas Close Cumb 108 E4
Thomastown Aberds 160 E2
Thompson Norf 68 E2
Thomshill Moray 159 D6
Thong Kent 29 B7
Thongsbridge W Yorks 88 D2
Thoralby N Yorks 101 F5
Thoresway Lincs 91 E5
Thorganby Lincs 91 E6
Thorganby N Yorks 96 E2
Thorgill N Yorks 103 E5
Thorington Suff 57 B8
Thorington Street Suff 56 F4
Thorlby N Yorks 94 D2
Thorley Herts 41 C7
Thorley Street Herts 41 C7
Thorley Street I o W 14 F4
Thormanby N Yorks 95 B7
Thornaby on Tees Stockton 102 C2
Thornage Norf 81 D6
Thornborough Bucks 52 F5
Thornborough N Yorks 95 B5
Thornbury Devon 9 D6
Thornbury Hereford 49 D8
Thornbury S Glos 36 E3
Thornbury W Yorks 94 F4
Thornby Northants 52 B4
Thorncliffe Staffs 75 D7
Thorncombe Dorset 11 D8
Thorncombe Dorset 13 D6
Thorncombe Street Sur 27 E8
Thorncote Green Beds 54 E2
Thorncross I o W 14 F5
Thorndon Suff 56 C5
Thorndon Cross Devon 9 E7
Thorne S Yorks 89 C7
Thorne St Margaret Som 11 B5
Thorner W Yorks 95 E6
Thorney Notts 77 B8
Thorney P'boro 66 D2
Thorney Crofts E Yorks 91 B6
Thorney Green Suff 56 C4
Thorney Hill Hants 14 E2
Thorney Toll Cambs 66 D3
Thornfalcon Som 11 B7
Thornford Dorset 12 C4
Thorngumbald E Yorks 91 B6
Thornham Norf 80 C3
Thornham Magna Suff 56 B5
Thornham Parva Suff 56 B5
Thornhaugh P'boro 65 D7
Thornhill Caerph 35 F5
Thornhill Cumb 98 D2
Thornhill Derbys 88 F2
Thornhill Dumfries 113 E8
Thornhill Soton 15 C5
Thornhill Stirl 133 E5
Thornhill W Yorks 88 C3
Thornhill Edge W Yorks 88 C3
Thornhill Lees W Yorks 88 C3
Thornholme E Yorks 97 C7
Thornley Durham 110 F4
Thornley Durham 111 F6
Thornliebank E Renf 120 D5
Thorns Suff 55 D8
Thorns Green Ches 87 F5
Thornsett Derbys 87 F8
Thornthwaite Cumb 98 B4
Thornthwaite N Yorks 94 D4
Thornton Angus 142 E3
Thornton Bucks 53 F5
Thornton E Yorks 96 E3
Thornton Fife 134 E4
Thornton Lancs 92 E3
Thornton Leics 63 D8
Thornton Lincs 78 C5
Thornton Mers 85 D4
Thornton M'bro 102 C2
Thornton Northumb 125 E5
Thornton Pembs 44 E4
Thornton W Yorks 94 F4
Thornton Curtis N Lincs 90 C4
Thornton Heath London 28 C4
Thornton Hough Mers 85 F4
Thornton in Craven N Yorks 94 E2
Thornton-le-Beans N Yorks 102 E1
Thornton-le-Clay N Yorks 96 C2
Thornton-le-Dale N Yorks 103 F6
Thornton le Moor Lincs 90 E4
Thornton-le-Moor N Yorks 102 F1
Thornton-le-Moors Ches 73 B8
Thornton-le-Street N Yorks 102 F2
Thornton Rust N Yorks 100 F4
Thornton Steward N Yorks 101 F6
Thornton Watlass N Yorks 101 F7
Thorntonhall S Lnrk 121 D5
Thorntonloch E Loth 124 B3
Thorntonpark Northumb 124 E5
Thornwood Common Essex 41 D7
Thornydykes Borders 124 E2
Thoroton Notts 77 E7
Thorp Arch W Yorks 95 E7
Thorpe Derbys 75 D8
Thorpe E Yorks 97 E5
Thorpe Lincs 91 F8
Thorpe Norf 69 E7
Thorpe Notts 77 E7
Thorpe N Yorks 94 C3
Thorpe Sur 27 C8
Thorpe Abbotts Norf 57 B5
Thorpe Acre Leics 64 B2
Thorpe Arnold Leics 64 B4
Thorpe Audlin W Yorks 89 C5
Thorpe Bassett N Yorks 96 B4
Thorpe Bay Sthend 43 F5
Thorpe by Water Rutland 65 E5
Thorpe Common Suff 57 F6
Thorpe Constantine Staffs 63 D6
Thorpe Culvert Lincs 79 C7
Thorpe End Norf 69 C5
Thorpe Fendykes Lincs 79 C7
Thorpe Green Essex 43 B7
Thorpe Green Suff 56 D3
Thorpe Hesley S Yorks 88 E4
Thorpe in Balne S Yorks 89 C6
Thorpe in the Fallows Lincs 90 F3
Thorpe Langton Leics 64 E4
Thorpe Larches Durham 102 B1
Thorpe-le-Soken Essex 43 B7
Thorpe le Street E Yorks 96 E4
Thorpe Malsor Northants 53 B6
Thorpe Mandeville Northants 52 E3
Thorpe Market Norf 81 D8
Thorpe Marriot Norf 68 C4
Thorpe Morieux Suff 56 D3
Thorpe on the Hill Lincs 78 C2
Thorpe Park, Chertsey Sur 27 C8
Thorpe St Andrew Norf 69 D5
Thorpe St Peter Lincs 79 C7
Thorpe Salvin S Yorks 89 F6
Thorpe Satchville Leics 64 C4
Thorpe Thewles Stockton 102 B2
Thorpe Tilney Lincs 78 D4
Thorpe Underwood N Yorks 95 D7
Thorpe Waterville Northants 65 F7
Thorpe Willoughby N Yorks 95 F8
Thorpeness Suff 57 D8
Thorrington Essex 43 C6
Thorverton Devon 10 D4
Thrandeston Suff 56 B5
Thrapston Northants 53 B7
Thrashbush N Lnrk 121 C7
Threapland Cumb 107 F8
Threapland N Yorks 94 C2
Threapwood Ches 73 E8
Threapwood Staffs 75 E7
Threave Gardens Dumfries 106 C4
Three Ashes Hereford 36 B2
Three Bridges W Sus 28 F3
Three Burrows Corn 3 B6
Three Chimneys Kent 18 B5
Three Cocks Powys 48 F3
Three Counties Showground, Malvern Worcs 50 E2
Three Crosses Swansea 33 E6
Three Cups Corner E Sus 18 C3
Three Holes Norf 66 D5
Three Leg Cross E Sus 18 B3
Three Legged Cross Dorset 13 D8
Three Oaks E Sus 18 D5
Threehammer Common Norf 69 C6
Threekingham Lincs 78 F3
Threemile Cross Wokingham 26 C5
Threemilestone Corn 3 B6
Threemiletown W Loth 122 B3
Threlkeld Cumb 99 B5
Threshfield N Yorks 94 C2
Thrigby Norf 69 C7
Thringarth Durham 100 B4
Thringstone Leics 63 C8
Thrintoft N Yorks 101 E8
Thriplow Cambs 54 E5
Throckenholt Lincs 66 D3
Throcking Herts 54 F4
Throckley T & W 110 C4
Throckmorton Worcs 50 E4
Throphill Northumb 117 F7
Thropton Northumb 117 D6
Throsk Stirl 133 E7
Throwleigh Devon 9 E8
Throwley Kent 30 D3
Thrumpton Notts 76 F5
Thrumster Highld 169 E8
Thrunton Northumb 117 C6
Thrupp Glos 37 D5
Thrupp Oxon 38 C4
Thrushelton Devon 9 F6
Thrussington Leics 64 C3
Thruxton Hants 25 E7
Thruxton Hereford 49 F6
Thruxton Motor Racing Circuit Hants 25 E7
Thrybergh S Yorks 89 E5
Thulston Derbys 76 F4
Thundergay N Ayrs 119 B5
Thundersley Essex 42 F3
Thundridge Herts 41 C6
Thurcaston Leics 64 C2
Thurcroft S Yorks 89 F5
Thurgarton Norf 81 D7
Thurgarton Notts 77 E6
Thurgoland S Yorks 88 D3
Thurlaston Leics 64 E2
Thurlaston Warks 52 B2
Thurlbear Som 11 B7
Thurlby Lincs 65 C8
Thurlby Lincs 78 C2
Thurleigh Beds 53 D8
Thurlestone Devon 6 E4
Thurloxton Som 22 F4
Thurlstone S Yorks 88 D3
Thurlton Norf 69 E7
Thurlwood Ches 74 D5
Thurmaston Leics 64 D3
Thurnby Leics 64 D3
Thurne Norf 69 C7
Thurnham Kent 30 D2
Thurnham Lancs 92 D4

Thurning Norf 81 E6
Thurning Northants 65 F7
Thurnscoe S Yorks 89 D5
Thurnscoe East S Yorks 89 D5
Thursby Cumb 108 D3
Thursford Norf 81 D5
Thursford Collection, Fakenham Norf 81 D5
Thursley Sur 27 F7
Thurso Highld 169 C6
Thurso East Highld 169 C6
Thurstaston Mers 85 F3
Thurston Suff 56 C3
Thurstonfield Cumb 108 D3
Thurstonland W Yorks 88 C2
Thurton Norf 69 D6
Thurvaston Derbys 76 F2
Thuxton Norf 68 D3
Thwaite N Yorks 100 E3
Thwaite Suff 56 C5
Thwaite St Mary Norf 69 E6
Thwaites W Yorks 94 E3
Thwaites Brow W Yorks 94 E3
Thwing E Yorks 97 B6
Tibbermore Perth 134 B2
Tibberton Glos 36 B4
Tibberton Telford 61 B6
Tibberton Worcs 50 D4
Tibenham Norf 68 F4
Tibshelf Derbys 76 C4
Tibthorpe E Yorks 97 D5
Ticehurst E Sus 18 B3
Tichborne Hants 26 F3
Tickencote Rutland 65 D6
Tickenham N Som 23 B6
Tickhill S Yorks 89 E6
Ticklerton Shrops 60 E4
Ticknall Derbys 63 B7
Tickton E Yorks 97 E6
Tidcombe Wilts 25 D7
Tiddington Oxon 39 D6
Tiddington Warks 51 D7
Tidebrook E Sus 18 C3
Tideford Corn 5 D8
Tideford Cross Corn 5 C8
Tidenham Glos 36 E2
Tideswell Derbys 75 B8
Tidmarsh W Berks 26 B4
Tidmington Warks 51 F7
Tidpit Hants 13 C8
Tidworth Wilts 25 E7
Tiers Cross Pembs 44 D4
Tiffield Northants 52 D4
Tifty Aberds 160 D4
Tigerton Angus 143 C5
Tigh-na-Blair Perth 133 C6
Tighnabruaich Argyll 128 C4
Tighnafiline Highld 162 F2
Tigley Devon 7 C5
Tilbrook Cambs 53 C8
Tilbury Thurrock 29 B7
Tilbury Juxta Clare Essex 55 E8
Tile Cross W Mid 63 F5
Tile Hill W Mid 51 B7
Tilehurst Reading 26 B4
Tilford Sur 27 E6
Tilgate W Sus 28 F3
Tilgate Forest Row W Sus 28 F3
Tillathrowie Aberds 159 F8
Tilley Shrops 60 B5
Tillicoultry Clack 133 E8
Tillingham Essex 43 D5
Tillington Hereford 49 E6
Tillington W Sus 16 B3
Tillington Common Hereford 49 E6
Tillyarblet Angus 143 C5
Tillybirloch Aberds 151 D5
Tillycorthie Aberds 151 B8
Tillydrine Aberds 150 E5
Tillyfour Aberds 150 C4
Tillyfourie Aberds 150 C5
Tillygarmond Aberds 150 E5
Tillygreig Aberds 151 B7
Tillykerrie Aberds 151 B7
Tilmanstone Kent 31 D7
Tilney All Saints Norf 67 C5
Tilney High End Norf 67 C5
Tilney St Lawrence Norf 66 C5
Tilshead Wilts 24 E5
Tilstock Shrops 74 F2
Tilston Ches 73 D8
Tilstone Fearnall Ches 74 C2
Tilsworth Beds 40 B2
Tilton on the Hill Leics 64 D4
Timberland Lincs 78 D4
Timbersbrook Ches 75 C5
Timberscombe Som 21 E8
Timble N Yorks 94 D4
Timperley Gtr Man 87 F5
Timsbury Bath 23 D8
Timsbury Hants 14 B4
Timsgearraidh W Isles 172 E3
Timworth Green Suff 56 C2
Tincleton Dorset 13 E5
Tindale Cumb 109 D6
Tingewick Bucks 52 F4
Tingley W Yorks 88 B3
Tingrith Beds 53 F8
Tingwall Orkney 176 D2
Tinhay Devon 9 F5
Tinshill W Yorks 95 F5
Tinsley S Yorks 88 E5
Tintagel Corn 8 F2
Tintagel Castle Corn 8 F2
Tintern Abbey Mon 36 D2
Tintern Parva Mon 36 D2
Tintinhull Som 12 C3
Tintwistle Derbys 87 E8
Tinwald Dumfries 114 F3
Tinwell Rutland 65 D7
Tipperty Aberds 151 B8
Tipsend Norf 66 E5
Tipton W Mid 62 E3
Tipton St John Devon 11 E5
Tiptree Essex 42 C4
Tir-y-dail Carms 33 C7
Tirabad Powys 47 E7
Tiraghoil Argyll 136 F4
Tiree Airport Argyll 136 F1
Tirley Glos 37 B5
Tirphil Caerph 35 D5
Tirril Cumb 99 B7
Tisbury Wilts 13 B7
Tisman's Common W Sus 27 F8
Tissington Derbys 75 D8
Titchberry Devon 8 B4
Titchfield Hants 15 D6
Titchmarsh Northants 53 B8
Titchwell Norf 80 C3
Tithby Notts 77 F6
Titley Hereford 48 C5
Titlington Northumb 117 C7
Titsey Sur 28 D5
Tittensor Staffs 75 F5
Tittleshall Norf 80 E4
Tiverton Ches 74 C2
Tiverton Devon 10 C4
Tivetshall St Margaret Norf 68 F4
Tivetshall St Mary Norf 68 F4
Tividale W Mid 62 E3
Tivy Dale S Yorks 88 D3
Tixall Staffs 62 B3
Tixover Rutland 65 D6
Toab Orkney 176 F4
Toab Shetland 175 M5
Toadmoor Derbys 76 D3
Tobermory Argyll 137 C6
Toberonochy Argyll 130 E3
Tobha Mor W Isles 170 G3
Tobhtarol W Isles 172 E4
Tobson W Isles 172 E4
Tocher Aberds 160 E3
Tockenham Wilts 24 B5
Tockenham Wick Wilts 37 F7
Tockholes Blkburn 86 B4
Tockington S Glos 36 F3
Tockwith N Yorks 95 D7
Todber Dorset 13 B6
Todding Hereford 49 B6
Toddington Beds 40 B3
Toddington Glos 50 F5
Todenham Glos 51 F7
Todhills Cumb 108 C3
Todlachie Aberds 151 C5
Todmorden W Yorks 87 B7
Todrig Borders 115 C7
Todwick S Yorks 89 F5
Toft Cambs 54 D4
Toft Lincs 65 C7
Toft Hill Durham 101 B6
Toft Hill Lincs 78 C5
Toft Monks Norf 69 E7
Toft next Newton Lincs 90 F4
Toftrees Norf 80 E4
Tofts Highld 169 C8
Toftwood Norf 68 C2
Togston Northumb 117 D8
Tokavaig Highld 145 B6
Tokers Green Oxon 26 B5
Tolastadh a Chaolais W Isles 172 E4
Tolastadh bho Thuath W Isles 172 D8
Toll Bar S Yorks 89 D6
Toll End W Mid 62 E3
Toll of Birness Aberds 161 E7
Tolland Som 22 F3
Tollard Royal Wilts 13 C7
Tollbar End W Mid 51 B8
Toller Fratrum Dorset 12 E3
Toller Porcorum Dorset 12 E3
Tollerton Notts 77 F6
Tollerton N Yorks 95 C8
Tollesbury Essex 43 C5
Tolleshunt D'Arcy Essex 43 C5
Tolleshunt Major Essex 43 C5
Tolm W Isles 172 E7
Tolpuddle Dorset 13 E5
Tolvah Highld 148 E4
Tolworth London 28 C2
Tomatin Highld 148 B4
Tombreck Highld 157 F7
Tomchrasky Highld 147 C5
Tomdoun Highld 146 D4
Tomich Highld 147 B6
Tomich Highld 157 B7
Tomich House Highld 157 E6
Tomintoul Aberds 149 E7
Tomintoul Moray 149 C7
Tomnaven Moray 159 F8
Tomnavoulin Moray 149 B8
Ton-Pentre Rhondda 34 E3
Tonbridge Kent 29 E6
Tondu Bridgend 34 F2
Tonfanau Gwyn 58 D2
Tong Shrops 61 D7
Tong W Yorks 94 F5
Tong Norton Shrops 61 D7
Tonge Leics 63 B8
Tongham Sur 27 E6
Tongland Dumfries 106 D3
Tongue Highld 167 D7
Tongue End Lincs 65 C8
Tongwynlais Cardiff 35 F5
Tonna Neath 34 E1
Tonwell Herts 41 C6
Tonypandy Rhondda 34 E3
Tonyrefail Rhondda 34 F4
Toot Baldon Oxon 39 D5
Toot Hill Essex 41 D8
Toothill Hants 14 C4
Top of Hebers Gtr Man 87 D6
Topcliffe N Yorks 95 B7
Topcroft Norf 69 E5
Topcroft Street Norf 69 E5
Toppesfield Essex 55 F8
Toppings Gtr Man 86 C5
Topsham Devon 10 F4
Torbay Torbay 7 D7
Torbeg N Ayrs 119 D6
Torboll Farm Highld 164 E4
Torbrex Stirl 133 E6
Torbryan Devon 7 C6
Torcross Devon 7 E6
Tore Highld 157 D7
Torinturk Argyll 128 D3
Torksey Lincs 77 B8
Torlum W Isles 170 E3
Torlundy Highld 139 B5
Tormarton S Glos 24 B2
Tormisdale Argyll 126 D1
Tormitchell S Ayrs 112 E2
Tormore N Ayrs 119 C5
Tornagrain Highld 157 E8
Tornahaish Aberds 149 D8
Tornaveen Aberds 150 D5
Torness Highld 147 B8
Toronto Durham 110 F4
Torpenhow Cumb 108 F2
Torphichen W Loth 122 B2
Torphins Aberds 150 D5
Torpoint Corn 6 D2
Torquay Torbay 7 C7
Torquhan Borders 123 E7
Torran Argyll 130 E4
Torran Highld 152 E6
Torran Highld 157 B8
Torrance E Dunb 121 B6
Torrans Argyll 137 F5
Torranyard N Ayrs 120 E3
Torre Torbay 7 C7
Torridon Highld 154 E5
Torridon Ho. Highld 154 E4
Torrin Highld 153 G6
Torrisdale Highld 167 C8
Torrisdale-Square Argyll 118 C4
Torrish Highld 165 C6
Torrisholme Lancs 92 C4
Torroble Highld 164 D2
Torry Aberdeen 151 D8
Torry Aberds 159 F8
Torryburn Fife 134 F2
Torterston Aberds 161 D7
Torthorwald Dumfries 107 B7
Tortington W Sus 16 D4
Tortworth S Glos 36 E4
Torvaig Highld 153 E5
Torver Cumb 98 E4
Torwood Falk 133 F7
Torworth Notts 89 F7
Tosberry Devon 8 B4
Toscaig Highld 155 G3
Toseland Cambs 54 C3
Tosside N Yorks 93 D7
Tostock Suff 56 C3
Totaig Highld 152 D3
Totaig Highld 155 H4
Tote Highld 152 E5
Totegan Highld 168 C3
Tothill Lincs 91 F8
Totland I o W 14 F4
Totnes Devon 7 C6
Toton Notts 76 F5
Totronald Argyll 136 C2
Totscore Highld 152 C4
Tottenham London 41 E6
Tottenhill Norf 67 C6
Tottenhill Row Norf 67 C6
Totteridge London 41 E5
Totternhoe Beds 40 B2
Tottington Gtr Man 87 C5
Totton Hants 14 C4
Touchen End Windsor 27 B6
Tournaig Highld 154 B4
Toux Aberds 161 C6
Tovil Kent 29 D8
Tow Law Durham 110 F4
Toward Argyll 129 D6
Towcester Northants 52 E4
Towcester Racecourse Northants 52 E5
Towednack Corn 2 C3
Tower End Norf 67 C6
Tower Knowe Visitor Centre, Kielder Water Northumb 116 F2
Tower of London London 41 F6
Towersey Oxon 39 D7
Towie Aberds 150 C3
Towie Aberds 161 B5
Towiemore Moray 159 E7
Town End Cambs 66 E4
Town End Cumb 99 F6
Town Row E Sus 18 B2
Town Yetholm Borders 116 B4
Townend W Dunb 120 B4
Towngate Lincs 65 C8
Townhead Cumb 108 F5
Townhead Dumfries 106 E3
Townhead S Ayrs 112 D2
Townhead S Yorks 88 D2
Townhead of Greenlaw Dumfries 106 C4
Townhill Fife 134 F3
Townsend Bucks 39 D7
Townsend Herts 40 D4
Townshend Corn 2 C4
Towthorpe York 96 D2
Towton N Yorks 95 F7
Towyn Conwy 72 B3
Toxteth Mers 85 F4
Toynton All Saints Lincs 79 C6
Toynton Fen Side Lincs 79 C6
Toynton St Peter Lincs 79 C7
Toy's Hill Kent 29 D5
Trabboch E Ayrs 112 B4
Traboe Corn 3 D6
Tradespark Highld 158 D2
Tradespark Orkney 176 F3
Trafford Park Gtr Man 87 E5
Trago Mills, Newton Abbot Devon 7 B6
Trallong Powys 34 B3
Tranent E Loth 123 B7
Tranmere Mers 85 F4
Trantlebeg Highld 168 D3
Trantlemore Highld 168 D3
Tranwell Northumb 117 F7
Trapp Carms 33 C7
Traprain E Loth 123 B8
Traquair Borders 123 F6
Trawden Lancs 94 F2
Trawsfynydd Gwyn 71 D8
Tre-Gibbon Rhondda 34 D3
Tre-Taliesin Ceredig 58 E3
Tre-vaughan Carms 32 B4
Tre-wyn Mon 35 B7
Trealaw Rhondda 34 E4
Treales Lancs 92 F4
Trearddur Anglesey 82 D2
Treaslane Highld 152 D4
Trebah Garden, Mawnan Smith Corn 3 D6
Trebanog Rhondda 34 E4
Trebanos Neath 33 D8
Trebartha Corn 5 B7
Trebarwith Corn 8 F2
Trebetherick Corn 4 B4
Treborough Som 22 F2
Trebudannon Corn 4 C3
Trebullett Corn 5 B8
Treburley Corn 5 B8
Trebyan Corn 5 C5
Trecastle Powys 34 B2
Trecenydd Caerph 35 F5
Trecwn Pembs 44 B4
Trecynon Rhondda 34 D3
Tredavoe Corn 2 D3
Treddiog Pembs 44 C3
Tredegar Bl Gwent 35 D5
Tredegar Newydd = New Tredegar Caerph 35 D5
Tredington Glos 37 B6
Tredington Warks 51 E7
Tredinnick Corn 4 B4
Tredomen Powys 48 F3
Tredunnock Mon 35 E7
Tredustan Powys 48 F3
Treen Corn 2 D2
Treeton S Yorks 88 F5
Tref-y-Clawdd = Knighton Powys 48 B4
Trefaldwyn = Montgomery Powys 60 E2
Trefasser Pembs 44 B3
Trefdraeth Anglesey 82 D4
Trefdraeth = Newport Pembs 45 F2
Trefecca Powys 48 F3
Trefechan Ceredig 58 F2
Trefeglwys Powys 59 E6
Trefenter Ceredig 46 C5
Treffgarne Pembs 44 C4
Treffynnon Pembs 44 C3
Treffynnon = Holywell Flint 73 B5
Trefgarn Owen Pembs 44 C3
Trefil Bl Gwent 35 C5
Trefilan Ceredig 46 D4
Trefin Pembs 44 B3
Treflach Shrops 60 B2
Trefnanney Powys 60 C2
Trefnant Denb 72 B4
Trefonen Shrops 60 B2
Trefor Anglesey 82 C3
Trefor Gwyn 70 C4
Treforest Rhondda 34 F4
Trefriw Conwy 83 E7
Trefynwy = Monmouth Mon 36 C2
Tregadillett Corn 8 F4
Tregaian Anglesey 82 D4
Tregare Mon 35 C8
Tregaron Ceredig 47 D5
Tregarth Gwyn 83 E6
Tregeare Corn 8 F4
Tregeiriog Wrex 73 F5
Tregele Anglesey 82 B3
Tregidden Corn 3 D6
Treglemais Pembs 44 C3
Tregole Corn 8 E3
Tregonetha Corn 4 C4
Tregony Corn 3 B8
Tregoss Corn 4 C4
Tregoyd Powys 48 F4
Tregroes Ceredig 46 E3
Tregurrian Corn 4 C3
Tregynon Powys 59 E7
Trehafod Rhondda 34 E4
Treharris M Tydf 34 E4
Treherbert Rhondda 34 E3
Trekenner Corn 5 B8
Treknow Corn 8 F2
Trelan Corn 3 E6
Trelash Corn 8 E3
Trelassick Corn 4 D3
Trelawnyd Flint 72 B4
Trelech Carms 45 F4
Treleddyd-fawr Pembs 44 C2
Trelewis M Tydf 35 E5
Treligga Corn 8 F2
Trelights Corn 4 B4
Trelill Corn 4 B5
Trelissick Corn 3 C7
Trelissick Garden, Feock Corn 4 F3
Trellech Mon 36 D2
Trelleck Grange Mon 36 D1
Trelogan Flint 85 F2
Trelystan Powys 60 D2
Tremadog Gwyn 71 C6
Tremail Corn 8 F3
Tremain Ceredig 45 E4
Tremaine Corn 8 F4
Tremar Corn 5 C7
Trematon Corn 5 D8
Tremeirchion Denb 72 B4
Trenance Corn 4 C3
Trenarren Corn 3 B9
Trench Telford 61 C6
Treneglos Corn 8 F4
Trenewan Corn 5 D6
Trent Dorset 12 C3
Trent Vale Stoke 75 E5
Trentham Stoke 75 E5
Trentham Gardens, Newcastle-under-Lyme Staffs 75 F5
Trentishoe Devon 20 E5
Treoes V Glam 21 B8
Treorchy = Treorci Rhondda 34 E3
Treorci = Treorchy Rhondda 34 E3
Tre'r-ddôl Ceredig 58 E3
Trerule Foot Corn 5 D8
Tresaith Ceredig 45 D4
Tresawle Corn 3 B7
Trescott Staffs 62 E2
Trescowe Corn 2 C4
Tresham Glos 36 E4
Tresillian Corn 3 B7
Tresinwen Pembs 44 A4
Treskinnick Cross Corn 8 E4
Tresmeer Corn 8 F4
Tresparrett Corn 8 E3
Tresparrett Posts Corn 8 E3
Tressait Perth 141 C5
Tresta Shetland 175 H5
Tresta Shetland 174 D8
Treswell Notts 77 B7
Trethosa Corn 4 D4
Trethurgy Corn 4 D5
Tretio Pembs 44 C2
Tretire Hereford 36 B2
Tretower Powys 35 B5
Treuddyn Flint 73 D6
Trevalga Corn 8 F2
Trevalyn Wrex 73 D7
Trevanson Corn 4 B4
Trevarren Corn 4 C4
Trevarrian Corn 4 C3
Trevarrick Corn 3 B8
Trevaughan Carms 32 C2
Treveighan Corn 5 B5
Trevellas Corn 4 D2
Treverva Corn 3 C6
Trevethin Torf 35 D6
Trevigro Corn 5 C8
Treviscoe Corn 4 D4
Trevone Corn 4 B3
Trewarmett Corn 8 F2
Trewassa Corn 8 F3
Trewellard Corn 2 C2
Trewen Corn 8 F4
Trewennack Corn 3 D5
Trewern Powys 60 C2
Trewethern Corn 4 B5
Trewidland Corn 5 D7
Trewint Corn 8 F4
Trewint Corn 8 E3
Trewithian Corn 3 C7
Trewoofe Corn 2 D3
Trewoon Corn 4 D4
Treworga Corn 3 B7
Treworlas Corn 3 C7
Treyarnon Corn 4 B3
Treyford W Sus 16 C2
Trezaise Corn 4 D4
Triangle W Yorks 87 B8
Trickett's Cross Dorset 13 D8
Triffleton Pembs 44 C4
Trimdon Durham 111 F6
Trimdon Colliery Durham 111 F6
Trimdon Grange Durham 111 F6
Trimingham Norf 81 D8
Trimley Lower Street Suff 57 F6
Trimley St Martin Suff 57 F6
Trimley St Mary Suff 57 F6
Trimpley Worcs 50 B2
Trimsaran Carms 33 D5
Trimstone Devon 20 E3
Trinafour Perth 140 C4
Trinant Caerph 35 D6
Tring Herts 40 C2
Tring Wharf Herts 40 C2
Trinity Angus 143 C6
Trinity Jersey 17
Trisant Ceredig 47 B6
Trislaig Highld 138 B4
Trispen Corn 4 D3
Tritlington Northumb 117 E8
Trochry Perth 141 E6
Trodigal Argyll 118 D3
Troed-rhiwdalar Powys 47 D8
Troedyraur Ceredig 46 E2
Troedyrhiw M Tydf 34 D4
Tromode I o M 84 E3
Trondavoe Shetland 174 F5
Troon Corn 3 C5
Troon S Ayrs 120 F3
Trosaraidh W Isles 171 J3
Trossachs Hotel Stirl 132 D4
Troston Suff 56 B2
Trottiscliffe Kent 29 C7
Trotton W Sus 16 B2
Troutbeck Cumb 99 D6
Troutbeck Cumb 99 B5
Troutbeck Bridge Cumb 99 D6
Trow Green Glos 36 D2
Trowbridge Wilts 24 D3
Trowell Notts 76 F4
Trowle Common Wilts 24 D3
Trowley Bottom Herts 40 C3
Trows Borders 124 F2
Trowse Newton Norf 68 D5
Trudoxhill Som 24 E2
Trull Som 11 B7
Trumaisgearraidh W Isles 170 C4
Trumpan Highld 152 C3
Trumpet Hereford 49 F8
Trumpington Cambs 54 D5
Trunch Norf 81 D8
Trunnah Lancs 92 E3
Truro Corn 3 B7
Truro Cathedral Corn 4 E3
Trusham Devon 10 F3
Trusley Derbys 76 F2
Trusthorpe Lincs 91 F9
Trysull Staffs 62 E2
Tubney Oxon 38 E4
Tuckenhay Devon 7 D6
Tuckhill Shrops 61 F7
Tuckingmill Corn 3 B5
Tuddenham Suff 55 B8
Tuddenham St Martin Suff 57 E5
Tudeley Kent 29 E7
Tudhoe Durham 111 F5
Tudorville Hereford 36 B2
Tudweiliog Gwyn 70 D3
Tuesley Sur 27 E7
Tuffley Glos 37 C5
Tufton Hants 26 E2
Tufton Pembs 32 B1
Tugby Leics 64 D4
Tugford Shrops 61 F5
Tullibardine Perth 133 C8
Tullibody Clack 133 E7
Tullich Argyll 131 D6
Tullich Highld 148 B2
Tullich Muir Highld 157 B8
Tullie House, Carlisle Cumb 108 D3
Tulliemet Perth 141 D6
Tulloch Aberds 143 B7
Tulloch Aberds 160 E5
Tulloch Perth 134 B2
Tulloch Castle Highld 157 C6
Tullochgorm Argyll 131 F5
Tulloes Angus 143 E5
Tullybannocher Perth 133 B6
Tullybelton Perth 141 F7
Tullyfergus Perth 142 E2
Tullymurdoch Perth 142 D1
Tullynessle Aberds 150 C4
Tumble Carms 33 C6
Tumby Woodside Lincs 79 D5
Tummel Bridge Perth 140 D4
Tunga W Isles 172 E7
Tunstall E Yorks 97 F9
Tunstall Kent 30 C2
Tunstall Lancs 93 B6
Tunstall Norf 69 D7
Tunstall N Yorks 101 E7
Tunstall Stoke 75 D5
Tunstall Suff 57 D7
Tunstall T & W 111 D6
Tunstead Derbys 75 B8
Tunstead Gtr Man 87 D8
Tunstead Norf 81 E8
Tunworth Hants 26 E4
Tupsley Hereford 49 E7
Tupton Derbys 76 C3
Tur Langton Leics 64 E4
Turgis Green Hants 26 D4
Turin Angus 143 D5
Turkdean Glos 37 C8
Turleigh Wilts 24 C3
Turn Lancs 87 C6
Turnastone Hereford 49 F5
Turnberry S Ayrs 112 D2
Turnditch Derbys 76 E2
Turners Hill W Sus 28 F4
Turners Puddle Dorset 13 E6
Turnford Herts 41 D6
Turnhouse Edin 122 B4
Turnworth Dorset 13 D6
Turriff Aberds 160 C4
Turton Bottoms Blkburn 86 C5
Turves Cambs 66 E3
Turvey Beds 53 D7
Turville Bucks 39 E7
Turville Heath Bucks 39 E7
Turweston Bucks 52 F4
Tushielaw Borders 115 C6
Tutbury Staffs 63 B6
Tutnall Worcs 50 B4
Tutshill Glos 36 E2
Tuttington Norf 81 E8
Tutts Clump W Berks 26 B3
Tuxford Notts 77 B7
Twatt Orkney 176 D1
Twatt Shetland 175 H5
Twechar E Dunb 121 B7
Tweedmouth Northumb 125 D5
Tweedsmuir Borders 114 B3
Twelve Heads Corn 3 B6
Twemlow Green Ches 74 C4
Twenty Lincs 65 B8
Twerton Bath 24 C2
Twickenham London 28 B2
Twickenham Stadium London 28 B2
Twigworth Glos 37 B5
Twineham W Sus 17 C6
Twinhoe Bath 24 D2
Twinstead Essex 56 F2
Twinstead Green Essex 56 F2
Twiss Green Warr 86 E4
Twiston Lancs 93 E8
Twitchen Devon 21 F6
Twitchen Shrops 49 B5
Two Bridges Devon 6 B4
Two Dales Derbys 76 C2
Two Mills Ches 73 B7
Twycross Leics 63 D7
Twycross Zoo, Ashby-de-la-Zouch Leics 63 D7
Twyford Bucks 39 B6
Twyford Derbys 63 B7
Twyford Hants 15 B5
Twyford Leics 64 C4
Twyford Lincs 65 B6
Twyford Norf 81 E6
Twyford Wokingham 27 B5
Twyford Common Hereford 49 F7
Twyn-y-Sheriff Mon 35 D8
Twynholm Dumfries 106 D3
Twyning Glos 50 F3
Twyning Green Glos 50 F4
Twynllanan Carms 34 B1
Twynmynydd Carms 33 C7
Twywell Northants 53 B7
Ty-draw Conwy 83 F8
Ty-hen Carms 32 B4
Ty-hen Gwyn 70 D2
Ty-mawr Anglesey 82 C4
Ty Mawr Carms 46 E4
Ty Mawr Cwm Conwy 72 E3
Ty-nant Conwy 72 E3
Ty-nant Gwyn 59 B6
Ty-uchaf Powys 59 B7
Tyberton Hereford 49 F5
Tyburn W Mid 62 E5
Tycroes Carms 33 C7
Tycrwyn Powys 59 C8
Tydd Gote Lincs 66 C4
Tydd St Giles Cambs 66 C4
Tydd St Mary Lincs 66 C4
Tyddewi = St David's Pembs 44 C2
Tyddyn-mawr Gwyn 71 C6
Tye Green Essex 55 F6
Tye Green Essex 42 B3
Tye Green Essex 41 D7
Tyldesley Gtr Man 86 D4
Tyler Hill Kent 30 C5
Tylers Green Bucks 40 E2
Tylorstown Rhondda 34 E4
Tylwch Powys 59 F6
Tyn-y-celyn Wrex 73 F5
Tyn-y-coed Shrops 60 B2
Tyn-y-fedwen Powys 72 F5
Tyn-y-ffridd Powys 72 F5
Tyn-y-graig Powys 48 D2
Ty'n-y-groes Conwy 83 D7
Ty'n-y-maes Gwyn 83 E6
Tyn-y-pwll Anglesey 82 C4
Ty'n-yr-eithin Ceredig 47 C5
Tyncelyn Ceredig 46 C5
Tyndrum Stirl 139 F7
Tyne Tunnel T & W 111 C6
Tyneham Dorset 13 F6
Tynehead Midloth 123 D6
Tynemouth T & W 111 C6
Tynemouth Sea Life Centre T & W 111 B6
Tynewydd Rhondda 34 E3
Tyninghame E Loth 124 B2
Tynron Dumfries 113 E8
Tynygongl Anglesey 82 C5
Tynygraig Ceredig 47 C5
Tŷ'r-felin-isaf Conwy 83 E8
Tyrie Aberds 161 B6
Tyringham M Keynes 53 E6
Tythecott Devon 9 C6
Tythegston Bridgend 21 B7
Tytherington Ches 75 B6
Tytherington S Glos 36 F3
Tytherington Som 24 E2
Tytherington Wilts 24 E4
Tytherleigh Devon 11 D8
Tywardreath Corn 5 D5
Tywyn Conwy 83 D7
Tywyn Gwyn 58 D2

U

Uachdar W Isles 170 E3
Uags Highld 155 G3
Ubbeston Green Suff 57 B7
Ubley Bath 23 D7
Uckerby N Yorks 101 D7
Uckfield E Sus 17 B8
Uckington Glos 37 B6
Uddingston S Lnrk 121 C6
Uddington S Lnrk 121 F8
Udimore E Sus 19 D5
Udny Green Aberds 151 B7
Udny Station Aberds 151 B8
Udston S Lnrk 121 D6
Udstonhead S Lnrk 121 E7
Uffcott Wilts 25 B6
Uffculme Devon 11 C5
Uffington Lincs 65 D7
Uffington Oxon 38 F3
Uffington Shrops 60 C5
Ufford P'boro 65 D7
Ufford Suff 57 D6
Ufton Warks 51 C8
Ufton Nervet W Berks 26 C4
Ugadale Argyll 118 D4
Ugborough Devon 6 D4
Uggeshall Suff 69 F7
Ugglebarnby N Yorks 103 D6
Ughill S Yorks 88 E3
Ugley Essex 41 B8
Ugley Green Essex 41 B8
Ugthorpe N Yorks 103 C5
Uidh W Isles 171 L2
Uig Argyll 129 B6
Uig Highld 152 C4
Uig Highld 152 D2
Uigen W Isles 172 E3
Uigshader Highld 152 E5
Uisken Argyll 136 G4
Ulbster Highld 169 E8
Ulceby Lincs 79 B7
Ulceby N Lincs 90 C5
Ulceby Skitter N Lincs 90 C5
Ulcombe Kent 30 E2
Uldale Cumb 108 F2
Uley Glos 36 E4
Ulgham Northumb 117 E8
Ullapool Highld 163 E5
Ullenhall Warks 51 C6
Ullenwood Glos 37 C6
Ulleskelf N Yorks 95 E8
Ullesthorpe Leics 64 F2
Ulley S Yorks 89 F5
Ullingswick Hereford 49 E7
Ullinish Highld 153 F4
Ullock Cumb 98 B2
Ulnes Walton Lancs 86 C3
Ulpha Cumb 98 E3
Ulrome E Yorks 97 D7
Ulsta Shetland 174 E6
Ulva House Argyll 137 E5
Ulverston Cumb 92 B2
Ulwell Dorset 13 F8
Umberleigh Devon 9 B8
Unapool Highld 166 F4
Unasary W Isles 171 H3
Underbarrow Cumb 99 E6
Undercliffe W Yorks 94 F4
Underhoull Shetland 174 C7
Underriver Kent 29 D6
Underwood Notts 76 D4
Undy Mon 35 F8
Unifirth Shetland 175 H4
Union Cottage Aberds 151 E7
Union Mills I o M 84 E3
Union Street E Sus 18 B4
University Museum, Oxford Oxon 39 D5
Unst Airport Shetland 174 C8
Unstone Derbys 76 B3
Unstone Green Derbys 76 B3
Unthank Cumb 108 F4
Unthank Cumb 109 E6
Unthank End Cumb 108 F4
Up Cerne Dorset 12 D4
Up Exe Devon 10 D4
Up Hatherley Glos 37 B6
Up Holland Lancs 86 D3
Up Marden W Sus 15 C8
Up Nately Hants 26 D4
Up Somborne Hants 25 F8
Up Sydling Dorset 12 D4
Upavon Wilts 25 D6
Upchurch Kent 30 C2
Upcott Hereford 48 D5
Upend Cambs 55 D7
Upgate Norf 68 C4
Uphall W Loth 122 B3
Uphall Station W Loth 122 B3
Upham Devon 10 D3
Upham Hants 15 B6
Uphampton Worcs 50 C3
Uphill N Som 22 D5
Uplawmoor E Renf 120 D4
Upleadon Glos 36 B4
Upleatham Redcar 102 C4
Uplees Kent 30 C3
Uploders Dorset 12 E3
Uplowman Devon 10 C5
Uplyme Devon 11 E8
Upminster London 42 F1
Upnor Medway 29 B8
Upottery Devon 11 D7
Uppark, Petersfield Hants 15 C8
Upper Affcot Shrops 60 F4
Upper Ardchronie Highld 164 F3
Upper Arley Worcs 61 F7
Upper Arncott Oxon 39 C6
Upper Astrop Northants 52 F3
Upper Badcall Highld 166 E3
Upper Basildon W Berks 26 B3
Upper Beeding W Sus 17 C5
Upper Benefield Northants 65 F6
Upper Bighouse Highld 168 D3
Upper Boddington Northants 52 D2
Upper Borth Ceredig 58 F3
Upper Boyndlie Aberds 161 B6
Upper Brailes Warks 51 F8
Upper Breakish Highld 155 H2
Upper Breinton Hereford 49 E6
Upper Broadheath Worcs 50 D3
Upper Broughton Notts 64 B3
Upper Bucklebury W Berks 26 C3
Upper Burnhaugh Aberds 151 E7
Upper Caldecote Beds 54 E2
Upper Catesby Northants 52 D3
Upper Chapel Powys 48 E2
Upper Church Village Rhondda 34 F4
Upper Chute Wilts 25 D7
Upper Clatford Hants 25 E8
Upper Clynnog Gwyn 71 C5
Upper Cumberworth W Yorks 88 D3
Upper Cwm-twrch Powys 34 C1
Upper Cwmbran Torf 35 E6
Upper Dallachy Moray 159 C7
Upper Dean Beds 53 C8
Upper Denby W Yorks 88 D3
Upper Denton Cumb 109 C6
Upper Derraid Highld 158 F4
Upper Dicker E Sus 18 E2
Upper Dovercourt Essex 57 F6
Upper Druimfin Argyll 137 C6
Upper Dunsforth N Yorks 95 C7
Upper Eathie Highld 157 C8
Upper Elkstone Staffs 75 D7
Upper End Derbys 75 B7
Upper Farringdon Hants 26 F5

Upper Framilode Glos 36 C4
Upper Glenfintaig Highld 147 F5
Upper Gornal W Mid 62 E3
Upper Gravenhurst Beds 54 F2
Upper Green Mon 35 C7
Upper Green W Berks 25 C8
Upper Grove Common Hereford 36 B2
Upper Hackney Derbys 76 C2
Upper Hale Sur 27 E6
Upper Halistra Highld 152 D3
Upper Halling Medway 29 C7
Upper Hambleton Rutland 65 D6
Upper Hardres Court Kent 31 D5
Upper Hartfield E Sus 29 F5
Upper Haugh S Yorks 88 E5
Upper Heath Shrops 61 F5
Upper Hellesdon Norf 68 C5
Upper Helmsley N Yorks 96 D2
Upper Hergest Hereford 48 D4
Upper Heyford Northants 52 D4
Upper Heyford Oxon 38 B4
Upper Hill Hereford 49 D6
Upper Hopton W Yorks 88 C2
Upper Horsebridge E Sus 18 D2
Upper Hulme Staffs 75 C7
Upper Inglesham Swindon 38 E2
Upper Inverbrough Highld 158 F2
Upper Killay Swansea 33 E6
Upper Knockando Moray 159 E5
Upper Lambourn W Berks 38 F3
Upper Leigh Staffs 75 F7
Upper Lenie Highld 147 B8
Upper Lochton Aberds 151 E5
Upper Longdon Staffs 62 C4
Upper Lybster Highld 169 F7
Upper Lydbrook Glos 36 C3
Upper Maes-coed Hereford 48 F5
Upper Midway Derbys 63 B6
Upper Milovaig Highld 152 E2
Upper Minety Wilts 37 E7
Upper Mitton Worcs 50 B3
Upper North Dean Bucks 39 E8
Upper Obney Perth 141 F7
Upper Ollach Highld 153 F6
Upper Padley Derbys 76 B2
Upper Pollicott Bucks 39 C7
Upper Poppleton York 95 D8
Upper Quinton Warks 51 E6
Upper Ratley Hants 14 B4
Upper Rissington Glos 38 C2
Upper Rochford Worcs 49 C8
Upper Sandaig Highld 145 B7
Upper Sanday Orkney 176 F4
Upper Sapey Hereford 49 C8
Upper Seagry Wilts 37 F6
Upper Shelton Beds 53 E7
Upper Sheringham Norf 81 C7
Upper Skelmorlie N Ayrs 129 D7
Upper Slaughter Glos 38 B1
Upper Soudley Glos 36 C3
Upper Stondon Beds 54 F2
Upper Stowe Northants 52 D4
Upper Stratton Swindon 38 F1
Upper Street Hants 14 C2
Upper Street Norf 69 C6
Upper Street Norf 69 C6
Upper Street Suff 56 F5
Upper Strensham Worcs 50 F4
Upper Sundon Beds 40 B3
Upper Swell Glos 38 B1
Upper Tean Staffs 75 F7
Upper Tillyrie Perth 134 D3
Upper Tooting London 28 B3
Upper Tote Highld 152 D6
Upper Town N Som 23 C7
Upper Treverward Shrops 48 B4
Upper Tysoe Warks 51 E8
Upper Upham Wilts 25 B7
Upper Wardington Oxon 52 E2
Upper Weald M Keynes 53 F5
Upper Weedon Northants 52 D4
Upper Wield Hants 26 F4
Upper Winchendon Bucks 39 C7
Upper Witton W Mid 62 E4
Upper Woodend Aberds 151 C5
Upper Woodford Wilts 25 F6
Upper Wootton Hants 26 D3
Upper Wyche Worcs 50 E2
Upperby Cumb 108 D4
Uppermill Gtr Man 87 D7
Uppersound Shetland 175 J6
Upperthong W Yorks 88 D2
Upperthorpe N Lincs 89 D8
Upperton W Sus 16 B3
Uppertown Derbys 76 C3
Uppertown Highld 169 B8
Uppertown Orkney 176 G3
Uppingham Rutland 65 E5
Uppington Shrops 61 D6
Upsall N Yorks 102 F2
Upshire Essex 41 D7
Upstreet Kent 31 C6
Upthorpe Suff 56 B3
Upton Cambs 54 B2
Upton Ches 73 C8
Upton Corn 8 D4
Upton Dorset 12 F5
Upton Dorset 13 E7
Upton Hants 14 C4
Upton Hants 25 D8
Upton Leics 63 E7
Upton Lincs 90 F2
Upton Mers 85 F3
Upton Norf 69 C6
Upton Notts 77 D7
Upton Notts 77 B7
Upton Northants 52 C5
Upton Oxon 39 F5
Upton P'boro 65 D8
Upton Slough 27 B7
Upton Som 10 B4
Upton W Yorks 89 C5
Upton Bishop Hereford 36 B3
Upton Cheyney S Glos 23 C8
Upton Cressett Shrops 61 E6
Upton Cross Corn 5 B7
Upton Grey Hants 26 E4
Upton Hellions Devon 10 D3
Upton House Warks 51 E8
Upton Lovell Wilts 24 E4
Upton Magna Shrops 61 C5
Upton Noble Som 24 F2
Upton Pyne Devon 10 E4
Upton St Leonard's Glos 37 C5
Upton Scudamore Wilts 24 E3
Upton Snodsbury Worcs 50 D4
Upton upon Severn Worcs 50 E3
Upton Warren Worcs 50 C4
Upwaltham W Sus 16 C3
Upware Cambs 55 B6
Upwell Norf 66 D4
Upwey Dorset 12 F4
Upwood Cambs 66 F2
Uradale Shetland 175 K6
Urafirth Shetland 174 F5
Urchfont Wilts 24 D5
Urdimarsh Hereford 49 E7
Ure Shetland 174 F4
Ure Bank N Yorks 95 B6
Urgha W Isles 173 J4
Urishay Common Hereford 48 F5
Urlay Nook Stockton 102 C1
Urmston Gtr Man 87 E5
Urpeth Durham 110 D5
Urquhart Highld 157 D6
Urquhart Moray 159 C6
Urquhart Castle, Drumnadrochit Highld 147 B8
Urra N Yorks 102 D3
Urray Highld 157 D6
Ushaw Moor Durham 110 E5
Usk = Brynbuga Mon 35 D7
Usselby Lincs 90 E4
Usworth T & W 111 D6
Utkinton Ches 74 C2
Utley W Yorks 94 E3
Uton Devon 10 E3
Utterby Lincs 91 E7
Uttoxeter Staffs 75 F7
Uttoxeter Racecourse Staffs 75 F8
Uwchmynydd Gwyn 70 E2
Uxbridge London 40 F3
Uyeasound Shetland 174 C7
Uzmaston Pembs 44 D4

V

Valley Anglesey 82 D2
Valley Truckle Corn 8 F2
Valleyfield Dumfries 106 D3
Valsgarth Shetland 174 B8
Valtos Highld 152 C6
Van Powys 59 F6
Vange Essex 42 F3
Varteg Torf 35 D6
Vatten Highld 153 E3
Vaul Argyll 136 F2
Vaynor M Tydf 34 C4
Veensgarth Shetland 175 J6
Velindre Powys 48 F3
Vellow Som 22 F2
Veness Orkney 176 D4
Venn Green Devon 9 C5
Venn Ottery Devon 11 E5
Vennington Shrops 60 D3
Venny Tedburn Devon 10 E3
Ventnor I o W 15 G6
Ventnor Botanic Garden I o W 15 G6
Vernham Dean Hants 25 D8
Vernham Street Hants 25 D8
Vernolds Common Shrops 60 F4
Verwood Dorset 13 D8
Veryan Corn 3 C8
Vicarage Devon 11 F7
Vickerstown Cumb 92 C1
Victoria Corn 4 C4
Victoria S Yorks 88 D2
Victoria and Albert Museum London 28 B3
Vidlin Shetland 174 G6
Viewpark N Lnrk 121 C7
Vigo Village Kent 29 C7
Vinehall Street E Sus 18 C4
Vine's Cross E Sus 18 D2
Viney Hill Glos 36 D3
Virginia Water Sur 27 C8
Virginstow Devon 9 E5
Vobster Som 24 E2
Voe Shetland 175 G6
Voe Shetland 174 E5
Vowchurch Hereford 49 F5
Voxter Shetland 174 F5
Voy Orkney 176 E1

W

Wackerfield Durham 101 B6
Wacton Norf 68 E4
Wadbister Shetland 175 J6
Wadborough Worcs 50 E4
Waddesdon Bucks 39 C7
Waddesdon Manor, Aylesbury Bucks 39 C7
Waddingham Lincs 90 E3
Waddington Lancs 93 E7
Waddington Lincs 78 C2
Wadebridge Corn 4 B4
Wadeford Som 11 C8
Wadenhoe Northants 65 F7
Wadesmill Herts 41 C6
Wadhurst E Sus 18 B3
Wadshelf Derbys 76 B3
Wadsley S Yorks 88 E4
Wadsley Bridge S Yorks 88 E4
Wadworth S Yorks 89 E6
Waen Denb 72 C5
Waen Denb 72 C3
Waen Fach Powys 60 C2
Waen Goleugoed Denb 72 B4
Wag Highld 165 B7
Wainfleet All Saints Lincs 79 D7
Wainfleet Bank Lincs 79 D7
Wainfleet St Mary Lincs 79 D8
Wainfleet Tofts Lincs 79 D7
Wainhouse Corner Corn 8 E3
Wainscott Medway 29 B8
Wainstalls W Yorks 87 B8
Waitby Cumb 100 D2
Waithe Lincs 91 D6
Wake Lady Green N Yorks 102 E4
Wakefield W Yorks 88 B4
Wakehurst Place Garden, Crawley W Sus 28 F4
Wakerley Northants 65 E6
Wakes Colne Essex 42 B4
Walberswick Suff 57 B8
Walberton W Sus 16 D3
Walbottle T & W 110 C4
Walcot Lincs 78 F3
Walcot N Lincs 90 B2
Walcot Shrops 60 F3
Walcot Telford 61 C5
Walcot Swindon 38 F1
Walcot Green Norf 68 F4
Walcote Leics 64 F2
Walcote Warks 51 D6
Walcott Lincs 78 D4
Walcott Norf 69 A6
Walden N Yorks 101 F5
Walden Head N Yorks 100 F4
Walden Stubbs N Yorks 89 C6
Waldersey Cambs 66 D4
Walderslade Medway 29 C8
Walderton W Sus 15 C8
Walditch Dorset 12 E2
Waldley Derbys 75 F8
Waldridge Durham 111 D5
Waldringfield Suff 57 E6
Waldringfield Heath Suff 57 E6
Waldron E Sus 18 D2
Wales S Yorks 89 F5
Walesby Lincs 90 E5
Walesby Notts 77 B6
Walford Hereford 49 B5
Walford Hereford 36 B2
Walford Shrops 60 B4
Walford Heath Shrops 60 C4
Walgherton Ches 74 E3
Walgrave Northants 53 B6
Walhampton Hants 14 E4
Walk Mill Lancs 93 F8
Walkden Gtr Man 86 D5
Walker T & W 111 C5
Walker Art Gallery Mers 85 E4
Walker Barn Ches 75 B6
Walker Fold Lancs 93 E6
Walkerburn Borders 123 F6
Walkeringham Notts 89 E8
Walkerith Lincs 89 E8
Walkern Herts 41 B5
Walker's Green Hereford 49 E7
Walkerville N Yorks 101 E7
Walkford Dorset 14 E3
Walkhampton Devon 6 C3
Walkington E Yorks 97 F5
Walkley S Yorks 88 F4
Walkley Clogs, Hebden Bridge W Yorks 87 B3
Wall Northumb 110 C2
Wall Staffs 62 D5
Wall Bank Shrops 60 E5
Wall Heath W Mid 62 F2
Wall under Heywood Shrops 60 E5
Wallaceton Dumfries 113 F8
Wallacetown S Ayrs 112 D2
Wallacetown S Ayrs 112 B3
Wallands Park E Sus 17 C8
Wallasey Mers 85 E4
Wallcrouch E Sus 18 B3
Wallingford Oxon 39 F6
Wallington London 28 C3
Wallington Hants 15 D6
Wallington Herts 54 F3
Wallington House, Ponteland Northumb 117 F6
Wallis Pembs 32 B1
Walliswood Sur 28 F2
Walls Shetland 175 J4
Wallsend T & W 111 C5
Wallston V Glam 22 B3
Wallyford E Loth 123 B6
Walmer Kent 31 D7
Walmer Bridge Lancs 86 B2
Walmersley Gtr Man 87 C6
Walmley W Mid 62 E5
Walney Island Airport Cumb 92 B1
Walpole Suff 57 B7
Walpole Cross Keys Norf 66 C5
Walpole Highway Norf 66 C5
Walpole Marsh Norf 66 C4
Walpole St Andrew Norf 66 C5
Walpole St Peter Norf 66 C5
Walsall W Mid 62 E4
Walsall Arboretum W Mid 62 E4
Walsall Wood W Mid 62 D4
Walsden W Yorks 87 B7
Walsgrave on Sowe W Mid 63 F7
Walsham le Willows Suff 56 B3
Walshaw Gtr Man 87 C5
Walshford N Yorks 95 D7
Walsoken Cambs 66 C4
Walston S Lnrk 122 E3
Walsworth Herts 54 F3
Walters Ash Bucks 39 E8
Walterston V Glam 22 B2
Walterstone Hereford 35 B7
Waltham Kent 30 E5
Waltham NE Lincs 91 D6
Waltham Abbey Essex 41 D6
Waltham Chase Hants 15 C6
Waltham Cross Herts 41 D6
Waltham on the Wolds Leics 64 B5
Waltham St Lawrence Windsor 27 B6
Walthamstow London 41 F6
Walton Cumb 108 C5
Walton Derbys 76 C3
Walton Leics 64 F2
Walton Mers 85 E4
Walton M Keynes 53 F6
Walton P'boro 65 D8
Walton Powys 48 D4
Walton Som 23 F6
Walton Staffs 75 F5
Walton Suff 57 F6
Walton Telford 61 C5
Walton Warks 51 D7
Walton W Yorks 88 C4
Walton W Yorks 95 E7
Walton Cardiff Glos 50 F4
Walton East Pembs 32 B1
Walton Hall Warr 86 F4
Walton-in-Gordano N Som 23 B6
Walton-le-Dale Lancs 86 B3
Walton-on-Thames Sur 28 C2
Walton on the Hill Staffs 62 B3
Walton on the Hill Sur 28 D3
Walton-on-the-Naze Essex 43 B8
Walton on the Wolds Leics 64 C2
Walton-on-Trent Derbys 63 C6
Walton West Pembs 44 D3
Walwen Flint 73 B6
Walwick Northumb 110 B2
Walworth Darl 101 C7
Walworth Gate Darl 101 B7
Walwyn's Castle Pembs 44 D3
Wambrook Som 11 D7
Wanborough Sur 27 E7
Wanborough Swindon 38 F2
Wandsworth London 28 B3
Wangford Suff 57 B8
Wanlockhead Dumfries 113 C8
Wansford E Yorks 97 D6
Wansford P'boro 65 E7
Wanstead London 41 F7
Wanstrow Som 24 E2
Wanswell Glos 36 D3
Wantage Oxon 38 F3
Wapley S Glos 24 B2
Wappenbury Warks 51 C8
Wappenham Northants 52 E4
Warbleton E Sus 18 D3
Warblington Hants 15 D8
Warborough Oxon 39 E5
Warboys Cambs 66 F3
Warbreck Blkpool 92 F3
Warbstow Corn 8 E4
Warburton Gtr Man 86 F5
Warcop Cumb 100 C2
Ward End W Mid 62 F5
Ward Green Suff 56 C4
Warden Kent 30 B4
Warden Northumb 110 C2
Wardhill Orkney 176 D5
Wardington Oxon 52 E2
Wardlaw Borders 115 C5
Wardle Ches 74 D3
Wardle Gtr Man 87 C7
Wardley Rutland 64 D5
Wardlow Derbys 75 B8
Wardy Hill Cambs 66 F4
Ware Herts 41 C6
Ware Kent 31 C6
Wareham Dorset 13 F7
Warehorne Kent 19 B6
Waren Mill Northumb 125 F7
Warenford Northumb 117 B7
Warenton Northumb 125 F7
Wareside Herts 41 C6
Waresley Cambs 54 D3
Waresley Worcs 50 B3
Warfield Brack 27 B6
Warfleet Devon 7 D6
Wargrave Wokingham 27 B5
Warham Norf 80 C5
Warhill Gtr Man 87 E7
Wark Northumb 109 B8
Wark Northumb 124 F4
Warkleigh Devon 9 B8
Warkton Northants 53 B6
Warkworth Northants 52 E2
Warkworth Northumb 117 D8
Warlaby N Yorks 101 E8
Warland W Yorks 87 B7
Warleggan Corn 5 C6
Warlingham Sur 28 D4
Warmfield W Yorks 88 B4
Warmingham Ches 74 C4
Warmington Northants 65 E7
Warmington Warks 52 E2
Warminster Wilts 24 E3
Warmlake Kent 30 D2
Warmley S Glos 23 B8
Warmley Tower S Glos 23 B8
Warmonds Hill Northants 53 C7
Warmsworth S Yorks 89 D6
Warmwell Dorset 13 F5
Warndon Worcs 50 D3
Warnford Hants 15 B7
Warnham W Sus 28 F2
Warninglid W Sus 17 B6
Warren Ches 75 B5
Warren Pembs 44 F4
Warren Heath Suff 57 E6
Warren Row Windsor 39 F8
Warren Street Kent 30 D3
Warrington M Keynes 53 D6
Warrington Warr 86 F4
Warsash Hants 15 D5
Warslow Staffs 75 D7
Warter E Yorks 96 D4
Warthermarske N Yorks 94 B5
Warthill N Yorks 96 D2
Wartling E Sus 18 E3
Wartnaby Leics 64 B4
Warton Lancs 86 B2
Warton Lancs 92 B4
Warton Northumb 117 D6
Warton Warks 63 D6
Warwick Warks 51 C7
Warwick Bridge Cumb 108 D4
Warwick Castle Warks 51 C7
Warwick on Eden Cumb 108 D4
Warwick Racecourse Warks 51 C7
Wasbister Orkney 176 C2
Wasdale Head Cumb 98 D3
Wash Common W Berks 26 C2
Washaway Corn 4 C5
Washbourne Devon 7 D5
Washfield Devon 10 C4
Washfold N Yorks 101 D5
Washford Som 22 E2
Washford Pyne Devon 10 C3
Washingborough Lincs 78 B3
Washington T & W 111 D6
Washington W Sus 16 C5
Wasing W Berks 26 C3
Waskerley Durham 110 E3
Wasperton Warks 51 D7
Wasps Nest Lincs 78 C3
Wass N Yorks 95 B8
Watchet Som 22 E2
Watchfield Oxon 38 E2
Watchfield Som 22 E5
Watchgate Cumb 99 E7
Watchhill Cumb 107 E8
Watcombe Torbay 7 C7
Watendlath Cumb 98 C4
Water Devon 10 F2
Water Lancs 87 B6
Water End E Yorks 96 F3
Water End Herts 40 C3
Water End Herts 41 D5
Water Newton Cambs 65 E8
Water Orton Warks 63 E5
Water Stratford Bucks 52 F4
Water Yeat Cumb 98 F4
Waterbeach Cambs 55 C5
Waterbeck Dumfries 108 B2
Watercress Line (Mid Hants Railway), Alton Hants 26 F4
Waterden Norf 80 D4
Waterfall Staffs 75 D7
Waterfoot E Renf 121 D5
Waterfoot Lancs 87 B6
Waterford Hants 14 E4
Waterford Herts 41 C6
Waterhead Cumb 99 D5
Waterhead Dumfries 114 E4
Waterheads Borders 122 D5
Waterhouses Durham 110 E4
Waterhouses Staffs 75 D7
Wateringbury Kent 29 D7
Waterloo Gtr Man 87 D7
Waterloo Highld 155 H2
Waterloo Mers 85 E4
Waterloo N Lnrk 121 D8
Waterloo Norf 68 C5
Waterloo Perth 141 F7
Waterloo Poole 13 E8
Waterloo Shrops 74 F2
Waterloo Port Gwyn 82 E4
Waterlooville Hants 15 D7
Watermeetings S Lnrk 114 C2
Watermillock Cumb 99 B6
Watermouth Castle, Ilfracombe Devon 20 E4
Waterperry Oxon 39 D6
Waterrow Som 11 B5
Water's Nook Gtr Man 86 D4
Waters Upton Telford 61 C6
Watersfield W Sus 16 C4
Watershed Mill Visitor Centre, Settle N Yorks 93 C8
Waterside Aberds 161 F7
Waterside Blkburn 86 B5
Waterside Cumb 108 E2
Waterside E Ayrs 112 D4
Waterside E Ayrs 120 E4
Waterside E Dunb 121 B6
Waterside E Renf 120 D5
Waterstock Oxon 39 D6
Waterston Pembs 44 E4
Watford Herts 40 E4
Watford Northants 52 C4
Watford Gap W Mid 62 D5
Wath N Yorks 94 C4
Wath N Yorks 95 B6
Wath N Yorks 96 B2
Wath Brow Cumb 98 C2
Wath upon Dearne S Yorks 88 D5
Watley's End S Glos 36 F3
Watlington Norf 67 C6
Watlington Oxon 39 E6
Watnall Notts 76 E5
Watten Highld 169 D7
Wattisfield Suff 56 B4
Wattisham Suff 56 D4
Wattlesborough Heath Shrops 60 C3
Watton E Yorks 97 D6
Watton Norf 68 D2
Watton at Stone Herts 41 C6
Wattston N Lnrk 121 B7
Wattstown Rhondda 34 E4
Wauchan Highld 146 F2
Waulkmill Lodge Orkney 176 F2
Waun Powys 59 D5
Waun-y-clyn Carms 33 D5
Waunarlwydd Swansea 33 E7
Waunclunda Carms 47 F5
Waunfawr Gwyn 82 F5
Waungron Swansea 33 D6
Waunlwyd Bl Gwent 35 D5
Wavendon M Keynes 53 F7
Waverbridge Cumb 108 E2
Waverton Ches 73 C8
Waverton Cumb 108 E2
Wavertree Mers 85 F4
Wawne E Yorks 97 F6
Waxham Norf 69 B7
Waxholme E Yorks 91 B7
Way Kent 31 C7
Way Village Devon 10 C3
Wayfield Medway 29 C8
Wayford Som 12 D2
Waymills Shrops 74 E2
Wayne Green Mon 35 C8
Wdig = Goodwick Pembs 44 B4
Weachyburn Aberds 160 C3
Weald Oxon 38 D3
Weald and Downland Open Air Museum, Chichester W Sus 16 C2
Wealdstone London 40 F4
Weardley W Yorks 95 E5
Weare Som 23 D6
Weare Giffard Devon 9 B6
Wearhead Durham 109 F8
Weasdale Cumb 100 D1
Weasenham All Saints Norf 80 E4
Weasenham St Peter Norf 80 E4
Weatherhill Sur 28 E4
Weaverham Ches 74 B3
Weaverthorpe N Yorks 97 B5
Webheath Worcs 50 C5
Wedderlairs Aberds 161 E5
Wedderlie Borders 124 D2
Weddington Warks 63 E7
Wedgwood Visitor Centre, Barlaston Staffs 75 F6
Wedhampton Wilts 25 D5
Wedmore Som 23 E6
Wednesbury W Mid 62 E3
Wednesfield W Mid 62 D3
Weedon Bucks 39 C8
Weedon Bec Northants 52 D4
Weedon Lois Northants 52 E4
Weeford Staffs 62 D5
Week Devon 10 C2
Week St Mary Corn 8 E4
Weeke Hants 26 F2
Weekley Northants 65 F5
Weel E Yorks 97 F6
Weeley Essex 43 B7
Weeley Heath Essex 43 B7
Weem Perth 141 E5
Weeping Cross Staffs 62 B3
Weethley Gate Warks 51 D5
Weeting Norf 67 F7
Weeting Heath NNR Norf 67 F7
Weeton E Yorks 91 B7
Weeton Lancs 92 F3
Weeton N Yorks 95 E5
Weetwood Hall Northumb 117 B6
Weir Lancs 87 B6
Weir Quay Devon 6 C2
Welborne Norf 68 D3
Welbourn Lincs 78 D2
Welburn N Yorks 96 C3
Welburn N Yorks 102 F4
Welbury N Yorks 102 D1
Welby Lincs 78 F2
Welches Dam Cambs 66 F4
Welcombe Devon 8 C4
Weld Bank Lancs 86 C3
Weldon Northumb 117 E7
Welford Northants 64 F3
Welford W Berks 26 B2
Welford-on-Avon Warks 51 D6
Welham Leics 64 E4
Welham Notts 89 F8
Welham Green Herts 41 D5
Well Hants 27 E5
Well Lincs 79 B7
Well N Yorks 101 F7
Well End Bucks 40 F1
Well Heads W Yorks 94 F3
Well Hill Kent 29 C5
Well Town Devon 10 D4
Welland Worcs 50 E2
Wellbank Angus 142 F4
Welldale Dumfries 107 C8
Wellesbourne Warks 51 D7
Welling London 29 B5
Wellingborough Northants 53 C6
Wellingham Norf 80 E4
Wellingore Lincs 78 D2
Wellington Cumb 98 D2
Wellington Hereford 49 E6
Wellington Som 11 B6
Wellington Telford 61 C6
Wellington Heath Hereford 50 E2
Wellington Hill W Yorks 95 F6
Wellow Bath 24 D2
Wellow I o W 14 F4
Wellow Notts 77 C6
Wellpond Green Herts 41 B7
Wells Som 23 E7
Wells Cathedral Som 23 E7
Wells Green Ches 74 D3
Wells-Next-The-Sea Norf 80 C5
Wellsborough Leics 63 D7
Wellswood Torbay 7 C7
Wellwood Fife 134 F2
Welney Norf 66 E5
Welsh Bicknor Hereford 36 C2
Welsh End Shrops 74 F2
Welsh Frankton Shrops 73 F7
Welsh Highland Railway, Caernarfon Gwyn 82 E4
Welsh Highland Railway, Porthmadog Gwyn 71 D6
Welsh Hook Pembs 44 C4
Welsh National Velodrome Newport 35 F7
Welsh Newton Hereford 36 C1
Welsh St Donats V Glam 22 B2
Welshampton Shrops 73 F8
Welshpool = Y Trallwng Powys 60 D2
Welton Cumb 108 E3
Welton E Yorks 90 B3
Welton Lincs 78 B3
Welton Northants 52 C3
Welton Hill Lincs 90 F4
Welton le Marsh Lincs 79 C7
Welton le Wold Lincs 91 F6
Welwick E Yorks 91 B7
Welwyn Herts 41 C5
Welwyn Garden City Herts 41 C5
Wem Shrops 60 B5
Wembdon Som 22 F4
Wembley London 40 F4
Wembley Stadium London 40 F4
Wembury Devon 6 E3
Wembworthy Devon 9 D8
Wemyss Bay Invclyd 129 D6
Wenallt Ceredig 47 B5
Wenallt Gwyn 72 E3
Wendens Ambo Essex 55 F6
Wendlebury Oxon 39 C5
Wendling Norf 68 C2
Wendover Bucks 40 D1
Wendron Corn 3 C5
Wendy Cambs 54 E4
Wenfordbridge Corn 5 B5
Wenhaston Suff 57 B8
Wennington Cambs 54 B3
Wennington London 41 F8
Wennington Lancs 93 B6
Wensley Derbys 76 C2
Wensley N Yorks 101 F5
Wentbridge W Yorks 89 C5
Wentnor Shrops 60 E3
Wentworth Cambs 55 B5
Wentworth S Yorks 88 E4
Wenvoe V Glam 22 B3
Weobley Hereford 49 D6
Weobley Marsh Hereford 49 D6
Wereham Norf 67 D6
Wergs W Mid 62 D2
Wern Powys 59 C6
Wern Powys 60 C2
Wernffrwd Swansea 33 E6
Wernyrheolydd Mon 35 C7
Werrington Corn 8 F5
Werrington P'boro 65 D8
Werrington Staffs 75 E6
Wervin Ches 73 B8
Wesham Lancs 92 F4
Wessington Derbys 76 D3
West Acre Norf 67 C7
West Adderbury Oxon 52 F2
West Allerdean Northumb 125 E5
West Alvington Devon 6 E5
West Amesbury Wilts 25 E6
West Anstey Devon 10 B3
West Ashby Lincs 79 B5
West Ashling W Sus 16 D2
West Ashton Wilts 24 D3
West Auckland Durham 101 B6
West Ayton N Yorks 103 F7
West Bagborough Som 22 F3
West Barkwith Lincs 91 F5
West Barnby N Yorks 103 C6
West Barns E Loth 124 B2
West Barsham Norf 80 D5
West Bay Dorset 12 E2
West Beckham Norf 81 D7
West Bedfont Sur 27 B8
West Benhar N Lnrk 121 C8
West Bergholt Essex 43 B5
West Bexington Dorset 12 F3
West Bilney Norf 67 C7
West Blatchington Brighton 17 D6
West Bowling W Yorks 94 F4
West Bradford Lancs 93 E7
West Bradley Som 23 F7
West Bretton W Yorks 88 C3
West Bridgford Notts 77 F5
West Bromwich W Mid 62 E4
West Buckland Devon 21 F5
West Buckland Som 11 B6
West Burrafirth Shetland 175 H4
West Burton N Yorks 101 F5
West Burton W Sus 16 C3
West Butterwick N Lincs 90 D2
West Byfleet Sur 27 C8
West Caister Norf 69 C8
West Calder W Loth 122 C3
West Camel Som 12 B3
West Challow Oxon 38 F3
West Chelborough Dorset 12 D3
West Chevington Northumb 117 E8
West Chiltington W Sus 16 C4
West Chiltington Common W Sus 16 C4
West Chinnock Som 12 C2
West Chisenbury Wilts 25 D6
West Clandon Sur 27 D8
West Cliffe Kent 31 E7
West Clyne Highld 165 D5
West Clyth Highld 169 F7
West Coker Som 12 C3
West Compton Dorset 12 E3
West Compton Som 23 E7
West Cowick E Yorks 89 B7
West Cranmore Som 23 E8
West Cross Swansea 33 F7
West Cullery Aberds 151 D6
West Curry Corn 8 E4
West Curthwaite Cumb 108 E3
West Darlochan Argyll 118 D3
West Dean Wilts 14 B3
West Dean W Sus 16 C2
West Deeping Lincs 65 D8
West Derby Mers 85 E4
West Dereham Norf 67 D6
West Didsbury Gtr Man 87 E6
West Ditchburn Northumb 117 B7
West Down Devon 20 E4
West Drayton London 27 B8
West Drayton Notts 77 B7
West Ella E Yorks 90 B4
West End Beds 53 D7
West End E Yorks 96 F5
West End E Yorks 97 F7
West End Hants 15 C5
West End Lancs 86 B5
West End Norf 68 D2
West End Norf 69 C8
West End N Som 23 C6
West End N Yorks 94 D4
West End Oxon 38 D4
West End S Lnrk 122 E2
West End Suff 69 F7
West End Sur 27 C7
West End S Yorks 89 D7
West End Wilts 13 B7
West End Wilts 24 B4
West End W Sus 17 C6
West End Green Hants 26 C4
West Farleigh Kent 29 D8
West Felton Shrops 60 B3
West Fenton E Loth 135 F6
West Ferry Dundee 142 F4
West Firle E Sus 17 D8
West Ginge Oxon 38 F4
West Grafton Wilts 25 C7
West Green Hants 26 D5
West Greenskares Aberds 160 B4
West Grimstead Wilts 14 B3
West Grinstead W Sus 17 B5
West Haddlesey N Yorks 89 B6
West Haddon Northants 52 B4
West Hagbourne Oxon 39 F5
West Hagley Worcs 62 F3
West Hall Cumb 109 C5
West Hallam Derbys 76 E4
West Halton N Lincs 90 B3
West Ham London 41 F7
West Handley Derbys 76 B3
West Hanney Oxon 38 E4
West Hanningfield Essex 42 E3
West Hardwick W Yorks 88 C5
West Harnham Wilts 14 B2
West Harptree Bath 23 D7
West Hatch Som 11 B7
West Head Norf 67 D5
West Heath Ches 74 C5
West Heath Hants 27 D6
West Heath Hants 26 D3
West Helmsdale Highld 165 C7
West Hendred Oxon 38 F4
West Heslerton N Yorks 96 B5
West Hill Devon 11 E5
West Hill E Yorks 97 C7
West Hill N Som 23 B6
West Hoathly W Sus 28 F4
West Holme Dorset 13 F6

First published in 2007 by Philip's
a division of Octopus Publishing Group Ltd
2–4 Heron Quays
London E14 4JP
An Hachette Livre UK Company
www.philips-maps.co.uk
First edition 2007
First impression 2007
Cartography by Philip's
Copyright © 2007 Philip's

Data for the speed cameras provided by PocketGPSWorld.com Ltd.

Information for Tourist Attractions shown on the mapping supplied by VisitBritain.

Information for National Parks, Areas of Outstanding Natural Beauty, National Trails and Country Parks in Wales supplied by the Countryside Council for Wales.

Information for National Parks, Areas of Outstanding Natural Beauty, National Trails and Country Parks in England supplied by the Countryside Agency. Data for Regional Parks, Long Distance Footpaths and Country Parks in Scotland provided by Scottish Natural Heritage.

Gaelic name forms used in the Western Isles provided by Comhairle nan Eilean.

Data for the National Nature Reserves in England provided by English Nature. Data for the National Nature Reserves in Wales provided by Countryside Council for Wales. Darparwyd data'n ymwneud â Gwarchodfeydd Natur Cenedlaethol Cymru gan Gyngor Cefn Gwlad Cymru.

Information on the location of National Nature Reserves in Scotland was provided by Scottish Natural Heritage.

Data for National Scenic Areas in Scotland provided by the Scottish Executive Office. Crown copyright material is reproduced with the permission of the Controller of HMSO and the Queen's Printer for Scotland. Licence number C02W0003960.

Printed in Italy by Rotolito

Photographic acknowledgments
Cover, page I and page VIII top: Brand X Pictures / Alamy
Page II left Design Pics Inc / Alamy • Page II right Bananastock / Alamy • Page III top thislife pictures / Alamy • Page VIII bottom Martin Blunt / Alamy • Page IX left Joe Bird / Alamy, right Wayne Linden / Alamy • Page X Denny Rowland / Alamy • Page XI Chris George / Alamy • Page XII Royal Borough of Windsor and Maidenhead • Page XIII Thomas Dobner / Alamy • Page XIV top left Albaimages / Alamy, bottom right Imagery and Imagination / Alamy • Page XV bottom left Neil McAllister / Alamy, top right Rob Rayworth / Alamy

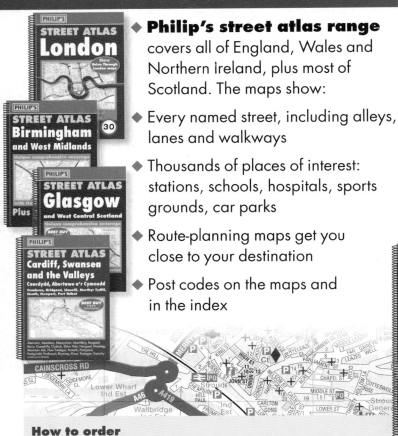
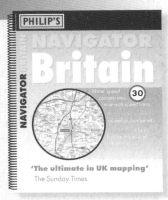